Writing Effectively

Beth S. Neman

Wilmington College

Charles E. Merrill Publishing Company
A Bell & Howell Company
Columbus Toronto London Sydney

To:
my students and
my family,
Albert, David and Dan

Published by
Charles E. Merrill Publishing Co.
A Bell & Howell Company
Columbus, Ohio 43216

This book was set in Garamond and Thompson Quillscript.
Production Coordination: Lucinda Ann Peck.
Text Designers: Lucinda Ann Peck and Tony Faiola.
Cover Art: Detail of "A Lady Writing": Jan Vermeer.
National Gallery of Art, Washington. Gift of Harry Waldron
Havemeyer and Horace Havemeyer, Jr., in memory of their father,
Horace Havemeyer.

Cover Design Coordination: Tony Faiola
Revision Guide: Coauthor, Nancy Bates
Exercises: Coauthor, Dan Neman

Library of Congress Catalog Card Number: 82–061567
International Standard Book Number: 0–675–20047–4
Printed in the United States of America
   2   3   4   5   6   7   8   9   10—86   85   84   83

Contents

Preface

You may wonder why another composition text is needed when we already have a number of fine books. The answer is that there is yet no really comprehensive text. Although many texts have thoroughly presented *individual* features of a writing program, no single volume has offered students and instructors the opportunity to study the *whole* field of expository writing. *Writing Effectively* does just that. It is a comprehensive text that offers both a thesis-support approach to structure and a stylistic-option approach to style (mainly through sentence-combining exercises). It also provides an anthology of twenty brief essays by highly regarded contemporary authors to give students models of good expository structure and style. Throughout the text this anthology serves as a source of examples and as the basis of many try-it-out-for-yourself exercises. In addition, *Writing Effectively* offers an alphabetical Revision Guide in which students can find easily accessible answers to their mechanical or stylistic problems. Furthermore, for those classes that wish to undertake research papers and critical analyses, *Writing Effectively* provides full and practical direction.

In addition to being a comprehensive composition text, *Writing Effectively* is student-centered, process-based, and rhetorically-oriented. It is student-centered in that its every feature is designed to meet specific student needs. I address the student-readers directly, taking them step-by-step through the whole writing process. I try to anticipate their questions, doubts, and problems and encourage them to explore alternative methods. Many exercises are provided so students can experiment with various theoretical strategies and assure themselves of the credibility of the principles the text endorses. *Writing Effectively* also discusses writing as process rather than end product, offering students practical guidance toward mastering all the steps of prewriting, writing, and revising. The text gives particular attention to prewriting, stressing the importance of discovering thesis and support; and it also emphasizes the necessity for revision. In addition, *Writing Effectively* is grounded in practical rhetoric. Throughout every step in the writing process, this text emphasizes the persuasive nature of writing. For example, I introduce the "although clause," a device that makes the latently argumentative nature of theses concrete by phrasing opposing ideas as a subordinate clause attached to the working thesis statement. This notion is surprisingly useful to students in delineating their working theses, in setting up the structure of their compositions, and in determining their approach to their readers. The text and exercises also encourage students to experiment with different structural and stylistic strategies and to consider their varying rhetorical effectiveness in particular contexts.

Writing Effectively is thus rooted in time-honored principles; but you will find that the development and treatment of these principles are innovative and exciting.

Part One, "Writing the First Paper," concisely introduces the essentials of the entire writing process. It aims to provide students the possibility of success on their first effort. Once students have worked their way through all the stages of the writing process, concentrating on the less familiar concepts of the vital prewriting stage, they should be able to produce a first composition they can take some pride in—especially if they are encouraged to rewrite.

Parts Two and Three, the heart of *Writing Effectively,* expose students to a wide range of rhetorical options, both structural and stylistic. Part Two, "Persuading through Structure," discusses the stages of the writing process, concentrating on prewriting in the first two chapters (Invention in Chapter 1 and Arrangement in Chapter 2), writing in the third, and revision in the fourth. Part Three, "Persuading through Style," discusses a writer's choice of syntactical and dictional options. Chapters 5, 6, and 7 present the major syntactical strategies and provide sentence-combining exercises. Chapter 8 emphasizes stylistic choices in diction.

The sentence-combining exercises in Chapters 5, 6, and 7 include both the limited (cued) and the contextual (noncued) varieties. Students are first given the opportunity to practice each new syntactic strategy by writing sentences in forms that limit their options to the newly introduced constructions. In addition, every major section concludes with several rhetorically contextual sentence-combining exercises. In these essays students are presented with a given context of ideas (phrased minimally in sentence kernels) and are asked to write paragraphs or essays from them by using whatever strategies they believe best express the given ideas. Having been a part of a carefully controlled experiment with contextual sentence-combining exercises at Miami University (Ohio) in 1976, I can add my personal endorsement of such exercises. (See Morenberg, Daiker, and Kerek, "Sentence-Combining at the College Level: An Experimental Study," *Research in the Teaching of English,* 12 Oct. 1978, 245–50.) I was impressed by the remarkably favorable results produced by the use of sentence-combining in this experiment and even more convinced by the improvement in the writing of my own students, who followed a combined structure-style curriculum similar to that suggested in *Writing Effectively.*

Part Four, "Writing Special Kinds of Essays," helps students apply the knowledge they have gained about writing expository essays in general to the two such essays most frequently assigned in college classes, the research paper (Chapter 9) and the critical analysis (Chapter 10). Both chapters offer detailed, practical guidance, and both include some especially helpful features. Chapter 9, for instance, introduces note-taking and documentation procedures that all but eliminate inadvertent plagiarism. Chapter 10 includes a section on close reading that gives students a definite sense of what the analytical process is really about.

Part Five offers a selection of brief essays chosen on the basis of the reputation of their authors, the variety of their topics, and the interest of their subject matter. Nineteen of these essays are quoted extensively throughout the text as examples; one is reserved from discussion so that it may be assigned for analysis. These essays make it possible for students to place the brief textual examples within the context of the essays from which they come. And they also permit students to check out against the practice of professional writers the validity of any point the text makes about writing. The collection also provides an excellent source for those instructors who like to teach composition partly through rhetorical analysis.

Part Six, "A Revision Guide," consists of alphabetically arranged, brief entries to answer any question a student is likely to raise about syntax, usage, capitalization, punctuation, spelling, and rhetorical figures. Because of the alphabetical arrangement, full exemplification, and extensive cross referencing, the Guide is easily accessible to students.

Writing Effectively is based on what I have learned about the needs of beginning writing students from my own years of classroom experience and from my research into the experience of other teachers. I hope that you who study from it and you who teach it will gain both knowledge and pleasure from using it.

Beth Neman

Acknowledgments

In writing this book I was assisted by Nancy Bates, whose extensive knowledge enlightens and whose quick wit enlivens the Revision Guide, and by Daniel Neman, whose intelligent curiosity and humor are largely responsible for the quality of the exercises. Other exercises and examples were penned by Laura Balster Rixey, Cynthia Manogue, and Christopher David Kelley. To all, my thanks.

Though the ideas expressed here are my own, they have been largely derived from the thought of others. I would therefore like to thank the authors of the works I have read in preparation and the teachers and researchers from whom I have learned at meetings of the Conference of College Composition and Communication and the National Council of Teachers of English. I am especially grateful to my colleagues and my students at Miami University and Wilmington College, whose thoughtful discussion has helped to shape this book. More specifically, I would like to thank William Guthrie and the students in his classes and mine at Wilmington, who class-tested earlier versions of *Writing Effectively,* as well as Lois Frankel, David Horn, Irene Margolin, Dominique Muller, and Daniel Nixon, students at other colleges who tested representative exercises.

Writing Effectively has benefited greatly from the wise advice and encouraging comments of scholars who kindly read the manuscript at its various stages. I am deeply grateful to George Bramer, Lansing Community College; Barbara Carson, University of Georgia; William Demaree, Del Mar College; Ron Fortune, Illinois State University; Tori Haring-Smith, Brown University; John Harwood, Pennsylvania State University; Frank Hubbard, University of Wisconsin, Milwaukee; Andrew Kerek, Miami University; Kim Moreland, Brown University; Robert Perrin, Indiana State University; Lucille Schultz, University of Maryland; Kathleen Stearns, Coastal Carolina Community College; Gerald Sullivan, California State University, Long Beach; and Joseph Trimmer, Ball State University.

My gratitude also goes to Elayne Bleill for her solid professionalism and skillful typing and to Donna McClughen for her warm and efficient secretarial service.

Writing Effectively has also had the advantage of caring and skillful editors. I greatly appreciate the work of Ellen Roush, who provided student perspective; and from Merrill, Cindy Peck, whose meticulous concern guided the book through publication, as well as Susan Glick, copy editor extraordinaire, and Beverly Kolz, a considerate, helpful, and most able editor, whose professional expertise and personal insight helped create this text.

Before
You Begin

Composition courses suffer from a bad press; there is no question about it. Many students actually believe the bad notices and thus come into the course thinking of learning to write as either an impossibly difficult or a worthlessly easy task. Some of these students think it is impossible to learn to write because they see writing ability as a talent a person either has or has not, a gift with which only a few lucky geniuses have been blessed. Others think that learning to write is too mechanical a procedure to bother very much about. They believe that to write well a person need only follow an easily memorized formula that they are certain all composition teachers know, but just fail to communicate. Though these views are widely held, they are both demonstrably false.

A well-written essay is derived neither from a stroke of genius nor from a mechanical formula. There is no magic formula with which to express each and every idea. There is no way just to "fill in the blank," just to "fulfill the specifications" and write anything but the dreariest of exercises. A glance at some of the articles in your favorite magazine (or at those in Part Five of this book) will convince you that no single formula or series of formulas could possibly account for the rich diversity of human thought they display. And although natural ability certainly helps a writer, the fact that a few people are particularly skilled does not suggest the futility of others trying to learn to write well any more than the performance of a superb Olympic diver should restrain the rest of us from learning to swim.

The truth is that writing—like swimming or bridge or driving a car—is a skill that can be learned; it is an activity that can be understood in terms of its overall purpose. The purpose of writing is to persuade readers that what the writer is telling them is true or right or good. Stripped of the mystique it has acquired, writing is simply the formulating of thought, the shaping of thought into sentences, and the arranging of thought into sentences on a page for the purpose of persuasion.

Although writing is thus as learnable as any other skill, the process is rarely easy. For writing is inextricably bound up with thought, and thinking is just about the hardest thing we do. Nevertheless, I will insist that learning to write, however strenuous the undertaking, will be worthwhile. First, if you learn to write effectively, you will be able to get your ideas across to others. Writing effectively will permit others not only to understand the essence of what you have to say but also to appreciate its merits, and that means that never again should lack of writing skill prevent you from being credited for what you know or what you have accomplished. Second, in the process of learning to write well, you will increase your ability to think clearly and logically, for this kind of thinking necessarily precedes or coincides with the writing of effective, well-organized prose. Furthermore, in forcing you to think, the process of writing will put you in touch with your ideas about a particular subject and thus will also provide you with the sort of practice in exploring and ordering your thoughts that will serve you well in the future.

Part One

Writing the First Paper

Although writing is a single process, it can be analyzed in terms of stages—prewriting, writing, and rewriting—stages followed in general by almost everyone who writes well. For purposes of study and discussion it is helpful to break these stages into steps that can be approached and understood one at a time. But despite the advantages of such a sequential approach, there would seem to be a catch to it when it is applied to a process as basically unified as writing. For although you can only study the steps one at a time, you will need to use them all for every composition you write—including the first!

This opening section, "Writing the First Paper," is provided to help you escape the catch. To prepare you for that first assignment, Part One introduces the most significant steps in the writing process. It emphasizes the essential early prewriting steps to get you off to a good start and presents a quick overview of the rest. In later chapters each of the steps will be covered in a fuller, more leisurely way.

Let's begin.

BEFORE YOU BEGIN
The Thesis and Its Importance

If I should ask you what is the most important part of an expository essay, the one thing it cannot really do without, you might very well say its *thesis*. And, of course, you would be right. Even so, you might not be totally sure what exactly a thesis is or why writers and teachers make such a fuss about it. For the thesis is a subject many people tend to be vague about. Many think of it only in such general terms as "the subject of a composition" or "what a paper is about," and thus they tend to underestimate its significance. The truth, however, is that the thesis is a good deal more than that.

The thesis embodies the purpose of the writer who sets out to write an expository article, essay, or book.

It embodies *your* purpose when you write any kind of expository prose.

Expository Writing Defined

The term *expository writing* may be unfamiliar to you. It is the sort of writing found in nonfiction books, in magazines, in many newspaper articles; the sort of writing you are called upon to perform in college exams and business reports; the workaday useful writing that makes the world's intellectual wheels go round. Expository writing expounds, explains, and sets forth information and ideas. Its function is not like that of poetry, to sing a lyric or a ballad, or like that of fiction or even news writing, to tell a tale. Rather, the function of expository writing is to make a statement. Its purpose, however, like that of all writing, is essentially persuasive.

All writing is an expression of an author's ideas, feelings, or view of the facts or the world. Whether consciously or unconsciously, authors write to persuade their readers of the truth of those ideas, feelings, or facts. Writers of tracts and satires can sometimes be fairly direct in their persuasive aim, but authors of every kind of writing use whatever devices are appropriate to their work to fulfill their purpose. Lyric poets bring all the charm of rhythm and metaphor to convince us of the power of their feelings. Humorists employ the comic tools of wit or farce to point out the funny inconsistency between what is and what should be in this world. Fiction writers present their view of life by narrating the actions of characters. And expository writers attempt to arrange and order their material so that the reader will come to understand and accept the truth of what they are setting forth, of the statement they are making.

Thesis Defined

The point expository writers set forth, that statement which contains the essence of what they mean to say, is the thesis. For a given work then,

the thesis is a concise statement of what the reader should come to believe.

The thesis statement is usually placed toward the end of the introductory portion of a piece of expository prose and/or somewhere in the concluding segment. Sometimes the thesis is not stated in so many words, and occasionally it is only implied; but there can be no good expository writing without it. Without a thesis, expository writing is, literally, pointless.

I have made these statements deliberately strong, even though a careful thinker is reluctant to remark that anything *always* or *never* happens. Yet even a very careful thinker can confidently assert that good expository writing *always* has a thesis, either stated or implied.

Form of the Thesis Statement

Just as there is great variety in what we call expository writing, there is also a great range in the theses that motivate these writings. Some theses offer assertions of scientific ideas, factually phrased, experimentally verifiable:

> The creeping, seemingly relentless spread of the earth's deserts. . . [has become] a major environmental danger. (Fred Golden, "Earth's Creeping Deserts," p. 432, *1*)*

Others seem to be declarations of a whimsical fancy:

> Children today not only exist, they have taken over. (Shana Alexander, "Getting Old in Kids' Country," p. 434, *2*)

Still others provide an author's insight into truth:

> To have that sense of one's intrinsic worth which constitutes self-respect is potentially to have everything: the ability to discriminate, to love and to remain indifferent. To lack it is to be locked within oneself, paradoxically incapable of either love or indifference. (Joan Didion, "On Self-Respect," p. 441, *11*)

But however varied the subject matter of the thesis or its author's approach to it, all theses, without exception, are statements that seem to demand development, explanation, demonstration, or in other words, persuasion.

This argumentative quality is fundamental to the nature of all theses. We can see it clearly in theses such as the following from Tom Wolfe who openly adopts an argumentative tone:

> So what this story is against . . . is the Sin Cult. I would like to put forth the thesis that if you want to sin, sin; but don't make so much noise about it. ("Down with Sin," p. 443, *6*)

It is clear, too, in the provocative accents of this thesis of George Will:

> The contagious crossness between Washington and Jerusalem that originated in Washington is a compound of Washington impatience and Israeli anxiety. The

---

*Examples from essays reprinted in Part Five of this text have been identified by page and paragraph number so that you may have the opportunity to see how the example works within the essay as a whole.

> anxiety is more reasonable than the impatience. ("Israel and Munich,"
> p. 446, *1*)

The three sample theses quoted first may not seem to demand demonstration and development quite as aggressively as these last two. But their readers will expect demonstration and development nevertheless. Every thesis requires explanation and support because, like the proverbial visitor from Missouri, every interested reader needs to be "shown." It is the writers' acknowledgment of this insistence of their readers that gives rise to all expository compositions—essays, articles, answers to test questions. For the whole of a composition goes to confirm or to further the point conveyed in its thesis. The thesis is thus both the basis for the persuasive strategy of a paper and the focus for its organization.

Try It Out

"Try It Out" exercises give you the opportunity to confirm for yourself the accuracy of this book's information. In some cases, as in question 1 below, you will be asked to refer to Part Five of this book, "A Selection of Essays." Part Five contains a group of essays selected as a fair sampling of good professional writing. These essays, adopted mainly because of their interest for readers, can also serve as a testing ground for statements made in the text. Use the selections to come to your own conclusions about good writing.

1. Browse through Part Five (beginning on p. 431) and see if you can find an essay that does not have a thesis. If you choose, go further afield and look into *Harper's* or the *Saturday Review* or articles of commentary in *Time* or *Newsweek* and continue your search. If you should find a thesis-less essay, record the title or bring it to class.
2. What kinds of subjects do people write about in articles like those in Part Five? What do they seem to be trying to accomplish in them?
3. How are their theses worded? Jot down the theses of three of the articles.
4. Where are the theses placed in the essays? Give the location of the three thesis statements you recorded in question 3.

Finding Your Working Thesis

You will need a "working thesis" to help you plan your writing. Even if you do not use the exact words of your working thesis anywhere in your final composition, you will find phrasing your central ideas into a definite statement and writing it down highly useful. How do you go about finding this thesis? There are two basic ways. The subject you will be writing on will either spontaneously suggest a thesis idea or it will not. If it should, then most of your prewriting time will be spent in developing and sorting out possible supporting ideas—that is, ideas that help make your point. As you work with these ideas, you will be refining and evaluating your thesis as well as building the structure of your paper. If no thesis immediately occurs to you, then you will want to discover one by making an inventory (a list) of your information or ideas on the subject, by analyzing the inventory into possible chains of supporting ideas, and then by deriving the thesis to which they lead.

Reasoning from Topic to Thesis

Although the quality of the thesis you develop will, of course, depend upon the quality of the ideas that go into it, the following list of steps may help direct your thinking toward finding a workable thesis to express what you want to say.

Step 1. Narrow Your Topic to a Workable Size. Unless your paper is to be a very long one indeed, almost any suggested topic from the proverbial "The Things I Did Last Summer" to "Water Buffalo" or "The Peloponnesian Wars" would be far too broad to be contained within it. More important, a paper written with no more focus than that of being "about" such a subject would be hopelessly diffuse. Furthermore, your readers wouldn't be able to find any purpose in your writing.

How do you go about narrowing your subject? By answering the question "What about it?" So ask yourself, What about last summer? ("Busy." "Lazy." "Satisfying.") What about it interests me most? What is most likely to interest others? ("The usefulness of the water buffalo." "Why the Athenians lost the Peloponnesian Wars.")

Step 2. Turn the Narrowed Topic into an Arguable Statement. Sometimes changing a topic into an arguable statement is just a matter of wording. The phrase "The usefulness of the water buffalo" easily converts to the full sentence "The water buffalo is useful," an arguable proposition. If the topic is phrased as a question or semi-question, the thesis lies in the answer to that question. "Why last summer was satisfying" becomes "Last summer was especially satisfying to me because I had a glimpse of self-knowledge that started me on the way to growing up." "Why the Athenians lost the Peloponnesian Wars" can be answered by the arguable statement "The Athenians lost the Peloponnesian Wars because they had a foolish foreign policy."

Step 3. Clarify Your Statement by Adding an "Although Clause."
The "although clause" is a group of words (usually a subordinate clause*) attached to and, in a manner of speaking, opposing the thesis. The structure of the "although clause" permits writers to clarify their persuasive purpose by defining the point of disagreement. Every thesis conveys the notion that something or someone opposes it, argues against it. After all, theses are by definition "arguable propositions." And if you think about it, it is this quality of *opposing* that gives the thesis its significance. For example, the statement about the usefulness of the water buffalo becomes worth discussing in view of the unlikelihood of real usefulness in a creature so awkward and ungainly. The loss of the Pelo-

---

*Terms such as *subordinate clause* are explained in Part Six, the Revision Guide.

ponnesian Wars becomes much more meaningful when we realize how much more highly civilized and intelligent than their opponents the Athenians were considered to be. Even the wonders of a summer of self-knowledge and growth are put into sharper perspective when considered together with the fact that to the rest of the family last summer seemed much like any other.

The "although clause" permits the writer to get a handle on such opposing arguments by phrasing them as a clause subordinate to the thesis statement. For instance, our three sample theses together with their "although clauses" might be worded as:

- *Although* the water buffalo is an ungainly beast, it is remarkably useful to the lives of many peoples of Asia.
- *Despite* the undeniable superiority of the Athenian civilization, the Athenians were foolhardy in their foreign policy and thus lost the Peloponnesian Wars.
- As far as the other members of my family are concerned, nothing special happened last summer—it was a vacation time much like all the others; *but* to me last summer was truly significant. For the first time, I got a glimmering of real knowledge about myself and I began the slow process of growing up.

In each of these cases, the addition of an "although clause" serves not only to sharpen the point of contention, but also to clarify the issues upon which the argument will depend.

Useful Facts about the "Although Clause"

- It need not contain the word "although."
- There is not, ordinarily, a single correct "although clause" for any given proposition. Usually you have a number of appropriate opposing perspectives from which to choose.
- As useful as the "although clause" part of the thesis is in constructing an essay, it need not appear in the finished composition. (In fact, though it is exceedingly useful to phrase your thesis exactly during the early stages of writing, you may decide that the thesis should not appear in the finished composition phrased in the original words of the working thesis.)

Step 4. Evaluate Your Thesis.
TESTS: • Is this proposition worth proving?
        • Do I have (or can I get) enough "evidence" to develop this thesis?

Formulating a potential "although clause" for a thesis you are considering can also be a useful way of evaluating whether the thesis proposition itself is worth writing about. Self-evident or clichéd theses do not make good compositions. Although a thesis certainly need not be blatantly controversial, a less-than-exciting composition will result from an attempt to argue that "Grass is green" when no one has ever proposed otherwise. Since you could not truthfully claim concerning the greenness of grass that "Despite its appearance to the contrary . . ." or that "Although noted authorities suggest differently . . ." or even that

"There is substantial reason for believing otherwise, but . . . ," the value of "Grass is green" as a thesis is, to say the least, questionable. Testing out your thesis in this way can save you from spending your time and energy working with an inherently uninteresting thesis. On the other hand, you should exercise some care not to discard a good thesis too quickly on these grounds. For the most exciting implicit opposition argument of all is "No one has ever pointed it out before, but . . . ."

You will also want to examine your potential thesis to see whether enough material is available to you to support it properly. There are many well-worded theses that would not make good compositions because they make an assertion about which little can be said. For example, "My roommate tosses our books on the floor" is an arguable statement; but after mentioning the dog-eared Calculus, the much underlined Western Civ text, and the brand new Rhetoric that litter the floor of the room, there is really little else left to say. Some statements, such as "The ptitze mold is a little-known organism," are self-limiting. For though they might serve well as an introductory remark or as a way of arousing interest, such statements cannot be illustrated and thus have little value as theses. Again, if you know nothing about ptitze mold and no information about it is accessible to you, the thesis "Ptitze mold is an interesting species" cannot yield you an adequate composition. By the same token, a statement such as "Grass is not green," though much more interesting than its opposite, must be discarded if, after investigation or serious thought, it turns out to be false.

There is an added dividend to evaluating a thesis in terms of possible support. At the same time you think through possible evidence to see if you have enough material to make your thesis worth pursuing, you also take the preliminary steps toward the lines of reasoning that you will use to develop and support your thesis.

Try It Out

1. The preceding section suggests four steps to help you find your thesis and word it in a useful way. Choose three of the following topics and take them through Steps 1, 2, and 3.

Peace with the Russians	Fraternities and Sororities
Elephants	Pizza
Women's Liberation	Crime in the Streets
Nuclear Power Plants	Vegetarianism
Digital Watches	The Great Wall of China
College Athletics	Computer Banking
Circuses	Capital Punishment

2. Evaluate the theses you have created by using both of the tests suggested in Step 4.

Reasoning from Informational Items to Thesis

The four steps suggested in the previous section are helpful in formulating your thesis statement if you have a general idea of what your thesis is going to be about, or after you come to that idea. But more often than not, when you set out to write, you may have only the most superficial notion of what you want to say. And if you attempt to formulate your thesis at this stage in your thinking, you may well end up with the most superficial of essays. Under these conditions, in order to discover your thesis you will need to explore your topic inductively—that is, by assembling all the ideas you can on the subject and drawing your thesis from this list of particulars.

Inventory of ideas.   Specifically, what you will need to do is to gather information on the subject and make an inventory of your ideas. You can gather the information by doing research of all kinds—by observing the world about you, by talking to people, by experimenting, by reading—or by summoning the information up from your own memory. When your subject takes you to outside resources, as it will in writing a research paper (see Chapter 9), then your inventory of ideas will probably be stored on note cards. When your ideas come mainly from your own thoughts, you can place them before yourself mentally or, better yet, jot them down in writing. However you assemble your inventory, you will need to play with the ideas: divide, stack, and restack the cards; draw lines between the ideas on the paper. Consider each notion or fact individually and relate them to each other. To do so, you will want to look for points of relationship. Which items are parallel or alike? Which items can be subordinated—that is, literally ordered or organized under others? You can form categories, eliminating some topics, adding others, until a pattern begins to emerge. At this point, since structure and thesis are so closely related, the emerging pattern will either suggest an organization that will in turn suggest a thesis or it will suggest a thesis from which you can derive an organization. Often as the pattern emerges and the thesis begins to shape itself, you will experience, with a sort of mental click, a sense that it is going to work out, that this particular combination will enable you to say something worth saying, something you would really like to say.

Example   Let me show you how one freshman class as a group made an inventory of their ideas and how they developed their thesis from it. They decided to work on the topic of "George Washington," which—though most did not consider it a particularly inspiring topic—did have the advantage of being one of the few subjects on which they shared a common knowledge. In pooling this knowledge, they assembled the list of items shown in Figure 1.

This class's inventory of ideas is as miscellaneous a collection as you would be likely to find; and yet, in its diversity, it is rather typical of the mixture of ideas in writers' minds as they start to compose. From just such miscellaneous collections come highly unified, logically structured compositions. First, however, the writer must discover the relationships among the diverse ideas. I'm not sure just what connections you would find among the "George Washington"

• White wig	✳ Mt. Rushmore	✓ Martha
• Wooden teeth	△ Military leader	▲ Farewell Address: strong union strong central govt.
✕ $ across the Potomac	△ Valley Forge	✓ Large plantation—slaves
✓ Surveyor	✕ Chopped cherry tree	✓ Born Feb. 22, 1732
▲ 1st Pres.	△ Crossed Delaware	✳ Birthday = natl. holiday
▲ Father of Country	✳ Washington Monument	▲ Refused crown
✳ Face on $	△ French & Indian War	✓ Kept slaves
• Death = being bled too often	▲ Vice Pres. = Adams	
	✳ Capital named Wash.	

FIGURE 1 Inventory of Ideas with Relationships Marked

ideas (though it might be fun for you to try and see), but this class, having first physically linked the items to one another by lines and symbols, came out with the clusters shown in Figure 2.

✕ cherry tree ✕ $ across Potomac	△ military leader △ French & Indian Wars △ Valley Forge △ Crossed Delaware	✳ U.S. Capital = Wash. ✳ Mt. Rushmore ✳ Wash. Monument ✳ Face on $ ✳ Birthday = holiday
• wig • teeth • bled/death	✓ surveyor ✓ Mt. Rushmore ✓ Martha ✓ Plantation ✓ Feb. 22, 1732 ✓ Slaves	▲ 1st Pres. ▲ Father of Country ▲ Farewell Address ▲ Adams = Vice Pres. ▲ Refused Crown

FIGURE 2 Inventory Grouped by Clusters

As the class worked, discovering parallels and relating items to one another, they began to perceive their clusters as categories, categories that were, in turn, also related (see Figure 3).

Homey Details		Private Life		Military Leader		Political Leader
wig teeth bled/death	←AND→	surveyor Mt. Vernon Martha plantation: slaves Feb. 22, 1732		French & Indian Wars Valley Forge Crossed Delaware	←AND→	1st Pres. Father of Country Farewell Address Refused crown
		Legends		**Monuments**		
		Cherry tree $ across Potomac	←AND→	U.S. Capital = Wash. Mt. Rushmore Wash. Monument Face on $ President's holiday		

FIGURE 3 Inventory Items in Categories

You may be wondering what these categories have to do with a thesis. Actually the connection is quite direct. Because an inventory of ideas contains what a writer knows about or how a writer thinks about a subject, it is the source that supplies the arguments that support the thesis, the material from which the thesis is developed. Writers are not, of course, limited to their original inventory of ideas. And they can (and often must) discard some original inventory items that are not directly relevant to their point as the thesis begins to make itself clear. Nevertheless, a writer's inventory of ideas on a subject is necessarily the raw material from which a composition by that writer on that subject must come. Thus, from the way you as the writer sort out this material, from the way you see the relationships among ideas and facts in your inventory, should emerge what you really want to say about the subject—in short, your thesis.

As for the class which generated the sample inventory of ideas on George Washington, they worked their thesis out in a long and rather heated discussion that produced a whole sequence of suggested theses. Here are the class's different working theses in the order they evolved:

- Washington was a great man.
- Washington was a hero in peace and a hero in war.
- Washington was a hero in the past and a legend in the present.
- Washington was a hero in his day and a legend in ours.
- Although Washington was a human being, even as we are, he was a genuine hero in his day and has become a legend in ours.
- √ Although Washington was not exempt from the flaws of humanity or the evils of his own culture, he became a genuine hero in his own day and a legend in ours.

This method (sometimes called "brainstorming") of taking an inventory of one's ideas and then focusing upon it to discover relationships between ideas takes much concentration and a certain agility of thought. When you learn how to do it well, you can be assured that you can almost always produce a worthwhile thesis and a strong supporting structure. In the next section, you will learn about developing that structure, an integral part of this process. And in Chapter 1 we'll consider some other, more formalized, methods for discovering theses and arguments.

Try It Out

1. Study the following inventory of ideas, relate the items in it to each other, and place them in categories. Consider the categories and try to develop a thesis that could be supported by the facts and ideas listed in them.

The Pilgrims*

Plymouth Rock	went to Holland
1625	children losing heritage
Indian friends	sailed to America
corn	Puritan religion
Mayflower	theocracy
religious freedom	cold winter
starvation	plain dark clothes
illness	strict observance of Sabbath
Mayflower Compact	rough voyage
peace pipe	restricting religious customs
taking Indian land	no celebration of Christmas
turkey	enforced Puritan religion on all
first Thanksgiving	stocks
fled England	punished by restricting food
religious persecution	unbelievers banished

2. Brainstorm one of the following topics and make your own inventory of ideas about it. Follow through to the thesis stage. Evaluate your thesis by the criteria suggested in Step 4 on page 8.

Daytime TV	Hijacking	ESP
Pornography	Blind Dates	Chinese Food

Structuring from the Thesis

However you discover your thesis, it is important to word it carefully—even if you never phrase it exactly this way in your paper. Try out two or three versions and see which one expresses your thought most precisely. Perhaps even more important, see which version will best help you design the structure of your paper. Since your thesis contains the essence of what you want to say, everything else in your paper must go to develop it or support it in some manner. Your thesis is what all parts of the composition depend upon and are subordinated to. We can conceive of the composition almost as an equation where the various parts combine to yield the thesis:

Part I + Part II + Part III + Part IV + · · · → THESIS

Thus the very wording of the thesis can provide you with the basis for your organizational plan.

Chapter 1 offers solid reasons why you will probably want to develop some

---

*This inventory of ideas, like that on George Washington, was suggested by the members of a composition class. After you have finished the exercise, if you would like to compare your thesis with those worked out by this class, turn to the end of Part One.

sort of written plan (or outline) for each composition. But for now when you are concentrating on your first essay, let me suggest only that a written plan, a shorthand way to designate organization, gives you a method of viewing the entire structure of the essay. It gives you a chance to think through your organization ahead of time, without taking away any of your freedom to make changes later in the writing process.

Making a working outline.

A plan of this sort is thus an indispensable tool for writing. How do you produce such a plan? You already know that the thesis wording itself can provide the major clues. It is possible literally to divide the thesis into its components and use the component ideas as your major topics. Briefly, you should:

1. Examine the language of your thesis carefully, and analyze its meaning.
2. Select the key words and phrases that point to the ideas in the thesis that will need support. Where the "although clause" is significant, find its key words too.
3. Find that support—in your inventory of ideas or, if necessary, beyond.
4. Subordinate the support under the appropriate idea. (The art of organizing is the art of subordinating.)

To see how this process would work in practice, let's try it out on the "George Washington" thesis that the class finally agreed upon:

Although Washington was not exempt from the flaws of humanity or the evils of his own culture, he became a genuine hero in his own day and a legend in ours.

1. Analysis: What exactly does this thesis commit its writer to prove?
   a. That Washington is justly considered a hero. (Subordinately: That Washington was also all too human.)
   b. To offer some explanation why.
2. What key words and phrases will need support?
   a. In the thesis itself:
      That W. was a hero in his time.
      That W. is a legend in our time.
   b. In the "although clause" where significant (as it clearly is here):
      That W. had human flaws.
      That W. reflected cultural evils.
3. The evidence to support these ideas. See the inventory of ideas categorized on page 11.
4. The support placed under the appropriate phrases (ideas).
   a. [Although] Washington was a fallible human mortal
      • He had human flaws
         ✓ subject to vanity: powdered wig
         ✓ subject to mortality: wooden false teeth
                                  death by overbleeding
      • He participated in cultural evils
         ✓ kept slaves
   b. [Still] Washington was heroic in his day

- He was a superb military leader
  - ⌣ in the French & Indian Wars
  - ⌣ at Valley Forge
  - ⌣ at the Delaware
- He was also an exceptional political leader
  - ⌣ father of his country
  - ⌣ first president
  - ⌣ wise adviser in his Farewell Address
  - ⌣ especially noble when he refused the crown

c. [Furthermore] Washington has become a legend in our day
- Glorified in cautionary tales
  - ⌣ for his honesty: the cherry tree
  - ⌣ for strength & skill: dollar across Potomac
- Memorialized in monuments
  - ⌣ in the name of U.S. capital
  - ⌣ with a holiday birthday
  - ⌣ on dollar bill
  - ⌣ with Mt. Rushmore
  - ⌣ with Washington Monument

d. Why? Washington is truly heroic because of a special quality: [Figure out for concluding portion—something about turning down the crown?]

Some sort of planning of this kind is essential. How extensive and how structured the planning needs to be depends upon the individual. Some people do best when they write it all out as fully as in our example. Others seem to need little written notation except when preparing very lengthy work. But the sort of plan I'm talking about should be written for use, not just for show. You should, therefore, experiment to find out what plan works best for you. As for me, if I were going to do the Washington paper, I would prepare the following brief plan to guide me along:

Thesis: Although W. was not exempt from the flaws of humanity or the evils of his own culture, he became a genuine hero in his own day and a legend in ours.

  I. Introduction
 II. W. as fallible human being
    A. Flaws & mortality
    B. Evils of his culture
III. But W. now a legend
    A. Tales
    B. Monuments
IV. Deservedly so: W. genuinely heroic
    A. Militarily
    B. Politically
 V. Conclusion: A special quality: Would not be king.

Did you notice that I reversed points III and IV? One of the greatest advantages in constructing a written plan is the flexibility it offers you. Like a blueprint, it gives you the opportunity to make your large structural mistakes in the plan, where they are easily corrected, rather than on the actual project, where change is achieved with much more difficulty.

Building your paper's structure from its thesis is a complex process. Perhaps additional examples would be helpful:

Thesis: Although the water buffalo is an ungainly beast, it is remarkably useful to the lives of many people of Asia.

1. Introduction: Description of ungainliness of w.b., leading to a statement of thesis.
2. Usefulness of w.b. as a source of food
3. Usefulness of w.b. as a beast of burden
4. Usefulness of w.b. as a source of power
5. Conclusion: Underrated animal, whose worth should be taken into account in plans for the region.

Thesis: Despite the undeniable superiority of the Athenian civilization, the Athenians were foolhardy in their foreign policy and thus lost the Peloponnesian Wars.

I. Introduction (poses the paradox)
II. Superiority of Athenian civilization
   A. Spartan culture
     1. Arts
     2. Philosophy
     3. Government   or
   B. Athenian culture   alternatively
     1. Arts
     2. Philosophy
     3. Government

   A. Arts
     1. Sparta
     2. Athens
   B. Philosophy
     1. Sparta
     2. Athens
   C. Government
     1. Sparta
     2. Athens

III. Foolishness of Athenian foreign policy
   A. Example
   B. Example
   C. Example
   D. Example
IV. Loss of Peloponnesian Wars
   A. Chronological account
   B. Evaluation (emphasizing point in III as the cause)
V. Conclusion (generalization)

There are a number of additional techniques for handling the specifics of organizing, as you will learn in the next chapter, but for now you might find helpful the accompanying boxed section called "Guidelines for Structure."

Guidelines for Structure

1. *Make your plan brief so that your mind can comprehend it as a whole.* Since the human mind reaches its outer limits for easy comprehension and memory with five or six items, you'll need to subordinate and coordinate ideas to keep within these limits.

- Restrict yourself to four to seven major headings (including the introduction and the conclusion).
- Restrict the subheadings as well. Resubdivide if a sequence becomes longer than five or six.

Remember: Your readers must be able to keep the plan in their heads too.

2. *Keep the plan (and thus the composition it will produce) unified and pointed toward its thesis.* Think of an organizational plan as a pie, for instance. The whole pie = the thesis. Divide it and all pieces are still part of the whole pie. Just as a slice of apple pie can be nothing but apple and a slice of cherry always remains cherry, so every part of a composition (and of the plan that shows its organization) is committed to explaining or supporting its point, its thesis.

The analogy can also be carried from the whole pie to its slices. Divide one of the slices into smaller portions and these small segments go to make up the larger piece just as the larger pieces go to make up the whole.

- Make sure, therefore, that all subpoints go to support or develop their points, and that all major points go to support and develop the thesis.

3. *Arrange your points (and subpoints) in the way that will most effectively support your thesis.*
- Deal with the "although clause" first—that is, clear the opposition arguments out of the way so that by the conclusion your point of view indisputably prevails.
- Arrange all items in a well thought out, logically defensible order.

4. *For a more tightly logical structure in the final composition, try wording your plan in phrases that are parallel in form.* For example, you might want to subdivide the point about Washington being genuinely heroic:

		BUT NOT
W. = Hero	W. = Hero	W̶.̶ ̶=̶ ̶H̶e̶r̶o̶
a. militarily	a. as a military leader	a̶.̶ ̶m̶i̶l̶i̶t̶a̶r̶i̶l̶y̶
b. politically	b. as a political leader	b̶.̶ ̶a̶s̶ ̶a̶ ̶p̶o̶l̶i̶t̶i̶c̶a̶l̶ ̶l̶e̶a̶d̶e̶r̶

Because of some oddity in the way our minds work, your finished composition will probably turn out to be less tightly constructed if you mix the terms in the plan.

Try It Out

1. Derive organizational plans (outlines) from the following theses:
   a. Although capital punishment has been proved to exert no deterrent effect upon crime, it should not be abolished because it serves some important economic and psychological needs of society.
   b. Despite the fact that capital punishment is still overwhelmingly popular in a country ideally run by the wishes of the majority, it should nevertheless be abolished because it serves no useful purpose and is inherently uncivilized.

2. Write two theses based on the following topics, and derive organizational plans from them. You may use the theses you created for the "Try it Out" exercises on page 13 if you wish.

Pilgrims   Modern Architecture
The Sixties   Blind Dates
Daytime TV   ESP
Pornography   Chinese Food
Hijacking   Little League Athletics

Establishing a Relationship with Your Readers

When you have discovered what you want to say and have found the material you will need to support or develop it, when you have formulated your thesis and have structured an effective organization around it, you still have one more important point to think about before you actually begin to write your essay. You will still have to consider your relationship to your reader.

A good way to think of writing is as a three-way relationship between writer, thesis, and reader, a relationship in which the *writer* tries to express ideas in such a way that *readers* are persuaded to accept the writer's view of the subject, the *thesis.*

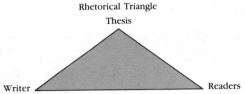

Rhetorical Triangle
Thesis
Writer   Readers

Your readers, then, are the people you will need to convince. And it is to them, to actual human beings, that you will direct your words. Exactly who are these readers? Sometimes they are very specific people. For example, if you have been asked to investigate an area of your company's operations and report back on your research, you will be writing for a particular group of individuals in the management of your company. Since you may know these people personally, you will be able to direct your message to fit both their interests and what you suspect their reactions might be.

Sometimes you will be writing to a specific group of people who share some important characteristics. Wayne Booth, for example, in "The Rhetorical Stance" (see p. 452), addresses an audience of English teachers and thus tailors his remarks to fit their special perspective. At present, I am writing to you and other college composition students. Though I may not know you personally, as I write I think about other students I know and thus try to speak to you (and them) in a natural way and try to address the ideas that you (and they) might be interested in learning about. Your instructors may sometimes assign a paper to be addressed to a particular audience, and then you will have to assess the special needs or personality of this audience and try to aim your writing to fit them.

Far more frequently, however, you will be writing for a less specific group of readers. Like all the authors whose work appears in Part Five (except Booth), you will be directing your writing toward a general audience of educated people, an audience like the readership of the newspapers and magazines for which most of our authors write, an audience of people, in short, much like yourself. Each of these readers is filled with the same sort of thoughts and emotions, the same quirks and eccentricities, the same capacity to be pleased—and to be irritated—that we all possess. Thus, to know yourself and your colleagues is to know your readers. Chapters 1, 4, and 8 detail specific techniques that authors have found helpful for reaching and convincing their readers.

Finding Your "Voice" as a Writer

We have not yet considered the third point in the rhetorical triangle: you the writer—perhaps the most significant part of the communication cycle. The assessment of Lou Kelly, writer and master teacher, is only a trifle exaggerated when she contends: "The content of composition *is* the writer—as he reveals himself, thoughtfully and feelingly in his own language, with his own voice." No subject can speak for itself. All content matter—scientific, historical, intellectual, as well as personal—of necessity is conveyed to the reader in the form of some sort of voice. That voice can be engaging or dull—or even the mechanical speech of a computer. Its tone can help readers along in their interpretation or understanding of the content or it can get in the way of their comprehension. Although readers are not always consciously aware of the writer's voice, it is always there in one form or another, influencing their attitude in a significant way, either openly or subliminally.

Try It Out

1. Look carefully at the opening paragraphs of Lewis Thomas's "Germs" (p. 461), J. H. Plumb's "De Mortuis" (p. 466), Ellen Goodman's "The Cult of Impotence" (p. 470), and Alan S. Katz's "The Use of Drugs in America" (p. 472). All of these essays are on scientific or sociohistoric matters, yet a distinctly personal voice speaks to its readers from each of them. As you read, consciously listen to the author's voice speaking to you through the written work.

   In a few well-chosen adjectives or brief descriptive phrases, try to characterize each of the authors' voices speaking through these samples and see if you can distinguish them from one another. Do you think, for instance, that a particular author reveals himself or herself to be

> compassionate? arrogant? intelligent? curious? knowledgeable? con-
> fused? authoritative? disagreeable? humble? angry? cynical? skeptical?
> foolish? well-educated?

Using the Appropriate Voice

All writing is conveyed through a particular voice and that voice influences the communication of the message it carries to the reader. How are you to make sure that the voice your writing projects carries the conviction you want it to have? The answer is twofold: (1) by making sure that your writing expresses YOUR OWN VOICE and (2) by using that voice of your own that is most appropriate to your approach to your subject and to the occasion.

Your writing should sound like you. It should not sound like an imitation of someone else, because the tones will not ring true. Your ideas will also lose their credibility if you clothe them in an artificial phraseology or express them in vocabulary inspired by Mr. Roget's thesaurus rather than your own experience. Nor should you attempt to abstract yourself from your writing so all that remains is that depersonalized, mechanical, often convoluted prose which is rarely seen anywhere but the classroom, the sort of writing English professor Ken Macrorie, having read hundreds of student compositions, has dubbed "Engfish." Your writing voice should instead incorporate those qualities you most like about yourself. Writing is, after all, a conversation with a reader held under ideal conditions: in writing you can always go back and clarify, go back and make amends, go back and insert that clever retort you never remember until the encounter is long over.

Your writing should also reflect the voice of yours that is most appropriate to your subject and to your audience. You may not often think of yourself as having more than one voice, but a moment's reflection should convince you that you instinctively speak quite differently when you're out with your friends than you do when you are applying for a job.

Professional authors speak in various voices, too. Two articles by George Will, for example, are included in Part Five, both typical examples of his work. And yet the voices behind the two essays are very different indeed. The voice in "The Chicago Cubs, Overdue" speaks in a playful, semi-ironic tone and addresses the reader in an almost intimate way:

> A reader demands to know how I contracted the infectious conservatism for which he plans to horsewhip me. So if you have tears, gentle reader, prepare to shed them now as I reveal how my gloomy temperament received its conservative warp from early and prolonged exposure to the Chicago Cubs. (p. 449)

By contrast, there is a hard, almost angry realism in Will's voice as he begins "Israel and Munich":

> Various Jewish religious observances commemorate calamities or narrow deliverance from calamities, and the short history of the Jewish state is replete with

such experiences. Today, friction between Israel and the Carter administration is building up a dangerous charge of static electricity. No Israeli government casually risks the U.S. government's displeasure: diminished support for Israel could lead to a calamity from which there would be no deliverance. But the contagious crossness between Washington and Jerusalem that originated in Washington is a compound of Washington impatience and Israeli anxiety. The anxiety is more reasonable than the impatience. (p. 446)

The essential point of difference between the voices talking to us from the two Will passages is "distance." In the first essay, Will seems to be very close to the reader. The tone is informal, and Will uses the first person "I" and the second person "you" in a familiar, conversational way. The distance between author and reader is far greater in the second essay. The I/you relationship is kept beneath the surface, providing a more objective tone. What Will writes is presented not as a matter of personal idiosyncrasy nor even as the individual opinion that an "I believe" or an "I should think" would suggest, but rather as a matter of soon-to-be-demonstrated fact: "The anxiety is more reasonable than the impatience." And despite such typical examples of Will's pertinent and witty diction as "contagious crossness," the tone of his voice in the second instance is far more formal than in the first, as befits its more serious subject.

Like Will, you too can employ widely varying voices. But how will you know what voice to use and how to use it? Fortunately, you already know very well. Without even thinking about it, you naturally adopt the tone, vocabulary, and syntax appropriate to the occasion—whether it is an outing with Grandma or an evening of romance. Though most of your ability in this respect is instinctive, you can learn to be more aware of this ability and thus become better able to manage it as you wish. The following tips for managing your written voice may be helpful:

1. Make sure that the voice that speaks from your composition is your own and that it represents your best self—that self you would most like others to know.
2. Determine the degree of distance you want to place between yourself and your reader and maintain that distance consistently.
3. If you have decided to write subjectively or informally or if the subject matter concerns your own life or opinions, feel free to speak in the first person. Much use of passive constructions and other sorts of unnecessarily complicated syntax results from writers struggling to avoid the natural use of "I." (You may have noticed that most of the writers of the essays in this text use "I" or "we" quite comfortably.) On the other hand, some uses of the first person can lead to pitfalls of which you should be aware. Therefore, a word of caution about:
   a. *Overuse of the pronoun.* Just as in conversation, beginning each sentence with an "I" or ending every phrase with a "me" tends to imply an unattractive self-centeredness.
   b. *Overqualifying your conclusions.* Adding an "I think" or an "I be-

When to use "I."

lieve" to your statements does not really identify the statement as your opinion. (The simple fact of your authorship does that.) Frequent use of these phrases, rather, introduces a hesitancy or a tentativeness to your writing. If such hesitancy (or the becoming modesty that this hesitancy sometimes implies) is your aim, well and good; but you must also realize that in creating such a tone, you lose a degree of persuasiveness from your statements.

c. *Forcing a personal thesis.* Ordinarily, a more interesting paper centers around a thesis formed from a generalization than from a first-person statement. The general thesis—backed by personal anecdotes when appropriate—offers a general rather than simply a personal appeal. "College breeds a sense of responsibility" would make a better thesis, for instance, than "I became a more responsible person when I came to college."

When to use "you."

4. Reserve the pronoun "you" only for those occasions when you want to address your readers directly. Using the "you" is appropriate in a "how to" work (such as this book) or when you have decided upon a very close distance to your reader or an unusually informal tone (as Will does so effectively in his Chicago Cubs essay). But for most expository writing, you would probably be wise to avoid the use of the second-person pronoun. "You" meaning "one" or an indefinite subject as, for example, in "Whenever you want to go out, it rains," is ordinarily incorrect in writing. Therefore—except in the most informal of essays—write "you" only when you truly mean "you, my reader."

5. Avoid slang and nonstandard dialect except when you have decided upon complete informality. Remember that writing is of itself more formal than speaking.

6. If you have any problem deciding upon the appropriate voice for your composition, you cannot really go wrong in using what used to be called "The Middle Style," the style that is neither "High" (formal, consciously eloquent) or "Low" (colloquial, slangy). The Middle Style has a conversational quality, but lacks the colloquialisms and carelessness of wording and sentence structure appropriate only to speech. It might be compared to the way you would talk to a group of friendly adults that you still do not know very well.

Try It Out

1. In how many of the essays included in Part Five do the authors use "I" and "me"? In how many do they use "we"? In how many, "you"?

2. Single out two specific uses of "I," one of "we," and one of "you" for analysis. What is the effect of this use of the personal pronoun upon the tone of the sentence or paragraph within which it occurs? Upon the author's voice in the article as a whole and the way that voice relates to the reader?

3. Try varying your voice by writing two brief paragraphs on the same subject. In both paragraphs discuss either "Dormitory Life" or "The First Days of the Freshman Year." But write one for private distribution to next year's students and the other for inclusion in the *Official Freshman Handbook.*

WHEN YOU WRITE
Beginning to Write

How should you begin to write an essay? The answer is "very quickly"! And that answer is more than a joke. For if you are like most of us, once you have written something on the page, almost anything at all, the "blank page jitters" begin to subside. Where should you start? There are differences of opinion on this point, but the wisest judgment holds that, for most people, it is best to begin at the beginning, that is, with the introduction. Ignoring for the moment the fact that you are free to change or erase anything you write, you should realize that with everything you say in your essay, you make a commitment to your reader—a commitment to follow up the statement, to explain, to support its premises. For this reason, it is usually wiser to write sequentially, to begin by writing your introduction.

But what should an introduction contain? What is it supposed to do? To discover the answer, let's look at the introductions to essays written by professional authors. The following excerpts, for instance, are introductions from some of the essays included in Part Five.

> The most obvious differences between different animals are differences of size, but for some reason the zoologists have paid singularly little attention to them. In the large textbook of zoology before me I find no indication that the eagle is larger than the sparrow, or the hippopotamus bigger than the hare, though some grudging admissions are made in the case of the mouse and the whale. But yet it is easy to show that a hare could not be as large as a hippopotamus, or a whale as small as a herring. For every type of animal there is a most convenient size, and a large change in size inevitably carries with it a change in form.   (J. B. S. Haldane, "On Being the Right Size," p. 480)

> Sometime after the Enlightenment, science and religion came to a gentleman's agreement. Science was for the real world: machines, manufactured things, medicines, guns, moon rockets. Religion was for everything else, the immeasurable: morals, sacraments, poetry, insanity, death, and some residual forms of politics and statesmanship. Religion became, in both senses of the word, immaterial. Science and religion were apples and oranges. So the pact said: render unto apples the things that are Caesar's, and unto oranges the things that are God's. Just as the Maya kept two calendars, one profane and one priestly, so Western science and religion fell into two different conceptions of the universe, two different vocabularies.

> This hostile distinction between religion and science has softened in the

last third of the 20th century. Both religion and science have become self-consciously aware of their excesses, even of their capacity for evil. Now they find themselves jostled into a strange metaphysical intimacy. Perhaps the most extraordinary sign of that intimacy is what appears to be an agreement between religion and science about certain facts concerning the creation of the universe. It is the equivalent of the Montagues and Capulets collaborating on a baby shower. (Lance Morrow, "In the Beginning: God and Science," p. 485)

Outside the great conference hall in Nairobi, 16 fountains sent up sparkling plumes of water, and black Mercedes limousines glistened in the bright East African sun. Inside, some 1,500 delegates from 110 nations sat in air-conditioned comfort. The splendid setting of the meeting could hardly have clashed more jarringly with its pupose. At the U.N.'s invitation, the representatives had gathered in the Kenyan capital last week to discuss and devise ways of containing what an increasing number of experts regard as a major environmental danger: the creeping, seemingly relentless spread of the earth's deserts. (Fred Golden, "Earth's Creeping Deserts," p. 432)

If we assume these examples are fairly typical, what can we say about introductions? Even on the basis of this limited sample, we can at least rule out a couple of deep-rooted bits of folklore about introductions:

- Clearly, an introduction is NOT always a single paragraph.
- The thesis is NOT always (or even usually) the first sentence in a composition.

We might even hazard some generalizations:

- Introductions (usually) contain a statement of thesis. In the examples:

  "For every type of animal there is a most convenient size, and a large change in size inevitably carries with it a change in form."

  "Religion and science . . . [now] find themselves jostled into a strange metaphysical intimacy [in their] . . . agreement . . . about certain facts concerning the creation of the universe."

  "The creeping, seemingly relentless spread of the earth's deserts . . . [is] a major environmental danger."

- Statements of thesis usually come at or toward the end of an introduction (with any material following the thesis merely restating or amplifying it).
- Introductions do not contain arguments or other kinds of support for the main point of the thesis.

From these introductions (and others you might want to take a look at), we can formulate some idea of the purpose of an introduction:

The purpose of the introduction to an expository work is to lead to a statement of its thesis (or at least to approach its central idea) in such a way that readers will want to continue reading.

How do writers manage to accomplish this purpose? Let me answer in terms of the three samples: Haldane tries to interest his readers in his thesis and at the same time leads to his statement of it by showing that not enough attention has yet been paid to it. Morrow points out that until relatively recently the opposite of his thesis has been the case. And Golden attempts to arouse interest in his little-known problem by demonstrating its current importance through his description of an international meeting recently held on the subject.

Each of these authors seems to have considered what interested him about the subject or what about the subject seems to make it relevant right now. Most striking perhaps is the fact that two of the three sample introductions appear to be a development of the "although clause" of their theses. The "although clause" to Haldane's thesis is surely that "Although zoologists have paid singularly little attention to size differences . . .," an idea that is amplified throughout the rest of the introductory paragraph up to the statement of the thesis. Similarly, Morrow's first paragraph is concerned with developing the "although clause" of his thesis: "[Although] science and religion [once] were apples and oranges" (that is, "hostile[ly] distinct"). Introductory use of "although clauses" is commonplace in professional writing, as a glance at the introductions of the other essays in Part Five readily confirms. And this use should not surprise us too much. After all, the reason behind much expository writing is the desire to refute a contrary opinion. There seems to be a natural tendency to want to begin an explanation at the point where the writer's mind first takes hold.

How can you follow in the footsteps of such professional writers? You can begin by searching for the same sort of reasons for reader interest concerning your own thesis. Then, by composing your introduction to lead from these reasons to the statement of your thesis, you will draw your reader into the ideas of the essay. You might, for instance, ask yourself such questions as these to get started:

1. What idea or event got me interested in this topic to start with? Might it not also be of interest to my readers?
2. What about my topic or my approach to my topic is relevant to readers at this time? Does my topic relate in some way to a subject of particular interest right now? (For example, to the women's movement? the election campaign? the coming of summer?)
3. Would expansion of the "although clause" of my thesis make an interesting introduction?

Once you have decided upon the approach to your subject that might most intrigue your reader, compose your introduction so that it leads quickly from the presentation of the ideas to the statement of your thesis.

Try It Out

1. Consider the introductions of four essays *other* than the three by Haldane, Morrow, and Golden sampled in the previous section and answer these questions about them:
   a. Do any of your samples state the thesis in the opening sentence? If so, which?

b. How many paragraphs long is each of your sample introductions?

c. Is there a statement of thesis in each of your samples? If not, which?

d. Exactly where does each statement of thesis occur? What is the nature of any material following it?

e. Can any of your sample introductions be considered expansions of the "although clauses" of their theses? Which ones?

2. Work out a suitable introduction for a thesis developed from one of the following topics. You may use a thesis you wrote for an earlier "Try It Out" exercise if you wish.

The Seventies	Hijacking	Chinese Food
Daytime TV	Blind Dates	Little League Athletics
Pornography	ESP	The Woman's Role
Pilgrims	Modern Architecture	

Writing the Body of Your Essay

Your introduction will interest readers in your subject and pave their way to your thesis. In the body of your paper, your task will be to develop and support that thesis. If you have thoughtfully carried out your prewriting procedures, the actual writing of your paper should not be too troublesome. After all, you will have already thought through the kinds of ideas you will use to support your thesis, and you will have already mapped out a logical way to organize that support. Your written plan or outline can be invaluable help to you. In fact, you could almost think about the actual writing of your paper as a process of fleshing out your outline, giving substance and body to your plan.

Though your plan can be a most useful guide to rely upon, it is neither sacred nor unchangeable. Despite the good thinking that went into formulating it, you have not carved it in stone. An outline chiseled in granite would certainly be a millstone about your neck, holding you back from making needed changes. So, as you write and have the opportunity to explore your ideas more fully, keep your mind open to any other thoughts that may come to you, adjusting your plan to accommodate changes in your thinking. At the same time, do guard yourself against writing about things only indirectly related to what you really mean to say. Remember that any new plan you come up with should be at least as logical and reasonable as the old.

Topic Sentences   Exactly how do you use your plan (or outline) to write the body of your essay? You take the thesis-supporting ideas, briefly noted as the points (and perhaps the subpoints) of your plan, and build them into the paragraphs or paragraph clusters that will make up the body of your paper. In fact, you will probably want to derive the topic sentences of these paragraphs from the ideas set forth in the points or subpoints of your plan.

The topic sentence of a paragraph, like the thesis of a composition, is that statement of the idea which all the rest of the sentences of that paragraph explain, support, or define.

Sometimes the topic idea is not completely spelled out in the topic sentence and sometimes it does not fill the entire sentence, but whether hinted indirectly or stated in full, the topic idea awakens the reader's expectations of what is to follow. Thus, if you are to guide your reader with understanding through the development of what you want to say, each of your paragraphs (or paragraph clusters) should have a topic sentence at or near its beginning, a topic sentence that should be followed by other sentences that either redefine or develop its point.

You may be surprised at my recommending topic sentences so unhesitatingly, for if you have ever come across the rule that "Every paragraph must be headed by a topic sentence," you may well have dismissed it as just another bit of folklore. But the truth is that, unlike other such dogmatic statements, this rule usually turns out to be valid. Research into the writing of professional authors has demonstrated that these authors control the direction of their writing by topic sentences at or near the start of most paragraphs or at the beginning of most content-linked paragraph clusters. (For a fuller discussion, see Chapter 3's section on "Supporting Your Point.")

The fact that professional writers regularly employ topic sentences should not surprise us because such sentences are remarkably useful to both writer and reader. We comprehend what we read mostly through our processing of a series of clues. Topic sentences provide perhaps the most important of these clues, for they alert us to what will immediately follow. When we read a sentence, we subconsciously expect the next one to amplify, explain, or illustrate it. When we read the beginning sentences of a paragraph, we look for their explanation and support in the rest.

Concrete Support Support for topic sentences is also important. The persuasive power of an essay in large measure lies in the strength of its supporting material. Sometimes, however, beginning writers fail to appreciate this fact. Having made their point and rephrased it to their satisfaction, they often feel ready to get on to the next order of business without realizing that their readers may be left unconvinced and dissatisfied. But *all* good writing must "show" as well as "tell." A topic sentence such as "Capital punishment does not act as a deterrent" clearly needs, for example, to be documented with such evidence as statistical studies, quotations from court transcripts, or criminal case histories. But it is no less urgent to back up less argumentative topic or sub-topic sentences such as "My brother keeps a messy room." Yes, Brother's room is messy, the reader might concede, but what is messy about it? In what specific way is it untidy? It is your job as writer to supply the answers—to explain and describe, to give examples and illustrations. You might, for instance, use anecdotes or bits of conversation:

> Ever since the day the frog jumped out at her, my mother avoids his room altogether. She claims she is afraid to go in.

Or you might support your statement with specific sensory details:

> Tossed on top of the rumpled sheets and blankets on Brother's unmade bed, and weighing down the limp heap of yesterday's soiled clothing, were a spelling notebook, a Snoopy-bedecked lunch pail, two nearly shredded *Mad* magazines, and a gym shoe with a broken lace.

Be careful not to rely too heavily on adjectives and adverbs. "The man was impatient," for instance, is far less effective than such persuasive documentation as:

> The man tapped nervously on the arm of his chair and every forty or fifty seconds glanced at his wristwatch.

When you write the body of your paper, you will write most effectively if you provide your readers with ample concrete and detailed information. Some of the sources for documentation of this sort that you may find most useful include:

Sources for concrete and detailed information.

- Facts
- Statistics
- Anecdotes
- Analogies and comparisons
- Well-reasoned arguments
- Evidence of the five senses (such as the details demonstrating the gentleman's impatience in the earlier example)
- Quotations

The more specific your examples, the more convincing your writing will be. Walter Williams in "Blacks and a Free Market" (p. 491, 7), for instance, makes his strong point about the excluding character of licensing even stronger when he provides his readers with the exact cost of a taxi license: $60,000. Don't hesitate to cite specific names—even when they may be unknown to most of your readers. Judith Crist, for example, in her essay "Gentlemen and Scholars of the Press," is not content just to explain that "Time was, a mere 20 years ago or so . . . when two telephone calls could solve any midnight [newspaper] emergency." She adds the particulars that give the situation reality: "One to Bleeck's downstairs and another to Chumley's in Greenwich village" (p. 494, 5).

You will find a much fuller discussion of these ideas in the section on "Supporting your Point" in Chapter 3.

Try It Out

1. Check to see if the research that showed that professional authors tend to place topic sentences at or near the head of their paragraphs (or paragraph clusters) holds true for the essays in Part Five. Excluding introductory and concluding paragraphs, or those paragraphs that shift

the focus from one topic to another (transitional paragraphs), look for topic sentences in these essays. You might want to begin with the two central paragraphs of E. B. White's "The Distant Music of the Hounds" (p. 498). What are their topic sentences? Shana Alexander's "Getting Old in Kids' Country" (p. 434), having been written originally to fit the narrow columns of *Newsweek,* consists of many very brief paragraphs. Some of these paragraphs, therefore, are likely to be parts of a cluster, controlled by the topic sentence of the lead paragraph of the cluster (usually the one directly above). With this thought in mind, what are the topic sentences of the third, fourth, fifth, sixth, and seventh paragraphs of "Kids' Country"?

2. What sort of concrete evidence do these authors provide to back up the ideas they express in their topic sentences? (You may find the terms listed on p. 28 helpful here.)

   a. In White's second paragraph? In his third?
   b. In Alexander's third? In her fourth?

3. Having considered the function of topic sentences, why do you think so few compositions begin with their thesis sentence?

Concluding Your Paper

The conclusion of a composition has but one purpose: to bring the work to a satisfying end. The reader should be brought to experience a feeling of finality, an understanding of the author's point, and a generally positive—or at least open-minded—attitude toward that point. Sometimes this goal is accomplished within the body of the composition—especially in a very short essay; but more often an author feels the need to conclude more formally in a brief paragraph or two. Although from time to time you may come across compositions that do not have formal conclusions, you'll find that all of the essays included in Part Five do have them. The conclusion is located, after all, in the most influential position in a written work. It is the last thing the reader will read and will probably be the part most readily remembered. It thus should contain the essay's strongest, most persuasive phrasing of the writer's point of view.

How then should you approach the ending of your own paper? I would urge you to finish writing introduction and body . . . and then pause. Clear the cobwebs from your mind, then read back trhough your composition and get a real sense of what you have written. You have worked hard on the paper part by part, and you need an opportunity to get a feeling for your essay as a whole. Read it aloud if you can; savor its rhythms; make the revisions that seem indicated. After taking this pause, an appropriate way to end the work almost always suggests itself. Through this approach, you are able to draw from the essay itself an understanding of what still needs to be said.

Some papers conclude by evaluating or interpreting the arguments or ideas they have presented; others offer the reader constructive suggestion for action or further thought. But the most frequently included element in well-written conclusions is an eloquent statement of thesis. This statement can be even more effective if it echoes the ideas or phraseology of the points supporting the thesis argument throughout the paper. The accompanying material in the rest of the conclusion might also contain such echoes. Through restatement or echoing, the reader not only experiences a more satisfying sense of wholeness and unity, but also receives a subtle reminder of the most persuasive points of the essay and all they had implied.

Thesis and echoes.

Try It Out

1. Read through E. B. White's "The Distant Music of the Hounds" (p. 498) to discover what phrase or phrases in the conclusion are echoes of what has gone before. Which sentence rephrases White's thesis?
2. Does Walter Williams's conclusion to "U.S. Blacks and a Free Market" (p. 490) tend most to evaluate, interpret, or restate the ideas of the essay or does it offer suggestions for further thought?

AFTER YOU WRITE

Reconsidering

Let's assume you have completed the first draft of your paper. If writing were exactly like a conversation, your act of communication would be over. However, because you are writing, you have the added opportunity to make sure that you have said exactly what you want to say and, perhaps even more important, that your reader will understand what you have said exactly as you intended it. If you can possibly arrange it, it is best to let some time elapse between your writing and your revising. The more time the better, because when you next look at your paper, you will be trying to see it not through the eyes of its anxious author but through those of an interested reader. So put it away for a couple of days. Or sleep on it. Or at least munch on a peanut butter sandwich and think about something else. And then very, very carefully read through your paper again.

Chapter 4 offers a thorough discussion of the copy-editing and proofreading skills you will want to develop as you become a more experienced writer. But for your early papers, let the accompanying checklist guide you in revising.

Checklist for Revision

Check for persuasiveness of thesis and structure.
1. Does your overall organization permit your points and ideas to support your

thesis? Could any parts be changed or adjusted to make your point more convincing or more appealing?

2. Is there a logical order behind the arrangement of your points?

3. Does every paragraph (or paragraph cluster) have a topic sentence that contributes to the development of your thesis?

4. Does every sentence contribute to the development of the topic sentence of its paragraph? Or would the ideas expressed in some sentences serve better to support the point of another paragraph? Are the sentences within each paragraph arranged in a logical order?

5. Is there any material in the essay that is, on the whole, irrelevant to the support of your thesis? (Be merciless on this one.)

Check for effectiveness of voice and tone.

1. Is the voice that speaks through the composition truly your own? Are the tone and distance of that voice appropriate to the subject? Are they appropriate to the relationship you want to achieve between yourself and your reader? Does this degree of distance remain consistent throughout the composition? Can any possible inconsistencies be eliminated?

2. Do you put your best foot forward in this composition? Do your most agreeable qualities come through? Do you let your genuine interest in or enthusiasm for the topic show?

Check for mechanics.

1. Have you checked in the dictionary for correct spelling of any word you're unsure about?

2. Have you checked in the Revision Guide (Part Six) any mark of punctuation or any point of grammar you are not certain about?

ASSIGNMENT

Using your personal experience as the basis for your generalizations, write on one of the following suggestions (or on another your instructor may provide). Check the list of steps following these suggestions for a useful approach to the assignment.

1. The transition between high school and college is often a crucial one— at least, it certainly feels that way to most of us at the time. In a well-organized essay, try to define the freshman experience as you are encountering it.

   If you would prefer, choose instead to focus on how it feels to be a member of your particular college or university community.

2. Have you read a book or seen a movie recently that seemed to speak to you in a personal way? In a well-organized essay, carefully describe the fictional action or idea that reached you; tell why it happened to move you in this way, and what came of the experience.

3. Drawing from your own personal experience or that of your friends or relatives, make a statement about the problem of discrimination based upon race or religion or sex or age or ethnic origin.

4. Many students (and a good number of educators as well) object to the sort of education that consists primarily of students repeating back what an instructor has taught. If you are among these critics, write an

essay justifying your objections from your own experience. You might
also want to suggest an alternative educational style.

5. Take as your topic "Fear of Flying" (or "of Driving" or "of Public Speaking" or ??) and, using the methods suggested, develop from it a strong
working thesis. Support your thesis in an interesting and persuasive essay.

6. Develop one of the theses you worked with earlier in this part into a
full composition. Remember to draw on your personal experience.

The steps suggested in this first part of *Writing Effectively* offer one good
approach to writing a composition. Try writing your first paper by working
consciously through the following summary of these steps.

Steps in Writing a Composition

1. Narrow your subject. (See p. 7.)
2. Find the point you are interested in making about your subject by reasoning
either from a general topic (p. 7) or from a group of particulars (p. 10). Phrase
your point as an arguable statement. Include an "although clause" that ac-
knowledges another approach to your thesis (p. 7).
3. Check your statement against the tests suggested on page 8, and if it still
satisfies you, write it down as the working statement of your thesis.
4. Analyze your thesis statement (as suggested on p. 13) to determine exactly
what you will need to demonstrate. Select from your thesis the key words and
phrases that will need to be supported, and compose an organizational plan
based upon these key ideas. Find that needed support (in your inventory of
ideas or elsewhere) and in your written plan subordinate that support under
the appropriate points (see p. 14).
5. Give some thought to the relationship you want to maintain with your reader
in discussing this particular subject and to the voice most appropriate for this
essay to project (see p. 18). Begin to write your essay.
6. Decide upon a meaningful and/or appealing way to introduce your subject (p.
23), and lead into a statement of your thesis toward the end of your introduction.
7. Support your thesis in the body of your paper by composing paragraphs from
the ideas outlined in your organizational plan. Each of your supporting or
amplifying points should be stated clearly in a topic sentence at or near the
head of a paragraph (or paragraph cluster). Be sure to demonstrate and/or
develop each of these points concretely and specifically (p. 26).
8. Read through what you have written. Reconsider and perhaps revise.
9. Draw your conclusion out from what you have already written (p. 29). Your
ending should probably include restatement of your central point.
10. Edit your paper. Revise. Correct. Rewrite.
11. Proofread.

Pilgrim Theses (see p. 13)

The theses the composition class created for the Pilgrim exercise are:

- Although the Pilgrims encountered many hardships, they were able to overcome them because of the strength of their character, a strength rooted in their deep religious faith.
- Although the Pilgrims believed in freedom, especially religious freedom, in America they set up a theocracy and restricted the religious freedom of others.

Part Two

Persuading through Structure

You are about to begin a detailed, step-by-step guide to the writing process. Throughout Part Two you will have the opportunity to experiment with a variety of practical strategies that will help you discover the point you want to make and find ways of supporting it. You will read about other techniques that can help turn ideas on a chosen subject into a well-structured, clearly written essay. Specifically, the four chapters of Part Two will direct you through all the stages of the writing process: the creative thinking and planning of prewriting (Chapters 1 and 2), the strategies and decision making of writing itself (Chapter 3), and the evaluating and revising of the final rewriting stage (Chapter 4).

Underlying all the strategies and techniques to be learned in these chapters is the central notion that you as writer should always be conscious of your readers. You should hear your voice talking to them as you write, and you should constantly keep their needs in mind. This awareness is probably the most significant means to effective writing. To write well is to communicate persuasively. Since no communication can take place in a vacuum, communication necessarily involves getting the ideas of the writer into the mind of the reader. As Wayne Booth points out in "The Rhetorical Stance" (see p. 452), even talented writers cannot write well for some vague disembodied audience. Only when writers fully understand that every composition they write is really a conversation with those who will read it are they able to make their writing come alive and be worth reading.

Throughout the writing process, then, as you make decisions about how to approach your topic and how to arrange your material, what to write and where to revise, train yourself to be aware of your readers as people. Conceive of your purpose for writing each essay in terms of the real human beings who will read your essay and interact with it.

1

Prewriting: Inventing

Let's begin our discussion of the prewriting process with the thesis because here you come face to face with the persuasive purpose of expository writing: Your thesis *is* the central point you want your readers to come to believe.

THE POINT IN HAVING A POINT

The concept of thesis was introduced in Part One, but in order to give an overall view we covered the material so quickly there you may have been left with some questions unanswered. Although thesis is a concept of the greatest importance to the writing process, people sometimes have difficulty accepting all that it implies. Here are some challenges most often raised about it:

- Why must I have a thesis? Why can't I just write about my subject?
- Surely some expository works don't have theses. Very long works must have many theses and very short ones don't really need one.
- Why must a thesis necessarily be phrased as a statement? One sort of wording should be about as good as another.
- Why must a thesis be argumentative?

Perhaps you have been asking some of these questions yourself. In the following sections I will suggest some answers.

Why You Shouldn't Just Write "About" a Subject

Have you ever heard someone tell a story (or describe a movie) and just go on and on? He'll say, "and then. . .and then. . .and then. . .and then. . . ." And you will be thinking, "Come to the point, won't you—just come to the point," all the while wishing for some convenient opening to get away. Readers experience much the same frustration in trying to read an essay that just talks "about" a subject. Our minds cannot assimilate a quantity of unrelated ideas except with great difficulty—and then only by finding some focus that will relate the ideas to one another. As readers, we have a right to expect the writer to discover the focus for us. For this reason, good writers do not decide they would just like to talk about, say, animals. Rather, they select in advance the particular point they want to make about animals and then direct all their attention toward making that point. Imagine for example what J. B. S. Haldane's article (p. 480) would be like if that noted zoologist had decided just to "write about" animals. He could have told all the interesting things he does tell about graceful gazelles, long-legged giraffes, and clumsy land crabs, and yet if he had not focused our attention on his point about the rightness of the size of these animals, we would finish reading the essay and say, "It's nice to know all these facts about animals, but *so what?*"

Why Every Expository Work Has a Thesis

Because of the possibility of every reader's "So what?" all well-written expository works do indeed have theses. There truly is no point in writers writing unless they have a point to make. And this necessity for a thesis is not a factor of length. Essays as brief as one paragraph must have a point—though in the case of single paragraphs, the thesis is usually called a "topic sentence." Even works as long as the multivolumed *The Decline and Fall of the Roman Empire* are organized around a single thesis. Of course, works of any real length must have subtheses too. In *The Decline,* for instance, the basic thesis of the author, Edward Gibbon, is that Rome was brought down by moral decadence, and every word in every volume goes to illustrate this idea. But, in discussing most of the major events of thirteen centuries of Western civilization, Gibbon also develops a number of subordinate theses, including, for example, the well-known idea for which Gibbon was severely criticized: that the rise of Christianity tended toward a negative rather than a positive overall moral effect.

From time to time, you may come across an expository composition that seems to have no single sentence which sums up the point of the whole. Nevertheless, if it is a well-written piece, you will invariably find that there is a single idea that underlies the whole, one around which the entire composition has been organized. In such works, the thoughtful reader has no difficulty identifying the author's point—the implied thesis—nor even in putting it into words.

Why the Thesis Must Be a Statement

It is true that within a finished composition the writer may choose to phrase the thesis in a variety of ways and occasionally may not state it there at all, but only imply it. Nevertheless, if the thesis is to be of any use at all in the composing process, the writer must phrase it as a statement, a proposition to be developed or demonstrated. If a composing writer plans just to "talk about" a topic, the topic can be embodied in a phrase: "animals," "capital punishment," or even "the size of animals" or "the evils of capital punishment." Or it can be posed as a question or semi-question: "How animals differ in size" or "Is capital punishment good or bad?" But if the writer is actually going to say something about the topic, is going to make a point about it, that point needs a statement to express it. It needs, for instance, a statement such as Haldane's about animal size, "For every type of animal there is a most convenient size," or simply "Capital punishment is evil."

Phrased in this way, your central idea becomes a thesis, a proposition that can be supported, developed, argued. Furthermore, you can use such a statement to organize your paper. As we discussed on pages 13–15, in the wording of the thesis itself you can find the clues to the points you will want to make and to the way you will want to develop these points. If you phrase your thesis statement carefully, you may be able to draw from it the organization of your entire composition. Therefore, however you decide to word your thesis in your finished essay, in the prewriting period you need to be very clear about your point in your own mind. In fact, ordinarily you would be wise to write it down, phrased explicitly as a statement, as an arguable proposition.

Why the Thesis Must Be Argumentative

The challenge most often raised about the concept of thesis concerns its argumentative nature. Experts certainly agree that this is its essence:

> Lucille Payne: "The thesis of your essay is your opinion boiled down to one arguable statement."
> Sheridan Baker: "Put an argumentative edge on your subject—and you will have found your thesis."
> Frederick Crews: "Your thesis doesn't have to be openly antagonistic, but it should . . . defend one position against possible alternatives to it."*

Yet even with the opinion of these experts and the concurring summary of the subject in Part One, you may still find it difficult to believe that *all* expository papers must "contain," in Crews's words, "a thread of argument." You may feel that some assignments, such as "Defend or Oppose Capital Punishment" or "Women's Liberation," can be viewed in this way but, candidly, may still not be convinced that Baker's "argumentative edge" must hold true for "Freshman Year at College" or "My Dog Spot." You may think that you are being advised to view all assignments as opposition papers; and you may find the notion frankly preposterous.

In voicing this concern, you are touching upon the crux of the whole thesis matter. Odd as it may seem, I really am suggesting—at least for purposes of argument—that you regard all expository writing in this light. I am asking you to consider *all* expository writing as if it were, in a manner of speaking, persuasive writing, to understand that the downright persuasive paper is just a more blatant example of what all good expository writing actually is.

Rhetoric, the art of persuasion. To demonstrate what rhetoricians actually mean by *persuasive* (and *rhetoric* is most accurately defined as "the art of persuasion"), let's take an example from a mode of writing removed as far as possible from the argumentative. Here

---

*Lucille Payne, *The Lively Art of Writing* (Chicago: Follett, 1965), p. 26; Sheridan Baker, *The Complete Stylist* (New York: Thomas Y. Crowell, 1966), p. 20; Frederick Crews, *The Random House Handbook* (New York: Random House, 1974), p. 23.

are some undeniably lyric lines from a poem, the beginning of Wordsworth's sonnet, "It Is a Beauteous Evening":

> It is a beauteous evening, calm and free;
> The holy time is quiet as a Nun
> Breathless with adoration; the broad sun
> Is sinking down in its tranquility;
> The gentleness of heaven broods o'er the Sea;
> Listen! the mighty Being is awake
> And doth with His eternal motion make
> A sound like thunder—everlastingly.

Even the most confirmed rhetorician would not dare claim that a lyric like this is obliged to have a thesis at all. And yet, if you look at the verse in these terms, you will notice that Wordsworth begins with something very like a thesis: "It is a beauteous evening . . . [and] holy," a contention that he argues most persuasively throughout the first eight lines. Wordsworth "argues" his "thesis" not only with factual statements, but also with all the devices of poetry at his command—with rhyme and meter, with simile:

> The holy time is quiet as a Nun
> Breathless with adoration;

with alliteration and personification:

> The broad sun / Is sinking down in its tranquility:
> The gentleness of heaven broods o'er the Sea;

with onomatopoeia:

> Listen! the mighty Being is awake
> And doth with His eternal motion make
> A sound like thunder—everlastingly.

Through these devices, Wordsworth has not simply described an evening, but has offered powerful emotional arguments to prove its beauty and its holiness.

If you can concede that there is something very like a thesis at work here, then perhaps you can also agree that what is going on in even the least controversial of expository compositions is the proving of the author's point. It is in this sense that all expository writing must be considered persuasive and all theses argumentative.

Creating Tension through an "Although Clause"

Your writing will benefit if you view it as persuasion in this way and approach your thesis as an argumentative statement. You see, your readers are likely to be a bit difficult to please or convince, skeptical, ornery (even as you and I). Therefore, if you—like Wordsworth—are writing about the beauteous holiness of an evening, you have the burden of somehow persuading your readers both of the evening's beauty and of its holiness. Besides being skeptical, these readers are likely also to be easily distracted or bored and thus may not continue reading if they suspect you are simply rehearsing the commonplace or the self-evident. They will, however, grow interested at the hint of controversy. Judge from your own experience. Don't you like to read about ideas that make waves and destroy the calm of the ideological ocean around you? Given the danger of boring readers, there is a tremendous advantage for writers who can acknowledge the fundamentally argumentative nature of even the least controversial of theses. These writers build into their theses the tension between their main statement and their "although clause" (whether implied or expressed) that will attract and maintain their readers' interest. And an interesting paper almost always results from the resolution of such tension.

See page 7 for discusssion of "although clause." How do you create such tension? You think of the point you want to make in terms of any contradictions that exist about it. To return to a familiar example, let's suppose you were assigned to write the paper on Washington discussed in Part One. You might very well survey the original inventory of ideas (p. 11) and come to the thesis "George Washington was a great man." However, since this statement is likely to turn out a paper every bit as exciting as that produced by the thesis "Grass is green," you would probably next want to consider working with its opposite: "Washington was not a great man." You would recognize quickly that this statement, although more interesting, is untrue—or at least not supportable by the facts in the inventory of ideas. Being left with the "great man" thesis, then, you would search for whatever contrasting ideas might exist within it that would make this conclusion worth the saying. Two such contrasts were suggested earlier in this book:

- Great man, despite the fact that he was merely human like ourselves (problems with his teeth and with his family)
- Great man, despite the recent anti-heroic approach of revisionist historians

Since the well-accepted idea often bores while the paradoxical notion almost invariably intrigues, you would probably choose one of these contradictions for your thesis or else find another similar contrast.

The quality of tension between what we have been calling the "although clause" and the main statement of thesis is present in every one of the essays in our collection. It accounts to a large extent for the appeal Lewis Thomas's "Germs" exerts upon even the nontechnical reader:

ALTHOUGH: "We still think of human disease as the work of an organized, modernized kind of demonology, in which the bacteria are the most visible and centrally placed of our adversaries. . . .

YET: In real life, however, even in our worst circumstances we have always been a relatively minor interest of the vast microbial world." (pp. 461, *2, 4*)

Tension is present even in a source as unlikely as the thesis of Plumb's "De Mortuis," which is given no explicit statement until the conclusion: "What is tasteless and vulgar in one age becomes tender and moving in another" (p. 468, *13*). Rephrased to emphasize the tension, the statement becomes:

ALTHOUGH: we may consider the funerary customs of our age tasteless and vulgar,

YET: we think of similar expressions from another age as tender and moving.

William Stegner, in his "Good-bye to all T--t," exploits this tension by phrasing his thesis in frankly paradoxical terms: "Some of us object [to the overuse of strong language] precisely because we value it" (p. 500, *1*):

ALTHOUGH: (Because) I value strong language,

YET: I object to its overuse.

If there is any single factor that all good expository essays have in common, it is probably this hint of argument that creates a tension, the resolution of which keeps the reader attentive to the end of the essay. And thus I would recommend that you adopt the point of view of the best of expository writers and approach your own writing in these terms.

Try It Out

1. Evaluate the following for their usefulness as *working* theses, checking them against the evaluation tests on page 8. Bear in mind that a good working thesis must be phrased as an arguable statement or proposition.

   a. I plan to discuss the effect of the Federal Reserve Bank on the stock market.
   b. Why John Donne wrote "A Hymn to God the Father."
   c. The sadness of life.
   d. Thomas Jefferson was the third president of the United States.
   e. My thesis asks about the problem of unemployment.
   f. The differences between the French and English political systems.
   g. Should inflation be defeated at the expense of full employment?
   h. A. A. Milne influenced Shakespeare.
   i. Sunsets are beautiful.
   j. The effects of gamma rays on man-in-the-moon marigolds.
   k. How the ancient alchemists tried to turn base metals into gold.

2. Choose from number 1 four items that you think have thesis potential. Then phrase them as good working theses.

3. Do the theses you have worked out for number 2 have explicit "although clauses"? If not, rephrase them so that they do.

FINDING YOUR POINT AND DISCOVERING SUPPORT

Since writing without a thesis is literally pointless, it follows that good writing is produced only when writers have something they truly want to express. Finding something significant to say, then, becomes the first major problem for a writer. You may have seen the problem firsthand: A paper is assigned and instantly all student sparkle fades and youthful eyes go blank and worried. Perhaps you have experienced this blank feeling yourself. Except for those miraculous moments when inspiration—or something akin to it—seems to strike, all writers at this stage have to give some serious thought to what is called the "invention" of ideas.

Invention

Although "invention" is the term that has been used since the days of the ancient Greek philosopher Aristotle, it is not really an accurate word for the process of finding ideas. Nobody really *invents* ideas; people discover them. They bring ideas out of their own subconscious minds into the light where their conscious minds can examine and work with them. There are two ways—not counting inspiration—that such invention can be accomplished. One is brainstorming, the strategy for encouraging the free flow of thought we discussed in Part One. The other is the use of more formalized schemes called **heuristics** (from the Greek word meaning "to find out"). Both approaches offer techniques that writers have found highly useful. The following sections describe a number of these techniques so that you can try them out and discover for yourself which one, or which combination, you personally find helpful.

Brainstorming through Free Writing   In "Writing the First Essay," we discussed the sort of brainstorming that begins with taking an inventory of your ideas. Closely related to the inventory of ideas—actually another way of approaching it—is a method called "free writing." Free writing is, as its name implies, totally unrestricted writing. Only one thing is required of the free writer: to keep writing until the time is up. Free writers must not stop to think, to rest their fingers, to relax their muscles; they must just keep writing. They should not look back at what they've written, should not make corrections. When you are free writing and you cannot think what to say, just repeat the last phrase over and over until a new idea comes.

To use free writing as an invention technique, concentrate on your topic or subject as you begin, and write for a specified amount of time. Let the wording of the topic suggest ideas to you and follow those ideas wherever they might lead you. Make no effort to direct your thinking into logical channels; just scribble down whatever thought comes into your head. When your time is up (and the alarm rings or the teacher calls a halt), read over what you have written. Even then make no effort to correct your writing or to turn it into a regular composition. Instead, use it as a storage bank of ideas. Underline or circle ideas that might be worth pursuing. Also be sure to look for and mark any particularly graceful turns of phrase that you might want to incorporate when you actually write your essay.

Use your annotated free writing as you would use an inventory of ideas, and think it through. Does a single principle begin to emerge that seems to incorporate most of the ideas or to which most of them can be subordinated? In short, does a thesis begin to take shape? Can you structure some of the other material around it?

Often it is helpful to try another free-writing session as a follow-up to the first. This time you begin by writing down the idea (or ideas) that seem central to your first free writing and then let your mind wander from there. The second attempt will probably turn out to be more structured than the first. From it you may be able to work out a plan that will lead directly to your first draft.

Free writing is not for everybody at all times. It is a good technique to try, however, if your mind feels especially blank or if you are confused about the subject you must write on. And many people find it a helpful way to begin on those days when even the thought of writing seems disagreeable.

The Five "Ws" of Journalism   If the purpose of brainstorming is to put writers in touch with their ideas, the purpose of the various heuristics is to help writers clarify their ideas and get a firmer grasp on their material.

One of the most useful of all the heuristics is derived from a memory device used by journalists. Reporters learn from their cub days to consider the *W*s, the traditional journalistic questions: Who? What? Where? When? Why? and, if applicable, How? Every good news story builds its "lead" around the answers to these questions. But these questions can be just as effectively asked by an expository writer during prewriting. Using the *W*s almost guarantees a fairly thorough survey of one's information. If the class working with "George Washington" had used the *W*s, their inventory of ideas might have been far more extensive. "Who?" for example, should have brought to mind not only "Martha" and "slaves" but probably also a number of other people important in Washington's life.

You can use the *W*s not only to expand your inventory of ideas, but also to narrow a topic and channel it in a specific direction. You can pose any one of the questions, answer it with whatever first comes to mind, and then ask the other questions in terms of that answer. Let's say, for example, that your topic is "First Love." You can start with the question "When?" and answer it "When I was 12." Thinking now in terms of that particular incident, you will answer the question "Where?" with "At summer camp." "Who?" will bring "Bill" or "Lisa," which should carry you on to the crucial exploration of "What?" and "Why?"

Some writers combine the questions for deeper probing. The "Why" combinations are especially penetrating. "Why this particular person?" for example. "Why at this particular place at that time in my life?" If this heuristic works for you, it should help you to narrow your subject to a workable size, to review all aspects of it, and to delve deeply enough into it to discover its significance.

Aristotle's "Topics"   Almost 24 centuries ago, Aristotle worked out a strategy for discovering and developing relationships between ideas, a technique so useful that many writers find it hard to equal even today. Aristotle suggested that support for any subject could be discovered by considering that subject in relation to five major "topics" (which he further subdivided into 17 subtopics).

The idea was for orators (or writers) to ask themselves questions about their subject that the "topics" suggested to them. For example, they were to consider their subject in terms of its class or grouping, its cause and its consequences, or its similarities to and differences from other comparable things. The "topics" of Aristotle that are most useful to writers today include:

1. *Definition:* What kind of thing is my subject? To what grouping or category does it belong? How is it distinguished from other members of that group?
2. *Comparison:* How is this subject similar to others in its group? How does it differ from them?
3. *Causal relationships:* What does this subject cause or bring about? What are the effects of this subject?
4. *Authority:* What do the experts have to say about my subject?

How might you use these "topics" to invent theses and support? Let's go back to the George Washington example. If the class working with the Washington topic had reasoned from Aristotle's "topics" with their same ideas in mind, they would probably have arrived at a thesis rather similar to the one they found by freely associated thought. But it might very well have been a more sophisticated and sensitive version of that thesis, and it would almost certainly have been backed by stronger and more convincing arguments. Here's one way their reasoning might have gone had they used the "topics":

   I. Questions of definition
     What category does George Washington belong to?
     • Man
     What kind of man was he?
     • A good man
     • A leader of men
     What kind of good man?
     • Good; but flawed, like all others
     What kind of leader?
     • Great soldier
     • Revolutionary hero
     • Became chief executive of his nation
  II. Questions of comparison
     What other good, but flawed, men were also great soldiers, revolutionary heroes, capable leaders of men, and became their countries' chief executives?
     • Napoleon; Mao Tse Tung; Castro
     How does George Washington differ from these other leaders?
     • Washington turned down the crown and voluntarily retired.
      —No other revolutionary leader ever voluntarily stepped down.
      —All others attempted to perpetuate their power.
 III. Questions of causal relationship
     What were the consequences of Washington's turning down the crown?
     • America became a truly constitutional republic, under elected leadership, unlike any other country of revolutionary origin.

- Washington became legendary for his "honesty."

IV. The opinion of experts

What do the authorities say about George Washington?

- In the past, historians have been almost unanimous in their praise. Recently, however, some have debunked Washington along with other national heroes.

Thinking through this dialogue, the following thesis might emerge:

Thesis: Although there has been a tendency in recent years to debunk our national heroes, George Washington, who was after all merely a man, subject to all the flaws and weaknesses that flesh is heir to, remains after reexamination a hero among leaders; for his special qualities contributed directly to that which makes America so great a country.

The usefulness of Aristotle's technique is not limited to factual material. It can work with equal creative power on more personal matters as well. Take, for example, the perennial subject "My Vacation."

- Definition
    Free time
    Learning experience
- Comparison (with other kinds of free time, other learning experiences)
    More time
    More solitude
    Different way of being with friends, family
    Sun and sand and sea
- Effects
    Vacation threw new light on my relationships with others
    Gave me more time alone to think about them
    The background of the great eternals lent everything new perspective
    I learned some important things about myself

Despite the triteness of the assignment, there is a thoughtful theme in the making here once each idea is supported by specific details.

As effective as the "topics" are for generating and developing theses, they were designed originally for finding arguments to support controversial positions. Even now this is the area where they can achieve their greatest effectiveness.

Let us look, for example, at positions for and against legislation relating to equal rights for women, and see how the "topics" might help a partisan develop arguments:

QUESTION: Should equal rights for women be recognized by law?

ANSWERS: Yes   No

ARGUMENTS

From Definition: Women, like men, are people and, therefore, should be regarded so in the eyes of the law.

From Definition: Men are men and women are women; and although neither should be favored, the difference should be legally recognized.

From Comparison:

1. Psychological difference: In the past women found their entire sense of identity and worth through the service they rendered to parents, husband, and children. Today more women recognize that they need something from life in their own right. The law must, therefore, grant them personhood and equality so that they will have an equal chance to achieve their desires.

2. Economic difference: In the past women had economic security. If they remained single, they remained a part of a larger family circle which would provide for them. If they married, their husbands took care of them financially. But now only the nuclear family remains, and it does not offer support to the unmarried relative. Married women now have to accept the possibility of divorce; and even if they remain married, the rise in the cost of living often requires two breadwinners. Women, therefore, now need to be economically effective just as men are.

From effect: If legislation is passed, justice will be served and the promises of "freedom and justice for all" will at last be fulfilled.

From Authority:
The Declaration of Independence
The Constitution (especially the 14th Amendment)
Betty Friedan, Gloria Steinem, Bella Abzug

From Comparison:

1. Psychological difference: In the past women found fulfillment in their traditional role. Now women who choose to continue in that role suffer a sense of degradation and many women feel so degraded that they believe they must work outside the home, thus contributing to the downfall of the family and disintegration of the moral fabric of society itself.

2. Economic difference: In the past, when men were the major breadwinners with most women content to be helpmates at home, massive unemployment existed only during infrequent periods of economic depression. But now many women have been persuaded to seek "personal fulfillment" with a job outside the home. In neglecting their own families, these women are also displacing other heads of families from their work, and our society suffers the ills of continuous unemployment. The legislation will further all these destructive trends.

From effect: If passed, all that is unnatural will triumph. Women will lose all their special privileges; they will be required to serve in combat, they will be forced to share lavatories with men, and they will lose all special financial protection in divorce and special physical protection in factories.

From Authority:
The Bible
Phyllis Schlafly, Marabel Morgan

Any one of these heuristics—Aristotle's topics, the five *W*s, or others you may discover—may keep you from the discouraging situation of not knowing what to say or how to go about supporting it. The following "Try It Out" section will give you a chance to experiment with these techniques for "inventing" ideas.

Try It Out

1. Choose one of the following topics and free write about it for twelve minutes.

The draft	Scholarships for athletes
The women's movement	Japanese automobiles
UFOs	Violence on television

   Does a central idea begin to present itself from your writing? If so, could this central idea be developed to serve as a thesis?

2. Take one of the above topics and ask yourself the five *Ws* about it. Write down your answers. Do the beginnings of an essay seem to emerge? What is its thesis?

3. Take one of the topics from number 1 (but *not* the one you used for number 2) and work it through Aristotle's "topics." Try to write a thesis from the results.

4. Which of the strategies we have discussed (including the traditional inventory of ideas you learned about in Part One) seems to be of most value to you? Why?

DISCOVERING STRATEGIES FOR MAKING YOUR POINT

Once you have distinguished the point you want to make, you have gone a long way toward determining the substance and, as Chapter 2 will discuss, the structure of your composition. But in order to develop your point effectively, it is important not to lose sight of your persuasive purpose. If you are writing a job application and your purpose is to secure an interview, or if you are composing a letter of complaint about a faulty product and your purpose is to get a refund, you are probably in little danger of disregarding the correspondent you are trying to influence. Your audience may be much easier to overlook when you are writing the sort of papers likely to be assigned in college classes, but your purpose is still persuasive and the relationship between you and your readers remains crucial. Your purpose in such papers will probably be a variation of one of the following:

Remember your persuasive purpose.

- To convince your readers that your explanation of the topic (as summed up in your thesis) is accurate and well thought out.
- To persuade your readers that your insights into the subject matter are well founded.
- To bring your readers to your point of view on your topic.

In general, the degree of persuasiveness required in a paper varies with the controversiality of your thesis; but in every case, the effectiveness of your writing depends upon your keeping this persuasive purpose in mind.

Dealing with "Although Clause" Material

It may be helpful to think of the element of controversy in your paper as "although clause" material, the portion of your paper in which you support and develop the "although clause" of your thesis. (You'll remember that the "although clause" is the part of your *working* thesis statement that represents information or a point of view contrary to the main thrust of your thesis.) Though an "although clause" is by nature contrary, it need not suggest that your thesis is particularly controversial. It can, for instance, merely imply that the thesis idea is newly discovered or probably little known to the reader. The Katz article, recounting his scientific study of drug abusers (p. 472), is based on such a model. Or an "although clause" might hint that "Although this material is well enough known (or accepted), I have a new angle, approach, or interpretation to bring to it." Shana Alexander's development of her thesis that "Children today not only exist, they have taken over" (p. 434) has this implication. The "although clause" might even suggest "Although I am sure you will agree with me once I tell you or remind you of the conditions . . .," as does Fred Golden's description of "Earth's Creeping Deserts" (p. 432). When you add such "although clauses" to your theses, you are not making them controversial. At least, you do not put your readers in an adversary position.

On the other hand, sometimes your "although clause" can indicate that your thesis is controversial indeed. In such cases, your "although clause" voices an opinion in total disagreement with your thesis. To determine just how controversial your thesis is, ask yourself how far your readers are likely to agree with it. You should be able to place them somewhere along the continuum shown in Figure 1.

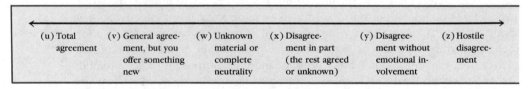

| (u) Total agreement | (v) General agreement, but you offer something new | (w) Unknown material or complete neutrality | (x) Disagreement in part (the rest agreed or unknown) | (y) Disagreement without emotional involvement | (z) Hostile disagreement |

FIGURE 1   The Controversy Continuum

The amount of agreement you expect from your readers should help you decide to what extent you will want to emphasize your "although clause" material and how you will handle it.

Strategies for Handling Noncontroversial "Although" Material

When the "although clause" of your working thesis does not set up an adversary relationship with your readers, you are not obliged to include the "although" material in your finished composition. There are, however, a number of reasons why you still might want to do so.

Justifying Your Purpose One reason to use "although" material in the finished composition is to justify your purpose in writing. J. B. S. Haldane, for instance, in choosing to discuss the varying size of animals in "On Being the Right Size," realizes that he might be accused of working with rather commonplace material. Despite the fact that his "although clause" is not at all controversial ("Although my way of looking at the material has been underemphasized . . . ."), he uses it in the first sentence of his introductory paragraph to ward off possible reader objections:

> The most obvious differences between different animals are differences in size, but for some reason the zoologists have paid singularly little attention to them. (p. 480)

Reviewing Earlier Work or Discussion Many scholarly articles begin with a summary of earlier research. We might think of this summary as "although" material ("although this is what has been discovered or thought already") since it points up the variation of the present concept and thus justifies the composition. Some writers do not include the "although" material, however, when it amounts to the fact that the ideas to be expressed in the thesis have been unknown until now. Nevertheless, Alan Katz begins his article with:

> When we at Boston University's Mental Health Clinic were first confronted five years ago with the drug scene, we knew very little about it; all the pharmacology books were of little help. . . . (p. 472)

By using the material in this way, Katz takes us readers into his confidence and lets us share his excitement at the discoveries he will unfold.

Opening a Way to Your Thesis Noncontroversial "although" material can also furnish an interesting or off-beat approach to your thesis. It can, for instance, let you contrast what you are discussing with the way it was at another time or place. If your thesis is concerned with a historical time or a faraway place, you might attract your readers' interest by opening with "although" material that would relate it to the here and now. Or if your thesis is contemporary, you might let your "although" material emphasize its uniquely modern character. Shana Alexander uses this strategy, for example, when she contrasts her modern thesis with a description from the past:

> Children are a relatively modern invention. Until a few hundred years ago, they did not exist. In Medieval and Renaissance painting, you see pint-size men and women wearing . . . grown-up expressions, performing grown-up tasks. (p. 434)

With this final strategy, then, you have three ways to use your "although" material to lead your readers into even noncontroversial compositions. But when your thesis is not particularly contentious, you will seldom want to continue the "although" matter beyond your introduction—except perhaps to give an echo of it just at the close (see "Frame or Circle Conclusions," p. 111).

Strategies for Handling Controversial "Although Clause" Material

While the main problem with noncontroversial theses is that your readers may wonder why you are taking the trouble to rehash known and accepted material, you confront a strikingly different challenge from your readers when your thesis is openly controversial. With controversial theses, you face the problem of winning over your readers from attitudes of disagreement ranging from indifference to hostility. The greater the disagreement, the greater care you will need to take with the "although clause" material expressing that disagreement, and the greater the attention you will need to pay to the feelings and needs of your readers.

Aristotle's advice that we must regard our readers as worthy opponents is often useful. And frequently as you determine your thesis and define its support, you will want to think of your readers as intelligently antagonistic people with "show me" attitudes. But this approach may not always be the most effective one when you are concerned with convincing readers of the value of what you have to say. Carl Rogers, a contemporary psychologist, has added modern psychological insights to Aristotle's ancient ones on the question of writer-reader relationships. Rogers advises us to reach readers through those areas where agreement might be worked out, to try for some commonality of ideas as a start. He writes:

> Mutual communication. . .leads to a situation in which I see how the problem appears to you, as well as to me, and you see how it appears to me as well as to you.*

In other words Rogers recommends putting yourself in your readers' place. His advice is similar to the folk wisdom of native Americans that suggests "walking a mile in the other person's moccasins."

From Your Readers' Moccasins   In order to put yourself in the place of those readers who strongly disagree with your thesis, try to remember how you felt when you read or heard something that challenged your most deeply held opinions. If you can do so, you will recall that the feelings such challenges aroused were not comfortable. You will also remember how easily an opponent of some idea you valued could overstep the line and make you defensive—or angry.

It may be easier to put yourself in the place of your uncommitted readers. If you try to remember the last time you were reading tensely controversial material that you had not yet made up your mind about, I'm sure you will recall your desire to weigh matters for yourself and not be unduly influenced by the writer. Perhaps you found yourself in sympathy with the side you considered the underdog—that is, the side the writer opposed, the side that could not argue back. If these memories of yourself as a committed or uncommitted

---

*Carl Rogers, "Communication: Its Blocking, Its Facilitation," in *On Becoming a Person* (Boston: Houghton Miflin, 1961), p. 336.

reader are at all vivid, they should lead you to two important conclusions about handling the "although clause" material. First, when you are urging a controversial thesis, you cannot afford to disregard or give only fleeting attention to the ideas of the opposition. And second, it is to your advantage to deal with their views fairly.

Presenting Controversial "Although" Material Fairly   You cannot expect to ignore the views opposed to your thesis and hope that your readers will be unaware of their existence. These views are bound to be passing through the minds of those readers who have been acquainted with the controversy. Further, you can be fairly certain that those who have not yet learned of it will be raising some of the opposition issues in their minds as you present your case. In order to make your own views persuasive, then, you will probably have to expand your discussion of the opposition ideas beyond an introductory sentence or two. You would also be wise to accord these views some portion of respect. For however you may feel about the opposing point of view or about those who hold it, you will not be able to reach your readers—let alone convince them—except by scrupulous fairness. Because your readers expect you to give the other side a fair hearing, name-calling, sarcasm, snide remarks, or an abusive or a superior tone in your discussion of that side will assuredly backfire. No matter how justified writers feel such tactics may be, readers tend to react negatively to these attacks unless they already hold a deep conviction supporting the thesis. Recall your own reactions as a reader.

In speaking strongly for fairness, I do not mean that you need to give the illusion of neutrality. For one thing, if you manage to present all positions equally, you will leave your readers confused and dissatisfied. For another, fairness itself demands that your readers learn where you stand. Thus, the idea is to identify your own position and present the other side's arguments in terms of your position without distorting the views of either side.

Let's look at George Will's "Israel and Munich" (p. 446) and Walter Williams's "U.S. Blacks and a Free Market" (p. 490). Neither author attempts to hide his viewpoint. Both can afford to be blunter and less tactful than is usual for an advocate because neither is personally identified with the view he is defending. Will is a Christian American arguing against American foreign policy and for the policy of the Jewish state of Israel, while Williams is a black arguing a position unpopular in much of the black community. Both authors state their position early in their essays. Will writes "The [Israeli] anxiety is more reasonable than the [American] impatience" (p. 446). And Williams admits that his "point *is* to question propositions concerning black socioeconomic progress which have now received an axiomatic status" (p. 490).

Both authors devote a fair proportion of their essays to presenting the opposition point of view. Although I believe that both effectively refute that view by careful, well-reasoned argument, it seems to me that one handles the "although" material in a fairer—and thus more successful—way. Compare these two early presentations of the opposing standpoint (I have placed brackets around the authors' own views):

Be fair but not neutral.

For a decade, since the Six Day War of 1967, U.S. policy has been that Israel should trade territory for peace. As President Ford put it, Israel should "dare the exchange of the tangible for the intangible." [The secure are always exhorting Israel to be daring.] Similarly, the governments of the world constantly insist that Israel be more forthcoming [than those governments ever are.]   (Will, p. 446, *2*)

Does black socioeconomic progress necessarily depend upon whether blacks are liked by whites? Does it depend on the continuance of massive federal expenditures?

   Well, if you asked the [self-appointed] black spokesmen, the answer to these questions would be "yes." [But before we all agree, there are some important issues that must be raised.]   (Williams, p. 490, *1–2*)

Few people could disagree with Will's statement of his "although" position. His summary of government policy is phrased as it was in public pronouncements, and the Ford quotation, of course, speaks for itself. Williams, on the other hand, could be accused of asking loaded questions similar to the unanswerable "When did you stop beating your wife?" If Williams did not later raise the issues he promises and answer them fairly, we might even accuse him of setting up a "straw man," a weak argument proposed only so the writer can shoot it down. This is a notoriously unfair tactic. What Williams has actually done here, however, is to take the opposition point of view—that the black community will prosper best when the government provides regulation of business and help for the needy—and phrase that view as unappealingly as possible. In so doing, Williams takes the risk of offending some of his readers. Secure in his belief that he can win them back by the soundness of his later argument, he chooses to use a striking opening that catches his readers' attention and challenges their beliefs.

Working with Controversial Material

1. Be sure to give adequate coverage to the opposition viewpoint.
2. You may, however, present their opinions from your own partisan point of view.
3. It is, nevertheless, to your rhetorical advantage to present the opposition viewpoint fairly.

Conceding What Can Be Conceded   The heart of Carl Rogers's persuasive strategy (see p. 50) is to root your points of controversy in as broad a base of agreement as can be managed. Your readers are far more likely to give serious consideration to your differing viewpoint if you show your basic good will and your eagerness for theirs by conceding to their side whatever points you can honestly concede. Notice how skillfully William Raspberry employs this technique in his opening to "Children of Two-Career Families":

Maybe you have to be crazy to argue with two Harvard psychiatrists—particularly two such insightful psychiatrists as Barrie Greiff and Preston Hunter.

So before I register my small objection to their article in the May-June issue of *Harvard Magazine,* let me say that nearly everything these two doctors have to say about the strains and stresses of dual-career families makes sense to me. (p. 502, *1–2*)

Carll Tucker's article "On Splitting" offers another example of how you might make your readers more open to persuasion by gracefully conceding that the opposition has some right on its side too. Tucker, who argues against divorce, begins his article by describing how angry he felt when two couples among his friends called to tell him they were getting divorced. He follows up this description by conceding that divorce may not have been a bad idea in the case of his friends:

> I did not feel anger at my friends personally: Given the era and their feelings, their decisions probably made sense. (p. 504, *3*)

Following this concession, he presents his "although" material in a fair—though, of course, not completely impartial—manner. Tucker is even willing to concede that, to a certain extent, his opposition is right:

> In some respects, this freedom [to divorce without stigma] can be seen as social progress. Modern couples can flee the corrosive bitterness that made Strindberg's marriages nightmares. Dreiser's Clyde Griffiths might have abandoned his Roberta instead of drowning her. (p. 504, 505, *6*)

Tucker's concessions doubtlessly take some of the sting out of his controversial position and, in so doing, help him argue his side more effectively. This strategy should be helpful to you as well.

Anticipating and Answering Possible Objections

When you are discussing an issue face-to-face, the other discussants have the opportunity to question your ideas or raise objections to your arguments. At the same time, you have the opportunity to answer each objection as they raise it and to put their minds to rest about whatever idea of yours may distress them. Writing denies you this opportunity for immediate interchange. Putting yourself in your readers' place, however, can help you to overcome this disadvantage. For, in trying to think as your readers might think, you should be able to anticipate their questions and supply answers, to foresee their objections and quiet them. Although covering possible reader objections is of major importance to argumentative theses, it can also be an effective technique when you do less controversial writing. For an example, glance again at the first section of this chapter (p. 36). You will see that I have tried there to speak to the sort of objections to the thesis concept that you might be harboring in your thoughts.

Whenever you are writing, try to see your work through your readers' eyes and try to figure out the issues they may have difficulty understanding and the ideas they may have problems accepting. Then raise these issues and ideas yourself and answer them in order to satisfy your readers' unspoken questions.

Strategies for Arguing Your Point Persuasively
1. Define the opposition material fairly.
2. Set forth your own position.
3. Concede what can be conceded.
4. Raise and answer possible objections—that is, argue what must be argued.
5. Present your own case.
NOTE: Points 1 and 2 and points 4 and 5 may be handled in reversed order, depending upon circumstances.

Presenting Your Own Case Persuasively

Your readers' concerns must be central in your handling of "although clause" material. They should also influence the way you support your own side of your thesis. In Chapter 3, we will talk about the kinds of support that should be most convincing. Here the focus is on planning the strategies that will help you present your thesis persuasively. Probably the most useful way of thinking of these strategies is to return to the idea of the rhetorical triangle (see Figure 2) and think of the relationships between you, your thesis, and your readers in terms of your persuasive purpose.

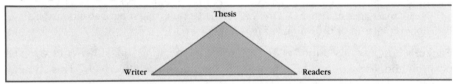

FIGURE 2   The Rhetorical Triangle

In order to persuade as a *writer,* you will have to give your work enough personal authority to make it convincing. You will best be able to persuade your *readers* if you can get them to identify with you and your ideas. And what you need to do to make your *thesis* itself persuasive is to give it the kind of intellectual validity that will make it credible to your readers. Let's consider these three tasks individually in order to find strategies to help you accomplish them.

Giving Authority to Your Writing

An effective way to make your point convincingly is to give it the weight of personal authority. How can you do that? You can start by letting your readers know what your intellectual and moral qualifications are for the job you have undertaken as their guide to the subject.

Establishing Intellectual Authority   If you have special expertise in your subject field, there is no reason to disguise it. Readers of Alan Katz's "The Use of Drugs in America" (p. 472) learn immediately of his credentials as a psychiatrist at Boston University's Mental Health Clinic. Because he fits this information in as a necessary part of his text rather than as an extra fact attached to it, we readers do not perceive Katz as immodest.

> When we at Boston University's Mental Health Clinic were first confronted five years ago with the new drug scene, we knew very little about it. . . . Although we were well-trained psychiatrists, drugs other than for therapeutic purposes were not part of our training. (p. 472)

Wayne Booth opens his essay "The Rhetorical Stance" with a similar strategy. He writes:

> Last fall I had an advanced graduate student, bright, energetic, well-informed, whose papers were almost unreadable. (p. 452)

The reader can easily infer that Booth is a professor in a graduate department of English. As readers, we tend to give additional credit to what Katz writes on psychiatry and what Booth writes on English teaching because of our knowledge of their expertise.

Even if you choose to be less personal or less specific, your readers will be able to discern the expertise that gives your work authority if you handle your material in a competent, knowledgeable way. For example, although Lewis Thomas gives no overt clues to his profession, every paragraph in his essay "Germs" demonstrates that he is a scientist in full command of his subject:

> Some bacteria are only harmful to us when they make exotoxins, and they only do this when they are, in a sense, diseased themselves. The toxins of diphtheria bacilli and streptococci are produced when the organisms have been infected by bacteriophage; it is the virus that provides the code for toxin. Uninfected bacteria are uninformed. When we catch diphtheria, it is a virus infection, but not of us. Our involvement is not that of an adversary in a straightforward game, but more like blundering into someone else's accident. (p. 462, 5)

When you have to write on a subject where you've had little previous understanding, it is hard to project such intellectual authority. Nevertheless, if you are careful to master the subject well enough to be able to speak knowledgeably about it, you will be able to write on it convincingly.

Establishing Moral Authority   Another important way to add to your personal authority as a writer is by projecting strength of character. For your readers to believe you, they need to understand that you are the sort of person they can trust. You can win this trust in a number of ways. One of them is by being fair to the opposition—in the still-partisan way mentioned earlier. Another is to be absolutely precise in your use of reference material. If you quote as much as a brief phrase from another writer, designate it as a quotation and credit its author. If you borrow an idea, never neglect to credit its source. (Chapter 10 will give you firm guidance in documentation.) Remember, unless you tell them otherwise, your readers have the right to believe that every word you write and every idea you discuss are original with you. Should you give them reason to suspect differently, their faith in you and in what you write will be severely shaken.

Another way to give moral authority to your work is to approach your subject in the stance of the Objective Observer and/or the Impassioned Advocate. The most effective writers have usually relied upon a combination of these roles.

FIGURE 3   Combining Objectivity
with Impassioned Advocacy

You may choose to approach your subject with the dry objectivity of Sergeant Friday of the 1950s television show *Dragnet*—"Just the facts, ma'am, just the facts." If you do, your readers will appreciate your insistence upon the unembellished facts and may be drawn to your interpretation of them. On the other hand, the righteous indignation of an Impassioned Advocate speaking out for justice carries a moral authority too. So if you can demonstrate with the objective facts that your indignation is indeed justified, you can wear your advocacy like a banner, and you just may be able to carry your readers with you. For a skillful example of such mingling, look again at that paragraph of Will's quoted earlier:

> [Voice of the Objective Observer]: For a decade, since the Six Day War of 1967, U.S. policy has been that Israel should trade territory for peace. As President Ford put it, Israel should "dare the exchange of the tangible for the intangible." [Voice of the Impassioned Advocate]: The secure are always exhorting Israel to be daring. Similarly, the governments of the world constantly insist that Israel be more forthcoming than those governments ever are. (p. 446, *2*)

Identifying Your Readers with Your Point

All people tend to respond more favorably to ideas they can identify with. You can use your knowledge of this human tendency to make your writing more persuasive. First, find some common ground with your readers and then present your thinking in these terms. If you know exactly who your readers are likely to be, you should have little trouble finding common ground. Wayne Booth, for instance, speaks as one English teacher to another and shows his familiarity with the struggles of his fellows:

> As we are all painfully aware when our 1:00 section goes miserably and our 2:00 section of the course is a delight, our own rhetoric is not entirely under control. (p. 453, 6)

In showing that he has "been there," struggling with the same problems as his readers, Booth lends a validity to his suggested solutions to some of these problems.

New Journalism   Booth's technique is to identify with his readers; New Journalists, like Tom Wolfe, pursue the opposite strategy of getting the reader to identify with them. They explain a circumstance or a thing vividly by describing both their own experiences with it and the impressions those experiences made upon them. These authors hope that readers will share the experience described and then adopt the accompanying interpretation of it. (See Tom Wolfe's essay "Down with Sin," p. 443.) If you should decide to work with this technique, however, you should be aware of one danger it can pose. Inexperienced writers must be careful not to use the method to excess and turn an essay about a topic into a story about themselves.

Irony   Another effective way you can get your readers to identify with you and your point of view is to use irony. In writing ironically, you say or imply the opposite of what you believe to be true. By requiring your readers to understand your actual intentions, you create a sly bond of conspiracy. It is as if you give a broad wink to your readers and flatter them by saying, "Those of you who are in the know will realize I am joking. I don't dare say how dreadful I think this matter is, but with *your* intelligence you will understand the strong criticism hidden in my words." For example, Tom Wolfe is very far from meaning that he thinks wholesomeness is a bad characteristic when he writes

> One of the worst insults kicking around today is any word that means, in effect, "wholesome." You are a wholesome person. How would you like to be called that? ("Down with Sin," p. 443, 3)

Here Wolfe hopes to bring his readers into an alliance with him against those who have so twisted the traditional values that *sin* takes on a positive value and *wholesomeness* a negative one.

If you lay the groundwork carefully, you can also turn your opponents' own words against them, "hoist them by their own petard," as Shakespeare would say. Ellen Goodman, for instance, in ironically quoting such pseudo-psychological catch phrases as "doing their own thing," "finding themselves," and "getting in touch with their feelings," gets her readers to agree that the therapists who urge such behavior are actually counseling selfishness. She makes her readers examine the literal meaning of those phrases when she writes, "The West Coast greeting, 'What are you into?' is most aptly answered with one word: myself" (p. 470, 7). Just as Goodman tries to debunk John Lilly's phrase "the universe within" (p. 470, 2,3) with dramatic irony, so does George Will ironically highlight the diplomatic phrase "the conscience of the West." (p. 447, 448, 7, 11). Through dramatic irony, Goodman's readers come to understand that she thinks the more important universe is "without" and Will's readers see that the conscience of the West may not be very conscientious.

Though irony is not easy to handle, you may find it a useful tool. When you use it, however, be careful not to be either too broad or too subtle. If your irony is too broad and sarcastic ("The cafeteria food here is just grrreat!" for instance), you are in danger of having your readers accuse you of being unfair or simplistic. If, on the other hand, you are too subtle and do not give adequate clues to your real meaning, your readers may very well take you seriously and think you mean just the opposite of what you intend.

Appeal to Emotion   The way writers most frequently use to get their readers to identify with a particular point of view is an appeal to their common humanity. After all, only rarely will you have the opportunity to address a group of readers as specifically defined as Booth's fellow English teachers. But whoever your readers may be, you can know for sure that they are human, and this knowledge can offer you insight into ways to persuade them.

You can, for instance, appeal to the feelings and sympathies that we all share. I am not, of course, suggesting that you add to those dismal appeals to greed and envy that are the shame of our television programming and much advertising. Rather, I am advising that you reach your readers through your understanding of such universal human experiences as love, fear, sympathy with the young, the helpless, and the oppressed, and indignation against the violators of fairness and justice. Joan Didion's essay "On Self-Respect" (p. 438), for instance, gains its strength from Didion's ability to involve her readers in her struggles with self-doubt. In getting her readers to remember personal moments of self-doubt, she secures the kind of identification that makes us readers tend to agree with her interpretation of these feelings—the idea that is, after all, her thesis. Or take a different sort of example, laughter. We all like to laugh and most of us admire the sort of cleverness and wit that make Will's Chicago Cubs essay (p. 449) and Plumb's cemetery essay (p. 466)) so delightful—and at the same time so persuasive.

Case Studies   You can win your readers by exemplifying your point in human terms. As impressive as statistics can be, they lack the human touch. For example, the number 6.5 million, when it refers to human deaths in the Nazi camps, is a terrifying figure. But that number becomes far more meaningful when it is backed by a single case history, such as Anne Frank's diary, for Anne was a human being like ourselves.

Sensuous Detail   You can make this emotional identification more complete by including the sort of vivid sensory detail that brings all your readers' senses into play. You might, for instance, follow the example Fred Golden sets when he leads his readers into his rather technical article, "Earth's Creeping Deserts," with this sense-stimulating sentence:

Outside the great conference hall in Nairobi, 16 fountains sent up sparkling plumes of water, and black Mercedes limousines glistened in the bright East African sun. (p. 432)

Imagery   Some other good ways to secure your reader's emotional agreement are detailed in Chapter 8, which offers suggestions on how to use language and imagery persuasively. See especially pages 315–27.

Problems   All these strategies for relating to your readers on an emotional level can be highly effective, but you can encounter serious problems in using them as well. The problems are those of excess. If you adopt an approach with too great an emphasis on feelings, your work may strike your readers as sentimental or mawkish. If you are too powerful in your use of language and imagery, they may think of you as heavy-handed or insincere. The topic you are writing about should enter into your decision. The amount of emotional charge that might be completely appropriate for an essay on nuclear destruction could only be ludicrous when you applied it to a composition on intramural soccer.

Giving Your Work Intellectual Validity

There is yet a third set of strategies to help you persuade your reader. Besides those techniques that help establish your moral and intellectual authority as a writer on a particular theme and those that aid in getting your readers to identify with what you are saying, there are techniques which should help you provide intellectual validity for the work itself.

No Unsupported Statements   Most important, you must be absolutely sure to give support for every point and every subpoint you make. You cannot expect your readers to believe your unconfirmed word. Every time you put forth a generalization, such as a conclusion about a broad class or category, you are making a silent promise to your readers that you will soon supply them with particulars that show the truth of what you have concluded. What are they to think when one unsupported generalization follows another with no particulars forthcoming for either one? Nor can any amount of restatement satisfy readers' hunger for detail, for specific evidence. Your evidence may be as insubstantial as a personal anecdote: "I had not been elected to Phi Beta Kappa. . . and I was unnerved by it. . ." (Didion, p. 438, 2). It may be as indisputable as statistics or an authoritative quotation: "Washington's Worldwatch Institute estimates that the lives of perhaps 50 million people are jeopardized . . . . Warns U.N. Secretary General Kurt Waldheim: 'We risk destroying whole peoples in the afflicted area'. . ." (Golden, p. 432, 4). But you will need to supply specific evidence of some kind or you will assuredly lose both your readers' confidence and their interest. There is no way of getting around it: Supporting your every point is an inviolable rule of good writing.

In order to be persuasive, however, that support—of whatever variety—must be intellectually valid.

Valid Authority/Appropriate Source   If you choose to support your idea by a quotation, that quotation will have only the authority that the person you are quoting brings to it. In the example just presented, for instance, Golden's use of a Secretary General of the United Nations to supply information about world drought supports his point most effectively. Will gains similar authority for his thesis in "Israel and Munich" by citing Theodore Draper, "scholar and journalist," Norman Podhoretz, "editor of *Commentary* magazine," and Saul Bellow, Pulitzer Prize–winning novelist, all of whom have made special studies of Israel and its problems.

Simply having a well-known name does not make a person an authoritative source outside of his or her own field, however. I might be willing to take the word of athletes, for instance, on the merits of athletic equipment or the fine points of a game, but their opinions on breakfast cereal or soap products or, for that matter, politics are of no more value than the rest of ours. Nor will you find a self-serving quotation effective. Readers give little weight to a comment that is clearly in the self-interest of the person being quoted. They would tend to discount, for instance, the views of the president of Exxon on deregulating oil prices.

Logically Valid Support

In order to persuade your readers, the support you offer for your points must be logically valid. That is, there should be a logical relationship between each of your points and the material you use to support them. Notice the clear-cut connection in this paragraph of Shana Alexander's:

Point:
Support:
> *In Kids' Country, every day must be prize day.* Miss America, Miss Teen-Age America, Miss Junior Miss America, and probably Miss Little Miss America trample each other down star-spangled runways. Volume mail-order giveaways will shortly silt up our postal system entirely. All day long TV shows like *Concentration, Dating Game, Hollywood Squares,* and *Jackpot* hand out more toys: wristwatches, washing machines, trips to Hawaii. (p. 434, 435, 6, emphasis mine)

Fred Golden uses a more complex kind of support. Yet there is sound logic in the connections he draws as he relates his point about "modern factors," along with his two examples of these factors, to his conclusion about the eventual disaster resulting from these factors:

Point:
Example 1
Example 2

Results:
Final
result:
> Droughts and crop failures have always been a harsh fact of life in arid regions. *But the Sahel's calamity was worsened by distinctly modern factors.* Improvements in public health had vastly expanded population. New wells lulled the Africans into thinking they were no longer so completely dependent on the slim rainfall. They enlarged their herds and planted more cash crops like cotton and peanuts. For a while, the land withstood the strains. But when the rains ceased, the crops failed and the cattle stripped the fields of virtually every blade of grass around the overworked wells. Soon the thin layer of topsoil vanished, and there was nothing but rock, sand, and dust. The Sahara had won. (p. 433, 6, italics mine)

Support that involves argument (the sort of support Golden uses) can be particularly effective. For inexperienced writers, however, it can also offer dangers. There are a number of logical pitfalls that you can easily slip into. The most dangerous of these include circular reasoning, false assignment of cause, false analogy, drawing conclusions from insufficient evidence, and thinking in terms of *all* and *never.* Let's examine each of these briefly to help you escape such pitfalls.

Circular Reasoning   When you reason circularly, you base your point on an argument that is itself rooted in your point. For example:

> Why is the team having such a losing season? The trouble is with Coach Sosnoski. It is clear that if Coach Sosnoski were any good at all, he would not be coaching a losing team.

FAULTY

Circular reasoning amounts to saying "I believe my argument is true because I say it is true." If you are careful to provide specifics to back up your reasoning, you will avoid circular arguments.

False Assignment of Cause   This logical pitfall is often called the *post hoc, ergo propter hoc* fallacy, a title that translates from Latin as the "after this, therefore because of this" fallacy. It involves arguing that just because one event is related to another by time or place or circumstances, it must be the cause of that other event. Using this reasoning, a strong case can, for instance, be made for the disease of cancer being carried by telephone. In fact, if you look at graphs made from perfectly valid statistics, you will find that the increase in cancer in the United States almost directly parallels the increase in this country's use of telephones. Such support may be impressive until you realize that the same evidence can just as easily prove that increased incidence of cancer causes growth in the holdings of AT&T. Always examine your own arguments for possible false causal connections. You may be sure that your readers will.

Faulty Analogy   Drawing analogies, or showing your readers one situation in terms of another, can be persuasive. But if your comparison is based upon too few similarities or upon a false assignment of causes, your analogy will be faulty. For example, early in this century the state of Maine acquired a reputation for giving the majority of their ballots to the presidential candidate who was elected by the country at large. Politicians began to regard the state of Maine as prophetic and to put their faith in the political analogy, "As Maine goes, so goes the nation." But in 1936 Maine was one of the only two states who chose Alf Landon over Franklin Roosevelt. Comedienne Gracie Allen pointed to the demonstrated weakness of the analogy when she quipped: "As Maine goes, so goes Vermont."

When you reason by analogy, be sure that the two compared events, people, or objects have a good number of significant points in common. (A good example is Will's comparison of the situation of Czechoslovakia just before World War II to that of Israel today.) But even when you find valid points of comparison, realize that the argument that you can draw from such a comparison is limited, and do not try to extract a definitive conclusion from it.

Drawing Conclusions from Insufficient Evidence   Readers are wary of conclusions that are drawn from weak or limited evidence. If, for example, you wish to claim effectively that a disillusionment with conservative politics has set in, you should argue upon more substantial grounds than the personal disillusionment of your dentist, Dr. Silvester, who had voted for Ronald Reagan in 1980. On the other hand, if you can show that Dr. Silvester is typical and if you can add other such examples to his, you will be arguing by the case study method, a kind of argument that can be persuasive indeed (see p. 58). You must exercise a good deal of caution if you employ this method, however, because it is difficult to determine just how typical your sample is.

Weighted samples are confusing because they may or may not be true. For instance, a poll of the readers of *Playboy Magazine* a few years ago not unsurprisingly revealed a noted liberalization in sexual standards. Such a poll, though probably valid for readers of that magazine, can give us no solid information about the nation in general. What is more, a very limited sample may be characteristic only of itself. If, for instance, you base your point that your town had a beautiful spring last year upon the fact that Aunt Julia's dahlias were especially abundant, don't expect the unqualified agreement of those of your readers who remember that a good portion of the town was wiped out by flood last spring.

Another problem with insufficient evidence is that it can promote stereotypical thinking: "Zulu tribesmen have bad breath because my cousin once met FAULTY a Zulu who—he told me confidentially—had bad breath."

Arguing in Terms of All or Never   Closely related to the sort of thinking that judges a whole category by a few examples is thinking that insists upon choosing between limited alternatives. Very few things are all or nothing, always or never. Few problems have a single cause or a single solution. Writers, like scientists, can get into trouble by oversimplifying. For example, an early study seemed to show that by drinking coffee during pregnancy, a woman increases the risk that her baby will be born underweight or will have birth defects. Later research revealed that most of the coffee-drinking mothers with defective infants in the original study were also smokers. It is possible that coffee is not a factor in birth defects at all because the negative effects of smoking on newborn babies are already well established.

Be careful, therefore, not to argue in absolutes. You can try to prove that lack of discipline in the schools is one of the causes (or even the greatest cause) of the decline in the quality of education. But if you say lack of discipline is the only cause, your readers will immediately become skeptical. Leave the door open for other possibilities. Readers are suspicious of claims that *all* members of any group *always* (or never) behave in any particular fashion. After all, some beer drinkers don't have large bellies, not all professors are absent-minded, and some blondes actually have less fun.

Supporting Your Point with a Logically Sound Structure

Perhaps the most important way you can give your paper intellectual validity is by providing it with a logically sound structure. Chapter 2 suggests methods for planning such a structure.

Try It Out

1. On the basis of their degree of controversiality, place the theses of the following articles from Part Five on the controversy continuum on p. 48.
   a. Stegner's "Goodbye to All T--t" (p. 500)
   b. Raspberry's "Two-career Families" (p. 502)
   c. Will's "The Chicago Cubs Overdue" (p. 449)
   d. Williams's "U.S. Blacks and a Free Market" (p. 490)
2. How much attention do the authors of the four works cited in number 1 pay to their "although clause" material? Be as specific as you can.
3. Will's "Israel and Munich," Williams's "U.S. Blacks and a Free Market," and Tucker's "On Splitting" have controversial theses. Choose one of these articles and list the persuasive strategies discussed in this chapter that the essay employs.
4. How effectively does your author handle these strategies? How persuasive is the result?

ASSIGNMENT

Using some or all of the techniques for invention and persuasion you have studied in this chapter and in Part One, carefully work through the prewriting process with one of the following topics. Remember that the most crucial part of prewriting is developing an effective working thesis. When you have completed your thorough prewriting, go on to write a polished, revised essay as outlined in Part One.

1. Attend a college cultural or sporting event, keeping a journalistic eye open as you participate. Then write an essay about what you observed among the audience members and/or among the participants as they sat on the sidelines. (Suggestion: Use the 5 *W*'s and concentrate on letting your observations build up to "why?" to lead you to your thesis.)
2. Write an essay for or against the proposition: Life is harder for men. Working through Aristotle's topics, develop the arguments you will need to support your thesis—and to present your "although clause" too.

3. Use one or more of the heuristics presented in this chapter to explore the notion of a four-day work week. How would more leisure time benefit or hurt an individual or society as a whole? How would the economy be affected? After you find your thesis and discover the ways you will support it, develop your material into a well-organized essay.

4. It is a common belief that youth is the best time of life. Yet a number of recent studies suggest that the forties is the age preferred by most people. Write an essay incorporating your response to these surveys.

5. Freewrite on one of the following topics:

Fly Fishing
Semis (tractor-trailer trucks)
Medical Research
Hydroelectric power
Cable TV
Phobias
Jazz

Freewrite again to help you come to a working thesis. Then write an essay using elements of your freewriting to support your thesis.

6. Develop into a finished essay any of the topics you began working with in one of the Try It Out sections earlier in this chapter.

$\mathcal{P}$rewriting: $\mathcal{A}$rranging

The argumentative nature of the thesis discussed in the previous chapter is not the only part of the writing process that inexperienced writers sometimes have difficulty accepting. Many sometimes also question the usefulness of a written plan. Although such a plan is almost universally said to be important, it is far from universally employed—except, of course, by professional writers and publishing scholars. You yourself have probably heard someone say, "Oh, yes, the outline is undoubtedly very important. Certainly. I never use it myself, though. Never have. I'm one of those who can do just as well without one." But if the 871,731 citizens who voted to elect the justly forgotten Millard Fillmore President of the United States could be mistaken, so can a large proportion of inexperienced writers. Using some sort of written plan is truly essential for constructing anything but the very shortest work of writing; and if you will try a brief experiment, you can prove it to yourself. This is an experiment that Albert Joseph uses to convince the sophisticated—and highly skeptical—business people who enroll in his Industrial Writing Institute. (See accompanying boxed section.)

Experiment

Directions: Answer the following questions. But *do not use pen or paper.* (The answers may be found at the conclusion of this chapter.)
1. What combinations can be made from the letters A and B? (If you think of the letters side by side as they would be typed, you shouldn't have much difficulty in discovering the two possible combinations.)
2. What combinations can be made of A, B, and C? (This one is harder. Were you able to find the six without resorting to pencil and paper? Most people cannot.)
3. Name all the combinations that can be made from the letters A, B, C, and D. (If you were able to name the 24 combinations correctly without using any kind of visual aid, congratulations. Research has shown that only one out of one hundred intelligent adults can match that accomplishment.)

The point of the experiment is that using memory alone to keep track of items of any complexity is extraordinarily difficult for most of us. And the moral is that if the composition you are going to write will have three or four ideas at least as complicated as A, B, C, D, you are well advised to order these ideas on paper before you start. In other words, you will do much better in organizing your writing if you rely upon some sort of written plan.

USING AN OUTLINE

Using an outline need not be burdensome. If the word "outline" summons up in your mind a picture of an unending list of items numbered I to XXVI or of three painstakingly typed pages of topic sentences, we are not talking about the same thing at all. The kind of outline I have in mind is a written plan genuinely meant to guide you in constructing your composition. An outline that is too long is more hindrance than help, and an outline that is too tidy or too fancy is not a working outline at all. Since your outline is to be a working tool for your personal use, how you construct it is essentially an individual matter.

Individual Variations

Although almost any kind of notation that you find helpful is probably good, I do have some general advice to offer. First, even if you are usually most comfortable with complete sentences, you probably should be somewhat wary of sentence outlines (outlines composed of topic sentences). These plans usually take so much time to write that students who make them often develop a vested interest in the phrasing of the sentences. Thus in using sentence outlines, students often compose their ideas to fit the words already established instead of composing their words to suit their ideas. A paper written from preconceived topic sentences tends to be not only inflexible in its thinking, but also stiff and awkward in its phrasing.

Second, since your outline is your own personal notation, meant basically for your eyes alone, its form is really up to you. What form you choose for your outline depends on how intricately your ideas relate to one another. Specifically, it depends on how much subordination—that is, how much ordering of one item under another—your outline will need to show. As long as an outline provides for little or no subordination, how you signify points really doesn't matter very much. All that is important is internal consistency. Bullets (•), dashes (—), or asterisks (*) before the points will do. But once you subordinate some ideas to others (and subordination is central to structure), you will find your outline simpler to make and clearer to use if your organize your points according to some system. What system you use is immaterial as long as the subordination is clearly designated.

Over the years, one system of outlining conventions has become fairly standard, and you might want to employ it. This system begins with roman numerals (I, II, III, IV), under which it places capital letters (A, B, C), and then arabic numerals (1, 2, 3), and then lowercase letters (a, b, c), and then, if needed, lowercase roman numerals (i, ii, iii, iv). (See Figure 1.) Traditional outline conventions call for parallel indentation for parallel levels of subordination. That means that if two minor points directly support the same major point, they are indented an equal amount under that major point. Where possible, parallel points should also be phrased in parallel wording.

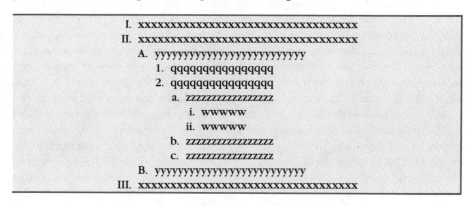

FIGURE 1 Traditional Outline Format

What is most important to remember when making your outline—however you choose to designate the points—is that all of its points must go to develop the thesis. All the subpoints of a point must go to develop that point. And all the subsections of a subpoint must go to develop that subpoint.

ORDERING YOUR IDEAS

Besides showing the importance of writing down your ideas to arrange them meaningfully, the experiment with the ABCD combinations on page 65 illustrates another significant point: the necessity for logical arrangement. People who were unable to figure out some logical sequence for combining the letters (for example, ABC, ACB, BAC, BCA, and so on) probably didn't come close to getting all the combinations, while those who were able to find a pattern were well on their way to achievement. The experiment demonstrates, then, that in order for our minds to grasp the meaning of a series of ideas, we need to understand their relationship to each other in a logical manner.

Subordination

The most important kind of logical ordering involves appropriate subordination. To subordinate is to decide what point supports, or can be categorized under, another point. Organizing is almost impossible without subordination. It is the key to the solution of both of the major problems in constructing a piece of writing: the key to the problem of organizing a large number of diverse items and to the problem of organizing a broad, undivided topic. Although the principles of subordination seem to come quite naturally to some people, others find this subject—as central as it is—obscure and difficult to understand.

Organizing Diverse Items One simple way to understand the principle involved here is to compare it with that of the "common denominator" in fractions. If you want to add 1/2, 1/3, and 1/6, you know that all three numbers have to be converted to a common denominator—that is, into sixths—in order to be combined. The same principle applies if you are trying to work with a number of diverse ideas. If you want to consider *mice* and *men* and *tigers,* for instance, you need to look for a common denominator for them, a category that all would fit into. In this case, you might decide to consider them all in the category of *mammals.* In the language of organizing, you would be, in both mathematic and zoological cases, *subordinating* the specific items under the general heading. Adding *canary* and *eagle* to your list would complicate the problem a little, since these animals are not mammals. But, just as you would

Seek a "common denominator."

broaden the common denominator to twelfths if 1/4 were added to the list of 1/2, 1/3, and 1/6, so you would search for a broader category—*warm-blooded animals,* perhaps—to handle your new additions.

In making these decisions, you are developing an organization. Subordinated in the conventions of the outline, these examples look like this:

I. Twelfths	I. Warm-blooded animals
A. Halves	A. Mammals
B. Thirds	1. Mice
C. Fourths	2. Men
D. Sixths	3. Tigers
1. Halves	B. Birds
2. Thirds	1. Canary
	2. Eagle

Even though the ideas you will be dealing with in your writing are more complicated than simple fractions or kinds of animals, the principle remains the same. In order to treat diverse ideas in a single paragraph, or even in a single essay, you have to discover their common base and work with them in those terms. Think back on the process which our example class used to bring order out of their jumble of facts about George Washington (p. 14). Despite the complexity of those items compared to fractions or categories of animals, the process the class went through was identical to the one just summarized.

Organizing the Undivided Topic The analogy to working with fractions also holds true when you are faced with the opposite organization problem: the large undivided topic, such as "Nuclear Disarmament" or "Freshman Year." Here you already have your common denominator, the topic itself. Your problem, just as it would be in mathematics, is to find appropriate categories to divide it into. Just as in mathematics you would have to find the "factors that go in evenly," so in organizing you have to discover divisions that encompass all the material.

Seek logical factors or divisions.

How does this principle work in practice? If, for instance, we continue with our analogy from zoology, we might take a look at "On Being the Right Size" (p. 480) to see how J. B. S. Haldane handles the problem. Haldane's thesis is: "For every type of animal there is a most convenient size. . . ." "How would I prove this point?" Haldane must have asked himself. Surely he knew he must use examples. But how should he arrange the examples to present the case most effectively? If you check the article, you will discover that Haldane first divides his subject into the disadvantages and advantages of increasing size. He then subdivides each of these categories into those specific bodily functions that would be affected adversely and those that are affected advantageously by increasing the size of the animal. And finally, he provides examples and explanations for each of these points. In short, Haldane probably worked from an outline much like the following:

Thesis: For every type of animal there is a most convenient size.
  I. Introduction
 II. Problems of increasing size
     A. Support
     B. Gravity
     C. Pumping blood
     D. Surface of organs
     E. Flying
III. Advantages of greater size (where necessary)
     A. Warmth
     B. Eyes
     C. Brains
 IV. Conclusion: Each size is right for its animal.

If you follow the subordinating processes discussed here, you should experience few difficulties in organizing your compositions. When you are faced with the problem of organizing diverse specific instances, look for appropriate common denominators. When you are confronted with the problem of structuring a general, unstructured topic, search for logical factors or divisions into which to divide it.

Keeping Sequences Short   One other point is worth remembering about the subordinating process: Try not to let any sequence contain more than five (or at the most six) items before subordinating again. Any greater number of points in a sequence is hard to retain in the memory. Further, as your readers would find, when developed in paragraphs, more than five or six points in a series become exceedingly tedious to read. But you will find as you write that there are very few lists of six or more points that cannot be regrouped and considered under subheads. American wars, for instance, are much more effectively ordered in either of the following (or other similar) ways than as a single grouping of ten:

NOT:	BUT:	OR:
III. American Wars	III. American Wars	III. American Wars
A. French-Indian	A. 18th Century	A. Major Conflicts
B. Revolutionary	1. French-Indian	1. Revolutionary
C. War of 1812	2. Revolutionary	2. Civil War
D. Civil War	B. 19th Century	3. World War I
E. Mexican War	1. War of 1812	4. World War II
F. Spanish-American	2. Civil War	B. Minor Conflicts
G. World War I	3. Mexican War	1. French-Indian
H. World War II	4. Spanish-American	2. War of 1812
I. Korean	C. 20th Century	3. Mexican War
J. Viet Nam	1. World War I	4. Spanish-American
	2. World War II	5. Korean
	3. Korean	6. Viet Nam
	4. Viet Nam	

Try It Out

1. Finding common denominators. In what group does each of the individuals in each of these sets belong?
   a. Reggie Jackson, Pete Rose, Joe Dimaggio, Babe Ruth
   b. Mohammed Ali, Joe Louis, Sugar Ray Leonard
   c. Chris Evert-Lloyd, Tracy Austin, Bjorn Borg, Jimmy Connors
   d. O. J. Simpson, Franco Harris, Roger Staubach, Terry Bradshaw
   Considering all the answers (a, b, c, and d) as a set, to what group would they all belong? Subordinate the items in number 1 appropriately and arrange them according to the conventional outline pattern.
2. The following is another list of specific items, but included within it are also some more general (or categorical) terms. Find the common denominators (you may use some of the included terms, if you wish) and construct a conventional outline by appropriate subordination.
   > John Travolta, Stevie Wonder, Singers, Jane Fonda, The Beach Boys, Gene Wilder, Actors, Steve Martin, Rock Groups, Robert Redford, Comedians, Paul McCartney, Tim Conway, Entertainers, The Beatles, The Rolling Stones, John Denver, Richard Pryor, Lily Tomlin
3. The following exercise is similar to one used by James M. McCrimmon at the University of Florida. It includes a list of contemporary English words and their original meanings. Language changes over the years, as you can see, and linguists have discovered that it changes in regular ways. They have noted regular patterns or principles to account for the change. Four of these principles have been at work on the words on this list. For example, words like (a) *chest* have become more general in meaning, and words like (b) *constable* have been upgraded in their meaning. Identify the four principles of change that apply to these words.

		Word	Original Meaning	Principle of Change
(1)	a.	chest ◀——— coffin		1. generalization
(2)	b.	constable ◀— stable caretaker		2. upgrading
	c.	minister ◀— servant		3.
	d.	immoral ◀— not customary		4.
	e.	meat ◀——— food		
	f.	lewd ◀——— ignorant		
	g.	starve ◀——— die		
	h.	knight ◀——— a rustic, country person		
	i.	girl ◀——— young person (either sex)		
	j.	virtue ◀——— manliness		
	k.	lust ◀——— pleasure		
	l.	pretty ◀——— sly, deceitful		
	m.	undertaker ◀— doer		
	n.	go ◀——— walk		

4. Consider the material in number 3 a fair sampling of a larger research project. What can you generalize on the basis of this research? Incorporate your generalization into a thesis that could be supported by the evidence within this exercise. Construct an outline to reflect the structure of a paper that you might write from that thesis. (Be sure to include the above items, appropriately subordinated.)

ARRANGEMENT

Logic is also essential when, in organizing your paper, you go beyond subordination of ideas to decide upon the sequence for ordering the categories and the examples within the categories. You may wonder whether the order of points and subpoints matters very much. The answer is that although the order of the subpoints is rarely of crucial importance to the finished composition, the order of the main topics can often make a real difference. In any case, you will necessarily have to select some items to be first and some to be last. And it is certainly better to make these decisions deliberately and logically rather than in a haphazard way. The following sections describe some of the principles for making structural decisions.

Organizing from the Rhetorical Principle

Probably the most important general guideline is the rhetorical principle, the principle of persuasion. The sole test for arrangements based upon this principle is their degree of persuasiveness. In organizing you ask yourself, How do I arrange this material to demonstrate or develop my thesis most effectively? In a way, then, this principle underlies all the others. For whatever arrangement you choose, whatever other principle you might follow, your decision should reflect your notion of the way to present your ideas most clearly and most appealingly. Subordinate

One important specific guide founded on this principle is: Place the mate- clause rial in the subordinate clause of the thesis first. Whenever the final thesis has material first.

anything approaching an "although clause" or other subordinate clause, the material this clause contains should be given less weight. The subordinate clause is subordinate to the main part of your thesis in fact as well as in grammar. It either states the opposition to your point of view or suggests an idea of far less importance in terms of your paper. You certainly will not want to have this idea lingering in your reader's mind and clouding the effect of your main point when the reader reaches the end of your paper. It is wisest then to get this material out of the way as early as possible. Furthermore, as we have seen, the "although" material can offer an effective opening for your composition.

Often, however, you will find that the subordinate clause of your thesis contains material that will need to be developed in some fullness in order to strengthen and clarify the main point. Organizing in these cases can be a little trickier. By and large it becomes a matter of using a comparison and contrast structural pattern. Such patterns are outlined and exemplified in the next section. The principle at stake, however, remains rhetorical:

- To refute the opposition ideas early in the paper
- Then to bring in your own arguments
- To finish up with the undistracted reader committed to your point of view

Organizing from the Comparison Principle

Among the most useful ways of organizing material are arrangements that compare and contrast ideas. A surprising number of theses lend themselves to such treatment, either for particular parts or for the whole structure. When you are interested in making an out-and-out comparison, in supporting one side of a controversial issue, or in exploring the differences between the main part of a thesis statement and its "although clause," you may very well find one of the comparison structural patterns the best arrangement.

Despite the enormous variation of possible subjects, there are only two basic comparative patterns. You might organize a controversial issue, for instance, in either of these two patterns:

I. Their side		I. Point 1
A. Point 1		A. Their side
B. Point 2		B. Our side
C. Point 3	OR	II. Point 2
II. Our side		A. Their side
A. Point 1		B. Our side
B. Point 2		III. Point 3
C. Point 3		A. Their side
		B. Our side

You would face a similar choice if your paper involved looking at one subject in terms of another. If, for example, you were interested in developing the thesis "Although high school and college offer courses in the same subjects, the college courses are much more difficult," you would probably set up your structure in one of these ways:

I. Introduction		I. Introduction
II. High school		II. Math
A. Math		A. High school
B. English		B. College
C. History	OR	III. English
III. College		A. High school
A. Math		B. College
B. English		IV. History
C. History		A. High school
IV. Conclusion		B. College
		V. Conclusion

For an example of the comparative pattern serving to guide the development of a single portion of a composition, recall the outline model about Athens and the Peloponnesian War on page 16. In order to show how remarkable it was that Athens should lose those wars to a place like Sparta, the writer was obliged first to demonstrate Athens' superiority over Sparta:

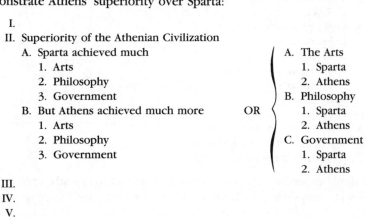

I.
II. Superiority of the Athenian Civilization

A. Sparta achieved much		A. The Arts
1. Arts		1. Sparta
2. Philosophy		2. Athens
3. Government		B. Philosophy
B. But Athens achieved much more	OR	1. Sparta
1. Arts		2. Athens
2. Philosophy		C. Government
3. Government		1. Sparta
		2. Athens

III.
IV.
V.

Each of these arrangements has its advantages—and its drawbacks. If there are quite a number of points or if the points are not strongly distinguished from one another, the alternating (second) arrangement can become repetitive, somewhat tedious, and sometimes even confusing. On the other hand, this arrangement does allow for a direct interplay between the two ideas that the first way does not offer. In some cases, a combination of the two is also possible. What you choose to do should be determined by the nature of your material. You might want to think your subject through both forms before deciding.

Some of the essays in Part Five show how these forms work out in actual practice. In "De Mortuis" (p. 466), J. H. Plumb relies for the most part on the first method. Briefly outlined, the structure of his essay includes:

1. Introduction: Presentation of the comparison of excessive modern and ancient funerary practice.
2. Description of modern excesses
   —Example
   —Example
   • Analysis

3. Description of ancient excesses
   —Example
   —Example
   —Example + a comparative speculation
   —Example
   —Example
4. Conclusion: Excesses of the modern day are more understandable in terms
   of those of ancient times.

George Will, on the other hand, arranges his essay, "Israel and Munich" (p. 446), by the second method:

Thesis: [Israel's] anxiety is more reasonable than [Washington's] impatience.
 I. Introduction
 II. The controversy
   A. Washington argument #1
     1. Presented
     2. Refuted
   B. Washington argument #2
     1. Presented
     2. Refuted
   C. Washington argument #3
     1. Presented
     2. Refuted
 III. Israel's position
   A. Defended by straight argument
   B. Defended by historical analogy
 IV. Conclusion: Witty summary of III B

Organizational plans based upon comparison are so frequently applicable that you'll want to keep these patterns in mind when you are planning your compositions.

Organizing from the Principles of Formal Logic

There are also a number of useful ways of constructing compositions that are grounded in the science of logic.

Cause and Effect   One logical arrangement is based upon cause and effect. You might, for instance, start with an effect—such as World War I—and, one by one, trace the causes leading to it. Or you might start with a cause—such as World War I—and consider individually the effects which it produced. You might even want to construct a chain of cause and effect: a cause leading to its effect, which in turn becomes a cause leading to other effects.

Ellen Goodman, for example, organizes her article "The Cult of Impotence" (p. 470) on a variation of this cause-and-effect principle. When she sets out to examine our society's glorification of the "isolation tank" existence, she first explores the causes of this turning self-ward, which she sees as a by-product of "the current condition of our lives" (p. 470, 6). Then she examines its effects:

"But then where are you? Then what?" (p. 471, 9). The basic structure of this essay involves:

- Introduction: We make a cult of individual isolation
- Causes of this "self-centering"
- Effects of "self-centering"
- Conclusion: Critical evaluation of "self-centering"

Problem and Solution   The problem-solution structure is another way of organizing that takes its impetus from logic and science. Using this method, you might set out a problem in your introduction, analyze it in the body of your paper, and offer a solution in your conclusion. Alternatively, you might consider your subject as a number of problems which you would explain and solve throughout. Alan Katz's article "The Use of Drugs in America" (p. 472) is based primarily on a problem-solution scheme. He presents the problem of drug abuse among young people, analyzes it in terms of his research, and offers his tentative psychiatric solutions based upon his clinical experience:

   I. Introduction
      Problem: Inexperienced psychiatrists face an epidemic of campus drug abusers.
  II. Analysis
     A. Purpose of drug abuse
     B. Personality of the abusers
        1. Personality trait
        2. Personality trait
        3. Personality trait
 III. Solution: A method of treatment
        1. Step
        2. Step
        3. Step
        4. Step
 IV. Conclusion: Theoretical explanation

You may find the problem-solution structure a practical tool to use when you want to write a letter of complaint or suggestion. You might use it, for example, to persuade the people in charge to accept your solution to a problem you have discovered with some campus service or at one of the stores in your neighborhood shopping center.

Classification   Classification, a logic-based system for organizing in general, is especially helpful for organizing compositions. The method consists of dividing up material by assigning it to classes of some kind. For our purposes, this usually means breaking down a subject so that it can be analyzed in terms of its parts. You will probably find this approach particularly useful for organizing your subpoints. Katz, for instance (see the outline in the previous section), uses this method twice in his essay: once to classify the personality traits of the drug abuser and again to divide up his method of treatment.

Classification can also be an important way of structuring an entire composition. Wayne Booth, for instance, in "The Rhetorical Stance," having defined his title subject, structures the rest of his essay to demonstrate that subject's importance by classifying the various corruptions of it. Since Booth suggests that an effective stance is achieved by "maintaining . . . a proper balance" (p. 453, 4) among the three rhetorical elements (subject, audience, and speaker), he classifies the unbalanced stances in terms of which element is overemphasized at the expense of the others: (1) the pedant's stance that is overdependent upon subject matter, (2) the advertiser's stance that concentrates overmuch on the effect on the audience, and (3) the entertainer's stance that subordinates everything to the personality of the writer.

The classification method works best when the categories chosen appear to be a natural outgrowth of the subject or of the author's approach to it. Some subjects do seem to fall into categories as a matter of course, as, for example, executive, legislative, and judicial branches of government; animal, vegetable, and mineral; staff officers, line officers, and enlisted men and women; elementary school, high school, and college. More often, however, you will have to impose classifications upon your material. Such divisions should be made in terms of your thesis and influenced by your own way of looking at the world. For example: "There are four approaches to this argument," or "Those who knew this great woman remember her chiefly for one of these three qualities." What may look like obvious classifications in retrospect are rarely cut-and-dried, however. Although Wayne Booth's categories, for example, seem almost uniquely appropriate to his subject, other writers might just as naturally choose other classification systems—for instance, the traditional Aristotelian categories of Invention, Arrangement, and Style.

Syllogistic Organization   A more formal approach to logic yields other more formal arrangements. The syllogism, a tool in deductive reasoning, can also serve as a basis for organizing your writing. A *syllogism* is a method of logical analysis consisting of three parts: a major premise (usually a generalization), a minor premise (usually a specific of that generalization), and a conclusion that follows from it. Some examples of the more common kinds of syllogisms include:

Syllogism	*Symbolic Expression*
1. • All Philosophers are wise.	All A is B.
• Socrates is a philosopher.	X is A.
∴ Therefore, Socrates is wise.	Therefore X is B.
2. • No giraffes are green.	No A is B.
• Joey is a giraffe.	X is A.
∴ Therefore, Joey is not green.	Therefore, X is not B.
3. • John's remark is meant either as a joke or an insult.	Either A or B.
• John never tells jokes.	Not A.
∴ Therefore, John meant to be insulting.	Then B.
4. • If a horse wins the triple crown, he should sire good racers.	If A, then B.

| • Secretariat won the triple crown. | A is true. |
| ∴ Therefore, Secretariat should be a good stud horse. | Therefore, B is true. |

Syllogistic reasoning can be persuasive. But when you use it, be certain that both your premises are true. Your conclusion can only be as true as the premises from which it is derived. The major premise in sample number 1, for instance, is on shaky ground in saying that *all* philosophers are wise. Thus, even though the logic of syllogism 1 is valid, you cannot safely conclude from it whether or not Socrates is wise. Besides evaluating your premises, you need to make sure that your syllogism itself is valid. The forms exemplified here are all valid, but many an argument that looks like a syllogism is not. For example, no positive conclusion is valid when one or both of the premises are negative. In terms of the second sample, for instance, you cannot argue conclusively that since no giraffes are green and Joey is not a giraffe, Joey is green.

The valid syllogism can, however, make an effective base for ordering your ideas in a tightly reasoned paper. If, for example you were writing a paper to argue that "Capital punishment should be abolished because it serves no useful purpose and is inherently uncivilized," you might base a portion of your paper on a syllogistic structure such as this:

II. Capital punishment is purposeless.
    A. Deterrence is its only conceivably useful purpose.
    B. Capital punishment is not a deterrent.
        1. Proof
        2. Proof
        3. Proof
    C. Therefore, capital punishment is not useful.

Dialectical Structure   "Dialectics" is a word that once signified a broad range of methods of logical analysis. In our time, however—primarily because of the work of Hegel and Marx—the term has come to mean the sort of reasoning that involves combining or compromising two valid or accepted contrasting positions. In dialectics, the *thesis* is a statement of the first position (→), the *antithesis* the statement of the opposing position (←), and the *synthesis* the statement of the combined position (↔). Surprisingly enough, the thesis, antithesis, synthesis format of dialectical reasoning can be put to good use in organizing compositions. Consider, for example, the following plan:

→ I. (Thesis, an accepted idea) To be educated a student needs some acquaintance with "the best that has been known and said in the world."
    A. Proof
    B. Proof
        etc.
← II. (Antithesis, valid objection to I) But to be professionally qualified, a student must have a large quantity of specialized knowledge.
    A. Proof
    B. Proof
        etc.

↔III. (Synthesis, a compromise) Therefore many colleges insist on two years of undergraduate general studies in the liberal arts and two years of specialization in a major field.

The synthesis that concludes this plan might then go on to become the thesis in yet another cycle of reasoning—perhaps, for example, a plan that argues for the additional years of specialization offered in a graduate course of study.

Wallace Stegner's essay, "Good-bye to All T--t" (p. 500) is organized by dialectic reasoning. If you search for its skeletal structure, you will find something like the following:

- Introduction: Some of us object to strong language precisely because we value it.
- → Words of themselves are not obscene and no words need be avoided (thesis, accepted idea).
- ← Excessive use of strong language robs it of its strength (antithesis, valid objection).
- ↔ One should, therefore, save strong language for the appropriate situation (synthesis, compromise).
- Conclusion: Ancecdote supporting the synthesis.

Organizing from the Principle of Progression

A progression is a succession of items ordered according to a linear scheme: first to last, closest to farthest, best to worst, for example. You will find the principle of progression particularly valuable when you are trying to decide upon the arrangement of subpoints under a topic.

Chronological Progression   Chronological arrangement, or arrangement in a time sequence, is one of the most useful of all progressions. So much of our lives is related in some way to the passing of time that a writer quite naturally looks to a time order for arranging material that would seem otherwise to be unfocused. In "De Mortuis," Plumb arranges his examples of ancient funerary practices from the earliest to the latest in time: beginning with those of the Paleolithic people and continuing through time with those of the people of Ur, the Egyptians, the Etruscans, and finally the nobles of medieval Europe. Similarly, when Katz needs an arrangement for his discussion of the development of the passive-dependent personality, he chooses the chronological sequence of newborn, infant, child, adolescent.

Though you also will doubtlessly find many occasions to use a time progression, it does offer some dangers you should be aware of. Just as thesis and argument is the basic structure of expository writing, chronological sequence is the basic structure of narrative writing or story telling. Story telling has primal appeal; it is the elemental composition, loved as much by primitive people and small children as it is by sophisticates. We all thus have a natural tendency to slip into story telling when we write. This natural tendency makes it all too easy for us to rely heavily upon chronological organization, sometimes employing it when it is not appropriate. When writers give in to this narrative urge, they find themselves developing every conceivable thesis in chronological order:

> Thesis: Many children suffer traumatic effects when they learn that Santa Claus is an imaginary figure.
>> I. Introduction
>> II. Santa's childhood
>> III. Santa's youth
>> IV. Santa's adulthood
>> V. Santa's old age
>> VI. Conclusion

FAULTY

Yes, the chronological principle is as useful an organizing method as we have; nevertheless, be warned.

Spatial Progression   If the items you want to discuss are spatially related—the different parts of a room, the places visited on a vacation, the states that may have off-shore oil—you may find it useful to order them according to their closeness to, or direction from, one another. You might, for instance, discuss them in the order that they occur going east (or north or south or west) from a particular point or going clockwise (or counter–clockwise). You might want to consider them according to their distance from a designated place, going from the farthest to the closest (or the other way around). Or you might think of them by their position up (or down) a mountain or along a river. Any sort of progression of sequential sites would help guide your reader's mind through the organization of your ideas.

Progression of Most to Least (Least to Most)   Logical progressions of the sort we have been discussing are not confined to time or space connections. We can also apply a logical progression to any quantitative or qualitative relationship, any sort of least to most or best to worst. You might, for instance, choose to organize your review of a museum collection by following a ranking of the most garish to the most subdued painting in the gallery; or you might want to make a zoological point by arranging your material in a sequence from the kind of caribou most likely to hibernate to the kind least likely to. J. B. S. Haldane, for instance, organizes his examples in "On Being the Right Size" from the most obvious to the least obvious and provides verbal clues to his procedure. When he begins his discussion of the disadvantages of increasing size, he writes: "Let us take the most obvious of possible cases" (p. 480, *2*). Similarly, he precedes his discussion of the advantages of size with the words "One of the most obvious is. . ." (p. 483, *10*). In "Earth's Creeping Deserts," Fred Golden clearly adopts the progression of least to most important when he orders his examples of ways of reclaiming the desert (p. 432).

Progression by the principle of importance is so useful an order that it deserves special attention. When no other arrangement seems suitable, you, like Golden, may well want to discuss your ideas according to the rhetorically sound strategy of beginning with those least important to your argument and ending with those most crucial to it. Under most circumstances, this strategy will serve you well. There are times, however, when it might be to your advantage to order your subpoints somewhat differently.* According to the findings of some psychological surveys, reader interest and reader memory are greatest for material at the end of a sample, next greatest for that at the beginning, and least for that in the middle. If you wanted to make your arrangement according to these findings, you would organize your points in order of importance: 2nd, 3rd, 4th, and 1st.

Final Thoughts on Arrangement

The list of ways to organize your compositions just detailed should be useful to you, but its usefulness should lie less in the knowledge it provides of the specific modes of ordering than in the glimpse it gives you of the richness and the variety of logical ways to organize. For the point is not that you select any particular strategy or combination of strategies, but that you choose some logically defensible order and that you know why you choose it.

The structure of your composition should seem organic. It should grow out of the material itself, not be forced onto it. Your most important consideration remains the presentation of your thesis. In selecting your strategies, ask yourself at each stage, What ordering will present my material most naturally and with the greatest degree of logical consistency? What sort of organization will develop my point and my supporting ideas most convincingly?

Try It Out

1. Included as examples in this chapter are the bare bones of outlines for articles by Katz (p. 75), Plumb (p. 73), and Will (p. 74). Using one of these essays, flesh out the given outline by specifying the subtopics merely suggested in the earlier outline and also by adding, where appropriate, examples from a further level of subordination.
2. The following is Judith Crist's thesis from "Gentlemen and Scholars of the Press":

   > Yes, the romance [of newspaper work] is gone—but only if romance is the stuff of economic insecurity and the personal, professional, and ethical carelessness bred by such insecurity. (p. 493, 4)

   Using the methods discussed so far in this book for organizing an undivided topic (pp. 68–69) and discovering a composition's structure

---

*In business letters and reports, for instance, it is usually wisest to progress from most important to least. Because of the press of time, business people customarily skim the beginnings and heads of most business documents, limiting their complete reading to those papers whose subjects coincide directly with their current needs. For further discussion of most to least progression, see pages 79–80.

from its thesis (pp. 13–18), derive a written plan to show the organization of the composition you might write from Crist's thesis.

3. Did Crist work from a plan similar to the one you constructed in number 2? (Try deriving her probable outline from her completed essay.) In what ways does the organization of the actual essay differ from yours? In what ways is it similar to yours?

4. Examine Shana Alexander's article "Kids' Country" (p. 434) and try to determine what principle(s) she uses in ordering her numerous examples. Would you have followed the same order she uses? If not, what principle would you have used?

5. Write a workable thesis about one of the following topics:

The draft	Scholarships for athletes
The women's movement	Japanese automobiles
UFOs	Violence on television

If you would prefer, you are welcome to use the thesis that came out of your work with these topics in the exercises on page 47. Or you may try one of the theses you developed in connection with the exercises on page 41. In any case, develop a working outline to structure support for this thesis. What strategy or combination of strategies did you use to order the points and subpoints of your outline? Why?

ASSIGNMENT

Paying particular attention to the prewriting process as outlined in "Writing the First Paper" and as discussed in the first two chapters, write a well-organized expository essay on the topic below that interests you most. Or, if you wish, you may take a topic you have worked on as an exercise in either of the two prewriting chapters and develop it into a full essay.

1. The feminist movement has tried to give women freedom of choice by emphasizing career and de-emphasizing family. Some critics (including Betty Friedan, a founding mother of the movement) feel that the de-emphasis of family has been too great and that now the choice of a completely family-centered life-style is being taken away from women. Write an essay explaining where you stand on the issue and why.

2. If you have recently changed your mind on an issue of some importance, write an essay explaining the change and persuasively setting forth your new point of view.

3. Compare your religious beliefs with those of a friend.

4. Do you agree with those who say that the process of growing up is harder today than it was a generation ago? Write a well-organized essay defending your point of view.

5. Write a thoughtful essay with a clearly defined thesis comparing and/or contrasting one of the following pairs:
   a. Video games/pinball games
   b. Soccer/rugby
   c. Riding a bicycle/jogging
   d. Biology lab/chemistry lab
   e. Two decades of life (twenties/thirties. teens/twenties. thirties/forties. etc.)

Before you begin to write your first draft, you should develop an interesting and supportable working thesis. Then construct a logically consistent organizational plan through which the thesis can be developed effectively. Both thesis and outline should be written down to be used and changed as your writing progresses.

A Further Hint:

Remember as you approach these comparative topics that a good thesis cannot be developed from "X and Y are different (or similar)" but should rather encompass your answer to the question "How" or "Why" or "In what ways . . . are X and Y different (or similar)."

Solutions to the Experiment (p. 65)

1. AB, BA   = 2
2. ABC, ACB, BAC, BCA, CAB, CBA   = 6
3. ABCD, ABDC, ACBD, ACDB, ADBC, ADCB
   BACD, BADC, BCDA, BCAD, BDAC, BDCA
   CABD, CADB, CBAD, CBDA, CDAB, CDBA   = 24
   DABC, DACB, DBAC, DBCA, DCAB, DCBA

3

Writing Your Essay

You have thought through the assignment and have made your decisions. You have, in short, completed the prewriting part of the writing process. And now you are supposed to be ready to write the essay itself. But there is that blank sheet of paper in front of you. I hope you are one of those who can plunge right into writing without too much concern. If you are not, you should understand that a large percentage of those who put pen to paper—including many professional writers—suffer a similar tension. Donald Murray, a well-respected writer, once admitted that he "feels more terror facing the empty page" than he did in leaping from a plane when he was a paratrooper.

The feeling of being "pen-tied" is not new. Sir Philip Sidney, who lived in Shakespeare's day, described this peculiar agony perhaps more accurately than anyone when he wrote:

> Loving in truth, and fain in verse my love to show . . .
> I sought fit words . . . her wits to entertain,
> Oft turning others' leaves to see if thence would flow
> Some fresh and fruitful showers upon my sun-burned brain.
> But words came halting forth, wanting Invention's stay;
> Invention, Nature's child, fled step-dame Study's blows,
> And others' feet still seemed but strangers in my way.
> Thus, great with child to speak, and helpless in my throes,
> Biting my truant pen, beating myself for spite . . .

Most of us (even those of us who make a special study of writing) know the feeling well. But the truth is that when you have finished your prewriting and have come at last to the point of actually writing your paper, the hardest part of your task is already behind you. You have your thesis; you have your supporting ideas; you even have a good notion of how you are going to structure them. All you have to do now is to find the words to express the ideas. All that remains is to introduce your point, develop it, and tie the essay all together persuasively.

INTRODUCING YOUR POINT

In "Writing the First Paper," we looked at the introductions of some essays by professional writers and from them determined that they have a double purpose: to set up the thesis and to capture the interest of the readers. This portion of Chapter 3 offers some specific ideas on how to approach both goals.

Setting Up Your Thesis

It might help to approach the problem of introduction writing from the point of view of your readers. Before they begin reading your essay, they can have no idea of its subject matter. As far as they are concerned, it could be about anything at all. They will, therefore, not want to read too far without at least some rather strong hints as to the topic you are pursuing. Your first problem, then, is to find a quick way to exclude from their consideration all else in the world except that small part of it which you will be discussing. Professional authors handle this problem in remarkably similar ways. A glance at the various essays in Part Five will show that whatever the style and whatever the introductory ploy, all of the authors follow the same procedure: (1) They manage to state the topic in so many words quite early on, (2) they find a way to particularize or expand upon the simple topic, and (3) by the end of the introduction, they reveal the approach they are going to take to this topic—that is, most of them state their thesis. The accompanying table shows just a few examples.

Title	Topic	Abbreviated Thesis
"Distant Music" (p. 498)	Perceiv[ing] Christmas through its wrapping	The miracle of Christmas is that . . . it [still] penetrates . . . the heart [despite everything].
"Kids' Country" (p. 434)	Modern . . . children	Children today . . . have taken over.
"In the Beginning" (p. 485)	Science and religion	Religion and science . . . are in agreement about certain facts concerning the creation.
"On Splitting" (p. 504)	Marriages [that] hadn't made it	What angered me was the loss of years and energy.
"Gentleman & Scholars . . ." (p. 493)	Newspaper business not what it was	Newspaper people [are] at last professionals.
"Israel and Munich" (p. 446)	Friction between Israel and the U.S. State Department	Israeli anxiety . . . is more reasonable than . . . Washington impatience.

From a practical standpoint, the question then becomes: How are you to suggest your topic and how are you to get from topic to thesis? Sir Philip Sidney, whose lines on the agony of starting to write were quoted at the beginning of the chapter, concludes these lines with some advice that has never really been matched:

"Fool," said my Muse to me, "Look in thy heart and write."

When it comes to writing introductions, *you* are your own richest resource. Think back and try to recall what first interested you in your subject. Is there a personal connection? Something that happened to you? A book you read? A movie or play that you saw? Is there something in the topic that connects to something currently in the news? Is there a subject much talked about just now that touches upon it? Is the topic an old subject that you have just seen in a new light? Is it a tried and true topic that you now understand from a new approach? Is there something about the topic that cries for attention? Do you disagree with the common view on the subject? Or with an important dissenting view? (These last questions, which lead into an "although clause" approach, can be particularly fruitful.)

Your experience, the richest resource.

　　Go over these questions in your mind or consider others like them that you may invent for yourself. Follow up your thinking on whichever questions appear most productive. Sharpen and develop this line of thought until it leads to a statement of your thesis. When you have put this reasoning on paper, you have written an introduction.

Interesting Your Readers

By getting at the root of what interests you in your subject and conveying it clearly and in an appealing way to your readers, you will probably be able to interest them too. This straightforward sort of introduction begins the great majority of professional essays. Sometimes, however, when the subject matter or the tone of their essays makes it appropriate, professional writers choose one of a variety of strategies or devices to add interest to their introductions. Journalists call these strategies "hooks." Although you would be unwise to rely upon hooks too often or in an artificial sort of way, they can add life and attractiveness to your approach to your thesis. The following examples from the essays in Part Five demonstrate some of the most frequently used hooks.

Using Introductory "Hooks"

Anecdotes　One of the most useful introductory strategies of all is the anecdote, the brief telling of an amusing or otherwise engaging incident. Most introductory anecdotes are the direct offspring of Sidney's "Look in thy heart" school of advice and are personal in character. They often relate the very event that brought the topic to the writer's attention. In using the anecdote, authors also take advantage of the universal appeal of stories and story telling. Carll Tucker, for instance, begins an essay of personal reflection in this way:

> One afternoon recently, two unrelated friends called to tell me that, well, their marriages hadn't made it. One was leaving his wife for another woman. The other was leaving her husband because "we thought it best." (p. 504, *1*)

Wayne Booth begins his rather technical discussion of rhetoric in much the same way:

> Last fall I had an advanced graduate student, bright, energetic, well-informed, whose papers were almost unreadable. He managed to be pretentious, dull, and

disorganized in his paper on *Emma* and pretentious, dull, and disorganized on *Madame Bovary*. On *The Golden Bowl* he was all these and obscure as well. Then one day, toward the end of term, he cornered me after class and said, "You know, I think you were all wrong about Robbe-Grillet's *Jealousy* today." We didn't have time to discuss it, so I suggested that he write me a note about it. Five hours later I found in my faculty box a four-page polemic, unpretentious, stimulating, organized, convincing. (p. 452, *1*)

Introductory Questions   Another hook which authors use to attract their readers is the question. When you choose to begin with a question, you take advantage of two possibilities that are natural to this sort of sentence. First, the question has an ability to involve your reader personally in whatever you have to say, because in itself it reflects direct communication between author and reader. Second, since a question asks, it presupposes an answering, which gives you a quick means into the thesis (or into the "although clause") by way of reply. Walter Williams sets up his "although clause" in this way:

> Does black socioeconomic progress necessarily depend upon whether blacks are liked by whites? Does it depend on the continuance of massive federal expenditures? (p. 490, *1*)

Pointedly Brief Statements   Like an introductory question, a pointedly brief statement catches the eye and, with luck, the interest of the reader by its contrast to the other kinds of sentences around it. Because most mature writing is expressed in complex sentences made up of clauses and phrases of various lengths, a blunt, affirmative statement containing only a few words can arrest the eye and startle the mind into attention. The simple phrasing of such brief statements gives them an almost proverb-like quality. The first words of Shana Alexander's essay are typical of this strategy:

> Children are a relatively modern invention. (p. 434, *1*)

Some writers inject an informal, conversational quality into their brief opening remark. William Raspberry's "Two-Career Families," for example, begins:

> Maybe you have to be crazy to argue with two Harvard psychiatrists . . . (p. 502, *1*)

Introductory Quotations   You might sometimes choose to introduce your essay with a quotation. In "Two-Career Families," Raspberry takes issue with a theory discussed in a book he recently read. He quotes the offending passage as part of his introduction:

> The only paragraph [from Barrie Greiff and Preston Hunter's article] that arched my eyebrows included this sentence: "Dual-career parents . . . shouldn't over-burden their children with responsibility for themselves or their siblings, or for running the household; that only cheats them out of their childhood and confuses them about parental roles." (p. 502, *3*)

Tom Wolfe uses a dash of irony in presenting the quotation which introduces his "Down with Sin":

The need for denunciation of sin occurred to me the other day when I read a remark by some young movie star, I forget his name, in defense of Doris Day. He had made a picture with Doris Day, and he felt it was time somebody *came to the defense of that girl.* He said, "You know, Doris is not the nice, sweet, wholesome, Mom's pie, All-American girl everybody makes her out to be. Actually, she is *quite a gal.*" (p. 443, *1,* emphasis Wolfe's)

Although both Raspberry and Wolfe slide into their quotations with some preliminary remarks, such a preface is not always necessary. Many authors who use this hook begin their essays with the quotation itself and offer their explanations later on. A typical article from the *Saturday Review,* for example, begins:

"The schools are the golden avenue of opportunity for able youngsters, but by the same token they are the arena in which less able youngsters discover their limitations." John Gardner's book, *Excellence,* has to do with this plain fact. He wishes to make it plainer, to have the country face up to it, and to have educators deal with it wisely. (Harold Taylor, "Quality and Equality," 44 [April 15, 1961], p. 72)

Introductory Analogies   Sometimes when you want to express a concept that is abstract or is difficult to understand, it is helpful to compare your concept with something that is more concrete or more readily understandable. This approach is called drawing an analogy. Because analogies can be witty and interest-provoking, they are an especially attractive introductory strategy. Wallace Stegner uses analogy in just this way in his "Good-bye to all T--t":

Not everyone who laments what contemporary novelists have done to the sex act objects to the act itself, or to its mention. Some want it valued higher than fiction seems to value it; they want the word "climax" to retain some of its literary meaning. Likewise not everyone who has come to doubt the contemporary freedom of language objects to strong language in itself. Some of us object precisely because we value it. (p. 500, *1*)

Wit and Humor   Some of the most appealing introductions are those that combine a clear setting out of the subject with an appropriately witty play on words. This quality of language, though highly effective, is difficult to pin down. Stegner's use of analogy certainly has it. So does E. B. White's subtle handling of the pun in his opening sentence:

To perceive *Christmas* through its *wrapping* becomes more difficult with every year. (p. 498, *1,* emphasis mine)

Judith Crist's ironic use of standard metaphors offers a more colorful example:

Much as I would like to be a keeper of my profession's flame, a herdsman of its sacred cows, a minstrel of its mythology, I think it is time to announce publicly that the newspaper business is not what it was. (p. 493, *1*)

J. H. Plumb, on the other hand, manages to intrigue us by his choice of only a few unexpected words (note italics) leading into his introductory question:

The British have *hilarious* fun over the *quaint* funerary habits of the Americans. The death of Hubert Eaton, the world's greatest *entrepreneur* of death, and the recent discovery of a funeral home for pets, by a wandering British journalist, released another *gale* of satirical laughter in the English press. The mockery was hearty and sustained; yet was it deserved? (p. 466, *1,* emphasis mine)

Using Hooks   Devices such as these do make an introduction more interest-provoking. But you must not feel that such pizzazz is necessary. If you should be inspired by an idea for such an opening that is both imaginative and appropriate to your subject, don't be afraid to experiment with it. But if such inspiration does not come, it is always a mistake to try to force it. For although you are right to admire a strikingly apt opening, you should not underestimate the value of a simple but solid lead into your thesis followed by a clear statement of the thesis itself.

Guidelines

Although good introductions are as various as good essays, there are a few practical suggestions which might be of help to you in composing yours. The accompanying guidelines combine suggestions offered in this chapter with those discussed in "Writing the First Paper."

Guidelines for Your Introduction

1. Overall purpose: To present the thesis interestingly
   a. Specific purpose: To lead into the subject and generally into some statement of thesis
   b. Persuasive purpose: To interest the reader in the subject
2. Include:
   a. (always) A lead into the subject
   b. (almost always) A statement of (or some expression of) thesis
   c. (often) A statement of the "although" clause or an explication of the "although" clause
   d. (sometimes) A clarification of approach or explication of structure
   e. (never) Arguments for the thesis
3. Arrangement
   a. Thesis statement (or expression) last or near the last
   b. If there is material after the thesis, it should be limited to
      i. Restatement or amplification of the thesis
      ii. A transitional sentence on structural matters

Try It Out

1. Examine six introductions from essays in Part Five or from another sampling of magazine essays or another collection of articles. Estimate what percentage of the introductions you studied are marked by the following:
   a. A straightforward lead into the thesis

   b. An "although" clause type of opening, leading to a contradictory thesis
   c. Some sort of hook or special strategy to attract the reader
   Describe the hooks that you have discovered. Do you find them effective?
2. Try constructing two effective one-paragraph introductions leading to two of the following theses. (Feel free to reword the thesis sentences to suit your own purposes.)
   a. The consumption of sugar creates more health problems than is usually acknowledged.
   b. Despite the corruption of the boss-run City Hall, there are those who long for restoration of the old-fashioned patronage system, abuses and all.
   c. As important as the computer is to our economy, it creates as many problems as it solves.
   d. Men and women of differing religions are unwise to marry each other.
   (or)
   e. The problems of inter-religious marriages are greatly exaggerated.

SUPPORTING YOUR POINT

Once you have completed the beginning of your paper, you have introduced and presented your point, your thesis. Now you have to support it. The ideas you have jotted down in your organizational plan, along with any thoughts they call to mind, should suggest the means of support and should help you structure that support. Your task at this stage is to explain, expand upon, and develop each of these ideas in order to present your thesis in the most convincing way.

The following sections offer suggestions about the form this support may take and include techniques and concepts to help you create the most effective sort of support for each idea. Give careful consideration to the ideas offered here and you'll gain some valuable insight into the writing process. Nevertheless, when you actually begin to write, you should not worry too much about keeping the precise particulars of this advice in mind. What you really want to do when you compose is to get your ideas flowing. Don't stop and consider every word, every sentence. Don't even be afraid occasionally to leave your plan behind and follow a thought wherever it seems to take you. Always realize YOU WILL HAVE THE OPPORTUNITY TO REVISE. You can stop and make changes at the end of each natural division if you like—or whenever the flow of your ideas begins to dwindle. You should certainly plan to revise when you reach the end. Remember your rewriting can be as extensive as you choose.

Bearing in mind, then, that everything you write is subject to change, use your plan as a general guide, and write as freely as you can.

Paragraphs and Paragraph Clusters

When we speak of writing the body of a composition, we are talking basically about composing paragraphs. "Paragraph" is, of course, a term familiar to you:

> A paragraph consists of material set off by spacing and indentation on a page of print, type, or script.

Although this definition is quite straightforward, the concept represented by the term "paragraph" is surprisingly problematical. The problem is that, in most respects, paragraphs are arbitrary divisions determined as much by the way a body of written material will look on a page as by the meaning of the words they contain. Where a paragraph ends is usually based upon readability. Since the space following each paragraph offers a rest for the reader's eye and mind, how many words to include before that rest is needed becomes a decision greatly dependent upon such variable conditions as the width of the column of print and the size of the lettering. For example, a good editor might decide to break up a passage of, say, 200 words on the popularity of soccer into three paragraphs if it were to be printed in a narrow newspaper column or into two paragraphs for printing on the pages of a small book with large print, while that same editor might leave it as a single paragraph if the material were to appear in a wide-column journal.

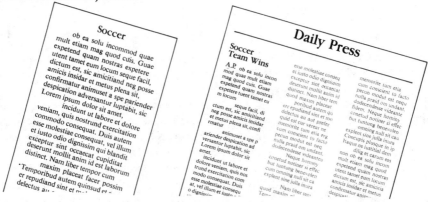

Printing Format
Affects Paragraphing

With such inconsistent division of material, you may well wonder how any consistent advice can be given to help you compose good paragraphs. The truth is that if we insist upon talking about the literal paragraph as it is variously printed on a page, no advice could be valid because no unvarying description can be made. The form of the middle paragraph in our example's newspaper column on soccer will probably have little in common with the form of the single 200-word soccer paragraph as it would appear in the wide-spaced journal. On the other hand, if we can look beyond the arbitrary mechanics of printing and concentrate on the 200-word passage as a whole—whether it appears as a single paragraph or a paragraph cluster of variable parts—we can recognize features in it that are characteristic of paragraphs or paragraph clusters in general.

What we are really talking about here (and what is often called "a paragraph" in rhetoric books) is *a section of prose in which a limited topic is stated and developed,* a unit of meaning for which there is no universally recognized English term. But it is this unit, whether it is found as a single paragraph or as a paragraph cluster, that is the major building block in expository compositions. And a very useful unit it is too. Scholarly research (which you can duplicate for yourself by studying the paragraphs in this book and elsewhere) shows that topic paragraphs (or paragraph clusters) in expository prose share the characteristics described in the accompanying boxed section on well-written paragraphs.

Paragraph or cluster as unit of meaning.

Well-written Expository Paragraphs (or Paragraph Clusters)

1. These units almost always contain a topic sentence (or sentence segment) that presents the subject of the paragraph (or cluster).
2. The rest of the sentences of the paragraph (or cluster) relate to the topic sentence in one of the following ways:
   a. Lead into it
   b. Explain it, by expanding or restricting its meaning
   c. Support it
   d. Or support or explain a supporting sentence
3. The placement of the topic sentence can vary, but in paragraphs or clusters that are *not introductory,* the topic sentence ordinarily occurs at or near the beginning.
4. Introductory passages generally have these characteristics:
   a. The topic sentence ordinarily occurs (as we have said) at or near the conclusion.
   b. In "although clause" introductory paragraphs (or clusters), the topic sentence often occurs somewhere near the center, following the "although" material. There it often has the effect of altering, even reversing, the meaning of the paragraph to that point.
   c. These introductory patterns sometimes occur within the body of an essay as well. In particular, they provide the pattern for some transitional paragraphs that introduce new sets of ideas.

What can you take from this knowledge of how good writers construct their paragraphs (or clusters) that should be useful to you in constructing your own? First, you can understand the importance of the topic sentence for communicating your points to the reader. (See p. 26 for a definition and discussion of the topic sentence.) You can also learn to help your reader by placing this extremely important sentence in the conventional position where your reader expects to find it. The other sentences in the paragraph unit can then perform their function of explaining or supporting your point. You will want to make sure that every sentence in the paragraph (or cluster) relates directly to your point and eliminate any that do not.

Topic Sentences

Most of your topic sentences should be effective statements of the points or subpoints in your organizational plan. As such, these sentences serve two functions:

- They set forth your point or subpoint clearly in a way that leads into or demands explanation or support.
- And they reflect back or tie into or support the thesis of your essay.

Consider, for example, the topic sentence of the fourth paragraph in Shana Alexander's essay, "Kids' Country";

> The food we live on is kids' food: pizza, hot dogs, fried chicken, ice cream, hamburgers. (p. 434, 4)

This sentence, like all good topic sentences, "looks before and after." At the same time it both supports Alexander's thesis that America has become a "kids' country" and it stimulates the statistics on American eating habits that make up the rest of the paragraph it heads.

Support

A contract with your readers. Topic sentences, no less than theses, make commitments to readers. When you write a topic sentence near the beginning of a paragraph, you are indicating to your readers that you will satisfy any question that might come to their minds about what the statement means or why it is true. That is, you agree to explain the statement or its key terms, to define them, to illustrate them until your readers find them clear. You also agree that you will provide enough supporting data, enough convincing examples, to make your readers follow your point and, if not agree to it, as least understand your reasons for thinking it is so.

You are probably wondering how you can keep this commitment. Here some definite advice can be offered: First, let your mind play over your topic sentence. Perhaps add another sentence or two to clarify it—to make it more specific or to expand it. Do not, however, fall into the danger, so common to writers, of building a paragraph consisting of repeated restatements of or generalizations on your topic sentence. When you are satisfied that you have made your point clearly, then see what supporting information comes to your mind to illustrate it or to back it up. Perhaps you will think of a series of examples, as Judith Crist does, for instance, in this paragraph from "Gentlemen and Scholars of the Press":

Topic sentence
Support by examples
Concluding thought

> *But none of the fun has gone out of newspapering either.** If anything, the company is better, the wit is more sophisticated, the joking less juvenile, the iconoclasm more judicious, and the occasional bender all the better for its occasion. And something has been added, a sense of service beyond one's self and a consciousness of craft: in short, professional pride. (p. 497, 24)

---

*This topic sentence, like those in the examples that follow, has been italicized for clarity.

Perhaps a single example that you can elaborate upon would back up your point more effectively. George Will uses this technique in this paragraph from his essay on the Chicago Cubs:

> Every litter must have its runt, but *my Cubs were almost all runts.* Topps baseball bubblegum cards always struggled to say something nice about each player. All they could say about the Cubs' infielder Eddie Miksis was that in 1951 he was tenth in the league in stolen bases, with eleven. (p. 450, 7)

Topic sentence

Support by a single example

Or perhaps you can find the best illustration for your point by relating an incident, as Wayne Booth does in this paragraph from "The Rhetorical Stance":

> One could easily discover *other perversions of the rhetorician's balance*—most obviously what *might be called the entertainer's stance—the willingness to sacrifice substance to personality and charm.* I admire Walker Gibson's efforts to startle us out of dry pedantry, but I know from experience that his exhortations to find and develop the speaker's voice can lead to empty colorfulness. A student once said to me, complaining about a colleague, "I soon learned that all I had to do to get an A was imitate Thurber." (p. 458, *22*)

Topic sentence

Developing material

Support by anecdote

Finding Support (Or Back to Aristotle Again) But what should you do when appropriate examples and illustrations do not come immediately to mind? You might try out Aristotle's "topics" (p. 43) to see if you could find some good supporting ideas by considering questions of definition, contrast, cause and effect, and authority. The following list offers a few such questions.

1. **Thinking in terms of definition and classification.** Ask yourself, Does my point or any key term in my topic sentence need to be defined? If so, what do I really mean by it? Can I classify it or analyze it into its parts? What examples could I give to illustrate its meaning?

   In the following example, Lance Morrow builds his paragraph by defining what is meant by "The Big Bang Theory."

   > [Transition sentence] That absolute expanse might be difficult, even unbearable, to contemplate, like an infinite snow field of time, but the conception at least carried with it the serenity of the eternal. *In recent decades, however, the Steady State model of the universe has yielded in the scientific mind to an even more difficult idea,* [*The Big Bang Theory*]*, full of cosmic violence.* Most astronomers now accept the theory that the universe had an instant of creation, that it came to be in a vast fireball explosion 15 or 20 billion years ago. The shrapnel created by that explosion is still flying outward from the focus of the blast. One of the fragments is the galaxy we call the Milky Way—one of whose hundreds of billions of stars is the earth's sun, with its tiny orbiting grains of planets. . . . (p. 486, *4*)

   In another paragraph, Williams defines by classifying and supports his topic sentence by giving examples from each of his classifications.

   > One of the most distinguishing features of American society is that we are a nation of racial minorities. What's more, casual reading of Amer-

ican history will show that *none of these minorities was welcomed to our shores with open arms.* They all faced varying degrees of open hostility and disadvantage. One need not go back too far in history to see in ads, "No Irish need apply," or, "Any color or country, except Irish." At one time Orientals were denied land ownership through the Alien Exclusion Act. Japanese citizens were imprisoned. Jews faced centuries of persecution and discrimination which was not completely relieved when they came to our country. (p. 490, *3*)

2. **Thinking in terms of comparison and analogy.** Ask yourself, Could my point, my topic sentence, become more clearer or more convincing if I compared it (or key terms within it) to something else? What analogy might I draw to it? Does my topic sentence already imply a comparison? If so, how does one portion relate to the other? What sort of examples might I give to illustrate both ideas or positions?

In the following example, Williams backs up and explains the idea put forth in his topic sentence by comparing the past with the present difficulties faced by newcomers to the American economy. He focuses here on a single instance, describing what is required to become a taxi driver:

> *One of the major differences between blacks and other minorities is the kind of economic system they faced when they became franchised and urbanized.* Minorities of the past faced a system of unfettered free enterprise. For example, a poor uneducated Italian immigrant in the 1920s in New York could own and operate a taxi as a means of upward mobility. All he needed was industry, ambition, and a used car with the word "Taxi" written on it. Today, a black, Hispanic, or for that matter anyone else, seeking the same path to upward mobility would find that he needs more than a car, industry, and ambition. He would have to buy a taxi license which costs $60,000. (p. 491, *7*)

Paragraphs developed comparatively include both those, like Williams's, in which a comparison included in the topic sentence is exemplified and those whose point is illustrated by drawing an analogy to it—that is, by setting up a comparative example. Such analogies usually involve finding a concrete example to stand for an abstract idea. J. B. S. Haldane, for instance, uses an airplane analogy to explain the flight problems enlarged birds would be likely to face:

> *Exactly the same difficulties attach to flying.* It is an elementary principle of aeronautics that the minimum speed needed to keep an aeroplane of a given shape in the air varies as the square root of its length. If its linear dimensions are increased four times, it must fly twice as fast. Now the power needed for the minimum speed increases more rapidly than the weight of the machine. So the larger aeroplane which weighs sixty-four times as much as the smaller needs one hundred and twenty-eight times its horsepower to keep up. Applying the same

principles to the birds, we find that the limit to their size is soon reached. An angel whose muscles developed no more power weight for weight than those of an eagle or a pigeon would require a breast projecting for about four feet to house the muscles engaged in working its wings, while to economize in weight, its legs would have to be reduced to mere stilts. (p. 482, 9)

Literary analogy is another sort of comparison that writers often find useful. Here abstractions set forth in the topic sentence are exemplified by allusion to concrete cases from literature. Carll Tucker develops one of his paragraphs in this way:

> *In some respects this freedom* [*to divorce casually*] *can be seen as social progress.* Modern couples can flee the corrosive bitterness that made Strindberg's marriages nightmares. Dreiser's Clyde Griffiths might have abandoned his Roberta instead of drowning her. (pp. 504, 505, 6)

3. **Thinking in terms of cause and effect.** Ask yourself, Would my point make more sense if its causes were explained? Or if the results it would lead to were pointed out? What examples would best show its causes or effects? When a topic sentence seems to demand an answer to the reader's unspoken question, "Why should this be so?" the author is committed to answer. Such answers usually require you to explain the reason or the cause behind the statement. Golden develops a number of the paragraphs in his essay, "Earth's Creeping Deserts," in this way. Among them:

> *The deserts' cancerous growth came to worldwide attention in the early 1970s with the great drought and famine in Africa's Sahel,* the band of impoverished land across the Sahara's southern flank. More than 100,000 people perished before the rains finally came in 1974, and that was not the end of the tragedy. Hundreds of thousands of tribesmen remain in camps, and the desert's encroachment has not halted. Senegal told the U.N. meeting that it feared its coastal capital, Dakar, would soon be engulfed. (pp. 432, 433, 5)

Judith Crist supports one of her topic sentences by exemplifying the effects of the ideas contained within it:

> *Financial and professional insecurity turned the newspaperman into a bohemian* who made a virtue of his lack of worldly status, a vice of such personal securities as education or professional training or even domesticity. If only for lack of money, the typical reporter was unmarried, an habitue of furnished rooms and cheap saloons, seeking solace among his fellows. He tended, naturally enough, to repay in kind the insecurity his employer offered, by moving on from job to job, by insouciance and prankishness that was charming but often disastrous, by kicking in the competitive clinches for temporary survival, and by an irresponsibility that caused him to regard his work as an end unto himself alone. The tramp printer of an earlier era was godfather to the tramp newspaperman. (p. 494, 8)

4. **Thinking in Terms of Authority.** Ask yourself, Would my point be clearer or more persuasive if it were restated or backed up by an authority (or authorities) in the field? What quotation(s) might be effective? What research or what statistics might bear it out or explain it more clearly?

Lance Morrow often quotes authorities to exemplify or substantiate his points in his essay, "In the Beginning: God and Science." The following paragraph is typical:

> A number of theologians concur that *the apparent convergence of religious and scientific versions of the creation is a coincidence from which no profound meaning can be extracted.* "If the last evidence for God occurred 20 billion years ago," asks Methodist W. Paul Jones of Missouri's St. Paul School of Theology, "do we not at best have the palest of deisms?" Jesuit Philosopher Bernard Lonergan goes further: "Science has nothing to say about creation, because that's going outside the empirical. The whole idea of empirical science is that you have data. Theologians have no data on God." (p. 488, *10*)

Shana Alexander supports her point in the following paragraph with the authority of facts and statistics:

> *The food we live on is kids' food:* pizza, hot dogs, fried chicken, ice cream, hamburgers. This bizarre diet is the reason we have such trouble maintaining our kids' bodies. The stuff we now drink has thrown the beverage industry into turmoil. Our consumption of soft drinks has risen 80 percent in a decade. Americans not only are switching *en masse* from hot coffee to iced tea, and from bitter drinks to sweet. The popularity of alcoholic soda pop—the so-called "fun" wines like Thunderbird and apple wine—has jumped 168 percent in five years. (p. 434, *4*)

Combined Support   As these sample paragraphs demonstrate, you may well find questions based on Aristotle's "topics" helpful to you in developing examples and illustrations to serve as "arguments" to "prove" your topic sentences. These samples are not totally representative, however, and it would be misleading to imply that most paragraphs are developed by following a single line of reasoning in this way. The truth is that the great majority of paragraphs written by professional writers are the result of combined reasoning. More typical than the examples above are such paragraphs as the following:

Comparison, Definition, and Effect

Yesterday's disadvantaged could effectively acquire skills. Many jobs used a piece rate as a form of compensation and there was no federally mandated minimum-wage law. What this meant was that a person could be low-skilled and still employable. Being employable meant a chance of upgrading skills and income. For today's disadvantaged minorities such a chance is reduced. The minimum-wage law has the full force of a law which says, "If you cannot produce $3.10 worth of goods or services per hour, you shall never be employed." The effect of this law is revealed by the scandalous rate of unemployment among black youths.   (Walter Williams, p. 491, *8*)

Definition and Authority

This self-centering is not only a retreat from the world, but a by-product of the current condition of our lives. The newest definition of American individualism is aloneness.

In the years since 1960, the number of "primaries"—people living alone—has risen only by 23 percent. Fifteen million of us live alone. Fifty million of us are single, widowed or divorced. At least partially in response to this, the new therapies—from the isolation tank on—offer us ways to "get into ourselves." Those who aren't "doing their own thing" or "finding themselves" are "getting in touch with their feelings." The West Coast greeting, "What are you into?" is most aptly answered with one word: myself.   (Ellen Goodman, p. 470, *6 & 7*)

Definition (Classification) and then Effect

Droughts and crop failures have always been a harsh fact of life in arid regions. But *the Sahel's calamity was worsened by distinctly modern factors.* Improvements in public health had vastly expanded population. New wells lulled the Africans into thinking they were no longer so completely dependent on the slim rainfall. They enlarged their herds and planted more cash crops like cotton and peanuts. For a while, the land withstood the strains. But when the rains ceased, the crops failed and the cattle stripped the fields of virtually every blade of grass around the overworked wells. Soon the thin layer of topsoil vanished, and there was nothing but rock, sand and dust. The Sahara had won. (Fred Golden, p. 433, *6*)

In order to activate what Agatha Christie's detective, Hercule Poirot, calls "the little grey cells," ask yourself the sort of questions of definition, comparison, cause and effect, and authority that we have been discussing over the last several pages. But do not limit yourself to any single line of reasoning. Instead, let your mind range freely among all the questions. Perhaps the best approach is to try to decide just what expectations your topic sentence would arouse in your readers, what questions it would create in their minds. Then plan your support to answer all of their unasked questions.

Try It Out

1. First, write topic sentences for three of the following topics. Then compose paragraphs supporting these topic sentences. Use the Guidelines on p. 91 to help you with paragraph form. Develop the material (at least in part) according to three of the four sets of Aristotelian questions: definition (or classification), comparison (or analogy), cause and effect, or authority.

   Murder mysteries or detective fiction   Sickle-cell anemia
   Cross-pollenization   Adoption
   Adolph Hitler   The Indianapolis 500
   San Francisco   Indians of the Great Plains

2. What questions do the following topic sentences raise in your mind? How would you suggest that a writer go about answering them in paragraph form?

a. Mononucleosis, a disease affecting the liver and spleen, is an uncommonly disagreeable affliction that attacks many college students.
b. Learning to write is not easy.
c. Many educators have become disillusioned with what used to be called the "new math."
d. Chicago is rightly known as the "Windy City."
e. Ronald Reagan was much admired for the gallant way he acted after the attack on his life.

Specific and Vivid Support

You are probably now convinced that in order to write an effective essay you need to develop your thesis with paragraphs or paragraph clusters whose topic sentences support the thesis and are in turn each convincingly supported. When you're involved in the writing process and have reviewed some of your options for developing that support, you may still wonder about the content of the support. Initially, professional writing may seem to offer little help. If you examine the sample paragraphs cited in the last section, other paragraphs from the essays in Part Five, or other examples of professional writing, your overall impression must be one of overwhelming variety. You will find that supporting material comes from literature (classical, popular, and historical); from statistical data and recorded facts; from memories or everyday knowledge; from personal observation or fantasy; from conversations, interviews, books, plays, television; from knowledge derived from a whole alphabet of scholarly disciplines from archaeology, botany, chemistry all the way to zoology. Nevertheless, in the midst of all this diversity, supporting material in well-written paragraphs does seem to have two important characteristics in common: the illustrations, from whatever source, are always both specific and vivid. It may even seem to you, as you examine writing samples, that an abundance of vivid and specific detail is what makes expository writing effective.

Unrelieved generalization, in fact, may well be the chief hallmark of the inexperienced writer. For example, approaching J. H. Plumb's idea that the wealthy of all ages have used their wealth to gain them something akin to immortality, an inexperienced person might write:

> Many ancient peoples believed that after death they merely passed from one life to another. They felt that the life hereafter was but a copy of life on earth. In order to enjoy their idea of heaven fully they took with them everything they had needed on earth. The graves of the ancient wealthy are thus filled with a greater display of wealth than even the showiest of modern cemeteries.

Although this is not a bad paragraph, it is far less effective than it could be. Instead of twice repeating the generalizations of the topic sentence, that sentence could be far better supported by the addition of details specific enough to explain it convincingly and vivid enough to involve the imaginations of its readers. Here is the paragraph as Plumb writes it:

The rich and the powerful, high priests and kings, could not die; they merely passed from one life to another. Because the life hereafter was but a mirror image of life on earth, they took with them everything they needed—jewels, furniture, food, and, of course, servants. In the Royal Graves at Ur, some of the earliest and most sumptuous of tombs ever found, a row of handmaidens had been slaughtered at the burial—death's necessities were life's. No one, of course, carried this elaboration of funerary activity further than the Egyptians. And the tombs of the Pharaohs and the high officials of the Egyptian kingdom make Forest Lawn seem like a cheap cemetery for the nation's down-and-outs. (p. 467, *8*)

Comparison of the two paragraphs reveals the sources of the second's strength. Instead of the general term *ancient peoples* in the first paragraph, Plumb tells us specifically that he takes his examples from "the Royal Graves at Ur" and "the tombs of the Egyptian Pharaohs." For the generality of *modern cemeteries,* he substitutes a particular one, "Forest Lawn." Plumb makes *the wealthy* more vivid by calling them "the rich and the powerful" and more specific by describing them as "high priests and kings." Not content to describe the grave articles as *everything they needed,* Plumb cites "jewels, furniture, food and, of course, servants." He is even more specific and vivid about the servants: "A row of handmaidens had been slaughtered at burial." In short, Plumb has made his point convincing in this paragraph by supporting it with vivid, specific detail.

What works for professional writers should also work for you. How effective you are in creating expository paragraphs depends upon how well you can think up vivid, specific detail and how appropriately you can use it. Two skills are especially important in this effort:

- The ability to observe in the particular rather than just in the general
- The ability to find relationships, to uncover similarities within your diverse experiences and memories

Both of these are the sort of skills that can be helped along by practice. The following ten exercises are designed to provide you with such practice.

Observing Visually There are two ways that you can train yourself to be an intelligent observer: Observe the object, person, or scene (1) as a whole in relation to its surroundings and (2) as a sum of its parts. In other words, think of yourself as first viewing it from afar and then examining it at close range. Try it out.

Try It Out

1. a. Select an object to observe carefully. (Take, for example, a particular tree or a particular typewriter.)
   b. Look at it from a distance. See how it relates to the space and other objects around it.

  c. Record your observations. What can you say about its size? Its proportions? Its color? Its relative importance to its own context?

  d. Does it remind you of anything from your own experience, from life, reading, movies, or television? Record also (however farfetched they appear at first) the ideas the distant object calls to your mind.

  e. Examine the object closer up. Describe it carefully. List at least ten specific details about it. (You may include details derived from senses other than the visual if you choose.)

  f. Record also any comparisons that the close-up examination might call from your memory.

2. a. Choose a small segment of landscape to observe carefully. Get some perspective on the scene. Observe it from afar or think how it would look if you were viewing it from a distance. (You might imagine how you would view it from a telescope.)

  b. Describe it carefully in relation to its surroundings.

  c. Record also any ideas that this scene might suggest to you.

  d. Record your observations taken at a middle distance.

  e. Place yourself within the scene and closely examine its various parts. You might even put some features of it under a mental microscope.

  f. List at least twelve specific details about it. (You may record details derived from senses other than visual if you choose.)

  g. Record also any comparisons that this close-up examination might call to your mind.

Observing by Hearing and Smelling Although there can be no question that for most of us the visual sense is the dominant observing power, good writers do not neglect any of their senses. Hearing and smell can be particularly useful. The following exercises will help you practice.

Try It Out

1. Choose three different locations. You may include the scene you used earlier if you wish.

  a. Close your eyes and listen.

  b. Then write down every sound that you hear. (If you have trouble describing a sound, use a comparison or an analogy that will communicate what you have heard.)

  c. What association(s) do the sounds call up in your mind?

2. a. Breathe deeply or sniff about at each of the three locations you used for the hearing exercise. (Or choose others if you prefer.)

  b. Identify the predominant odor(s) if you can. In any case, describe it (them) specifically.

  c. If you cannot make the odor clear by descriptive words alone, use comparisons or analogies.

  d. What association(s) do the odors bring to mind?

Selecting Intelligently

"Not being able to see the forest for the trees" is an old saying that sums up the problems that inexperienced writers sometimes face when they have learned how to observe well enough to gather a great number of details, but have not yet learned how to use those details discriminatingly. In your use of details, as in almost anything else, there can be too much of a good thing. You need to narrow down the dozens of sense impressions that are part of every situation to those few telling details that convey the sense of what you want to say. Specifically, in composing each of your paragraphs or paragraph clusters, focus in on the meaning of your topic sentence and select only those details that serve to support it. The following exercises offer an opportunity to practice this skill.

═══ Try It Out ═══

1. a. Return to the scene you used for observation in the visual exercise (and possibly also in the later exercises). What is the overall impression the place leaves in your mind? Perhaps it is a mood you sense there. Perhaps it is a thought that the place brings to your mind.
    b. Compose a sentence in which you express this impression, this mood, or this thought.
    c. Examine your list of specific details describing the place, and check only those details that have to do with the ideas expressed in your sentence.
    d. Making this sentence your topic sentence, write a paragraph (or

"The Bathers" by
Georges-Pierre Seurat (1859–1891)

paragraph cluster) in which you support your topic sentence with the details you have checked on your list.

2. a. Study the accompanying picture. What do you think the artist is trying to say by it? Phrase your answer as a sentence.

b. Jot down all of the details you can find in the picure that suggest that your interpretative sentence is correct. (If you find details that do not fit with your theory, be sure to revise your theory.)

c. Write a paragraph interpreting the picture, using your revised interpretative sentence as its topic sentence and the details you have noted as its support.

Thinking Specifically   Specific details can make a paragraph not only more convincing but also clearer and less ambiguous. General terms are almost always subject to a number of interpretations, and these interpretations can vary widely. The word "cruelty," for example, has been used to describe the effects of such completely different causes as the medieval torture rack and an indifferent lover. The following exercises are meant to help you learn to select appropriately specific support.

Try It Out

1. In three to five sentences, distinguish one middle-aged lady standing at a bus stop from another middle-aged lady standing at the same stop. Select your specific details carefully.

2. Choosing specific details, describe one yard in the country so as to distinguish it from another such yard.

Seeing Relationships, Drawing Connections   Sometimes good writers do not draw the details with which they support their points directly from sense impressions or even from facts and figures. Sometimes they take them instead from memory. When Wayne Booth, for example, wanted to back up his point that good writing springs only from a real desire to communicate, he remembered his frustrations over a particular student's progress and illustrated his point with a story about it (p. 85 in this chapter). When Walter Williams wanted to prove that it was much easier for a person to achieve economic security in the past than it is now, driving a taxi was the illustration that occurred to him. With this idea in mind, he researched the appropriate licensing facts and gave vivid and specific proof (p. 94). When George Will needed support for his statement that the Chicago Cubs of his youth were a laughably inferior team, he remembered an old bubblegum baseball card that couldn't find anything to praise about one of the team members (p. 93).

All of these illustrations illuminate the idea expressed in the topic sentences of these paragraphs so well that they may appear to be natural outgrowths of the statements that prompted them. In reality they came about because their authors have the ability to see relationships, to make connections between what they want to say and the relevant portions of their experience or memories. The ability to use imagination and memory to convey ideas to readers in this way is one of the important skills involved in writing effectively. The following exercises should help you practice it.

Try It Out

1. a. Think of someone you know. What character in a book or in a movie or on television does he or she remind you of? In what *specific* ways are they alike? What are their points of difference?
   b. Write a paragraph describing your acquaintance (or friend or relative) in terms of the fictional (or historic) character so that a reader familiar with the character will be able also to understand your friend or acquaintance as well.

Picture A   "Madame Moitessier Seated"   **Picture B**   "Portrait of Greta Moll"
  by Jean-Auguste-Dominique Ingres   by Henri Matisse (1869–1954)
        (1780–1867)

2. a. Carefully study pictures A and B. There may well be an underlying resemblance in the features of the women who sat as models for these two portraits. The works, however, were painted by artists widely separated in time and in artistic technique, who were influ-

enced by widely differing ideas of fashion and beauty. Do you see the pictures as similar or as very different? Upon what do you base this judgment?

b. In deciding upon what you base your judgment, you should discover a major point of comparison between the two pictures. What is it?

c. Phrase your point of comparison as a topic sentence.

d. Illustrate and demonstrate the truth of your topic sentence in a paragraph built on details actually in or suggested by the two pictures.

TYING IT ALL TOGETHER

Inexperienced writers often worry about how they are going to end their papers. They are concerned because they are aware of the importance of endings. They realize that their conclusions will provide readers with a final impression, but they often just don't know what to say. Many are not sure what a conclusion is expected to do. It might be a good idea, therefore, to see how professional writers bring their essays to a close. If you examine the essays in Part Five or check over others in books or magazines, you should discover the facts about conclusions listed in the accompanying boxed section.

Facts about Conclusions

Length
Conclusions vary in length as much as introductions do. A few essays have no separate closing paragraphs at all, but simply end the final paragraph in the body of the essay with a sentence that sounds a note of finality. (See, for example, Will's essay, p. 451.) Some end with a single brief paragraph. Other essays conclude with a long paragraph or a paragraph cluster. Still others—especially those where there is no early statement of thesis—end with a concluding paragraph cluster of substantial length. (See the Didion and Plumb essays, pp. 441, 442, and 468, 469.)

Content
Despite the variation in length, concluding paragraphs (or paragraph clusters)—where they exist—tend to be built on similar patterns. They consist of:

1. A final statement of the essay's thesis, along with
2. Additional material that either
   a. Helps to define the thesis more completely or to develop its implications or
   b. Suggests to the reader constructive ways of viewing the thesis or of applying it.

Placement of Thesis
Most concluding paragraphs (or paragraph clusters) begin with a restatement of the essay's thesis, now phrased in terms that include what has gone before. Some

concluding paragraphs end with such a rephrasing of thesis. (See, for instance, Raspberry, p. 503.) Sometimes, longer conclusions both begin with a statement of thesis and end with a rephrasing of the same idea, often in metaphorical terms. (See Plumb, pp. 468, 469, or Tucker, p. 505.)

Style

Concluding paragraphs (or paragraph clusters) are usually marked by a tone in which there is at least some increase in emotional intensity, a heightening of conviction. This heightening is achieved by an underlying excitement expressed in such devices as rhythmic language, metaphor, paradox, and other imagery; quotations, anecdotes, irony, or humor. Often the final sentence is especially involved in this sort of emphasis.

It would seem, then, from this information, that the purpose of a conclusion is to tie a composition together by a final and perhaps emotionally charged restatement of its thesis and, often, to lead the readers' thoughts beyond the theoretical thesis into the real world where that thesis might be applied.

How are you to accomplish these purposes in your own closing? The rest of the chapter offers some practical suggestions.

Rereading Your Paper

Much has been said in this book about the importance of planning ahead. Chapters 1 and 2, in fact, are completely devoted to the advance thinking that is the essence of the prewriting part of the writing process. Nevertheless, when it comes to writing the conclusion of your essay, I want to suggest that you do *not* plan it exactly beforehand. When you have finished writing the first draft of the introduction and body of your composition, you should take time out and read carefully through what you have written. Having reread and reconsidered, you can then let your ending flow out of what you have already said. There are a number of reasons why this procedure is a good one.

To begin with, it is possible that when you have reread your composition, you may find that you have already said all you have to say, that anything else would just be filler. Especially in a very brief paper, a formal conclusion can be repetitive and unnecessary. It may be that instead of writing a concluding paragraph all you will need to do is to be sure that the last paragraph of the body of your essay ends with a note of finality. Then too, you cannot know before you have written the essay just what its conclusion should say. Writing itself is part of the invention process. Unless you follow your original outline in a totally robot-like way, the chances are that you will be reshaping some of your ideas while you are writing them. You want to leave yourself free to find the most effective way of concluding the composition you have actually written. Furthermore, rereading your paper as a whole will probably rekindle your enthusiasm for your point so that you will find yourself rephrasing it in language that reflects your inner excitement.

But most important of all, drawing your conclusion from your rereading of the rest provides your essay with a sense of wholeness. When you write your closing after rereading, you will not be tempted to add on a pat ending. Instead, you will give your final reflections upon your thesis, your final coloring of the point your paper makes and the ideas you have discussed in making it. You can achieve this sense of wholeness and completion by employing two basic concluding techniques: (1) You can restate your central point, your thesis, in terms of the ideas through which you have developed it, and (2) you can provide echoes of these ideas and even of the language in which you have phrased them earlier. Let's look more closely at both these techniques.

Echoes   When you write the closing of your paper with the ideas and phrasing of the rest of it fresh in your mind, you are likely to echo the ideas and phrasing in your conclusion. Not only do such echoes give your readers a sense of unity that is both satisfying and persuasive, but they can also provide an under-the-surface summary of your most persuasive points. I am not, of course, recommending that you build your conclusion out of the last part of the old saw that says "Tell them what you're gonna say; say it; and then tell them you've said it." Closings such as "I have argued (1) . . . , (2) . . . , and (3) . . . ; and therefore, . . . " can be deadly, especially in a brief or nontechnical paper. It is quite a different matter, however, for these points to express themselves to the reader through connecting links with the rest of the paper.

What exactly are these connecting links? Echoes are difficult to explain by means of brief quotation alone since by their very nature they reflect the whole. But let me suggest a way you can explore them for yourself. Examine the conclusion of one of the essays in Part Five. When you have selected the key words within it, trace them or their counterparts throughout the whole work. If you should try, for example, the closing paragraph cluster of Judith Crist's "Gentlemen and Scholars of the Press," you might focus in on its first phrase, "For sane, sober, and secure though this business has become" with its clear implication of an earlier insanity, insobriety, and insecurity. If you should choose to follow up the key words "sober" and "secure" from this phrase, you would be able to find, among others, the following network of early references to these ideas and their opposites. The page numbers listed at the right show that these references appear throughout the essay:

"Sober"

Echo Networks
- Fedora-topped drunkards tippling from desk drawer bottles (p. 493, *2*)
- Shaven, sober commuters . . . my colleagues (p. 493, *3*)
- Bleeck's downstairs . . . Chumley's in Greenwich Village (p. 494, *5*)
- [Now] found in saloons only [for] . . . special celebrations (p. 494, *5*)
- Tribe of assorted drunkards. . . (p. 495, *10*)
- Arrogant and sodden (p. 495, *10*)
- Shoptalk in the nearby saloon is regulated by his commuting-train schedule (p. 495, *12*)

"Secure"
- Romance is the stuff of economic insecurity (p. 493, *4*)
- Carelessness bred by such insecurity (p. 493, *4*)
- A vice of such personal securities as education (p. 494, *8*)
- Repay in kind the insecurity his employer offered (p. 494, *8*)
- Pays for his security with skill (p. 495, *13*)
- Economic security has proved a magnet (p. 496, *16*)
- The "security system" works (p. 496, *18*)
- As much by pride as by liking for security (p. 496, *20*)

Other key words in the conclusion would yield similar linkage patterns.

Networks of echoes like this one are perhaps most clearly seen in essays that employ a framelike structure. In such essays, the author picks up an idea or image put forward in the introduction and builds the conclusion around it, pulling the paper together in a sort of a frame. The technique of the frame is one of the more formal closing strategies discussed later in this section (see p. 111).

Final Statement of Thesis. . . and Beyond   Besides recalling echoes of earlier parts of your essay for use in its closing, rereading your essay should help you with the most important element of your conclusion, the final presentation of your central point. The whole of your essay focuses upon setting forth this idea. Your readers will expect that in closing you will give your thesis its clearest and most persuasive statement. When you reread your essay before writing your conclusion, you can phrase the thesis so that it will follow naturally from what you have written earlier. You can phrase it so that it summarizes, without repeating your ideas monotonously. The conclusion of Judith Crist's essay serves as a good instance of thesis restatement:

> For sane, sober, and secure though this business has become, it has lost none of the glory that is its essence, the glory of transmitting the fact, of telling the truth so that the people will know it, and—one must confess—of being on the inside when news is made. (p. 497, *23*)

Crist could have ended her essay here. Having her main point persuasively stated (and having used echoes to unify her essay in the process), she could have considered her essay complete. Brief endings of this sort can be highly effective. But Judith Crist, like many professional authors, in this case chose to carry her conclusion beyond the reformulation of its thesis. Her conclusion begins with a restatement of her point and continues on to an evaluation of it.

Specifically, Crist has convinced us readers throughout her essay that the newspaper business has given up much of the shabby lifestyle from which nostalgic stories of journalism still take their color and has instead become civi- *Add an evaluation or application.*

lized. In her final words, she wants to persuade us that the change has been for the good:

> But none of the fun has gone out of newspapering either. If anything, the company is better, the wit is more sophisticated, the joking less juvenile, the iconoclasm more judicious, and the occasional bender all the better for its occasion. And something has been added, a sense of service beyond one's self and a consciousness of craft: in short, professional pride. (p. 497, *24*)

In finishing off your essay, you might wish to take your readers a step beyond your thesis, just as Judith Crist does. In doing so, you may also want to offer some evaluation of your point.

On the other hand, you may want to apply your point in some practical way as does Walter Williams. This author, whose central point involves explanation of why black people have a harder time than did low-income groups in earlier historical periods, clearly states his thesis at the beginning of his concluding paragraph cluster:

> Therefore, what has happened is that when blacks received the franchise, they found that many markets were closed and hence the traditional sources of upward mobility. (p. 491, *10*)

In the final paragraph of the cluster, he applies this explanation in order to offer a solution to the problem:

> What disadvantaged people need are freer markets and a return to the principles of the Bill of Rights—principles which the Supreme Court of the 1930s threw out when they gave the state and federal governments greater control over the individual's economic life. Black people need a fair chance to compete—nothing more and nothing less. (p. 492, *11*)

Suggest change or action.   Similarly, in writing your own conclusion, you may want to suggest that your readers change their thinking or take action on your point. Scholars, for instance, often close articles or reports with suggestions of further scholarly work to be undertaken in the field they have just explored. Lance Morrow ends his essay on "God and Science" in just this way:

> If it has done nothing else, however, the new coincidence of scientific and theological versions of creation seems to have opened up a conversation that has been neglected for centuries. . . . The theory of the Big Bang is surely not the last idea of creation that will be conceived; it does suggest that there remain immense territories of mystery that both the theologian and the scientist should approach with becoming awe. (pp. 488, 489, *13*)

Although endings that go beyond the present thesis to a future application or beyond a theoretical thesis to a practical application can be highly satisfying, you should *not* feel obliged to conclude in this way. Brief conclusions may be even more effective, especially for brief essays. Avoid "filler." Avoid wordiness. Often when you have expounded your thesis clearly and persuasively, there is nothing more to say. At such times it is best simply to conclude. Both Golden and Raspberry close with simple but strongly worded reaffirmations of their theses:

> Some scientists feared that the document placed too much faith in technological—rather than "human"—solutions, but the plea nonetheless represents a milestone. For the first time, the international community is committing itself to the fight against the growth of deserts. While the document leaves action up to individual countries, the incentive to collaborate—perhaps even with old enemies—is great. *To many countries, doing battle against the deserts is the only alternative to poverty, starvation and chaos.* (Golden, p. 433, *8*, thesis in italics)

> The Harvard psychiatrists worry about cheating children out of their childhood. *I worry about cheating them out of something more profoundly important: their self-respect as responsible, contributing human beings.* (Raspberry, p. 503, *16*, thesis in italics)

Heightened Language

The purpose of a conclusion is to conclude, to tie the whole experience of reading the essay together and to leave the reader with something to remember or ponder. Because all writing is essentially persuasive, the reader should also be left with a certain sense of conviction. To gain this sense of conviction, authors often close their essays with language that has more emotional intensity than they include earlier in the piece. They word their conclusions in a prose that is more rhythmical in its phrasing and more metaphorical in its content. Examples abound. There is scarcely an essay in the Part Five collection in which the emotional impact of the writing does not intensify through the final sentences. Sometimes it is in the almost poetic rhythms created by parallel structure and the use of "and": *Use rhythm and metaphor.*

> It is there we perceive Christmas—and the sheep quiet, and the world waiting. (White, p. 499, *4*)

Sometimes it is in the contrast of a final very brief sentence with the lengthy ones preceding it:

> Hildy Johnson never had it so good. (Crist, p. 497, *25*)

Sometimes it is in a rousing exhortation:

> Black people need a fair chance to compete—nothing more and nothing less. (Williams, p. 492)

Or sometimes the impact can come from the use of emotional language and metaphor:

> We tear ourselves to pieces because of symbols, and we are more vulnerable to this than to any host of predators. We are, in effect, at the mercy of our own Pentagons, most of the time. (Thomas, p. 465, *15*)

> There is great joy in watching a tree grow. (Tucker, p. 505, *10*)

You may want to try to bring this sort of color to your endings. The chapters on style later in the book (see especially Chapters 7 and 8) should give you some concrete ideas about heightening language. And rereading your essay should also help. For rereading can rekindle your enthusiasm for your subject and thus prompt you to convey that sense of excitement to your readers.

More Formal Concluding Strategies

In concluding some essays—though by no means all—authors may go beyond the simple heightening of language to employ more formal strategies. You should feel under no compulsion to try out these techniques. Sometimes they can, in fact, lead to excess. Yet, when the devices are appropriate to the subject and tone of an essay and they are not overdone, these strategies can be highly effective. Let us examine some that you might employ.

Concluding Quotations   You might close your paper with a quotation. Sometimes another author states your point in a particularly telling way. Sometimes you can find a quotation that adds the kind of ringing phrases to your conclusion that you feel shy about using yourself. If the author you quote is well known, you have the additional advantage of providing authoritative weight to your restatement of thesis. William Raspberry concluded an essay on equal opportunity by quoting from a recent book:

> Should blacks be given preferential treatment? Dorn finds the answer easy: "If equal opportunity is to produce racial equality, then it is clear that a period of compensatory inequality is required. . . . It simply makes no sense to pretend that 'equal' opportunity, as we now practice it, will lead us toward racial equality." (*Washington Post,* April 20, 1981)

Since one of your reasons for ending with a quotation would be to heighten the language and intensify the emotional quality of your conclusion, you might try concluding with a line or two of poetry. The language of poetry is, almost by definition, heightened. Quoting poetry is not an unusual way to close, although none of the essays in Part Five adopt this technique. A typical example may be found in an article from *Time* reviewing the effect of the counter-culture of the sixties. The closing poetic lines are from W.B. Yeats' poem, "The Second Coming":

> Ultimately, the great danger of the counter-culture is its self-proclaimed flight from reason, its exaltation of self over society, its Dionysian anarchism. . . .
> The Second Comings of history carry with them no guarantees of success, and a revolution based on unreason may just as easily bring a New Barbarism rather than the New Jerusalem. As Yeats so pointedly asked:
> > And what rough beast, its hour come round at last,
> > Slouches toward Bethlehem to be born?
> > ("The Message of History's Biggest Happening," *Time,* 94 [August 29, 1969], 32–33.)

Quoting from a poem can enhance your thesis by lending to your prose the appealing qualities of poetry. Similarly, you can draw on the narrative appeal of the story form to create interest and add persuasiveness to your conclusion. Ellen Goodman, for instance, found an anecdote appropriate to her thesis in an article she had read and closed her own essay by quoting it:

> I am reminded of a brief exchange Peter Marin had with a man "into" mysticism, and which he repeated in a piece written for *Harper's* last year. He wrote: "He was telling me about his sense of another reality. 'I know there is something outside of me,' he said. 'I can feel it. I know it is there. But what is it?' 'It may not be a mystery,' I said, 'Perhaps it is the world.'" (p. 471, *10*)

Concluding Anecdotes   All good anecdotes are not, of course, found in the writing of others. You might very well dicover a brief incident in your own experience that you could relate as a closing for your essay. Wallace Stegner, for example, concludes his essay with an anecdote that captures his point in narrative form:

> I remember my uncle, a farmer who had used four-letter words ten to the sentence ever since he learned to talk. One day he came too near the circular saw and cut half his fingers off. While we stared in horror, he stood watching the bright arterial blood pump from his ruined hand. Then he spoke, and he did not speak loud. "Aw, the dickens," he said.
>
>   I think he understood, better than some sophomore girls and better than some novelists, the nature of emphasis. (p. 501, *9–10*)

Tom Wolfe also uses an anecdotal conclusion. To reinforce his point about the strange attraction for the violent that middle-class sophisticates have recently acquired, he tells a story about Bongo, a professional killer at a sophisticated cocktail party (p. 445). In closing with personal anecdotes such as these, you can take advantage of the almost universal appeal of the story form. When your anecdote is completely appropriate, you will make your thesis more understandable by translating it into other terms.

Frame or Circle Conclusions   A particularly satisfying sort of conclusion is the kind that seems to complete a circle of ideas begun in the early sentences of an essay. The essay thus seems to be framed by a unifying introductory and concluding idea. Judith Crist, for instance, begins "Gentlemen and Scholars of the Press" with a reference to Hildy Johnson, the hero of *The Front Page,* Ben Hecht's and Charles MacArthur's famous play that romanticized and helped create the public view of old-time journalism:

> Hildy Johnson is no more and *The Front Page* is history. (p. 493, *1*)

Having worked through her thesis about the improvements in newspaper work, in closing she reminds us of her beginning allusion:

> Hildy Johnson never had it so good. (p. 497, *25*)

Although a frame construction does not necessarily require it, Crist also used other references to Ben Hecht or to the play in the body of the essay, all of which serve to strengthen the frame. You will find similar framing images in a number of the articles in this text, including the UN conference in Golden's

"Earth's Creeping Deserts" and the Harvard psychiatrists in Raspberry's "Children of Two-Career Families."

Paradox Conclusions   Authors often take advantage of the fact that paradoxes are endlessly fascinating by closing their essays on a paradoxical note. Often such endings involve a twist on an image presented earlier and thus can be thought of as "reverse-frame" conclusions. For example, Shana Alexander begins her essay with the notion that

> Children are a relatively modern invention. Until a few hundred years ago, they did not exist. (p. 434, *1*)

By the time she reachs her closing, she has reversed her earlier conclusion:

> If in the old days children did not exist, it seems equally true today that adults as a class have begun to disappear, condemning all of us to remain boys and girls forever, jogging and doing push-ups against all eternity. (pp. 436, 437, *16*)

Plumb uses much the same strategy with the image of Nixon's late dog Checkers whose interment in a special pet section of Forest Lawn Cemetery he at first treats derisively. After working through his anthropological explanation of our funerary customs, however, Plumb concludes his essay with:

> How right, how proper, that Checkers should be waiting in Slumberland. (p. 469, *14*)

Conclusions: Final Advice

As exciting as such formal conclusions can be, most essays do not employ such flourishes. On the other hand, a great number do achieve, as we said, an intensification of meaning by a heightening of the language. What should *you* do? You should read your paper through and permit yourself to be—well, let's call it by its name—inspired in a quite natural way by what you have written in the introduction and the body. Then, if the rereading works as it can, you may find that without any artificial striving, you can achieve a genuinely effective conclusion. In any case, you should draw from your rereading a final statement of your thesis that has both solidity and clarity. That in itself is no small achievement.

The Title

When you have finished your essay, you should give it a title that will suggest its content or, where appropriate, comment upon it in a clever way Since a title may appear on a separate page, it should never be considered an integral part of the essay. Never depend upon the title to introduce the topic of your paper. A paper that begins, "This idea will lead to no good" arouses unnecessary curiosity while the reader fumbles for the title page to find out whether the writer is referring to capital punishment or kissing on the first date. Think of a title as a nice completing touch. It is rather like the frosting on a cake: Though it does not really affect the texture of the product, it gives gloss and finish.

Try It Out

1. Choose one of the following phrases from the conclusion of an essay and trace its echoes throughout the work:
   a. "perversions of . . . the rhetorical balance" from Wayne Booth's "The Rhetorical Stance." (p. 452)
   b. "say shit before a lady" from Wallace Stegner's "Goodbye to All T--t." (p. 500)
2. Staple or tape paper over the conclusion of your last (or next) composition and exchange it with that of a classmate whose conclusion is similarly covered. Read through your classmate's essay and write an appropriate ending for it. Compare the new closings with the original ones in terms of features discussed in this section.
3. Suggest alternative titles for two of the essays in Part Five.

ASSIGNMENT

Following the suggestions set forth in Part One and the first three chapters, write an effective essay on one of the following topics, a topic suggested in one of the "Try It Out" sections (pp. 88, 97), or one suggested by your instructor.

1. There is (or there is not) a body of knowledge that people must have to be considered educated. Therefore, courses in ------ should be required for college graduation.
2. An employer hiring college graduates should give particular weight to the applicant's grade point average, or choice of curriculum, or campus activities, or ------.
3. The English language, as it is used today, has an abundance of sexist overtones, and (but) these do (do not) reinforce discriminatory attitudes toward women (men).
4. Comic movies, plays, or television programs are often more profound than serious ones.
5. Video games that fill "family fun arcades" these days do (do not) serve a useful purpose in the lives of young people.
6. Choose a quotation—perhaps a humorous one—that appeals to you in some way and use it to give focus to your essay.

   a. Write an introduction using the quotation you have chosen. The quotation should lead to your statement of thesis.
   b. Work two references to the quotation into the body of your essay.
   c. Use a further quotation from the same source to write your conclusion, creating a "frame" that ties your essay together.

4

Revising Your Essay

You have finished writing your paper, and you certainly have earned a hearty sigh of relief. Nevertheless, if you have done a good job of composing this first draft, your work is not yet over. For if you have been able to let your ideas flow freely, if you have been able to push aside questions of mechanics and just let yourself write, then there will probably be a number of ways you will be able to improve your initial effort. Although the revising stage of the writing process is, on the whole, not as difficult as either the prewriting or the writing stage, it is at least as important. After all, during this final stage you create the essay your readers will actually see.

Probably the best way to go about revising is to work from large to small, from overall to the parts, from structure to style. This ordering saves a good deal of effort; for in making major revisions, you may very well eliminate material where smaller revisions would have been needed. Furthermore, research has shown that when a writer clarifies the thinking behind an awkwardly worded passage, more often than not the syntactical problems take care of themselves. Chapter 4 will help you look at the possibilities for revising, first for structure, then for persuasiveness, and finally for correctness.

REVISING FOR STRUCTURE

Traditionally, when writers have worked on revising the structure of their compositions, they have evaluated them in terms of unity, coherence, and emphasis. These remain the most useful criteria. Here is how Donald Murray defines them:

> [Your essay] must have unity; it should all be about the same subject. It must have coherence; each point should lead to the next point. And it must have emphasis; the most important points should be in the most important places.
> (*A Writer Teaches Writing* [Boston: Houghton Mifflin, 1968], p. 11)

The following sections offer suggestions on how you can review your first draft to make sure that it has the appropriate unity, coherence, and emphasis. They also advise you on ways you can revise your paper to correct any such deficiencies you might discover.

Unity

Your thesis is your best tool for achieving unity. If you have focused your entire paper upon demonstrating your thesis, your paper will automatically be unified. How can you tell? Why not read over all the topic sentences of your paragraphs to make sure that they somehow relate to "proving" your thesis. If they do, then your paper has an overall focus. However, your essay needs internal unity as well. To check for this, you will need to reread those topic sentences to be certain that each one also sets up the subject matter of its particular paragraph. Then, within each paragraph unit, check to see if all the supporting material contributes to backing up the topic sentence.

If you should find some paragraphs that do not directly support your thesis or some material within a paragraph that does not relate to the idea suggested in its topic sentence, I strongly urge you to eliminate it. No matter how interesting this extra material might be, if it distracts from the line of thinking you are pursuing in this paper, it can only do harm. If you cannot bear to give up *Save unrelated* a particular passage, you might try to find another point to which it relates *material for a* more directly or to which it can be subordinated. But if it is truly unrelated to *future paper.* your present thesis, do not try to include it. Consider instead jotting the passage down in a notebook or journal so that you can develop it in another paper some day.

If you sense a lack of focus in your essay, but are having trouble locating the source of the problem, there is an almost mathematical way to look for the difficulty. Go back to your outline and revise it, if necessary, so that it corresponds exactly to the structure of your paper as you have actually written it. Then check the corrected outline for unity using the modified versions of the following equations that are appropriate to your own situation:

- Do points I + II + III + IV . . . = Your Thesis?
- Do subpoints IIA + IIB + IIC . . . = Point II?
- Do sub-subpoints IIA_1 + IIA_2 + IIA_3 = Subpoint IIA? And so on?

Where you find a discrepancy, rework your outline to correct it. And then revise your paper accordingly.

Professional writers have invented a handy technique for making major revisions of this sort that you also might find useful. It's called "cut-and-paste." What you do is cut out the portions of your first draft that seem to be out of *A practical* order, and staple or tape them to scratch paper in the new positions before *hint.* making the necessary internal revisions.

Try It Out

It is often easier to spot elements of disunity if they are not of your own making. The following two exercises offer you practice in this sort of editing. The skill you gain can transfer over to your own work.

1. Distracting sentences have been introduced into the following professionally written paragraphs. Identify these sentences and explain how they clutter a paragraph and interfere with its unity.

A. Revise the following paragraph back to the lean, strong prose Martin Luther King, Jr., originally intended:

> Sometimes a law is just on its face and unjust in its application. Justice is the goal we all strive for. For instance, I have been arrested on a charge of parading without a permit. And arrest is a degrading and humiliating experience. Now there is nothing wrong in having an ordinance which requires a permit for a parade. Parades are enjoyed by children on the Fourth of July. They love to decorate their tricycles with red, white, and blue crepe FAULTY paper. They love to wave their miniature flags and beat their miniature drums. When veterans parade on Memorial Day, they remind us of our great debt to those who sacrificed for our country. Of course, the police need to establish some order on parade days, so licensing ordinances need to be required. But such an ordinance becomes unjust when it is used to maintain segregation and to deny citizens the First Amendment privilege of peaceful assembly and protest. (Adapted from "Letter from Birmingham Jail," Apr. 16, 1953. In *Why We Can't Wait* [New York: Harper & Row, 1958])

B. Edit out the unrelated material that was inserted into this article by John Holt:

> We learn to write by writing, not by reading other people's ideas about writing. Some excellent suggestions on how to write are given by Maxine Hairston in *Successful Writing* and by Don Murray in *A Writer Teaches Writing*. What most students need above all else is practice in writing, and particularly in writing about things that matter to them. Children care about their own experiences in the classroom and on the playground. Their excitement FAULTY ment runs especially high when there is a fight on the playground. Then some of the children will shout, "Fight, Fight," and they will all gather round gawking until the playground monitor comes out and separates the miscreants. Children should be able to write about such subjects. They will then begin to feel the satisfaction that comes from getting important thoughts down in words and will care about stating these thoughts forcefully and clearly. (Adapted from "How Teachers Make Children Hate Reading," *Redbook*, 130 [Nov. 1967], p. 50)

2. Exchange your last essay (or your next one) with one of your classmates, and examine it for problems of unity or focus. Discuss how these problems might be remedied.

Coherence

Many inexperienced writers have a serious problem with coherence that stems from an inability to put themselves in the reader's place and read their own work through a reader's eyes. Sometimes what these writers want to say is so clear in their own minds that they have a hard time perceiving that they have left out the connecting material that will make sense of two seemingly unrelated ideas. And sometimes they are so taken up with the order in which a set of ideas came to them, that they do not realize that these ideas would be more logical if they were ordered in another way. Because of this common difficulty in identifying with the reader, I suggest that you postpone your search for problems of coherence until the paper is less fresh in your mind, until the precise details of its composition have faded from your memory—at least to a degree.

Overall Coherence   You should begin your search for coherence by examining your overall structure to determine if all of your points and subpoints are in the order that supports your thesis most logically. If you have any serious uncertainty at this point, ask others to look your paper over to see if they can easily follow your chain of thought. If you discover a problem, do not hesitate to cut and paste until the difficulty is eliminated.

Coherence in Paragraphs   Logical ordering of ideas is also important at the paragraph level. Scholars such as Francis Christensen and Alton Becker have conducted research to determine exactly what makes for coherent paragraphs. To further their research, each scholar has developed an apparatus of analysis. You may find their apparatus valuable in your editing as well. When you sense that a coherence problem exists within one of your paragraphs, but are unable to point to it precisely, the apparatus may be a useful diagnostic tool to employ.

TRI   Alton Becker developed a relatively simple approach to the paragraph. He sees it in terms of the statement of a (T)opic, a (R)estriction on or a development of that topic, and an (I)llustration of the topic. More informally, his schema is known as TRI. He would analyze a paragraph in this way:

(T) Rhetoric is the art of persuading, not the art of seeming to persuade by giving everything away at the start.

(R) It presupposes that one has a purpose concerning a subject which itself cannot be fundamentally modified by the desire to persuade.

(I) If Edmund Burke had decided that he could win more votes in Parliament by choosing the other side—as he most certainly could have done—we would hardly hail this party-switch as a master stroke of rhetoric. If Churchill had offered the British "peace in our time," with some laughs thrown in, because opinion polls had shown that more Britishers were "grabbed" by these than by blood, sweat, and tears, we could hardly call his decision a sign of rhetorical skill. (Wayne Booth, "The Rhetorical Stance," p. 458, *21*)

Although most good paragraphs fit the TRI structure, Becker's system also allows for an occasional TIRI, ITR, TRIT, or even IRT. Furthermore, Becker enhances the usability of his system by adding the symbols Q(uestion) and A(nswer) along with P(roblem) and S(olution). They work in this way:

(Q) But has any such confirmation occurred?

(A)(T) Robert Jastrow, director of NASA's Goddard Institute for Space Studies, has published a small and curious book called *God and the Astrono-*

mers, in which he suggests that the Bible was right after all, and that people of his own kind, scientists and agnostics, by his description, now find themselves confounded.

(R) Jastrow blows phantom kisses like neutrinos across all chasms between science and religion, seeming almost wistful to make a connection. Biblical fundamentalists may be happier with Jastrow's books than are his fellow scientists.

(I) He writes operatically: "For the scientist who has lived by his faith in the power of reason, the story ends like a bad dream. He has scaled the mountains of ignorance; he is about to conquer the highest peak; as he pulls himself over the final rock, he is greeted by a band of theologians who have been sitting there for centuries." (Lance Morrow, "In the Beginning: God and Science," p. 487, *8*)

Christensen's Method Although you may find the TRI method a useful tool for analyzing the structure of a paragraph you are concerned with, you may feel that you need a more precise guide for recognizing the source of a particular problem in coherence. Francis Christensen's more complex method may serve you better in this case. Like Becker's, Christensen's research led him to focus on the topic sentence, which Christensen defines as "the sentence on which the others depend, . . . the sentence whose assertion is supported or whose meaning is explicated or whose parts are detailed by the sentences added to it."* Except for paragraphs which begin with transitional material, Christensen found that paragraphs generally open with a topic sentence. This topic sentence is then developed in two possible ways: by sentences that are either coordinate with it or subordinate to it. By "coordinate" sentences, Christensen means sentences that explain or restate the matter in the topic sentence. By "subordinate" sentences, he means those that exemplify, modify, or develop the topic material. He believes that each of the rest of the sentences in a good paragraph is also developed in either of the two ways—in relation to the topic sentence or to the sentence immediately before it.

Christensen suggests a paragraph analysis that permits you to understand this structure visually. In the following example, note that coordinate sentences are assigned the same number. A subordinate sentence is given one number less than the sentence to which it is subordinate. The topic sentence is always numbered one. Note also the parallel indentation.

(Transition) Just as there is a best size for every animal,
1. So the same is true for every human institution.
 2. In the Greek type of democracy all the citizens could listen to a series of orators and vote directly on questions of legislation.
  3. Hence their philosophers held that a small city was the largest possible democratic state.
 2. The English invention of representative government made a democratic

---

*"Generative Rhetoric of the Paragraph," in *Notes Toward a New Rhetoric* (Harper & Row, 1978), pp. 79–80.

   nation possible, and the possibility was first realized in the United States,
   and later elsewhere.
2. With the development of broadcasting it has once more become possible
   for every citizen to listen to the political views of representative orators,
   3. And the future may perhaps see the return of the national state to the
      Greek form of democracy.
2. Even the referendum has been made possible only by the institution
   of daily newspapers. (J. B. S. Haldane, "On Being the Right Size," p.
   482, *14*)

   For a paragraph to be truly coherent, every statement must be either coordinate or subordinate with the topic sentence or with the statement preceding it. If a sentence does not fit in this way, it is clearly out of place—either in
the sequence it occurs in or in the particular paragraph (or cluster) as a whole.
Christensen's system of analysis thus offers a practical method for discovering
the exact source of problems you may sense in the coherence of your paragraphs.

Transitions and Linkages   Structural coherence of the sort we have been
discussing is basic to the coherence of your essay. But what if you have
checked your paper thoroughly and, though you have found it structurally
sound, it still does not read as smoothly and coherently as you would like? Your
problem then might very well be a lack of appropriate linkage between your
ideas.* Besides an underlying coherence, you have to give your readers surface
clues to help them connect your ideas together so that they can understand
them. You can give these clues in two basic ways: repetition and transitional
devices.

   If you think about it, all sentences in the context of a paragraph or an essay
ought to consist of old material and new material. The old material is necessary
to provide continuity of thought and to prevent confusion. The new material is
needed to develop ideas and to avoid monotony. Check, for example, the sentences in the commonplace paragraph preceding this one, the one headed *Transitions and Linkage,* (or, for that matter, in almost any professionally written
paragraph), and you will see that this principle holds true:

Old, Linking Material	New Ideas
1. Structural coherence of the sort we have been discussing is basic to the coherence of your essay.	But what if you have checked your paper thoroughly and, though you have found it structurally sound, it still does not read as smoothly and coherently as you would like?
2. Your problem then	might very well be a lack of appropriate linkage between your ideas.

---

*For a discussion of concluding "echoes" to link your conclusion with the ideas you
have expressed throughout your essay, see pages 106–07.

| 3. Besides an underlying coherence, | you have to give your readers surface clues to help them connect your ideas together so that they can understand them. |
| 4. You can give these clues | in two basic ways: repetition and transitional devices. |

In every case, repetition of what is known makes for coherence.

Clues through repetition.   Sometimes you can achieve this reinforcement by an exact repeating of words or phrases (for example, the repetition of "coherence" and "coherently" in the sample paragraph). Sometimes you will want to repeat the idea, but would rather change the wording to avoid monotony (as I did with the interchanging of "linkage" and "connect[ion]" in the example). Sometimes you will want to substitute an appropriate pronoun in order to avoid endlessly repeating the same word (for instance, *it* for *paper* and *them* for *clues*). Whichever of the methods of repeating you use, you can think of the idea to be repeated as a colored thread that you weave through the tapestry of your essay, both to create the pattern of your ideas and to hold those ideas together. In checking over your paper for coherence, you need to make sure that these important threads are in place.

Clues through transitional devices.   The English language is rich not only in words and phrases that help writers tie ideas together, but also in those that point the reader to the particular relationships that hold among a writer's ideas. The brief paragraph on "Transitions and Linkages" just examined (though it certainly was *not* composed as an exemplary paragraph) offers a number of instances of these devices as well. "But" suggests a mild contradiction of the preceding idea. "What if" implies speculative possibility. "Though" suggests a concession to another point of view. "Still" implies that despite the obstacles raised, the concept expressed remains true.

Using devices such as these to help tie your work together will smooth out your transitions between sentences and between paragraphs and will make your essay read more fluently. The accompanying box of transitional words and phrases is a partial list of such devices and the general relationship to which each points.

Transitional Words and Phrases

Phrases of affirmation: in fact, actually, indeed, certainly

Phrases of negation: nevertheless, on the contrary, notwithstanding, on the other hand, despite, still, however, but, yet, conversely

Phrases of concession: although, though, granted that, no doubt, to be sure, whereas, of course, doubtless, certainly

Phrases of illustration: for example, for instance, to illustrate, in particular, specifically

Phrases of addition: and, also, moreover, or (nor), furthermore, next, again, too, second (third, etc.), another, finally

Phrases of qualification: frequently, often, usually, in general, occasionally, provided, in case, unless, when, since, because, for, if

> *Phrases of summation:* therefore, thus, in conclusion, to sum up, so, consequently,
>   accordingly, all in all, in short, on the whole, in other words, then
> *Phrases of sequence:* then, after, since, before, when, whenever, until, as soon as,
>   as long as, while, in [1923, the summer, and so on], at [Christmastime, the end
>   of term, and so on]

The section on adverbials in Chapter 6 (p. 202) will give you the opportunity to make creative use of transitional devices such as these in the composing process. But now, while you are thinking in terms of revising for coherence, you should be aware of what these phrases can contribute to improving an incoherent passage. Perhaps even more to the point, you should also understand the damage that faulty use of these transitional words and phrases can do to writing. Since these phrases point to very specific relationships, they cannot easily be interchanged. For instance, examine the following:

Jane held the smoking gun in her hand.

> *Furthermore,* she was not the   FAULTY
> murderer.
>
> *Consequently,* she was not the   FAULTY
> murderer.

"*Nevertheless,* she was not the murderer" would be a more reasonable choice of words. *Furthermore, consequently,* and *nevertheless* are all equally useful transitional words, and the sentence each is used in is syntactically correct. In relation to the first sentence, however, these two words make their sentences ridiculous. To save your work from equally disastrous results, be very sure that each of your transitional words lends your sentence precisely the meaning you intend. If you should have any question about what your transitional phrase implies, ask someone else to read through the passage.

──────────────────────────────────**Try It Out**──

1. Analyze the following paragraphs by the TRI method.

   A. One could easily discover other perversions of the rhetorician's balance—most obviously what might be called the entertainer's stance—the willingness to sacrifice substance to personality and charm. I admire Walker Gibson's efforts to startle us out of dry pedantry, but I know from experience that his exhortations to find and develop the speaker's voice can lead to empty colorfulness. A student once said to me, complaining about a colleague, "I soon learned that all I had to do to get an A was imitate Thurber." (Wayne Booth, p. 458, *22*)

   B. Seen in the context of history, Forest Lawn is neither very vulgar nor very remarkable, and the refrigerators at Phoenix are no more surprising than a pyramid in Palenque or Cairo. If life has been good, we, like the rich Etruscans, want it to go on and on, or at the very least to be remembered. Only a few civilizations have evaded expensive funerary habits for their illustrious rich, and these usually poverty-stricken ones. For all their austerity, the Hindus, burning bodies and throwing the ashes into the Ganges, have maintained distinction in their pyres. Not only were widows coaxed or thrown into the flames, but rare and perfumed woods were burned to sweeten the spirit of the rich Brahman as it escaped from its corrupt carapace. Cremation a la Chanel!   (J. H. Plumb, p. 468, *12*)

C. But has any such confirmation occurred? Robert Jastrow, director of NASA's Goddard Institute for Space Studies, has published a small and curious book called *God and the Astronomers,* in which he suggests that the Bible was right after all, and that people of his own kind, scientists and agnostics, by his description, now find themselves confounded. Jastrow blows phantom kisses like neutrinos across all chasms between science and religion, seeming almost wistful to make a connection. Biblical fundamentalists may be happier with Jastrow's books than are his fellow scientists. He writes operatically: "For the scientist who has lived by his faith in the power of reason, the story ends like a bad dream. He has scaled the mountains of ignorance; he is about to conquer the highest peak; as he pulls himself over the final rock, he is greeted by a band of theologians who have been sitting there for centuries."   (Lance Morrow, p. 487, *8*)

2. Analyze paragraphs B and C above according to Christensen's numbering and indenting method.

3. The following paragraph has been annotated to highlight its use of the

Notes

Paragraph Structure:
Topic sentence (1) in question form with 3 parallel answers (sentences 2, 3, 5)

Meaning:
The linkage of sentences 2 & 5 by means of the discovery in 3 is the "validation," which is the paragraph's point.

Structural Linkage:
(2) "We learned that"
(3) "And we learned what"
(5) "Conversely, we also found"
summary phrase (5)"this development"

Internal Linkage:
(2) "drug was used," "it was being used," "it was being used"
(5) "non-drug reasons," "involved with drugs"
(2) "tension, anxiety, & depression"
(5) "underlying anxieties"
(2) "ward off or deal with"
(5) "sought relief by"
(3) "specific personality type"
(4) "passive dependent personality"
(5) "passive dependent personality"

Paragraph

(1) What did all of this teach us? (2) We learned that no matter what drug was used, if it was being used for other than occasional social fun purposes, . . . it was being used to ward off or deal with tension, anxiety, and depression. (3) And we learned what had been theoretically formulated in classical psychiatric literature: that we were dealing with a specific personality type. (4) In psychiatry, we call this the passive dependent personality. (5) Conversely, we also found the passive dependent personality types whom we were seeing for non drug reasons, . . . were tending to become more involved with drugs as their underlying anxieties started to come out in the course of therapy and sought relief by turning on in order to turn off: for us this development again was a validation. (Katz, p. 473, *5*)

strategies of coherence: underlying structure; repetition of ideas, phrases, and words, or pronoun substitution for these words; and transitional words and phrases.

Study the sample. Then trace the patterns of coherence in a similar manner in the following paragraph:

(1) To perceive Christmas through its wrapping becomes more difficult with every year. (2) There was a little device we noticed in one of the sporting-goods stores—a trumpet that hunters hold to their ears so that they can hear the distant music of the hounds. (3) Something of the sort is needed now to hear the incredibly distant sound of Christmas in these times, through the dark, material woods that surround it. (4) "Silent Night," canned and distributed in thundering repetition in the department stores, has become one of the greatest of all noisemakers, almost like the rattles and whistle of Election Night. (5) We rode down on an escalator the other morning through the silent-nighting of the loudspeakers, and the man just in front of us was singing, "I'm gonna wash this store right outa my hair, I'm gonna wash this store . . . ." (E. B. White, p. 498, *1*)

4. Apply this method of analysis to a paragraph of your own choosing.

Emphasis

Because even the simplest composition contains a number of ideas competing for your readers' attention, it is important that you give the most significant of these ideas the most emphasis. There are two main ways to achieve emphasis structurally: by the proportion of your work that you devote to an idea and by where you place it in your essay.

Emphasis by Proportion   To achieve a quantitative sort of emphasis, it is a good rule of thumb to assign the space in your essay roughly in proportion to the importance of each idea to your thesis.

> The greater the importance of an idea to your overall point, the more space you should devote to it.

This principle may seem obvious to you; but, unfortunately, it is one inexperienced writers sometimes disregard. Too often, inexperienced writers begin their compositions with enthusiasm and cover the early points fully, only to find themselves running out of steam with only the energy to summarize their final points briefly. Though this mode of writing is certainly understandable, it creates disappointing papers, papers that often do not reflect their authors' intentions. If, for example, a writer organizes an essay's ideas in the usually effective order of least to most important, the most important ideas, occurring later, will be the ones slighted should a decline in energy set in. The results are particu-

larly disastrous when the problem occurs in an essay based upon the "although clause" structure, where the "other side" is explicated first with the writer's point of view following and refuting it. The effect of "Writers' Fatigue" here is to emphasize the "although" side at the expense of the writer's own.

Revising damage from "Writer's Fatigue."

There are three good strategies to choose from if you should discover the results of "Writers' Fatigue" in your own essay:

1. When the early part of your first draft pleases you, you can leave it pretty much as you have written it, and rewrite the final section(s) with the same care and spirit with which you began.
2. If the early part now seems wordy or overdone, you can cut it down and do less rewriting with the later parts. Be careful if you choose this alternative, though. Very often when the first portions are too profuse, the latter portions tend to be too scanty.
3. A third alternative is to shift your thesis itself to match the emphasis that your writing has taken. Let's say that in writing about the "although" position you have worked up so much interest that you would prefer to take another stance. Unless such a move would contradict your assignment, there is no reason why you cannot do so. In such a case, you would want first to write a new introduction and beginning section(s) and then to revise what you had written earlier to serve as the main focus of your paper.

Since all of these alternatives involve fairly extensive revision, it would probably be better to guard yourself against "Writers' Fatigue" in the first place. Thus, when you are writing your first draft and sense fatigue creeping over you, stop. Rest and refresh yourself before continuing.

Emphasis by Position   Another way to put emphasis on certain ideas is to give them a prominent position in your paper. Beginnings and endings are the sections readers are most impressed with and remember longest. They are the parts, therefore, that make the best showcase for your most important ideas. When you check over your paper, you will want to make sure that your thesis is either stated or prepared for early in your paper and that it is given a resounding declaration toward the end. You will also want to check your supporting paragraphs so that no idea of importance is permitted to get lost in midparagraph or midsentence. Be sure that all points of any prominence have at least a sentence or two of their own and that you position those important ideas at the beginning or end of the paragraph.

Whether first or last is most important depends a good deal on whether you expect your composition to be read in its entirety. Since few pieces of business writing get every reader's complete review, writing for business is a matter of saying the most important ideas at the very beginning—of the composition and of each paragraph. When you write for your classes in college or for magazines or journals, on the other hand, you can expect those readers you win over in the beginning to stay with you to the end. For this audience, you can regard the essay as a whole unity and build toward a persuasive conclusion. (See pp. 71 and 80.)

For our present purposes, then, the ending of your paper is the point of greatest emphasis. You will want to give it an especially close look before making your revisions. Guard particularly against shifting your emphasis at the close. For example, watch that you have not included any "By the way, I forgot to mention earlier . . ." sort of material in your conclusion. And be equally careful not to allow your "although clause" ideas to reenter at the end. Avoid:

> In closing, therefore, it is clear that *my point* is true. On the other hand, there   FAULTY
> is much to be said for *the alternative* point of view.

If you decide to continue on from your final statement of thesis, make sure that what you write follows naturally from and completes your main point. When you are certain that your reader will come away from your paper with a clear final idea of what you have been trying to say, your conclusion needs little further revision.

Revising For Structure: A Summary Checklist

Key: Keep your thesis in mind.
Try to achieve:

Unity

1. Check to see that every paragraph, every sentence, contributes to supporting the thesis.
2. Be sure that the sentences in each paragraph support the paragraph's topic sentence.

Coherence

1. Read your essay carefully to see if your ideas come across clearly and that they follow one another in a logical manner. If you are not completely certain, ask someone else to examine your paper with these questions in mind.

2. If your rereading discovers coherence problems in the presentation of your major ideas, return to your outline and shift its points about until you discover a logical ordering. Then reorder the sections of your paper to fit it. Do not hesitate to "cut and paste."

3. If your rereading discovers problems of coherence within your paragraphs, reorganize the offending paragraphs. Discard any intruding material. If you have difficulty locating the specific problem, try the TRI or the Christensen method of analysis.

4. If your ideas are logically placed and yet your paragraphs still do not seem to hang together properly, examine your linkage systems.
   - Check to see if there is enough repetition to guide the reader through the pattern of your ideas.
   - Check to see that your transitional words and phrases relate your ideas to each other appropriately.

Emphasis

1. Make sure that the amount of space you have allotted to each idea coincides with its importance.

2. Be especially careful that your "although" material does not overpower your own point.

3. Make sure that you have placed your discussion of your major points at the end and/or the beginning of your essay and that you have not buried them in midparagraph or mid-sentence.

Try It Out

Revise the following paragraph for structural problems. The statement given before the paragraph is the thesis of the paper from which the paragraph is taken. Use the thesis as a guide for your editing. (You may find it helpful to refer to the revision checklist as you work.)

Thesis: *High unemployment disrupts the social fabric.*

FAULTY

All too often, a teenager will see keys in a car and decide to steal it. And he might break into a house and steal all of the valuables located there. Additionally, there is a high unemployment rate for teenagers which is turning them to a life of crime. Many crimes take place because they're committed by teenagers; nevertheless, they are restless from unemployment, and they lack the money they need for things like beer, junk food, video games, movies, their cars, records, sometimes college tuition, books, and drugs, which are furthermore against the law. However, frustration results, and he turns to specific acts of theft and violence.

REVISING FOR PERSUASIVENESS

Many sections in this book have already focused on techniques for making your work persuasive, and the chapters on style in Part Three discuss this purpose even more. But at this point, when you are concerned with revising your essay, you are probably more interested in the opposite side of the question, What might keep your writing from being as persuasive as it could be? From this point of view, as you go over the first draft of your paper, you should search for any elements of your paper that might interfere with your readers' accepting what you have to say. To find these elements, you must make yourself acutely aware of your readers as people—as real human beings who can be both pleased and offended.

It is possible that you object to this kind of approach. You may be thinking that if your facts are sound and well supported, nothing else should matter. And perhaps nothing else would matter if your essay were to be processed by a machine. But the truth is that your writing will be read by people whose judgments are humanly illogical enough to be influenced by their impression of you, the writer. Without even being aware of it, readers take in signals that help them make up their minds, signals quite apart from the merits of your arguments. They can be offended by the tone of an article, by its language, or by underlying attitudes they think it reveals. They can become bored by it or annoyed because they find it difficult to read or because it contains mechanical errors such as poor spelling or incorrect punctuation. Any or all of these conditions can distract your readers from what you are trying to say. Let us look into these problems more specifically.

Offenses Against Taste

Taste is, as you know, an extremely slippery concept to grasp. The saying "One man's meat is another man's poison" is no less true because it is too often quoted. Your problem as a writer who must make choices based partly on your readers' taste is increased because in most cases you do not know your prospective readers well enough to be sure of their taste. You certainly cannot know them precisely if you are writing for a journal or magazine (though reading a few issues can give you real insight into the values and ideas shared by the readership). And even if you write only for your teacher and your classmates, you can count on no clear uniformity of taste. You are better off, therefore, to avoid language that large numbers of your potential readers would find offensive.

Racial Slurs   Foremost among expressions which revision should rule out of your writing are slurs against racial, religious, or national groups or against any other group that has been subject to stereotyping. This is not to say that you cannot take issue with the opinions shared by a particular group. You can, for instance, express strong disapproval of the terrorist tactics of the Palestine Liberation Organization (PLO) without implying that "All Arabs are . . . ." In fact, except for some stories told in dialect, I can think of no occasion where the use of an ugly slang term for a member of a racial, religious, or national group would be appropriate. Nor are there many occasions where a legitimate rhetorical purpose would be served by including stereotypical details about any particular group. No group has a monopoly on any characteristic, either good or bad, and it is not only false, but also boring to imply that it does.

Sexist Slurs   As offensive as are the sort of stereotypes that claim that all politicians take bribes and that all athletes are dumb, we need not take up each kind individually. But one sort of stereotypical thinking must be singled out for special mention because more than half the population is involved. I am referring, of course, to stereotypes about women. More and more we are coming to understand how tasteless sexist references can be. We need not dwell on the boorishness of such terms as "broad" or "chick" or on the contradictory notions that all women are weak and helpless and all women are domineering nags. Such lapses are easily rooted out. Unfortunately, some sexist thinking seems to be built into the language itself. And it is here where it is possible for you to offend quite unawares. The following hints may be helpful:

1. Use plurals wherever possible to avoid having to choose a sex-marked pronoun. For example, if you write "Students should complete *their* exams," you avoid the awkward "A student should complete *his or her* exam." (The old rule that suggested turning all neutral pronouns masculine is now outdated, and the practice is offensive to many.)
2. Avoid the use of expressions such as "lady lawyer" which carry the insulting implication that a professional who is a woman is somehow less of a professional than a man is. Prefixing such terms as "lawyer" or "doctor" or "engineer" with "lady" assumes that the occupational term by itself refers exclusively to men. When you write simply "Susan is an engineer," there is no lack of clarity.
3. Wherever possible, use such terms as "humankind" instead of "mankind" and more general words, such as "person", instead of "man" (as in "We had a five-person chess team" or "a five-member team").

Profanity and Obscenities   Think very carefully before you permit a word many people consider profane or obscene to reach the final draft of your paper. Wallace Stegner (in "Goodbye to All T--t," p. 500) makes a good case for saving such terms for moments of extreme emphasis. But I would caution you thoroughly to consider the readers to whom you are directing your work before including such expressions at all. Those who are offended by this language make such a sizable group that unless you feel certain that you cannot achieve the desired effect without the expression, you would probably be wise to delete it.

Editing for Offensive Tone

Tone is the sound of the writer's voice talking to the reader. It is a particularly difficult element for writers to check themselves. In fact, if you have a serious question about the tone of a paper, you might consider asking a friend to read it aloud to you. When you read it aloud to yourself, you may hear only the tone you meant rather than the one that the paper actually imparts.

Much of what is offensive in writing tone is similar to the tones that most people find irritating in conversation. Conversations make us uncomfortable when they make us feel inadequate. In writing as in conversation, then, it is better to avoid an overbearing tone or a show-off manner. Conversation also becomes difficult when a speaker's bearing is unpleasant or when the emotional atmosphere becomes overcharged. Thus, again in writing as in conversation, a sneering tone does not make us share in the disapproval expressed. It rather leads us to believe that the writer (or speaker) is mean-spirited, not to be trusted on this point, and probably not very sound in general. Similarly, a gushy tone does not convince us that the subject deserves such effusions, but rather that the writer (or speaker) is insincere and, again, not to be trusted. We tend to shy away in the same way from an angry tone. David Worcestor, an insightful critic, once explained why tones that seem overemotional tend to backfire:

> It is acute discomfort to be present where a man has fallen into a furious passion. If you are in such a situation, and the object of your acquaintance's rage has no connection with you, you will experience an instinctive craving to turn the painful situation into a ludicrous one. This is done by withdrawing all sympathy from the blusterer and by taking a more relativistic view of him as a lobster-faced baboon in a fit. (*The Art of Satire* [Harvard Univ. Press, 1940], pp. 17–18)

In order to avoid consequences such as Worcestor imagines, you should listen carefully for any trace of an overemotional tone coming into your paper. If you should find any, more often than not you will be able to correct the flaw by omitting a word or two or by substituting words of a less inflammatory character. Should the problem go deeper and the questionable tone pervade your essay, you may want to reword the whole piece so that it reflects a more objective point of view. No matter how strongly you feel about a subject, if you can present the material objectively, you will be more convincing. There is much persuasive force in restraint.

Editing Out Confusion

One of the easiest ways to earn the ill will of your readers is to confuse them. Lack of clarity is probably the most important fault you should look for when you read through your draft to plan revision. Rewrite any passage that you have reason to think might not be clear. Do not hesitate to explain it thoroughly— even if you secretly think it will sound a bit as if you were explaining it for a six-year-old. Although you may understand your subject completely, chances are that it is unfamiliar to your reader.

Vague Reference   Sometimes the confusion can be even more deep-seated. Occasionally, writers compose a passage without having taken the effort to be fully clear on the matter themselves. We all fall into such vagueness unconsciously from time to time. But you can uncover such passages when you reread your essay by looking for the give-away signal of a "this," "that," "it," or "which" appearing without any definite word to refer back to (antecedent). The following example is typical:

FAULTY

> Jan had long wanted to spend a summer in Italy. *This* was on her mind all the time. *It* kept interfering with her studies. She finally made up her mind to take the trip, *which* surprised no one.

The italicized pronouns are used here—as similar ones are used in all such writing—to mean, vaguely, "all the stuff I just said." Readers find indefinite reference of this sort exasperating because they sense that the writer is not completely sure about what is intended and is lazily relying upon the pronouns in order to escape having to be more specific.

In order to revise sentences such as these, you first have to give a name to the vague idea you are referring to. You have to ask yourself, What exactly do I mean by that pronoun? When you have decided, an easy solution is to use a demonstrative pronoun ("this," "that") as an adjective pointing to the name you have chosen:

> Jan had long wanted to spend a summer in Italy. *This desire* . . .

An alternative is to substitute a specific idea for the indefinite pronoun. Let's continue with the example and revise "*It* kept interfering . . .":

> Jan had long wanted to spend a summer in Italy. This desire was on her mind all the time. *Dreams of Roman fountains and Venetian canals* kept interfering with her studying.

Although using "which" in the vague way of the sample ("*which* surprised no one") is a more serious error than the others, you can correct it by similar means. You can name the idea it stands for:

> She finally made up her mind to take the trip, *a decision which* surprised no one.

Or you can rephrase to edit out the "which" entirely:

> • That she finally made up her mind to take the trip surprised no one.
> • When she finally made up her mind to take the trip, no one was surprised.

Often when you search for a way to edit out instances of confusing reference, you come to firmer grips with what you want to say, and your work improves all around.

Inconsistency   Be careful also to present your ideas in a manner that is logically consistent. A confusing inconsistency of presentation is more difficult to avoid than you think. In trying for objectivity, for example, many inexperienced writers will seem to advocate each idea in turn, leaving readers totally confused about the point of the writing. If in your revising you uncover such a situation, you can correct it by making your position clear at the outset. You can either explain that you will be presenting the best case for each alternative or you can include in each presentation a clue to your own preference. Note, for example, how the word "well," which Carll Tucker interjects into the following statement, leaves his readers with no doubt as to where he stands on the situation he narrates:

> One afternoon recently, two unrelated friends called to tell me that, well, their marriages hadn't made it. One was leaving his wife for another woman. The other was leaving her husband because "we thought it best." (p. 504, *1*)

Inconsistency of voice is another way to confuse your readers, who are entitled to a sure sense of the voice that addresses them. For them to gain this sureness, you will need to provide a degree of unity of tone, time, and mode of address. If, for example, you begin your paper rather formally and then suddenly lapse into a style that is full of neighborhood dialect and slang, your readers will not know what to make of it. It would almost be as if Thomas Jefferson had begun the *Declaration of Independence* in this way:

> When in the course of human events, a bunch of baddies start to throw their weight around with some of their relatives, it becomes necessary for those relatives to dissolve the political bands which have connected them.   FAULTY

Your readers will also be distracted by inappropriate shifts in tense. There is a dizziness built into writing that hops about between the past and present. Examine, for instance, the following bad example:

> We *had begun* our trip when we *see* a tree. The tree *is growing* right in the middle of the road, which *was divided* at that spot and *heads* on the left for   FAULTY
> Burlington while it *wound* round to Clarksville on the right.

You can further confuse your readers by shifting back and forth in your point of view:

> *I* visited the mountains and *it* was much enjoyed. *You* get all choked up when *you* see so much beauty. *Mother and Uncle Joe* said *they* had never had so   FAULTY
> much fun. *There* is a plan to go back some day.

You need not strive for a total unity. (Chapter 8, pp. 305–15, in fact, points out effective ways to *vary* your tone.) But an overall consistency is necessary if you are to avoid confusing your reader. When you edit, you should, therefore, keep a sharp eye out for inconsistencies like those in the preceding bad examples, and be ready to make whatever revisions are needed. The following exercise should give you some practice.

Try It Out

Edit the following paragraph from a student essay. Watch especially for vague references and inconsistencies.

FAULTY

The almost dialectically cryptic syntax and high-faluting imagery of James Joyce's *Ulysses* makes it difficult to read but added to your pleasure. Often, the narrative flow of a paragraph sometimes is stopped short by a sentence fragment, pun, or an only slightly connected idea. That is called *stream of consciousness* writing, and he used it to show the way his main character, Leopold Bloom, thought and acts. Furthermore, Joyce is using this to write about its other main characters, Stephen Dedalus and Molly Bloom. It bestows upon both of them their thoughts just as they would think them. Ergo, in this way, you can really get into his characters' thoughts and understand what it is that makes each of them tick.

Editing Out Boredom

There is no doubt in my mind that writers lose more of their readers through boredom than through any other cause. For every reader who tosses an article aside in a huff because of the presence of foul language, there must be twenty whose minds simply drift away because of the dullness of the work. To revise your composition effectively, you should be on the lookout for a variety of possible sources of boredom.

Boredom from Long-windedness   The most obvious cause of boredom is the presence of too much and too many:* too much writing, too many unrelated ideas, too many over-related sentences, too many words, too many flowery adjectives. Good editing strives for succinctness. If you can convey an idea in two sentences, there is no need to use three. Eliminate any sentence that adds nothing new to your presentation, or combine three sentences into two where there is overlap. If you can say something in ten words, why use fifteen? Cross out any word that does not contribute to the meaning of your sentences. Be especially wary of stock phrases with built-in redundancies (that is, phrases that say the same thing twice). Common examples include: *adequate enough, past experience, consensus of opinion, the fact that, my own personal . . ., each individual person.* (See p. 574 of the Revision Guide for a list of common redundancies.) Always use the simpler expression. If wordiness or long-windedness is a habitual problem for you, pretend that space is rationed and you have been given only so many lines. To economize on your limited space, select only the most essential words or change grammatical constructions so that the lengthier terms are eliminated. *-Ing* nouns, for instance, are one syllable and two letters shorter than their corresponding *-ation* nouns, and their use requires fewer supporting words. Compare:

*For a fuller discussion, see Chapter 8 first section.

Irrigating the desert has made it bloom.
The irrigation of the desert has made it bloom.

One of the most boring aspects of long-windedness is repetition. Although repetition is one of the most important tools for producing emphasis in your writing (see p. 120), nonpurposeful repetition can be dull. Have you ever been in conversation with an eagerly talkative sort of person who says everything twice to make sure you heard it and once again because he is beginning to like the sound of it? If so, you can appreciate just how boring repetitive writing can be. Repeated ideas, repeated words, repeated sentence structure can all be the source of this boredom.

When you are editing and discover a passage where you have *repeated an idea,* you must decide whether the repetition provides the emphasis or clarity you want or whether it merely clutters your work. Often in striving to explain an idea in a first draft, a writer tries out a number of different phrasings and ends up getting rather attached to them all. The best approach when this is the case is to rewrite the idea a final time, including in your new wording those phrases from earlier efforts that you find especially appealing.

Editing for repeated ideas.

Similar criteria hold for *repeated words.* Ask yourself, Does repeating this word help give coherence to the paragraph or emphasis to the idea? Does the repetition tend to become monotonous? If you decide that using the word again adds nothing to the style of your paper, it would probably be better to substitute a synonym. But before you run to your *Thesaurus* or dictionary of synonyms, a word of caution is in order. Do not choose a word unless you're completely sure of its meaning and appropriateness in the context of your paper. Especially avoid lengthy words of obscure significance. It is far better to repeat three or four times a term whose meaning precisely fits your intentions than to vary your vocabulary with words whose meanings are even a speck off what you want them to say. (See p. 299.)

Editing for repeated words.

Repetition of sentence structure is more difficult to spot than repetition of words or ideas. But if the rhythms of your words begin to drum monotonously in your ears when you read your paper aloud, you should look closely at the structure of your sentences to make sure that you have not fallen into a habit of using the same pattern over and over. For an example of over-repetitive syntax, try reading this passage aloud.

Editing for repetition of sentence structure.

Rising quickly, Jan went outdoors. Seeing the sunshine, she smiled to herself. Stooping to pick some flowers, she began to whistle. Whistling merrily, she returned to the house.

FAULTY

Chapters 5 and 6 will show you ways you can keep your sentence structure from becoming monotonous in this way. And Chapter 7 points out methods of repeating grammatical constructions to your advantage.

Boredom from Lack of Specific Detail
Another sort of "too much" that results in reader boredom is too much generalization without enough specific support. When you edit your paper, make sure that you have not left a single

generalization unsupported. Watch, for instance, for such sequences as the following from a student paper, where one generalization follows another without a hint of support:

FAULTY
> Sports are enjoyable and exciting because of the physical competition. Politics casts a shadow upon the real pleasure in sporting events.

Most of the time your readers will not object if you need to take an extra sentence or two to restate or clarify an especially difficult concept. But when you have amplified your point until it is crystal clear, you will still be obliged to offer some support for it. The first two sentences in the following paragraph from the same student paper, for example, leave the reader hungering for the detailed support that the rest of the paragraph never delivers:

FAULTY
> Coaches should judge their players only on ability and not involve themselves in politics. Political considerations do not offer a fair base for judgment and can only hurt the players—and eventually the team. When politics interferes with sports, it has a way of destroying one's confidence and making an athlete feel useless. Politics may be the reason why some of the best players lose all interest in the game. Coaches should always pick players on the basis of their athletic ability rather than on politics.

If you should come across this sort of accumulation of generalities in your own work, supply concrete support for those generalizations that add to the paragraph's point (see p. 92). Then eliminate the others or save them for another part of your essay. By adding detail in this way, you create interest in your subject and save your readers from boredom.

Try It Out

1. Rewrite the student's paragraph on politics in high-school athletics presented in the previous section and, by specific examples and detail, provide it with the interest it now lacks. Eliminate anything that does not add to the overall effectiveness of the paragraph.
2. Edit the following paragraph from another student's essay. Be especially careful to remove errors of repetition.

   FAULTY
   > In Joseph Heller's *Catch-22,* he says that in the army, officers are all uncaring murderous monsters, unthinking purveyors of death and destruction, mad makers of murder and mayhem, unintelligent workers of slaughter and death, and lunatic referees of massacre. The army officers are also shown to be incompetent fools, blundering idiots, and insensible morons. Additionally, some of the enlisted men, too, are seen to be selfish dolts and mindless ninnies. But, in contrast, Yossarian, the hero of the book, on the other hand, along with a few of his friends, are thinking men, reasonable, considering, logical, and properly questioning of their officers' authority and judgment.

Boredom from Overfamiliarity   Readers also get bored when they feel that they can just about finish a writer's every phrase or, when given a topic sentence, they can accurately guess the contents of the next few paragraphs. Although in both these cases the readers' boredom results from the predictability of the context, there are two quite different editing problems here.

The solution to the first problem is to get rid of all *stock phrases* and *clichés*. They can only detract from your work. (This problem is analyzed in more detail in the section on "Lazy Thinking" in Chapter 8, p. 331.) If the words of your phrase seem to belong together like "torrential rain" or "raining cats and dogs," you should make an attempt to keep your readers awake by substituting a word or phrase that accurately describes the situation but that they probably would not have thought of themselves. You will also want to think twice about clichés resulting from stereotypical thinking. After all, the sort of thinking that decrees that all princesses must have blond curls and blue eyes and that all villains must twirl their moustaches is closely related to the sort of thinking responsible for the uglier stereotypes discussed earlier.

Eliminate clichés and stock phrases.

Determining whether to edit out *ideas* that some consider commonplace or even trite is not as automatic as deciding to eliminate stock phrases and clichés. In dealing with ideas, you need to bring another sort of judgment to bear. As you edit your text, you should certainly question your conventional statements. Ask yourself, Am I making a statement that is commonly accepted to be true? Am I repeating a bit of folk wisdom? Am I simply expressing the sort of thing people like to hear? That the answer to any of these questions is "yes" does not necessarily mean you have to eliminate the statement from your essay. What a "yes" answer does mean is that you are working in an area where your writing may be subject to criticism for either lack of sincerity or lack of purpose. You therefore need to look at your ideas yet more closely.

Evaluate platitudes.

First, examine yourself to be sure that you really mean the statement in question. Conventional wisdom is difficult to make interesting even when you sincerely believe it. If you disbelieve it or are indifferent to it, there certainly is no point in writing it. More likely, however, you do believe that the conventional statement you have written is true, at least to some extent. You may believe, for instance, that "All babies are cute" or that "Playing football builds character" or that "Spring is a happy time." The problem here may well be one of overstatement. The solution is to qualify your remarks. There are very few statements to which "always" or "never" apply. *Most* babies are cute. Playing football *can* build character. Spring is *sometimes* the happiest season. And do not cheapen your genuine feelings by overstating them as did the student who once wrote: "I did not stop crying for a week after my dog died." Wherever you can, make your statement specific to the facts.

After you have phrased the well-accepted value in a way that removes any concern for your sincerity, you still have to deal with the problem of purpose. Since your readers most probably have come across the idea you are stating before, you will have to be sure that you have something to add about it that is

worth their reading. Even if that something is only your assurance that the notion, common though it is, needs occasional reinforcing, go ahead with it. But
if you really have no reason for expressing commonplace ideas, they are better
edited out.

Boredom through Overpersonalizing

Boredom through Overpersonalizing   Self-centered people are among
the most boring of conversationalists. Nor do they do much better as writers.
On the other hand, the sound of a personal voice is one of the keys to effective
writing. Drawing the distinction between a tone that has a strong sense of self
and one that is self-absorbed is a difficult editing problem. You can base part of
your decision on the nature of your composition. If you are writing a personal
essay or even if your expository essay is on a personal theme, this issue need
not become a problem. But when you are called upon to discuss a topic of
external interest—as is usually the case with college writing—you can scarcely
avoid the question of just how much personalizing is *too* much. It is a difficult
question to answer theoretically, so let me give you a specific example of an
approach that I judged too personal.

A student came in for a conference about a paper he planned to write on
the relationship between science and sexual behavior in the Laputa Voyage segment of Swift's *Gulliver's Travels* and in Huxley's *Brave New World.* I tried to
convince him that his thesis must include a comparison of the authors' intentions in setting up these relationships and must be supported by examples from
the books demonstrating the relationship in each case. The student, on the
other hand, wanted to write a thesis giving his opinion of the relationship in
both cases and supporting it with details of how he came to have that opinion.
There is no question in my mind that a paper based on such premises would be
boringly personal (quite aside from my concern over just what a recital of how
he came to his opinion on sex and science would amount to). The paper, you
see, would be about the student—and not really about Swift's Laputa and Huxley's brave new world at all.

As for a personal approach that might pass your editor's pencil, let me
suggest the anecdote just narrated. Although what is acceptable in tone is, as
we have said, very much a matter of private taste, more readers would probably
agree that the personal tone in the anecdote about the Swift-Huxley paper
works out all right because it contributes rather than detracts from the point
the example is intended to make. Whether or not you agree in this case, this is
the sort of criterion you should use to test for the overpersonal as you edit your
essay.

Boredom through Underpersonalizing

Boredom through Underpersonalizing   No matter how dull overper-
sonalized writing can be, the writing whose tone is the most offensively boring
is that which seems to have no personal author at all. Underpersonalized writing
speaks to its readers in the dehumanized drone of a machine, with no identifiable human author addressing the human reader. Nobody really does anything
in such writing, or at least nobody seems willing to take responsibility for doing

anything. It is as if everything that happens is compelled by some vague, nameless force:

It has been thought that . . .	FAULTY
It has been brought to mind . . .	FAULTY
There can be no doubt that . . .	FAULTY

Nobody ever complains:

Complaints have been made.	FAULTY

Nobody receives letters:

Letters are received.	FAULTY

Nobody conducts business:

Business is conducted.	FAULTY
"Yours of the fifth inst. received and contents duly noted."	FAULTY

What is more, the vocabulary used in this mechanized writing is not the sort that conveys information from one human mind to another in a natural manner. It is composed instead of the stock phrases, words, and popular jargon you find programmed into computers.

GOOSEMYER   by parker and wilder

GOOSEMYER by Parker and Wilder © 1980 Field Enterprises, Inc. Courtesy of Field Newspaper Syndicate.

Whatever could possess anyone to write such nonsense as "Yours of the fifth inst. received" or "A logistical interface of management referendums"? Inexperienced writers fall into machinelike writing of this sort partly through a misinformed desire to avoid using "I" and partly in an equally misguided attempt to sound businesslike. If you have any doubts at all that such attempts are misguided, let me reassure you. All effective communication of the world's business—whether in industry, in the classroom, or in people's lives—is conducted by a thoroughly human "I" or "we" to an equally human "you," in language they all can understand and be affected by. Should you fall into the habit of machinelike usage, you must be especially vigilant in your editing.

Editing Out Jargon and Pseudo-Jargon   Properly speaking, jargon is the specialized vocabulary of a technical field—of computer science or psychology, for instance. Pseudo-jargon is an imitation of this vocabulary. Both of these, when used to "sound impressive," are important sources of machinelike writing. Be sure you can recognize their excesses so that you can eliminate them. Except for those times when you need to use this vocabulary to communicate technical ideas within a specialized field, jargon and the stock phrases that form a pseudo-jargon will mar your written work. For a full discussion of this subject, see page 334.

Editing Out Unnecessary Passive Constructions   Much of the unappealing nonpersonal quality we have been discussing stems from structuring sentences too often in the passive voice. In English, the basic sentence has what is called an *active* structure; that is, it is composed of a subject doing something to an object:

> The boy *hit* the ball.

Most such sentences can also be constructed in the *passive* structure by switching object for subject and turning the verb passive (by adding on a form of the verb "to be"):

> The ball *was hit* [by the boy].

But now the new subject remains passive, being acted upon; and the actor, relegated to a phrase at the end, no longer seems necessary. As a matter of fact, the actor is often dropped from the sentence.

Of course, there are times when passive sentences—though on the whole less interesting—can convey your meaning more precisely. Sometimes, to continue the example, it is not the boy but the ball you want to concentrate upon:

> The *ball* was hit. It soared and soared.

Sometimes the active construction is simply inappropriate. Only the passive can get across what you wish to say:

- The site of the accident was as devastated as a battlefield.
- The president was elected by a large plurality.

Nevertheless, if you use the passive habitually, your writing will probably become both dull and awkward. There are three reasons for this result.

1. The passive encourages that curious absence of an agent or actor, of a human being in charge.
2. Because the passive is not the natural construction in English, it often leads to long and convoluted (twisted) sentence structures. Compare:

Passive	Active
A question is raised whether . . .	Professor Jones questions whether . . .
There exists the reason that . . .	The reason is . . .
It was the understanding of this committee that . . .	The committee understood that . . .

3. The kind of twisted prose that passive sentences set up often involves turning verbs into nouns that are elongated and sometimes pretentious, the words that give this sort of writing its tone of pompous clutter. Compare:

- *A reduction* in paper work *would be brought* about by this plan. (long, FAULTY *passive* phrasing)
- This plan *would reduce* paper work. (short, direct *active* phrasing)

Habitual users of the passive form pile up such constructions in awkward abundance. The four passive convolutions in the following example are typical:

> *The suggestion is made* (1) *that the utilization of company money* (2) to pay for executive vacations in Hawaii *could appear suspicious to the Internal Revenue Service* (3) and make them think that *there may have been an improper disbursement of funds* (4). FAULTY

To edit this sentence you would first turn all of the passive constructions into the active voice:

> *We suggest* (1) that if *the company uses its money* (2) to pay for executive vacations in Hawaii, *the IRS might suspect* (3) that *the company has disbursed its funds improperly.* (4)

Next, in editing, you would compare your new sentence with the original one and decide whether it conveys the meaning you intended in a more direct way. In the case of the sample sentence, the revised version clears up the awkwardness, indirectness, and pretension of the original without changing its meaning.

Editing to eliminate the boredom of the impersonal style, then, requires first eliminating jargon and then evaluating passive constructions for effectiveness, rephrasing into the active voice where necessary.

Revising for Persuasiveness: A Summary Checklist

Key: Keep your readers in mind
Try to avoid:

Offenses against taste
1. Edit out slurs against special groups (racial, religious, national, and so on).
2. Edit out sexist slurs. Avoid sexist use of pronouns and general terms that use "man" instead of "human" or "person."
3. Edit out profanity or obscenity unless you're sure of a receptive readership.

Offensive Tone
1. Revise to avoid a tone that is overbearing or self-congratulatory.
2. Avoid an excessively emotional tone, whether it's angry and disapproving or gushy and overly effusive.

Confusion
1. Rewrite any passage that may not be clear.
2. Make sure every pronoun points to *a particular word,* for which it is the substitute.

3. Be consistent in your presentation of ideas, especially in conveying your point of view.
4. Be consistent in the voice with which you address readers.

Boredom
1. Revise to eliminate "too much and too many." Simpler is better.
2. Edit out unnecessary repetition of ideas, words, or sentence structure.
3. Make sure every generalization is fully supported by specific detail.
4. Edit out clichés; evaluate platitudes.
5. Avoid overpersonalizing or underpersonalizing your writing.
6. Edit out unnecessary jargon and all pseudo-jargon.
7. Edit out unnecessary passive constructions.

Try It Out

1. Revise the following awkwardly written paragraphs from student papers. How can you eliminate the awkwardness of the impersonal style? Ask yourself, Who is doing what? Try to get most of your sentences into an appropriate subject-verb-object relationship. (Don't forget also to prune any unnecessary words or awkward phrasing.)

A. One of the biggest problems today that modern students seem to have concerns a perceived inability on the part of these students to write papers and indeed lower sub-sections of papers—paragraphs and even sentences—that are clearly intelligible by the reader. One of the biggest and chief problems that arises in these hard-to-read papers is that of verbosity, wherein the modern student will use many too many words in his paper to be easily understood, while actually the idea he is hoping and trying to express is, under close examination, shown to be in actuality quite simple.

FAULTY

B. This country is being taken over by a revolution. It's not a revolution with guns or coups or military juntas, but rather it is a video revolution. The craze for video games was given birth to by television—more satisfaction is apparently derived by youths today in watching an image on a screen than by controlling the erratic moves of an actual physical ball in a pinball machine. Not too long ago, money would be well spent by people who would watch the ball be bounced from bumper to bumper. Today, however, there are few of these machines around. The same money is now foolishly wasted by youths in front of TV screens. Spaceships are shot at, aliens are destroyed, and cars are recklessly driven by a vacant-faced, unblinkingly blindless mass of quick reflexes. There can be but little hope left for Western civilization.

FAULTY

2. Write a paragaph without using a single passive sentence.

REVISING FOR CORRECTNESS

Yet another important way writers manage to offend or annoy their readers is by not conforming to the accepted standards for written English. It is true that errors in spelling, capitalization, punctuation, sentence structure, and grammatical usage can only be considered minor compared to those difficulties of structure and tone we have been discussing. And it is equally true that such errors (with the possible exception of those in punctuation) rarely interfere with the actual communication of a writer's ideas. Nevertheless, for a large proportion of readers these errors present an almost inpenetrable block between themselves and the writer's message. In fact, research has shown that certain errors cause readers to form such negative judgments about the writer of a composition that they disregard the merits of the content. Readers who react this way are not just English teachers. Actually, as Professor Maxine Hairston discovered in a recent survey,* professionals such as engineers, judges, bankers, architects, lawyers, and corporation executives tend to be even more distressed by errors in the "mechanics" of writing than are college instructors. There can be no question but that the presence of errors in a finished composition can severely damage its impact.

If errors in mechanics are relatively unimportant to your overall composition and yet if they are of tremendous significance to an important segment of your readers, what are you to do? Let me recommend that you go through the process of prewriting, writing, and rewriting your paper without giving the mechanics too much thought. Many of the errors in your original draft will vanish when you revise for structure and clarity, for these errors tend to creep in when you are still not completely sure of the ideas you want to express. But before you copy over your composition to present it to your readers in its final form, you should make as sure as you possibly can that it is free from errors and that it conforms to the standards of written English.

Readers do not find all errors equally disturbing. Professor Hairston's study confirmed earlier research that among the kinds of errors that are most distressing are errors of the sentence—especially run-on sentences and fragments. Other errors that seem to be almost as offensive are certain errors of capitalization and punctuation—in particular, commas that violate the logic of the sentence and uncapitalized proper nouns. Spelling errors also appear to be troublesome when they are too abundant. Although there are many other areas where errors can occur,† the ones just mentioned seem to be by far the most important to readers. In these closing sections on editing then, we will concentrate on those specific areas and suggest strategies for their correction. (The Revision

---

*As reported in a paper read at the annual meeting of the National Council of Teachers of English in Cincinnati, Ohio, November, 1980, and more formally in *Successful Writing* (New York: W.W. Norton, 1981), pp. 244–46.

†Professor Hairston's research also recognized the importance of errors due to nonstandard dialects and other errors of usage. Such errors are examined at length in the Revision Guide.

Guide, Part Six of this text, offers a more complete discussion of the rules you need to know to help you avoid or correct these and other errors.)

Editing Out Errors of the Sentence

A capital letter signals readers that a sentence is beginning and triggers their expectations for all that conventionally goes on in the English sentence. A period (sometimes a question mark or exclamation point) lets readers know that the sentence has come to an end. When their expectations for the sentence are not fulfilled in the usual way, readers often find themselves so puzzled that their minds wander from the writer's ideas and struggle instead with the form. The kind of sentence fragments and run-on sentences that can distract readers in this way are ordinarily caused by a lack of understanding of what actually constitutes a sentence. The old definition that "a sentence is a complete thought" does not help much in deciding where to put the capital letters and the periods. Run-ons occur when a writer mistakes two or more complete sentences for one "complete thought" and punctuates accordingly:

FAULTY   • The day was bright the birds sang.
FAULTY   • Joe crammed himself into the car, it was bursting already with passengers.

A fragment appears when a writer mistakes a nonsentence (usually a clause or a phrase) for a "complete thought" and punctuates it as a sentence:

FAULTY   • Janet decided to accept the position. *Having given the matter real consideration.*
FAULTY   • *Although the fish were biting that day.* Henry gathered up his gear and trudged home. *Which he really had not wanted to do.*

If you have any doubt at all about what is wrong with these examples, studying Chapter 5 (p. 156–62) will help you understand better the nature of the sentence, especially how it differs from clauses and phrases.

Avoiding Run-on Sentences

Wherever you are suspicious that you might have been treating more than one sentence as if they were only one, test each part by asking yourself: Does it have a subject? Does the subject control the verb? Is there nothing added on to keep this subject-predicate combination from standing on its own? Each time you can answer yes to all three questions, you have a complete sentence. You cannot leave two or more of these sentences running together without punctuation, as in the example above:

FAULTY   The day was bright the birds sang.

Nor can you splice them together with commas:

FAULTY   Joe crammed himself into the car, it was already bursting with passengers.

But you do have three editing options which will not involve any change in wording:

1. You can write the two as separate sentences:

- The day was bright. The birds sang.
- Joe crammed himself into the car. It was already bursting with passengers.

2. If you feel that the two ideas are so closely related that you do not wish to separate them, you can keep them both in one sentence by placing a semicolon between them:

   - The day was bright; the birds sang.
   - Joe crammed himself into the car; it was already bursting with passengers.

3. Or if you would like to divide them only by a comma, you can do so if you add a coordinating conjunction *(and, but, so, for)* to the second sentence (clause):

   - The day was bright, *and* the birds sang.
   - Joe crammed himself into the car, *but* it was already bursting with passengers.

Please note that only coordinating conjunctions will work with a comma in this way. If you want to include a word like "however" or "nevertheless," you will have to select one of the alternative choices:

- The day was bright; *furthermore,* the birds sang.
- Joe crammed himself into the car. *However,* it was already bursting with passengers.

You might also consider a fourth option—surbordinating one of the two sentences to the other:

- *Because* the day was bright, the birds sang.
- Joe crammed himself into the car *that* was already bursting with passengers.
- Joe crammed himself into the car *although* it was already bursting with passengers.

Avoiding Sentence Fragments   When a group of words lacks a subject or its verb (or both), or when it has a word or two attached that prevents it from standing on its own (*that* birds fly, birds *which* fly, *although* birds fly, *when* birds fly, and so on), it is only a fragment of a sentence. As a rule, such fragments should not be punctuated as sentences.

Once you have identified the fragments in your own work, you will usually have little trouble revising them. Ordinarily the fragment will attach quite naturally to the sentence that either precedes it or follows it. Let's look at the examples given at the beginning of this section.

Janet decided to accept the position. *Having given the matter serious consideration.*   FAULTY

This revises easily into:

Janet decided to accept the position, having given the matter serious consideration.

The way to edit the next example is just as clear:

FAULTY
- *Although the fish were biting that day.* Henry gathered up his gear and trudged home.

REVISED
- Although the fish were biting that day, Henry gathered up his gear and trudged home.

Occasionally, however, the fragment will need to be reworded, perhaps changed into a sentence to stand on its own. The end of the second sample is a case in point:

FAULTY
- Henry gathered up his gear and trudged home. *Which he had not really wanted to do.*

REVISED
- Although the fish were biting that day, Henry gathered up his gear and trudged home. He had not really wanted to leave that early.

Unintentional fragments can mar your work. Nevertheless, you will find that fragments do sometimes have a place in serious writing. Experienced authors deliberately use sentence fragments for emphasis or to provide an informal tone:

> What's wrong with simple nondiscrimination, with just plain fairness? *Two things really.* (William Raspberry, "Equal Opportunity May Solve Nothing," *Washington Post,* Apr. 19, 1981)

> There is a great fascination with evil today. *There always has been . . . .* (Tom Wolfe, p. 444, 7)

Subject and Verb Agreement A third sentence error that jars many readers almost as much as fragments and run-ons occurs in the sentence or clause whose subject and verb do not agree in number. Singular subjects take singular verbs and plural subjects take plural verbs:

When our *cat is* outside, the *birds have* to be careful.
 (singular)   (plural)

Notice the curious fact that although singular nouns have no *-s* endings, their appropriate present-tense verbs do; and while plural nouns end in *-s,* plural verbs in the present tense do not.

Unless you speak a nonstandard dialect, you should not have much trouble with subject-verb agreement in most sentences. However, prepositional phrases complete the subject of many sentences, and the nouns in those phrases may cause confusion. You should remember that the subject of a sentence cannot be in a prepositional phrase. If figuring out proper agreement is a problem for you in such cases, mentally cross out all prepositional phrases and concentrate on the words that remain to find the subject that will give you the proper form for your verb:

         (singular)   (plural)

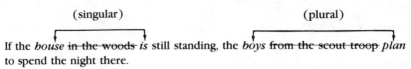

If the *house* in the woods *is* still standing, the *boys* from the scout troop *plan* to spend the night there.

Compound subjects, pronoun subjects, and single subjects that end in *-s* also can cause you problems when you must decide whether a verb should be singular or plural. For a list of rules governing these situations, check the Revision Guide section, "Agreement: Subject and Verb."

Try It Out

Revise the following student paragraph. Watch especially for sentence errors.

Trivia

Much has been made of trivia in recent years. Which makes it look like the desire of students to have more knowledge about utterly useless things than your friends are going to keep on spreading and never stop. Many colleges, radio stations, and other organizations are now holding contests where they ask questions on all subjects. From sports to television, from political history to movies and music. Many a team of eager students get together to face each other in the competitions, they are asked such ques-   FAULTY
tions as "What was the name of Gene Autry's horse?" Vying to be the first to answer them. Some easier questions like "Who holds the record for most home runs?" But with all of the questions being asked; and all the eager, trivia-minded people dying to answer the likes of "In *Casablanca,* what was the color of Ingrid Bergman's dress the day the Germans marched into Paris?" It's interesting that no one ever answers the question, "Why bother?"

Editing for Correct Capitalization and Punctuation

You can make errors in capitalization and punctuation both by omitting these symbols and by placing them wrongly. Although inexperienced writers worry a good deal about excluding punctuation marks and capital letters from where they rightfully belong, they should probably be more concerned about including them where they should not be. Naturally, readers find certain omissions distressing—omissions such as the lack of a capital at the beginning of a sentence or of a person's name, for instance. But if they should discover capitals or commas or other symbols randomly punctuating the text, they will not be able to follow the flow of ideas. A good rule to follow, therefore, when you have editing questions about capital letters and punctuation marks (and are unable to look up the answers), is "When in doubt, leave them out."

Capital Letters Always begin each sentence with a capital letter. Always capitalize "I" when you are referring to yourself. And always use a capital for the initial letter of a proper name. (If you have any doubt as to what is a proper name, look in the Revision Guide under "Capitalization.") You will rarely need to use capital letters outside of these occasions. Do not use them for emphasis.

Some writers develop the habit of absent-mindedly beginning some of their words with capital letters. If you are among this group, take care to edit out these random capitals from your final drafts.

Commas   Some writers also scatter commas about. Readers find unnecessary commas especially intrusive, for a comma interrupts the flow of the text. A single purposeless comma placed between a subject and its verb or a verb and its object can make a sentence almost incomprehensible:

FAULTY
- She and her friends, knew that he would come.
- She and her friends knew, that he would come.

Edit out any commas that intrude in this way.

On the other hand, commas ensure that interrupting material (parenthetical remarks, interjections, transitional words and phrases, appositives, nonessential relative clauses, and other sorts of explanatory phrases) are separated off. Thus such interruptions do not interfere with the readers' understanding of the central subject-verb-object flow in the sentence. When you edit your work, make sure that all such material you use in midsentence is marked off *on both sides* by commas. When such material occurs at the beginning or the end of a sentence (or of an independent clause), you will, of course, need to use only one comma. The examples in the accompanying boxed section can serve as models.

Using Commas to Set Off Interrupting Material

- Even the civilization of Sumer, *the birthplace of written language,* declined and vanished.
- *Nevertheless,* artifacts of this civilization can still be found in museums.
- The Oriental Museum at the University of Chicago, *for example,* has an impressive collection; *unfortunately,* it is little-known.
- May the class take a field trip to Chicago, *Professor Marx?*
- Professor Marx, *who had long believed in the benefits of field trips,* booked reservations for his group on the first bus heading for Chicago.

The final instance in the boxed section shows the use of commas in a nonessential relative clause. The interesting distinction between nonessential relative clauses, which require commas because of the material's semi-parenthetical nature, and essential relative clauses, which do not, is discussed in detail in Chapter 5, p. 182.

Closely related to the comma's use to separate interrupting material from the main sentence flow is its use to set off lengthy introductory material. (See the next boxed section.)

Using Commas to Set Off Introductory Material

- *When you begin a sentence with an adverb clause,* add a comma before you begin your main clause.
- You need not use a comma, *when the adverb clause concludes your sentence.*
- *Having begun your sentence with a participial phrase,* you will also want to use a comma.
- *In the case of a number of prepositional phrases at the beginning of your sentence,* you have the option to clarify with a comma.

Other Essential Comma Uses   When you edit your compositions, make sure that you have used commas to mark the divisions in dates and addresses and to separate the words or phrases in a series. (The final comma before the "and" in a series is optional.) The examples shown in the next boxed section should be helpful as models.

Using Commas in Series, Addresses, and Dates

- *On Sunday evening, April 10, 1983,* a soccer match was held on the beach at Santa Barbara, California.
- *Joe, John, and Ellen* all went to the match.
- *Having sunned themselves on the beach, having splashed in the waves, having consumed an excellent supper, and even having watched a little of the match,* they pedaled home.

You will find a more detailed discussion of the use of the comma in the Revision Guide under "Comma."

Semicolons   The semicolon, which consists of a period on top of a comma (;), is related to both marks. It signals a strong interruption—somewhat less than that of the period, but much more than that of the comma. Because its purpose is to interrupt the text in such a definite way, misplaced semicolons are particularly distracting to readers. The examples in the boxed section model their appropriate use.

Using Semicolons to Separate and to Tie Together

- The semicolon is like the period; its function is to separate independent clauses (sentences) from one another.
- But unlike the period, the semicolon also unites; it ties independent clauses together in a compound sentence without the necessity for conjunctions like *and* or *but.*

- The semicolon also acts as a stronger comma, dividing the sentence in a masterly way when commas are already present⊙ and thus it is appropriate, if you have employed commas within the segments, to use semicolons to substitute both for the commas that divide items in a series and the commas that join with *and* or *but* to divide independent clauses in compound sentences.

Further Examples

- The moon rose⊙ the stars came out⊙ a coyote howled.
- The desert seemed empty⊙ nevertheless, danger lurked everywhere.
- Some children enjoy cantaloupe, of course⊙ but you can't really go wrong on ice cream for a kiddie party.
- Among the attendants at the zoo that summer were college kids on vacation, who had a sentimental attachment to animals but no particular desire for hard work⊙ ambitious young men and women, just out of veterinary school, eager to make their mark⊙ and old, grizzled veterans, who signed on some thirty years ago when times were hard and nobody had ever heard of scientifically trained animal keepers.

The purposes exemplified in these guidelines are the only ones for which the semicolon should be used. To keep from distracting your readers, make sure in your editing that all the semicolons in your paper are used in one of these ways.

Colons, Dashes, and Parentheses   This discussion of editing and punctuation has emphasized eliminating excess. Some marks of punctuation, though useful in their way, seem to have a special tendency to be overused by inexperienced writers. The exclamation point (!), for instance, has little place in expository essays. Ellipses (. . .), too, while essential to indicate omissions in quoted material (see Chapter 9), have no other use in expository prose. You may find, however, that dashes, parentheses, and colons, though equally subject to overenthusiastic use, can be helpful in your serious writing—providing you do not rely upon them too heavily.

These three kinds of punctuation have some overlapping functions. Sometimes, then, you will have to make a choice among them. Here your sense of style must be your chief guide. To give you a sense of how professional authors make these decisions, all of the examples in this section are from the professional work included in Part Five.

Using Colons, Parentheses, and Dashes to Add or Explain

Colons signify "namely," "to wit," "that is," or "let me explain."
- The food we live on is kids' food⊙ pizza, hot dogs, fried chicken, ice cream, hamburgers. (Shana Alexander)
Translate the colon, "namely."
- None of this is cheap⊙ the capsule costs four thousand dollars, and then there are the freezing costs. (J. H. Plumb)
Translate the colon, "that is."

- The American way of death is not novel: seen in proper historical perspective, it reaches back not only down the centuries but down the milleniums, for it is a response to a deep human need. (J. H. Plumb)

Translate the colon, "Let me explain."

Dashes can be used as an informal sort of colon. They also can be used to include incidental information or digressions. And they can provide emphasis or contrast or can help change the direction of a sentence.

As an informal colon:

- Because the life hereafter was but a mirror image of life on earth, [the Egyptians] took with them everything they would need— jewels, furniture, food, and, of course, servants. (J. H. Plumb)

To include incidental information:

- Some scientists feared that the document placed too much faith in technologi-cal— rather than "human"— solutions. (Fred Golden)

To include digressions:

- By September [the Cubs] had set a mark for ineptness at which others— but not next year's Cubs— would shoot in vain. (George Will)

To provide ironic contrast:

- Only a handful of reporters still live in Manhattan, and they can be found in saloons only in the event of special celebrations— if, that is, a babysitter has been found for the occasion. (Judith Crist)

To change the direction of a sentence:

- This week many will be reminded that no explosion of atoms generates so hopeful a light as the reflection of a star, seen appreciatively in a pasture pond. It is there we perceive Christmas—and the sheep quiet, and the world waiting. (E. B. White)

Parentheses, which are ordinarily more formal than dashes, are used to include scholarly apparatus or comment on a text. But, like dashes, they are also used to include incidental information and digressions.

As comment on a text:

- The hippies and the students whom I have seen and who have used LSD in the largest quantities (such as over 200 times) were in fact the most passive, non-destructive, turned-off group of all drug abusers. (Alan S. Katz)

To include incidental information:

- But even if Israel were to withdraw in exchange for full peace (recognition of its right to exist plus free movement of people, ideas and commerce in the region) there would still be an inherent asymmetry of risk in a trade of the physical for the political. (George Will)

To include digressions:

- If you want to do your kitty proud, you can spend three hundred dollars or so on a stately layingout, a goodly coffin (if you're worried about its fun in the afterlife, you can put an outsize rubber mouse in with it). (J. H. Plumb)

As effective as an occasional usage of this sort can be, relying too extensively on dashes and parentheses will give your paper an informality of tone that can border on the haphazard. Too frequent asides and digressions can seriously interfere with the flow of your ideas. Each time you come to one of these constructions as you edit your work, ask yourself, Would this information or digression be more effective if it were removed from the dashes or parentheses that enclose it and presented in a more straightforward way? If the answer is yes, make the appropriate changes.

Try It Out

1. Edit the following student paragraph, paying particular attention to your use of capital letters and commas.

College

FAULTY

Last Fall, when I went to College I did not know, what to expect, from the New Life, I was entering in. Was it going to be all reading Books, studying French, and writing Papers, or was it going to be just one big Party, with Beer, raucous Dormitory Life, and friendly meetings, with Members of the Opposite Sex? As it turns out College Life has been, a combination of these. Sure I have to Study, a lot; especially my Capitalization and Punctuation but I have Time for fun too. Just last last week, a Paper I had written on, Arthur Miller's *Death of A Salesman,* got ruined in a Water Fight. This proves I suppose, that one cannot mix, Business with Pleasure.

2. The student who wrote this next paragraph relied totally on the comma to punctuate his work. Some of the commas are appropriate, but others might better be exchanged for semicolons, colons, dashes, or parentheses. Edit the paragraph, giving special emphasis to punctuation.

A "Mute, Inglorious Milton"

FAULTY

Many people think it's easy to write a novel. God knows I've tried to enough times, but it is, in fact, hard work, a rough estimate would be that only one-tenth of all people who start a novel finish it, and a smaller percentage yet, of which I am not unhappily a member, actually get published. Face it, most of us just aren't destined to be Great Authors, like Great Authors past, Fielding, Jane Austen, Hawthorne, Hemingway. But oh, what would I give, and I would give a lot, I assure you, for just a little of the fame, the glamour, the glitter, that attends even a lesser author, a Horatio Alger, an Agatha Christie, a Ford Maddox Ford. But no, no, my pen is likely, fated, you might say, to achieve no greatness other than winning at tic-tac-toe.

Editing for Correct Spelling

Misspellings, especially multiple misspellings, are another of the sort of error that is likely to distract your readers. Unfortunately, English is a notoriously difficult language to spell. "Sounding it out" does not always work with English because there are many discrepancies between sound and spelling. Most such problems stem from the tendency of English over the centuries to simplify its sounds. For example, in the days when there really were knights in armor, "knight" was pronounced "ka-ni-ckt." Today, the spelling still reflects the medieval sound, even though the modern pronunciation no longer offers a key to it. Furthermore, as time has passed, all unstressed vowels in English words have tended to draw toward the single sound "uh." Though no doubt the following examples of unstressed vowels were once clearly distinguishable in speech, now they are all pronounced "uh":

oct@gon fun©ral intell©gent oct©pus diffi©lt plat©pus

These examples are typical. Thus, when you are faced with spelling the "uh" sound in a word that you do not have fixed in your visual memory, you have few grounds upon which to base an intelligent guess.

English also owes much of its confusing spelling to the source of its amazing richness, the numerous words it has borrowed from foreign languages. A line from comedian Shelley Berman's skit, "Franz Kafka on the Telephone," demonstrates the confusion brought to English spelling by the presence of these foreign sound systems. In this line, Berman attempts to identify the letters that spell *pokerface:*

> POKERFACE. P as in *Psychosis.* O as in *Oedipus.* K as in *Knicknack.* E as in *Euphemism.* . . .

Despite the difficulties caused by an evolving language, correct spelling remains important to the success of your written work. To keep your writing free from spelling errors, it is best to be a reader with a natural eye and memory for the formation of words. Failing that, second best is to be conscious of the fact that you are not a naturally good speller and be willing to check out every word you are not as sure of as you are, for instance, of C-A-T. When editing your final draft, circle all the words whose spelling you are not certain of, look them up, and correct where necessary. You will find the words most commonly misspelled or confused listed at the end of the spelling section in the Revision Guide, Part Six of this text.

In addition, despite the irregularities of the English language, there are a number of spelling rules that might be helpful to you. Under "Spelling" in the Revision Guide, you will find rules for placement of vowel pairs (piece, pour, and so on), for adding suffixes (mopping, moping, stopped, marries), for combined words (roommate), and for special problems with K, C, and S. Spelling with apostrophes is also discussed under that heading. And should you have any doubts about the spelling of particular homonym*s* or sound-alikes (*there, their, they're; accept, except;* and the like), you'll find them in the Revision Guide as well, alphabetically listed.

Revising for Correctness: A Summary Checklist

Key: Look up the correct form whenever you are unsure.
Try especially to correct:
Errors of the Sentence
1. Edit run-on sentences.
2. Revise unnecessary or inappropriate sentence fragments.
3. Check for subject-verb agreement; be particularly careful of subjects that include prepositional phrases.

Faulty Capitalization and Punctuation
1. Check for initial capitals and final periods.
2. Make sure every proper name is capitalized.
3. Edit out absent-minded capitals and those meant only for emphasis.
4. Edit out commas that interrupt the flow of the text.
5. Make sure interrupting material is set off by a *pair* of commas.
6. Add a comma after introductory subordinate clauses or other lengthy introductory material.
7. Check for needed commas in series, in addresses, and in dates.
8. Be sure to **use** a semicolon to separate the independent clauses in a compound sentence where there is no linking *and* or *but* or where either of the clauses contains commas.
9. To keep the structure clear, use semicolons to divide a series where the components contain internal commas.
10. Use colons, parentheses, or dashes to make your meaning clear; but check to be sure you are not over-using them.

Spelling Errors
1. In this area of revision, it's best to know your weakness. "When in doubt, look it up."
2. Learning spelling rules may help. Check under "Spelling" in the Revision Guide.

Editing for Correctness

Only those errors that are most distracting to readers have been singled out for discussion in this chapter. They are, of course, only a small fraction of potential errors. Since errors are such an individual thing, the problems discussed here may not be yours. In editing for correctness, the most important thing you can do is to come to an awareness of your *own* areas of weakness. Then you can train your editing eye to focus on those writing situations where you are likely to run into difficulty. If you find any points where you are uncertain, turn to the Revision Guide for clarification. The alphabetically arranged entries offer concise explanations and practical advice. You should find the guide a reliable tool for successful editing.

ASSIGNMENT

Write a thoughtful essay on one of the following topics (or another that your instructor suggests). Before you write, give your ideas a chance to grow and mellow and then organize them carefully. When you write your essay, concentrate on getting your ideas written down as clearly as you can.

When you have finished your first draft, edit your paper carefully and revise it according to the suggestions given in this chapter.
1. Write about:
   • Something of genuine importance to you, though not necessarily to others.
   • Something of tremendous importance to others, but not to you.

- Something that once seemed important to you, but does no longer.
- Something you believe to be unfair.

Although these topics are phrased in personal terms to help you begin your thinking, you would probably be wiser to take a less personal approach to the essay itself.

2. Respond to a recent article in the newspaper or in a newsmagazine such as *Time, Newsweek,* or *U.S. News and World Report.*

3. Read Tom Wolfe's "Down with Sin" (p. 443). Analyze Wolfe's ideas expressed in the essay. Then, relating what he has to say about sin to behavior on your campus or in your neighborhood, develop your own thesis on the subject. Revise your essay thoroughly following the guidelines in this chapter.

4. Look through the titles of the Part Five essays. Choose one to direct a free-writing. Use that free-writing to arrive at a thesis through one of the methods described in Chapter 1 or Part One. Write an essay on that topic. Set it aside for a minimum of 24 hours. Then revise it thoroughly accordingly to the three-step method you learned in this chapter.

Part Three

Persuading through Style

The early parts of this book concentrated, to a large extent, on ideas and the organization of those ideas. This part focuses instead upon the expression of ideas—in short, upon style. For though thesis and structure are the nuts and bolts of expository writing, the style in which this material is expressed is no less important. The style of a passage, after all, largely determines the readers' reactions to it.

In Part Three you will learn to think of style as a matter of writer's choice. Its chapters discuss the specific stylistic decisions you must make—consciously or unconsciously—whenever you write. The text and exercises are designed to help you become aware of these decisions and learn to choose effectively. Chapters 5, 6, and 7 are concerned with choices within the structure of the sentence. They use a technique called "sentence combining." Chapter 8 deals with choice of words and phrases. All the chapters in Part Three mean to help you develop your own style of writing, your own way of expressing your ideas persuasively.

5

Creating Your Style by Making Decisions: Sentence Combining

Style can never be totally distinguished from content, the expression from the expressed. But by looking closely at the *form* of the language used, we can nevertheless isolate style—at least in a particular passage—for separate consideration and study. If we can keep the content of two passages relatively constant, whatever differences emerge must be attributable to style. Say, for example, you wanted to suggest that a girl you were writing about had negative feelings about leaving a place. Among many possible ways of expressing this thought you might choose to write either

Defining style.

- The girl was reluctant to leave.

    or

- She just didn't want to go nohow.

The actual content of the statements—the girl and her feelings—remains the same in both sentences. But the styles of the two statements—the way the girl is observed and reported and, consequently, the way she will be perceived by the reader—are entirely different. The style of neither sentence accounts for the sentence's meaning, but the difference in the styles of the two sentences does account for the differences in meanings and the differing effects of the two sentences upon the reader.

Viewed in this way, style can be considered a matter of the writer's choice—basically a choice of words (diction) and of sentence structure (syntax). Improving your writing style, then, becomes a matter of learning to make these choices wisely.

STYLE AND SENTENCE COMBINING

The technique of sentence combining has been developed to give writers like you the opportunity to concentrate on making syntactic stylistic choices (that is, choices in sentence structure) without having to worry about inventing ideas. Exercises provide the content. You provide the style. For instance, an exercise might ask you to combine such sentences as these:

- The team committed a serious error.
- The coach talked earnestly to the team.

In working the exercise, you might consider creating such sentences as the following:

- After the team made a serious error, the coach talked to them earnestly.
- The coach talked earnestly to the team after their serious error.
- The team, having made a serious error, were talked to earnestly by the coach.
- The coach talked earnestly to the team that had made the serious error.

To complete the exercise, you would then decide which sentence works best in the given context. By keeping content and wording more or less constant, sentence-combining exercises free you to think about the shape of your sentences and give you practice in using syntax persuasively.

You will not need special training to do sentence-combining exercises, for you are already something of an expert in the English language. You already have inside your brain the kind of rules that prevent you from ever creating such nonsentences as "Over game was the." Being a speaker of English you have an intuitive knowledge of the patterns of the English sentence and the ability to fit the thousands of words you know into these patterns. The purpose of sentence-combining exercises is to strengthen your ability to do what you already do well by making you more aware of the process while you are doing it.

Although you will not need any traditional grammar drill to help you do these exercises, some review of the vocabulary of grammar may be useful for the discussion that is an integral part of sentence combining. After you try each exercise, you will probably have the opportunity to compare your solutions with those of your classmates and instructor. If you share the same vocabulary, understanding and discussion should both flow more easily. To this end, the next section, "The Building Blocks of Style," will take you through a quick review of grammatical terms and help you recall syntactical concepts that may have faded from your memory.

THE BUILDING BLOCKS OF STYLE

The Essential Sentence: Subject-Verb-[Complement]

Since we are about to begin a study of *sentence* combining, we ought to be fairly certain of what exactly a *sentence* is. The actual essence of the sentence becomes clearest when we reduce the sentence to its basics. Let's examine some examples of the shortest possible sentences:

- Birds fly.
- Babies coo.
- [You] Smile!
- Garbage smells.

These brief examples (the last included to avert any charges of sentimentality) contain everything a verbal structure needs to be a sentence. They each contain a subject and a verb: *something doing or being.* The requirements for a sentence are met whether it is phrased as a statement:

Birds will fly
(subj.) (verb)

or as a question:

(subj.)
Will birds fly?
(verb)

or even as a command where the subject, "you," is understood:

[You] Jump down!
(subj.)(verb)

> In essence, a sentence is an independently existing group of words arranged to express something doing or being.

Actually, as we know, very few sentences are as sparse as these. Most English sentences also include an object or quality needed to complete the verb (a complement) and thus instead express *something doing or being something.* Some examples of this sort of sentence—again cut to the bare bones—include:

- Bats   hit   balls.
  (subj.) (verb) (obj.)

- The   girl   picked   a   daisy.
      (subj.) (verb)   (obj.)

- The squirrel will climb the tree.
      (subj.)   (verb)   (obj.)

- (subj.)
  Will the squirrel climb the tree?
                           (obj.)
          (verb)

And that's really all there is to it. The configuration Subject-Verb-[Complement (Object)] is at the heart of the English syntactical system, and almost everything within that system can be explained in its terms.

Clauses and Phrases Defined

Clauses and phrases might both be defined as *meaningfully arranged groups of words* within a sentence. They are distinguished from each other by the presence or absence of subject and verb. *Phrases* do not have subjects or verbs:

- in the wind
- blowing in the wind

- blown in the wind
- to blow [in the wind]

But *clauses,* like sentences, must include both a subject and a verb.

An *independent clause* (also called "main clause") is of itself a sentence, though it exists within a larger structure. Given initial capital and end punctuation, it could stand alone, as for instance in the sentence:

The wind blows, and the waves pound.

Both "The wind blows" and "the waves pound" are independent clauses and can be transformed into true sentences by appropriate capitalization and punctuation:

- The wind blows.
     (subj.) (verb)
- The waves pound.
     (subj.) (verb)

A *dependent clause (subordinate clause)* also must possess a subject and a verb. The subordinate clause cannot stand alone, however, because it is hindered by an extra word (a *subordinating conjunction** or a *relative pronoun*) that attaches it to its main clause and signals its dependent relationship. For example, although "The wind blows" is a main clause, it can become a subordinate clause simply by adding a subordinating conjunction: "*That* the wind blows," "*When* the wind blows," and "[The wind] *which* blows" are all subordinate clauses. Incorporated with appropriate main clauses into sentences, they become:

- He   told me *that* the wind blows.*
  (subj.) (verb)   (subj.) (verb)
- The waves pound *when* the wind blows.*
     (subj.) (verb)   (subj.) (verb)
- The wind *which* blows* makes the waves pound.
     (subj.)   (subj.) (verb) (verb)

Parts of Speech

The Subject-Verb-[Complement (Object)] configuration explains the functions of the parts of speech—and the functions of the various kinds of phrases and clauses as well. *Nouns* are words that serve as the subjects or objects of sentences, clauses, or phrases. Observe, for instance, the functions served by the nouns in the following constructions:

Defined by function.

- The *waves* pound the *shore.*
     (subj.)   (obj.)
- *Jack* told the *boy*   the *tale.*
  (subj.) (indirect obj.)   (obj.)

---

*Subordinating conjunctions (see also pp. 183, 202 and 217).

- in the *wind*
    (obj. of phrase)
- to sail the *ship*
    (obj. of phrase)
- Jack, a *man* after my own heart,
    (subj. of phrase)

Pronouns serve the same functions when they substitute for nouns:

- *They* [the waves] pound the shore.
(subj.)
- *Who* has seen the wind?
(subj.)
- To *whom* do you wish to speak?
    (indirect obj.—or obj. of phrase)

Verbs are the words that express the doing or being of the subject. By changing their spelling or adding on an auxiliary, they also tell *when* the subject does or is:

The wind *blows.* The waves *pounded* the shore. The beach *will be* sandy.

Adjectives describe or modify subjects or objects—that is to say, nouns:

The *rough* waves pound the *sandy* shore.

Adverbs similarly describe or modify the verb:

The waves *roughly* pound the shore.

Adverbs also mark the sentence for time, place, manner, or frequency by telling when or where or how often the subject acts or is:

Then the waves pounded the shore *again* and *again.*

Nouns (and pronouns), verbs, adjectives, and adverbs carry the basic meaning. The remaining parts of speech (variously named depending upon the authority) are *function words* which serve primarily to shape sentences, clauses, and phrases and to hold them together. These function words include three kinds of *conjunctions:*

Coordinating conjunctions (*and, but, or,* etc.) join groups of words together in more or less equal balance.

Subordinating conjunctions (*after, because, when,* etc.) attach a dependent group of words (clause or phrase) to an independent one.

Connectors (*therefore, however, nevertheless,* etc.) combine an adverbial with a conjunctive function.

Prepositions (*under, over, around, in, out, above, to, from,* etc.) should also be considered function words. They link their object, a noun, and its modifiers to the rest of the clause or sentence.

Phrases

Phrases and subordinate clauses function within the sentence exactly as the single-word parts of speech do.

Prepositional phrases, for instance, can serve as either adjectives or adverbs, depending upon whether they describe a noun:

> The child *with the shovel* . . .
>> (noun)

or a verb:

> . . . played *in the garden*.
>> (verb)

Participial phrases, that is, phrases headed by the *-ing* or the *-ed* forms of the verb, act as adjectives because they describe nouns:

> The ship, *sailing swiftly, managed by its crew* . . .
>> (noun)

Infinitive phrases, phrases headed usually by the "to" form of the verb, behave mainly as nouns, where they serve as subjects:

> *To err* is human.

or as complements:

> He learned *to swim.*

Gerund phrases, phrases headed by the *-ing* form of the verb, also serve as nouns. They act as subjects:

> *Playing chess* is lots of fun.

or as objects (here of a prepositional phrase):

> . . . by *swimming competitively.*

Appositive phrases, though they consist of a noun and its modifiers, actually have an adjectival function because they modify another noun and its modifiers:

> • The haunted house, *a dilapidated Victorian monstrosity,* . . .
> • Professor Offenbach, *my teacher,* . . .

And *adverbial phrases* serve, of course, as adverbs. Adverbial phrases are adverb clauses with their subject and verb removed. You might also think of them as participial phrases headed by an adverbial subordinating conjunction:

> • *While sitting by the road* . . .
> • *When drenched with rain* . . .

Defined by function.

Subordinate Clauses

The three kinds of subordinate clauses (adverb, adjective, and noun) are called by the name of the particular part of speech they function as in a sentence.

Defined by function.

Adverb clauses are headed by adverbial subordinating conjunctions ("when," "while," "since," "because," "if," and so on). These clauses mark the sentence for time, place, manner, or frequency—or, in short, they behave like adverbs:

- *When the dance was over,* the band stopped playing.
- The band stopped playing *because the dance was over.*

Adjective clauses are the "who," "which," "that" clauses that describe nouns:

- Sally, *who was dressed in red,* answered the door.
- The clock *that was always late* chimed three times.

Adjective clauses are sometimes called *relative clauses* because the words they are introduced by are *relative pronouns.* (These pronouns are *relative* because they relate or connect the clause to the rest of the sentence; they are *pronouns* because, by substituting for the modified noun, they usually serve as the subject of the clause.)

Noun clauses, which are introduced by words like "that," "where," and "what," act as subjects or objects, the whole clause taking the place of a single noun:

- She told me *that she was happy.* (as object of sentence)
- *That she was happy* was all too clear. (as subject of sentence)
- He was afraid of *what he could not understand.* (as object of preposition)
- *Where my love laughs* is *where I want to be.* (as subject and as object of sentence)

Try It Out

The preceding summary gives you a systematic way of approaching syntax, but it has been extremely concentrated and intense. Fortunately, there are two exercises for reviewing grammar that are helpful but not at all intense, and most students seem to have a good time working them. The Diamond Paragraph exercise requires knowledge of the structure of simple, compound, complex, and compound-complex sentences. The Add-It-On exercise, which comes first, is designed to provide this information.

Add-It-On Exercise

Though you can work this exercise alone as you might work a puzzle, most people find it more fun to try it in groups.

The serious purpose of the Add-It-On is to explore the possibilities of the simple sentence and to distinguish it from the compound, complex, and compound-complex varieties. We have already discovered the minimal boundaries of the simple sentence. This exercise will help you push the simple sentence to its maximum contours. In so doing, you will find just how much you can add to a simple sentence before it becomes complex or compound. For the most successful solution to this exercise, follow the directions with as much imagination as you can summon up. The sample solution shows you how one freshman class worked it out.

The Simple Sentence

1. Create a simple sentence in the unadorned subject-verb-object pattern—the more absurd the subject matter, the better.
   Sample: Armadillos eat fig newtons.

2. Add adjective modifiers.
   a. Add at least one adjective.
      Sample: *Clumsy* armadillos eat *burnt* fig newtons.
   b. Add at least one adjectival prepositional phrase.
      Sample: Clumsy armadillos *with growling stomachs* eat burnt fig newtons.
   c. Add at least one participial phrase (either past *-ed* or present *-ing*).
      Sample: Clumsy armadillos with growling stomachs eat burnt fig newtons *dipped in paste-like catsup.*

3. Add adverbial modifiers.
   a. Add at least one adverb.
      Sample: Clumsy armadillos with growling stomachs *slowly* and *carefully* eat burnt fig newtons dipped in paste-like catsup.
   b. Add at least one adverbial phrase or adverbial prepositional phrase.
      Sample: Clumsy armadillos with growling stomachs slowly and carefully eat burnt fig newtons dipped in paste-like catsup *while falling off a cliff.*

(We are still dealing with nothing but a SIMPLE SENTENCE!)

4. Compound the subject by adding at least one other subject.
   Sample: *Little lemmings and* clumsy armadillos with growling stomachs slowly and carefully eat burnt fig newtons dipped in paste-like catsup while falling off a cliff.

5. Compound the object by adding at least one more complement to the verb.

Sample Little lemmings and clumsy armadillos with growling stomachs slowly and carefully eat *popcorn and* burnt fig newtons dipped in paste-like catsup while falling off a cliff.

6. Compound the verb by adding at least one other main verb.

Sample: Little lemmings and clumsy armadillos with growling stomachs slowly and carefully eat popcorn and burnt fig newtons dipped in paste-like catsup *and play stud poker* while falling off a cliff.

All this and THE SENTENCE IS STILL A SIMPLE SENTENCE!

The Compound Sentence

How then can you make a compound sentence? Not by adding another subject or another verb, but by adding another *complete* sentence. The two main clauses can be joined by a coordinating conjunction, such as "and" or "but," or by a semicolon.

7. Make a compound sentence by adding another sentence to the first (and thus turning them both into the main clauses of a compound sentence).

Sample: Little lemmings and clumsy armadillos with growling stomachs slowly and carefully eat popcorn and burnt fig newtons dipped in paste-like catsup and play stud poker while falling off a cliff, *but they are silly beasts.*
                              (subj.)(verb)(obj.)

The Complex Sentence

A complex sentence is a sentence that has a main clause and at least one subordinate clause. How do you turn your simple sentence into a complex one? One way is by changing your sentence into a subordinate clause by adding a subordinating conjunction. Amazing as it may seem, the entire concoction of lemmings and armadillos and catsup and poker and cliffs can be turned into a dependent clause—and thus no sentence at all—by the addition of a single word: "*When* little lemmings. . . ," "*After* little lemmings. . . ," "*Although* little lemmings. . . ," "*Until* little lemmings. . . ," and so on.

8. *Complex Sentence with Adverb Clause.* Create a complex sentence by turning your original sentence into an adverb clause and attaching it to a suitable main clause—either before or after.

Sample: Because little lemmings and clumsy armadillos with growling stomachs slowly and carefully eat popcorn and burnt fig newtons dipped in paste-like catsup and play stud poker while falling off a cliff, they are silly beasts.

9. *Complex Sentence with Noun Clause.* Create a complex sentence by adding a "that" (or comparable expression) to your original sentence and use it as a noun clause to serve as the subject or the object of a verb.

> **Sample:**   That little lemmings and clumsy armadillos with growling stomachs slowly and carefully eat popcorn and burnt fig newtons dipped in paste-like catsup and play studpoker while falling off a cliff means they are silly beasts.

10. *Complex Sentence with Adjective Clause.* The whole sentence cannot be turned into an adjective clause, but the original sentence can become complex if an adjective clause is inserted into it. Any adjective—word or phrase—is at base an adjective clause with the relative pronoun and verb "to be" removed. Restore the pronoun and verb (*is, are, was, were,* or other forms of "to be") and the clause is created. The sentence then automatically becomes complex. Use this technique to turn your original sentence into a complex sentence with an adjective clause.

> **Sample:**   Little lemmings and armadillos, *which are clumsy and have growling stomachs,* slowly and carefully eat popcorn and burnt fig newtons dipped in paste-like catsup and play stud poker while falling off a cliff.

The Compound-Complex Sentence

The compound-complex sentence is a compound sentence with one or more subordinate clauses.

11. Create a compound-complex sentence, using the material from your original sentence.

> **Sample:**   Little lemmings and armadillos, which are clumsy and have growling stomachs, slowly and carefully eat popcorn and burnt fig newtons dipped in paste-like catsup and play stud poker while falling off a cliff; they are silly beasts.

Diamond Paragraph Exercise

Within the following diamond-shaped syntactic pattern, develop a thesis of your own choosing. Feel free to vary the position of the three dependent clauses or to add a second compound-complex sentence in the center if you need more room to develop the content.

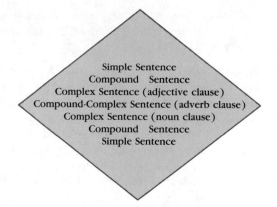

Simple Sentence
Compound   Sentence
Complex Sentence (adjective clause)
Compound-Complex Sentence (adverb clause)
Complex Sentence (noun clause)
Compound   Sentence
Simple Sentence

Please note that although the diamond sets up an interesting exercise, it is in no way recommended as the ideal form for a paragraph.

INTRODUCTION TO SENTENCE COMBINING

The sentence-combining approach assumes that all the sentences we actually speak or write are derived from simple basic sentences: subject, verb, object. Our minds combine these minimal sentences in complex ways to create an infinite number of possible sentences. In this view, the sentence "A troubled Hamlet gazed thoughtfully at the skull" is derived from these three basic sentences (sometimes called "kernels"):

- Hamlet gazed at the skull.
- Hamlet is troubled.
- Hamlet's gaze is thoughtful.

These same kernels could also produce:

- Hamlet, who was troubled, gazed at the skull thoughtfully.
- Thoughtfully, a troubled Hamlet gazed at the skull.
- The skull was gazed at thoughtfully by a troubled Hamlet.
- Hamlet, who was troubled, gazed thoughtfully at the skull.

Sentence-combining exercises provide sets of such kernels and thus offer you a way to duplicate consciously the theoretical sentence-forming process. In trying out various combinations, you can become aware of the range of your stylistic choices and through this awareness learn to make these choices more effectively.

Abundance and Variety of Possible Combinations

In the sections that follow, you are asked to make effective sentences out of sets of simple kernels such as the following:

- The game was over.
- The crowd was excited.
- The crowd left the stadium.
- The crowd filled the streets.
- The streets were narrow.

The most direct combination of these kernels gives you

The game was over, and the excited crowd left the stadium and filled the narrow streets.

But whether this is the most pleasing or most suitable sentence these kernels can yield, you can't know until you experiment with other options. The following possibilities come immediately to mind, but I'm sure that if you think about it you can find several more.

1. The game was over, and the excited crowd left the stadium and filled the narrow streets.
2. After the game was over, the crowd, which was excited, left the stadium and filled the narrow streets.
3. Leaving the stadium after the game was over, the crowd excitedly filled the narrow streets.
4. The narrow streets were filled by the excited crowd who left the stadium after the game.
5. Because the game was over, the excited crowd left the stadium and filled the narrow streets.
6. The game being over, the crowd left the stadium excitedly and filled the narrow streets.
7. As they left the stadium, the after-game crowds filled the narrow streets with excitement.
8. The game was over; the excited crowd left the stadium, filling the narrow streets.
9. The streets, which are exceedingly narrow by the stadium, are always filled with excited crowds when games are over.
10. The streets were filled with an excited crowd who had left the stadium. The game was over.

This set of sentence kernels about the stadium crowd—like every such set—offers the writer a remarkable number of options. In order to explore these options, you should feel free to experiment in the following ways:

- To combine the kernels in any order that sounds good to you
- To add appropriate function words (for instance, *after* as in examples 2, 4, and 7; *because* as in 5; *as* as in 7; *who* as in 4 and 10; *which* as in 9; and so on)
- To change the form of words (for instance, *excited* to *excitedly* in examples 3 and 6 and to *excitement* in 7; *filled* to *filling* in 8 and to *were filled* in 4 and 10)
- Not to combine at all (occasionally to let a kernel sentence stand as is, as in 10)

- To add or to delete a detail (for instance, the addition of *exceedingly narrow* and *always filled* in 9)

Don't hesitate to be creative. The more kinds of sentence structure you can learn to use comfortably, the richer your writing style will become.

═══ Try It Out ═══

Combining Kernels

In how many different ways can you combine the following sentences without changing the content? Experiment with these kernels.

Paris at Sundown

1. The sun sank.
2. It sank over the river Seine.
3. A girl sat at a sidewalk cafe.
4. The girl was American.
5. The girl finished her coffee.
6. She finished idly.
7. The girl watched the passersby.
8. She watched eagerly.

Were you able to create at least eight different combinations of these kernels? If so, you have done very well indeed. Even so, there may well be as many as twice eight more combinations waiting to be discovered—the English language is that rich in possibilities.

Evaluating Combinations

Having discovered the abundance of possibilities in combining even the simplest set of kernels, you may already understand that there can be no single "right" way to combine them and that there is *no* single "correct answer" to any sentence-combining puzzle. Still, you have probably also determined that some ways are better than others, and you may be wondering if there aren't some objective criteria to help you distinguish the best combinations. Clearly there are criteria, but they are rather subjective. And that is why comparing your work with others and discussing the results is so important in sentence-combining practice. For through this sort of discussion, you will be able to develop a surer sense of what is effective with your readers and thus become more confident in your own judgment.

In order to determine just how effective a particular combination is, you may safely rely on these three standards:

- Clarity and directness of meaning
- Rhythmic appeal
- Intended emphasis

Clarity   The standard I judge most important is clarity. Since communication is the fundamental aim of expository writing, a sentence is good when it clearly conveys its meaning and weak when it is ambiguous or difficult to understand. In applying this standard, you might ask whether the subject, verb, and object of a particular sentence are immediately perceivable. Sometimes too many, or oddly placed, interrupting words and phrases between these three vital elements of the sentence act to obscure the sentence's meaning. Sometimes added phrases or clauses, which would otherwise work to the sentence's advantage, cause problems by faulty punctuation. (Remember to surround such unessential interruptions with a pair of commas or dashes or parentheses—never use just one.) Moreover, clarity demands a certain logic of content. Of the American girl in the earlier exercise, you might say, for instance, that she

> . . . finished her coffee idly because she eagerly watched the passersby.

But it would be illogical for you to write the equally grammatical statement that she

> . . . eagerly watched the passersby because she idly finished her coffee.   FAULTY

Rhythmic Appeal   A second criterion, rhythm, exerts a subtle yet important influence on readers. In evaluating, therefore, it is fair to judge a sentence as better when it is more rhythmically pleasing. A sentence will be rhythmically pleasing when its parts are harmoniously balanced, when related elements are kept parallel, and when the syntax is not awkward or convoluted. A sentence usually loses its rhythmic appeal and becomes awkward, for instance, when the main clause is sandwiched between two adverbials:

> When the American girl idly finished her coffee,
> she sat at the sidewalk cafe
> while she eagerly watched the passersby.

A lack of proper parallelism is an even greater offender against harmony. For an unparallel example, read this version. Note the miscellaneous mixture of grammatical elements.

> The American girl sat idly at the cafe,   FAULTY
>   was finishing her coffee, and
>   she watched the passersby eagerly.

A harmonious sentence is pleasing, but a sentence that builds a compelling rhythm through repetition (rhythm *is* patterned repetition) can stir the emotions. The appeal seems to be universal, tied up with something that is deep and primitive in human nature. Such sentences are useful for beginnings, for endings, and for building to a climax of persuasiveness. At times when you want to create an emotional response, you should judge your sentences for their rhythmic qualities. Watch for syntactic parallels such as:

> id ly   finish ing   her coffee
> eager ly   watch ing   the passersby

Read the construction aloud and listen for the accented beats of each sentence as you would for those in a piece of music. And notice contrasts between the lengths of phrases—that of a long, rolling preliminary segment, for example, and its abrupt conclusion. High in rhythmic appeal, for instance, is the following combination with its parallel -*ing* phrases and its long dominant clause contrasting with the single-syllable beat of its relatively brief climactic finale. Note also how the repetition of the *s* sound contributes to the rhythm.

> The American girl sat at the sidewalk cafe, idly finishing her coffee and eagerly watching the passersby, while the sun sank down over the river Seine.

Intended Emphasis   A third standard for judging the quality of a combination of kernels is whether it has appropriate emphasis. What emphasis is appropriate depends upon the exact meaning intended. Such exactness of meaning must take precedence over all other considerations. In most cases, for example, you would choose to call the subject of the sentence on the Paris cafe simply "an American girl." The construction is both direct and smooth and easily meets the other two standards. But if the purpose of your sentence were to emphasize the girl's nationality—to distinguish her from girls of other lands, for instance— then you would more appropriately write "The girl, an American, . . ." or "the girl, who was American, ..."

To give you another example, suppose you were interested in directing your readers' attention to the girl's relationship with the passersby—perhaps in order to develop her characterization or to foreshadow some later event. In such a case you would probably not use the parallel structure that rhythmic considerations might otherwise dictate (see p. 242). Instead you might select a sentence with this emphasis:

> While the sun sank quietly over the river Seine, an American girl, who was idly finishing her coffee at a sidewalk cafe, watched the passersby with great eagerness.

Putting "watched the passersby" in the main clause, subordinating all the rest of the material to it, as well as giving it the important final position focuses the readers' interest squarely where you want it. Substituting the more emphatic adverbial prepositional phrase "with great eagerness" for the adverb "eagerly" also helps achieve a greater consequence for the girl-passersby relationship.

Sentences written from the Paris-cafe kernels usually focus on the girl, therefore placing her as the subject. But you could choose other emphases. For example, if the aim of the sentence were to give the reader a glimpse of one of a series of little Parisian scenes that will set the stage for later action, then you might choose to use the sun as the subject and write a sentence like this:

> The sun, as it sank down over the river Seine, also cast its glow upon an American girl who sat at a sidewalk cafe, idly finishing her coffee and eagerly watching the passersby.

There are, in fact, times when you might even choose to write a sentence in the passive (to write "The girl was lit by a glow from the setting sun" instead of the usually preferable active construction used in the previous example).

Despite the excellence of advice to avoid the passive in order to achieve directness and clarity, the passive is a legitimate English construction and occasionally has its appropriate uses. If you want to put the emphasis on the object (rather than on the subject), and especially if you want to stress the action that is being done to the object ("The girl was illuminated . . ."), you would select the passive option. For instance, if you wanted the sentence on the Paris cafe to serve as one example in a paragraph developing a thesis about the universality of coffee not only as a beverage, but as a medium of social exchange, you might choose to write it with a passive emphasis:

> Coffee, for instance, is the beverage consumed by idle American girls eagerly watching passersby from sidewalk cafes as the sun sinks over the river Seine.

In summary, make your writing choices and evaluate your sentences and those of your classmates by how clearly and directly the wording conveys the intended meaning—including how precisely they reflect their intended emphasis—and by how smoothly and effectively the sentences sound their rhythms.

Evaluating Combinations in Context   As useful as these three criteria can be, they take on real meaning only in terms of a specific writing situation. In fact, most evaluating questions can only be answered: It depends. Is a long sentence better or worse than a short sentence? It depends. Is it better to begin a sentence with a participial or with an adverbial phrase? It depends. Is it better to put adverbial clauses at the beginning or at the end of sentences? Again it depends. What it depends upon is where the sentence in question fits into its paragraph, what its purpose is within the paragraph, and what its relationship is to the other sentences in that paragraph. For instance, a composition filled with brief sentences of the subject-verb-object variety would surely give the impression of immature writing—rather like that of a first reader:

> Here is a dog.
> His name is Spot.
> Run, Spot, run.

But such sentences can also provide an impressive note of contrast after a series of longer and more complicated sentences. See, for example, combination 10 on page 167. With the proper contrast, short sentences can also add a surprisingly dramatic note:

> While the sun was setting in all its glory over the river Seine, an American girl sat in a sidewalk cafe watching the passersby with great eagerness. *The sun sank. The girl finished her coffee.*

Purpose, balance, and variety are the important considerations. And these qualities are all dependent upon the larger context.

Furthermore, a phrasing that would make a good topic sentence for a paragraph might well be inappropriate for a supporting sentence. And certainly a sentence that is meant to serve as a transition should have a different phrasing from one that is intended to be climactic. The answer to what makes a good sentence, then, is largely dependent upon the purpose of that sentence within the context of a whole composition. Good sentences build upon one another, as we have seen. Their rhythms and their meanings should flow from one to the other.

For these reasons, most of the sentence-combining exercises in this text give you the opportunity to choose your options within the context of paragraphs and short essays.

As you do the exercises, you will become familiar with the stylistic possibilities of a good number of sentence strategies. At the same time, you will have done that stylistic experimenting with an eye to the necessities of particular expository situations—good practice for real-life writing.

The following is typical of the exercises you will be asked to do in the remainder of Part Three, "Persuading through Style."

Try It Out

Combining Kernels

Combine the following kernels into strong sentences making up an effective paragraph. The kernels are grouped to help you decide upon the size of individual sentences, but you may disregard these groupings if you wish.

The Pizza Parlor

1. Sam is the pizza chef.
2. The pizza chef removes the pizza.
3. The pizza is hot.
4. The pizza is steamy.
5. He removes it from the oven.
6. The oven is oversized.
7. He removes it deftly.

8. The cheese is yellow.
9. The cheese bubbles.
10. It bubbles over the tomato sauce.
11. It bubbles over the pepperoni.

12. The pizza cools.
13. The waitress eyes the pizza.
14. She eyes it with hunger.
15. She eyes it with envy.
16. The waitress inhales the odors.
17. The odors are delicious.

18. The pizza is ready (finally).
19. The waitress delivers the pizza.
20. She delivers it with resignation.
21. She delivers it to the customers.
22. The customers are eager.
23. The customers are accepting.

To work through this exercise, write down the various possibilities, read them aloud, and decide upon the particular options you feel will make the most effective paragraph. Then you will be ready to discuss your decisions and compare them with those others have made. Your instructor will probably ask three or four students to share their versions in some way. If your class tries out "The Pizza Parlor," some of the versions may be similar to the four following paragraphs.

A. Sam, who is the pizza chef, removes the pizza deftly from the oversized oven. The pizza is hot and steamy. The cheese is yellow, and it bubbles over the tomato sauce and over the pepperoni. As the pizza cools, the waitress eyes it with hungry envy. She also inhales the delicious odors. When the pizza is finally ready, the waitress delivers it with resignation. The customers accept it with eagerness.

B. Sam, the pizza chef, deftly removed the hot, steamy pizza from the oversized oven. The yellow pizza cheese bubbled over the tomato sauce and the pepperoni. While the pizza cooled, the waitress, hungrily eyeing it with envy, inhaled the delicious odors; and when it was finally ready, she delivered it with resignation to the eager, accepting customers.

C. The hot, steaming pizza is deftly removed from the oversized oven by Sam, the pizza chef. The cheese bubbles over the tomato sauce and pepperoni. Hungrily, the waitress enviously eyes it, inhaling the delicious odors, while it cools. Finally it is ready, and she resignedly delivers it to the eagerly accepting customers.

D. Yellow cheese bubbles over tomato and pepperoni as Sam, the pizza chef, deftly removes the hot and steamy pizza from the oversized oven. Hungrily the waitress eyes the cooling pizza, and enviously she inhales the delicious odors. With resignation she delivers the pizza to the customers, who accept it eagerly.

After you have had a chance to hear these paragraphs read aloud, the differences among them should become clear to you. In order to discover how these stylistic differences have been achieved—and how some might be avoided—you may want to ask yourself questions such as the ones in the accompanying lists.

Overall Impression

1. Which of the versions do you think is the best? Why?
2. Which do you like the best? Are they the same? If not, why?
3. Which versions seem to handle the material most creatively? Have any of them changed or added to the original wording? If so, do the changes make an improvement? Why? Or why not?
4. Which versions offer the most variety in sentence structure? Which have tried the most unusual or interesting structures?
5. Which is the most rhythmically effective version? How is this effectiveness achieved?

6. Are any of the versions weak in coherence or in unity? How might these flaws be corrected?

7. In what major ways do the versions differ?

Purpose and Point

1. Do all the versions seem to have the same purpose? If not, how do they differ? If yes, what is that purpose?

2. Do the differences in style reflect a difference in purpose? Or simply different approaches to the same purpose?

3. How well do the various stylistic strategies serve their purpose? (If the point of "Pizza Parlor," for instance, is to focus on the pizza and the reactions it evokes, is it better achieved through the emphasis in C and D or in A and B?)

4. How might some versions be changed to communicate their points more effectively?

Part by Part

The point of this last group of questions is to help you examine in close detail any paragraph or essay under discussion, to look at it specifically part by part and even sentence by sentence. Because of the specificity of this sort of study, general questions are less helpful. Therefore, I've substituted representative questions dealing specifically with the "Pizza Parlor" sample paragraphs.

1. *Which begins best?* Do you prefer the Sam openings (A and B) or the pizza openings (C and D)? If you like the Sam openings, how do you feel about the "who" clause in version A? Does it add desirable emphasis? Or does it detract from a concise, direct approach? If you think the initial emphasis belongs on the pizza itself, do you like the passive method in C? Or do you prefer the way the D version manages to focus upon the appetizing "bubbling yellow cheese" by subordinating Sam to a dependent clause placed later in the sentence?

2. *Which version has the most effective conclusion?* Do you like the conclusive ring of the brief final sentence in A? How do you feel about the directness in A's use of "accept" as an active verb and about the final parallelism A achieves with

> . . . delivers it with resignation.
> . . . accept it with eagerness.

Do you prefer that ending to B's ending where the waitress delivers the pizza:

> . . . with resignation to the eager, accepting customers

or to C where she delivers it:

> . . . resignedly to the eager, accepting customers?

Do you find "resignedly" or "with resignation" the more effective term in this context? Or do you prefer D altogether, where the first phrase of the final sentence, "With resignation," parallels the "Hungrily" and "enviously" beginnings of the preceding clauses? And how effective do you find D's concluding "who" clause?

> With resignation she delivers the pizza to the customers, *who accept it eagerly.*

3. *What about the use of verbs?* Does turning the opening sentence passive in C help to advance the meaning? Or does it make it vaguely indirect or awkward? Does changing the verb tense to the past (in B) seem to improve or detract from the paragraph?

4. *What about the length and complexity of the sentences?* Do you find the third sentence in B too long and complex? If so, where would you suggest breaking it up? How could it be better phrased? A has a number of very brief sentences. Are they effectively employed? Would some be more productively combined? If so, which ones? And how? Or is there already sufficient variety in length and structure?

5. *How do the paragraphs stack up in a close analysis of stylistic features?* Let's compare the different handling of these two important kernels:

   - She eyes it with hunger.
   - She eyes it with envy.

A handles the situation in a single striking phrase: "hungry envy." Do you find this phrase impressive? Why? How do you feel about C's surrounding the subject with adverbs:

   - *Hungrily* the waitress *enviously* eyes it.

Do you think this construction is excessive or awkward? If so, how would you suggest revising it? Do you prefer the alternative construction in B?

   - The waitress hungrily eyes it with envy.

Do you find the parallelism of the treatment in D especially effective?

   - Hungrily, the waitress eyes the cooling pizza.
   - Enviously, she inhales the delicious odors.

Note that D is a bit creative with the text. Do you feel that the changes and additions offer improvements?

More Practice   The following exercises offer more opportunity to explore the possibilities of sentence combining. They should help you become familiar with the thinking involved in building sentences and paragraphs and should give you valuable experience in comparing the effectiveness of various constructions as well.

Try It Out

Combining into Paragraphs

Combine the following sentence kernels into an effective paragraph. Experiment. The spaces between the clusters of kernels are meant to help you to form your sentences, but feel free to disregard them.

Beatlemania

1. The Beatles appeared in the 1960s.
2. Then the English-speaking world was seized by something.
3. This was called "Beatlemania."
4. It was seized immediately.

5. Teenaged girls heard a song.
6. They would swoon.
7. The song was by the Beatles.
8. The girls fell in love.
9. The love was mad.
10. The love was with John
11. The love was with Paul.
12. The love was with George.
13. Or the love was with Ringo.

14. Teenaged boys would not be outdone.
15. They copied the haircuts.
16. The haircuts belonged to the Beatles.
17. The haircuts were new.
18. They copied the clothing.
19. The clothing belonged to the Beatles.
20. The clothing was new.

21. The Beatles went on tour.
22. Then they would be met.
23. They would be met at the airport.
24. They would be met by a horde.
25. The horde was screaming.
26. The horde was of thousands.
27. The horde was fans.
28. The fans wanted a memento.
29. The memento was an autograph.
30. The memento was a lock of hair.
31. The memento was even a shred of clothing.

32. The Beatles managed somehow.
33. The Beatles managed this.
34. They survived these attacks.
35. They went on.
36. They enjoyed their fame.
37. They enjoyed their fortune.

Combining into Essays

Compose effective brief essays by combining the following set of kernels. Don't hesitate to be creative.

Arson

1. Arson is a crime.
2. The crime is one of the worst.
3. The crime should be considered this.
4. The crime arises.
5. It arises solely from greed.

6. The crime results.
7. The only result is death.
8. The only result is destruction.
9. The destruction is of homes.
10. The homes belong to people.
11. The people are innocent.

12. Arson is widespread.
13. There is an example.
14. There were 114,000 fires.
15. The fires were in 1979.
16. The fires were in New York.
17. Nearly 10,000 fires were set.
18. The setting was intentional.
19. Fifty people were killed.

20. There were arson fires nationwide.
21. The fires were in the same year.
22. The fires killed 1,000.
23. The fires caused damage.
24. The damage was three billion dollars.

25. Police believe this.
26. Accidents cause some fires.
27. Pyromaniacs set some fires.
28. The profit motive causes most fires.
29. Property owners order most fires.
30. These property owners are heavily insured.

31. One big city landlord had an interest.
32. The interest was in 250 buildings.
33. The 250 buildings burned down.
34. The burning was over a five-year period.
35. The landlord had associates.
36. They collected over five million dollars.
37. The dollars were from fire insurance claims.

38. Arson fires are a crime.

39. The crime is especially frustrating.
40. The reason for this frustration is a fact.
41. The fact is this.
42. Prosecution is difficult.
43. Only 5 percent result in conviction.
44. The 5 percent is of all arson investigations.

Try It Out

Dreaming Cats

1. Studies were conducted.
2. They were in France.
3. They were recent.
4. Studies confirm the beliefs.
5. The beliefs are of many pet owners.
6. Cats dream while sleeping.

7. The research discovered this.
8. Some cats suffer minor brain damage.
9. These cats sleep.
10. The sleep is deeper than the sleep of normal cats.
11. These cats do not merely visualize their dreams.
12. They act out their sleeping thoughts.
13. They seem to perform like a human.
14. The human is sleepwalking.
15. These cats groom themselves.
16. They stalk prey.
17. The prey is imaginary.

18. How do researchers know this?
19. Do they know that the cats were really asleep?
20. Do they know that the cats were really dreaming?
21. They observed the performance of the cats.
22. The performance was mechanical.
23. They tested the cats with stimuli.
24. A piece of paper was stuck in their fur.
25. These cats were like all sleeping cats.
26. The paper did not arouse a scratch.
27. The paper did not arouse a lick.

28. Yet the damaged cats groomed themselves.
29. The grooming was without external stimulation.
30. The stimulation must have been internal.
31. The stimulation must have been a dream.
32. The dream must have been about grooming.
33. Damaged cats surely dream.

34. Then all cats must dream.
35. The research was conducted by Professor Michel Jouvet.
36. The professor is from the Claude-Bernard University.
37. Professor Jouvet has yet to tackle another question.
38. The question is pressing.
39. The question is of the adoring pet owner.
40. The question is this.
41. Do Jouvet's little cats dream in French?

Trying Out Specific Strategies

Now that you have a general idea of how sentence combining can work to help you mold your writing style, let's examine some of the specific strategies of the sentence you can select to make your writing more persuasive to your readers. We'll start here with adjectival constructions. In Chapter 6 we'll take up adverbial, noun, and absolute constructions. And in Chapter 7 we'll discuss the more sophisticated strategies of parallelism and cumulative and periodic sentences. At the end of Chapter 7, in "Sentence Combining to Help Prove Your Point" we'll take a look at the way you can put all of these syntactic techniques together to give stylistic support to your particular theses.*

Let's begin by exploring the possibilities adjectival constructions can offer you.

CHOOSING ADJECTIVAL CLAUSES AND PHRASES

The adjectival function is one of the most important syntactic functions. It consists of modifying, describing, and developing the nouns that serve as the subjects and objects of sentences—and of clauses and phrases. The adjectival function not only is important, but also allows varied approaches to expression—though this fact is not generally known to inexperienced writers. Such writers tend to restrict their use of adjectival modifiers to two positions, either using them as adjective complements:

- The baritone is *plump.*
- The baritone is *lusty.*

or sandwiching them in between the article and its noun:

- The *plump* baritone
- The *lusty* baritone
- The *singing* baritone
- The *red-bearded* baritone } participial adjectives

———————————

*See Chapter 8 for strategies with words.

Both these uses can be effective, but the adjectival option is by no means limited to these two. Two other positions for adjective placement, for instance, are equally appropriate though less frequently employed. These positions are directly before or directly following the noun and its article:

> *Plump and lusty,* the baritone . . .
> The baritone, *plump and lusty,* . . .

Yet another way of describing the baritone would be to do so through the use of an adjective clause:

> The baritone, *who is plump and red-bearded,* . . .
> The baritone, *who was singing happily,* . . .
> The baritone, *who was a lusty singer,* . . .

Or you might prefer to employ a prepositional phrase:

> The baritone, *in his red beard,* . . .
> *With his lusty singing voice,* the baritone . . .

Another alternative is to use an appositive, a descriptive phrase that stands as an equivalent to the noun described:

> The baritone, *a lusty singer,* . . .
> *A plump and red-bearded man,* the baritone . . .

The appositive is an interesting mix: it is noun-like in form and adjectival in function.

One of the most useful of all adjectival modifiers is the participial phrase, a phrase denoting the *-ing* or *-ed* form of a verb and used adjectivally immediately preceding or immediately following the word described:

> *Singing lustily,* the baritone . . .
> The baritone, *singing lustily,* . . .
> *Red-bearded and bronzed by the sun,* the baritone [sang lustily].
> [Yesterday we caught a glimpse of] the baritone, *red-bearded and bronzed by the sun.*

In the exercises later in the chapter, you will have the opportunity to experiment with all of these options. And you will be able to discover which constructions you feel are most appropriate to particular contexts. But first, let's examine each of these adjectival possibilities more closely.

Choosing Adjective Clauses

The purpose of the adjective clause is to add descriptive or explanatory information about a person, place, animal, or object in a way that subordinates this information to that in the rest of the sentence or clause. According to sentence-combining theory, such sentences are created from two kernel sentences about the same person, place, animal, or object by embedding the sentence to be subordinated into the other one and by linking them together with a relative pronoun *(who, which, that, whose,* or *whom).* Let's take, for example, these two sentences* about Theodore Roosevelt:

A. Theodore Roosevelt had been a colonel in the Puerto Rican campaign of the Spanish American War.
B. Theodore Roosevelt became one of our most colorful presidents.

Depending upon which aspect of Roosevelt's career you prefer to focus upon, you could turn either sentence A or sentence B into a relative clause and embed it in the other. If, for instance, you wanted to emphasize Roosevelt the soldier, you would subordinate sentence B:

Theodore Roosevelt, *who became one of our most colorful presidents,* had been a colonel in the Puerto Rican campaign of the Spanish American War.

But if you wanted to focus upon Roosevelt the president, you would subordinate sentence A:

Theodore Roosevelt, *who had been a colonel in the Puerto Rican campaign of the Spanish American War,* became one of our most colorful presidents.

You may be wondering what point there is in forming adjective clauses. After all, both sentences A and B are pretty good sentences on their own, and they seem to be typical of their kind. Actually, there are a number of advantages to this construction. Some are listed in the accompanying boxed section.

Advantages of Using an Adjective Clause

1. It links related ideas more closely together and reveals that relationship.
2. It helps to structure the ideas in a paragraph by subordinating one to another.
3. It tightens the writing by combining two related sentences; and by eliminating duplication of the modified word or phrase, it helps to avoid nonpurposeful repetition.
4. It varies the sentence structure within a paragraph and enhances the rhythms of the paragraph. Often it provides a pause within the structure of the sentence and thus also offers variation in the rhythm of the sentence.

Although you would not wish to put an adjective clause into every sentence, it is a useful construction to have in your repertoire.

The use of the adjective clause involves judgment about appropriate punctuation and appropriate connecting pronouns. Since inexperienced writers often run into some confusion in making such judgments, these topics are worth exploring here.

---

*To simplify matters, I will sometimes use extended kernels (as in A and B) for examples and exercises.

Punctuating Adjective Clauses   Sometimes adjective clauses should be enclosed in commas and sometimes they should not be. The distinction is important not only because it goes to the heart of a major function of the comma, but also because placement of commas can change the meaning of such sentences. Take, for example, this pair of sentences:

A. Little boys who have bubble gum on their faces are in need of a bath.

FAULTY   B. Little boys, who have bubble gum on their faces, are in need of a bath.

Since pairs of commas indicate parenthetical or interrupting material not essential to the main meaning of the sentence, sentence B makes two unintended implications: (1) *all* little boys have bubble gum on their faces and (2) *all* little boys are in need of a bath. Despite the possibility that these implications contain some degree of truth, they are clearly *not* what the author has in mind. The author obviously intends to limit those little boys in need of a bath to the ones who have bubble gum on their faces and thus should omit the commas.

In summary, one of the main purposes of the comma is to indicate visually the pause which in speech distinguishes the essential from the not-completely-essential portions of a sentence. Pairs of commas enclose what, roughly grouped together, might be called "parenthetical material." If the following image helps you to visualize the comma's function, you can think of comma pairs as handles with which nonessential matter can be lifted from a sentence leaving the essence of the sentence untouched.

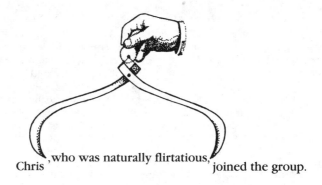

Chris ,who was naturally flirtatious, joined the group.

Here, as in all such parenthetical material, the writer seems to be confiding something to the reader in a comma-enclosed aside while the real business of the sentence continues unimpeded. A peculiarity of adjective clauses is that sometimes they contain parenthetical material (such as the description of Chris here) and sometimes they contain material that is absolutely essential to the sentence's message, with a meaning that must not be interrupted by punctuation (such as in the little boys and bubble gum sentence earlier).

How do you determine whether you should use commas or not? You must discover whether or not the described noun is limited or restricted by the

Guidelines for Punctuating Adjectival Clauses with Commas

1. Always use commas when the adjectival clause describes a proper noun. Since the noun is already limited to a single entity, further descriptive material is always "extra." For example, "O'Hare Airport" does not need the description "which is the busiest in the world," to distinguish it from other airports, so the following punctuation is appropriate:

    > O'Hare Airport, which is the busiest in the world, is located just outside Chicago.

2. When in doubt, try adding the commas and, mentally removing the clause, see if the remaining sentence still carries your meaning. For instance, consider the sentence:

    > Automobiles that have faulty brakes should not be permitted on the highway.

    Surrounding the adjective clause, "that have faulty brakes," with commas would, metaphorically speaking, give it handles and make it liftable from the sentence. With commas, then, the sentence would state, "Automobiles should not be permitted on the highway"—a curious sort of statement.

3. If your particular sentence still does not come clear, ask yourself: "What do I actually mean? Do I mean to limit the noun or don't I?" For example, in the sentence: "John saw the priest who was standing in the garden," do I want to say that a point of interest about the priest John saw was that he happened to be standing in the garden:

    > John saw the priest, who was standing in the garden.

    Or do I want to distinguish the priest standing in the garden from another priest—say, chatting by the sweets table?

    > John saw the priest who was standing in the garden, [walk over to speak to the priest at the sweets table].

description. If it is not, if the description is "extra," then add the "extra" commas. You'll find further guidelines in the accompanying boxed section.

Selecting the Appropriate Relative Pronoun   Sometimes writers find themselves confused about which pronoun they should use to introduce their adjective clauses. There are a number of possibilities—*who, whom, whose, which* and *that*—and they are similar to one another. But though the confusion is understandable, it need not be troublesome. Let us look, for example, at the following sentence, which contains several relative clauses:

> On October 3, a hunter, *who had a habit of carelessly fingering the trigger of his gun,* just missed murdering one of Farmer MacGregor's cows *that happened to be ambling by,* almost demolished the patchwork quilt *which was hanging on Mrs. MacGregor's clothesline,* and actually hit two of the MacGregor piglets, *whose pathetic oinking could be heard for miles.*

Did you notice the particular pronoun that introduced each of the clauses?

- "the hunter *who*" (*Who* refers to a person.)
- "the cow *that*" (*That,* which can refer to either person or object, is particularly appropriate here for an animal.)
- "the patchwork quilt *which*" (*which* always refers to an object.)
- "piglets *whose* pathetic oinking" (*Whose* is the possessive pronoun. It stands in for nouns that take an apostrophe as "piglets" would here: "piglets' oinking," "the oinking of the piglets.")

The other relative pronoun, *whom,** the objective form of *who,* is seldom used now. More and more it is being replaced by *that* in such constructions as "the partner *that* she chose" (instead of "the partner *whom* she chose"). Except for very formal usage, such prepositional constructions as "the person *to whom* he spoke" are being replaced by the now mostly acceptable "the person he spoke to."

One more point on this subject: *That* is usually preferred to *"which"* when the material introduced is not extra and doesn't require commas:

The home *that* I knew so well . . .

not

The home *which* I knew so well . . .

In fact, some good writers find *which* awkward and try to avoid using it too frequently.

Try It Out

Combining Kernels

Combine each set of the following kernel sentences into a single sentence using at least one adjective clause.

Sample Problem:

- The earthquake set the dishes rattling in the cupboard and the chandelier swinging from the ceiling.
- The earthquake registered 6 on the Richter Scale.

Some Sample Solutions:

- The earthquake, *which registered 6 on the Richter Scale,* set the dishes rattling in the cupboard and the chandelier swinging from the ceiling.
  or
- The earthquake, *which set the dishes rattling in the cupboard and the chandelier swinging from the ceiling,* registered 6 on the Richter Scale.

---

*For a more technical discussion of *whom,* see its entry in the "Revision Guide" in Part Six.

1. Babe Ruth hit sixty home runs in 1927.
   Babe Ruth started his baseball career as a pitcher.
2. I watched a man suspiciously all day.
   The man with beady eyes turned out to be the president of a major corporation.
3. Thomas Glidden died in obscurity.
   Thomas Glidden's invention of barbed wire changed the way of life in the west.
4. Some aspirin costs twice as much as other aspirin.
   Some aspirin is packaged under an advertised brand name.
   Some aspirin is simply labeled "aspirin."
5. Some babies' limbs were deformed by thalidomide.
   Many of these babies have grown up to lead useful and productive lives.
6. Franklin Delano Roosevelt signed the bill calling for the creation of the Tennessee Valley Authority.
   The TVA in later years has been both savagely condemned as an important step toward state socialism and extravagantly praised as the noblest experiment in history.
7. Ludwig Von Beethoven was completely deaf for a substantial part of his mature life.
   Ludwig Von Beethoven wrote some of the most glorious music the world has ever known.
8. I threw some wadded paper in the wastebasket.
   The wastebasket was already overflowing with the discards and refuse of the academic life.

Try It Out

Compose Your Own

Compose your own sentences by adding at least one adjective clause to each of the following sentences. Be as creative and imaginative as you can.

Sample Problem:

The famous detective put down his pipe and concentrated upon the evidence.

Some Sample Solutions:

The famous detective, *whose exploits had been faithfully recorded by his friend, Dr. Watson,* put down his pipe and concentrated upon the evidence.
or
The famous detective put down his pipe and concentrated upon the evidence *that was laid out upon the table before him.*

1. The old auto worker walked to the bank to cash his Social Security check.
2. Tom never finds enough time to do his laundry.
3. Jim reluctantly put down his magazine and picked up his homework.
4. The defendant pleaded not guilty to all the charges.
5. Tina thinks that her school is the best one in the country.
6. Carlos clutched his foot in pain.
7. Adam Smith can be considered the first capitalist.
8. As he was trained to do, the gorilla practiced daily on his symbol typewriter.

Reducing the Adjective Clauses

Adjective clauses are, as we have seen, highly useful. On the other hand, at times they can be wordy and cumbersome, even awkward. To achieve an economy of language, an appealing leanness in your prose, you may sometimes want to reduce an adjective clause to a briefer—and perhaps stronger—adjectival construction. Wherever the adjective clause uses the verb "to be" *(is, are, was, were),* you can almost always reduce it to such a structure by eliminating the relative pronoun and the verb. For example,

> Sherlock Holmes put down his pipe, which was a blackened veteran of many investigations.
> can become
> Sherlock Holmes put down his pipe, a blackened veteran of many investigations. (appositive phrase)

> Sherlock Holmes put down his pipe, which was blackened by much long and thoughtful use.
> can become
> Sherlock Homes put down his pipe, blackened by much long and thoughtful use. (participial phrase)

> Sherlock Holmes put down his pipe, which was black and sooty from many earlier investigations.
> can become
> Sherlock Homes put down his pipe, black and sooty from many earlier investigations. (adjective cluster and prepositional phrase)

In every case, both versions are good; both versions are correct. Many readers, however, would prefer the conciseness and directness of the second alternatives.

Another advantage of reducing adjective clauses wherever possible is that while these clauses normally follow the noun described, the reduced adjectival constructions—whether participial phrases, adjective phrases, or appositives— can either precede or follow the noun they modify. In short, these reduced combinations offer all of the benefits suggested for adjective clauses (p. 181) plus conciseness and a greater flexibility of placement. The rest of the chapter provides an opportunity for you to experiment with these adjectival alternatives.

Choosing Adjective Clusters and Phrases

Adjective clusters and prepositional phrases offer some interesting, less traditional constructions. For example, sentences—sometimes even paragraphs—can be effectively begun with initial adjective construction. A grouping of prepositional phrases can lead rather dramatically to the described subject:

> *With sunshine in her eyes and moonlight in her smile,* Mary Ellen approached the gathering.

An adjective cluster can be used in the same way:

> *Solemn and stately,* the mansion had stood there on Yorkshire Moor for nearly three centuries.

On the other hand, you might prefer to use such phrases immediately following the term modified:

- Mary Ellen, *with sunshine in her eyes and moonlight in her smile,* approached the gathering.
- The mansion, *solemn and stately,* had stood there on Yorkshire Moor for nearly three centuries.

Try practicing with a few such combinations in the following exercises to get the flavor of the construction and the placement.

━━━━━━━━━━━━━━━━━━━━━━━━━━━━━━━━ **Try It Out** ━━━

Combining Kernels

Combine each set of the following kernel sentences into a single sentence using at least one adjective cluster or adjectival prepositional phrase.

Sample Problems:

A. • Mary Ellen had sunshine in her eyes.
   • Mary Ellen had moonlight in her smile.
   • Mary Ellen approached the gathering.
B. • The mansion was solemn.
   • The mansion was stately.
   • The mansion had stood on Yorkshire Moor.
   • The standing was for nearly three centuries.

Some Sample Solutions:

See the preceding section on "Choosing Adjective Clusters and Phrases."

1. The gnat was tiny.
   The gnat was elusive.
   The gnat darted erratically.
   The darting was around my head.
2. The dictator had a forcefulness of expression.
   The dictator had a power of persuasion.

The dictator held his subjects' attention.
The attention was unswerving.

3. James was lithe.
   James was sprightly.
   James was like a deer.
   James bounded through the meadow.

4. The tenement was old.
   The tenement was decrepit.
   The tenement collapsed unnoticed.
   The collapsing was into a pile.
   The pile was of bricks.
   The pile was of dust.

5. Gloria was like a statue.
   Gloria was in the sunlight.
   The·statue was graceful.
   The statue was still.

6. The speaker was pompous.
   The speaker was uninspired.
   The speaker bored his audience.
   The boring was with details.
   The details were trivial.

Try It Out

Compose Your Own

Compose your own sentences by adding at least one adjective cluster or adjectival prepositional phrase to each of the following sentences. See what effects you can achieve.

Sample Problem:

The ocean liner pulled away from the dock.

Some Sample Solutions:

- *With its flags waving, its whistle blowing, and its passengers cheering,* the ocean liner pulled away from the dock.
- The ocean liner *under cover of darkness* pulled away from the *dark and deserted* dock.

1. The hypocrite pretended to scorn what she really enjoyed.
2. Sir Gawain battled the Green Knight.
3. My sister is almost always a pest.
4. The preacher gave his sermon on sin.
5. The television executive cancelled the only show she really liked.
6. The actor fumbled his way through *Hamlet.*

Choosing Appositive Phrases   Appositive phrases offer other interesting options for sentence construction. An appositive phrase is a different sort of modifier, one dominated by a noun (the appositive). The appositive phrase is equivalent to—and thus helps define—the noun (or noun phrase) to which it refers. For example:

> Abraham Lincoln, *a tall, angular, awkwardly moving man,* aroused mixed emotions in his constituents.

Appositive phrases can be used in a variety of ways. Although the placement in the Lincoln illustration (directly following its equivalent noun) is the one most frequently employed, appositive phrases can also be effective preceding their nouns:

> *A tall, angular, awkwardly moving man,* Abraham Lincoln aroused mixed emotions among his constituents.

Appositives can also express a negative equivalence—defining what the referent noun is not:

> Juliet tried to convince Romeo that he had heard a nightingale, *not a lark.*

Appositive constructions offer an effective means of adding specific detail—especially those appositive phrases introduced by such expressions as *for instance, for example, particularly, especially, namely, including,* and *mainly.* For example:

- Although the service songs, *such as "The Marines' Hymn," "Anchor's Aweigh," and the "Caisson Song,"* are memorized by every school child in times of war, they are rarely heard in peacetime.
- College freshmen—*particularly those who are the only children in their families*—sometimes have difficulty in adjusting to the hubbub of dormitory life.

Another important use of the appositive phrase is to build to a rhetorical climax, as in the following sentences:

- He went without eating. He fretted and fumed and worried for hours. Then *it* finally came: *a knock on the door.*
- Little Elmer waited all day for *the sound* that to him was as melodic as the playing of any symphony orchestra—*the sound of the ice cream truck.*

Note that in this last example, the appositive, *sound,* repeats its noun. You may want to repeat in this way to provide clarity or emphasis. The pattern is especially useful when (as in this case) other modifiers separate the appositive phrase from its noun. The appositive repetition of its noun is also useful in sentences such as the following, where it heads an otherwise ambiguous relative clause:

> She had spent half her life in a search for her true identity—*an identity that she hoped would rid her forever of her sense of shame.*

If you do not wish to repeat the referent noun, you can substitute a more general appositive term for it, one such as *some* [*of which*], *one* [*of which*], *something* [*that*], *the latter, the kind* [*of*], *the sort* [*of which*], *the fact that,* and the like. For example:

- The plans were finally complete for the family's trip to the Rockies—*something they had long dreamed about.*
- Jo spent the summer reading horror stories, *few of which ever engaged either her intellect or her imagination.*

Continuing this line of thought, the appositive is an excellent device to rid your work of those bothersome indefinite references, those annoying *this's* without specific antecedents so common in academic writing. Take, for example, the following typical passage from a student paper:

Faulty

> The national emotional state evolved into the progressive movement in an attempt to harmonize the modern industrial age with traditional values. *This* is reflected in the thesis of Robert H. Wiebe's book, *The Search for Order 1877–1920.*

Most of us know very well that *this* cannot really refer to "all that," but we have trouble thinking of ways to avoid it. The appositive construction offers one graceful solution to the problem:

> The national emotional state evolved into the progressive movement in an attempt to harmonize the modern industrial age with traditional values—*a fact that is reflected in the thesis of Robert H. Wiebe's book, The Search for Order 1877–1920.*

Appositive phrases are almost always enclosed by punctuation. But you will want to decide for each use whether the matter-of-fact commas, the more dramatic or the more informal dashes, or the very formal colon is the most appropriate punctuation to use.

You will find the appositive phrase a useful construction—especially for closely reasoned explanatory writing such as was needed for the paragraphs in this section on appositive phrases. Before trying the phrases out yourself in the following exercises, read back over this section and note how often the appositive construction has been used.

Try It Out

Combining Kernels
Combine each set of the following kernel sentences into a single sentence using at least one appositive phrase.

Sample Problem:

- The Charge of the Light Brigade was a battle of the Crimean War.
- It was immortalized in a poem by Alfred Lord Tennyson.
- It was a combination of unimaginable folly and heroism.
- It will stand forever as a symbol of the absurdity of war.

Some Sample Solutions:

- The Charge of the Light Brigade, *a battle of the Crimean War immortalized in a poem by Alfred Lord Tennyson,* was a combination of un-

imaginable folly and heroism that will stand forever as a symbol of the absurdity of war.
or
- The Charge of the Light Brigade, *a combination of unimaginable folly and heroism,* having been immortalized in a poem by Alfred Lord Tennyson, will stand forever as a symbol of the absurdity of war.

1. The pope is the spiritual leader of millions.
   The pope issued an important papal decree.
2. My girl friend is the most wonderful person in the whole wide world.
   My girl friend is coming to visit soon.
3. The bank robber lied to the police.
   The bank robber was never an honest man.
4. My broken watch is a worthless piece of workmanship.
   It always reads the same time.
   The time is always 3:27.
5. Lee Harvey Oswald was the man who shot President Kennedy.
   Jack Ruby killed Lee Harvey Oswald.
   The killing was on national television.
6. The first rock-and-roll hit was *Rock-around-the-Clock.*
   Rock-around-the-Clock was by Bill Haley and the Comets.
   The first rock and roll hit is still the biggest selling rock single ever.
7. The comedian's monologue focused on what seem to be the central subjects of all comic routines.
   The central subjects of all comic routines seem to be sex and alcohol.
8. My congressman appeals to the values deepest in the heart of all Americans.
   Truth, justice, and freedom are the values deepest in the heart of all Americans.
9. *La Traviata* is an opera by Verdi.
   Verdi's opera will be performed this year by many opera companies.
   Examples of these companies are La Scala and The Chicago Lyric Opera.
10. Many Americans have made heroes of lawyers.
    Clarence Darrow and Perry Mason are lawyers.
    The latter is a fictional character.

Try It Out

Compose Your Own

Compose your own sentence by adding at least one appositive phrase to the following sentences. Experiment with creative ideas.

Sample Problem:

Last Wednesday the century-old tree in the center of the market square was destroyed by lightning.

Some Sample Solutions:

- The century-old tree, *a sturdy, large-leafed oak that long had shaded the market square,* was destroyed by lightning last Wednesday.
  or
- Last Wednesday the century-old tree in the center of the market square was destroyed by lightning, *some of which also set fire to Farmer MacGregor's barn.*

1. The *Washington Post* first broke the story of the Watergate affair.
2. My dentist filled two cavities, causing me much pain.
3. The carrier delivered only half the mail assigned to him that day.
4. My teacher always gives good grades.
5. The laser is now being used in surgery.
6. Steve knew that when he opened the door he would see the one thing he was most afraid of.
7. The mechanic began to repair the car.
8. Rembrandt painted his famous "The Syndics of the Clockworkers Guild" in 1662.

Choosing Participial Phrases   Like the other adjectival modifiers, participles and participial phrases can help you make your writing tighter by combining related ideas, clearer and more logical by subordinating less important to more important ideas, and more interesting by eliminating repetitive patterns. Your use of participles can also help make your writing more lively and informative because these phrases, like other adjectival structures, provide an excellent medium for the addition of specific detail. Note, for instance, how much more effective the following kernels are when combined as participials than when written as simple sentences:

- The athletes strained. The athletes tugged. The athletes pulled at the rope. Their muscles rippled.
- *Straining and tugging,* their muscles rippling, the athletes pulled at the rope.

A sense of action and time.

Unlike the other adjectival modifiers, however, participles are related to verbs, and thus they can bring their own verbal quality to your sentences. We have seen that, since appositives are nouns functioning as adjectives, they can give a sense of equivalence and definition to the subjects and objects they modify. Similarly, since participles are verbal adjectives, they can provide a sense of action and a sense of time to the subjects and objects they modify. Phrases dominated by the present participle (the *-ing* form of the verb) lend a quality of immediate and continuing action to their descriptive function:

Whistling merrily, the boy walked to the end of the pier.
The witch, *riding high above on her broomstick,* looked out at the black night.

Phrases dominated by the past participle (the *-ed* form of the verb) add a sense of completed action to their descriptive function:

- *Accomplished and poised,* the ballerina stepped out onto the stage.
- The young man clearly was a dandy, *top-hatted and affected in his speech.*

The more distant past participles (the *having* and the *having been* forms of the verb), besides describing a noun, convey a sense of action having taken place before the time of the sentence:

- *Having heard the tragic news,* the once joyful comedian sat down and wept.
- The trainer, *having been badly mauled by the lion,* decided not to return to the cage for a few days.

All in all, participles and participial phrases can become an important part of your writing style.

Try It Out

Combining Kernels

Combine each set of the following kernels into a single sentence, using at least one participial phrase.

Sample Problem:

- The hordes of Attila the Hun rode out of the East.
- They pillaged.
- They raped.
- They terrified the inhabitants of the land.

Some Sample Solutions:

- *Pillaging, raping, and terrifying the inhabitants of the land,* the hordes of Attila the Hun rode out of the East.
  or
- *Riding out of the East,* the hordes of Attila the Hun pillaged, raped, and terrified the inhabitants of the land.

1. Dan mowed the lawn.
   Dan silently cursed his mother.
   Dan's mother made him work hard.
2. Maria cried steadily.
   Maria broke up with her boyfriend.
3. The mourners went to the graveyard.
   The mourners were shaken by the tragedy.
   The mourners were stunned by the tragedy.
4. Willy Loman was confronted by the knowledge of a hopeless life.
   Willy Loman killed himself.
5. The journalist eyed the politician coldly.
   The journalist asked pressing questions.

6. The butterfly sought a flower.
   The butterfly fluttered about merrily.
7. The storyteller spent his days weaving fascinating tales.
   The storyteller was loved by all the children.
8. Marie Antoinette did not realize what trouble she would be causing herself.
   Marie Antoinette said, "Let them eat cake."

Try It Out

Compose Your Own

Compose your own sentences by adding at least one participial phrase to each of the following sentences. Don't be afraid to experiment creatively.

Sample Problem:

The clown silently wiped away a tear.

Some Sample Solutions:

- *Ridiculously costumed, jauntily capped, and smiling painfully,* the clown silently wiped away a tear.
  or
- *Having remembered the days of his youth,* the clown silently wiped away a tear.

1. The teacher could not explain to the class what he wanted them to do.
2. The author graciously accepted the award.
3. The child ran home from school.
4. My brother read the sports section of the paper from beginning to end.
5. Pericles addressed the Athenians.
6. Her dentist skillfully filled the cavity.
7. The patient lay down on the psychiatrist's couch.
8. Every vacation Jean rereads her high school yearbook.

A Word of Warning

If there is anything more uncomfortable than to tell a joke and have it met by serious lips and unsmiling eyes, it is to be perfectly serious about a statement and have it greeted by chuckles. Just such is the almost universal reaction to dangling or misplaced modifiers. I would be less than honest if I did not warn you that along with all the exciting possibilities adjectival constructions offer, in their use lurks the potential pitfall of the dangling modifier, a pitfall into which all of us stumble from time to time. Misplaced modifiers are modifying words or phrases that are so positioned in a sentence that they seem to apply to a noun to which they are not intended to refer. They range from the hilarious to the only mildly amusing, depending upon the degree of inappropriateness of the match. The following examples include modifiers of all the kinds we have been discussing thus far (the modifiers are italic; the words they modify are circled):

- *Walking upside down on the ceiling,* (I) saw a huge black fly.
- *Studious and bright,* (the examination) was a snap for Charley.
- *A serious student,* (Charley's teacher) praised her highly.
- *Having studied Roman history,* (not just one, but many coliseums) still remain standing throughout what was once the Roman world. *Misplaced modifiers.*
- The briefcase was the favorite possession of (Lawyer Brown,) *being cracked with age and filled with a jumble of papers and official documents.*
- *Badly in need of repair and rattling at every window,* (I) still find that old ramshackle house appealing.

Dangling and misplaced modifiers, though immensely distracting to the reader, are easily corrected. You can remove the error simply by placing the modifier near its appropriate referent, taking care to supply the referent if it has been omitted. If the resulting sentence sounds awkward, you may want to rephrase it further. You might, for instance, edit our sample sentences in this way:

- I saw a huge black fly walking upside down on the ceiling.
- The examination was a snap for Charley, who was studious and bright.
- A serious student, Charley was praised highly by her teacher.
- Having studied Roman history, I know for a fact that not just one, but many coliseums still remain standing throughout what was once the Roman world.
- Cracked with age and filled with a jumble of papers and official documents, the briefcase was the favorite possession of Lawyer Brown.
- I still find that old ramshackle house appealing—though it is badly in need of repair and rattles at every window.

You can always correct such errors when you edit and revise your compositions, so you need not worry about dangling modifiers while you write your first drafts. Still, in order to avoid such danglers in the first place, here are some rules to bear in mind:

1. Keep all modifiers as close as possible to the noun described. *Rules for*
2. When you begin a sentence with a modifying phrase, make sure it refers to the main subject of your sentence. *modifiers.*

Try It Out

Combining into Paragraphs

Write an effective paragraph by combining these sentence kernels as you choose. Include the adjectival constructions that most effectively develop the point of the paragraph.

Master of Ceremonies

1. The Master of Ceremonies is fresh-scrubbed.
2. The Master of Ceremonies is smiling.
3. He greets the contestants.
4. The greeting is warm.
5. The contestants are underneath the lights.
6. The lights are hot.
7. The lights are placed for a reason.
8. The contestants' eyes and teeth shine.
9. The contestants' eyes and teeth sparkle.

10. The Master of Ceremonies is smiling.
11. He is always smiling.
12. He explains the rules of the game.
13. He explains them to the contestants.
14. He explains them to the television audience.
15. He apparently thinks this:
16. The audience has intelligence.
17. The intelligence belongs to a golf club.
18. The club is dull.

19. The Master of Ceremonies is still smiling.
20. He asks questions of the contestants.
21. The questions are easy.
22. Their answers are correct.
23. Then lights light.
24. Then bells sound.
25. Then an amount of money is flashed.
26. The amount has been won.
27. The flashing is on a board.
28. The board is big.

29. The board looks fancy.
30. But the board is like the Master of Ceremonies.
31. The board is like all the proceedings.
32. The board is only a facade.
33. The facade is plastic.

Try It Out

Combining into Essays

Combine one of the following sets of sentence kernels to create an effective essay. Try to include some adjective clauses, appositives, participial phrases and other adjective phrases within it.

Aztec Cannibalism

1. The Aztec Indians were a tribe.
2. Their tribe had an empire.
3. The empire was important.
4. The empire was influential.
5. The empire once occupied a part of Central America.
6. The occupied part was substantial.
7. The Aztecs practiced cannibalism.
8. The practice was during the fifteenth and sixteenth centuries.
9. Accounts provide evidence of this cannibalism.
10. The accounts were contemporary.
11. The accounts were by Spanish conquistadors.
12. Piles of skeletons provide evidence.
13. The skeletons are limbless.
14. The evidence is irrefutable.

15. The Aztecs were lightning fast.
16. The Aztecs were efficient warriors.
17. The Aztecs would attack their enemies.
18. The Aztecs would capture a number of their enemies.
19. The Aztecs would then swiftly retreat.

20. The Aztecs were excited.
21. The excitement was from the battle.
22. The excitement was from their own religious fervor.
23. The Aztecs marched their captives.
24. The march was to the top.
25. The top was of one of their temple-pyramids.
26. The Aztecs performed a rite there.
27. The rite was one of the most important in their religion.
28. The rite was the sacrifice of the prisoners.

29. They would cut out the prisoners' hearts.
30. They would offer them to the gods.
31. There would be a feast.
32. They would give three limbs to each successful warrior.
33. The successful warriors had captured the prisoners.
34. They would give the remaining limbs to the priests.
35. They would give the remaining limbs to the elite class.
36. The elite class were the rulers of the Aztecs.
37. They fed the torsos to the animals.
38. The animals were hungry.
39. The animals were waiting.
40. The animals were carnivorous.
41. The animals were kept in the Royal Zoo.

42. Anthropologists believe this:
43. This system of cannibalism was ritualistic.

44. It was used by the Aztecs.
45. It was used for a purpose.
46. The purpose was nourishment (of themselves).
47. The nourishment was during periods.
48. The periods were frequent.
49. The periods were of famine.
50. The famine was in Central America.
51. The famine was throughout the fifteenth and sixteenth centuries.

Try It Out

The Contradictory Dr. Johnson

1. Samuel Johnson was an English author.
2. Samuel Johnson was a critic.
3. Samuel Johnson was a conversationalist.
4. Samuel Johnson was a man of extremes.
5. Samuel Johnson was a man of contradictions.

6. Dr. Johnson's life spanned most of the eighteenth century.
7. During this life he could be lazy.
8. He was lazy at times.
9. He could be hardworking.
10. This was at times.
11. He could be devout.
12. This was at times.
13. He could be confused.
14. This was at times.
15. He could be childishly loyal.
16. This was at times.
17. He could be wisely critical.
18. This was at times.

19. There is an example.
20. Dr. Johnson could barely raise himself from bed.
21. The rising was for breakfast.
22. The breakfast was at two P.M.
23. The same Dr. Johnson wrote the English Dictionary.
24. The dictionary was the first.
25. The dictionary was comprehensive.

26. This was a feat.
27. The feat was of remarkable speed.
28. The remarkable speed should be understood.
29. We must remember something.
30. The entire French Academie took forty years.

31. The forty years was to complete the same task.
32. The task was in their own tongue.

33. This speedwriting was not untypical for a man.
34. The man wrote newspaper columns at parties.
35. The man wrote in one week.
36. The writing was of a novel.
37. Yet, Dr. Johnson could go into a depression.
38. The going was just as quickly.
39. The depression would stop the writing.
40. The stopping would be for months.
41. Dr. Johnson had every excuse for these behaviors.
42. These behaviors are schizophrenic.
43. Johnson was brilliant.
44. He was impoverished.
45. He was self-educated.
46. He was paranoid.
47. He was deformed.
48. He was spastic.
49. He was nearly blind.
50. He was married to an alcoholic.

51. Nevertheless, Dr. Johnson became a man.
52. The man was one of the most respected.
53. The respect was in England.
54. The respect was of his time.

ASSIGNMENT

1. Choose one of these issues involving values and write an effective essay. Use adjectival constructions as they seem appropriate. The following pairs of contradictory words of wisdom show that even the very wise can differ over values. Choose the pair that comments upon the values you wish to explore and write a well-organized, rhetorically effective, expository essay supporting one of the suggested positions. Do not simply try to illustrate the proverb or quotation you select, but discuss the issue, analyze the values in question, and develop concrete evidence to support your position. Use adjectival constructions as they seem appropriate.

   a. Look before you leap.
      He who hesitates is lost.

   b. It matters "not that you won or lost, but how you played the game." (Grantland Rice)
      Winning isn't everything—it's the only thing. (Vince Lombardi)

    c.   War alone brings up to its highest tension all human energy and puts the stamp of nobility upon the peoples who have the courage to face it.   (Anonymous)
War is hell.   (William Tecumseh Sherman)

    d.   Absence makes the heart grow fonder.
Out of sight; out of mind.

2.   In "Chicago Cubs: Overdue" George Will constructs an essay around his definition of *Conservatism,* and in "Self-Respect" Joan Didion creates an essay based on her definition of the title phrase. Choose a similar abstract concept that is especially meaningful to you and, being careful to back up your thesis with concrete and specific support, write an essay in which you define and explain this concept.

6

Making Other Stylistic Decisions: More Sentence Combining

In the last chapter you learned the fundamentals of sentence combining and applied that technique in your writing practice with adjectival clauses, phrases, and other adjectival constructions. In this chapter you will again use sentence combining to gain skill—this time skill in writing adverbial constructions, noun clauses and phrases, and absolutes. By learning to manipulate these writing tools, you should be able to add a good deal of sophistication to your writing style.

CHOOSING ADVERB CLAUSES AND PHRASES

The adverbial function is more complex than the adjectival. The adverb not only modifies and describes the verb in the way that the adjective does the noun, but it goes beyond. For the adverbial function also includes placing the verb's action in time and space, marking it for degree and frequency, and providing it with causal, conditional, contrastive, and other such relationships. Learning to use adverbial clauses and phrases in your writing will thus enable you to make many important connections for your readers.

Choosing Adverb Clauses

You will find adverb clauses among the most useful of all constructions because, on the one hand, you can use them to convey all the information of the most sophisticated sentence. On the other hand, you can also use them to express a highly specialized relationship to information in another sentence. This relationship is expressed by means of adverbial conjunctions that connect and subordinate the adverb clause to the other sentence. Among the most useful of these adverbial conjunctions are those shown in the accompanying boxed section—grouped there in terms of the general relationships they express.

Adverbial Conjunctions

Relating by *time:*	Relating by *cause:*	Relating *conditionally:*
When	Because	If
Whenever	Since	Only if
Before	In view of the fact that	Provided that
Even before		Unless
Until	**Relating by *contrast:***	Not unless
Once	Although	Whether or not
As soon as	Even though	Assuming that
As long as	While	In case
While		Only
After		
Since		**Relating by *place:***
		Where
		Wherever

The following sets of sentences show something of the power of these adverbial subordinators and give a sample of the tremendous variety of the relationships they make possible—even between very simple concepts. Suppose you are working with these two ideas:

- Chris walked away.
- Robin was angry.

Taken by themselves, and unsubordinated, they permit the reader only to speculate on the nature of the event they both describe. But if you combine them with an adverbial conjunction, you can make the meaning unmistakable.

Time   For example, you can let the reader know in what order the actions took place. If Chris walked away first, you could write:

- *After* Chris walked away, Robin became angry.
  Robin became angry *after* Chris walked away.
- Chris walked away *before* Robin became angry.
  Before Robin became angry, Chris walked away.

Which one you chose would depend upon which of the participants you wanted to focus upon and upon what exactly you wanted to imply about the nature of the quarrel. You could be even more precise about the timing of the quarrel. For instance, you could advance the time of Robin's anger by writing

Once Chris walked away, Robin became angry.

And advance it yet further by

As soon as Chris walked away, Robin became angry.

Or you could lengthen the duration of the anger with

Ever since Chris walked away, Robin has been angry.

Or stress its recurring nature with

> *Whenever* Chris walks away, Robin becomes angry.

You can even use the adverb clause to tell the sequence of events in such a way as to assign a cause:

- Robin was angry *even before* Chris walked away.
  or
- Chris walked away (or kept walking away) *until* Robin became angry.

Cause Actually there is some causal implication inherent in almost all of these time relationships, for by revealing the time sequence, you also hint at the reason for the action. But if you wish, you can use a conjunction to be completely direct about the cause. Let's say that Chris's walking away caused Robin's anger. Then you might write:

- Robin became angry *because* Chris walked away.
  or
- *Since* Chris walked away, Robin became angry.

Condition But what if the action has not taken place, yet you want to assert that if the conditions were right, the event certainly would happen. You would write

- *If* Chris walks away, Robin will be angry.
  or
- Robin would be angry *if* Chris should walk away.

Or you might want instead to make a negative prediction:

> *Unless* Chris walks away, Robin will not become angry.

Or, on the other hand,

> Robin will become angry *whether or not* Chris walks away.

Contrast And if this last prediction proved false, you might want to express the contradiction involved in such a turn of events:

- *Although* Chris walked away, Robin did not become angry.
  or
- Robin did not become angry *even though* Chris walked away.

Despite the length of this list, we have by no means exhausted the possible relationships you might create by using adverbial conjunctions. By becoming sensitive to the subtle distinctions involved in these relationships, you can learn to choose the wording that most accurately reflects each relationship as you perceive it.

Adverb Clause Strategies

In using adverb clauses you will find that you have two important options besides the choice of an appropriate adverbial conjunction. You have to decide which of the two ideas to put into the adverb clause and where to place the adverb clause in the sentence. In our simple example, this meant we had to choose between the Robin and Chris clauses and, once we had decided which was to be the adverb clause, we had to decide whether to put the subordinate clause at the beginning or end of the sentence.

Subordination   Fortunately, in most cases, there is a sure way of determining which idea to put in the adverb clause. An adverb clause is a subordinate clause; and, in a sentence, the main clause is meant to carry the major thrust. By the very nature of English grammar, then, the main clause will be perceived as containing what the sentence "really" says. The rest, however interesting or important, will be seen to be of lesser significance. So, in the act of putting material into an adverb clause, you are making a subtle statement about the comparative importance of that material to the information contained in the main clause.

Put main idea in main clause.

Position in Sentence   The question of where to put the adverb clause is not nearly so cut and dried as the question of which clause to subordinate. There are a number of considerations to take into account. The English sentence has a natural order, as we have seen:

> Natural sentence order = Subject (and its modifiers) + verb (and its modifiers)

Since adverbial constructions are considered verb modifiers, we can suppose that when a sentence is written in its natural order, the adverb clause will be at the end. This supposition is supported by the punctuation rule that traditionally advises you to separate the two clauses with a comma when the natural order is inverted—that is, when the adverb clause opens the sentence:

- When the moon is full, some men go mad.
- Some men go mad when the moon is full.

The principle of emphasis would then seem to suggest that you use the "natural" order of main clause + adverb clause when you intend no special emphasis and when you want to be as simple and direct as possible. Even an emotional statement such as the following appears more matter-of-fact in the natural sequence:

A question of emphasis.

> She might never see him again if the train came late.

On the other hand, if you should want to emphasize this sentence, you can get your reader to pause at the comma—and perhaps ponder the implications of the statement—by reversing the order:

> If the train came late, she might never see him again.

Such an order also has the effect of giving added significance to the *if,* the adverbial conjunction which would otherwise be buried midsentence. To focus greater importance upon the adverb clause, you might place it back in the emphatic end position but break the quick rhythm of the natural order with a pause-inducing comma—or better yet, an emphatic dash:

> She might never see him again—if the train came late.

There are other reasons besides emphasis for breaking the natural order. One reason occurs when the internal logic of the sentence seems to demand that you place the adverb clause first. Not reversing the "normal" order in the following sentence, for instance, would violate the actual chronological sequence:

> After a volcano explodes, a geyser of lava is released and, flowing irresistibly, destroys everything in its unpredictable path.

Another reason to switch the order of a sentence is to achieve a smooth and logical transition to the sentence following. Such alterations occur frequently because the material in the main clause, usually composed of ideas directly related to the focus of the paragraph, is often echoed in the next sentence. In order to achieve an uninterrupted flow of ideas, the clause containing this material should be as close as possible to the new sentence. For example, you would probably avoid using the "normal" order if the following sentence were part of a paragraph discussing Arab influence:

> *Although the United Nations began so hopefully,* its very nature has been perverted by such occasions as PLO chieftain Yasser Arafat's machine-gun-adorned address. The very fact that this address was permitted to take place vividly illustrates the power that the oil-rich Arab countries can exert in the world.

> The United Nations' very nature has been perverted by such occasions as PLO chieftain Yasser Arafat's machine-gun adorned address *although the United Nations began so hopefully.* . . .   FAULTY

In this example the "normal" order violates the internal logic of the sentence itself. Placing the adverb clause first not only makes more sense, but also permits an appropriate follow-up sentence.

Try It Out

Combining Kernels

Combine each of the following sets of kernel sentences into effective sentences containing at least one adverb clause. In each case, don't hesitate to try a number of subordinating conjunctions and differing placements of the clauses to find the one you feel most precisely expresses the suggested ideas.

Sample Problem:

- The pizza has shrimp and anchovies.
- I am determined to eat the pizza.

Some Sample Solutions:

- *Even if* the pizza has shrimp and anchovies, I am determined to eat it.
- I am determined to eat the pizza *whether or not* it has shrimp and anchovies.

1. Louis B. Leakey was looking for the remains of early man.
   Louis B. Leakey made an astounding discovery.
2. The violinist tunes his A string too sharp.
   The A string will surely break.
3. I can't have the work done for you by Tuesday.
   I will work all night.
4. Drunken drivers frequently cause automobile accidents.
   Drunken drivers have impaired reactions.
5. The price of oil increases.
   Inflation will rise.
6. It seemed a ridiculous thing to do.
   The daredevil was resolved to go over Niagara Falls in a barrel.
7. Lindbergh toured the world.
   Lindbergh drew cheering crowds.
8. The wide receiver can run with the ball.
   The wide receiver must catch the pass.
9. I chose a dorm room.
   My room has a good view of the quads.
10. My father hears Reverend Green preach a sermon.
    My father falls asleep.

Try It Out

Compose Your Own

By using different adverbial conjunctions and thus adding differing adverbial clauses, create from each of the following sentences three interesting sentences that differ from one another in meaning and intent.

Sample Problem:

The train whistle blows at night.

Some Sample Solutions:

- *Whenever* the train whistle blows at night, my dog scampers under my bed.
- The train whistle blows at night *whether or not* there are cars waiting at the crossing.

1. Popeye continued to eat his spinach.
2. The *New York Times* pledges to publish "all the news that's fit to print."

3. Many people believe in the presence of poltergeists.
4. There is scarcely a village in England that does not have a memorial recording the human devastation of the First World War.
5. The dance had been the happiest evening of her young life.
6. Snoopy may well be the world's most beloved cartoon character.

Reducing Adverb Clauses

Adverb clauses are exceedingly useful for establishing the subtle relationship between ideas that can contribute crucial meaning to your composition. Sometimes, however, you can achieve the same effects more economically and more concisely by reducing adverb clauses to phrases. If the subject of an adverb clause is the same as that of its main clause and the verb is some form of the verb "to be" (such as *is, are, was, were, had been*), the subject and verb of the adverb clause can be eliminated and a phrase created from the condensed clause:

- *Although Doreen had once been a frequent visitor to the Governor's mansion,* now she was seldom invited.
  reduces to
  Although once a frequent visitor to the governor's mansion, now Doreen was seldom invited.

- Don said he would be glad to help out at the newspaper office *whenever he would be needed.*
  reduces to
  Don said he would be glad to help out at the newspaper office *whenever needed.*

If you wish to condense an adverb clause where the verb is *not* a form of "to be," you still can do so—providing the subject is the same as that of the main clause. If both clauses have the same subject, you can reduce the adverb clause by eliminating its subject and changing the verb to its participial form:

- *After the soprano sang the solo,* she collapsed in a faint.
  reduces to
  After singing the solo, the soprano collapsed in a faint.

Sometimes you can achieve an economy of wording by changing adverb clauses into adverbial prepositional phrases. By doing so, you may also be able to achieve a greater precision of meaning. Here are some examples of the alternatives that adverbial prepositional phrases can offer to the standard adverb clause construction:

- While the preparations for the picnic were going on . . . (Clause)
  reduces to
  During the preparations for the picnic . . . (Phrase)

- Although the sky was overcast and thunder threatened in the distance . . . (Clause)
  reduces to
  Despite the overcast sky and the threatening sound of distant thunder . . . (Phrase)

- *Since the patient had a cheerful heart,* she would come through her illness. (Clause)
  reduces to
  With her cheerful heart, the patient would come through her illness. (Phrase)

Try It Out

Reducing Clauses

Reduce the adverbial clauses in the following sentences to an adverbial phrase or to an adverbial prepositional phrase.

Sample Problem:

Although Jenny had always wanted to be a lawyer and legislator, she gave in to her family's pressure to adopt a less taxing profession.

Sample Solution:

Despite Jenny's lifelong desire to become a lawyer and legislator, she gave in to her family's pressure to adopt a less taxing profession.

1. Since Charisse had come as a counselor to the camp, she had learned a great deal about the psychology of little children.
2. While Henry waited for the plane, he made up lists in his mind of all the things he had to do in Poughkeepsie.
3. Stanley was content to remain at home until he discovered that most of his friends had found good summer jobs.
4. Even though James Dean made only three movies in his short life, he is considered one of Hollywood's great actors.
5. Ever since Grandma had her operation, she has been cautious in climbing stairs.
6. Before Caesar took his troops across the Rubicon, he carefully assessed the political situation.

Using Adverbials Like adjectival constructions, adverbials can be single words,

quickly	seldom
luckily	often
affectionately	indoors

phrases,

in the garden	with candor
at the stroke of noon	although tired
while singing	after bathing

or clauses,

When she was happy, . . .
Before the game ended, . . .
Because I love you, . . .

Adverbial constructions differ from the adjectival, however, in their movability. When you let an adjective construction stray too far from the noun it modifies, the sentence can suffer from a dangling modifier. In contrast, you have a great deal of freedom in placing adverbials. For many adverbials, almost any position will do:

Frequently, the invalid turned to her window to look at the birds.   Beginning

The invalid *frequently* turned to her window to look at the birds.   Middle (after subject)

The invalid turned *frequently* to her window to look at the birds.   Middle (after verb)

The invalid turned to her window *frequently* to look at the birds.   Middle (mid-complement)

The invalid turned to her window to look at the birds *frequently.*   End

Even adverbial clauses, which are regularly placed at the beginnings and ends of sentences, can be used effectively midsentence. Directly after the subject is a position that offers an interesting—almost adjectival—effect. Compare, for instance:

- Greg, *though he was quaking with fear,* climbed to the very top.
- *Though Greg was quaking with fear,* he climbed to the very top.
- Greg climbed to the very top *though he was quaking with fear.*

Furthermore, although you may let a misplaced adjectival get by you once in a while, if you are a native speaker of English, you should have no such trouble with misplaced adverbials. You will catch them right away because they will sound "funny." A popular song of a few years ago played on the quaint humor inherent in the misplaced adverbial with such lines as "Throw mama from the the train a kiss."

Placement   If almost all positions in a sentence—except the downright ludicrous—are correct for the placement of adverbials, then you may be wondering what to base your placement decisions upon. The answer is to base them on the principles of sound, coherence, and emphasis. First, check on the general   Listen to the sound of the sentence. Does the order you selected sound awkward when you   sound. read it aloud? Does it sound awkward when you read it together with its neighboring sentences in the paragraph? If so, how might you reorder it to give it a comfortable sound?

Next check for coherence. If the adverbial construction in question looks back to the last sentence, place it near the beginning of your sentence:

> She sought refuge in a cabin in the remote hills of Kentucky. But *through those hills* stalked a brooding stranger.

If it refers to the next sentence, place it at the end:

> She sought refuge in a cabin *in the remote hills of Kentucky.* But through those hills stalked a brooding stranger.

Finally, seriously consider the matter of emphasis. As you will recall from Chapter 4, the end of a sentence is the part that ordinarily receives the most attention from readers. The beginning of the sentence is second in importance. And the middle of the sentence draws the least of the readers' notice—except, that is, when internal punctuation interrupts and gives the sentence other beginnings and endings within. (See page 204 for examples of how the emphasis can be modified by the use of commas or dashes.) How do these principles apply specifically to the placement of the mobile adverbials? First, they can remind you to make sure that an unimportant adverbial does not occupy the focal final spot in the sentence. For instance, though the "invalid's window" sample sentences listed earlier are all grammatically correct, the one with "frequently" in the final position has an awkward ring not present in the other versions. The final "frequently" creates an anticlimactic sort of effect you might wish to avoid:

The invalid turned to her window to look at the birds *frequently.*

Then, if you want to create interesting dramatic effects, try clustering prepositional phrases at the beginning of a sentence. The old Thanksgiving song makes good use of just such a strategy:

> Over the river and through the woods, to Grandmother's house we go.

Adverbial prepositional phrases not only can set a sentence in place and time, but when clustered in this way can also provide the sentence with a rhythm that may be compelling. This sort of opening can be especially effective in introducing a passage or an essay:

> *On the eastern shores of the Mediterranean, amid the ruins of an ancient civilization,* the embattled nation of Israel continues her struggle to exist.

In summary, after all other considerations have been met and you still cannot decide where to place your adverbial constructions, ask yourself, How important is the idea contained in this adverbial to the purpose of the sentence? Just how much emphasis do I want to give it? And then, guided by the principles of emphasis, find it an appropriate home.

Combining Kernels

Combine the following kernel sentences into effective sentences containing adverbs, adverb prepositional phrases, and other adverb phrases.

Sample Problem:

- Something was according to Wordsworth.
- The daffodils fluttered.
- The fluttering was in the breeze.
- The daffodils danced.
- The dancing was in the breeze.
- The daffodils were beside the lake.
- The daffodils were beneath the trees.

Some Sample Solutions:

- Beside the lake, beneath the trees, daffodils were fluttering and dancing in the breeze, according to Wordsworth.
  or
- According to Wordsworth, some daffodils, while fluttering in the breeze, danced beside the lake and beneath the trees.

1. A political strategy was planned.
   The strategy was interesting.
   The planning was on the Republican side.
   The side was of the aisle.
2. A small colony carried out its life processes.
   The colony was made up of antibiotic cells.
   The colony was in a petri dish.
   The colony was on top.
   The colony rested on some agar-agar.
3. The snow fell.
   The falling was soft.
   The falling was quiet.
   The falling was unending.
4. The flood obliterated everything.
   It obliterated along its path.
   This happened after it pushed past the dam.
   The pushing was ruthless.
   This also happened after it rushed downstream.
5. Washington crossed the Delaware.
   The crossing was while Washington was standing.
   He stood in a boat.
   The boat was filled.
   The cargo was men.
   The men were ragged.
   The men were hungry.

6. Napoleon's army proceeded.
   The progress was on the frozen steppes of Russia.
   The progress was dogged.
   Then it was halted.
   The halt was irretrievable.
   The halt was in snow.
   The halt was in blood.

Try It Out

Compose Your Own

Compose your own effective sentences by adding adverbs, adverb phrases, and adverb prepositional phrases to the following sentences.

Sample Problem:

Abraham Lincoln faced the crowds.

Some Sample Solutions:

- *While standing precariously on a makeshift platform, in the heat of the summer's sun, shyly* and *awkwardly* the young Abraham Lincoln *first* faced the crowds.
  or
- *On a quiet day, not long after the roar and the blood of the great battle,* a weary Abraham Lincoln stood *on the very field of the battle* and *sadly* but *triumphantly* faced the crowds.

1. The General Assembly of the U.N. passed a resolution.
2. The broadcaster delivered the news.
3. The 35-year-old pitcher haggled for a raise in pay.
4. The grandfather's clock struck the hour.
5. A haggard Woodrow Wilson battled Congress.
6. The brown bear roams Admiralty Island.

Try It Out

Combining into Essays

Combine the following sets of sentence kernels into effective essays. Make use of adverbial constructions where they seem appropriate. Feel free to experiment.

Black Holes in Space

1. An astronomer knew something was unusual.
2. He had turned his telescope to the skies.
3. He saw something near the constellation Cygnus.

4. There seemed to be a space.
5. An empty space was in the heavens.

6. Something was even stranger.
7. The astronomer watched.
8. He saw a star.
9. The star orbited around the empty space.

10. Astronomers have dubbed this phenomenon.
11. They call it a "black hole."
12. The reason for the name is its appearance.
13. The hole appears to the viewer.
14. It appears to be something.
15. There is an empty hole in space.

16. No one knows for certain.
17. What is a black hole?
18 What is it actually?
19. Yet most astronomers hold to a basic theory.
20. They hold some variation of this therory.

21. They theorize.
22. There are some cases.
23. A star has expended most of its nuclear energy.
24. Then it collapses.
25. The collapse is under its own weight.

26. The collapse happens.
27. Then the star becomes a core.
28. The core is relatively small.
29. The core is composed of material.
30. The material is extremely dense.
31. The core has a gravitational pull.
32. The pull is tremendous.
33. There is a reason for the pull.
34. The reason is the core's size and density.

35. Is this indeed the case?
36. Then something would happen to any object.
37. The object is floating in space.
38. The object comes near the hole.
39. This object would be drawn into the gravitational field.
40. This object would be pulled to the core.
41. The object would make the core even denser.
42. The object would expand the gravitational field.
43. The expansion would be consequent.

44. One assumes something.
45. The particle theory of light is true.
46. At least part of this theory is true.

47. Then the core would draw in even rays of light.
48. The pull would be so powerful.
49. The gravity would prevent any reflection.
50. There is no reflection.
51. Therefore the astronomer would see a void.
52. The astronomer is on earth.
53. The void is all the astronomer sees.
54. The void is a black hole.
55. The black hole is in the heavens.

Try It Out

On ESP

1. Many people call extrasensory perception "hogwash."
2. They are skeptical.
3. A number of cases of ESP have been reported.
4. These cases seem to indicate experiences.
5. Some people have had experiences.
6. These experiences were psychic.
7. These experiences were real.

8. These experiences take a form.
9. The form occurs frequently.
10. The experience is a person knowing something.
11. The person is extra perceptive.
12. He or she knows it suddenly.
13. He or she knows it somehow.
14. A loved one is in danger.
15. A loved one is in pain.

16. There is an ordinary case.
17. The perceptive person will have a dream.
18. The perceptive person will have a hallucination.
19. The perceptive person will have a vision.
20. The perceptive person will have a sudden impulse.
21. The perceptive person will have an intuition.
22. The intuition may be a certain feeling.
23. Something is wrong.
24. Or the intuition may be a different feeling.
25. A friend needs help.

26. There was an instance.
27. The instance was during World War II.
28. A lady dreamed this.
29. The dream was of her brother.

30. Her brother asked a nurse something.
31. The nurse should not touch his leg.
32. A bullet had just been removed.
33. The bullet had been in his leg.

34. The lady found out something.
35. The discovery came later.
36. Her brother had been shot.
37. The shooting had been on that very day.
38. The wound was in the leg.
39. Her brother had undergone surgery.
40. The surgery removed the bullet.

41. There is another example.
42. This example is also authenticated.
43. A 19-year-old planned to attend a funeral.
44. He went home instead.
45. He felt something.
46. He felt it for some reason.
47. He must see his mother.

48. He arrived home.
49. He called to his mother.
50. His mother left her chair.
51. His mother came to him.
52. A truck crashed.
53. The crash was at that very instant.
54. The truck came through the living room wall.
55. The truck smashed a chair.
56. His mother had been sitting in that chair.

57. There are volumes of evidence.
58. The evidence is similar.
59. Many people still are skeptical.
60. They do not believe in ESP.
61. They have had no personal experience with ESP.

62. Only a few people have had experiences with ESP.
63. This is a fact.
64. This fact gives ESP its special value.

Try It Out

The Fabled Phoenix
1. The phoenix is fabled.
2. The phoenix has remarkable habits.
3. Thus it has been an emblem.

4. It represents immortality.
5. The emblem holds in several cultures.

6. The phoenix is a legendary bird.
7. It probably originated in ancient China.
8. Yet its "wingspan" stretched.
9. It stretched across ancient Egypt.
10. It stretched across ancient Greece.
11. It stretched across ancient Rome.
12. Later it stretched into Christian lands.

13. The plumage of the phoenix is gold and scarlet.
14. The cry of the phoenix is eerily beautiful.
15. The phoenix is enormous.
16. The phoenix must be a spectacle indeed.

17. Moreover, only one phoenix exists at a time.
18. Thus one glimpses the creature.
19. Then one has a stroke of fortune.
20. The stroke of fortune is rare.

21. Egyptian mythology, for one, describes the phoenix.
22. Here the phoenix lives for 1,000 years.
23. Then the bird senses the end of its time.
24. Then the bird builds a great nest.
25. The nest is of spices and boughs.
26. The spices and boughs are fragrant.

27. Then the phoenix huddles within its nest.
28. It sets its nest on fire.
29. It is consumed by the flames.
30. The old bird dies.
31. Then a new phoenix rises from the soot.

32. The following account is according to the Egyptian legend.
33. The fledgling phoenix embalms its parent's ashes.
34. The embalming takes place in an egg of myrrh.
35. The fledgling carries the ashes.
36. It flies to Heliopolis.
37. Heliopolis is the City of the Sun.
38. The fledgling places the ashes.
39. The location is on the altar.
40. The altar is to the Sun God, Ra.

41. The phoenix has a cycle.
42. The cycle is eternal.
43. The cycle is of death and rebirth.
44. Therefore our conclusion is easy.
45. We can see why.

46. The phoenix was adopted as a symbol.
47. The adoption was frequent.
48. The symbol is of resurrection.

CHOOSING NOUN CLAUSES AND PHRASES

Choosing Noun Clauses

A noun clause is a clause that functions like a noun by serving in its entirety as the subject or object of a sentence, clause, or phrase. In some ways the advantages of using noun clauses are similar to those you gain in using adjective or adverb clauses. In enabling you to combine two sentences, all subordinate clauses permit you to relate two ideas together more precisely and to subordinate one to the other. The noun clause, which joins the rest of the sentence by means of "that" or a question word (*why, how, what, who, whose, where, whatever, whoever, wherever,* and so on), accomplishes this end by standing in for the subject or object of a sentence that is indefinite or not clearly defined. For instance:

- Pedro wanted her to know something.
  Pedro loved her.
  can become
  Pedro wanted her to know *that he loved her.*
  or
  That he loved her was *what Pedro wanted her to know.*
  or
  What Pedro wanted her to know was *that he loved her.*
- Pedro also wanted her to know something else.
  Why did Pedro love her?
  can become
  Pedro also wanted her to know *why he loved her.*
  or
  Why he loved her was something else that Pedro wanted her to know.
  or
  Why he loved her was also *what Pedro wanted her to know.*

In addition to the advantages shared with all subordinate clauses, noun clauses (and noun phrases) offer some special benefits. Most important, perhaps, noun clauses provide a good way to avoid using "this" to mean "All that I have just said"—the sort of indefinite pronoun reference that readers often interpret as sloppy thinking. Consider these examples:

- Leslie had copied from René's paper.
  René was very angry about *this.*
  can become
  René was very angry *that Leslie had copied from his paper.*

• How did Houdini do his famous disappearing elephant trick? No one ever found *this* out for certain.

can become

No one ever found out for certain *how Houdini did his famous disappearing elephant trick.*

Although you may be less familiar with the possibilities of noun clauses than with those of the other clauses, they can be truly useful additions to your stylistic repertoire.

Try It Out

Combining Kernels

Combine the following sets of sentence kernels into effective sentences containing at least one noun clause.

Sample Problem:

• I think this.
• I know something.
• Whose woods are these?

Some Sample Solutions:

• I think *that I know whose woods these are.*
  or (more poetically as Robert Frost originally wrote it)
• *"Whose woods these are,* I think [*that*] *I know."*

1. National Guardsman PFC Albert Amos wondered this:
   Was his battalion going to train at Camp Grayling in Michigan?
2. On her wedding night, the bride told her new husband this:
   She had been married before.
3. The migrant worker did not know this:
   When would he have a chance to work again?
4. The Burger Doodle waitress sweetly informed her customer something about the menu.
   Escargot is not on the menu.
5. The society matron lost all her money.
   This fact did not keep her from putting on aristocratic airs.
6. Who will be elected student body president?
   I can't begin to guess.
7. She would never go hungry again.
   Scarlett O'Hara swore this to herself.
8. There was no water in the pool.
   This did not keep my friend from trying to swim.
9. Maria forgot to tell me something about the party.
   Where is the party going to be?
10. Two objects cannot occupy the same space.
    This is a law of physics that cannot be refuted.

11. Lenin's brother was executed by the czar.
    This execution led, in part, to Lenin's radicalization.
12. How is it done?
    I will show you.

Try It Out

Compose Your Own
Create effective sentences by adding at least one noun clause to each of these sentences.

Sample Problems:
- I would not have directed you that way if I had known that . . . .
- The pilot flew . . . .

Some Sample Solutions:
- I would not have directed you that way if I had known that the bridge was out.

  or

  If I had known that your co-star was coming down with the mumps, I would not have directed you that way.
- The pilot flew *wherever his imagination took him.*

1. Alice had a dream that . . . .
2. Napoleon wondered whether . . . .
3. Plato pondered why . . . .
4. Edison explained how . . . .
5. . . . is a well-known fact.
6. . . . is where I want to be.
7. . . . drives men wild.
8. . . . is the reason that . . . .

Noun Phrases

In many situations where you can use a noun clause, you also have the option of employing a noun phrase—either a gerund phrase or an infinitive phrase. The gerund is the *-ing* form of the verb when it is used as a noun: the *singing,* the *climbing.* Gerund phrases are phrases that are dominated by a gerund:

- *The singing of the Vienna Boys Choir* filled our hearts with joy.
- *Climbing the peaks of the Colorado Rockies* is strenuous fun.

The infinitive is the "to" form of the verb: *to sing, to climb.* It too can be substituted for a noun:

- *To climb the peaks of the Colorado Rockies* is strenuous fun.
- It fills our hearts with joy *for the Vienna Boys Choir to sing.*

Noun phrases share with noun clauses the advantage of avoiding the indefinite pronoun. After all, the samples above might just as easily be written:

FAULTY   • The Vienna Boys Choir sang. *This* filled our hearts with joy.
FAULTY   • *You* climb the peaks of the Colorado Rockies. *It* is strenuous fun.
           or
FAULTY   *One* climbs the peaks of the Colorado Rockies. . .

So if you catch yourself using the usually too colloquial "you" or the usually too formal "one" or the indefinite referents "this" or "it," you might think through what you want to say and see if the sentence wouldn't be more effectively phrased with a gerund or an infinitive. These examples illustrate some alternatives:

• Children watch violence on television. *This* is harmful.
  can be phrased
  Watching violence on television is harmful to children.
  or
  For children to watch violence on television is harmful.
• *You* buy beer and peanuts in college. *It* is an old custom.
  can be phrased
  An old college custom is *buying beer and peanuts.*
  or
  To buy beer and peanuts is an old college custom.

Another important advantage to using infinitives and gerunds arises from their verbal nature. They partake in the "acting" or "doing" which is the essence of the verb, and they thus impart a vitality to the sentence that nouns cannot match. Examine, for instance, the following comparable sentences:

• Against all odds, Carolyn continued *the maintenance of her position.* (nominalization)
  Against all odds, Carolyn continued *to maintain her position.* (infinitive)
  Against all odds, Carolyn continued *maintaining her position.* (gerund)

• *Construction of a home* is deeply rewarding work. (nominalization)
  Constructing a home is deeply rewarding work. (gerund)
  To construct a home is deeply rewarding work. (infinitive)

• If the sun disappeared, *our existence* would cease. (nominalization)
  If the sun disappeared, we would cease *to exist.* (infinitive)

In every case, as I think you will agree, the sentence containing the nominalization seems static and weak compared to the sentences with the gerund and infinitive phrases.

You should find that gerund and infinitive phrases come in handy when you want to infuse the vitality of verbs into your writing. But try them out for yourself.

━━━━━━━━━━━━━━━━━━━━━━━━━━━━━ **Try It Out** ━━━

Combining Sentences

Combine each of the following sets of kernels into effective sentences containing at least one gerund or infinitive phrase.

Sample Problem:

- Octavian would seize control of the western part of the empire.
- This was his goal.

Some Sample Solutions:

- Octavian's goal was *to seize control* of the western part of the empire.
- *Seizing control* of the western part of the empire was Octavian's goal.

1. The magician diverts the attention of the audience.
   This is the most important ploy of the magician.
2. Jane Ace, radio's tongue-twisting comedienne, claimed she hoped for something.
   She wanted the attainment of the "pinochle of success."
3. The children would swim and play in the sun all summer.
   This is the desire of every school boy and school girl.
4. One drives on the expressways.
   It requires the utmost in concentration.
5. One should write well.
   It is a prerequisite in journalism.
6. One keeps the wounds of minor surgery from becoming infected.
   It is one of the most important aspects of podiatry.
7. People slice carrots.
   It can be a dangerous activity if one doesn't know how.
8. Some people have climbed Mt. Everest.
   This has always been Margaret's dream.

━━━━━━━━━━━━━━━━━━━━━━━━━━━━━ **Try It Out** ━━━

Compose Your Own

Substitute a gerund phrase or an infinitive phrase for the blank in each of the following sentences.

Sample Problem:

_____ was a foolish thing for Van Gogh to do.

Some Sample Solutions:

- *Sending his ear* to the prostitute who had mocked him was a foolish thing for Van Gogh to do.
- It was foolish *for Van Gogh to send his ear* to the prostitute who had mocked him.

1. _____ can be very dangerous.
2. The Marine sergeant said he wanted all of his recruits _____.
3. _____ requires courage, bravery, skill, and a certain amount of stupidity.
4. _____ is not liked by most professors.
5. _____ is Ralph's secret wish.
6. Next to completing these exercises, my favorite activity is _____.
7. Fred gets upset whenever he finds _____ necessary.
8. The National Safety Council has found _____ one of the leading causes of accidental death.

Try It Out

Combining into Essays

Compose effective essays from the following three sets of sentence kernels. Use noun clauses and phrases where they will enhance the writing. Don't hesitate to experiment with your constructions. Be creative.

Escaping the Tower

1. The Tower of London is huge.
2. The Tower of London is solid.
3. It seems an impenetrable prison.
4. These facts would seem to suggest something.
5. No one could escape from this prison.
6. Yet this idea is not precisely so.

7. The Tower has had a long history.
8. Some prisoners have managed.
9. They have escaped.
10. But such escapees have been few.

11. The escape requires strength.
12. It requires daring.
13. It requires courage.
14. It requires a great deal of luck.

15. Some escaped.
16. Almost all of these managed it in the following way.
17. They used a rope.
18. They scaled down the wall.
19. They swung across the moat.
20. They accomplished this somehow.

21. Bishop Rannulf Flambard escaped by this method.
22. He was the first.
23. Henry I imprisoned Bishop Flambard.

24. Henry I was a son of William the Conqueror.
25. The escape was in 1100.

26. What did Bishop Flambard do to escape?
27. He got the guards drunk.
28. He supplied them with wine.
29. His act was gracious.
30. He slipped out.
31. He slipped between the bars.
32. The bars were on his window.
33. He slid down.
34. He slid on a rope.

35. Others tried to escape.
36. They were not so fortunate.
37. It was less than a century later.
38. Griffin was the son of Llewellyn.
39. Llewellyn was Prince of Wales.
40. Griffin also tried to escape.
41. He also used a rope.
42. His rope was made of knotted sheets.
43. Griffin was midway down.
44. The rope broke.
45. Griffin fell to the ground.
46. Griffin broke his neck.

47. There is a fear.
48. Prisoners might suffer a fate.
49. The fate would be the same as Griffin's.
50. There is also another fear.
51. The Tower has a size.
52. That size is imposing.
53. So most prisoners do not attempt this:
54. They do not escape.

Try It Out

Shrewd Sharks
1. Sharks have a sixth sense.
2. That sense is electric perception.
3. Humans do not have this sense.
4. This is a fact.
5. This fact has been confirmed.
6. The confirmation is recent.
7. Research confirmed it.

8. Scientists discovered something.
9. The discovery was nearly fifty years ago.
10. The discovery was the following.
11. Sharks avoid something.
12. They avoid it every time.
13. The sharks are blindfolded.
14. A steel wire is placed in their path.
15. The steel wire is rusty.
16. The sharks do not swim into the steel wire.

17. Scientists were at a loss.
18. They were for a long time.
19. They could not explain this phenomenon.
20. Then Adrianus J. Kalmin and Kenneth Jon Rose determined something.
21. They determined it by experiment.
22. Sharks respond to an electric field.
23. The electric field is very weak.
24. The electric field is put out by the wire.

25. Virtually every living thing creates an electric field.
26. The electric field is weak.
27. The living things are in water.
28. Scientists then reasoned something.
29. Sharks have an ability.
30. Sharks can sense weak electrical impulses.
31. Sharks might use this ability.
32. They might select possible sources of food.

33. Researchers would test this theory out.
34. Then they would cut up some dead fish.
35. The dead fish would have a strong odor.
36. The dead fish would not have an electric field.
37. The researchers would put the dead fish in a shark tank.
38. The placement would be some distance from some live electrodes.
39. The researchers' hypothesis might be correct.
40. Then the smell of fish would attract the shark first.
41. But the shark would attack the electrodes.
42. The shark would presume something about the electrodes.
43. The electrodes were its food.

44. What did the hypothesis predict?
45. That did in fact happen.
46. More experiments showed something about sharks.
47. Sharks are attracted.
48. The attraction is definite.
49. The attraction is to electric fields.
50. The electric fields can be produced by living creatures.

51. The electric fields can be produced by electric gadgets.
52. The electric gadgets are made by men.
53. Then the researchers concluded something about sharks.
54. Sharks use their sixth sense of electric perception.
55. They use it wherever possible.
56. They use it for this reason.
57. They find their prey.

Try It Out

Conspiratorial Mother Goose

1. Many aspects of life exemplify a maxim.
2. This maxim is well known.
3. "Things are not always what they seem."
4. Even Mother Goose rhymes exemplify this maxim.

5. There was a method.
6. The method was common.
7. One could disguise political opinions.
8. The opinions were dangerous.
9. One could phrase the opinions as nursery rhymes.
10. The nursery rhymes were harmless.
11. One could avoid official censure.
12. One could avoid possible imprisonment.
13. The censure and imprisonment would be for this:
14. One would publish these opinions.
15. Many Mother Goose rhymes have this origin.
16. These rhymes are familiar.

17. Scholars have pointed something out.
18. "Who Killed Cock Robin?" is an example.
19. Its original authors intended something with "Who Killed Cock Robin?"
20. It should be an allegory.
21. The allegory was on intrigues.
22. The intrigues attended the end.
23. The end was of a career.
24. The career was political.
25. The career was Robert Walpole's.
26. Robert Walpole was prime minister.
27. He was Britain's first prime minister.

28. "Little Miss Muffet" is a rhyme.
29. It is even more inflammatory.

30. Scholars agree.
31. Little Miss Muffet has a meaning.
32. She signifies Mary Queen of Scots.
33. Mary was Catholic.
34. Some significance was meant by the spider.
35. The spider tormented Miss Muffet.
36. The spider signifies the Reverend John Knox.
37. Knox was fervently Protestant.

38. What is the most fascinating instance?
39. Perhaps it is the identity of the baby.
40. The baby is in "Rock-a-Bye Baby."
41. Some scholars claim:
42. The baby is James Francis Edward Stuart, the Pretender.
43. The baby is the infant son of King James II.
44. The scholars may be right.
45. Rhyme reflects the public sentiment.
46. The public sentiment was of that time.
47. The public sentiment was restless.
48. The rhyme would also anticipate a revolution.
49. The revolution was called the "Glorious Revolution."
50. The revolution was in 1688.
51. The revolution overthrew King James II.

52. One can learn the stories behind the Mother Goose rhymes.
53. Then these rhymes assume a perspective.
54. The rhymes are beloved.
55. The perspective is new.

CHOOSING ABSOLUTES

Although you may never have heard of the absolute construction before, it is a favorite with some of our best-regarded authors. And though it is possible that you may never even have used it in your writing before, once you try it, you may find it especially appealing and helpful to your work.

Just what is an absolute? Here, printed in italics, are some examples:

Examples
- The 1968 Rambler was badly in need of repair, *its motor knocking, its radiator leaking, and its body rusted through.* (a)
- The Russian dolls sat smugly on the mantle, *each of their painted faces forever fixed in a mirthless smile.* (b)
- Santa laughed, *his nose a cherry, his stomach a bowl of jelly.* (c)
- *The concert over,* the orchestra gathered up their instruments and left the stage. (d)
- The loser hobbled away from the fight, *nose still bloody, arm in a makeshift sling.* (e)

Absolutes are modifiers attached to their sentences only by a comma (or occasionally by a dash). You can think of them as clauses without verbs:

- Clause = subject + verb + complement
- Absolute = subject + complement

Or you might think of them as phrases with their own subjects:

- subject + participle phrase [as in examples (a) and (b)]
- subject + prepositional phrase [as in example (e)]
- subject + adjective [as in example (e)]
- subject + adverb [occasionally, as in example (d)]
- subject + appositive [as in example (c)]

However you choose to view them, you can form absolute constructions in one of two ways. If the sentence from which you want to derive the absolute contains the verb "to be" (*is, was, are, were,* and so on) either as the main verb or as an auxiliary, you simply eliminate that word and you have your absolute ready to attach to another sentence. For instance:

- The sky ~~was~~ sunny———→the sky sunny
  or
- The birds ~~were~~ chirping ———→ the birds chirping

If there is no verb "to be" in the sentence, then you change whatever verb is there to a participial form:

The bees buzzed merrily from flower to flower ———→ the bees buzzing merrily from flower to flower. (absolute)

Attached to a sentence, the above absolutes would produce the following:

The day was perfect for a picnic, *the sky sunny, the birds chirping,* and *the bees buzzing merrily from flower to flower.*

Note that since absolutes have their own subjects, misplaced modifying is not such a problem with them.

Although you will usually want to attach your absolutes to the end of your sentences, as in the preceding examples, occasionally you may want to use them to introduce a thought, as in example (d). The introductory absolute is useful for establishing a sense of finality, a sense of something having been concluded or accomplished before the main action of the sentence can take place. For example:

- *The lawn mowed, the bushes trimmed,* and *the dishes washed and put away,* Greg went guiltlessly off to the movies.
- *His swim concluded,* the polar bear violently shook the water off his fur.

Though the introductory absolute can help you vary the structure of your sentences from time to time, do not rely upon it too frequently. To begin with, it is essentially a passive construction, as you probably have noticed. As such, it suffers the disadvantages of the passive. Many people would therefore prefer an active phrasing of the polar bear example, for instance, using a participle phrase:

Having concluded his swim, the polar bear . . .

Then, too, the introductory absolute may also suffer from having its roots in an ancient Latin construction (the "ablative absolute"), a construction that is not entirely at home in English. If you have studied Latin, you will surely recall such memorable sentences as

> The enemy having been smitten, Caesar marched his troops again.

If you use the introductory absolute awkwardly or too often, as Sheridan Baker* points out, you run the risk of having your writing sound like a bad translation.

The danger of creating this sort of stilted syntax is much less when you attach your absolutes to the end of your sentences. And here, when employed skillfully, absolutes can be used to quite telling effect. You can use them to narrow in from a broader focus, much as a movie camera can zoom in to focus on a particular scene. And they are a good way of adding specific detail to a more general statement. For example:

> The old woman lay in her hospital bed, her skin drawn and sallow under the rouge, her painted lips parched.

Because of their capacity for including detail, absolutes are especially useful for developing your arguments descriptively or narratively. But they can also provide an impressive ring for more strictly explanatory points you may want to emphasize:

> The bill had finally passed the House, every article as originally proposed, every amendment intact.

Absolutes can be impressive because they combine well in series, because they easily fit into the pattern of cumulative sentences (which you'll learn about in the next chapter) and because they can build the sort of rhythm from which you can create effective climaxes. But like some of the other constructions which can lend a tone of sophistication to your writing, absolutes are most effective when used sparingly.

Try It Out

Combining Kernels

Combine the following sets of sentence kernels to form effective sentences using absolute constructions.

Sample Problem:

- The mother duck groomed herself for half an hour.
- The mother duck swam smugly across the pond.
- Each of her feathers was in place.
- Her ducklings glided in a silent parade behind her.

The Complete Stylist and Handbook, 2nd ed. [New York: Harper & Row, 1980], p. 150.

Some Sample Solutions:

- After half an hour's grooming, the mother duck swam smugly across the pond, *each feather in place, her ducklings gliding in a silent parade behind her.*
- *A half hour's grooming accomplished,* the mother duck, *each feather in place,* swam smugly across the pond, *her ducklings gliding in a silent parade behind her.*

1. The dawn heralded the start of a new day.
   The birds sang.
   The dew glistened on the grass.
2. The terrorist ran down the dark street.
   The terrorist's gun glinted blue-grey in the moonlight.
3. Lady Jane Grey was resigned to her fate.
   Lady Jane's courage was unwavering before the scaffold.
4. The hammers were flying.
   The nails were bending.
   The wood was splitting.
   The inept carpenters tried to build the house.
5. Dr. Frankenstein set out to create his monster.
   There was an evil glint in Dr. Frankenstein's eye.
6. The baboons bounded.
   The lions stalked.
   The veldt itself seemed almost alive with activity.
7. Dracula singled out his victim.
   Dracula got ready to drink her blood.
8. Mark Twain prepared to write his essay.
   His cigar was lit.
   His whiskey glass was in his hand.
9. The violinist played the concerto.
   His fingers were flying.
   The violin was singing.
10. Nathan Hale said, "I regret that I have but one life to give for my country."
    Nathan Hale's voice was ringing with fervor and conviction.

Try It Out

Compose Your Own

Use your imagination and create interesting, effective—perhaps climactic—sentences by adding one, two, or a series of absolutes to the following sentences.

Sample Problem:

The elderly British lady returned to her study.

Some Sample Solutions:

- *Her guests refreshed, and the tea things put away,* the elderly British lady returned to her study.
- The elderly British lady returned to her study, *a new mystery plot on her mind, a thesaurus by her elbow, and murder in her heart.*

1. Marc Antony addressed the Roman Senate.
2. The fireman worked earnestly to save the burning building.
3. The health department inspector closed down the outdoor food store.
4. Bob prepared to go on his first date.
5. Hank Aaron watched the ball go over the center-field fence.
6. Joan returned the overdue book to the library.
7. Noyes's Highwayman rode back over the moor to see Bess, the landlord's daughter.
8. Ron explained to his father how the car came to be dented.

Try It Out

Combining into Essays

Compose effective essays by combining the following sets of sentence kernels. Try to use at least one or two absolute constructions.

The First Transatlantic Flight

1. Everyone "knows" this:
2. Charles Lindbergh was the first.
3. He flew across the Atlantic.
4. He flew nonstop.
5. But this is the fact:
6. Lindbergh was the 81st person.
7. Other people flew the Atlantic nonstop.
8. (Lindbergh's was the first solo flight.)

9. The first team flight was for a prize.
10. A newspaper offered a prize.
11. The offer was in 1913.
12. The newspaper was English.
13. The newspaper was *The Daily Mail.*

14. The prize was £10,000.
15. £10,000 was then about $50,000.
16. The prize was for a flight.
17. The flight was to be across the ocean.
18. The flight was to be nonstop.
19. The flight was to be the first.

20. No plane was ready.
21. The readiness was not immediate.

22. No plane could make the trip.
23. The newspaper increased the prize.
24. The increase was after World War I.
25. A number were eager.
26. They were pilots.
27. They would try.
28. They would fly nonstop.
29. The flight would be from Newfoundland to Ireland.

30. Two attempts ended.
31. They were the first.
32. The endings were disastrous.
33. One plane went down in the ocean.
34. Its radiator was clogged.
35. The other plane was handicapped by its fuel tanks.
36. The fuel tanks were extra large.
37. The handicap was fatal.

38. A plane was ready on May 18, 1919.
39. The pilot of the plane was Jack Alcock.
40. The navigator of the plane was Teddy Brown.
41. Alcock and Brown felt confident of success.
42. But the plane was 1,000 pounds overweight.
43. Alcock and Brown felt compelled.
44. They must bring along their two cats.
45. The cats were toys.
46. The cats were for luck.

47. The exhaust pipe split away.
48. The split was shortly after takeoff.
49. The flames shot behind them.
50. The noise rang in their ears.

51. Then they flew into a cloud bank.
52. The bank was heavy.
53. They were battered about.
54. The battering was by high winds.
55. Their dials were invisible.
56. Their controls were useless.
57. The dials and controls could not guide them.

58. The plane stalled.
59. The stalling was inevitable.
60. It went into a spin.
61. Then the plane broke through the clouds.
62. It came out of the spin.
63. They were only 100 feet above the water.

64. They caught their first glimpse.
65. The glimpse was of Ireland.

66. Then the air-intake valve iced over.
67. The valve was on one of their two engines.
68. The engine coughed.
69. The engine sputtered.

70. Alcock shut off that engine.
71. He slowly glided to an atmosphere.
72. The atmosphere was lower.
73. The atmosphere was warmer.
74. Here he hoped this:
75. The ice would melt.
76. The melting would be enough.
77. It would restore the engine.
78. The ploy worked.
79. The adventurers flew the rest of the way.
80. This flying was without incident.

81. They landed in an immense Irish bog.
82. They had set out 16 hours and 28 minutes before.
83. The flight had crossed the Atlantic.
84. The flight was nonstop.
85. The flight was the first.

Try It Out

The Abominable Snowmen

1. A small number of creatures exist in the Himalayan Mountains.
2. The mountains are in Tibet.
3. The creatures exist high up.
4. The existence is apparent.
5. These creatures are primitive humans or anthropoid apes.
6. They are called "Abominable Snowmen."

7. Major L. A. Waddell first described large footprints in the snow.
8. Major Waddell was a member of the India Army Medical Corps.
9. His description was in 1899.
10. The footprints were made by these creatures.
11. These creatures were "hairy wild men."
12. This was according to the native Tibetans.
13. The "wild men" live in the mountains.
14. Waddell's interest was aroused.
15. Waddell asked other Tibetans a question.
16. Did they know of such creatures?
17. The Tibetans all spoke casually about them.
18. But no Tibetan claimed anything.
19. They had not seen them.

20. Waddell's report was dismissed.
21. Other reports followed.
22. These other reports were also dismissed.
23. They were dismissed by most members.
24. The members were of the scientific community.
25. The reports were dismissed as speculation.
26. The speculation may have been only imaginative.
27. The speculation may have been caused by bears.
28. The bears were large.
29. The bears sometimes walked upright.
30. The speculation may even have been caused by humans.
31. The humans were fugitives.
32. The humans were hiding in the mountains.

33. The natives still insisted on something.
34. The insisting was nevertheless.
35. The footprints belonged to a hairy race.
36. They called the hairy race "Yeti."

37. Only a few Western men claimed something:
38. They have actually seen the Abominable Snowmen.
39. One Western man told Jean Marquis-Rivière this.
40. Marquis-Rivière is a French author.
41. The man saw a group of Yeti.
42. The group was large.
43. The group was in a circle.
44. They were beating tom-tom drums.
45. They were swaying back and forth.
46. This evidence is hearsay.
47. This evidence is unreliable.

48. The testimony of Sen Tensing is much more reliable.
49. Tensing is the Sherpa guide.
50. Tensing guided the climbs of Mt. Everest.
51. These climbs were the most famous.
52. Tensing saw a Yeti.
53. Tensing was at a Tibetan festival.
54. A Yeti appeared.
55. The appearance was sudden.
56. The Yeti was a human-apelike creature.
57. The Yeti was standing 5½ feet tall.
58. The Yeti was covered with hair.
59. The hair was reddish brown.
60. The face was not covered with hair.

61. Eric Shipton took a photograph.
62. This was in recent years.
63. Shipton is an explorer.

64. The explorer is renowned throughout the world.
65. The photograph was of fresh Yeti tracks.
66. The tracks prove something.
67. The proof is conclusive.
68. The creature is not a bear.
69. The creature is not a human.

70. Most scientists have had a skepticism.
71. This skepticism has been allayed.
72. The scientists have concluded something.
73. Some human-ape creature exists.
74. Travelers and scientists in that part of the world have a belief.
75. The belief has thus been kept alive.
76. Travelers and scientists will continue the following:
77. They will nourish hope of this:
78. The encounter will be one day.
79. The example will be living.
80. The example will be of a missing link.
81. The link is in the evolution of humankind.

VARYING YOUR CHOICE

The exercises in the remainder of this chapter give you the opportunity to try out combinations of the various constructions we have been working with. Try to keep them in mind as you work, but in composing every essay or paragraph, your main concern should be to discover the most effective way to get the point across to the reader.

Try It Out

Combining into Paragraphs
Combine the following sentence kernels into an effective paragraph.

Delicatessen Warfare
1. My neighborhood is in Chicago.
2. My neighborhood has a war going on.
3. The war is not between countries.
4. The countries use sophisticated weapons.
5. The war is rather between delicatessens.
6. The weaponry is advertising slogans.

7. One delicatessen is Morey's.
8. Morey's specializes in corned beef sandwiches.
9. The other delicatessen is The Flying Lox Box.

10. The Flying Lox Box is only a block away.
11. The Flying Lox Box makes rival corned beef sandwiches.
12. The sandwiches are even better than Morey's.

13. Morey's posts the slogan, "Catering to the Stars."
14. The slogan has been posted for a long time.
15. At first The Flying Lox Box could not find a slogan to compete.
16. The Flying Lox Box tried many slogans.
17. The Flying Lox Box tried for many months.
18. Now The Flying Lox Box posts the slogan, "Catering to Nobel Laureates."

19. I do not know something:
20. Are the slogans true?
21. But once I saw a man eat at Joe's.
22. The man was a Nobel laureate.
23. I never saw a person eat at Morey's.
24. The person was a star.

Try It Out

Combining into Essays

Using your knowledge of noun, adjective, adverb, and absolute constructions, compose effective essays from the following sets of sentence kernels. Try to be creative in your syntax.

Einstein's Uncertainty about Heisenberg's Principle

1. Certainty came slowly.
2. The certainty was about the Uncertainty Principle.
3. The principle is Werner Heisenberg's.
4. The principle is famous.

5. Werner Heisenberg first postulated his Uncertainty Principle.
6. Then it became a center of controversy.
7. The controversy was among scientists.
8. The controversy was immediate.

9. Physicists were everywhere.
10. They came to see something about the principle.
11. Heisenberg was correct.
12. The correctness was in fact.
13. The recognition was gradual.

14. One scientist was a holdout, however.
15. The holdout was notable.
16. Albert Einstein was that scientist.
17. He was the most respected of all.

18. Einstein would suggest a possibility.
19. The suggestion would be made every morning.
20. One could not apply the Uncertainty Principle to the possibility.

21. Heisenberg would ponder the problem.
22. The pondering would take all afternoon.
23. Heisenberg would be able to do something.
24. He would be able to do it by dinnertime.
25. He could explain this:
26. How did his principle hold true in the case?
27. Einstein had proposed the case.

28. Then Einstein would have all night.
29. He would think of a way.
30. The way would be new.
31. He would try to do something.
32. He would disprove the Uncertainty Principle.

33. Heisenberg would win out.
34. This happened each time.
35. Einstein came to a belief.
36. All of science came to this belief.
37. They all accepted the Uncertainty Principle.
38. The acceptance was as fact.
39. The acceptance came in this way.

Try It Out

Master of the Wisecrack

1. George S. Kaufman was growing up in the 1890s.
2. He was a weak child.
3. He was a sickly child.
4. He was constantly challenged to fight.

5. He could not fight with his fists.
6. He developed another weapon.
7. His weapon was much more powerful.
8. His weapon was words.

9. He kept this skill.
10. He sharpened this skill.
11. He refined this skill.
12. He used this skill.
13. The using was to make his mark.
14. The mark was in theatre.
15. The mark was as a playwright.

16. Kaufman was one of the most significant playwrights.
17. The significance was of this century.

18. He wrote 45 plays.
19. He wrote the plays in 37 years.
20. 27 plays were huge hits.

21. Kaufman became the first playwright.
22. The first playwright won two Pulitzer Prizes.
23. The prizes were for plays.
24. The plays were *Of Thee I Sing* and *You Can't Take It With You.*

25. Success came.
26. The reason for the success was the new style of wit.
27. Kaufman introduced the new style of wit.
28. He introduced it to the stage.

29. His characters thrived on the wisecrack.
30. The wisecrack is a device.
31. Kaufman uses the device abundantly in his plays.
32. Kaufman used the device abundantly in the movies.
33. He wrote movies for the Marx Brothers.

34. Kaufman was the master of the wisecrack.
35. This fact is not really surprising.
36. One remembers something:
37. Kaufman had once been a sickly child.
38. Kaufman learned fighting.
39. The fighting was with words.
40. The fighting was not with his fists.

Try It Out

The Red Scare of 1919–20
1. The Bolsheviks seized power.
2. The seizure was in Russia.
3. The seizure was in 1917.
4. Communists were convinced of something.
5. Socialists were convinced of something.
6. The Communists and Socialists were American.
7. A revolution could take place.
8. A revolution could be successful.
9. The revolution could be in America.
10. These radicals joined the Communist party for a reason.
11. These radicals joined the Socialist party for a reason.

12. They consolidated their power.
13. They pursued their goals.
14. Their pursuits were mainly peaceable.

15. Many of these radicals were immigrants.
16. Many could not speak English.
17. This gave an intensity to the fears.
18. The nation had these fears.
19. The intensity was special.

20. What caused further problems?
21. A number of anarchists caused problems.
22. The number was small.
23. The anarchists were violent.
24. The anarchists were also immigrants.
25. The populace mistook the anarchists.
26. They thought the anarchists were Communists.
27. They thought the anarchists were Socialists.

28. Much of the nation was upset.
29. The upset was caused by the radical immigrants.
30. Much of the nation overreacted.
31. They started a campaign in 1919.
32. The campaign was for getting rid of the "Red Menace."
33. The campaign represented a disregard of civil rights.
34. The disregard was blatant.
35. The disregard was the most since the time of slavery.

36. Attorney General A. Mitchell Palmer believed something about all immigrants.
37. All immigrants pose a threat to the nation.
38. The threat was serious.
39. Attorney General A. Mitchell Palmer instituted a series of raids.
40. The raids were against aliens.
41. Palmer questioned the loyalty of the aliens.

42. Palmer arrested thousands.
43. Palmer held thousands for deportation.
44. Palmer had the support of the country behind him.
45. He did not have the support of the constitution behind him.

46. Three hundred people were arrested.
47. The arrests were in Detroit.
48. The arrests were on charges.
49. The charges were false.
50. Three hundred people were deprived of food.
51. The deprivation was for 24 hours.
52. Three hundred people were forced to sleep.
53. They slept on the floor.

54. Three hundred people were held in jail.
55. The imprisonment was for a week.
56. The week was before the following findings:
57. All three hundred were innocent.

58. The public was appalled.
59. It was by the end of 1920.
60. It was at last.
61. Public sentiment turned against Palmer.
62. Public sentiment ended the violation.
63. The violation was of civil rights.
64. The violation was widespread.

65. The "Red Scare" of 1919–20 ended.
66. The Red Scare was a mixture of panic.
67. The Red Scare was a mixture of zeal.
68. The zeal was patriotic.
69. It was destroyed by its own excesses.

Try It Out

Milk and Mankind

1. Americans consume a glass or two of milk each day.
2. These Americans are average adults.
3. They consume milk by the glass.
4. They consume it on cereal.
5. They consume it in coffee.
6. They consume it as ice cream.
7. Yet the majority of adults in the world differ.
8. This majority considers milk a substance.
9. But the substance is not edible.

10. These adults are residents of East Asia.
11. They are residents of Africa.
12. They are residents of South America.
13. Many of these residents believe this:
14. An infant stops drinking milk.
15. The milk is its mother's.
16. Then it should drink no more milk.

17. These people feel a certain way about drinking milk.
18. We would feel the same in the following situation:
19. We would be offered a glass.
20. The glass would be full of blood.

21. After all, blood is a liquid.
22. The liquid is life-giving.

23. Milk is a liquid.
24. The liquid is life-giving.

25. Furthermore, there are many cases.
26. Some people's stomachs cannot tolerate milk.
27. They are not used to milk.
28. They consume milk.
29. Or they consume milk products.
30. Then the result would be distress.
31. The distress would be of the stomach.

32. There is another reason.
33. Many South Americans throw out milk.
34. These South Americans are impoverished.
35. The milk is powdered.
36. The milk has been sent to them.
37. North Americans sent it.
38. The North Americans are well intentioned.

39. However this reaction may seem strange.
40. The strangeness is to us.
41. This reaction is quite understandable.
42. Most adult mammals do not drink milk.
43. Most adult mammals cannot digest milk.

44. A person should digest milk properly.
45. Digestion requires substantial amounts.
46. The amounts are of the enzyme lactase.
47. The amounts must be in the stomach.
48. Most mammals stop something:
49. They do not produce lactase.
50. The change is at an early age.

51. But Americans and Europeans live in areas of high production.
52. The production is of dairy goods.
53. Americans drink much milk.
54. Europeans drink much milk.
55. They drink milk throughout their lives.

56. We are in the West.
57. We can therefore continue throughout our entire lives.
58. We can enjoy.
59. We can pour cream.
60. The cream is thick.
61. We can pour it over strawberries.
62. We can pour it into coffee.
63. We can slurp our ice cream sodas.
64. We can slurp them with pleasure.

ASSIGNMENT

Choose one of the following and write an effective essay. Include some of the constructions you have been working with.

1. In a letter to the editor of your college newspaper, your city or hometown newspaper, or the editor of a national magazine or journal, comment upon a recent item in that publication, or support or take issue with an opinion expressed there.*

2. Imagine a place you've been that made a great impression on you. As your memories of that place flood back, take notes on the elements of the place or scene that created that impression. Use those notes to develop a thesis and then an essay in which description of that place forms about half of the essay.

3. Using free-writing or other prewriting techniques, describe an experience that had an important effect on you. Arrive at a thesis; then write an essay that includes description of the original experience.

---

*Note: I would be most interested in hearing about the letters that the newspapers and magazines accept for publication.

7

Making Sophisticated Stylistic Decisions: Still More Sentence Combining

This chapter will help you learn to create rhythmic effects through special managing of the basic constructions discussed in Chapters 5 and 6. Rhythm can exert extraordinary emotional power. All human beings respond to the patterned repetition that is rhythm—whether it is in the form of a primitive drumbeat, a sophisticated symphony, or rhythmically persuasive prose. Its appeal would seem to be basic to human nature. Some research indicates, for example, that newborn infants gain weight better and cry less when a recording of a beating heart plays in their nursery, perhaps reminding them of the security of the womb. And rhythm also satisfies intellectually. It imposes pattern and order upon otherwise disordered impressions. In this chapter you will have the opportunity to experiment with a variety of rhythmical arrangements so that you can learn to add some of this emotional power and intellectual appeal to your own writing.

PARALLELISM

Parallelism is at the heart of rhythmic sentences. It can be a telling technique not only because of the emotional impact of the rhythms it can create, but also because it gives you a way of linking ideas to reveal their essential relatedness. How is this parallelism achieved? Through repetition. The trick is to make sure the elements you wish to emphasize are repeated and are arranged in such a way that the repetition is instantly clear to the reader. Notice the repetition in the following well-known examples of parallelism:

Serial Parallelism
- I came,
  I saw,
  I conquered.   (Julius Caesar)

- We cannot dedicate—
  we cannot consecrate—
  we cannot hallow—this ground.   (Abraham Lincoln)

Balanced Parallelism

- Spare the rod and spoil the child.   (English and biblical proverb)
- Hear the instruction of thy father and forsake not the teaching of thy mother.   (Bible)

Contrasting Balance

- To err is human, to forgive divine.   (Alexander Pope)
- Every sweet has its sour; every evil its good.   (Ralph Waldo Emerson)

Although achieving such parallel effects involves repetition of both sound and meaning, you will find that the most significant repeated element is syntax. To put it in terms of sentence-combining theory, you can make the ideas you wish to link together parallel by making sure you have changed their basic kernels of meaning into identical constructions and by combining them in one of the two ways that emphasize this identity: in a series (vertical parallelism) or in a balance (horizontal parallelism).

Serial Parallelism

When you have a number of ideas you want to tie closely together, you can do so most impressively by forming them into parallel constructions and linking them together in a series. In doing this you can exercise a great deal of freedom. You have the choice of phrasing your series items into any kind of sentence element you want. You can choose single words or words and their modifiers from any of the parts of speech. For example, nouns:

- A *rag* and a *bone* and a *hank* of hair . . .   (Rudyard Kipling)
- A *keeper* of my profession's flame, a *herdsman* of its sacred cows, a *minstrel* of its mythology.   (Judith Crist)

Or adjectives:

- A *real* and an *irresistible* and an *inexorable* and an *everlasting* enemy.   (John Donne)
- The *clean-shirted, barbered, shaven,* and *sober* commuters, who are my colleagues.   (Judith Crist)

Or verbs:

- I shall never *ask,* never *refuse,* nor ever *resign* an office.   (Benjamin Franklin)

Or adverbs:

- We are swallowed up, *irreparably, irrevocably, irrecoverably, irremediably.*   (John Donne)

Or you can choose to form the ideas into parallel phrases. For example, participial phrases:

- . . . any nation so *conceived* and so *dedicated* . . .   (Abraham Lincoln)

Or infinitive phrases:

- The problem for modern parents is to find ways *to give their children a sense of usefulness, to make them feel that they are a vital part of a general family enterprise . . . .* (William Raspberry)

With prepositional phrases you have two choices. You can keep the objects identical and vary the prepositions:

- . . . that government *of the people, by the people, for the people . . . .* (Abraham Lincoln)

Or you can vary the objects and keep the prepositions constant:

- *With* malice toward none, *with* charity for all, *with* firmness in the right as God gives us to see the right. . . . (Abraham Lincoln)

Clauses of all kinds also can be used in parallel constructions. For example, noun clauses:

- We hold these truths to be self evident: *that all men are* created equal; *that they are* endowed by their creator with certain inalienable rights; *that among these rights are* life, liberty, and the pursuit of happiness . . . (Thomas Jefferson)

Or adverb clauses, such as these "unless" clauses:

- For *unless all the citizens* of a state are forced by circumstance to compromise, *unless they* feel that they can affect policy but that no one can wholly dominate, *unless by* habit and necessity *they have* to give and take . . . (Walter Lippman)

Or these "if" clauses:

- *If we wish* to be free; *if we mean* to preserve inviolate these inestimable privileges for which we have been so long contending; *if we mean* not basely to abandon the noble struggle in which we have been so long engaged . . . (Patrick Henry)

Or adjective clauses, as for example, those in the same Henry sentence from which we have just quoted:

- . . . privileges *for which we have been* so long contending . . . struggle *in which we have been* so long engaged, and *which we have pledged* ourselves never to abandon . . .

You can also put ideas into parallel main clauses. The parallel elements may be partial main clauses:

- We cannot dedicate—we cannot consecrate—we cannot hallow—this ground. (Abraham Lincoln)
- We have petitioned; we have remonstrated; we have supplicated; we have prostrated ourselves at the foot of the throne . . . (Patrick Henry)

Or they can even be full sentences:

- Journalism is my profession; factual reporting is my function; and my mission, for the moment, is iconoclasm. (Judith Crist)

In constructing parallel series, you also have a variety of connecting elements to choose from. You can join the parallel parts together with commas or semicolons or periods. Each of these kinds of punctuation is exemplified in the previous examples. Or if you choose to use conjunctions, you have your choice of the whole array of coordinating and subordinating conjunctions. What is more, you can decide exactly how often you want to use conjunctions. You might choose to use the conventional sequence of items that concludes with a conjunction:

- Life, liberty, *and* the pursuit of happiness.
- Never ask, never refuse, *nor* ever resign . . .
- A jug of wine, a loaf of bread, *and* thou . . .

In another case you might want to depart from the norm and eliminate the conjunction in order to instill a note of urgency and achieve a brisk, no-nonsense approach:

- I came, I saw, I conquered.
- We have petitioned; we have remonstrated; we have supplicated; we have prostrated ourselves at the foot of the throne . . .

To see just what is achieved by this omission, try adding a conjunction at the conventional place: for example, "I came. I saw. And I conquered."

On the other hand, you might prefer to achieve the emphasis that goes with departing from the norm by instead adding conjunctions between each of the parallel items. These additions have the effect of slowing the rhythm of the sentence and giving extra weight to each of the items:

- *Neither* snow, *nor* rain, *nor* heat, *nor* gloom of night . . .
- A real *and* an irresistible *and* an inexorable *and* an everlasting enemy . . .

If Donne had used the conventional system, he would have lost most of the force of his phrase: "A real, irresistible, inexorable, and everlasting enemy." In most cases you should be completely consistent with repeated conjunctions, adding the same one between all items in the series you choose to connect in this way. Nevertheless, you have the freedom occasionally to add them selectively and thus arrange your series in groups. Note, for example, how Lewis Carroll groups the items by his intermittent use of "and" and "of" in this line:

Of shoes—*and* ships—*and* sealing wax—of cabbages—*and* kings.

For so formal a construction as parallelism, you thus have a surprising amount of freedom. There are, in fact, only two rules to follow when you work with this strategy:

1. Make the elements in the series as equivalent as possible.
2. Put the most important element last.

Making the Terms Equivalent   To achieve parallelism, the major term in all of the items in a series must be of identical parts of speech, or as we said earlier, all the items must have "identical constructions." But the technique loses much of its force if the parallelism is not extended further. The modifiers, for instance, should also be equivalent. Think how much less effective Kipling's line would have been if he had not described the vamping woman as

• *A* rag, *a* bone, and *a* hank of hair

but had instead called her

Less effective   • Rags, a bone, and the hank of hair
                        or
Less effective   • A rag, the bone, and hanks of hair

Though it is often neither feasible nor wise for you to carry a total parallelism through every portion of every element in a series, still you should try for at least a measure of parallel construction throughout. Take, for example, Patrick Henry's "if" clauses cited earlier (p. 244). They differ in many respects. The first is brief, the others more lengthy; the last is negative, the others positive; the first is passive, the others active; and so on. Yet these constructions have much more than the initial "if" in common:

If we wish to be free;	
If we mean to preserve . . .	for which we have been so long . . .
If we mean not basely to abandon . . .	in which we have been so long en-gaged
	and which we have . . .

It is also usually a good idea—for the sake of clarity as well as for rhetorical effectiveness—to repeat an introductory word throughout the series. Note, for example, that Lincoln did not write

Less effective   • With malice toward none, charity for all, and firmness in the right . . . .

But rather

• *With* malice toward none, *with* charity for all, *with* firmness in the right . . . .

Building to a Climax   One of the major advantages in using serial parallelism is the possibility the technique offers of working toward a climactic point. Almost every one of our samples illustrates the fulfillment of this possibility. And you should find it worthwhile to organize climactically too. Furthermore, if you are not careful to arrange your items in order of importance, you run the risk of creating the sort of anticlimax that your readers may find ludicrous. If Patrick Henry, for instance, had been less careful in ordering his clauses, his great plea for independence might have petered out in this way:

FAULTY   • We have prostrated ourselves, we have remonstrated, we have even petitioned.

You can avoid running into similar problems by remembering to conclude your series with the item you want your readers to consider most important.

When you master the subtleties of creating parallel structures, you should find this technique a highly effective way to demonstrate the relatedness of a group of ideas, to organize these ideas in a creative sequence, and to develop a pleasing rhythmic quality in your prose.

━━━━━━━━━━━━━━━━━━━━━━━━━━━━━ **Try It Out** ━━

Combining Kernels
Combine the following sets of kernels into effective sentences by creating parallel structures and arranging them in series.

Sample Problem:

- No matter how you look at the automobile question, it would seem that Japan continues to dominate the automobile market.
- You can look at the thriftiness of gas mileage in Japanese cars.
- Japanese cars are also more economical to manufacture.
- The engines of Japanese cars tend to last longer.

Some Sample Solutions:

- Whether you look at the thriftiness of the gas mileage in Japanese cars or at the economy of their manufacture or at the durability of their engines—however you choose to look at the automobile question, it would seem that Japan will continue to dominate the automobile market.
- Because Japanese car engines tend to last longer, because they are more economical to manufacture, and because they are more thrifty to run, it would seem that Japan will continue to dominate the automobile market.

1. Doug could not understand the following things.
   Claire would not go out with him.
   Martina would not speak to him.
   Annette would not look at him.
2. I am going to finish these exercises.
   Then I am going to kick off my shoes.
   Then I am going to throw myself.
   I'll throw myself on my bed.
   I'll throw myself down for a well-deserved rest.
3. The spy stole slowly.
   The spy stole quietly.
   The spy stole stealthily.
   The spy stole up the darkened steps.
   The spy knocked on the door.
   The knocking was three times.
   The door was heavy.
   The door was oaken.
4. Sheila is arrogant.
   Sheila's husband is rude.
   Sheila's baby is just plain obnoxious.
5. The piano player took one last drag.
   He took it on his cigarette.
   The piano player sat down.
   He sat at the bench.

The piano player began.
He banged out the blues.
6. Pericles spoke a funeral oration.
The oration is famous.
He spoke with force.
He spoke magnetically.
His speech was convincing.
He spoke about the advantages of the Athenian life.
7. Carol put on her boots.
Carol opened up her umbrella.
Carol stepped out into the rain.
8. The tornado struck Kansas.
Dorothy and Toto were swept up in the air.
Dorothy and Toto were deposited in Oz.
9. They were climbing on the walls.
They were dancing on the ceiling.
They were hiding under the beds.
The imbiber's room was crowded with pink elephants.
10. Hamlet ponders.
The earth is this goodly frame.
The earth seems a sterile promontory.
It seems so to me.
The air (sky) is this most excellent canopy.
The air (sky) is this brave o'erhanging firmament.
The air (sky) is this majestical roof.
It is fretted with golden fires.
The air (sky) appears no other thing to me than a congregation.
It is a congregation of vapors.
The congregation is foul.
The congregation is pestilent.

Balanced and Contrasting Parallelism

The other form of parallel structure you might try is balanced parallelism. You can use balanced parallelism to reinforce a statement by repeating a particular sentence structure in a parallel way or by dividing the statement into balanced halves. For example:

- Eat not to dullness; drink not to elevation.   (Benjamin Franklin)
- What we attain too cheap, we esteem too lightly.   (Thomas Paine)
- A man's heart deviseth his way, but the Lord directeth his steps.   (Bible)

Although the two kinds of parallelism distinguished in this chapter are alike in that they both are composed of similar items linked together by similar placement, they differ in structure. If you picture serial parallelism vertically as a column of parallel items, then you might picture balanced parallelism horizontally as a balance scale or a teeter-totter with a single item (or group of items) on each side of the balance point. The balance point, which can be a mark of punctuation or a conjunction or simply a pause, separates the balanced items.

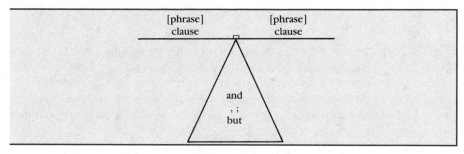

FIGURE 1   Balanced or
Contrasting Parallelism

As with serial parallelism, the similarities in the balanced pairs usually go beyond repetition of function words and syntax to include an actual similarity of sound. The pairs of words balanced for their meanings in the preceding examples, for instance, are similar in number of syllables and in initial and final sounds: *attain/esteem, deviseth/directeth, his steps/his way.*

Balanced parallelism not only is useful for pointing up the correspondence of like statements, but also is particularly effective in revealing the contrast that lies at the heart of some concepts. In such contrasting parallelism, the balanced halves are the contradiction or the antithesis of one another. For example:

- We must all hang together or, assuredly, we will all hang separately. (Benjamin Franklin)
- Hatred stirreth up strifes; but love covereth all transgressions. (Bible)
- It matters not how a man dies, but how he lives. (Samuel Johnson)
- Faith defies proof; science demands it. (Lance Morrow)
- The urge to obliterate death is the urge to extend life. (J. H. Plumb)

Contrasting parallelism.

Because balanced (especially contrasted) parallels express ideas so succinctly and neatly, and often so wittily, many proverbs and maxims are written in this style. But you must not think that the writing of short, pithy statements is the only—or even the primary—use of parallelism. By imposing a proverb-like quality upon a sentence, parallelism can add an air of wisdom to the content and make it memorable. In this way, balanced constructions can often contribute rather substantially to the persuasiveness of your own writing and to the great bulk of expository writing that does not strive for an especially proverbial sound. The following passages from essays in Part Five exhibit the typical effect.

- The Harvard psychiatrists worry about cheating children out of their childhood. I worry about cheating them out of something more profoundly important; their self-respect as responsible, contributing human beings. (William Raspberry, p. 503, *16*)

- We have discovered that when you cure typhoid, you get overpopulation and when you raise the standard of living, you destroy the environment.   (Ellen Goodman, p. 470, *5*)
- Financial and professional insecurity turned the newspaperman into a bohemian who made a virtue of his lack of worldly status, a vice of such personal securities as education or professional training or even domesticity.   (Judith Crist, p. 494, *8*)

Paired Conjunctions   One important strategy for building balanced constructions is to employ paired conjunctions: both . . . and . . . ; not only . . . but also . . . ; neither . . . nor . . . ; more . . . than . . . ; less . . . than . . . , among others. The pairs offer even inexperienced writers a useful form upon which to construct a balanced sentence. But professional writers also employ paired conjunctions to good advantage:

- Seen in the context of history, Forest Lawn is *neither* very vulgar *nor* very remarkable.   (J. H. Plumb, p. 466, *12*)
- We *not only* wear kids' clothes and eat kids' food; [*but*] we [*also*] dream kids' dreams, and make them come true.   (Shana Alexander, p. 436, *15*)
- Shallow understanding from people of good will is *more* frustrating *than* absolute misunderstanding from people of ill will.   (Martin Luther King)
- After four wars, Israelis are unmoved by the idea that their security depends *less on* their toughness *than on* their malleability.   (George Will, p. 447, 7)

Special Effects   Because of its highly structured nature, balanced parallelism lends itself to some rather spectacular effects. For instance, with appropriate subject matter you can achieve a double pairing, such as this by Disraeli:

- Man is not the creature of circumstances; circumstances are the creatures of men.

Or this by Emerson:

- For everything you have missed, you have gained something else; for everything you gain, you lose something.

John F. Kennedy employed the strategy to remarkable effect:

- . . . ask not what your country can do for you; ask rather what you can do for your country.

Or you can work for the round-robin sort of balance that characterizes this famous adage:

- For want of a nail a shoe was lost;
  For want of a shoe a horse was lost;
  For want of a horse a soldier was lost;
  For want of a soldier a battle was lost;
  For want of a battle the war was lost.
  All for the want of a horse-shoe nail.

Such balance may also appear more prosaically:

- Experience is the child of thought, and thought is the child of action. (Disraeli)

Variations   On the other hand, you need not feel bound by the rigidity of the balanced parallel form, for variations not only are permitted, but in many cases also enhance the effectiveness of the construction. You should feel free, for instance, to interrupt the parallelism with an aside or a parenthetical phrase:

> We must all hang together or, assuredly, we will all hang separately. (Benjamin Franklin)

And although, as we have seen, balanced parallelism demands the pairing of elements on both sides of an imaginary balance point to achieve the balanced effect, it is not necessary—indeed, it is sometimes damaging—to spell out the parallelism between every element. You will notice that the authors of many of the statements cited here have substituted a pronoun for an important noun in the second half of the pairing. In doing so they avoid the awkward and somewhat ponderous effect that repetition would involve. Compare, for example, the way Lance Morrow actually phrased his statement with the way he might have phrased it:

- Faith defies proof; science demands *it.*
  Faith defies proof; science demands *proof.*

Similarly, you have the option of skipping some of the wording in the second half of the balance, as was done in these examples:

- Pride goeth before destruction, and a haughty spirit [goeth] before a fall. (Bible)
- Character is much easier kept than [it is] recovered. (Thomas Paine)
- Every sweet has its sour; every evil [has] its good. (Ralph Waldo Emerson)
- Financial and professional insecurity turned the newspaperman into a bohemian who made a virtue of his lack of worldly status, [and who made] a vice of such personal securities as education or professional training or even domesticity. (Judith Crist, p. 494, *8*)

Decisions on just how much of the pattern to repeat require the sort of subtle judgment that comes with practice and experience.

When you have acquired this experience, you should find that contrasting and balanced parallelism are techniques that can add to the wit or profundity of what you are trying to say and can also enhance the rhythmic effectiveness of your writing.

━━━━━━━━━━━━━━━━━━━━━━━━━━━━━━━ **Try It Out** ━━

Combining Kernels
Combine the following kernels to create pleasingly balanced sentences.

Sample Problem:

- Do you believe that peace can endure in a world filled with nuclear armaments?
- If you do, you deny history's evidence that war has always come when the world has been saturated with weapons.

Some Sample Solutions:

- To believe that peace can endure in a world filled with nuclear armaments is to deny history's evidence that war has always come when the world has been saturated with weapons.
- That peace can endure in a world filled with nuclear armaments is widely believed; yet history's evidence that war has always come when the world has been saturated with weapons cannot be denied.

1. Rachel got her law degree.
   Sarah is Rachel's twin.
   Sarah got married.
2. You make your bed.
   It is expected.
   You do not make your bed.
   It is an unforgivable sin.
3. Sandy has a favorite American novel.
   It is *Huckleberry Finn.*
   Dan has a favorite American novel.
   It is *Catch 22.*
4. Television news programs show the story.
   They show the visual aspects.
   Newspapers go further into the story.
   They go into it in depth.
5. Beth and Betsy are sisters.
   Beth is a blond.
   She is short.
   She has green eyes.
   Betsy is a brunette.
   She is tall.
   She has deep brown eyes.
6. Ada does not know something.
   Darielle does not know something.
   Frederick goes out with them both.
7. Camille makes pizza.
   It is the best this side of the Mississippi.
   Camille also serves pizza.
   She serves it with style.
   She serves it with grace.
   The style and grace are exceptional.
8. Lord Byron characterizes Don Juan in a light.
   The light is decidedly favorable.
   Mozart sees his Don Giovanni in a light.
   It is an uncompromisingly unfavorable one.

Try It Out

Compose Your Own

Compose your own balanced sentences by filling in the blanks with a pair of parallel clauses, phrases, or words.

Sample Problem:

During the Civil War the North had not only _____, but also _____.

Some Sample Solutions:

- During the Civil War the North had not only a just purpose in their support of the Union, but also a moral cause in their opposition to slavery.
- During the Civil War the North had not only superiority of arms, but also dominance in manufacture and industry.

1. Both _____ and _____ are cherished traits I have tried to develop.
2. I consider myself knowledgeable not only about _____, but also about _____.
3. For there to be a prolonged period of true world peace, there would have to be either _____ or _____.
4. In the past ten years people have been concerned more with _____ than with _____.
5. Not only is Otis _____; he is also _____.
6. Next summer I would much rather _____ than _____.

Combining Serial and Balanced Parallelism

We have discussed the two kinds of parallelism separately so that you might understand the structures more clearly. But in actual practice, writers tend to build these constructions into one another in complementary ways—especially where they want to heighten the rhetorical excitement. In working through the exercises that follow, you will have the opportunity to integrate both kinds of parallelism into the structure of expository essays. But first, examples from writings in Part Five can serve as useful models for the sophisticated stylistic tools parallelism offers:

- Children today not only exist; they have taken over.
  God's Country has, to an astonishing degree, become Kids' Country—
      in no place more than in America, and at no time more than in the period
      Halloween-to-New Year's Day. (Shana Alexander, p. 434, *2*)
- Because he has tenure, he can weigh values beyond the cutthroat competitive
      scoop of the moment;
  because he has a future, he can devote himself to the refinement of his craft,
      to specialization and expertise,
  so that not only does his value to his employer increase, but also his own
      opportunities for advancement broaden. (Judith Crist, p. 495, *13*)

- To have that sense of one's intrinsic worth which constitutes self-respect is potentially

  to have everything: the ability to discriminate, to love and to remain indifferent.

  To lack it is to be locked within oneself, paradoxically incapable of either love or indifference.   (Joan Didion, p. 441, *11*)
- Liberals are temperamentally inclined to see the world as a harmonious carnival of sweetness and light,

  where good will prevails, good intentions are rewarded,

  the race is to the swift, and

  a benevolent Nature arranges a favorable balance of pleasure over pain. . . .

  Conservatives know the world is a dark and a forbidding place

  where most knowledge is false, most improvements are for the worse, the battle is not to the strong, nor riches to men of understanding, and an unscrupulous Providence consigns innocents to suffering. (George Will, p. 449, *2, 3*)

Try It Out

Combining Into Essays

Write effective essays from the following sets of sentence kernels. Use parallel constructions when they seem appropriate.

Identical Behavior from Identical Twins

1. Identical twins are physically identical.
2. They are also behaviorally identical.
3. This identity is in many ways.
4. It is apparent.
5. A study shows something.
6. The study is recent.
7. The study is of identical twins.
8. Some twins were separated at birth.
9. Some twins were separated shortly after birth.
10. These twins show many of the same behavior traits.
11. These twins show many of the same mannerisms.
12. These twins show many of the same likes.
13. These twins show many of the same fears.
14. But these twins did not grow up together.

15. There are examples.
16. Take one set of twins.
17. Both twins bit their nails.
18. They bit them to the quick.
19. Take another set of twins.
20. Both punctuated their remarks.
21. They punctuated them with giggling.

22. The giggling was nervous.
23. Take yet another set of twins.
24. Both counted everything.
25. The counting was compulsive.
26. They counted everything in sight.

27. Identical twins even tend toward other things.
28. They share the same phobias.
29. They both express these fears.
30. But their way of expressing is not always the same.
31. In one pair of twins both twins were claustrophobic.
32. Both twins refused something.
33. They refused interviewing.
34. The interviewing should not be in a room.
35. The room could not be small.
36. The door must be kept open.

37. In another pair of twins both were afraid.
38. The fear was of escalators.
39. One twin would not ride escalators.
40. The other twin rode escalators.
41. But she rode in fear.

42. Some separated twins share the same likes.
43. Others share the same dislikes.
44. Here is one instance.
45. The twins are English.
46. The twins are women.
47. The twins are identical.
48. The twins like to sit in a way.
49. This way is identical.
50. Their pose shows off their hands.
51. Their hands show off their rings.
52. Both twins also like rings.
53. Each twin wears seven rings.
54. They wear them habitually.

55. Twins often have life-styles.
56. The twins are identical.
57. The life-styles are identical.
58. An extraordinary example is this:
59. Both twins in one set were married on the same day.
60. The day was in 1965.
61. The twins were not reunited then.
62. The reuniting was several years later.

63. Dr. David Lykken was one of the researchers in the study of identical twins.
64. Dr. Lykken analyzed the results of the study.

65. Then Dr. Lykken commented.
66. He said the following.
67. "It is very likely a lot more behavior is genetically influenced than we had previously thought."

Try It Out

Snake Charmers

1. Indian snake charmers make their living.
2. They charm snakes.
3. The snakes come out of their baskets.
4. The charmers charm coins.
5. The coins come out of the pockets.
6. The pockets belong to the onlookers.

7. Charmers like to be called "snakers."
8. The "snakers" are trained from childhood.
9. The training is in an art.
10. The art is of snake catching.
11. The art is of snake charming.
12. The art is of snake showmanship.

13. They have passed down these arts.
14. The passing down has been through the snaker castes.
15. The passing down has been for thousands of years.
16. Egyptian pyramid texts mention serpent charming.
17. The texts date from about 2350 B.C.
18. Buddhist writings indicate something.
19. Serpent charming was a profession.
20. The profession was established by 300 B.C.

21. A long time has passed.
22. The technique has changed little.
23. The snakers themselves have heightened the mystique.
24. The snakers themselves have encouraged the mystique.
25. The mystique surrounds the snakers.
26. The mystique surrounds their profession.
27. But the mystique is just part of the show.

28. What is important?
29. What brings in money?
30. The show is important.
31. The show brings in money.
32. The snakers claim this:
33. They have power.
34. The power is magical.

35. The power is over the snakes.
36. But these claims are just part of the show.
37. The snakers use snakes.
38. Nearly all of them are nonpoisonous.
39. Some snakes are truly poisonous.
40. They divert the venom of these snakes.
41. The venom never reaches the fangs.

42. The snakers play music.
43. The music is on their flutes.
44. The snakes rise up.
45. The snakes sway.
46. The snakes bare their fangs.
47. But snakes have no ears.
48. They do not respond to the sound.
49. The sound is of the music.
50. They respond to the feel.
51. The feel is of the air.
52. The air rushes through the pipes.
53. The air blows on their backs.

54. The snakes rise up.
55. They rise in alarm.
56. But what intimidates them?
57. It is only the motion.
58. The motion is weaving.
59. The motion is of the flute.

60. Tourists are impressed.
61. Onlookers are impressed.
62. They think there is danger.
63. The danger is from the snakes.
64. They think the snakers are calm.
65. They think the calm is magical.
66. The tourists pay to see the show.
67. The onlookers pay to see the show.
68. They pay well.

_____ **Try It Out** _____

Desensitizing

1. Our society has become brutalized.
2. Murder fills it.
3. Rape fills it.
4. Theft fills it.
5. Other violent crimes fill it.

6. We have become insensitive.
7. Our insensitivity is to tragedies.
8. The tragedies are real-life ones.
9. There is a cause for our insensitivity.
10. Our ears are barraged.
11. The barrage is of violence.
12. The barrage is constant.
13. The barrage is in the news.
14. There is another cause.
15. Our eyes are assaulted.
16. The assault is by death.
17. The death is staged.
18. The assault is by mayhem.
19. The mayhem is staged.
20. The assault is on television.

21. We have reached a point.
22. At this point a crime does not lead to shunning.
23. The crime is well publicized.
24. The crime is violent.
25. The shunning would be general.
26. The shunning would be by the public.
27. The shunning would be of such crimes.
28. The crime leads rather to an occurrence.
29. The occurrence is increased.
30. The occurrence is of crimes.

31. A study shows something.
32. The study is recent.
33. The study is from Northeastern University.
34. The death penalty functions.
35. The function is less as a deterrent.
36. The deterrent is to violent crimes.
37. The function is more of an encouragement.
38. The encouragement is to violent crimes.

39. A study was made in New York.
40. The study covered the years 1907 to the present.
41. The study found this:
42. A month follows each execution.
43. Two more homicides take place in that month.
44. Two is on the average.
45. These homicides are more than an uncommon occurrence.
46. The occurrence is usual.
47. The month is ordinary.

48. Researchers conducted the study.
49. Researchers attribute this situation.

50. The attribution is to the "brutalizing effect."
51. The effect is on society.
52. The violent event has a "brutalizing effect."
53. The event is publicized.
54. It is publicized highly.

55. The researchers observed another effect.
56. People commit suicide.
57. The people are visible.
58. The people are admired.
59. The people are famous.
60. Then other people commit suicide.
61. They follow the example.
62. Here is an instance.
63. Marilyn Monroe committed suicide.
64. This provoked over 250 suicides.
65. The 250 is estimated.
66. The suicides were in her own country.
67. This provoked another 100 suicides.
68. The 100 is estimated.
69. The suicides were in Britain.

70. Thus our senses become desensitized.
71. Then each tragedy spurs suffering.
72. Each tragedy is new.
73. Then each violent event spurs suffering.
74. Each violent event is new.
75. The suffering is additional.
76. The suffering is innocent.

Faulty Parallelism

You will be pleased, I'm sure, with most of the effects you achieve when you consciously create parallel constructions. And you may be even happier with the effects that seem to develop spontaneously out of the material itself without your really setting your mind to it. But sometimes, when you are not in conscious control of these effects, the constructions that form are not completely parallel, but only semi-parallel. Because these semi-parallels (or faulty parallels) are so common, you will need to watch for them in your proofreading. And when you revise your work, you will want to give these constructions true parallel character by providing equivalent form for equivalent ideas. The following are examples of the sort of mistakes in parallelism that creep into every writer's work:

1. Among Peter's ambitions were a good job, to do well in college, and learning to fly a plane.   FAULTY

FAULTY

2. The tourists were unsure whether to unpack and settle in their hotel or if they should go out and see the sights of the town.
3. Brent's uneasiness was due to his being late and because he had forgotten the speaker's name.
4. Decide upon a goal that is reachable with a clear direction and purpose and which offers real satisfaction.
5. The politician's tour included munching on such ethnic delights as pizza and bagels and spanokepeta and some adorable Sicilian-American babies whom he kissed.

Think through how you might edit out such faulty parallelism; then read the following possible solutions:

1. Among Peter's ambitions were to get a good job, to do well in college, and to learn to fly a plane.
   or
   Among Peter's ambitions were getting a good job, doing well in college, and learning to fly a plane.
2. The tourists were unsure whether to unpack and settle in their hotel or to go out and see the sights of the town.
3. Brent's uneasiness was due to his being late and to his having forgotten the speaker's name.
4. Decide upon a goal that is reachable, that has a clear direction and purpose, and that offers real satisfaction.
5. The politician's tour included munching on such ethnic delights as pizza, bagels, and spanokepeta, and kissing some adorable Sicilian-American babies.

Try It Out

Revising Parallelism

Correct the errors in the following sentences by turning faulty parallelism into the genuine article.

1. Having had a good night's sleep, our hotel manager was especially pleasant and the food was delicious.
2. Angela liked black-eyed Susans, ambling in the meadows, and to pick buttercups.
3. Simon P. Pettifog, a sleazy lawyer, was disbarred and charming.
4. I long to return to the cry of the loon, waking with the sun, and where the waves beat against the shore.
5. Vladimir Ilich Ulyanov had quietly practiced law in St. Petersburg, is an accomplished hunter, was reading revolutionary authors, and would become the man known as Nicolai Lenin.
6. The Village Inn Hotel was dingy, the rooms were dark and in disrepair, and they cheated on their bill.

7. In the morning she was happy, in the springtime, she was delighted, and she always enjoyed being in Poughkeepsie.
8. The fine restaurant served tournedos, escargots, and the waitress was nice.

COMPOSING CUMULATIVE AND PERIODIC SENTENCES

In arranging your ideas into sentence form, you have, in addition to the options we have already discussed, the choice of composing two special kinds of sentences: the *cumulative* (sometimes called *loose*) sentence and the *periodic* sentence. Though you would probably not want these forms to make up the majority of your sentences, you may find them exceedingly useful for varying the internal structure of your paragraphs, for building satisfying rhythms, and for creating desired emphasis. Cumulative and periodic sentences are opposite to each other in structure. The sentence base (subject–verb–complement) of the cumulative sentence occurs at or near the beginning of the sentence and is followed by a number of modifiers, either assorted or parallel. In the case of the periodic sentence, the modifiers come first and lead into the sentence base.

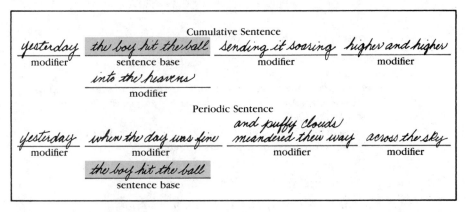

Cumulative Sentences

Cumulative sentences have been much praised in recent years. Scholars have discovered that this sort of sentence is an important strategy in the stylistic repertoire of many contemporary writers. Some praise it for its natural, almost conversational quality. Others find it a useful way to compose, since it is developed by adding details to describe and expand an already stated central idea. On the other hand, some writers—such as E. B. White—warn that loose sentences can easily be overused and that writers should therefore take care to vary them with other forms.

When you begin to study cumulative sentences, probably the first thing that will become apparent to you is the rich variety of constructions that can be used to expand your base. These expansions can be dominated by any of the descriptive or adjective-like constructions. You can choose present or past participial phrases, appositives, prepositional phrases, or absolutes. Each of these constructions can, in turn, itself be expanded by an even wider variety of elements, including infinitive phrases, gerund phrases, prepositional phrases, and adjective clauses. The following cumulative sentences, taken from the essays in Part Five, exemplify this variety. They are arranged schematically, with the base sentence in italics to make analysis easier.

Expansions can be dominated by past participial phrases:

Watching television,
you'd think we lived at bay,
in total jeopardy,   (prepositional phrase)
surrounded   (past participle)
on all sides   (prepositional phrase)
by human-seeking germs,   (prepositional phrase)
shielded   (past participle)
against infection and death   (prepositional phrase)
only by a chemical technology   (prepositional phrase)
that enables us   (adjective clause)
to keep   (infinitive)
killing them off.   (gerund)
(Lewis Thomas)

By present participials—here supported by past participials:

Many choose to think that romance has gone out of newspapering,
taking with it all the life and lust and adventure   (present participle)
immortalized by Ben Hecht and Charles   (past participle)
MacArthur and
perpetuated in old men's tales   (past participle)
of escapades and capering characters.   (prepositional phrase)
(Judith Crist)

Here the present participial is supported by infinitives:

So this day and this century proceed toward the absolutes of convenience, of complexity, and of speed
only occasionally holding up the little trumpet   (participial phrase)
to be reminded of the simplicities and   (infinitive phrase + prepositional phrase)

(as at Christmas time)   (adverb phrase)
to hear the distant music of the hounds.   (infinitive phrase + prepositional phrase)

(E. B. White)

Other expansions are dominated by appositive phrases:

What disadvantaged people need are freer markets and a return to the principles of the Bill of Rights,

principles   (appositive phrase)
   which the Supreme Court of the 1930s threw   (adjective clause)
   out
      when they gave the state and federal gov-   (adverb clause)
      ernment greater control
         over the individual's economic life.   (prepositional
             (Walter Williams)   phrase)

Another element useful in the expansion of cumulative sentences is the absolute. Here it is employed to good advantage by J. H. Plumb:

There they lie,
   larger than life,   (adjective phrases)
   grave,
   portentous,
   frozen in death,
a wife, sometimes two, rigidly posed beside them,   (absolute)
and beneath, sorrowing children, kneeling in filial piety   (absolute)
the whole structure made more pompous   (absolute)
with heraldic offerings.   (prepositional phrase)

The expansion part of the cumulative sentence can also be dominated by prepositional phrases:

He tended, naturally enough, *to repay in kind the in-*
security his employer offered,
   by moving on from job to job,   (prepositional phrases)
   by insouciance and prankishness
     that was charming but often disastrous   (adjective clauses)
   by kicking in the competitive clinches   (prepositional phrases)
   for temporary survival and
   by an irresponsibility
     that caused him to regard his work as an end   (adjective clause)
   unto himself alone.
                (Judith Crist)

Besides showing the use of prepositional phrases, this last Crist example also demonstrates the vigorous parallel effects that are possible in the cumulative sentence. E. B. White is another author who adds parallel effects to his cumulative sentences with considerable success:

It was the night, and the excitement of the note of
the hound,
   first heard and   (past participial phrases)
   then not heard.
It was the natural world,
   seen at its best and most haunting,   (past participial phrases)
   unlit
     except by stars   (prepositional phrase)

impenetrable   (adjective phrase)
    except to the knowing and the sympa-   (prepositional phrase)
        thetic.

(E. B. White)

But as the other examples should make amply clear, whether or not a cumulative sentence includes overt parallelism, this construction, when skillfully conveyed, almost invariably provides naturally graceful rhythms. By using it, you can increase the effectiveness of your writing.

Try It Out

Combining Kernels

Combine the following sets of kernels to compose effective cumulative sentences.

Sample Problem:

- The buttercup opened.
- The opening was gradual.
- The sepals bent back.
- The bending was slow.
- The sepals exposed the petals.
- The petals spread.
- The spreading was languid.
- The spreading revealed the stamen and anthers first.
- The spreading revealed the carpels.
- The revealing was eventual.
- The carpels were visible now.
- The carpels were ready for the ministering bee.

Sample Solution:

The buttercup opened gradually: the sepals slowly bending back to expose the petals, the petals spreading to reveal first stamen and anthers and eventually the carpels—now visible and ready for the ministering bee.

1. Mario jumped up.
   He spun the ball.
   He fired the ball at the basket.
2. Monica carried her baby home.
   She carried it from the hospital.
   She carried it with a proud air.
   She carried it with an almost haughty air.
3. Brenda likes something:
   She reads romantic novels.
   Each page is filled with torrid love.

Each page is filled with wild passions.
Each page is filled with uninhibited emotions.
These emotions are quite unlike any emotions.
Brenda herself had never experienced such emotions.

4. I often like camping.
I camp out on the beach.
The campfire glows.
The salt spray fills the air.
The call of a seagull splits the night.
The seagull is lonely.

5. The bowling ball rolled down the alley.
It rolled with a hum.
The hum was menacing but controlled.
The ball reached the end of the alley.
It exploded there.
The exploding was with an energy.
The energy was furious.
The energy blasted the lifeless pins.
The pins went in all directions.

6. Hamlet's father's ghost delivered a message.
The message was chilling.
The message informed Hamlet of his murder.
The message commanded Hamlet to take revenge by certain means.
Hamlet should confront the new king, Claudius.
Hamlet should kill the new king, Claudius.
Claudius was Hamlet's uncle.

7. The artist paints the mural.
The artist mixes the colors.
The artist swirls the paint.
Then he has a feeling.
He has painted a representation of life itself.

8. The Peace Corps worker flew off to Zambia.
She flew with a heart full of hope.
She flew with a head full of ideas.
She flew with a soul full of anticipation.

Try It Out

Compose Your Own

Compose your own cumulative sentences by adding appropriate expansions to the following sentence bases. Try to vary from sentence to sentence the kind of expansions you use.

Sample Problem:

Sportcasters aim to excite their viewers . . . .

Some Sample Solutions:

- Sportcasters aim to excite their viewers, those bored and weary people around their sets at home, who watch the programs out of lack of something better to do, and who wait impatiently for the commercials so that they can get a snack or use the restroom.
- Sportscasters aim to excite their viewers, giving suspense to every pitch, intrigue to every huddle.

1. Amelia Earhart started her long journey, . . .
2. The soft drink machine hisses and sighs, . . .
3. The businesswoman entered the elevator, . . .
4. Jose put on his ski boots, . . .
5. The mathematicians pored over their figures, . . .
6. Yesterday Bob wrote Sue a letter, . . .
7. The grocer put the turnip greens on sale, . . .
8. The Mr. Softee truck turned the corner and tinkled its bell. . . .

━ Try It Out ━

Combining into Essays

Combine the following sets of sentence kernels into essays. Use the cumulative construction where it would be effective.

The Venerable, Variable Tale of Don Juan

1. The story of Don Juan has been told.
2. The story of Don Juan has been retold.
3. The telling and retelling has been for hundreds of years.
4. Each new writer adds details.
5. Each new writer shifts the characterizations.
6. The adding and shifting are for a reason.
7. The writer presents an outcome.
8. The outcome fits the writer's moral vision.

9. There was a first literary treatment of the tale.
10. The treatment was by Tirso de Molina.
11. The treatment was in 1630.
12. The treatment gives the basic outline of the story.
13. The story is of Don Juan.
14. Don Juan is a young nobleman from Seville.
15. Don Juan is a seducer of women.
16. His seducing is unscrupulous.
17. Don Juan is slain.

18. The slaying is by a statue.
19. The statue is of a man.
20. Don Juan killed this man.

21. Molière provides the next important handling.
22. The handling is of the theme.
23. The handling was in 1665.
24. The handling is in Molière's play *Don Juan.*
25. The play turns the story into a comedy of manners.
26. Molière turns it by introducing characters.
27. He turns it by introducing actions.
28. The characters and actions are humorous.

29. Mozart's opera *Don Giovanni* is perhaps the best-known version of the story.
30. The opera is of 1787.
31. The hero of the opera is witty.
32. The hero of the opera is charming.
33. The hero of the opera is persuasive.
34. But the hero of the opera is flawed.
35. The flaw is his tendency.
36. The tendency is giving himself to excess.
37. The flaw causes his end.
38. The end is sudden.
39. The end is painful.

40. Lord Byron makes Don Juan his hero too.
41. He does so from 1819 to 1824.
42. He does so in his poem, *Don Juan.*
43. The poem is long.
44. The poem is mock-heroic.
45. Byron's hero is a rake.
46. The rake is lovable.
47. The rake is sympathetic.
48. The rake gets involved in adventures.
49. The adventures are numerous.
50. The adventures are exciting.
51. The adventures are romantic.

52. The huge work is incomplete.
53. The incompleteness was at the time of Byron's death.
54. Still there is no indication of something.
55. Byron did not intend his hero to die.
56. The death was not to be at the hands of a statue.
57. The death was not to be at the hands of anyone else.

58. Jose Larilla changed the story.
59. Jose Larilla is a Spanish playwright.

60. The change was marked.
61. The changing was in 1804.
62. The changing was to a morality play.
63. The change portrayed Don Juan.
64. The portrayal is as a corrupt man.
65. The corruption is clear.
66. The man is riddled with evil.
67. The man is sent to his end.
68. The end is terrifying.
69. The end is everlasting.
70. The sending is by the forces of good.

71. George Bernard Shaw wrote a "Don Juan in Hell" sequence.
72. The sequence is in his play, *Man and Superman.*
73. This is the most recent major adaptation of the story.
74. The story is of Don Juan.
75. There Shaw tells of events.
76. The events were after Don Juan's death.
77. Don Juan was in hell then.
78. Don Juan's last mistress was in hell then.
79. His mistress's father was in hell then.
80. The statue was also in hell then.

81. Shaw portrays a paradox.
82. Don Juan is supposedly sensuous.
83. Shaw portrays him as a philosopher.
84. Shaw portrays him as a thinker.
85. The thinker wishes something.
86. He would exchange hell.
87. Life in Shaw's hell is pleasantly sensual.
88. Life in Shaw's hell is sociable.
89. But Shaw's Don Juan prefers Shaw's heaven.
90. Life in Shaw's heaven is austere.
91. Life in Shaw's heaven is intellectual.

92. Authors have manipulated the saga of Don Juan.
93. The manipulation has been repeated.
94. The manipulation has been through the centuries.
95. The manipulation has produced a variety.
96. The variety is of thematic points of view.
97. The variety has been remarkably wide.

98. One cannot help wondering something.
99. What will the next version be like?

Try It Out

The Restless Dead

1. Revolutionary War heroes led active lives.
2. This was generally so.
3. But many Revolutionary War heroes have found activity in death.
4. The activity was almost as much as in life.
5. Graves have been dug up.
6. Bodies have been removed.
7. The graves and bodies are of these war heroes.
8. Their number is surprising.
9. The removing has been to other parts of the country.
10. The removing has been by family members.
11. The removing has been by historians.
12. The removing has been by communities.
13. The communities compete.
14. The competing is in their display of local pride.

15. Mad Anthony Wayne is a case in point.
16. Mad Anthony Wayne was a hero of the Revolutionary War.
17. Mad Anthony Wayne was a hero of the Indian Wars.
18. Mad Anthony Wayne survived the dangers of many fierce campaigns.
19. Mad Anthony Wayne finally succumbed.
20. The succumbing was to complications.
21. The complications arose from a case of gout.

22. Wayne was buried.
23. The burial was in accordance with his wishes.
24. The burial was in a frontier blockhouse.
25. Wayne died in this frontier blockhouse.

26. Wayne stayed there for thirteen years.
27. Then his son decided something.
28. The general would rather have had a different resting place.
29. His resting place should have been closer to his home.

30. Wayne's son opened the grave.
31. Wayne's son found his father.
32. Mad Anthony was almost perfectly preserved.
33. Mad Anthony was thus much too bulky.
34. He could not be carried in the carriage.
35. The carriage was small.
36. The carriage was a one-horse carriage.
37. Wayne's son had provided the carriage for the trip.

38. Wayne's son enlisted the help of a surgeon for something.
39. The surgeon separated the skin from the skeleton.
40. Wayne's son had the skin reburied.
41. The reburial was in the blockhouse.

42. Wayne's son had the bones transported.
43. They were transported back home.
44. Home was in Radnor, Pennsylvania.
45. The bones were buried there.
46. The burial was with much ceremony.

47. John Paul Jones is another example.
48. John Paul Jones was a flamboyant ship captain.
49. John Paul Jones was the Father of the American Navy.
50. John Paul Jones is now recognized as this.
51. John Paul Jones died in France.
52. John Paul Jones was buried in France.
53. The burial was in 1792.

54. The American government decided something.
55. They decided it in 1899.
56. They would move John Paul Jones's body.
57. The moving would be back to America.
58. They found his grave.
59. They opened his grave.
60. This was six years later.

61. Jones had been buried in a lead coffin.
62. Jones had been buried in straw.
63. The straw was sloshed with alcohol.
64. This combination kept him remarkably well preserved.
65. Photographs attest to this preservation.
66. The photographs are rather gruesome.
67. The photographs show Jones's face and features.
68. The face and features are only slightly distorted.

69. Jones's coffin was brought to America.
70. The move was by ship.
71. The move was in 1905.
72. Jones's coffin was shelved.
73. They waited until an elaborate ceremony could be arranged.
74. The wait lasted for eight years.

75. John Paul Jones was buried.
76. He was buried in his own country.
77. The burial was final.
78. The burial was in 1913.
79. The burial was 121 years.
80. The years were after John Paul Jones had died.

Periodic Sentences

Some rhetoricians insist that periodic sentences are the most difficult of all sentences to write because you should know how a sentence will come out before you begin to compose it. It seems to me, however, that whether you find the cumulative or the periodic sentence the more difficult to compose depends on your accustomed way of thinking. If you are one of those people who like to qualify and explain before committing themselves—who like to hedge their bets—or if you find yourself often beginning your written or spoken statements with such expressions as "Although this" or "Because of that," then you may find yourself quite comfortable with periodic sentences (like this one).

In periodic sentences, clauses and phrases—especially adverbial ones—pile up on one another at the beginning of the sentence, often in a parallel manner, until they are followed by a succinct statement of the main thought. The following examples occur in the essays of Part Five.

These first are dominated by adverbial prepositional phrases:

- For clinical sexual observation,   (prepositional phrases)
  for full acceptance
      of the natural functions,
  for boldness
      in the use of words
          that it should take courage   (adjective clause)
              to say before a lady,   (infinitive)
  give me a sophomore girl every time.
                              (Wallace Stegner)

- Out in central Illinois,   (prepositional phrase)
      where men are men and I am a native, (adjective clause)
  in 1948,   (prepositional phrase)
  at age seven,   (prepositional phrase)
  I made a mad, fateful blunder.
                              (George Will)

- At any rate,   (prepositional phrases)
      in a century
          of Einstein's relativity,
          of Heisenberg's uncertainty principle
              (the very act of preserving nature (parenthetical statement)
              disturbs and alters it),
          of the enigmatic black holes   (prepositional phrase)
              ("Of the God who was painted as a (parenthetical statement)
              glittering eye, there is nothing now
              left but a black socket," wrote the
              German Romantic Jean Paul),
  science is not the cool Palladian temple of ra-
  tionality
      that it was in the Enlightenment.
                              (Lance Morrow)

The following examples of periodic sentences are introduced mainly by adverb clauses (and phrases):

- When the early development fosters tremendous (adverb clauses)
  dependency and does not allow for indepen-
  dent exploration, error making, and correction,

> when all tensions are relieved by the parent,
> *the child holds on very intensely to the total*
> *parent,*
>> whose image he has stored in his mind.
> To grow,   (adverbial infinitives)
> to find his own style,
> to achieve his own goals and destiny,
> *he must selectively give up parts of the parental*
> *image.*
>> (Alan S. Katz)

- No matter how earnestly the former spouses try   (adverb clause)
-- to "keep in touch,"   (infinitive)
  no matter how generous the visiting privileges   (adverb clause)
  for the parent who does not win custody of the
  children,
  the continuity of their lives has been broken.
>> (Carll Tucker)

Because of the rhythmical quality of the periodic sentence, and because of the compelling thrust in such sentences toward the words in the sentence base, and even because of the strategic concluding position of that base, writers often use the periodic sentence to express climactic passages in works of impassioned rhetoric. Take, for example, the following famous statements:

- Just as the prophets of the eighth century B.C. left their villages and carried their "thus saith the Lord" far beyond the boundaries of their home-towns, and Just as the Apostle Paul left his village of Tarsus and carried the Gospel of Jesus Christ to the far corners of the Greco-Roman world, *So am I compelled to carry the gospel of freedom beyond my home-town.* (From "Letter from a Birmingham Jail" by Martin Luther King, Jr.)

- If we wish to be free;
  if we mean to preserve inviolate those inestimable privileges for which we have
      been so long contending;
  if we mean not basely to abandon the noble struggle
      in which we have been so long engaged, and
      which we have pledged ourselves never to abandon
          until the glorious object
          of our contest shall be obtained—
  we must fight! (From "Address to the Virginia House of Burgesses" by Patrick Henry)

In the second example, Patrick Henry takes advantage of the possibilities periodic sentences afford for contrasting long constructions with short ones. Notice how effectively he contrasts his series of long preliminary clauses with the abrupt three-word main clause that concludes the sentence. Henry goes on to emphasize the contrast by following up his long sentence with the brief (and repetitive) "I repeat sirs, we must fight!" You can achieve a similar—though perhaps less flamboyant—effectiveness by following up some of your own periodic sentences with brief and simple ones. A number of the authors quoted here have done so.

If you learn to formulate effective period sentences, and if you use them discreetly and in moderation, you will have a useful tool for adding variation, rhythm, and perhaps fire to your prose.

Try It Out

Combining Kernels
Compose effective periodic sentences by combining the following sets of extended kernels.

Sample Problem:

- Computerized typing systems can store past work in their memories.
- Computerized typing systems can call forth the past work when needed.
- Computerized typing systems can permit the typist to correct errors.
- The typist can omit or add material without retyping.
- Computerized typing systems save secretarial time.
- Computerized typing systems save company money.
- Many businesses seriously consider adopting some kind of computerized typing system.

Some Sample Solutions:

- Because computerized typing systems can store past work in their memories and can call it forth when needed, because they permit the typist to correct errors—to omit or add material without retyping—and because these systems can thus save secretarial time and company money, many businesses are now seriously considering adopting some kind of computerized typing system.
- When businesses discover that computerized typing systems can store past work in their memories and can call it forth when needed, that they permit the typist to correct errors—to omit or add material without retyping—and that they can thus save secretarial time and company money, these businesses seriously consider adopting such a system.

1. The sheriff deliberately put on his mirrored sunglasses.
   The sheriff wiped the sweat off his brow.
   The sheriff spit a fine stream of tobacco juice.
   The tobacco juice was deep-brown.
   The sheriff approached the speeder.
2. Socrates worked for no pay.
   Socrates earned only the scorn of his countrymen.
   This scorn eventually led to his condemnation.
   This scorn eventually led to his death.
   Socrates tore down pretenses.
   The pretenses were of those who feigned great knowledge and insight.

3. Lois went to Europe.
   She went last year.
   She went to make her friends jealous.
   She went for no other reason.
4. All is said and done.
   There is only one way to avoid using clichés.
   Clichés are a dime a dozen.
   That way is expressed as follows:
   "Keep them under your hat."
5. Mrs. Byatt opened her home to houseguests.
   The guests came from around the country.
   They attended a wine-tasting festival.
   The festival was in Mrs. Byatt's small city.
   Mrs. Byatt deserves the hospitality award of the year.
6. The dentist had a cold, hard glint in his eye.
   The dentist had a slight, tight-lipped smile.
   The smile played on his face.
   The dentist raised his drill.
   The dentist was ready for the attack.
7. Maggie's hair was disheveled.
   Maggie's makeup was only half put on.
   Maggie ran to open the door.
8. Beatrice and Benedict were assured of their hatred for one another.
   Their assurance was in Shakespeare's *Much Ado About Nothing*.
   They were assured by much sardonic wit.
   They were assured by many barbed jests.
   Then Benedict and Beatrice fell in love.

Try It Out

Fill in the Construction

Expand the following sentence bases into periodic sentences by composing appropriate additions in the suggested grammatical form.

Sample Problem:

Although _____ , and although _____ , (optional "when" clause),
King Henry VIII had his queen executed.

Some Sample Solutions:

- Although he had once loved Ann Boleyn deeply, and although he had even challenged the power of the Pope to marry her, when he tired of her willful ways, King Henry VIII had his queen executed.
- Although Catherine Howard's screams echoed through the elegant hallways of Hampton Court, and although she swore she would come back

and haunt the palace forever, when the appointed day arrived, King Henry VIII had his queen executed.

1. After . . ., when . . . and . . ., the Greene family boarded up their house and never returned to Lakewood.
2. Until . . ., which . . ., Arthur could not speak to Merlin.
3. Having . . . but still hoping for . . ., Marilyn kept her appointment with the dean.
4. Because . . . and because . . .—and since . . . (clause)—Jonah was certain someone had tampered with the election.

=============== **Try It Out** ===============

Compose Your Own

Compose your own periodic sentences by adding appropriate expansions to the following sentence bases. Try to vary the kind of expansions you choose to use.

Sample Problem:

. . . it is time to call the doctor.

Some Sample Solutions:

- If a child seems listless and his appetite is poor, if his usual cheerfulness gives way to irritability or moodiness, and if his temperature approaches 101—even in the absence of any other symptoms—it is time to call the doctor.
- When you are awakened at 2:00 A.M. by the blaring rock and roll from the all-night party of the doctor's kids next door, and when you put two pillows over your head but you can't block out the thump, thump, thump of the percussion, and when all you can think about is that 8:00 exam in the morning, then it surely is time to call the doctor.

1. . . . Gwendolyn despised her job.
2. . . . the sandy beaches stretched to the shore.
3. . . . Reva celebrated her birthday.
4. . . . the car swerved off the road.
5. . . . Jose walked away from his friends.
6. . . . the shoe would not fit.
7. . . . the ambulance arrived at the hospital.
8. . . . the distressed citizen wrote a letter to the editor.

A Warning

Writing cumulative and periodic sentences can give full range to your imaginative and syntactic powers. And, as I have pointed out, they can be exceedingly useful in creating special rhetorical or dramatic effects. But a word of caution is in order, too. These sentences can tend to become long and complicated. If relied upon too often, they can make your prose dense and difficult to understand. Thus, by all means, do use cumulative and periodic sentences—but use them wisely and discreetly.

Try It Out

Combining into Essays
Combine these sets of kernels into sentences to construct effective essays. Use periodic sentences where appropriate.

"Chop Shops"
1. It is no longer only the result of simple maliciousness.
2. It is no longer only the result of kleptomania.
3. More and more, car-theft is becoming big business.
4. The business is well organized.

5. There has been an advent of "chop-shops."
6. "Chop shops" are places where stolen cars are stripped down.
7. The stripping is for essential parts.
8. The stripping is for specially requested parts.
9. Car theft has now become an industry.
10. The industry is multibillion dollar.

11. Over one-third of all stolen cars are taken immediately to a "chop-shop."
12. This is happening today.
13. The cars are stripped of their parts.
14. The parts are marketable.
15. The price of any piece of a car from a "chop-shop" is considerably less.
16. The comparison is with the same piece new.
17. Therefore, even some legitimate dealers deal with "chop-shops."
18. Even some legitimate garages deal with "chop-shops."
19. They pass the savings on to their customers.

20. The stolen cars are stripped beyond recognition.
21. Most stolen parts are unmarked and difficult to track down.
22. Thus the police find it hard.
23. Breaking up auto theft rings is hard.
24. There is a fact.
25. 86% of all car thieves are never captured.

26. The "chop-shops" started out as small-time operations.
27. Yet it is the case with any illegal business.
28. The business is financially successful.

29. Organized crime has moved into the "chop-shop" business.
30. Many "car butchers" have been found executed.
31. The executions are in the traditional gangland fashion.

32. Ordinary drivers are now the prey of criminals.
33. These criminals are professional.
34. These criminals operate on a large scale.

Try It Out

Biology or Something Else?

1. We have seen something.
2. We have seen it all our lives.
3. We have seen it at home.
4. We have seen it in church.
5. We have seen it in school.
6. We have seen it while walking down Wall Street.
7. Men control society.
8. Men spin the globe.
9. Women fry the eggs.

10. Men repair to the drawing room.
11. There they are safe from clatter.
12. The clatter is of knitting needles.
13. The clatter is of pans.
14. The clatter is annoying.
15. There men discuss the reason for their superiority.

16. The reason is biology.
17. The reason is the legacy of the womb.
18. The mothering instinct ennobles a woman.
19. The mothering instinct etches roses.
20. The roses are on a woman's cheeks.
21. Still the mothering instinct does not build skyscrapers.
22. Only men build skyscrapers.

23. Yet we can search far enough behind us.
24. We can turn back the yellowed pages.
25. The turning back can be to preclassical times.
26. Then we encounter some facts.
27. The facts are shocking.
28. Patriarchy has not always been the rule.

29. The ancient scholar Diodorus traveled far.
30. Diodorus studied many cultures.

31. Diodorus was Greek.
32. Diodorus was accustomed to male dominance.
33. What did Diodorus see?
34. It surprised him.
35. It surprises us today.
36. Diodorus reported on the ancient Libyans.
37. The ancient Libyans practiced a division of labor.
38. Their division of labor was neatly reversed.
39. The men did the housework.
40. The men cooked the meals.
41. The men reared the children.
42. The women conducted business.
43. The women ran the government.

44. Early Egyptian society was similar.
45. Early Egyptian society was matrilineal.
46. Early Egyptian society was matriarchal.

47. There is another example.
48. The Amazon warriors galloped down the battlefield.
49. The Amazon warriors screamed.
50. The Amazon warriors brandished their weapons.
51. Their screaming and brandishing were as frightening.
52. Their screaming and brandishing were as deadly.
53. The comparison is to any male army.

54. Historians believe something:
55. This opposite state of affairs was deeply rooted in these ancient systems.
56. The systems were based on laws and customs.
57. The laws and customs were designed for a reason.
58. They were meant to keep men in their place.
59. These ancient systems had a pro-female bias.
60. These ancient systems therefore were probably no fairer than the systems today.
61. The systems today are pro-male.

62. The existence of these systems proves something, however.
63. Biology is not destiny.
64. Woman may be smaller.
65. Woman may be more openly expressive of emotion.
66. Woman may be the childbearer.
67. But woman is as fully inventive.
68. Woman is as fully analytical.
69. Woman is as fully capable.
70. The comparison is to woman's partner, man.

SENTENCE COMBINING TO HELP PROVE YOUR POINT

These sentence-combining chapters have given little emphasis thus far to what may be the most important criterion for your stylistic decision making. That criterion is your answer, in each specific situation, to the question, Which stylistic choice will contribute most effectively to making my points, to supporting my thesis? Chapters 1, 2, 3, and 4 can provide the bases for your answers. The exercises that conclude this chapter offer contexts to give you practice in making these stylistic choices.

Using a Paragraph to Make Your Point

The following exercises ask you to construct an effective paragraph by creating a strong topic sentence from the given kernels and then, by composing supporting sentences, to develop the point of that topic sentence as effectively as possible.

━━━━━━━━━━━━━━━━━━━━━━━━━━━━ **Try It Out** ━━━

Combining into Paragraphs

In this first exercise, concentrate on phrasing the ideas expressed in the kernels so as to emphasize those that are most pertinent to the point of the paragraph and to create the tone most appropriate to the subject matter. There has been no attempt to scramble the ideas in this paragraph, but feel free to rearrange them if you choose.

The Decline and Fall of the Tomato

A. 1. Today's tomato may be rosy.
    2. Today's tomato may be attractive.
    3. It is bland.
    4. It is dry.
    5. It tastes like cardboard.

B. 1. Mechanization, technology, and a rise in the size of farms have combined.
    2. The mechanization is increased.
    3. The technology is dramatic.
    4. The rise in farm size is impressive.
    5. The combining has been in recent years.
    6. The combining has contributed to cultivation.
    7. The cultivation is of a bland, processed-tasting tomato.

C. 1. Mechanization was introduced fifteen years ago into tomato cultivation.
    2. The coming of the mechanical harvester reduced the number of human harvesters.

      3. The number was reduced by 80%.

      4. The human touch lends a certain loving tenderness.

      5. That human touch is all but gone.

D.   1. The human touch was also part of the small tomato farm.

      2. Small tomato farms are a thing of the past.

      3. A sudden demand for tomatoes has forced American farmers.

      4. They must strive for quantity.

      5. They can no longer strive for quality.

      6. They must increase the size of their farms.

      7. They must produce 50.5 pounds of tomatoes a year for every American.

      8. In 1920, they had to produce only 18 pounds of tomatoes for every American.

E.   1. There have also been spectacular breakthroughs in technology.

      2. These breakthroughs have allowed a certain way of breeding.

      3. Geneticists can now breed tomatoes for uniform ripeness.

      4. They can now breed tomatoes for high yield.

      5. They can now breed tomatoes for thick walls.

      6. They can now breed tomatoes for low acidity.

      7. Chemists have also manufactured a substance.

      8. The substance ripens and reddens tomatoes.

      9. The ripening and reddening is faster than nature's.

F.   1. Now we eat tomatoes.

      2. These tomatoes have been mass produced.

      3. These tomatoes have been artificially ripened.

      4. These tomatoes have been mechanically harvested.

      5. It is not a wonder.

      6. Such tomatoes no longer appeal.

      7. They do not appeal to our taste buds.

Try It Out

Supporting the Topic Sentences

In this exercise, compose an effective paragraph by combining the kernels into sentences supporting a topic sentence. Since the supporting ideas have been scrambled to give you practice in ordering, you will probably want to rearrange them. That is, when you compose your own paragraph you will not necessarily want to place the contents of section B before that of C, nor that of C before D.

Hair-Trigger Trickery

Topic sentence

A.   1. History has traditionally condemned Aaron Burr.

      2. He was the cold-blooded murderer in the duel.

      3. The duel was fatal.

    4. The duel was with Alexander Hamilton.
    5. New evidence suggests something:
    6. Hamilton, in fact, tried something in the duel.
    7. Hamilton rigged the duel.
    8. Hamilton died.
    9. His death was from his own scheming.

B. 1. Hamilton provided the pistols.
    2. The pistols were borrowed.
    3. The borrowing was from John B. Church.
    4. John B. Church was Hamilton's brother-in-law.
    5. But Hamilton owned a set of pistols himself.
    6. Hamilton's pistols were perfectly proper.
    7. They were dueling pistols.

C. 1. Many historians now believe something.
    2. Hamilton deliberately set the hair trigger of his gun.
    3. Hamilton lowered his gun for a reason.
    4. He aimed his gun at Burr.
    5. Hamilton applied too much pressure.
    6. The pressure was on the sensitive trigger.
    7. The sensitive trigger caused a misfire.
    8. The gun fired several feet over Burr's head.
    9. Burr would not have known something.
  10. He would not have set his gun's hair trigger.
  11. Burr then had an opportunity.
  12. He could take proper aim.
  13. He could fire.

D. 1. Hamilton and Burr concluded their feud.
    2. Their feud was long-standing.
    3. The concluding was with a duel.
    4. The duel took place on July 11, 1804.
    5. The duel was in the morning.
    6. The duel was in Weehawken, New York.
    7. Hamilton's shot struck a tree.
    8. The striking was 12 feet above Burr's head.
    9. Burr's shot hit Hamilton in the liver.
  10. Burr's shot mortally wounded Hamilton.

E. 1. Church's pistols have survived.
    2. A recent study of these pistols shows something.
    3. These pistols have a trick mechanism.
    4. The trick mechanism is a hair trigger.
    5. The mechanism can be set.
    6. The set mechanism makes something much easier.
    7. The gunsman can pull the trigger easier.
    8. The gunsman can thus fire the gun faster.

F. 1. It happened this way.

2. Hamilton's trickery led to the result.
3. Hamilton had a downfall.
4. It was his own.

Try It Out

Identifying the Topic Sentence

Before you can compose a paragraph from the following sets of sentence kernels, you will have to decide which set (or portion of a set) will make the most effective topic sentence and then arrange the others to support your choice.

Squelching Snores

A.   1. Robert Crossley has invented a cure.
2. The invention is recent.
3. The cure is over 90% successful.
4. Its success is apparent.
5. The invention is a plastic collar.
6. The collar sends electrical impulses.
7. The impulses go into the sleeper's neck.
8. The impulses go with each snore.
9. Crossley claims something.
10. The collar acts as a punishment.
11. The punishment is very mild.
12. The collar builds up a mental block.
13. The block is against snoring.

B.   1. Over 100 devices have been patented.
2. The devices differ.
3. The devices are designed for a purpose.
4. They should stop snoring.
5. Most of these devices do not work.
6. Some of these devices have straps or springs.
7. Some of these devices have flaps or prongs.
8. These seem like punishment.
9. The punishment is cruel.
10. The punishment is unusual.
11. The offense is minor.
12. The offense is only snoring.

C.   1. There have been countless attempts.
2. The attempts have been throughout the years.
3. The attempts have been for a purpose.
4. They would combat a problem.
5. The problem is snoring.
6. Snoring is an affliction.
7. The affliction is shared by one in every eight persons.

8. This number is estimated.

D.   1. Many colonial soldiers were told something.
     2. It was during the American Revolutionary War.
     3. They should put musket balls in the backs of their night clothes.
     4. There was a purpose.
     5. The balls should discourage the soldiers.
     6. Soldiers should not sleep on their backs.

E.   1. Columnist Ann Landers gives advice today.
     2. It is much the same advice.
     3. Ann Landers substitutes table tennis balls.
     4. The substitution is for the musket balls.

Try It Out

Combining into Essays

Compose an effective essay from the following sentence kernels. The kernels are grouped for placement in the introduction, the body, or the conclusion of the essay. It is up to you to order the ideas within these parts. Be sure that you understand from the start what your thesis will be. Arrange the introduction to introduce the thesis idea in the best way. Compose effective topic sentences within the body to develop this idea, and compose good sentences within each paragraph to support the paragraph's topic sentence. Finish off your essay with a persuasive conclusion.

Cowboys and Astronauts

Introduction

1. The purple sage is conquered.
2. The lonely wagon ruts are paved.
3. No new frontiers are left to humankind.
4. Do you believe that?
5. You do not.
6. Then there is a chance you are aware.
7. You have been reached by some hints.
8. There have been many hints about a new age.
9. The space age is upon us.
10. There is a fact.
11. NASA and scientist Gerard K. O'Neill have conducted a study.
12. One can judge by that study.
13. The "final frontier" may be just around the bend.

Body

V.   1. The space colony could staff solar power satellites.
     2. The space colony could act as a permanent laboratory.
     3. The space colony could serve as a base for mining expeditions to the moon.
     4. These are all plausible functions of the space colony.

W.   1. O'Neill has designed space colonies.
      2. The colonies are permanent.
      3. The colonies could house 10,000 people.

X.   1. O'Neill's cylinder boasts a circumference.
      2. The circumference is over a mile.
      3. O'Neill's cylinder includes terraced hillsides.
      4. It includes verdant valleys.
      5. It even includes lakes.
      6. The lakes are ample enough for boating.
      7. A pattern of light could be simulated.
      8. The pattern could be natural for day and night.
      9. The simulation would be by means of reflective mirrors.
     10. The mirrors would be outside the cylinder.

Y.   1. "Sounds great!" you may say.
      2. "For my grandchildren," you may say.
      3. Yet the hypothesis of space colonization is not particularly far-fetched.
      4. Only a relatively brief time has elapsed since the Industrial Revolution.
      5. Technology tends to progress at an exponential rate.
      6. Cars and airplanes have been around for less than a century.
      7. Rockets were daydreams.
      8. This was in the 1930s.
      9. The next 50 years could witness the construction.
     10. The construction could be of orbital space settlements.
     11. There is nothing in O'Neill's design that goes beyond the capacity of technology.
     12. That technology exists this very day.

Z.   1. These colonies would be anchored in a libration point.
      2. The point could be between the earth and the moon.
      3. Libration points are locations.
      4. At the locations gravity and centrifugal force cancel each other out.
      5. Librations insure a stationary position for the colonies.
      6. They would be stationary in respect to the earth and the moon.

Conclusion
      1. One thing is certain.
      2. The certainty is for whenever we get there.
      3. This last frontier will be more alien.
      4. This last frontier will call for more daring.
      5. This last frontier will have more profound results.
      6. The comparison is with any other frontier ever attempted.
      7. The first frontier attempted was when our ancestors struggled from the ocean onto the land.

━━━━━━━━━━━━━━━━━━━━━━ Try It Out ━━

Paragraphing Your Essay

The kernels in the following exercise are grouped for placement in the introduction, the body, or the conclusion of an essay. It is up to you to order the ideas within these parts to make the most effective essay possible. What will be your thesis? You will probably want to decide right away so that you can point your introduction toward expression of the thesis idea and construct the topic sentences of your body paragraph(s) to support it. And you will want to compose your conclusion to give your point its most persuasive expression.

The Cinderella Blue Jean

Introduction
A.   1. The blue jean is a symbol.
      2. The symbol is of American sturdiness.
      3. The blue jean came from beginnings.
      4. The beginnings were the humblest.
      5. The blue jean is a piece of wearing apparel.
      6. The apparel became desired.
      7. It is the single most desired.
      8. The desiring is in the world.

B.   1. A culture believes something.
      2. "Mighty oaks from little acorns grow."
      3. A culture holds the underdog in favor.
      4. The holding is perpetual.
      5. In this culture a story should have appeal.
      6. The story would be of the blue jean.
      7. The blue jean is lowly.
      8. The appeal is of a Cinderella.
      9. The Cinderella is from true-life.

Body
V.   1. The business was modest enough.
      2. This was at the start.
      3. Then Strauss bought the rights.
      4. The rights were for an idea.
      5. Then Strauss patented the idea.
      6. The idea was for a certain construction.
      7. He put rivets on the pockets.
      8. He put rivets on points of stress.
      9. The rivets were of copper.
    10. The rivets kept the pockets and the points of stress.
    11. They did not tear.
    12. Then business picked up.
    13. The increase was appreciable.
    14. Levi Strauss and Company supplied the clothing.
    15. The clothing was for most of the working West.

16. Some of the workers were lumberjacks.

17. Some of the workers were cowboys.

W. 1. Blue jeans began with a peddler.

2. The peddler was named Levi Strauss.

3. The peddler was impoverished.

4. The peddler was Jewish.

5. The peddler was an immigrant.

6. He decided on a move.

7. He would move West.

8. The move was in 1850.

9. The peddler took a quantity with him.

10. The quantity was of canvas.

11. Strauss hoped to sell the canvas.

12. It would sell for tenting.

X. 1. Strauss soon found something.

2. The canvas was the wrong kind.

3. The canvas was not for tents.

4. Strauss heard a miner.

5. The miner complained.

6. The miner could not find work pants.

7. The pants were not truly sturdy.

8. Strauss measured the miner.

9. The measuring was for six dollars in gold dust.

10. Strauss fitted the miner.

11. The fitting was with canvas trousers.

12. The miner liked the trousers.

13. The miner told all his friends.

14. Strauss made pants for the friends.

15. Strauss soon found himself in business.

16. Strauss was in the pants business.

Y. 1. In the 1960s there was a counterculture.

2. This culture was international.

3. This culture adopted blue jeans.

4. This culture took them as their own.

5. Blue jeans became ubiquitous.

Z. 1. Word spread.

2. The word was of the pants.

3. The pants had riveted pockets.

4. The pants were immensely popular.

5. The spread was to the East.

6. Eastern city folk vacationed.

7. They vacationed at western dude ranches.

8. They took the news back home.

9. The news was of the western Levis®.

10. Then easterners also started something:
11. They wore blue jeans too.

Conclusion

C. 1. Blue jeans are pants.
   2. They are unpretentious.
   3. But they are sturdy.
   4. Jeans originated in leftover canvas.
   5. Jeans have become the uniform.
   6. The uniform is worldwide.
   7. The uniform is of youth.

D. 1. Today more than 83,000,000 Levis® are sold.
   2. These Levis are genuine.
   3. The selling is each year.
   4. Imitations are also sold.
   5. Probably twice that number are sold.
   6. The selling is each year.

E. 1. There are fashionable shops.
   2. The shops are in Paris.
   3. The shops are in London.
   4. The shops sport jeans.
   5. The jeans are prefaded.
   6. The fading is to just the right intensity of blue.
   7. Sales are at prices.
   8. The prices go over £50.

F. 1. There is a traffic.
   2. The traffic is in blue jeans.
   3. The traffic is lively.
   4. The traffic is on the black market.
   5. The black market is in Russia.
   6. The black market is in the Eastern European countries.
   7. Some blue jeans are authentic American.
   8. These jeans bring a great deal of money.
   9. Sometimes these jeans bring over $200.

Persuading

The main problem in persuading others to adopt your point of view on an issue is that there are almost always valid points to be made on the other side. You can, of course, ignore the other side altogether, but you do so at your peril. For even if your audience has not heard of specific opposition arguments, they could hardly be fooled into thinking that the other side has no points to make at all. If you decide to include some of the opposition points, it is best to get them out of the way as soon as you can. First acknowledge what must be acknowledged gracefully, then refute soundly what can be refuted, and end with some rousing points of your own. In the course of your discussion, you will want to phrase the opposition ideas with as little emphasis as possible and give the most persuasive phrasing to your own views. (See also Chapter 1, p. 54.)

Try It Out

Arguing with Kernels

This exercise consists of two sets of sentence kernels arranged in columns representing alternative points of view on the issue in question. Combine the kernels into an effective essay arguing for *one* point of view. Although you will likely be using more material from one column than from the other, do not ignore the other column completely.

Pro–Gun Control Arguments

Introduction (Death Pre-Argument)

A. 1. Guns are instruments of death.
    2. Guns have but one purpose.
    3. Their sole purpose is this:
    4. They kill living beings.
    5. Guns carry with them a threat.
    6. The threat is inherent.
    7. The threat is of death.
    8. Guns are thus used for a purpose.
    9. They commit crimes.
   10. Their use for this purpose is easy.
   11. Their use for this purpose is frequent.

B. 1. There is therefore a need.
    2. The need is particularly urgent.
    3. We must ban handguns.
    4. At least we must register handguns.

Body (Crime Arguments: Anti-Handgun)

X. 1. Handguns are used to commit murder.

Anti–Gun Control Arguments

Introduction (Freedom Pre-Argument)

A. 1. Every American has a right.
    2. The right is constitutional.
    3. The American can keep arms.
    4. The American can bear arms.
    5. America was made great.
    6. America has this right.

B. 1. Americans conquered the wilderness.
    2. Americans fought.
    3. Americans kept America free.
    4. Today there is a controversy over gun control.
    5. This controversy is essentially a fight for something.
    6. Americans should retain this freedom.
    7. The freedom was hard-won.

Body (Crime Arguments: Pro-Handgun)

W. 1. Now there is a crime rate.
    2. The crime rate is soaring.

2. They are responsible for one murder.

3. The one murder is out of every two.

4. Approximately 72% of all homicides are not premeditated.

5. These homicides are committed by citizens.

6. These citizens were previously law-abiding.

7. These citizens kill their lovers.

8. These citizens kill their friends.

9. These citizens kill their relatives.

10. The killings are spur of the moment.

11. The killings are during arguments.

12. The arguments are passionate.

13. These murders would not take place without a gun.

14. The gun is readily accessible.

Y. 1. There are other forms of spur-of-the-moment violence.

2. These forms are less final.

3. Broken crockery can be swept up.

4. Bruises can heal.

5. Even stabbings are seldom fatal.

6. There are odds on surviving a stabbing.

7. These odds are five times greater.

8. The comparison is with surviving a gunshot wound.

Z. 1. There would not be any guns.

3. Now guns are a near-necessity.

X. 1. Guns are needed for good reasons.

2. People must defend their lives.

3. People must defend their property.

4. People must protect themselves against crime.

(Anti-Handgun Control Arguments)

Y. 1. One handgun is used in committing a crime.

2. This one handgun is out of every 4000.

3. The 4000 are in the United States.

4. Criminals commit these crimes.

5. These criminals would have acted in any case.

6. Even if guns had been outlawed.

7. Even if there had been no guns.

Z. 1. But this is unlikely:

2. Criminals would not go weaponless.

3. Guns would be outlawed.

4. Then only criminals would own guns.

(Pro-Rifle Arguments)

L. 1. Rifles are a kind of gun.

2. Rifles are needed to hunt animals.

3. Hunting is a legitimate sport.

4. Hunting is a means of obtaining food.

M. 1. Farmers use rifles.

2. Farmers use shotguns.

3. They keep predators away from their crops.

2. Then there would be far fewer murders.
3. There is an example.
4. Japan has a murder rate.
5. That rate is 200 times less than the U.S. rate.
6. Japan prohibits handguns.

(Anti-Rifle Arguments)

L. 1. The problem is not posed by handguns alone.
    2. Rifles are a favorite weapon.
    3. Terrorists favor rifles.
    4. Assassins favor rifles.

M. 1. Many hunters misuse rifles.
    2. They massacre animals.
    3. The massacre is to such an extent.
    4. Many species are now extinct.
    5. These species were hunted.
    6. Several hundred more species are in danger.
    7. The danger is of extinction.
    8. The species are hunted.

Conclusion (Danger Arguments)

C. 1. The ownership of guns is increasing in the United States.
    2. This ownership is becoming more widespread.
    3. There is little check on the mental state of gun buyers.
    4. There is little check on the criminal record of gun buyers.

D. 1. These guns serve no useful purpose.
    2. These guns instead pose a constant danger.
    3. They are a continuous threat.

4. They keep predators away from their livestock.

N. 1. There is a custom in many communities.
    2. They give a boy a gun.
    3. The gun is his first.
    4. The gun is a symbol.
    5. The symbol is of the boy's initiation.
    6. The initiation is into manhood.

Conclusion (Freedom Arguments)

1. Some people wish to control guns.
2. Some people wish to confiscate guns.
3. These people have a desire.
4. They may realize its meaning.
5. They may not realize its meaning.
6. They want to impose regulations.
7. The regulations would be on society.
8. This is a type of thinking.
9. This thinking can lead to a police state.

4. The threat is to nature.
5. The threat is to society.
6. The threat is to innocent life.
10. There is a defense against a police state.
11. It is the best defense.
12. Individual citizens should have access to guns.

Arrange the sentences you compose from the following kernels into an essay that will persuasively support one side of the issue of a peacetime draft. Feel free to omit any kernel that will not contribute to making your side convincing. You may also add details not given in the kernels where you feel they will help. Do not hesitate to rearrange the groups of kernels to your advantage. When in doubt, remember to put the "although clause" material first. Be creative and persuasive in your use of syntax.

Pro–Peacetime Draft Arguments

Introduction

1. America needs a draft.
2. The following is the reason.
3. There would be a threat to the security of this country.
4. Then an army would be already formed.
5. Then an army would be already prepared.
6. Our country would be ready.

Body (Practical Drawbacks of a Volunteer Army)

1. A volunteer army is often less competent.
2. A volunteer army tends toward something:
3. It is filled with misfits.
4. It is sloppily trained.
5. It is therefore grossly inefficient.
6. It cannot be relied upon in an emergency.
7. A volunteer army is too small.
8. A volunteer army is too weak.
9. A volunteer army cannot keep our nation safe.

Anti–Peacetime Draft Arguments

Introduction

1. A peacetime draft is not necessary.
2. A peacetime draft is not desirable.
3. A peacetime draft is not in keeping with the spirit.
4. American was founded in this spirit.

Body (Practical Benefits of a Volunteer Army)

X.
1. A volunteer army would better serve our needs.
2. A volunteer army is made up of soldiers.
3. These soldiers want to be in the army.
4. The volunteer army has an overall willingness.
5. The volunteer army has an overall desire.
6. The willingness and desire is shared by three million soldiers.
7. This shared will provides efficiency.
8. This efficiency is greater

(Practical Benefits of a Draft)

1. Expedience is needed in an emergency.
2. Efficiency is needed in an emergency.
3. A draft ensures expedience and efficiency.
4. A draft makes soldiers available for combat.
5. The soldiers would be in large numbers.
6. The soldiers would be qualified for service.
7. The soldiers would be well trained.
8. A draft can also prevent an emergency.
9. Enemy nations will know that we are conducting a draft.
10. Enemy nations will understand something:
11. Our draft provides us with a formidable army.
12. Enemy nations will respect our strength.
13. Enemy nations will therefore hesitate to attack.

(Ideational Benefits of a Draft)

1. The draft is also needed for something else.
2. It can contribute to the spirit of the country.
3. The spirit can become patriotic.
4. Serving our country can become an ideal again.
5. Self-discipline can become an ideal again.
6. Draftees can learn democracy.
7. Draftees are from all levels of society.

than that of a much larger army.

9. The larger army would not hold this attitude.

Y. 1. There is a matter of fact.
2. Enormous masses of soldiers are no longer needed.
3. Masses do not fight a modern war.
4. What is needed instead?
5. It is a relatively few people.
6. These people must be intelligent enough.
7. These people must be well trained enough.
8. They must handle the sophisticated equipment of today's army.

Z. 1. One would not need to draft everyone in sight.
2. Money could be saved.
3. This money could be spent for something else.
4. The spending could pay soldiers wages competitive with those of the civilian economy.
5. The spending could thus entice qualified and interested people into joining the army.
6. The spending could entice them into making the army their lifetime career.
7. America could be well defended.
8. The defending would be at last.
9. The defending would be with volunteer soldiers such as these.

(Practical Drawbacks of the Draft)

1. A draft is not desirable.

8. In the army they work together.
9. They work on equal terms.
10. Draftees gain a sense of duty.
11. They devote a year or two of their lives.
12. They help their country.
13. They help themselves.

2. A draft will build a large military force.
3. This large force could tempt power-hungry generals.
4. These generals could flex the nation's military muscles.
5. The flexing might occur on any pretext.
6. The flexing might include invading another country.
7. The flexing might bring us into war.
8. The war would be caused by dangerous thinking.
9. The thinking would be that the draft makes us invincible.

(Ideational Drawbacks of a Draft)

1. A draft installs a system of servitude.
2. The servitude is involuntary.
3. Draftees are made to serve in the army.
4. Draftees may or may not want to serve.
5. Draftees can be forced to do things.
6. Draftees can be forced to go places.
7. Draftees can even be forced to kill other people.
8. The forcing is against the draftees' will.

Conclusion

1. The draft makes something possible:
2. America will be ready.
3. America can thwart aggression.
4. Aggression occurs.
5. America can defend itself.

Conclusion

1. Our country is founded on principle.
2. The principle is of freedom.
3. We cannot protect freedom through a system of slavery.

6. America can defend its allies.
7. A draft will permit America something.
8. A draft will permit the world something.
9. That something is peace.
10. America and the world can remain at peace.

4. A peacetime draft amounts to using slavery to guarantee freedom.

Try It Out

Scholarly Persuasion

Although most of the compositions you are asked to write in college are not concerned with topics as overtly controversial as those in the last two exercises, you must remember that scholarly papers need to be persuasive too. The final exercise in this chapter should help you make the sort of decisions necessary for writing effective scholarly papers. Combine the kernel sentences in the next exercise to construct an essay discussing the discovery of America. The kernels are arranged in three sets of arguments. Each of these arguments contains a series of facts which points to a particular conclusion about the discovery of the American continents. The following suggested procedure may help you construct your essay from the three arguments:

1. Read over the arguments and come to your own decision on their relative merit. (They are all factual.)
2. Phrase your decision as a thesis. You may want to include an "although clause" to cover the subordinate arguments. Include your thesis in the introduction you construct from the kernels.
3. Organize the arguments to support your thesis in the best way.
4. Combine the kernels within each argument so as to make its point most effectively.
5. When your essay is complete, read it over carefully and write your own conclusion for it.

Who Discovered America?

Introduction

1. Tribes were already settled.
2. The settling was throughout North and South America.
3. The tribes were "discovered."
4. There is a question of who "discovered" the tribes.
5. This question may seem a moot point.
6. It would seem so to the tribes.
7. The question fans a spark, however.

8. The spark is competitive.
9. The competition is for people of non-American origin.
10. Who got there first?
11. Columbus is the best-known candidate for the prize.
12. But Columbus is not the only candidate.
13. Recent discoveries suggest . . .

(Read through the material in the succeeding arguments, form your opinion and *compose your own thesis*. Add your thesis to number 13 in the Introduction kernels or start a new sentence.)

The Columbus Arguments
1. It was two hours past midnight.
2. The night was dark.
3. It was at sea.
4. Three ships had been sailing unknown seas.
5. The ships were small and wooden.
6. The sailing had been for over two months.
7. A shout came suddenly.
8. The shout came from the prow of the *Pinta*.
9. The shout proved something.
10. The earth was round.
11. The shout was "Land Ho."
12. Christopher Columbus had discovered the New World.
13. This triumph was the culmination.
14. The triumph was on October 12.
15. The culmination was of a long personal struggle.
16. Columbus was Italian.
17. Columbus was fired by an unproven hypothesis.
18. Columbus was tempted by the tales of Marco Polo.
19. Columbus longed for something.
20. He would sail in search of India.
21. He had a quest for a patron.
22. The quest covered eight years.
23. King Ferdinand and Queen Isabella of Spain agreed.
24. They agreed at last.
25. They agreed in 1492.
26. They would sponsor his voyage.
27. The *Nina*, the *Pinta*, and the *Santa Maria* sailed.
28. They sailed out of Palos harbor.
29. They sailed on August 3.
30. The expense was justified.
31. The trust was justified.
32. The justification came two months and nine days later.
33. The Spanish sailors were unaware of something.
34. Their lack of awareness was ironic.

35. They trod a soil.
36. This soil was completely unfamiliar to European civilization.
37. Columbus leaped ashore.
38. Columbus claimed the small Bahama island.
39. The claiming was in the name of Spain.
40. Then Columbus set off blithely.
41. He searched for Japan.
42. The treasures of the Orient were nowhere in sight.
43. Of course, this was true.
44. But a bounty lay at Europe's feet.
45. It was a far greater bounty.

The Chinese Arguments
1. The sun sinks down beyond the ocean.
2. The sun is a red dragon.
3. A Buddhist monk turns his gaze.
4. The turning is resolute.
5. The turning is from the sun's flaming passage.
6. The passage is homeward to China.
7. The monk's ship sails east from China.
8. Morning comes.
9. The shores of a new continent stretch.
10. The stretching is in the haze.
11. The monk calls the new continent "Fusang."
12. Today "Mexico" is the name of the new continent.
13. Fang Zhongpu is a navigational historian.
14. Fang points out something:
15. Chinese merchants traveled.
16. The traveling was beyond the Phillippines.
17. The traveling was as early as the 11th century B.C.
18. The Chinese Kingdom of Wu had ships.
19. They had the ships by the 3rd century B.C.
20. These ships could carry 3,000 passengers.
21. The Chinese had the ability.
22. The ability is evident.
23. The ability is not the only supporting clue.
24. Two stone anchors have been found.
25. The anchors are of a type.
26. This type was carried on Chinese ships.
27. The ships were of the 5th century.
28. The finding was in American waters.
29. The finding was recent.
30. The first anchor was recovered near the Palos Verdes peninsula.
31. The second anchor was recovered off Point Mendocino at about 1,000 fathoms.

The Viking Arguments

1. The Viking longship drifted.
2. The ship was slender.
3. The ship was wooden.
4. The drifting was aimless.
5. The drifting was through the churning mist.
6. The drifting was through the chunks of glacier.
7. The chunks were perilous.
8. The chunks filled the Northern Sea.
9. Ice and fog conspired.
10. They formed a soup.
11. The soup was thick.
12. The soup was frozen.
13. The soup was swallowed up by night.
14. The worried sailors could not glimpse their home.
15. Their home was a sea-road.
16. "Lucky Leif" Ericson beached his ship and his crew.
17. He beached them safely.
18. He beached them once again.
19. The sculpted sea-monster bedded down.
20. The sculpting was on the prow.
21. The sea-monster was savage.
22. The bedding down was tame.
23. The bedding down was beside the Labrador coast.
24. The Labrador coast was rocky.
25. Ericson had been bored by the prospect.
26. The prospect was of another routine journey.
27. The journey would be from Iceland to Greenland.
28. Ericson had decided something:
29. He would try an unusual route.
30. The unusual route would be by way of the Hebrides.
31. The storms cleared from the unknown shore.
32. Ericson realized this:
33. He had lost his way.
34. He turned his ship.
35. He sailed toward his Nordic home.
36. Ericson arrived.
37. He announced his discovery.
38. The discovery was of a new continent.
39. He called the new continent "Vinland."
40. Thorfinn Karlesefini was Ericson's countryman.
41. Karlesefini organized a colonizing expedition.
42. He organized it shortly after Ericson's return.
43. The expedition was complete.
44. It had three ships, 160 people, and some cattle.

45. The colonists stayed in their new home.
46. They stayed for three years.
47. They stayed until the natives drove them out.
48. They called the natives "Skraelings."
49. This tale is related in the "Saga of Eric the Red."
50. The saga is famous.
51. The tale has long been intriguing.
52. The tale has long been unverified.
53. Helge Ingstad is an archaeologist.
54. Helge Ingstad excavated eight house sites.
55. The excavation was in 1960.
56. The excavation was successful.
57. The sites are on the northern tip of Newfoundland.
58. Carbon dating proves something.
59. The ruins are Norse.
60. The ruins are from houses built around the year 1000 B.C.
61. The ancient saga has been confirmed.
62. The confirmation is at last.

ASSIGNMENT

Using all the persuasive strategies now at your disposal, convince an indifferent or neutral reader that your position on one of the following issues (or other similarly controversial ones) is best.

College athletic scholarship
Test-tube babies
Alimony
Patenting of scientifically created life forms
Use of public parklands
Premarital chastity
National health insurance
Life support machines/ Euthanasia

8

Creating Your Style
by Making Decisions
About Words

Chapter 5 pointed out that writers create their writing styles through their choices of sentence structure (syntax) and words (diction). In the intervening chapters, sentence-combining exercises offered you experience in making syntactic decisions by providing you with a ready-made diction, thus relieving you of the problems involved in making decisions about words. Yet words are the basic building blocks of style, and in your effort to improve your style, you should probably also give some serious thought to your choice of words. For this reason, Chapter 8 explores the practical considerations involved in making your stylistic decisions about words.

FINDING THE PRECISE WORD

Although deciding upon words would seem to be a complex process, there is but a single, overriding consideration behind every choice: precision of meaning. Without a doubt, that word or phrase is best which most precisely conveys your intended meaning to your readers.

To get some notion of the significance of precise diction, let's examine the key words in a professional sentence or two. Note, for example, the italicized words* in the sentence with which Wallace Stegner begins his essay in Part Five:

> Not every one who *laments* what contemporary novelists have done to the sex act *objects to* the act itself or to its mention.   (p. 500.)

Try interchanging the roughly synonymous terms *laments* and *objects to*. Such a change weakens the sentence substantially. Or try to substitute another word

---

*Italics are used throughout this chapter to call attention to particular words. Unless otherwise indicated, you may assume that italics in quotations are mine and not the original authors'.

for *laments. Deplores* comes close, but it carries with it the sort of moralistic overtones that Stegner clearly wants to avoid. *Deplores* also does not have that aura of sorrow that colors the sentence and helps to establish Stegner's tone of "more in sorrow than in anger." To replace *laments* with *mourns, grieves over,* or *bewails,* on the other hand, would be excessively sorrowful—sorrowful almost to the point of irony. Even such a partial analysis of one word choice should point up the careful judgment Stegner exercises in choosing his diction as well as the importance of such care.

And Stegner's prose is not unique. The principle holds with all effective writing—even with rather commonplace sentences like this one by Lance Morrow:

> Roman Catholic theologian Hans Kung *detects* the beginning of a new period . . . *of mutual assistance* between theologians and natural scientists. (p. 488, *13*)

To understand just how well the words *detects* and *mutual assistance* carry the exact sense of what Morrow wants to convey, try replacing them. The following substitutes might come to mind:

> Kung *predicts* that there will be a new period of *greater helpfulness* . . .
> or
> Kung *declares* the beginning of a period of *lessening antagonism* . . .

As close as these replacements are to Morrow's in meaning, the original writing is clearly superior. Examining instances such as these should convince you that a large part of writing well is the ability to find the word or phrase that most exactly suggests your meaning.

The Richness of the English Vocabulary

When it comes to finding the expression that exactly indicates the thought, we who write in English are particularly blessed. Many believe that the English vocabulary is more eloquent than that of any other language because of its abundance. English has come to encompass a great number of the words and phrases that enrich and enliven other languages. The English that we speak and write today is basically a mixture of the language of the Anglo-Saxon inhabitants of the British Isles (Old English) and that of their Norman conquerors (Old French). Latin, the language of the church and the universities, enriched this mixture, as did a generous smattering of Hebrew and Greek from the same sources, along with some remainders of Danish and Celtic that survived from earlier times. The early disposition of English to gather to itself the linguistic treasures of other cultures continues to this day and has produced the extraordinarily rich vocabulary from which we can choose our words and phrases.

Synonyms   There is scarcely a concept for which there are not at least two or three forms of English expression. That with which we think, for example, is variously called *mind* (Old English derivation), *reason* (Old French), *intellect* (Latin), or even *psyche* (Greek). But this multiplicity of synonyms does not fully account for the richness of English. Even more important is the variety of nuances and shades of meaning offered by these synonyms. Competing words of identical meaning do not exist long in a language together. Either one word becomes dominant and drives the other out of use, or their meanings differentiate enough so that both are needed to give a full range of expression to a concept. Thus, though synonyms can substitute for one another in certain contexts, they can not be interchanged in all situations. If, for example, you want to write about *publicizing* something, you would have a wide range of synonyms from which to choose: *broadcast* (OE),* *publish* (OF), *propagate* (L), *spread* (OE), *promulgate* (L), *disseminate* (L). Which you would choose would depend a great deal upon the nature of the material you wished to publicize. You might, for instance, *broadcast* a game, but you wouldn't *promulgate* it. You might *promulgate* a doctrine, but you would not *spread* it. And although you might *spread* fertilizer, you surely would not *propagate* it.

Synonyms not only vary in the identity of what they refer to (their denotation), but they also differ in the tone they convey and in the value judgments they imply (their connotation). The Latin-derived *promulgate* or *disseminate* suggests a more formal tone than the Old English *spread* or *broadcast,* which, like most Anglo-Saxon derived words, carry with them the informality of ordinary speech. And these words do not suggest the casualness of other synonyms of *publicize* such as *ballyhoo* or *hawk about.* On the other hand, even the Latinate words are less formal or less ennobled than the Biblically allusive synonym *give tongue.* This list of words, more or less synonymous with *publicize,* can also illustrate the fact that synonyms do not have equivalent emotional weight or moral value. Ask yourself, for example, what is likely to be more important: that which is *promulgated* or that which is *bandied about?* Which is more likely to be believed? Or even more likely to be true?

Denotation and connotation.

Since synonyms are thus clearly *not* interchangeable, their abundance in English offers you great room for choice. Within this abundance, you can find just the word or phrase that will most precisely (1) express your exact thoughts, (2) indicate the level of formality and tone of voice you mean to project, and (3) imply the moral and emotional value you intend. These elements of meaning overlap, of course, in every word; but because each is a truly significant consideration in your choice of diction, let us examine each element individually.

Choosing Words for Exact Expression (Denotation)

It would, I know, be helpful if I could supply some absolute rules to guide you in choosing the words that will most effectively express every idea that you might want to write about. The problem is that in stylistic matters there is almost no "always," almost no "never." A way of writing that one good author is careful to avoid, another uses to eloquent advantage. Consequently, though I

---

*The abbreviations after these synonyms follow the conventional manner of signifying a word's linguistic derivation: Old English (OE), Old French (OF), Latin (L).

can offer you two precepts to follow, these precepts are only *usually* useful; and I suggest that you follow them with thoughtful reservations.

Rule 1. Choose the Most Specific Term.   When you are writing about concrete ideas, select the word or phrase that most accurately summons up the sense picture (not necessarily visual) that you have in your mind's eye and will best convey it to your reader. Ordinarily, use the most specific term available. For most purposes:

> "Joey took a picture of *an animal* at the zoo" is weak.
> "Joey took a picture of *a bear* at the zoo" is better.
> "Joey took a picture of the zoo's *polar bear cub, Whitey*" is good.

In most circumstances, you should probably avoid using a word (like *animal* in the sentence about Joey) that does not call up a specific mental image. And you should be particularly wary of words like *nice* that, despite their original specific meanings, have now fallen into a vague general use.

An Important Reservation   By emphasizing the importance of finding the specific term, I do not mean to say that good writers should always shun words signifying general concepts. For instance, although Lewis Thomas often refers in his article (see Part Five) to such specifics as "the diphtheria bacilli or strepto-cocci" and "bacteriophage," he does not hesitate to write "vast microbial world" when the generality is his immediate concern. You, too, should follow his example. The term you choose should be specific to the subject matter—however general or specific that subject happens to be.

The point, then, is not to be vague. If you use a general term, choose it deliberately. You might decide to use a general word such as "building," for example, if you are working toward suspense and want to withhold the exact type of building for a time ("The blindfolded man was ushered into a building"); or if you are speaking generically in architectural terms ("Buildings should be constructed to fit into the existing landscape"); or if you have already used the appropriate specific terms to the extent that you do not want to repeat them again. But if—as is usually the case—generality is *not* your purpose, then good writing requires that you select the particular word that most specifically holds your meaning.

Finding the Appropriate Specific Expression   You can use questions to guide your search for the right specific word. If you are working with a concept like "building," you first would probably want to think of a word that expresses function. Do you want to refer to a *residence? a church? a tavern? a factory? a hotel? a hospital?* or a *store?* You might even want to choose a word yet more particular in function. Having selected a term, you would then try to make it more specific: Is the *residence,* for instance, an *apartment building? a two-family house (duplex)? a farmhouse? a county seat?* Is the *church* a *mosque? a meeting house? a temple? a synagogue?* Is the *tavern* an *inn? a restaurant? a bar? a pub?* On the other hand, you might prefer to distinguish the building by size: Is the *residence* a *high-rise? a mansion? a cottage? a bun-galow?* or a *hut?* Is the *church* a *cathedral?* or a *chapel?* You might even want to distinguish the building by the nationality of its occupants. If so, you might choose to call it an *igloo,* a *hogan,* a *hacienda,* or a *chalet.* Perhaps the building you want to discuss is not intended for human occupation; you might then decide to refer to it as a *kennel,* an *aviary,* a *stable,* a *barn,* a *dovecote,* or even a *garage.* The more precisely the word you choose fits your idea, the better you will be able to communicate that idea, and the better your writing will be.

Rule 2. Prefer Strong Verbs and Vivid Nouns; Be Sparing with Modifiers.   If you admire a spare, clean style of writing, you would be wise to let strong verbs carry much of your meaning wherever feasible. Verbs such as *laments, objects, detects* in the Stegner and Morrow sentences quoted earlier directly express action and are described as "strong." In contrast are verbs grammarians describe as weak: the various forms of the verb "to be" (*is, are, was, were, has been,* and so on) and other such verbs that must be completed by an adjective or a noun (*seem, appear, become,* and so on). Most authorities consider the weak verb-complement construction to be less forceful. For example, note the vigor of J. B. S. Haldane's choice of *compress* and *stretch out* in the following sentence:

> Or it [the suddenly large gazelle] can *compress* its body and *stretch out* its legs
> obliquely to gain stability, like the giraffe.   (p. 480, *3*)

Surely the sentence is more satisfying as Haldane phrases it than it would be if he had used a "weak" verb construction:

> It could *make* its body *smaller* and its legs *longer* to gain stability.

Effective writing is also built upon vivid and explicitly suggestive nouns. Examine, for instance, the following sentence from William Raspberry's essay:

> [The] *sense* of *uselessness,* I am convinced, lies behind the shocking *statistics*
> on teen-age *pregnancy,* youthful *homicide* and *suicide, crime, alcoholism,* and
> *drug abuse.*   (p. 502, *9*)

Raspberry's sentence is a strong one mainly because of the force of its precisely chosen nouns. Sentences like Haldane's and Raspberry's gain much of their leanness from the absence of optional adjectival and adverbial modifiers. Where strong verbs and vivid nouns carry the meaning, few modifiers are required. Excessive use of these modifiers can add a bulk or a wordiness to your prose. Raspberry's one optional adjective *shocking* works well because it is a persuasive word in this context—and because it is alone. A writer must resist the temptation to embellish every noun with an adjective and every verb with an adverb. Think what such a method might have done to Raspberry's sentence:

> The futile sense of *utter* uselessness, I am *firmly* convinced, lies *dangerously*
> behind the *startling* and shocking statistics on *aimless* teen-age pregnancy, *ma-*   FAULTY
> *levolent* homicide and suicide, *miserable* crime, *wasteful* alcoholism, and *de-*
> *plorable* drug abuse.

Though every modifier in this revision is completely appropriate to its context, the overkill lends a ludicrous—almost ironic—tone, even to a subject as serious as Raspberry's. Similarly, you will find that qualifiers like *very* and *really* often weaken where they are meant to make expression more emphatic. The best way to avoid problems with excessive modifiers is to take care in your choice of nouns and verbs to make these essential words as vivid and explicit as possible.

An Important Reservation Unquestionably, thoughtless or excessive use of modifiers can cause writing difficulties. Yet good writers often put modifiers to vigorous use. Some fine writers, like Judith Crist, have developed a style firmly rooted in the use of adjectival constructions. (See her essay in Part Five.) And even in authors who tend toward leaner prose, sentences like the following by J. H. Plumb are not atypical:

> The British have *hilarious* fun over the *quaint* funerary habits of the Americans.   (p. 466, *1*)

Few readers would prefer:

> The British have mocked the American funerary customs.

And yet *hilarious* and *quaint* are clearly optional modifiers. Furthermore, *have fun* is just the sort of weak verb construction that critics deplore. Nevertheless, most readers would agree that Plumb's sentence is effective and a worthy opener for his article.

As a further caution in advising the use of strong verbs, it is only fair to point out that such constructions do not predominate in the main clauses of most professional expository writers—including those represented in this text. The verb "to be" and the other linking verbs (for example, *become, appear, seem, feel, believe, think,* and so on) are among the most useful building blocks of our language. Perhaps because of their very colorlessness, they provide an all-purpose serviceability, which even professional authors employ in a high proportion of sentences. I would not, therefore, suggest that you avoid these verbs, but recommend rather that when you use "weak" verbs you are careful to make your nouns, adjectives, and adverbs as precisely meaningful as possible. Note the precision with which these parts of speech convey the subtleties of their author's meaning in the following examples:

- Perhaps the most *poignant victim* of the twentieth century is our sense of continuity.   (Carll Tucker, p. 505, *8*)
- We still think of human disease as the work of an *organized, modernized demonology,* in which the bacteria are the most *visible* and *centrally placed* of our adversaries.   (Lewis Thomas, p. 461, *2*)

Try It Out

Classifying Words
Classify the following sets of words as directed. Use your dictionary wherever needed.

Sample Problem:

> Classify the following beds by their occupants: cradle, crib, sofa-bed, sleeping bag, bunk, berth.

Sample Solution:

cradle, for an infant	sleeping bag, for a camper
crib, for a toddler	bunk, for a sailor
sofa-bed, for a guest	berth, for a passenger

1. Classify the following ways of imbibing by their appropriate beverage (example, "sip tea"): sip, drink, chug-a-lug, quaff, take-a-nip, swallow.
2. Classify the following kinds of wood by their function (example: "posts, for building fences"): posts, lumber, boards, timber, beams, cords.
3. Classify the following adjectives in terms of the nouns they might appropriately describe (example: "extinct dinosaurs"): extinct, obsolete, archaic, old-fashioned, passé, antiquated.
4. Classify the following verbs in terms of their appropriate objects (example: "predict future"): predict, prophesy, give prognosis, foretell, dope out, forecast.

Distinguishing Synonyms

Though Roget's *Thesaurus* implies that the words in the following pairs are synonymous, there are subtle distinctions in their meanings. Write a sentence for each in which these distinctions are apparent. Don't hesitate to use your dictionary.

1. ample/excessive
2. ecstatic/happy
3. answer/explain
4. old/venerable
5. weather/climate
6. vitality/animation
7. eager/anxious
8. prejudice/bias
9. repudiate/deny
10. suppress/repress

Distinguishing Confusing Word Pairs

These pairs of words are often confused. Write a sentence using each in which you distinguish their meanings.

1. affect/effect
2. principle/principal
3. credible/credulous
4. flaunt/flout
5. persecute/prosecute
6. climactic/climatic
7. imply/infer
8. proceed/precede
9. assume/presume
10. elicit/illicit

Choosing Words for Appropriate Implication (Connotation)

If denotative meanings of the sort we have been discussing were the only meanings words had, then your task of choosing words would be much less complicated. Unfortunately, then, your language would also be far less expressive. But almost all words, in addition to signifying a particular object or concept, are also rich in implications and hidden nuances. In short, they *connote* as well as *denote* meaning.

To distinguish between the concepts of connotation and denotation, let's examine two lines from Alfred Noyes's poem about a dashing, young highwayman and Bess, the girl he loves. Noyes describes the highwayman's sweetheart as

> Bess, the landlord's daughter,
> The landlord's *red-lipped* daughter.

The denotative meaning of the italicized phrase is that the blood vessels near Bess's oral orifice are close to the surface—hardly an adequate summation of a key phrase in a romantic poem. Nevertheless, most readers would agree that the phrase is poetically apt, for readers instinctively know that "red-lipped" *means* a good deal more than it denotes. Clearly, in addition to their denotative meaning, the words "red" and "lipped," when used together in this way, have sensual connotations so descriptive that Noyes, having only two syllables in which to sum up his heroine, justifiably chose these two. The connotative meaning of words and phrases is an important factor to keep in mind when you make your decisions about diction.

Beyond the surface meaning.

Connotations of Formality and Informality

One important kind of connotation that words convey is the notion of degree of formality. Often the formality that a word connotes determines the situation where it can be appropriately applied. For instance, you might use connotations of formality to guide your choice from among the various words that express *haste*:

- The diplomats *hastened* from the room.
- Mother *hurried* home from the grocery.
- When the sergeant said, "Snap to it," the soldiers *snapped to it.*
- "Take the loot and *scram,*" hollered the masked man.

A set of synonyms for almost any noun, verb, adjective, or adverb can be arranged on a scale of levels of formality, from the ceremonial and learned terms of the formal style to the colloquialisms and slang of the extremely informal style. Connotations of formality correspond fairly well to the traditional concept of levels of usage: the High, Middle, and Low Styles. The writers and rhetoricians of times past believed that it was important to adapt the level of their language to the "kind" of speech they were giving or literature they were writing. They used the High Style for epics and tragedy and the Low Style for farcical comedy. (Think, for example, of the contrast between the language of Shakespeare's heroes and that of his clowns.) The Middle Style was the basic language of satire and of expository prose. Although the "Doctrine of Kinds," with its insistence on a strict match between level of usage and literary genre (or "kind") has long since been discarded, the traditional concept continues to be a useful tool in the study of diction to this day. For example, it is still convenient to divide synonyms into categories representing the modern equivalents of the three major stylistic levels. The accompanying table shows six scales that reflect these levels of style.

Formal/Learned Style	Middle Style	Colloquial Style
hasten	hurry	snap to it scram
intrepid valiant	courageous brave	plucky spunky gutsy
pedagogue educator	instructor teacher	grinder crammer
peruse contemplate	study learn	grind bone up
astutely	cunningly shrewdly	slickly
arduous	difficult	tough

FIGURE 1   Three Stylistic Levels

By developing an ear for connotative levels, you can control much of the tone of your writing. But what level of words should you choose?

The Middle Style   For most of your expository writing, the Middle Style is best—the clearest and the least pretentious. Not surprisingly, the majority of expository writing is still in this style. Since Middle-Style expressions are the common language of most of our thinking, these words usually come naturally to mind. Ordinarily, you will think and write *hurry,* for example, rather than *hasten, go* rather than *scram,* and there will be no problem in making your choice.

Nevertheless, there will be times when your first thoughts will not reflect the middle level. At these times a more formal or a more colloquial term will seem to conform most closely—most precisely—with what you want to say. It is then that the stylistic question arises: Should you go with the most precise term? The answer in most cases* would be yes.

The Learned Style   On the formal side, if you are addressing a scholarly subject and are writing for an audience that will understand your terminology, use the terms, however technical, that will most accurately convey your meaning. Similarly, if you find a word precisely reflecting your meaning that carries connotations appropriate to a more formal tone than the one you are trying to convey, then go with accuracy of meaning. Professional writers almost always do. Alan Katz, for instance, in "The Use of Drugs in America" (p. 472) does not hesitate to emphasize the term "passivity," though the word is not widely known in its technical meaning. Nor do other professional authors writing for the most part in the middle style avoid the formal, or even the learned, word when it best expresses their thoughts. E. B. White, for example, who is famous for his simple, lucid prose, consistently chooses the most precise expression—whatever level it might connote. In one sentence of his "Distant Music of the

---

*For a discussion of exceptions, see page 315.

Hounds" White enriches his prose with several rather learned expressions without ever abandoning the basic Middle Style he maintains throughout the essay:

> Christmas in this year of crisis must compete as never before with the dazzling complexity of man, whose *tangential* desires and *ingenuities* have created a world that gives any simple thing the look of *obsolescence*—as though there were something *inherently* foolish in what is simple or natural. (p. 498, *3*)

For another example, Shana Alexander, whose style is more informal than White's, does not hesitate to vary it with a learned word where appropriate. She describes chess champion Bobby Fischer, for instance, as "the *quintessential* smart boy of every school". (p. 436, *10*)

You should feel free to follow the example of these professional writers and choose your words because of the precision with which they express your meaning—even if from time to time you must use expressions that are more formal or more learned than the Middle Style.

The Colloquial Style Similarly, you may occasionally take the option of choosing words that are more colloquial than the rest of your prose. Sometimes a colloquial word or even a slang expression can come closer to your meaning than any other term. Or sometimes when you feel the tone of your work getting too stuffy—perhaps too scholarly, perhaps too intense—you can regain a more conversational flavor by including an informal expression or two. Professional authors vary their writing in this way. George Will, for instance, occasionally uses a colloquial word or phrase to relieve the intense tone of his argument or to add a conversational intimacy to his otherwise serious prose. In his deadly serious "Israel and Munich" article, for example, he writes

To add a conversational tone.

> Now, diplomacy always involves a lot of solemn nonsense, but Carter went a *tad* far. (p. 447, *8*)

Joan Didion similarly breaks the formality and the emotional emphasis of her balanced and metaphorical style in "Self-Respect" with the addition of an occasional colloquial phrase:

> To say that Waterloo was won on the playing fields of Eton is not to say that Napoleon might have been saved by a *crash program* in cricket. (p. 441, *10*)

Note that both *tad* and *crash program* convey their intended meaning with singular precision and that both phrases tend to enhance, rather than detract from, the established tone.

Your Decision Precision of meaning and of tone should be your criteria for deciding whether to include an expression that momentarily raises or lowers the general level of your style. If a word or phrase is not precisely to the point, or if it seems awkward in context, you risk having readers perceive it as affectation, a product of questionable motives. A word or phrase will also trigger similar criticisms in your readers if it seems to depart too abruptly from the tone you have established throughout the composition. If it appears inappropriately learned or technical, it will be judged (and its author will be judged) as pompous or pretentious. If you go too far in the other direction and select terms that your readers judge off-color or too slangy, your seriousness and your taste will be open to question. These are the dangers. And yet, in the past, a judiciously mixed style was warmly approved by no less an authority than Aristotle; and in the present, it can be a real delight—as a number of the essays in this book demonstrate.

To Control Your Tone

1. When you write expository prose, try to choose your words from a vocabulary rooted in the Middle Style.
2. Do not be afraid from time to time to select a more learned or a more colloquial word or phrase
   • when it allows you to express your thought more precisely.
   • when it offers an appropriate variation in your tone.
3. Be especially careful when you choose words and phrases from the extreme ends of the formality continuum (either very learned or slang). Such words can add pungency to style, but they are also capable of spoiling the overall effect.

━━━ Try It Out ━━━

Classifying Synonyms
Place the synonyms in these lists on a continuum according to the formality of their connotations. For at least two of the words, write sentences that clearly express their meanings and are internally consistent in tone.

Sample Problem:

Difficult, arduous, tough

Sample Solution:

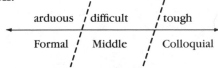

arduous / difficult / tough

Formal / Middle / Colloquial

• After his *arduous* climb, the hiker removed his boots and relaxed his weary limbs.
• It had been a *tough* day for all the kids.

1. skeert, fearful, skittish, timorous, timid
2. ease, effortlessness, facility, piece of cake
3. dexterity, skill, adroitness, savvy, know-how, ability
4. quibble, pussyfoot, bicker, dodge, equivocate
5. drink, imbibe, wet-the-whistle, quaff, tipple
6. effervescence, fizz, froth, foam

▬ **Try It Out** ▬▬▬▬▬▬▬▬▬▬▬▬▬▬▬▬▬▬▬▬▬▬▬▬▬▬▬▬

Rewriting for Level of Style

The following sentences are written in exaggerated versions of either the Formal (Learned) Style or the Colloquial Style. Rewrite them in the Middle Style by selecting words and phrases appropriate to that stylistic level.

Sample Problems:

- Cool it man. He's really with it.
- You tend to obfuscate the significance of your conceptualizations by utilizing unintelligible encoding.

Sample Solutions:

- Don't get angry. He understands the situation.
- You tend to blur the meaning of your thoughts by using language difficult to understand.

1. The butterfingered oaf seemed bound and determined to louse up the job.
2. Hang loose, Jack. I'll catch you on the backtrack.
3. Your inordinate capacity for public expectoration tends to nullify certain of your aspirations toward upward social mobility.
4. The incomparable absurdity attending your gyroscopic maneuvers makes you a farcical partner on the dance floor.
5. Your old lady's a real trip!
6. As I enumerate the unpalatable consequences of your proposed endeavor, I begin to abhor the entire prevailing circumstance.

Connotations of Value and Intensity Almost every English word not only expresses a particular connotation of formality or informality but also evokes a positive or negative response. This built-in value judgment varies widely. Synonyms of almost any noun, verb, adjective, or adverb can be arranged along a scale from highly positive to extremely negative and probably cover a number of gradations in between. Take, for example, this list of words roughly synonymous with "understanding" or "wise":

sagacious astute discerning knowing shrewd canny cunning sly slick

$\longleftarrow$

(positive)   (negative)

Should you want to use a word to represent an *odor,* you would have to decide just how good or bad a *smell* you intended before choosing one of the following:

fragrance bouquet aroma scent redolence rankness putrescence stench stink

$\longrightarrow$

(positive)   (negative)

Sometimes a scale of values is not so much a measure of good or bad as of the intensity of the value connoted. All of the following, for instance, have a connotation that is at least somewhat negative, yet there is a wide variance in the emotional intensity that is conveyed:

dishabille   disarray   disorder   messiness   dirtiness   sloppiness   squalor

←——→

(less intense)   (more intense)

Slant   Our outlook on any subject is expressed by the evaluative connotations of the words in which we choose to discuss it. As columnist Sydney Harris suggests,

> I am opposed to your "newfangled ideas" because I believe in "the value of tradition," but you are opposed to my "sensible reforms" because you are "blindly clinging to the past."
>
> My outburst was "indignation"; yours was "anger"; his was "petulance."
>
> I am "cautious"; you are "timid"; he is "cowardly."
>
> My crude friend is "a diamond in the rough"; yours is "a touch on the common side"; his is "a loudmouthed boor."
>
> The ceremony I approve of had "dignity and grandeur"; the ceremony I disapprove of had "pomp and ostentation."
>
> Our country is engaged in "security measures"; your country is engaged in an "arms race"; his country is engaged in "stockpiling weapons."
>
> I am a "realist" when I am doing to you that which, if you were doing it to me, I would call "ruthless."   ("Antics with Semantics: 5," *Leaving the Surface* [New York: Houghton-Mifflin, 1968], pp. 269–70.)

Harris's gentle irony points to the subjective quality of our language. This subjective quality is also known by the more negatively evaluative words "slant" or "bias." Since this quality is so universal—practically inevitable—I am not sure much is gained by strongly criticizing it. After all, an outlook may be biased and still be correct. A reasonable approach is first to acknowledge that every piece of writing (or bit of oral language, for that matter) has a built-in point of view, a built-in bias. Then, whenever you read or listen, you should try to discover the author's point of view as quickly as possible, so that you can take it into account as you form your own reactions to it. And whenever you write, you should be conscious of the slant inherent in your own words as you choose them.

You can even make your biases work for you. First, be aware of your own prejudices. Before attacking any writing job, examine your own thinking on the matter and determine exactly where you stand. If you are going to write about a legislative investigation, for instance, decide whether you regard it (to quote Harris again) as a "probe," a "fishing expedition," or a "witch hunt." If you are planning to analyze the beliefs of a social, political, or religious group, be straight with yourself as to whether you think of their ideas as "creed," "dogma," or "superstition" (p. 269). However you answer, acknowledge to yourself that this answer is inevitably slanted—at least to some extent—by the sum total of your life experiences. Then, having decided how strongly you want to project this point of view, select the words and phrases that will convey the particular slant you want to project.

Words and phrases selected in this way should both express your specific meaning and suggest the value you wish to put upon it. If, in addition, they can withstand the following qualifications, your chosen terms should serve you well.

Evaluating for slant.

Choosing Words and Phrases: A Checklist

1. Is the term appropriate to the subject you are writing about and the tone you have established?
2. Do you have sufficient evidence to support the value connotations your term suggests, as well as its specific meaning?
3. Will this term be so offensive to your audience that they will not be able to give a fair consideration to the thrust of your argument? (Chapter 4 goes into detail on the question of what is offensive language.)
4. Does this term both denotatively and connotatively reflect the truth as you view it? The answer to this question is important, even if you would wish to sidestep the questions of morality (though I am not convinced that a writer ever *can* sidestep such questions). Even the suspicion of insincerity in your reader's mind can rob you of your persuasive power—not only for the point at issue, but often for the entire composition.

When you can control the value connotations of the words you choose, you will command one of the most powerful features of rhetoric, since much of the persuasive ability of your prose lies here.

With power, however, should go responsibility. You should use this skill thoughtfully, for words can matter quite a lot. It can matter very much, for instance, to a careful worker whether she is evaluated as "conscientious" or as "meticulous" or as a "finicky fussbudget." And, for another example, it can matter to the conscience of a people whether they see their armies on foreign soil as "conquerors" or "liberators." It is thus truly important that you understand the value judgments inherent in the words you use and that you choose your words with care.

Try It Out

Arranging by Value

Arrange these sets of synonyms along scales from positive to negative *connotative value*. Then choose at least two words from each group and use them in sentences that clearly distinguish their meaning. Use your dictionary as needed.

Sample Problem:

scheme, plan, connive, conspire, plot

Sample Solution:

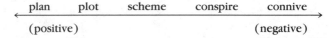

| plan | plot | scheme | conspire | connive |

(positive)   (negative)

- In an old inn where highwaymen once *conspired* together, the local Boy Scouts gathered to *plan* their next cookout.

1. sentimental, tender, warm-hearted, maudlin
2. generous, extravagant, unselfish, prodigal, wasteful
3. caution, cowardice, carefulness, plucklessness, chickenheartedness
4. inquire, question, examine, grill, interrogate, put through third degree
5. old, experienced, seasoned, senior, venerable, aged, senile
6. impulsive, capricious, impetuous, heedless, thoughtless, uncalculating, inconsiderate

Ordering by Intensity

Arrange the words in each of these sets in order of *intensity of meaning,* from the least to the most intense. Then use at least two of them in sentences that distinguish their meaning.

Sample Problem:

adversary, opponent, enemy, rival, antagonist

Sample Solution:

rival   opponent   antagonist   adversary   enemy

(least intense)   (most intense)

- The two boys were *rivals* in their studies, *opponents* on the sporting grounds, and in their maturity became deadly *enemies* on the field of battle.

1. apathy, indifference, callousness, dispassion, insensitivity
2. drizzle, downpour, rain, shower, deluge
3. falsify, lie, dissemble, be untruthful, fib
4. abandon, leave, forsake, withdraw, desert
5. interest, passion, concern, enthusiasm, absorption
6. disease, malady, pestilence, ailment, plague

Evaluating Synonyms

Find four synonyms for each of these words. Arrange the five terms in the order of least to most formal, least to most positive, least to most intense in meaning, or any other appropriate order. Clearly label the scale. Then choose at least two words from each set and use them in sentences that distinguish their meanings.

Sample Problem:

intemperate

Sample Solution:

immoderate   intemperate   indulgent   dissipated   debauched

(least intense)   (most intense)

- After many years of *intemperate* living, the Marquis de Sade surrendered himself completely to *dissipation.*

1. stale
2. competence
3. clumsy
4. curiosity
5. desire
6. flee

Try It Out

Rewriting For Connotation

Since words and phrases carry strong value connotations in addition to surface meanings, sentences with identical denotative meanings can evoke either positive or negative interpretations. Rewrite the following positive statements to convey an overall negative impression by substituting expressions with negative connotations.

Sample Problem:

- Thomas, who was included in neither gathering, was nonetheless concerned with the success of both enterprises.

Sample Solution:

- Thomas, who was invited to neither party, nonetheless officiously intruded in the planning.

1. The intriguing character of Laura's verse captivates her readers and wins their enthusiastic notice.
2. Jimmy danced about with eager anticipation as he breathed in the tangy fragrance of the bubbling stew.
3. As she slipped lightly into the puddle, Jan exclaimed with surprise.

Rewrite the following negative statements to convey positive impressions by substituting appropriate positively charged words and phrases.

4. The stubborn cop grilled the hapless suspect unmercifully.
5. Andrew took a cavalier attitude toward his scientific studies and, though able enough, performed his experiments in a frivolous, disdainful manner.
6. Grunting with disgust, Nan hurled the book onto the sod.

Writing Job Evaluations

For each of the people described in the following summaries, write three 1- to 2-sentence job evaluations. In each set, one evaluation should be positive, one neutral, and one negative.

Sample Problem:

Millicent Smythe does tidy, careful work. Her clothing is always bandbox fresh with never a hair out of place. Except for current work and a small green plant, Ms. Smythe's desk is completely clear. She reworks each assignment until it meets her own high standard.

Sample Solution:

- Millicent Smythe is an unusually conscientious worker, whose extra care produces exceptionally reliable work.
- Millicent Smythe is meticulous in her concern with the details of her work, which she executes in a neat, tidy fashion.
- Millicent Smythe is a finicky fussbudget, who concerns herself almost excessively with minutiae.

1. Jerome M. Caldwell is quick to accept the decisions of his supervisors and is diligent in carrying them out. He is always ready with a compliment or a pleasantry when in contact with his superiors, and he is readily available for such encounters. Caldwell wears a carefully groomed moustache.
2. Jennifer L. Peterson is the first to come in the a.m. and last to leave in the p.m. She brown-bags it at lunch with the most recent edition of the journal in her field. She socializes very little at the coffee machine. Ms. Peterson usually wears well-tailored tweed suits.
3. B. Michael Pennington has a hearty manner, a sturdy handshake, and a full knowledge of the latest stories and jokes. He always wears a vest and is often difficult to find at his desk. Both his expense account and his volume of sales are high.

ACHIEVING PRECISION THROUGH IMAGERY

So far this chapter has advised you to choose the words and phrases that most precisely capture the meaning of what you want to say. And this is good advice. But sometimes you cannot find a word or even a phrase that exactly conveys the meaning you have in mind. There are times when the word or phrase that could communicate exactly what you mean seems simply not to exist—especially when you are dealing with concepts that are not concrete (like "buildings," "huts," "two-toed sloths") but rather abstract (ideas such as "freedom"— to be "free," "freely"; feelings such as "love"—"to love," "loving," "lovingly"). If you question whether with all the abundant resources of the English language such a lack of vocabulary could actually be, then think of how you might describe, for instance, the feeling of nausea. Whenever I have asked students to try this experiment, they have always responded with facial grimaces, gestures of hands clutching throat or abdomen, and a chorus of moans and gargles sounding like "Yucch" or "Gwrrk." If someone starts a semimedical description ("There is a constricted feeling in my throat . . ."), he or she is inevitably booed down by those who feel that this sort of language is very far from what they are feeling. But when in frustration some people start sputtering "It's like . . . it's like . . .," they are coming very close to the answer. Because our language does not have the words and phrases to express all of our ideas and feelings directly, writers find that they sometimes need to be indirect, to tell instead what "it's like." They resort, in short, to comparison—to what we call "imagery" or "metaphor"—in order to communicate fully. Though imagery is the language of poetry, it can be very useful to the writing of prose as well.

The Objective Correlative

In order to use imagery effectively in your writing, you'll find useful a little technical understanding of what makes imagery work. The most helpful definition I know is T. S. Eliot's discussion of the objective correlative:

Definition.

> The only way of expressing emotion in the form of art is by finding an *objective correlative;* in other words, a set of objects, a situation, a chain of events which shall be the formula of that *particular* emotion; such that when the external facts, which must terminate in sensory experience, are given, the emotion is immediately evoked. ("Hamlet," in *Selected Essays 1917–1932* [New York: Harcourt Brace, 1932], pp. 124–25)

What Eliot is saying is that when you can't find the words to express a feeling or an abstract idea directly, you should look for something objective, something that can be understood by the senses, to compare your abstraction or feeling with. He calls this compared thing an *objective correlative.* (We'll call it "o.c." for short.) If you have chosen well, your o.c. will call up in your readers something very close to the indescribable feeling or idea you have been wanting to express.

How does it work? For example, let's take that feeling of nausea mentioned above. There is a stanza in "The Highwayman" where Noyes aims at conveying just such a feeling. In it he sets up an evil stablehand, a man full of sick fancies, as the betrayer of the dashing highwayman who is the hero of the poem. Noyes wants the image of Tim the osler literally to turn the reader's stomach:

> And dark in the dark old inn-yard, a stable-wicket creaked
> Where Tim the osler listened; his face was white and peaked;
> *His eyes were hollows of madness, his hair like mouldy hay,*
> But he loved the landlord's daughter, The landlord's *red-lipped* daughter,
> *Dumb as a dog he listened,* and he heard the robber say . . . .

If your response to these lines is similar to the way you felt when you attempted to express the feeling of nausea, then Noyes' objective correlatives of "mouldy hay" and "hollows of madness" worked for you.

The Forms of Imagery

Comparison is thus the basis of imagery. An image is a comparison. Writers have distinguished four forms of comparisons: metaphor, simile, connotative language, and symbol. Any image you compose will take shape in one of these forms. The forms differ because of the differences in the relationship of the o.c. to the idea it expresses. In **metaphor,** the o.c. is *equated* to the idea or feeling.

Directly or subtly there is always an equal sign. The o.c. is said *to be* the idea or feeling. In **simile,** the relationship is a little more distant. The o.c. is shown rather to be *similar to* the subject. The writer uses the word "like" or "as" to convey this similarity. With **connotative language,** the comparison is only implied by the connotations of the words used to express the ideas. And in **symbolism,** the o.c. has both a literal and a symbolic meaning—that is, at one time the o.c. both means itself and stands for something else, just as the American eagle is both a bird and a symbol of American strength and freedom. The accompanying boxed section illustrates how each of these forms works.

Imagery

Definition: Imagery is comparison. The image centers on an **objective correlative** (o.c.) to which the writer compares an indescribable idea or feeling to evoke a similar idea or feeling in the reader.

Forms of Images	Subject	Comparison	Objective Correlative (o.c.)
METAPHOR:	*Subject*	=	*o.c.*
Example:	Tim's eyes	"were"	"hollows of madness"
SIMILE:	*Subject*	*like (as)*	*o.c.*
Examples:	Tim's hair	"like"	"mouldy hay"
	Tim's listening	"dumb as"	"a dog"
CONNOTATIVE			
LANGUAGE:	*Subject*	*implies*	*o.c.*
Example:	Landlord's daughter's sensual attractiveness	implied by	"red-lipped"
SYMBOL:	*Subject*	=	*itself*
		AND *stands for*	*o.c.*
Example:	Tim, the osler	=	the stablehand, a character in the poem
		AND *stands for*	stealthy, unseen evil

Using Imagery in Expository Prose

Our examples so far have been taken from a poem, and it is true that imagery is the language of poetry. Nevertheless, metaphor (used in its general sense to mean all kinds of imagery) is also extremely useful for prose writers. For prose writers, like poets, sometimes also want to convey an inexpressible feeling and, more often than poets, need to clarify an abstract idea. Furthermore, since prose writers are not confined to the condensed language of poetry, they are free to expand and elaborate upon an image they find useful for their explanation. Each of these expansions has its own uses and its own name:

Expanded Images
Expanded metaphor = Extended metaphor
Expanded simile   = Analogy
Expanded symbol   = Allegory

The following quotations show how the authors of the essays in Part Five make use of the various forms of imagery. The examples should give you some ideas about how you too might employ these forms. The italic type throughout highlights the objects of comparison.

Examples of Metaphor
Metaphor with Directly Indicated Comparison

> To do without self-respect . . . is to be an unwilling *audience* of one to an interminable *documentary* that details one's failings, both real and imagined, with fresh *footage spliced* in for every *screening.*   (Joan Didion, p. 439, *4*)
> [Watching a movie rerunning one's life (o.c.) =   Agonies of retroactive self-
> disapproval]

Metaphors with Subtly Indicated Comparison

> The desert's *cancerous* growth.   (Fred Golden, p. 432, *5*)
> [An ever-growing cancer (o.c.) = The ever-increasing desert]

> *Contagious crossness.*   (George Will, p. 446, *1*)
> [The contagious quality of disease (o.c.) = tendency of one anger to kindle
> another]
> [The crankiness of ill-health or childhood (o.c.) = Discord among nations]

Extended Metaphor (Excerpts)
Here the comparison is extended or elaborated on. Not only is the subject equated to the o.c., but its qualities are spoken of in terms of the qualities of the o.c.

> Our *arsenals* for *fighting* off bacteria are so *powerful,* and involve so many different *defense mechanisms,* that we are in more *danger* from them than from the *invaders.* We live in the midst of *explosive devices;* we are *mined* . . . We are, in effect, at the mercy of our own *Pentagons.*   (Lewis Thomas, pp. 463, *9,* 465, *15*)

The subject field of metaphor is warfare: human beings and germs are adversaries.

O.C.s	Subject
fighting	= resisting disease
invaders	= germs
defense mechanism	
explosive devices }	= the body's natural disease resistors
mines	
Pentagon	= system that sets the resistance in motion

Examples of Simile

Scattered across a page (like) chocolate chips through a Tollhouse cookie. (Stegner, p. 500, *3*)

Seal the toilet seats (like) state secrets. (Thomas, p. 461, *1*)

To be driven back upon oneself is an uneasy affair at best, rather (like) trying to cross a border with borrowed credentials. (Didion, p. 438, *3*)

Analogy

The analogy, an expanded simile, permits the reader to view one set of ideas in terms of another:

(Just as) the Maya kept two calendars, one profane and one priestly, (so) Western science and religion fell into two different conceptions of the universe, two different vocabularies. (Morrow, p. 485, *1*)

(As) Czechoslovakia, a democratic country, was accused of mistreating the German minority in the Sudeten regions, (so) Israel, also a democratic country, is accused of mistreating the Arab minority. . . . (As) the creation of the Czechoslovak state after World War I was called a mistake by Hitler and Neville Chamberlain, (so) the creation of the Jewish state after World War II is called a crime by contemporary totalitarians and their appeasers. The insistence by the Czechs that surrendering the Sudeten regions to Hitler would leave Czechoslovakia hopelessly vulnerable was derided . . . (as) a shortsighted reliance on the false security of territory and arms; (so) a similar insistence by the Israelis . . . is treated today with lofty disdain. . . . Made malleable by diplomatic pounding, Czechoslovakia, by spring 1939, had no shield except "the conscience of the West," and no deliverance. (Will quoting Norman Podhoretz, p. 448, *10*)

Examples of Connotative Language   Almost all words that are not simply function words project various connotative meanings in addition to their literal or denotative meanings, as you learned earlier in the chapter. Connotative language becomes imagery when writers use the connotations of a particular word or phrase to stand as an objective correlative for the feeling or abstract idea they are trying to express.

The *coy fig-leaved* art [of Forest Lawn Cemetery] gives one goose flesh. (Plumb, p. 466, *1*)

["Coy, fig-leaved art" (o.c.) implies pseudo, maudlin art because it conjures up in the readers' minds visions of imitation Greek and Roman figures, whose original vigor has been thwarted by the prudery and bad taste of those who commissioned them]

We were supermen with *soiled collars* and holes in our pants (Ben Hecht, as quoted by Crist, p. 495, *10*)

["soiled collars" (o.c.) implies down-and-out gentility]

Examples of Symbolism
Symbolism with Directly Indicated Comparison

The *"isolation tank"* is as good a symbol as any of a time when we are making a positive value out of our sense of impotence in the world, and a cult out of the fragmentation of society and missed connections of our personal lives. (Goodman, p. 470, *4*)

Follow-ups throughout the Goodman essay:

- The new therapies—from the isolation tank on—offer us ways to "get into ourselves." (p. 470, 7)
- The "isolation tank" seems to suggest that the road to happiness, peace, ful-fillment, understanding, is an internal route. (p. 471, *8*)
- At a time when we seem in almost perilous need of personal connections, the tendency toward the isolation-tank psychology can be a sad perversion of the old American individualism. (p. 471, *9*)

["Isolation tank" (o.c.) = "an enclosed tank, with 10 inches of water heated to precisely 93 degrees and room for exactly one person" (p. 470, *2*) and stands for total self-absorption]

Symbolism with Subtly Indicated Comparison

People used to grow up with *trees,* watch them evolve from saplings to fruit bearers to gnarled and unproductive grandfathers. Now, unless one is a farmer or a forester there is almost no point to planting trees because one is not likely to be there to enjoy their maturity. (Tucker, p. 505, *8*)

Follow-ups later in essay:

(Tucker discusses the break in continuity in the lives of the divorced and con-cludes:)
There is great joy in watching a tree grow. (p. 505, *10*)

[Tree (o.c.) = a large leaf-bearing, wooden trunked plant and stands for stabil-ity and continuity in a disconcertingly fragmented world]

Images of Content

Though all images take the shape of one of the basic forms—metaphor, simile, connotative language, or symbol—images can vary enormously in content, in the nature of their objective correlatives. Many o.c.'s refer to the sense impres-sions of ordinary experience: "like bees among flowers" (Tucker, p. 505, *8*), "as a rabbit track in snow leads eventually to the rabbit" (White, p. 499, *4*). But as a shaper of images, you also have a number of other kinds of o.c.'s available to you. Three of the most useful of these are called *hyperbole, personification,* and *allusion.*

Hyperbole   If the emotion or the idea you want to express seems inexpres-sible because it is so big, so vast, so overwhelming, that it makes any regular image an understatement, and if only an exaggeration will do to convey that vastness, then you can turn to hyperbole. In hyperbole, the objective correlative is wildly exaggerated. George Will used hyperbole with reckless abandon in his essay on the Chicago Cubs:

Spring . . . became for me an experience comparable to *being slapped around the mouth with a damp carp.* Summer was like *being bashed across the bridge* *of the nose with a crowbar—ninety times. . . . .*My youth was like *a long rainy Monday in Bayonne, New Jersey.*   (p. 449, *5*)

The italicized o.c.'s all relate to what Will considers the unspeakable agony of a boyhood as a devoted Cubs' fan. Will phrases his hyperboles as similes. But they, like the other images of content, can be phrased in any of the forms. Judith Crist, for example, uses a hyperbolous metaphor when she writes that

> The copy desk is no longer the *graveyard* of old reporters with nowhere else to go.   (p. 496, *17*)

Personification   In personification, another image of content, the objective correlative is human. Personification thus adds human appeal to nonhuman objects by endowing them with the characteristics of human beings. There are two kinds of personification. One kind turns an abstraction into a human being, like the characters in the old morality plays: Faith, Hope, Charity, and Bad Deeds. This form, though perhaps used more extensively in past centuries, is not uncommon even today, and it is employed especially effectively with ironic intent. Shana Alexander, for instance, in characterizing the youthful affectations of the middle aged, writes:

> New hair sprouts, transplanted, on *wisdom's* brow.   (p. 434, *3*)

This sort of personification can also be used quite seriously. George Will, for instance, quotes Saul Bellow:

> *Moral judgment,* a *wraith* in Europe, becomes a full-bodied giant when Israel and the Palestinians are mentioned.   (p. 446, *4*)

The other kind of personification attaches human characteristics to the nonhuman. Lewis Thomas, for example, ascribes uniquely human activity to bacteria when he suggests:

> Most bacteria are totally preoccupied with *browsing.*   (p. 463, *8*)

And Saul Bellow (quoted in Will's essay) assigns human attributes to the world in this metaphor:

> Where Israel is concerned, the world *swells with moral consciousness.* (p. 446, *4*)

Allusion   Another way you can expand the metaphoric universe of your writing is to tint your o.c. with the unmistakable color of another piece of literature. Thus, through *allusion,* you include the world of the other work within your own. With an allusion you provide your readers with a shorthand "memo" that will take them to the work in question for the relevant idea and then back to your writing again. Joan Didion, for instance, condenses a description of her early view of herself into an allusion:

> I had somehow thought of myself as a kind of academic *Raskolnikov.* (p. 438, *2*)

Those readers who are familiar with Raskolnikov, the hero of *Crime and Punishment,* can understand from a phrase what might otherwise have taken several paragraphs to explain.

Allusion also helps readers experience the pleasure of recognition and of sharing their author's knowledge. As long as reader and author actually do share in the knowledge alluded to, allusion can be a highly persuasive strategy. Lance Morrow, for example, wittily uses a number of allusions in order to convince his readers of just how diverse the worlds of religion and science used to be. He begins "In the Beginning: God and Science" with a well-known folk expression:

> Science and religion were *apples and oranges.*   (p. 485, *1*)

He then builds on this commonplace definition by working it into an especially appropriate Biblical quotation:

> So the pact said: render unto apples the things that are Caesar's and unto oranges the things that are God's. *(1)*

Once Morrow has convinced his readers of his premise, he can go on with yet another allusion to insist upon the enormous improbability of science and religion reaching any kind of agreement on a subject as fundamental as creation:

> It is the equivalent of the Montagues and the Capulets collaborating on a baby shower.   (p. 485, *2*)

Those of his readers who understand how unlikely it would be for Romeo and Juliet's parents to get together for any such occasion smile knowingly to themselves in agreement; and Morrow's point is made.

Allusion is not confined to literary objective correlatives alone. With it you may draw in historical figures and events as well. Joan Didion, for instance, writes:

> *Of course,* I will play Francesca to your Paolo, Helen Keller to anyone's Annie Sullivan.   (p. 441, *11*)

Or again:

> To say that Waterloo was won on the playing fields of Eton is to say that Napoleon might have been saved by a crash program in cricket.   (p. 441, *10*)

Allusion can also be highly effective when used ironically. Shana Alexander provides the pastime of jogging with an exaggeratedly noble allusion to "America the Beautiful":

> Sages jog *from sea to shining sea.*   (p. 434, *3*)

And William Stegner uses Tennyson's famous description of Sir Galahad ironically to challenge the purity of heart of his foul-talking sophomore:

> *Her strength is as the strength of ten,* for she assumes that if one shocker out of her pretty mouth is piquant, fifty will be literature.   (p. 501, *6*)

The only problem in selecting your objective correlatives from history or literature is that such images rely more than any other comparison upon your readers' having shared your experience. If readers have had no personal contact with *mouldy hay,* for instance, they can still imagine enough about it to find meaning in the metaphor; but if they know nothing about Napoleon or have never heard "My strength is as the strength of ten because my heart is pure," not only do the Didion and Stegner images fall flat, but their authors' points may be weakened as well. Thus the question emerges: Should you use an allusion that goes right to the heart of what you want to say even though you are not sure that it will be understood by all your readers? With my bias for placing precision of meaning above all other considerations, I would have to say, yes, use the allusion that will precisely carry your point. But hedge your bets. In the phrasing of your allusion (or in addition to your allusion) include enough hints of your intended meaning to be sure that your readers will take your point. George Will, for example, ends his essay on the Cubs with a wonderfully witty *tour de force* of allusions. Those readers who recognize every quotation undoubtedly enjoy it most. Those readers (and they are probably in the majority) who find vaguely familiar echoes in his phrases should enjoy it thoroughly. But Will provides enough clues so that even those readers who are unaware of the source of any of his quotations, can still understand his meaning and can find the passage a pleasure to read:

Allusion	Source
Do not go gently into this season, Cub fans: Rage, rage against the blasting of our hopes.	Do not go gentle into that good night./Rage, rage against the dying of the light. ("Do Not Go Gentle into that Good Night," Dylan Thomas)
Had I but world enough, and time, this slowness, Cubs, would be no crime.	Had we but world enough, and time,/This coyness, lady, were no crime. ("To His Coy Mistress," Andrew Marvell)
But I am almost halfway through my allotted three-score-and-ten, and you, sirs, are overdue. (p. 451, *15*)	The days of our years are three score years and ten. (Psalm 90, Bible) Overdue. (Radio announcer quoted earlier in essay)

Creating Images

This review of the metaphoric possibilities open to you demonstrates the kind of precision of meaning you might be able to achieve by using imagery in your writing. But you may still be in some doubt about how to go about actually composing such images. First, metaphors and similes, and certainly connotative language, may occur to you spontaneously as you write. When they do, be bold. Add them to your writing just as they occur to you, even if they seem a bit showy at first. Remember, you can always go back and revise or even delete.

But what about the times when the images do not come, yet you feel a certain precision is missing in your prose that a good metaphor might take care of? At these times, you have two good sources: your subconscious and your conscious mind.

Searching Your Subconscious Mind   Try freewriting (see p. 42) on a point that is troubling you. Then examine carefully what you have written for bits and pieces of metaphors and subconscious images that may have come to you unaware. If you do freewriting on a regular basis, you can accumulate a storehouse of imagery to turn to as you need it.

Similarly, if you keep a journal, you can read back over your recent entries for ideas and associations. Even if you do not keep a journal with any degree of regularity, it is a good idea to keep a small notepad in your pocket or purse, so that if a striking comparison should occur to you while you are going about your activities, you will be able to preserve it for future use.

The poet, Donald Hall, who is also a teacher, recommends daydreaming as a place to start building your images. Because dreams put you in direct contact with your own image-making faculty, Hall believes they can be an especially rich source of metaphoric material. Hall suggests that you analyze your dreams for images and the words that accompany them. The crazier they are, he feels, the more fruitful these images are likely to be. Hall writes: "We may start dreaming; we end up thinking."*

Searching Your Conscious Mind   Your first step in a conscious search for imagery is to take your topic—or a person, place, or situation important to your topic—and deliberately associate physical objects and sense impressions with it. Make these associations as concrete and specific as possible. For example, if you were writing about rioting in the inner city, you might feel the need for an image to describe the tensions that occur just before a riot breaks out. By consciously employing your senses and your imagination, you might produce these associations:

> a street smelling of melting asphalt
> obscene grafitti on crumbling walls
> lounging figures
> the feeling of boredom
> the feeling of restlessness
> the rank odor of sweat and unwashed underwear
> unmirthful joking
> oppressive heat

Your second step, then, is to find an objective correlative that would make your associations real to your reader. Returning to our example, you might single out the oppressive heat and its triggering effect upon the riot and try it for various comparisons. What first comes to mind? Perhaps "hotter than blazes." But you would probably want to discard all such hackneyed phrases because their o.c.'s are so familiar that they no longer evoke sense images in readers' minds. You

---

Writing Well, 3rd ed. (Boston: Little, Brown & Co., 1979), pp. 110–11.

might also want to discard "as hot as a blast furnace" because it also may not seem like a fresh comparison to you or because it is not really an accurate description of city heat (that is, unless you decide to strive for hyperbole).

How do you find a fresh comparison? Search your recent memory. Where have you felt heat recently? Perhaps in a plant conservatory. You might try out:

> The atmosphere was hot and heavy with unfallen rain, like the perpetual moist heat of a conservatory of plants.

The conservatory is indeed a fresh comparison, and one that accurately describes the feeling of heat. But is it as completely appropriate a reference to your basic subject as you could find? The best metaphors take the reader beyond a simple sense comparison into the heart of the concept being considered. So why not try again? Can you remember another recent experience with heat? How about the heat you may have felt when walking by piles of burning trash? Why not try:

> The air was oppressive with the sort of acrid heat that surrounds a heap of burning rubbish.

Here your image is directly related to your basic subject matter and could also foreshadow your descriptions of the wanton fire-setting that will follow.

Though you may find the totally appropriate image difficult to discover, the result is certainly worth the effort. Total appropriateness of metaphor is one of the hallmarks of the professional writer. You will find it again and again in our collection of essays. J. H. Plumb, for example, achieves it in his selection of an image to express the enormity of the refrigerators that contain the frozen dead. He could have conveyed the notion of great size alone if he had chosen to write, "Refrigerators huge as elephants" or "huge as football stadiums." But he underlines the comparison fundamental to his point by writing "Refrigerators *huge as pyramids*", (p. 467, 5). Similarly when Joan Didion wants a way to convey the emptiness of a person who has no self-respect, she selects a close-to-perfect metaphor in "One eventually runs away to find oneself and finds no one at home." (p. 442, 12) *Seek total appropriateness in metaphors.*

Hidden Metaphors   Yet another way to develop your imagery is to make use of the metaphors hidden in the very words that must be used to discuss the subject. Many words in common use are actually metaphors. George Will, for instance, writes about "friction" in the relations between Israel and the United States. "Friction" literally means "the rubbing of one surface against another." Will puns upon that meaning to develop this striking image:

> Today *friction* between Israel and the Carter administration is *building up a dangerous charge of static electricity.*   (p. 446, 1)

Similarly Lewis Thomas, as noted earlier, bases much of the metaphoric system of his essay "Germs" upon a vocabulary of military confrontation. This whole system of imagery stems from the metaphors hidden in our ordinary speech about the body's "defense system" and the ongoing "fight" against disease. Thus, if you are having difficulty uncovering appropriate imagery, you might check to see whether any of your key words actually have more than one meaning. Perhaps you will be able to derive some useful imagery from the literal sense of such words.

Negative Metaphors   When you are bogged down in your efforts to discover an appropriate image for conveying an important idea, you might try thinking in negative rather than positive terms. Lance Morrow, for instance, uses a negative metaphor:

> Science is ⟨*not*⟩ *the cool Palladian temple of rationality* that it was in the Enlightenment. (p. 486, *6*)

Judith Crist employs a similar technique:

> The copy desk is ⟨*no longer*⟩ *the graveyard for old reporters* with no place else to go.   (p. 496, *17*)

Reviving Dead Metaphors   Sometimes the only kind of image that comes to you will seem too trite and cliché-ridden to be of any use. And it is true that though such expressions as "red as a rose" or "as bitter as gall" were once sharply evocative, they have been so widely employed that today they have lost most of their metaphoric power. (See p. 333.) The problem is that such clichés often come so automatically to our minds that they crowd out other ideas. If you find yourself in this difficulty, you will be glad to know that there are ways to put such dead metaphors to good use. Sometimes it is possible to revitalize the dead expression and make your readers think it through as they would an original image. By subtly acknowledging its familiarity, you can make that familiarity work for you. It is a matter of adding a well-chosen word or two and sometimes a certain tongue-in-cheek quality that can give the worn-out expression back its power. Note how these professional authors make use of this technique:

Grow old ungracefully. (Judith Crist, p. 494, *9*)	(From "to grow old gracefully")
Pick the cream of the ever-flourishing crop of applicants. (Judith Crist, p. 496, *18*)	(From "the cream of the crop")
Barely advanced beyond the bib-and-cradle stage, I plighted my troth to a baseball team destined to dash the cup of life's joy from my lips. (George Will, p. 449, *4*)	(From "plight my troth," "cup of joy," "dash the cup from the lips")
Lie down alone in that notoriously uncomfortable bed—the one we make for ourselves. (Joan Didion, p. 439, *4*)	(From "You have made your bed: Now you can lie in it.")

Practice Makes Inspiration?   Composing effective images is, of course, to some degree, a matter of inspiration. But inspirations come more often to a mind that is ready to recognize them, knows what to do with them when they arrive, and even has ways of encouraging their coming. The following sets of exercises are offered as the sort of practice that can lead to such receptivity.

==================================== **Try It Out** ========

Composing New Images

The following images have long ago lost their impact. Find a new simile, metaphor, allusion, or other image to illustrate each of these abstractions. Suggest a context in which your image would be appropriate.

Sample Problem:

Red as a rose

Some Sample Solutions:

- She blushed a painful tomato-juice red. (for an essay on vegetarians)
- Red as the cover of a copy of "Quotations from Chairman Mao" (for an essay on radicalism)

1. Pure as the driven snow
2. Green as grass
3. Ugly as sin
4. Bitter as gall
5. Dead as a doornail
6. Jolly as old St. Nick
7. Life is the pits.
8. They were heavy into [modern dance, for instance].
9. Hungry enough to eat a horse
10. The room was wall-to-wall people.
11. Richer than Midas; or He has the Midas touch.
12. Stubborn as a mule

Describing with Metaphors

Describe five of your classmates in metaphoric terms. Make one description into an extended metaphor.

==================================== **Try It Out** ========

Creating Personification

Try turning the following abstractions into personifications.

Sample Problem:

Laughter

Some Sample Solutions:
- "Laughter holding both its sides" (Milton)
- Her laughter hung in the air as if waiting for its presence to be recognized.

1. The sea
2. Autumn
3. Joy
4. Thirst
5. A computer
6. A mosquito
7. A guitar
8. A football

Creating Hyperbole

Create a suitable hyperbole for each of the following superlative situations.

Sample Problem:

A truly excellent fiddle player

Some Sample Solutions:

- "He fiddled all the bugs off a sweet potato vine."
- "He fiddled up a whale from the bottom of the sea."
- "He fiddled down a 'coon from a mile high tree." (Stephen Vincent Benet)

1. A child's really grimy face
2. An enormous sandy beach
3. True love
4. A politician with disgusting ideas
5. A delectable meal

Creating Allusions

Create at least two metaphors or similes for each of the following. Try to include as many allusions as you can.

Sample Problem:

Your favorite toddler

Some Sample Solutions:

- Holding the big bat determinedly in his tiny hands, Jamie stood at the plate, *a miniature Babe Ruth.*
- Two-year-old Susie, *like the dormouse at the Mad Hatter's Tea Party,* had the habit of falling asleep at the table.

1. One of your professors
2. A basketball triumph
3. An elderly relative
4. A scene from a movie or television drama
5. Your room
6. An idea of your choice

AVOIDING IMPRECISION

This chapter has detailed ways in which you can achieve precision of meaning by carefully choosing your words, phrases, and imagery. This goal of precision is well worth striving for, but sometimes deep-rooted habits or desires can prevent you from achieving it. The two most destructive tendencies are the desire to be impressive and the habit of lazy thinking.

Resisting the Desire to be Impressive

Although the desire *to impress* is a natural human wish that can be useful in your writing, the desire *to be impressive*—though equally human—is misguided and can produce the opposite of the wished-for results. Trying to be impressive often backfires because inexperienced writers tend to be mistaken in their notions about what sort of writing actually is impressive.

The Size Misconception   Probably the most important such misconception can be summed up in the catch phrase "Big is better." Those who subscribe to this notion think that a greater number of long words give their compositions an impressive tone. And so they search for opportunities to ornament their writing with the likes of "antidisestablishmentarianism." If a word they want to use does not seem impressive enough, they pile prefixes and suffixes on it until it reaches a satisfying length. By this means they create such unnecessary monstrosities as "directionality" or "scrutinization" as in "Our goal is to establish directionality in the development of educational programs" or "He gave the summary careful scrutinization." To get a word like "directionality," the writer had to begin with the perfectly good noun "direction" (which is already an extension of the verb "direct"), add a suffix to turn it into the adjective "directional," and add yet another suffix to turn it back into a noun again. If the writers of the sample sentences had not used the elongated terms, they would have produced writing both more direct and more effective:

- Our goal is to establish direction . . .
- He gave the summary careful scrutiny.

Many of those who try to impress by size also try to impress by quantity. They like to pile up adjective upon adjective, adverb upon adverb. Not content to make their point soundly once, they restate it again and again. Those who hold with this way of thinking seem to believe that if one figure of speech in a sentence is good, three are better and six are really terrific. In their writing you would find long passages of what is usually called "purple prose." These writers seem to share the mistaken idea that, since effective writing often involves touching the readers' emotions, they can achieve even greater effectiveness by wringing their readers' hearts. And the believers in quantity do not seem to understand that they can lessen the impact of any idea or device, however effective, by overdoing it. They overlook altogether the remarkable persuasiveness of honest simplicity.

Moderation is best.

The Oddity Misconception   Some inexperienced writers not only believe that "bigger is better," but also that "the more singular, the more significant." Unfortunately, the only words people generally consider unusual are words that are not comfortably lodged in their own vocabularies. We all tend to think of words that we know well and use without self-consciousness as ordinary. Thus, writers who wish to strive for unusual diction often find themselves forced to select for their writing words and phrases with which they are basically unfamiliar. Such writers comb their thesauruses for synonyms and often seem unaware that synonyms cannot be interchanged in all contexts. Actually, interchanging synonyms without regard to connotations or other nuances of meaning can be the source of downright embarrassing sentences. The following examples are typical:

> The nurse was *interminably* helpful. (Did the writer mean "unceasingly"?)
> She was well known for her *soporific* conversational style. (Did the writer mean "relaxed"?)
> The graduate's father glowed with paternal *superciliousness.* (Could the writer have meant "pride"?)

Guide to Using a Thesaurus

1. Use your thesaurus to spur your memory when you have a word on the "tip of your tongue," but aren't able to bring it to your conscious mind.
2. Try your thesaurus when you have used a word several times and you feel you are beginning to establish a repetitive pattern.
3. Do not use your thesaurus to find a word that will seem more impressive than your original term.
4. And most importantly, NEVER select from a thesaurus a word that you do not already use comfortably and that you do not already have in your working vocabulary.

Simpler Really Is Best   Throughout this chapter I have insisted that your best choice is that word or phrase—whatever its length or degree of familiarity—which most precisely expresses your meaning. And such precision should remain your chief goal. Nevertheless, an important exception must be made: Since the whole purpose of precise wording is to communicate your thoughts, communication itself must always be your most important consideration. If, for instance, you know that a word like "antidisestablishmentarianism" most precisely conveys your meaning, but you have reason to believe that much of your readership would not have that expression in their vocabularies, then you would be wise to trade precision for understanding and select a briefer, more widely known, term.

In fact, because of the desire of most modern readers for speedy comprehension of their reading material, you should probably conclude that, where there is a choice, smaller and simpler is usually better. The eye takes in the small word quicker than the longer, and the mind decodes and processes the more familiar term faster than the more unusual word. For these reasons, large, long, and complex wordings not only do *not* impress but, by impeding reading, can actually annoy readers. Readers who feel bored, confused, or intimidated are not likely to see the writer as an impressive chap, but rather as an inconsiderate show-off. The truth is that even the best-chosen diction that aims at being impressive tends to divert its readers' attention and thus to distract from the subject matter. In general, therefore, good writing, like good acting, should move its audience without calling too much attention to itself.

Try It Out

Editing for Simplicity

Edit the following sentences by choosing words and phrases that are less pretentious or less emotionally charged.

Sample Problem:

> Insofar as excessive trepidation will incapacitate my vocational advancement, I will endeavor to vanquish this inadequacy.

Sample Solution:

> • I will try to get over my shyness because it may harm my career.

1. The fragile Dolly-Lou was rendered prostrate by the callous insensitivity, hard-heartedness, and searing cruelty of Joe's cold-blooded indifference.
2. The guilt-ridden child went back to school intending to obliterate, exterminate, eradicate, and annihilate all signs of yesterday's mischief.
3. Consequently, the operator of the motor vehicle determined that it would be advantageous to maneuver his conveyance to a position perpendicular to where it was now located.
4. He gazed into her eyes with fervent ardor, his limbs trembling, his heart beating wildly, forlornly hoping against hope that Susan would choose to sit at the empty desk next to his.
5. Last evening's frankfurter occasioned the production of intermittent cadences in my abdomen, a condition whose immediate cessation I profoundly coveted.

Lazy Thinking

Another important obstacle to using precise diction is the almost universal human tendency to be lazy in our thinking. Such laziness accounts for most of the repetitiveness and wordiness that mar so much written work. We don't want to make the effort to come out with the phrase that exactly expresses what we have on our minds, so we include a number of similar wordings, each of which comes near to what we really want to say. Careful editing should clear up this problem; but again out of sheer laziness, most of us don't bother to keep on striving for a single precise expression but settle instead for a half dozen near misses.

Clichés   Lazy thinking is also behind the unfortunate tendency of so many writers to compose in clichés. Clichés are automatic verbal responses that carry almost no meaning. They are the fixed phrases that come to mind before we *"Filler" clichés.* give a subject serious thought. Some clichés are fillers, empty words that hold the space while we wait for our ideas to come together:

- In this day and age. . .
- When all is said and done. . .
- As luck would have it. . .

Others are sets of words that seem "sort of to *belong* together," one word triggering the whole phrase. *The Harvard Lampoon** (with tongue in cheek) suggests the following as "phrases [that] occur only as indivisible units, even though they appear to be constructed of discrete words":

Avoid automatic phrases.

furtive glance
limpid pools
abject poverty
catlike quickness
lightning-quick reflexes
waning interest
insurmountable odds

Other such automatic phrases have the further disadvantage of being redundant (see p. 133); that is, part of the phrase necessarily implies another part. Nonetheless we continue to use the parts together because one word seems naturally to summon up the rest. Here are a few typical examples:

Redundant automatic phrases.

evening sunset (or "morning sunrise")
white snow
high mountains
at this point in time (Either "at this point" or "at this time" would do. Why use both?)

Lazy thinking of this sort can trigger responses so automatic that they border on gibberish. I have known writers lazy enough to produce such nonEnglish as "Doggy-dog world" and "Watch pot." These phrases resulted from incoherent attempts to recreate "Dog-eat-dog world" and "A watched pot never boils," themselves clichés of the most overused kind.

The Harvard Lampoon Big Book of College Life, Stephen G. Crist & George Meyer, eds. (Garden City, N.Y.: Doubleday, 1978), p. 108.

But clichés do not start out as clichés. On the contrary, when most of these phrases were introduced, they were so effective at conveying their points that they were used again and again. Over the years they simply lost their meanings. Many clichés are dead metaphors that had their origin in colloquial speech. You may recall that truly original way of describing an overcrowded room, that has already died from overuse: "wall-to-wall people." Other examples include:

bite the bullet
the name of the game
game-plan
heavy into
gross
sight for sore eyes
the pits

Dead metaphors.

Other clichés are made from words that have succumbed to the tendency of language to become more general in meaning. Though such terms have precisely defined meanings, these meanings are rarely intended by those who use them, as the accompanying table shows.

Word	Meaning	Usually used to mean
nice	precise	having a positive quality
classic	having stood the tests of time	very nice
adorable	fit to be worshipped	extremely nice
divine	fit to be worshipped	extremely nice
fantastic	having to do with fantasy	wildly nice

If you are to aim for precision in your diction, clearly you will have to learn to avoid such clichés. But how can you tell when you have written a cliché? Whenever a word or a phrase seems to come automatically to your mind, you should check it objectively for both literal and figurative meaning. If it evokes no specific or appropriate sense image in the context in which you want to use it, you can be fairly sure you are burdened with a stock phrase or a cliché.

Try It Out

Editing for Freshness
Test the following sentences for the presence of stock phrases or clichés. If you discover any, edit them out, and rewrite the sentence in a fresher, more effective way.

Sample Problem:
Meryl regretted that his chances for advancement were so *few and far between*.

> ### *Some Sample Solutions:*
>
> - Meryl regretted that he had such infrequent opportunities for advancement.
> - Meryl regretted that chances for his advancement came up so rarely.
>
> 1. Joe and Mabel were determined to devote their retirement to pursuing the finer things in life.
> 2. Although the mountain climber noticed the sky becoming dark and stormy, he resolved to stay on until the bitter end.
> 3. Felicia took advantage of this golden opportunity to get some rest, and so she went back to her room, where she turned on her radio and lounged around to her heart's content.
> 4. Last, but not least, we will discuss the bill pending in the state legislature.
> 5. After the 1980 election, Carter returned to Georgia, where he was gone but not forgotten.
> 6. In the months following each of Mt. St. Helens's eruptions, plastic vials of volcanic ash were selling like hotcakes.
> 7. Unlike her predecessors, Katherine Parr, Henry VIII's last wife, survived her experience in good spirits and went into her widowhood none the worse for wear.
> 8. The diplomat showed his true colors when he began playing fast and loose with his country's economic commitments.
> 9. Nowadays it goes without saying that getting involved in a deep and meaningful relationship is easier said than done.
> 10. As luck would have it, the newlyweds had many trials and tribulations trying to make ends meet in this day and age.

Gobbledygook

Authorities agree that the kind of diction that most interferes with precision of expression today is the pompous nonsense that has been humorously termed "gobbledygook." Gobbledygook has its roots in *jargon,* the inhouse terminology of a variety of disciplines that, even wrenched from its technical context, manages to maintain a pseudo-technical ring. Such terms, for instance, as *peer group, fixation, goal-directed,* and *function,* from the field of psychology, or *feedback, input, breakthrough,* or *interface,* from computer science, are characteristic of jargon. Gobbledygook results when such terms are combined (most often in twisted and unnecessarily complex syntax) with elongated words and forced diction. Typical of such expressions are

prioritize	utilize	render operative	take cognizance of
maximize	potentiate	causative factors	energize
facilitate			synergize

The use of gobbledygook presents one of the most persistent stylistic problems, because this imprecision combines both of the obstructive habits of thought we've discussed: lazy thinking and the desire to be impressive. Because of its "in" quality, such pseudo-technical vocabulary quickly becomes popularized, turning into the sort of readily available stock expressions so tempting to our lazy minds. This faddishness also reinforces the notion that the use of jargon provides its user with an impressive image. Inexperienced writers adopt it to enhance their authority.

The truth is that far from making an impressive show, the user of such gobbledygook has become something of a figure of fun, fair game for the comedian's and the cartoonist's barbs, as the accompanying Goosemyer cartoon shows.

GOOSEMYER   **by parker and wilder**

GOOSEMYER by Parker and Wilder © 1980 Field Enterprises, Inc. Courtesy of Field Newspaper Syndicate.

You are well advised to use a technical word when your purpose requires a technical meaning, but you should avoid a specialized term when a nontechnical word will convey all you mean to say. There are very few occasions, for instance, when "utilize" would convey your meaning more precisely than "use"; when "transmit" would be more meaningful than "send"; or when "terminate" would be preferable to "end."

━━━━━━━━━━━━━━━━━ Try It Out ━━━

Eliminating Gobbledygook

Edit the following sentences by eliminating the gobbledygook and rephrasing in a clear and meaningful way.

Sample Problem:

> Mr. Farnestock, I believe at this point in time that a logistical interface of management referendums would be of significant manifestation.

Sample Solution:

> • Mr. Farnestock, I think now would be a good time to discuss ways of putting management's proposals into practice. (See the cartoon on page 137.)

1. Multiple modular capabilities form the basis for a support system which contributes to the implementation of a variety of facilities.
2. A conceptual performance analysis would tend to maximize communications compatibility at this point in time.
3. Incremental opportunities for interface should yield dynamic operational capacities within the parameters of a conducive environment.
4. Professor Mason is cognizant that, performancewise, the overall facilitation of the input in this area will not obviate the necessity for a sequential utilization of the backup system.
5. The executive committee attempted to reconceptualize the implementation of the remuneration procedures pursuant to a multiplicity of contingencies.

A Final Word on Style

In these chapters on style, I hope you have come to see that an appealing style is neither accidental nor beyond your reach. You mold your style by the decisions you make in specific choices of syntax and diction. Those decisions are most successful that make your meaning clearer and more accessible to the reader. In choosing your syntax, you should construct your sentences with rhythms that are both harmonious and varied and with a rhythmical emphasis that coincides with your purpose and your point. In choosing your diction, you should select the words and phrases that most precisely express what you want to say. In general, when other considerations are equal, you should aim for the simpler, shorter, clearer word or structure. All this advice is fundamentally sound; yet it may well be that H. L. Mencken's counsel is even more useful:

> The essence of a sound style is that it cannot be reduced to rules—that it is a living and breathing thing, with something of the devilish in it. ("Literature and the Schoolma'm," *Prejudices: Fifth Series* [New York: Knopf, 1926], p. 197)

ASSIGNMENT

1. Write an essay in which you put into words an insight you have gained or a set of ideas you have come to understand in one of your other courses. Define your point carefully and explain and support it by specific reference to the facts upon which it is based.

    Because you will be dealing with ideas and the relationship of facts to ideas, you may be confronted with the problem of vagueness. It will, therefore, be especially important for you to choose your diction so as to express your meaning with as much precision as possible.
2. Choose one word that has interesting meanings—denotative and connotative—associated with it. Learn all you can about the word through dictionaries (especially the Oxford English Dictionary [O.E.D.]), dic-

tionaries of slang, histories of the English language, and other references available in your library. Draw associations with the word from your own experience (free-writing or brainstorming may help). Then formulate a thesis based on all the ideas you've gathered and write an essay. Here are some words that are interesting to me:

romance	spectacle	circus	guest
fantastic	deem and doom	chamberlain	

Here's a sample introduction and thesis for one such essay:

> I always thought what I'd been reading in the lawn swing over summer vacations were "romances." You know, those dollar novels with pictures of impassioned, embracing (or near-to-embracing) couples in a tidy, vine-scrolled frame on the cover. But when my medieval lit teacher assigned a "romance," I found that this kind of reading was another story altogether. Knights and legends and wan fair maidens were a far cry from a modern breezy couple finding each other among the dunes by a secluded beach house. Despite the obvious differences, though, there's still a touch of the medieval in the modern word "romance."

Part Four

Writing Special Kinds of Essays

"Here is the term paper assignment for the course. The topics listed will require some research, so I suggest you spend a lot of time in the library between now and the due date. I want the paper by . . . ." And so may begin the research paper assignment for any course you have. In literature courses this assignment may take the form of a "critical analysis" paper. In any case, you will need to know how to go about considering your topic, doing library research, reading critically and closely, taking notes, actually writing the paper, and documenting your sources.

The two chapters in Part Four will give you the background you need to complete this kind of assignment successfully. The guidance offered here is general enough to be applicable to all of your courses and specific enough to be of practical use in the actual preparation of your paper.

9
The Research Paper

There comes a time—sometimes quite early in your college career—when you can no longer write from your personal experience alone, when you must turn to books or other sources to find your information. And suddenly you are writing a research paper. You find that you are no longer in the freewheeling realm of individual writing but rather in the highly conventionalized territory of scholarly research. In this territory you are obliged to play by the scholars' rules. And, if you are like most inexperienced writers, you probably don't know these rules. This chapter aims to help you learn them.

THE PRINCIPLE OF THE THING

You might not even be sure of what exactly a research paper is. Let's begin with a definition:

A research paper is a specialized form of expository writing in which a writer attempts to add to the accumulation of the world's scholarship by making some definite statement based upon a careful study of already existing data or ideas on a particular topic.

Expository Nature of a Research Paper

The scholarly research paper, then, is basically an *expository essay,* the same sort of essay we have been discussing throughout this book. Its nature, like that of all expository writing, is the development of a point, a thesis. In most cases, writing a research paper is much like writing other sorts of expository prose— you set out your thesis in an introduction, support it logically in the body of the paper, and restate it most convincingly in the conclusion.

Expository Nature.

Scholarly Purpose of a Research Paper How then is the scholarly research paper distinguished from other expository writing? The difference lies partly in its purpose, for the goal of research is an attempt "to add to the accumulation of the world's scholarship." This goal may at first strike you as far-fetched. You may wonder how any paper you might produce right now could serve so lofty an end. Yet, when you think about it, you may discover that by finding out what has been said on a topic and by taking it one step further, or at least by considering it in writing from a new and individual point of view, you really do contribute to scholarship in general. And although you may never have considered yourself a scholar before, in doing research and writing it up, you in fact become one. For research is what scholars do, and writing research papers is one way scholars talk to each other. Although the chances may be slight that your first research paper will be among those few beginning papers each year that form the kernel of later dissertations or scholarly articles, still, by following the methods and conventions of research in writing these early papers, you are gaining the key that will open up the world of scholarship to you.

Special Sources of a Research Paper   The most important difference between the research paper and other forms of expository writing is the source of its subject matter. Instead of writing from personal knowledge, in the research paper you will be basing your work and your conclusions upon *a careful study of already existing ideas or data.* The most difficult part of writing a research paper is distinguishing between these ideas and your own comments and conclusions. Scholars have worked out research procedures and writing conventions to help you keep the distinguishing line clearly drawn. These procedures and conventions are what cause a research paper to appear to be so different from other sorts of expository prose. Yet they are the most helpful tools you have for writing a successful research paper.

A Basic Assumption—A Moral Obligation

With the research paper thus defined, there are practical principles to keep in mind as you set out to write. These principles concern the authorship of your paper. Who is the author of your research paper? You are. Whose point will you make in its thesis and support throughout the paper? Your own. Despite the fact that you will be working with other people's ideas, sometimes even with other people's words, you remain the single force, the unifying intelligence behind your paper. You are the only person sitting in the driver's seat.

Even if you are working with a subject that is completely new to you, a YOU are the subject so unknown that you necessarily find yourself heavily dependent upon author. the thoughts of others, in writing your research paper you must make yourself master enough of the new material so that the way you present the work, the way you structure the ideas, will be exclusively your own. And even if you find yourself quoting or paraphrasing extensively, your thesis statement (and ordinarily most of the surrounding introduction and conclusion) should be in your own words exclusively. Similarly, all of your topic and subtopic sentences as well as all of the sentences introducing your quoted or paraphrased source material must be completely your own. For better or for worse, you are uniquely the author of your research paper.

Because your research paper is so exclusively your own, its readers have every reason to assume that all phrasing and ideas not definitely assigned to someone else were created by you. You are thus obliged to acknowledge explicitly the source of all ideas and all wording that comes from someone besides yourself. To give you some notion of the seriousness of this obligation, I prefer to speak plainly. Permitting the words or ideas of others to pass as one's own is a particularly ugly form of theft called "plagiarism." Some people, in fact, view plagiarism as even more immoral than ordinary theft. They argue that while ordinary thieves steal only material objects, plagiarists steal thoughts and ideas—surely substances of far greater worth.

As a writer of a research paper you are under strong moral obligation not to quote so much as a two-word phrase without acknowledging the mind who created that phrase. But questions of morality aside, crediting your sources is of value to you because it makes your paper more persuasive. Every time you cite or refer to the author of a quoted or paraphrased passage, you add to your own so-far unrecognized voice the weight and authority of the voices of the well-known people who have influenced your thinking.

ESTABLISHING YOUR TOPIC

Your first major step in working on your research paper is choosing your topic. It is possible that your instructor has relieved you of this responsibility by assigning a specific topic. Or it may be that when you learned of the general subject, a specific question related to it, perhaps one that you have long been interested in pursuing, came immediately to mind. On the other hand, you may be approaching the whole problem with a blank mind. Research papers are often assigned before you have had an opportunity to become acquainted with the subject. In any case, there are at least five standards by which you can judge how good a research project is likely to develop from a particular topic:

1. The topic (an aspect of the assigned subject) should truly intrigue you. You should have enough genuine curiosity about this topic to continue your interest in it through much reading and over the considerable length of time you must expect to spend in its company.

2. Ideally the topic should be narrow enough for you to be able to consider all the available resources on it. If this goal cannot be met, then you can narrow your approach at least to the point that you can make yourself expert on that portion of your subject which most concerns you.

Standards for evaluating potential topics.

3. The topic you select for investigation should show potential for yielding a possible thesis. In fact, even at this early state you may want to project a supposed or presumed thesis (often called a "hypothesis"). But if you do start your investigations with a specific hypothesis in mind, always remember that it is only a hypothesis, and keep your mind open to other possibilities that may occur to you as you probe more deeply into your subject.

4. The topic you pick should be one for which the necessary resources are available to you. The books, magazines, or printed records you

need should be obtainable from the library you have access to. If your topic needs nonprint resources, they also should be where you can obtain them.

5. In particular, you should be able to see *primary source material* on your topic. Primary sources contain the material that is "straight from the horse's mouth." If you are writing on the Civil War, for instance, you might find primary source material in the official documents of the political leaders, the diplomats, and generals who supervised the war effort or in the diaries and letters of the soldiers who fought in it, or in the poems, stories, journals, or histories of contemporary observers, whether they were scholars, novelists, or the woman- or man-on-the-street. Primary source material is always the most direct, most relevant material. Usually, the more heavily a writer relies upon such sources, the more interesting will be the resulting paper.

6. It is also often useful to have *secondary source material* available on your topic. Secondary source material discusses or interprets primary sources. When you read a modern history of the Civil War or a critical study of *Hamlet*, you are reading secondary material. Your own research paper, if you base it mainly upon primary sources, will itself be a secondary source. Although you probably will not want to quote much from secondary material, you should find it useful in helping you interpret your topic. More important, secondary works sometimes offer the best opportunity you will have to examine the primary material that is not available to you locally. Although the secondary authors select the material they quote to fit their own theses, you may find much of the material they do quote valuable.

Beginning Your Search

Where do you begin to find information on your topic? Especially if you are unfamiliar with the assigned subject, you will need to get some preliminary information just as quickly as you can. A good starting place is an article on the subject in an encyclopedia. There you will most likely find a comprehensive survey of the subject, a list of related articles, and a bibliography for future research. In your library's card catalogue, another good starting point, you can discover what your library offers on the subject. After selecting a few likely books, you might browse through them and try to define a question on which to focus your research.

Preliminary browsing can help you define your research question in one of two ways. On the one hand, you might want to pursue one of the questions about your subject that has intrigued previous scholars. Even skimming material on a subject most often reveals the issues related to it that have been of greatest scholarly concern. Most of the writers on the subject of Shakespeare's *Hamlet*, for instance, have dealt with the critical question of what causes Hamlet's delay in revenging himself on his father's murderer. And many students of concentration-camp psychology have pondered why the victims of camp atrocities have so seldom risen up against their captors. If such central scholarly questions about your subject should interest you, you could devote your research to investigating the varying opinions put forth as answers to them, then evaluate these answers, and perhaps arrive at a comparable opinion of your own. If, on the other hand, such long-standing questions do not appeal to you, your preliminary readings may lead you to an aspect of your subject which, though it has attracted little earlier attention, is intriguing to you and about which you would like to learn more. In this case you would then need to define your own investigative question. In either case, your research project will be a search for a satisfying answer to your question. And the thesis of your paper will embody this answer.

Try It Out

1. Imagine that you have been assigned one of the following general subjects from which to choose your research paper topic. Your first task will be to narrow it to workable size.

   Hamlet   Quakers
   Nazi concentration camps   General Robert E. Lee
   The poems of Robert Frost   Dyslexia

   a. Read an article on one of these subjects in a major encyclopedia, and suggest three specific issues or questions that you feel would offer good possibilities for research.
   b. Browse through four books (or articles) listed in the bibliography accompanying the encyclopedia article or four listed in your library's card catalogue. Again suggest three potential research questions.
   c. Compare your sets of questions from exercises *a* and *b*. Are the sets identical? If not, how do they differ? Is the second set more narrowed, more precise?

2. Since primary source material is ordinarily the best source material, you will want to identify the primary sources for research on your topic. Where might you find primary source material to help you answer the following research questions?
   a. How did the critics first react to *Gone With the Wind* when it was originally shown in 1939?
   b. During her lifetime, was Madame Curie given the same recognition as her husband, Pierre?
   c. What were James Joyce's methods of writing?
   d. How did the beliefs of the early Puritans differ from those of the members of the traditional Church of England at that time?
   e. How will the most recent budget voted by Congress be likely to affect the U.S. economy?

THE CRUCIAL NOTE-TAKING STEP

Once you have a fairly clear notion of the specific question you want to investigate, you are ready to start taking notes. Note-taking is the most critical procedure involved in a research-writing project. In fact, failure to master this skill will almost certainly result in disaster. Let me tell you a sad story about a typical student who was confused about note-taking.

Tale of the Confused Notetaker

Once upon a time a research paper was assigned. The very next day we find a jean-clad figure sitting in the library hunched up over his notebook. Intensely concentrating, he pushes an unruly lock of hair out of his eyes and gets a firmer grip on his pencil. Several heavy books with dark covers and small print lie open before him, and he works with each in turn. "P. Q. Snerd, *The Vanishing Aardvark,*" he dutifully copies at the top of a page from a loose-leaf notebook and dutifully adds the name of a publishing house, its city and a date. "Pp. 86–93" finishes the heading. He then turns to page 86, glances at it and begins to scribble rapidly. Skipping *the, and,* and *however,* abbreviating lengthy constructions, and omitting difficult words and dull arguments, the student reproduces—more or less—what Snerd had written. As ideas come to him, the student, pleased with his understanding and insight, writes them on the same sheet. Once in a while he attempts to paraphrase a sentence, always carefully preserving its essential structure or its distinctive wording. When he has filled a loose-leaf page from the chapter by Snerd, he turns to a book by Smith and fills two more pages in the same way. He repeats the process with the works of Jones and Brown. Then, feeling shyly satisfied with his good day's work, he packs up his notebook and wends his way home. The days pass, filled with the usual college joys and sorrows, and suddenly the due date for his paper is very close. The student turns eagerly to his notes. But he finds he is no longer able to remember which words and ideas are his and which are Snerd's (or Smith's or Brown's). Nevertheless, the student knows that from these notes a paper must be constructed, and he begins writing.

*　　*　　*　　*　　*

This story of the beginning of a research paper has only two possible endings; both of them are sad. In one ending, the student reads over his notes and rather likes them. "Not bad at all," he thinks. And so, leaving the notes basically "as is," he corrects them for spelling and punctuation, affixes the appropriate footnotes, and creates his first draft. All that is needed further is to write transitional sentences connecting the sequence of sources to one another, to copy these pages neatly, and to turn in the finished research paper.

In the other ending to the story, the student reads over his notes and falls in love: "Snerd really has it. She is totally right. She says just what I have always thought!" (or "She says just what I have wanted to say.") But what to do? The prof insists that at least four sources be cited. The answer our student finds is to use Snerd as the base of the paper and to fit in a little of Smith and Jones and Brown where they seem most natural.

The first of these papers is organized according to the order in which our student chanced to read his sources. The second follows the structure of a botched version of a single author's arguments. Both papers, despite their footnotes, can be technically considered plagiarized. Since the poor student could not know where his words ended and those of his sources began, he could not mark off quotations. Thus, much of the wording that would seem to be his own was actually written by someone else. The structure of the second paper is also plagiarized. And the first paper has no structure at all. Neither paper, in short, offers anything to reward all the time and effort that went into its creation.

The bad news is that such papers as both of these are the almost inevitable results of the student's rather typical note-taking methods. The good news is that the proper use of notecards can solve the problems of random organization and unconscious plagiarism, which so badly mar many student papers. Skillful note-taking can also make research and writing a good deal easier.

Purpose of Notecards

The immediate purpose of notes is to serve as a memory aid, a way to keep the information you need readily available to you long after the source books, journals, and magazines have been returned to their shelves and the people you have interviewed are no longer available. Scholars do their note-taking on index cards (usually the 4×6 size). You may well wonder how the form in which you store your information could make any difference. Yet surprisingly, when you try to use note cards, you will find that they do make a remarkable difference. Only note cards permit you to record facts and ideas individually, separate from the original author's arguments. Only when each item can be considered on its own does it become the sort of raw material you can integrate with your own creative thinking on the issue you are yourself pursuing.

The eventual purpose for notes is to serve as the "inventory of ideas" (see Part One), from which you will define your thesis and organize your paper. *Individual items of raw material.* Only separate note cards can give you the advantage of relating ideas to one another in a physical way. You can arrange your cards in appropriate stacks. And you can test out the effectiveness of various organizational schemes by simply rearranging the stacks of cards. With note cards your inventory of ideas is in concrete form.

Note cards can, finally, be of great use to you when you credit your sources within your research paper, as well as when you document them in your footnotes and bibliography. Note cards are, in fact, the most effective way of keeping "what is mine" cleanly separate from "what is thine," the thorniest problem researchers face.

Basis for accurate documentation.

Fool-proof Note-taking

1. Make two different kinds of cards: Bibliographical Cards and Note Cards.
2. Bibliographical Cards are straightforward recording. They contain all the information you will need to make your bibliography plus the library code number. (See Figures 1 and 2.)

Author
Title of Book
City of Publication: Name of
Publisher. Copyright Date

Edition?
Editors?   Library
Translator?   Code Number

FIGURE 1. Bibliography Card for a Book

Author
"Title of Article"
Name of Magazine or Journal
Volume, Date, Pages

Library Code Number

FIGURE 2. Bibliography Card for a Journal or Magazine

3. Note cards, however, demand care. Give each of your note cards a three-part structure with an option for adding a fourth part. Figure 3 shows this structure.

Summary Heading
Author, p.

Me:

1. A brief heading summarizing the contents of the card
2. The author's last name and the number of the page on which the recorded material was found
3. The note itself
4. (Optional) Your own comment on the note

FIGURE 3. Four-part Note-card structure

4. Record only ONE idea on each note card.
5. Limit your note cards to one of these three forms: (1) exact quotations; (2) lists of facts or figures; and (3) (rarely) brief summaries of long passages.
6. Do NOT try to paraphrase quotations on your note cards.

Note cards can, in these ways, be as useful to you as they are to scholars in many fields of study all over the world. It is, however, important that you take your notes *exactly* according to the guidelines discussed in the following sections.

Note-taking Procedure

By following the conventions outlined in these six guidelines, you will have the sort of note cards from which you can write a well-organized, well-documented research paper. But these rules leave many questions of procedure unanswered. The following step-by-step discussion of the actual note-taking process should answer these questions for you.

Step 1. Making Bibliography Cards You go to the library and you assemble some books and/or articles on your subject. What then? The first thing you should do is glance through the material to eliminate anything that does not bear directly on the issue you have chosen to research. Then, before you write anything else, make a bibliography card for any book or article that seems to be even a remotely possible source. Even if you do not use the book during this day's note-taking, you'll have the bibliography card to help you find it again quickly. Just jot down all the pertinent bibliographical information (see Figures 1, 2)—and don't forget the library code number. Three sample cards appear in Figure 4.

Neman, Beth S. Teaching Students to Write Columbus, OH: Charles E. Merrill Company, 1980 79 92580	Booth, Wayne C. "A Report on the Failure of Idecom" College English Vol. 43, No. 2 (February 1981, 111-21.) 0010 0994
Book	**Journal Article**

Price, D.K.
"Staffing the Presidency" in
Outside Readings in American
Government Eds. H. Malsolm
Mac Donald and Wilfred D. Webb
N.Y.: Thomas Y. Cromwell Co., 1949
pp. 476-90

PX M 132

Article in a Book

FIGURE 4 Sample Bibliography Cards for a Book, a Journal Article, an Article in a Book

Alphabetize your bibliography cards for storage.

Step 2. Deciding What Information to Record You open a likely book, use the index or the table of contents to help you find the relevant material, and begin to read. How do you know when to take notes? As a rule of thumb, you can ask yourself, first, How closely does this passage touch on my topic? and second, Is it possible that I will need to use this material when it comes time to write the paper? You will probably want to take especially careful notes from your primary source material, even when it is quoted in your secondary sources.

As you continue your work and come closer to the formulation of your actual thesis, you will, of course, find much easier the decision about the relevance of a particular piece of material. But in the early stages when you are in doubt, go ahead and make the note. After all, discarding material that later becomes unrelated is far easier than trying to retrieve a passage you neglected.

Step 3. Deciding When to Copy a Direct Quotation You decide that a passage is important to your work and should be recorded: Should you quote it exactly? The answer almost always is yes, go ahead and get the author's exact words. At note-taking time you really can have no notion of how you will want to use particular material when you actually come to write your paper. You do not know whether you will want to quote it, paraphrase it, or discuss it in combination with material on other cards. You'll find you often want to have the author's exact words available when it comes time to make that decision. For a discussion of those circumstances when a quotation card is not your wisest choice, see Alternative Step 5.

Step 4. Deciding How Much to Quote Common sense assures that you will want to copy onto note cards as little material as you can. Consequently, what you need to do is to locate the significant part of a passage, the words or sentences in which the author sums up the essence of the idea you want to remember. Then you'll be ready to record, word for word, the significant words or sentences only. To streamline the note-taking, do not copy down extraneous material such as "as we said earlier" or "let us examine the facts" or even material important to the author's argument but not closely related to your concerns. Instead replace the omitted matter with marks of ellipsis: three periods (. . .)—or four (. . . .) if a sentence ending occurs in the omitted material. You may have to add or change a word or two to clarify the sense of a passage out of context. If so, enclose any material you add in [brackets].

Finally, in recording quotations be sure to limit yourself to one idea per card—even if several ideas important to your work appear on the same page of a source.

Step 5. Making Your Quotation Cards Leave the top line of your note card for the summarizing phrase that will label the recorded passage, and begin the next line by writing the last name of the source's author and the number of the page on which the quotation appears. Because you have already made a bibliography card for the book or article from which you are quoting, the last name of your author should be sufficient identification. If you use two authors of the same name, add identifying initials. If you use two works by the same author, include also a portion of the title.

Following author and page number, copy the passage, omitting irrelevant material and clarifying meaning as Step 4 describes. If the passage you are quoting runs onto another page, insert the new page number at the appropriate place in your recorded material.

When you have finished copying a quotation, carefully proofread your card for accuracy. Then summarize the contents of the card as precisely as you can, and label your card on the top line with this summary heading. The summary line will permit you to work with the card later by simply glancing at the heading rather than by having to take the time to read the entire card.

And we learned what had been theoretically formulated in classical psychiatric literature: that we were dealing with a specific personality type. In psychiatry we call this the passive dependent personality. Conversely we also found that the passive dependent personality types whom we were seeing for non-drug reasons, those of the first subcategory, were tending to become more involved with drugs as their underlying anxieties started to come out in the course of therapy and sought relief by turning on in order to turn off: for us this development again was a validation. (Katz, p. 473)

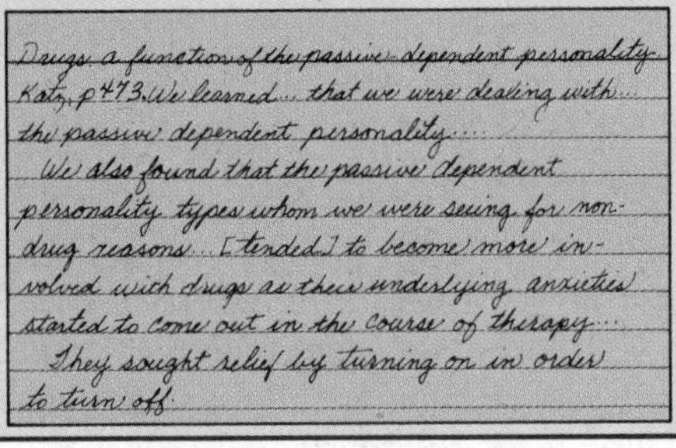
Drugs a function of the passive dependent personality
Katz, p.473 We learned... that we were dealing with...
the passive dependent personality....
We also found that the passive dependent
personality types whom we were seeing for non-
drug reasons... [tended] to become more involved with drugs as their underlying anxieties
started to come out in the course of therapy....
They sought relief by turning on in order
to turn off.

FIGURE 5 Source Passage and Quotation Card

Alternative Step 5. Making List Cards or Summary Cards What if you cannot foresee any possible future need to quote a particular passage exactly? And what if the information in question is strictly factual or numerical and would be more clearly recorded in a numbered list or a vertical column? In such cases, it is appropriate to make a list card rather than a quotation card. The headings remain the same. If you wish to quote an actual phrase of your author's when making your list, remember to enclose it in quotation marks. Here are some examples in Figure 6.

Occasionally you will read some background material that you want to remember, but that you do not expect to use directly in your paper. In this case, you may want to write a summary card. On such a card you would briefly summarize a much longer amount of material completely in your own words. If

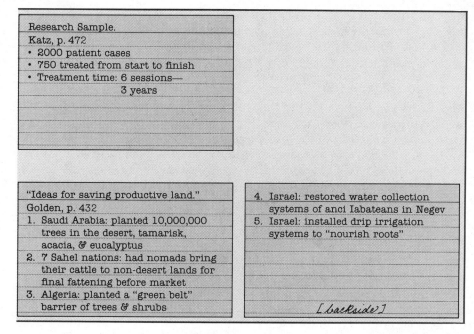

FIGURE 6 List Cards,
Simple and Complex

you should want to quote a phrase or two, you would surround it with quotation marks and be sure to include the page number. Figure 7 shows a sample summary card.

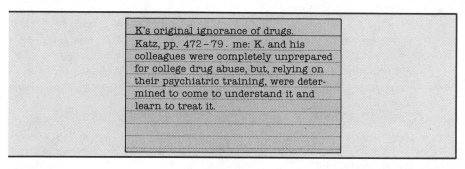

FIGURE 7
Summary Card

Step 6. Summarizing the Contents on the Top Line   Read over the material you have quoted on your notecard. Analyze it in terms of your research purpose and summarize it on the top line of the card. Making such a title line will not only serve you in a practical way when you organize your cards, but it can help you now. Even at this early stage it forces you to analyze the information you have discovered and to come to terms with it.

Step 7. Adding a Personal Notation   If quoted material inspires you with thoughts of your own, skip a line and jot them down. But make sure to add your initial or some other sign to indicate just whose thoughts they are. For example, you might add this kind of cryptic personal note:

Me: A.'s approach conflicts with other proofs at this point only.

Step 8. Storing Your Cards   As you finish your research for the day and prepare to encircle your cards with a rubber band and depart, you have one more step to complete. In order to keep your thinking on your topic open and flexible, it is a good idea to arrange your cards by ideas for storage. Because this ordering will often NOT coincide with arrangement by author, you will be more likely to think of the ideas as separate units to analyze and combine rather than as member parts of the original structures of their authors' arguments.

Arrange cards by ideas.

Usefulness of These Techniques

The note-taking conventions outlined in the preceding seven steps were developed by scholars to make their own research easier. Although the conventions may seem burdensome to you at first, if you follow them exactly, you will find that they make your work less difficult too. Here are some ways that specific conventions can speed up your work:

Advantages of following note-taking conventions.

1. Using separate bibliography cards keeps you from having to recopy the bibliographical information on every note card. These cards also make alphabetizing your final bibliography a breeze.
2. One idea per card makes your organizing task far easier, for you will be able to try out various combinations of structures simply by rearranging or reordering your cards.
3. Having a good summary of your material at the top of each note card saves you the time of repeatedly rereading each card during the process of "shuffling cards" to organize your paper.
4. Quoting most information exactly not only saves precious time during note-taking, but also gives you full information when you must decide how to use what your sources have to offer.
5. Writing the source's name on each card both refers you easily to the appropriate bibliography card and lets you know at a glance whose words you are working with. Having this information so handy should be helpful when you are composing your paper and want to include an author's name.

Try It Out

1. Write the information you would include on a bibliography card for each of the following:
   a. One of the books on your shelf

    b. An article in a current magazine

    c. An editorial in today's newspaper

    d. An essay in Part Five of this book (choose one)

2. Compose the sort of brief summary of the following quotations that would be useful later in organizing a research paper. Your summary should fit on the top line of a note card. Add the appropriate note.

    a. Subject of the paper: research into the causes of schizophrenia

       Quotation:

> Kay, p. 401. "Wheat gluten, when [experimentally] introduced into the diet of schizophrenics, had the effect of exaggerating the schizophrenic symptoms and retarding the response to treatment."

    b. Subject of the paper: research into Bible-based pro- and anti-slavery arguments before the Civil War

       Quotation:

> Jay, p. 626. "It is wholly immaterial whether the ancient Hebrews held slaves or not, since it is admitted by all that if they did, they acted by virtue of a special and express permission from God, while it is equally admitted that no such permission has been given to us."

    c. Subject of the paper: research into critical opinion on why Hamlet delayed killing the king.

       Quotation:

> Harrison, p. 109. "*Hamlet* is usually considered a play of problems; and the problem which has chiefly exercised the critics is why did he delay? To which the answer is that in the play which Shakespeare wrote there was no delay."

3. Take notes suitable for note cards on the following situation: You are investigating the broad question of the influence of writers of fiction upon American culture. Ben Hecht (as, for instance, with his play *Front Page*) seems to be a promising example of a writer who exerted a strong influence on his time. Read Judith Crist's Part Five essay "Gentlemen and Scholars of the Press" from this point of view and derive from it note cards appropriate to your topic. Remember the following conventions in making your cards:

- Identify each card by page number and author's last name.
- Limit each card to a single idea central to your concerns in this particular project.
- Quote the material accurately, replacing the phrases you omit with three periods (. . .) and enclosing words you need to add in [brackets].
- For each card compose a useful summary of the passage quoted and write this summary on the card's top line.

WRITING YOUR RESEARCH PAPER

Finding Your Thesis

Identifying a thesis for your research paper is not likely to cause you much difficulty. As you have been gathering your material, you have probably been testing out possible theses in your mind. If you began with a working hypothesis, you have probably been adding to it, changing it, or exchanging it for a thesis that would work better. If you began with a special question, you have probably found the answer to that question, and you should have little trouble formulating a thesis from that answer. In short, if you have been writing good theses for your other expository papers, you probably do not need additional advice on formulating an effective thesis for your research paper.

Nevertheless, two common thesis problems seem to plague research-paper writers. One is the overly combative "I think such-and-such is great" (or "terrible") thesis. And the other is its opposite, the bland, self-evident thesis of the "such-and-such is an interesting subject" variety. The latter type is usually meant to mask papers that simply "talk about" their topics rather than come to grips with the questions concerning them. Although there is no need for your research-paper thesis actually to be controversial, still a less than exciting paper will result from an attempt to assert that "George Washington was the first President of the United States," for instance, or that "The Grand Canyon is an impressive sight." Perhaps more to the point, the biographical summaries or geographical descriptions that result from such theses are not really research papers. They do not "add to the accumulation of the world's scholarship by making a definite statement based on careful study of . . . data." You can avoid bland, unfocused papers of this sort by making sure you have an arguable point to prove. Try using the "although clause" approach from Part One to help you arrive at that point.

On the other hand, by emphasizing the controversial aspects of the thesis statement, I don't want to imply that a combative thesis is required. In fact, such theses are best avoided. The propaganda tracts and personal pronouncements they tend to produce are rarely successful as research papers. When you think about it, you can find so many interesting nonpersonal statements to make about socialism, *Paradise Lost,* or Buddha that you should easily be able to avoid having the point of your paper amount to "I believe it is good" or "I believe it is bad."

Constructing Your Outline

Once you have found your thesis, constructing your outline or plan is perhaps the most vital step in the writing of your research paper. To begin you must think through the totality of your reading—and the ideas inspired in you by that reading—and then organize them into a clear and coherent whole.

Notecards as an Inventory of Ideas   In some ways organizing a research paper is easier than organizing other sorts of expository essays. Your stack of note cards gives you a ready-made inventory of ideas, with every idea concrete and movable. You can group and regroup your notecards until the topics on their summary lines fall into natural subdivisions, the five or six major points that will become your paper. Then you can arrange these groups or points into the best possible order for presenting your thesis. As you write your outline, coordinate your stack of note cards with it. Discard any cards that do not contribute to supporting your thesis. Be merciless in striving for a tight structure.

General Organizing Techniques How do you discover the structure that will present your thesis most effectively? Inasmuch as a research paper is a form of expository prose, you can use the same techniques to design its structure that you use to organize other expository essays. In fact, it would be a good idea to reread Chapter 2 and review the strategies suggested there.

A Specific Research-Paper Technique: F.D.R. To the extent that research papers form a distinct kind of writing, some special considerations also apply. Despite the great variety in research papers, they all share one important point: They are all grounded in fact. A good research paper is not simply a discussion of its writer's views. Its thesis must arise from a full consideration of the facts being examined. When you decide upon the structure of your research paper, then, you must be sure to keep the placement of your factual material foremost. One professor, who is also a history buff and an admirer of President Franklin Delano Roosevelt, suggests that the best way to organize a research paper is never to forget F.D.R. That is, always remember:

F acts
D iscussion
R ecommendations

What F.D.R. means is that your *Recommendations* or interpretations (that is, your final statement of thesis) must be based upon the *Facts* that you have presented clearly and have weighed and *Discussed* as objectively as possible.

In the sample outlines from student papers shown in the accompanying boxed section, you will notice a number of structures that were suggested in Chapter 2. But despite the variety, every sample outline demonstrates an understanding of the principle of F.D.R. Thus, when you are stacking your note cards into little piles that will form the structure of the outline for your research paper, be sure to keep F.D.R. in mind.

A final word of caution may be in order. Since organizing is a crucial step in fashioning your research paper, you may want to schedule a conference with your instructor before moving on to the writing itself.

Guidelines: Sample Outlines

Research Paper on a Literary Topic

Thesis: None of the major theories suggested by literary scholars completely answers the central critical question in Shakespeare's *Hamlet*, the question of why Hamlet delays in killing the king. Yet a combination of these theories can offer a plausible explanation.

I. Introduction—stressing the variety of critical answers to the question (Leading to) → Thesis
II. Detailed presentation of the most plausible theories.
   A. Theory of melancholia (A.C. Bradley)
      1. Explanation
      2. Facts in the play it accounts for
      3. Facts in the play in does not explain
   B. Oedipal theory (Lawrence Olivier's movie interpretation)
      1. Explanation
      2. Facts in the play it accounts for
      3. Facts in the play it does not explain
   C. Theory of practical impossibility (G. B. Harrison)
      1. Explanation
      2. Facts in the play it accounts for
      3. Facts in the play it does not explain
III. My theory. A combination of II A, II B, & II C.
   A. Explanation
      1. Hamlet's delay in Acts I, II, & III.
         Caused by Hamlet's melancholic (II A) and, to some extent, Oedipal (II B) preoccupation with the possibilities of his mother's guilt.
      2. Hamlet's delay in Acts IV & V.
         Caused by lack of practical opportunity (II C) until Hamlet actually does the deed.
   B. How this theory accounts for the facts in this play
   C. How it avoids the problems of the other theories
IV. Conclusion

Research Paper on a Scientific Topic

Thesis: Schizophrenia is caused by a chemical imbalance in the brain and thus should be treated chemically, not by psychotherapy.

- Introduction. Although clause—Until recently schizophrenia was treated through psychotherapy
Leading to → Thesis
- Presentation of research that shows schizophrenia to be the result of chemical imbalance in the brain.
   Farley's research
   Potkin's research
   Fisher's research
   Terensius's and Kline's research
- Possible cause for this imbalance
   diet
   virus
   genetic causes
- Failure of the psychoanalytic approach
- Recommendation: Drug therapy should replace psychotherapy for schizophrenia

Research Paper on a Historical Subject

Thesis: During the Civil War the Bible became the South's main justification for slavery and the North's foremost weapon against the institution.

1. Introduction: Setting up the paradox
2. Anti-slavery use of Bible
- Influenced the leaders

- Quoted at abolitionist meetings
- Quoted in abolitionist literature
3. Pro-slavery use of Bible
   - Biblical passages used as justification
   - Biblical history used as justification
     —The patriarchs
     —The Mosaic Law
4. Abolitionist rebuttal
   - Interpretation of cited passages
   - Explanation of allusions to Biblical history
     —The patriarchs
     —The Mosaic Law
5. Conclusions
   - The Bible was an effective weapon
   - The anti-slavery arguments prevailed

Writing the Paper

In writing your research paper, keep in mind that this paper is only a special kind of expository essay. You should, therefore, continue to think in terms of the usual three-part structure: introduction, body, and conclusion. All of these parts will function in much the same way they do in other kinds of expository writing. When you write your introduction, you will first approach and then set forth your thesis. You will take care not to bring any of your arguments into the introduction. And when you write your conclusion, you will read back over the rest of the paper and draw your final reflections on it, being sure to give your thesis its most thorough definition in the process. In your introduction and conclusion, you will be expressing your own ideas, and thus you will probably not include any quoted or paraphrased material—except possibly as a stylistic device.

The body of a research paper is also typically expository in that it consists of major points set forth in topic sentences, backed up by subpoints, defined in subtopic sentences, and supported by evidence of various kinds. As you write your paper, you will probably be even more conscious of this structure than usual because you will be working with a stack of cards that has been arranged to coordinate point-by-point with your outline. You will work down your outline, point by point, considering the cards that relate to a particular point and determining how you will approach each point from the sort of information the relevant cards contain.

It is possible that you will experience something almost akin to pleasure in this process. You may find a kind of delight in combining your well-organized outline and your well-coordinated note cards in a puzzle-building sort of way. And certainly there is a joy in watching the whole project fall into shape. Nevertheless, you must be careful not to let such pleasure lull you into thinking that writing a research paper is really just putting together the parts of a puzzle.

Such thinking can lead to a final paper that is merely a patchwork quilt of quotations. Where your mind should be focused instead, as you construct each section, is on these questions: What exactly do I want to say here? What point do I want to make? and How can I make it most convincingly? Your answers will determine in exactly what ways you will use the information the cards contain.

When to Quote or to Paraphrase (and When Not to)   There are two major ways you can make use of the material on your cards. The fact that you have the exact words of the author permits both options. On the one hand, you may want to read over the cards associated with a particular point, digest the information they contain until it becomes part of your own thinking, and— putting the cards completely aside—make your point about the subject in your own way. Depending, of course, upon the topic, you will probably write the greater part of your paper in this fashion.

On the other hand, there will be times when paraphrasing or quoting the material on your cards directly seems the right choice. Such may be the case when an author's words (or your version of them) are in themselves proof of whatever the passage is asserting. All primary source material can be quoted (or paraphrased) in this manner—whether it is a statistical chart for a scientific paper, a literary passage for a critical analysis, an expert opinion (when what is involved is weighing of scholarly views), or even the words of the man-on-the-street (when they are pertinent). To get a sense of the appropriate use of primary source material, read through the following quotations and corresponding paraphrases from a student's paper on the employment of Biblical arguments in the slavery dispute.

This first example uses quotation and paraphrase* to show the Abolitionists' dependence upon the Bible to reinforce their anti-slavery arguments:

Use of Quotation	Use of Paraphase
The Bible was the backbone of the Abolitionist cause. "Take away the Bible," William Lloyd Garrison said, "and our warfare with oppression and infidelity, intemperance and impurity, is removed—we have no authority to speak and no courage to act."[1]	The Bible was the backbone of the Abolitionist cause. William Lloyd Garrison felt that if the Bible could not be used, then they would lose their best weapon and best authority and would no longer have either the justification or the spirit to continue.[1]

The next example uses quotation and paraphrase to express the religious rationale of the slaveholders:

Use of Quotation	Use of Paraphrase
There was . . . a widespread belief [in the South] that [slavery] was	There was a widespread belief in the South that slavery was somehow

---

*Both quotations and paraphrases must be documented in footnotes. Footnote numbers are therefore included in the examples.

somehow good for the slaves. The Reverend Phillip Schaff considered slavery as "a wholesome training school for the Negro—taking him from the lowest state of heathenism and barbarism to some degree of Christian civilization."[2]

good for the slaves. Reverend Phillip Schaff, for instance, thought that slavery was a means of educating the slave in civilization and in Christianity.[2]

Both quotations and paraphrased material require footnotes, and in both cases the author must be identified within the text. Most of the time, as you can see from these examples, quotations and paraphrases are interchangeable and you should choose for yourself which would be the most effective for you to use.

There are times, however, when only a quotation can adequately make your point. Here is an instance from the same student paper:

Use of Quotation

[John Brown] studied the Bible with such zeal that his speech and writing acquired the flavor of the Old Testament. He was known throughout the land as a "Terrible Saint" or "God's angry man."[3]

And—very occasionally—you might want to use a quotation when your source employs a phrasing so much in point that you cannot resist repeating it yourself. For example:

The famous New England poets, who lashed out so strongly against slavery, did so with an enormous fund of Scriptural knowledge as background. Whittier, for example, according to Nelson, "wrote biblically as naturally as he breathed."[4]

The following set of guidelines should help you use quotations and paraphrases correctly and gracefully in your research papers.

Guidelines for Use of Quotation and Paraphrase

1. **Point.** Introduce your point in your own words. Use the quotation or paraphrase for support only. Never simply insert it to speak for itself. *Your paper should be able to make coherent sense with all quotations and paraphrases omitted.*
2. **Pertinence.** Use a quotation or a paraphrase only when your point could not be supported as well without it. Remember that too many quotations could give your research paper that patchwork quilt effect.
3. **Brevity.** Trim your quotations as closely as possible, leaving only the phrasing that is completely relevant to your point. Carefully shape the quotation to fit *your* context, but be accurate and true to the author's original meaning.
4. **Identification.** Give the quotation a source. Either name its author specifically ("William Garrison," "Reverend Phillip Schaff," "John Brown") or in general ("the famous New England poets"). A paper cannot simply burst into quotation as a singer bursts into song. Even when the paper is read aloud (so that quotation marks have no significance), a listener should be able to understand that a new voice is speaking and, for the most part, should be told whose voice it is.

Putting the Rules into Practice   Guidelines can suggest what you should do, but the individual context of each of your points and subpoints, your actual paragraphs themselves, must determine how you will put these suggestions into practice. Consider the following situation.

Your thesis is:	The problem of "pollutolescence" continues to be a serious one, despite a long series of governmental efforts to solve it; but the ideas being worked on by Professor Smarts of Urban University and by Doctors Vera and Very Smart at the National Institution appear promising and should be tried.
Your outline is:	

    I. Introduction
   II. Seriousness of problem
      A.
      B.
      C.
  III. Failure of government efforts
      A. Efforts from 1950 to 1965
         1. A project
         2. B project
         3. C project
      B. Efforts from 1965 to the present
         1. X project
         2. (The Boon-Doggle Project)
         3. Y project
         4. Z project
  IV. Promising new ideas
      A. The Smarts Idea
         1. Nature of plan
         2. Why it is promising
      B. The Very Smart idea
         1. Nature of plan
         2. Why it is promising
   V. Conclusion

Your present task is:	Write the section for point III. B. 2.
Your point, then, is:	Government attempts to solve the problem of "pollutolescence" have ended in disaster.
Your subpoint is:	The Boon-Doggle Project is a typical example.
Your note cards on this point include:	

Boon-Doggle Project: Information
Smith, pp. 46–48
1. Located outside of Pittsburgh, Pa.
2. Begun 1968
3. Completed 1973
4. Congress refused funding 1978
5. Congress investigated 1982
6. Overall cost $49,000,000

Boon-Doggle Warning
Snerd, p. 101
"I felt like Cassandra crying in the wilderness, but I could see no good coming from the planned Boon-Doggle Project. As early as Sept., 1967, I testified in Congress to that effect."

Boon-Doggle Warning
Green, p. 55
"There is no way such a project [i.e., Boon-Doggle] can succeed."

Boon-Doggle Evaluated (neg.)
Jones, p. 11.
"The facts of physics—if not common logic—had doomed the Boon-Doggle Project from the start."

Boon-Doggle Fails
NY Times (edit.) Dec. 2, 1979, p. 48
"This week with no fan-fare the ill-happed Boon-Doggle Project closed its doors for the last time. . . . Senator Budget regretted that $49,000,000 of the taxpayers' money 'seems just to have gone down the drain.'"

How would you combine the information on these cards to make your point? It would surely depend upon how much emphasis you wanted to put on this particular idea. Perhaps you want to use it in a rather minimal way as a single example among many. In that case you might use your information as a consensus view:

Example A
Another example of the government's mismanagement of the pollutolescence problem is the Boon-Doggle Project near Pittsburgh, Pennsylvania. It was begun in 1968 despite the warnings of the scientific community, and after struggling along for a number of seasons, it finally came to an inglorious close in 1979 to the tune of a $49,000,000 bill to the American taxpayers.[5]

The more specific you are, the more importance you give to the point:

Example B
. . . Although such recognized authorities as J. P. Snerd and Caroline Green warned that the project would fail,[5] the government persisted in its plan. . . .

If the point is one you truly want to emphasize, you might decide not only to paraphrase but also to quote directly:

Example C
The Boon-Doggle Project near Pittsburgh, Pennsylvania, should never have been undertaken. Nobel Laureate Caroline Green warned that such a project could never succeed[5] and Professor J. P. Snerd said he "felt like Cassandra crying in the wilderness"[6] while the government pointedly ignored his warnings. The professors' warnings proved all too correct. Five years and $49,000,000 later,[7]

it was all over. As Professor Janice C. Jones pointed out, "The facts of physics— if not common logic—had doomed the Boon-Doggle Project from the start."[8]*

As you become more experienced in research writing, you will begin to develop a surer intuition about what sort of approach to take.

The Mechanics of Quotation   A number of conventions have developed for transcribing quoted material. The purpose of these conventions is to make the quoted material instantly recognizable and to make the text as a whole easier to read. Therefore, follow the rules offered in the accompanying boxed section when you use quotations.

Guidelines for Using Quotations

1. **A brief quotation** should be enclosed in quotation marks:

   The power and force of the Old Testament were so much a part of Garrison that many associated the two together. Bates likens him to "a fiery Hebrew prophet"[7] and Wendell Phillips said that Garrison was "Taught of God . . . God endowed, and God-sent to arouse a nation."[8]

2. **A quotation that extends over three lines** should be indented and blocked off. (You do not need to use quotations marks when you use this form. The indentation of itself says "quoted material.") For example:

   Wendell Phillips, like so many of his time, used Bible language and imagery in the remarkable oratory of his Abolitionist addresses. For example, this excerpt from his "Dangers from Slavery" speech:

   > Then the wicked will walk on every side for the vilest of men will be exalted, and America, become the mock and scorn and hissing of the nations, will go down to worse shame than was ever heaped upon Sodom; for the lust of wealth, land and power, she will also have commmitted the crime against nature.[9]

3. **Poetry** should be quoted in lines:

   The prose of *The Liberator* is interspersed with poetry, most of which has more passion than art:

   > God is a God of mercy, and would see
   > The prison-doors unbarr'd—the bondmen free!
   > He is a God of Truth, with purer eyes
   > Than to behold the oppressor's sacrifice![10]

---

*In order to avoid writing too many notes, you can sometimes combine several into a single note. The four notes interrupting Boon-Doggle Example C, for instance, could be combined in this way:

[5]Green, p. 48; Snerd, p. 101; statistics from Smith, p. 48; Jones, p. 11.

4. **Brief portions of poetry** (under three lines) may be included within the text, but you should indicate the line divisions by slashes:

> According to Stephen Vincent Benet's Bible-reading slave-trader, "It's down there, Mister, / Down there in black and white."[11]

Punctuation

Punctuate your quotations according to the following rules:

1. Carefully copy the author's punctuation (and spelling and wording) within the quotation.
2. When you trim the quotation to meet the requirements of your own introductory sentences and the point that you are making, substitute three periods (. . .) for any omitted words. Any additions or changes in wording that you have to make so that the quotation will fit the demands of your own text should be included in brackets []. For example, if your quotation, taken out of context, should read, ambiguously:

> He was the first president.

You would quote it as:

> "[George Washington] was the first president," according to Professor DiAngelo.[12]

3. A quotation within a quotation is indicated by single quotation marks (that is, apostrophes):

> Professor Goldberg points out that "Edison tested out the first record player with 'Mary Had a Little Lamb.'"[11]

Double quotation is awkward, however, and (as in the example above) can usually be avoided.

4. All punctuation that is part of a quotation itself goes *within* the quotation marks. In addition, periods and commas *always* go within the quotation marks.
5. You have your choice of a variety of punctuation for introducing your quotation.
   a. You can make the quotation an integral part of the sentence by using no additional punctuation:

   > Thus both sides claimed to act "in strict accordance with the will of God."[12]

   b. You can introduce the quotation informally with a comma:

   > According to F. C. Stifler, "The great Lincoln was nurtured on the Bible as few men ever have been."[13]

   c. Or you can introduce it more formally with a colon:

   > Lincoln's actions on slavery, as on all important issues, were governed by his creed: "What doth the Lord require of thee, but do justly, to love mercy, and to walk humbly with thy God?"[14]

   d. You can use commas to interrupt the quotation by inserting its identifying tag:

   > "Take away the Bible," William Lloyd Garrison said, "and our warfare with oppression . . . is removed."[15]

e. Or you can use a comma to put the identifying tag at the end:

> The prophets were particularly outspoken on the subject. "Woe unto him . . . who useth his neighbor's services without wages," Jeremiah wrote (22:13).

Try It Out

1. The technique of quoting effectively is useful to know. To practice this technique, let's say that in a research paper you are writing you are working on a passage about the ancient Etruscan attitude toward death. Quote the following note card—or portion of it—as you would for such a passage. Remember to identify your author and be sure to introduce your quotation with a statement of your own. Include a footnote number.

Etruscan Tombs: gay, filled with enjoyment of life, Plumb, p. 466. A rich caste of princes built tombs of singular magnificence, filling them with amphorae, jewels, and silver. And they adorned their walls with all the gaiety they had enjoyed alive. . . . In their tombs they hunted, played games, performed acrobatics, danced, feasted; their amorous dalliance was	both wanton and guiltless. Deliberately they banished death with the recollected gusto of life. *[backside]*

2. Paraphrasing is an equally important research paper strategy. Rewrite the Etruscan passage by paraphrasing the material on the note card (or a portion of it). In order to paraphrase, restate the author's point in other words. If you need to use any of the original phrasing, be sure to enclose those portions in quotation marks. Ordinarily, you will be introducing your material with such phrases as "The author said *that*. . . ." (See examples on page 358.) Be sure to include a footnote number in the appropriate place.

3. Which version of your Etruscan passage (the quoted or the paraphrased) do you think is most effective? Why? Would you prefer a mixed version combining both quotation and paraphrase?

4. This final exercise gives you the opportunity to practice putting together the kind of paragraph you will be writing in your research papers. Imagine that you have collected the following note cards for a section of your research paper on contemporary American fads. Write a paragraph making use of the information they contain. You may quote and/or paraphrase or omit material as you choose. (See p. 360.)

Interest in partic. fad is short-lived
Tucker, p. 505. Today, the question
often is not "What do you do?" but
"What are you into?" Macrame one
week, astrology the next, health
food, philosophy, history, jogging,
movies, EST—we fly from "commitment" to "commitment" like bees
among flowers because it is easier . . .

to buy a new toy than to repair an
old one.

[backside]

The "Me" Fad
Goodman, p. 470. The new therapies—
from the isolation tank on—offer us
ways to "get into ourselves." Those
who aren't "doing their own thing" or
"finding themselves" are "getting in
touch with their feelings" . . . .
The range of the new therapies is
characterized by a frenzied search
inward.

Examples of "Me" Fad
Goodman, p. 471.
The hyperindividualism of a movement
like est . . . .
The "isolation tank" seems to suggest
that the road to happiness . . . is
an internal route.

The Hippy Fad
Wolfe, p. 443. In the women's
colleges . . . . there is a whole
generation of young buds with pre-
Raphaelite hairdos and black-muslim
stockings who worship Guitar
Players and Smoking Pot . . . [These]
girls all talk about going down to
the Village and having affairs
with coffeehouse pothead poets.

The Macho Fad
Wolfe, p. 444. [The men today] are
not only wacked-out, but tough. . . .
The evil that seems to fascinate
[them] most is violence. A lot of
men today have a kind of hairy sentimentality about violence that is
somewhat like the girls and Lady
Brett.

CREDITING AND DOCUMENTING
The Process Defined

When scholars talk about documentation, they mean the supplying of full bibliographical information about their sources. Basically, they are referring to footnotes and bibliographies and the identification of author and work inserted
within the text itself. Such bibliographical references are for most an unfamiliar
technical apparatus and are, frankly, odd-looking. They sometimes even arouse
feelings of panic in inexperienced writers. But as it is with unfamiliar dogs (and
other such things before they are known), the bibliographical bark is much
worse than its bite. Actually bibliographical notation is a kind of shorthand de-

signed by scholars in a particular field to share the necessary information as quickly and as easily as possible. This bibliographical information is necessary, both to give "credit where credit is due" and to allow readers the opportunity to obtain the sources themselves in order to get fuller information or to build upon the research. All bibliographical apparatus shares these purposes—though specific conventions differ. The conventions described in this chapter are used by students of the humanities (literature, language, history, philosophy, religion, and the fine arts), and they are somewhat different from those used in the natural, physical, and social sciences.

Number or note as you write.
Documenting sources is an important part of your research paper. Although most of the bibliographical details can be postponed until after the early drafts of your paper are written, you will need to keep the necessity for crediting well in mind as you write. You will want to incorporate footnote numbers into your working text as you go along and to record the appropriate number on the corresponding card or cards. An alternate plan is to include parenthetically in the text the abridged notations from the cards—for instance, "(Smith, p. 29)." When you have finished writing and are ready to make your footnote page, you can match the abbreviated reference with its corresponding bibliography card and get all the information you need for each footnote. If you have used the text-noting method during the writing process, you must scratch out all of the notations from your draft before making a final copy.

What Should Be Credited?

The question of what should be credited is not always easy to answer. Too many footnotes can be distracting and can leave the impression of a stuffy, fuddy-duddy sort of mind. But too few footnotes can amount to plagiarism. As you become more experienced in research, you will develop a feel for what should and what should not be credited. But until you develop this natural sureness, it is best to avoid the greater of the two evils. In other words: When in doubt, document. Here are the rules:

Rules for documentation.
1. All quotations MUST be credited.
2. All paraphrases MUST be credited.
3. Material that is not directly quoted or paraphrased from your source should be credited whenever it is, in any way, exclusive to its author. You do not need to credit it if it is common knowledge. The test should not be "Did I know this information before?" but rather "Can this information be found in an encyclopedia or in almost any book on the subject?" For example, you may not personally know the birthday of Czar Nicholas, but there would nevertheless be no reason to footnote such a fact because it is available in any number of sources. Information that needs documentation includes:
   - Interpretations
   - Opinions

- Challengeable data, including:
  - Statistics
  - Results of surveys
  - Results of studies

Remember the results of research are only as good as the people who did the work. Your reader has the right to know who they are.

There are, basically, three ways to credit the material you obtain from outside sources: in the text, in footnotes, and in a bibliography.

Making In-Text Notation

The documentation you include within the text itself is the most important because your reader absorbs it along with the rest of your discussion. You will want to introduce most of the quoted or paraphrased material that you use in the body of your research paper by mentioning the name of the person from whom you took the material. Such identification clarifies the distinction between your voice and that of your sources and also lends authority to your argument.

The first time you mention an author or informant, you should give the full name. At this first mention, you might also want to add an identifying tag such as "Jane S. Doe, Professor of Literature at Johns Hopkins University" or "John Q. Doe, Agronomist with the Department of the Interior." In this first reference it is also often useful to mention the name of the work from which you are quoting as well: "According to Leslie L. Snerd in *Poltergeists for Fun and Profit,* . . ." or "In *Poltergeists for Fun and Profit,* Leslie L. Snerd points out, ..." In later references, citing the last name alone is sufficient: "Doe argues that . . ." or "As Snerd explains, ..."

When you refer to Biblical passages or lines from well-known plays or poems, you may decide that including their brief citations parenthetically within the text is less distracting to the reader than giving each one of them a separate footnote. This decision is an especially wise one if the particular edition you are quoting from is immaterial to your point. Here are some sample citations of this sort:

Biblical Passage:
All through the Bible, the principles of freedom and equality are stressed: "Have we not all one father? Hath not one God created us?" (Malachi 1:10).

To give a Biblical citation, follow the name of the book by the number of the chapter and then the number of the verse. Separate chapter from verse by a colon. Use Arabic numbers for both.

Drama:
In his most famous soliloquy Hamlet reflects that "Conscience doth make cowards of us all" (III, i).

When citing a play, use a large Roman numeral to signify the act and a small Roman numeral to stand for the scene. Separate them by a comma.

Long Poems:
> At the end of Milton's *Paradise Lost,* Adam and Eve, "with wandering steps and slow,/Through Eden take their solitary way" (XII, 648–49).

Use a Roman numeral for the book (or other enumerated division) number, Arabic numbers to show the lines. Separate by a comma.

In-text references are also useful when you need to quote (or paraphrase) a particular source a number of times. Rather than bothering your reader with repeated footnotes it is better to include the page number parenthetically within the text. In cases of this sort, as well as those times when the name of the particular edition of the Bible or of a well-known poem or play is important to know, footnote the first reference to the work in this manner:

> [16]This and all subsequent references to *Hamlet* within this paper are taken from *Shakespeare: The Complete Works,* ed. G. B. Harrison, 3rd ed. (New York: Harcourt, Brace and World, 1968).

Writing Your Footnotes

As important as in-text notation is, it cannot replace footnotes altogether. Including full bibliographical references within the text would be much too distracting for the reader. So when you want to provide a quantity of information that might interrupt the argument you are pursuing in the text, use a footnote. Add a number (raised a half space above the line of print) referring to a note which will contain the additional information. The number in the text is a small distraction that gives your reader the choice of continuing on with your argument or of stopping to pick up the extra information along the way. Your instructor will tell you whether to place these notes at the "foot" of the appropriate pages in the traditional manner or whether to follow the newly accepted method (recommended by the Modern Language Association) of placing your notes in a list at the conclusion of the entire paper. The content of the footnotes will be the same in either case. And in both cases, you should number the notes consecutively throughout the paper.

Comment Footnotes   Most of the information your footnotes express will be bibliographical. Since the bibliographical format is, as we said, a sort of shorthand, it speaks for itself to those who can interpret it and usually needs no further comment. Yet there are times when further explanations do help to clarify a note. You should not hesitate to speak directly to the reader in situations like the following:

- When you have quoted an author who was quoted in your source:

> [17]Pattengill, *as quoted in* Gruen, p. 12.

- When you want to call your readers' attention to sources beyond those you refer to in the text:

[18]Schwartz, p. 38. *See also* Bloom, pp. 38–44, and O'Brien, pp. 109–117.

- When you base a paragraph on multiple sources (see Boon-Doggle Example A, p. 361):

[19]*The material in the above paragraph was derived from* Smith, pp. 46–48; Green, p. 55; Snerd, p. 101; and Jones, p. 11.

Feel free also occasionally to use footnotes to comment upon the text. You can elaborate upon a point, offer an opposing view, clarify an idea, or define a troublesome concept. Comment footnotes are also handy places to make use of that material from your note-taking that you found difficult to give up—even though it was not directly relevant to your thesis. You might phrase it briefly in an "It is interesting to note in this connection . . ." note, include its source, and attach it to the point in your paper most closely related to it.

Distinction Between First- and Later-Reference Footnotes The most important purpose of your footnotes, however, is to let your readers know the title of the work from which you are taking your material, its author's name, publishing information, and the page number of the original passage. This information is essential for your readers, yet you will not want to interrupt their reading any more than is necessary. Although you may very well find reason to refer more than once to a single text, there surely is no need to distract your readers by repeating the entire bibliographical entry. After all, the only item that changes from note to note is the page number. Consequently, scholars have adopted the convention of giving a complete bibliographical description the first time a source is referred to and only an identifying word or two (usually the author's last name) and the page number on all later notes. There is never any need to use such tags as *ibid.* and *op. cit.,* once widely used in later-reference notes. These labels not only are confusing for the writer, but also are unnecessary and intrusive for the reader. A note such as "Farley, p. 36" remains the clearest later reference. The abbreviated later-reference form is appropriate to all kinds of footnotes: single source, multiple source, or comment notes.

Models for Constructing Bibliographical Notes The accompanying boxed section offers footnote patterns based upon the *MLA Handbook.* It should give you working models from which to construct footnotes as well as bibliography entries.

Models for Footnotes and Bibliography Entries

Footnote Model: First Reference to a Book
[20]Author's Name, "Name of Article," <u>Title of Book,</u> ed.[itor's] Name, (or) trans.[lator's] Name, 3rd ed. (Place: Publisher, Date), p. 3 (or pp. 3–4).

Footnote Model: First Reference to a Magazine or Journal Article
[21]Author's Name, "Name of Article," Title of Journal, [volume] 3 (Month or Season, Year), [page] 3.
Footnote Model: Second Reference
[22]Author's Last Name, p. 3.
(If no author, substitute Abbreviated Title.)
(If author wrote more than one work, add Abbreviated Title.)
(If two authors share a name, add first name or initial.)
Bibliography Entry Model: Book
Name, Author's. "Name of Article." In Title of Book. Ed.[itor's] Name. (or) Trans.-[lator's] Name. 3rd ed. Place: Publisher, Date, (Only if limited to a specific article or section in a book) pp. 3–33.
Bibliography Entry: Magazine or Journal Article
Name, Author's. "Name of Article." Title of Journal, [Volume] 3 (Month or Season, Year), [pages] 3–33.

Since the formats offered as models are cumulative, you can expect to omit items. If there is no author, for example, you should begin with the title of the article; if that also is missing, with the title of the book. Because articles in books are rare, except in anthologies, that item will be frequently omitted. However, if the quotation you are working with is from an Introduction or an Afterword, you should treat it in the same way as an article. Do not be too concerned if an exception to these models should arise. Your own good sense will show you how to handle it in a way consistent with the format. You need not repeat information that has been given in the text.

The following samples should give you an idea of how various kinds of footnotes work out in practice.

First-Reference Footnote Samples

A Book with Two or Three Authors (first edition)
[23]Gerome Ragni and James Rado, *Hair* (New York: Pocket Books, 1969), p. 87.
An Article in an Anthology (later edition)
[24]Alan S. Katz, "The Use of Drugs in America: Toward a Better Understanding of Passivity," in *The Norton Reader: An Anthology of Expository Prose,* ed. Arthur M. Eastman et al., 3rd ed. (New York: W. W. Norton, 1965), p. 399.
(Note the handling of three or more editors or authors.)
An Unsigned Article in an Encyclopedia
[25]"Hygrometer," *Funk & Wagnalls Standard Reference Encyclopedia,* 1967, ed.
(You do not need to cite volume or page number of an encyclopedia if it is alphabetically ordered. When an encyclopedia article is signed with initials, look them up in the index of contributors and use the author's full name as you would the author of any article.)

An Article from a Journal

[26]Wayne C. Booth, "The Rhetorical Stance," *College Composition and Communication,* 14 (1963), 139–45.

An Unsigned Article from a Newspaper or Magazine

[27]"Majorette Allowed to March," *Cincinnati Enquirer,* 2 October, 1982, Sec. A, p. 4.

A Quotation from an Outside Source

[28]Norman Podhoretz, as quoted in George Will, *The Pursuit of Happiness and Other Sobering Thoughts* (New York: Harper & Row, 1978), p. 281.

Consolidation of References

[29]The material in this paragraph is derived from Kenneth L. Pike, "How to Make an Index," *PMLA* 83 (1968), 991; Robert L. Collins, *Indexing Books* (New York: DeGraff, 1963); and *The MLA Style Sheet* (New York: Modern Language Association Publications, 1970), p. 22.

Later-Reference Footnote Samples

Most Later References

[30]Smith, p. 45.

When Two of Your Sources Have the Same Name

[31]F. L. Jones, p. 56

and

[32]Janice Jones, p. 109.

When You Use Two Works by the Same Author

[33]Snerd, *Aardvarks,* p. 89.

and

[34]Snerd, *Poltergeists,* p. 109.

When the Work Is Anonymous

[35]"Hygrometer," p. 19.

Writing Your Bibliography

Your bibliographical entries should contain the same information as your first-reference footnotes, but there are a few conventional differences in the formats. The author's name is written last name first in a bibliography in order to make the alphabetizing clearer. The rest of the entry is indented under that name. There are also some changes in the punctuating conventions. While the three large divisions (author, title, and publishing data) are to be separated by commas in one long pseudo-sentence in the footnotes, each part is considered a little sentence of its own in the bibliography and so the parts are separated by periods. To understand the differences between the footnote and the bibliographical entry formats, compare the models on pp. 386–90.

Bibliographical Entry Samples

Journal Article

Thomas, Lewis, "Germs." *New England Journal of Medicine,* 287 (1972), 553–57.

Book

White, E. B. *The Second Tree from the Corner.* New York: Harper & Row, 1949.

Another Work by the Same Author

————. *Poems & Sketches of E. B. White.* New York: Harper & Row, 1981.

Anonymous Work

Education Directory: Higher Education 1967–68. Part 3. Washington, D.C.: Government Printing Office, 1968.

Article in an Anthology

Crist, Judith. "Gentlemen and Scholars of the Press." In *The Columbia University Forum Anthology.* Ed. Peter Spackman and Lee Ambrose. New York: Atheneum, 1968, pp. 227–30.

Try It Out

1. Using the sample first-reference footnotes as your list of sources, write a bibliography (Footnote numbers 23–29.)
2. Make up footnote entries for the following situations:
   a. A first reference to the second page of the Judith Crist article in this text
   b. A later reference to the first page of the same article
   c. A first reference to an anonymous article on Socrates on p. 8070 in volume 22 of *Funk and Wagnall's Standard Reference Encyclopedia* in the 1967 edition
   d. A later reference to the same article
   e. A first reference to an article on the front page of today's newspaper
   f. A later reference to the same article

A SAMPLE STUDENT RESEARCH PAPER

The Outline

The Influence of the Bible on the Slavery Question

Thesis: During the Civil War the Bible became the South's main justification for slavery and the North's foremost weapon against the institution.

I. Introduction

II. The Influence of the Bible on the Anti-Slavery Movement

    A. The influence of the Bible on the Northern Leaders

        1. Abraham Lincoln

        2. John Brown

        3. Wendell Phillips

        4. William Lloyd Garrison

    B. The Bible used to foster the Abolition movement

        1. Technique of a religious revival

        2. Poetry and novels

        3. The Liberator

III. The Influence of the Bible on the Pro-Slavery Movement

    A. Pro-slavery feeling aroused in the South

1. Former mild feeling

2. Apologies change to assertions

B. The Bible justification of slavery

1. "Cursed be Canaan"

2. Slavery sanctioned by God and prevalent among the Hebrew

people

a. Patriarchs

b. Mosaic Law

IV. The Abolitionist Rebuttal

A. Interpretation of "Cursed be Canaan"

B. Interpretation of slavery among the Hebrews

C. Slavery forbidden

D. Equality stressed

V. Conclusion:

A. The Bible an effective weapon

B. The North "prevailed"

The Paper

The Influence of the Bible on the Slavery Question

The will of God prevails. No doubt, no doubt—

Yet, in great contest, each side claims to act

In strict accordance with the will of God.

Both may, one must be wrong.[1]

    During the Civil War the Bible became the South's main justification for slavery and the North's foremost weapon against the institution. Thus both sides claimed to act "in strict accordance with the will of God." This was entirely possible for them to do, in all sincerity. There are ample grounds in the Bible upon which to base either a violently anti-slavery or a strongly pro-slavery point of view, for the Bible is in some ways a very contradictory book. With differing interpretations, the Bible can be made to prove many viewpoints. Both of the opposing sides in the slavery controversy realized the effectiveness of the Bible and put it to constant use.

    The Bible was the backbone of the Abolitionist cause. "Take away the Bible," William Lloyd Garrison said, "and our warfare with oppression and infidelity, intemperance and impurity, is removed—we

Use of epigraph.

Quotation from Benet epigraph.

THESIS

Quotation from a primary source.

2

have no authority to speak and no courage to act."[2] The powerful

leaders of the North were so thoroughly steeped in the Bible from the

days of their childhood that it naturally had a large influence upon

their lives. According to F. C. Stifler, "The great Lincoln was nurtured

Quotation from a secondary source.

on the Bible as few men ever have been."[3] His actions on the slavery

question, as on all important issues, were governed by his creed: "What

Biblical quotation and documentation.

doth the Lord require of thee, but to do justly, to love mercy, and to

walk humbly with thy God" (Micah 6:8).[4] The spirit of John Brown,

which legend tells us walked the night and could not rest until the last

slave was free,[5] was a direct product of the Bible, for this first and

most ardent of the Abolitionists followed the Scriptures to the point of

fanaticism. He studied the Bible with such zeal that his speech and

writing acquired the flavor of the Old Testament. He was known

throughout the land as a "Terrible Saint" or "God's angry man."[6]

Wendell Phillips, too, was influenced by the Holy Book. He believed that

Direct quotation and paraphrase combined.

the Bible was the "final authority on human bondage"; he even went so

far on these grounds as to curse the Constitution because it condoned

slavery.[7] Phillips, like so many others of his time, used Bible language

and imagery in the remarkable oratory of his Abolitionist addresses.

For example, this excerpt from his "Dangers from Slavery" speech:

3

Then the wicked will walk on every side for the vilest of men

will be exalted, and America, become the mock and scorn and

hissing of the nations, will go down to worse shame than was

ever heaped upon Sodom; for the lust for wealth, land, and

power, she will also have committed the crime against

nature.[8]

Long quotation indented and blocked off.

Perhaps William Lloyd Garrison did more with the Bible to further

his cause than any other Abolitionist, both in his fiery speeches and in

the Liberator, his daring newspaper. Even his first anti-slavery

address was marked by constant Biblical allusion:

Thus saith the Lord God of the Africans, Let this people go,

that they may serve me; I ask them to proclaim liberty to the

captives, and the opening of the prison to them that are

bound;—to light up a flame of philanthropy that shall burn till

all of Africa be redeemed from the night of moral death and

the song of deliverance be heard throughout her borders.[9]

Quotation from primary source.

The power and force of the Old Testament were so much a part of

Garrison that many associated the two together. Bates likens him to "a

fiery Hebrew prophet"[10] and Wendell Phillips in his beautiful eulogy

said that Garrison was "Taught of God . . . God endowed, and God-sent

Quotation from secondary source.

4

to arouse a nation."[11] Thus, the influence of the Bible was extended into the minds of the leaders of the Abolition movement, and their voices carried it to the people.

There were many ways in which the people received the spirit of Abolition, and in most of these the Bible played a major role. There were monthly prayer meetings. Songbooks and hymnals stressing Biblical phraseology appeared by the score. Time and time again the techniques of a religious revival and a fourth of July rally were intermingled.[12] Abolitionist propaganda was also spread through poetry and novels, and again the Bible influence was very apparent. The most stirring novel of the era, <u>Uncle Tom's Cabin,</u> was written by Harriet Beecher Stowe, members of whose family had been ministers for generations, and who, consequently, was brought up on the Bible.[13] The famous New England poets, who lashed out so strongly against

Secondary source credited with quotation.

slavery, did so with an enormous fund of Scriptural knowledge as background. Whittier, for example, according to Nelson, "wrote biblically as naturally as he breathed." In 285 of his poems are 816

Statistics footnoted.

passages drawn from the Bible.[14] For instance, as the controversy was coming to a head, he wrote:

He flung aside his silver flute,

5

> Snatched up Isaiah's stormy lyre,
>
> Loosened old angers pent and mute,
>
> Startled the iron string with fire;[15]

Lesser poets, too, drew from this unending source:

> Though hearts be torn asunder,
>
> For freedom we will fight:
>
> Our blood may seal the victory,
>
> But God will shield the right![16]

Poetry quoted in indented lines.

The publication that most aroused the ire of the pro-slavery enthusiasts and the admiration of the Abolitionists was William Lloyd Garrison's <u>Liberator.</u> It was a newspaper composed of a series of anti-slavery essays and poems. Throughout there are many Bible references and some of the writing style is reminiscent of the Old Testament. The prose is interspersed with poetry, most of which has more strength than style:

> God is a God of mercy, and would see
>
> The prison-doors unbarr'd—the bondmen free!
>
> He is a God of truth, with purer eyes
>
> Than to behold the oppressor's sacrifice![17]

Thus by words and actions the Abolitionist movement advanced in the

6

North with the Bible as the cornerstone of the whole effort.

Until so much anti-slavery sentiment had been aroused in the North, the Southerners had looked upon slavery as a necessary evil. They condoned it because they believed it an economic necessity, but were mildly apologetic toward the institution on moral grounds. There was, however, a widespread belief that it was somehow good for the

Short quotation included within text. slaves. The Reverend Phillip Schaff considered slavery as "a wholesome training school for the Negro—taking him from the lowest state of heathenism and barbarism to some degree of Christian civilization."[18] There was also a feeling that God had willed the superiority of the white race. After much reflection, Alexander Stevens came to this conclusion. He said:

Long quotation. No need for quotation marks in a blocked quotation.
> A proper subordination of the inferior to the superior race was the natural and normal condition of the former in relation to the latter. . . . The assignment of that position in the structure of society to the African race amongst us was the best for both races and in accordance with the ordinance of the Creator.[19]

More often, however, this belief was confined to a much vaguer feeling as expressed by Benet in his description of Mary-Lou Wingate:

7

In heaven, of course, we should all be equal,

But until we came to that golden sequel,

Gentility must keep to gentility

Where God and breeding had made things stable,

While the rest of the cosmos deserved civility

But dined in its boots at the second-table (p. 162).

Perhaps the South would have continued to apologize for slavery, but

for the denunciations of the Abolitionists; for few had ever before

considered it in the light of a "scriptural blessing," as historian Lloyd

terms it.[20] But after the severe attacks of Garrison and the others, the

South, on the defensive, thoroughly investigated the matter.

Elaborate proofs were prepared justifying slavery on Biblical

grounds. These were completed by intensive research and were

intricately planned. The Old Testament justification of slavery fell into

two principal arguments. The first: that from the beginning the Negro

race had been condemned to servitude; and the second: that God

Himself had expressly sanctioned the institution of slavery. The proof

of the first argument was found in Noah's angry prophecy to Canaan,

Ham's son:

Cursed be Canaan: a servant of servants shall he be unto his

Benet page number included in text. See footnote 1.

Phrase quoted for its stylistic appeal, appropriately credited.

Note effective lead in to Biblical point.

8

brethren (Genesis 10:25).

Because legend tells that Ham was the founder of the dark races, this point became quite influential. Even Benet's Bible-reading slave-trader used this as his excuse for his infamous work. The poem reads:

Literary evidence.

He touched the Bible. 'And it's down there, Mister,

Down there in black and white—the sons of Ham—

Bondservants—sweat of their brows.' His voice trailed off

Into texts. 'I tell you, Mister,' he said fiercely,

'The pay's good pay, but it's the Lord's work, too.

We're spreading the Lord's seed—spreading his seed—' (p. 15).

The second argument was put into a syllogism by Lloyd.

*Whatever God has sanctioned among any people cannot be in

 itself a sin.

*God did expressly sanction slavery among the Hebrews.

*Therefore, slavery cannot be in itself a sin.[21]

Topic sentence.

All that was needed to complete the argument was concrete

Explanation setting up quotation support.

Biblical evidence of the first and second points. Passages were found and pointed out in detail by the Southern clergy. Several quotations were always cited proving the existence of slavery in patriarchal times. Among the ones most often quoted were the commandment to

9

Abraham concerning circumcision, which particularly specifies, "he Biblical quotation.

that is bought with thy money" along with others listed (Genesis

17:13), and the advice of the angel to Hagar, Sarah's runaway servant:

"Return to thy mistress and submit thyself under her hands" (Genesis

16:19). The complicated proofs continued by placing emphasis on the

Mosaic law. Frequently stated were the long passages regulating the

conduct toward "bondservants" (Leviticus 25:44–46; Exodus 21:2–6,

20–21). But perhaps repeated with most regularity was this one

quotation, which stressed the property idea:

> And ye shall take them for a possession; they shall be your Southern Biblical arguments.
>
> bondmen forever: but over your brethren, the children of
>
> Israel, ye shall not rule one over another with rigour
>
> (Leviticus 25:46).

Thus, with no mention of the later sections of the Bible, the arguments

for the Old Testament justification of slavery were complete. Now

firmly convinced that slavery was consistent with the will of God, the

South sent out its challenge: "You cannot abolish slavery, for God is

pledged to sustain it!"

The North accepted the challenge and answered the South's every

argument with clear-cut logic. Their first point was that the pro-slavery evidence pertaining to the Mosaic law was really inconclusive

because it related exclusively to the "regulation of the Hebrew social

system."[22] William Jay said, "It is wholly immaterial whether the Jews

held slaves or not, since it is admitted by all that if they did, they acted

by virtue of a special and express permission from God, while it is

equally admitted that no such permission has been given to us."[23]

Several technical denials were made to the "Cursed be Canaan"

argument. It was pointed out that there is no reason to believe that

Noah's curse extended to the other children of Ham.[24] Furthermore,

the Old Testament tells of a vast Canaanite family in which there were

both Negroes and whites.[25]

The North's most conclusive arguments, however, were not

defensive. In the later sections of the Bible there are many passages

which actually forbid slavery; but even within the five books of Moses

several quotations may be found which prohibit slavery and slave

trade as well. Among these are:

Northern Biblical arguments.

And he that stealeth a man and selleth him, or if he be found

in his hand, he shall surely be put to death (Exodus 21:16).

and

Thou shalt not deliver unto his master a bondman that is

11

escaped from his master unto thee (Deuteronomy 23:15).

The prophets were particularly outspoken on the subject. "Woe unto

him . . . that useth his neighbor's services without wages," Jeremiah

wrote (22:13). And all through the Bible, time and time again, the

principles of freedom and equality are stressed:

Have we not all one father? Hath not one God created us?

(Malachi 1:10).

Thus the North argued that there is little to be gained in following

literally all of the ancient laws set down in the Bible for a specific

people in a particular set of circumstances, but that the ideas

expounded in the Scriptures are just and right.

The Bible thus proved to be an excellent weapon, not only because   Concluding
restatement of
of its variety in interpretations, but because of its widespread appeal.   thesis

As we have seen, the Bible arguments influenced all men from the very   leading to

lowliest to the greatest leaders of the time in both sections of our

country. As for the right of the matter, from our modern perspective,   author's
concluding
the Northern Biblical arguments would seem to have had the clear   evaluation.

logical and moral superiority; and, as we know, they prevailed.

The Footnotes

Footnotes

¹ Stephen Vincent Benet, <u>John Brown's Body</u> (Garden City, N.Y.: Doubleday Doran, 1928), p. 213. All subsequent textual references refer to this edition.

² As quoted in Lawrence Emerson Nelson, <u>Our Roving Bible</u> (New York: Abington-Cokesbury Press, 1945), p. 177.

Content notes.

³ Francis Carr Stifler, <u>The Bible Speaks</u> (New York: Duell, Sloan & Pierce, 1946), p. 42. In this regard, it is also interesting to note a conversation, which Stifler cites, that Lincoln once had with an agnostic friend: "You are wrong, Mr. Speed; take all of this book on reason that you can and the rest on faith, and you will, I am sure, live and die a happier and better man" (p. 42).

⁴ As cited by Nelson, p. 179.

⁵ John Brown's Body, passim [throughout].

First reference to book by single author.

⁶ Charles A. Madison, <u>Critics and Crusaders</u> (New York: Henry Holt, 1947), pp. 41, 43.

Subsequent reference.

⁷ Madison, p. 64.

First reference to anthology, multiple author.

⁸ <u>Old South Leaflets,</u> ed. Directors of the Old South Work (Boston: Old South Meeting House, 1896–1908), V, No. 79, 15.

Subsequent reference.

⁹ <u>Old South Leaflets,</u> VIII, No. 180, 10.

13

[10] Ernest Sutherland Bates, <u>American Faith</u> (New York: W. W. Norton, 1940), p. 454.

[11] <u>Old South Leaflets,</u> IV, No. 79, 7.

[12] Nelson, p. 176.

[13] Derived from an autobiographic passage by Harriet Beecher Stowe, as quoted in Nelson, p. 178.

Note the explicit citation.

[14] Nelson, p. 176.

[15] As quoted in Nelson, p. 176.

[16] Lucy Larcom, "The Nineteenth of April," in <u>Bugle Echoes: A Collection of Poems of the Civil War,</u> ed. Francis F. Browne (New York: White, Stokes, & Allen, 1886), p. 38.

Citing a poem from a primary source.

[17] "The Salvation," stanzas 10, 12, from <u>The Liberator,</u> (Jan. 1, 1831), 2 in <u>Old South Leaflets,</u> IV, No. 78, 6.

Citing a song from a primary source.

[18] As quoted in Arthur Charles Cole, <u>A History of American Life</u> (New York: MacMillan, 1934), VII, 256.

Primary reference quoted in a secondary source.

[19] Alexander H. Stephens, <u>Recollections of Alexander H. Stephens</u> (New York: Doubleday Page, 1910), p. 199.

[20] Arthur Young Lloyd, <u>The Slavery Controversy</u> (Chapel Hill: Univ. of N. Carolina Press, 1939), p. 164.

[21] Lloyd, p. 189.

14

[22] Henry Drisler, <u>Criticism of John H. Hopkins's "Bible View of Slavery"</u> (New York: C. S. Westcott, 1863), p. 3.

[23] William Jay, <u>Miscellaneous Writings on Slavery</u> (Boston: Jewett, 1853), p. 626.

[24] Drisler, p. 3.

[25] Agenor Etienne Gasparin, <u>The Uprising of a Great People</u> (New York: Scribner, 1862), p. 104

The Bibliography

Bibliography

Primary Sources

Benet, Stephen Vincent. John Brown's Body. Garden City, N.Y.:

Doubleday Doran, 1928.

Holy Bible. Authorized King James Version. Cleveland: The World

Publishing Company, 1955.

Browne, Francis F., ed. Bugle Echoes: A Collection of Poems of the

Civil War, Both Northern and Southern, Ed. Francis F. Browne.

New York: White, Stokes & Allen, 1886.

Drisler, Henry. Criticism of John H. Hopkins's "Bible View of Slavery."

New York: C. S. Westcott, 1863.

Gasparin, Agenor Etienne. The Uprising of a Great People. New York:

Scribner, 1862.

Jay, William. Miscellaneous Writings on Slavery. Boston: Jewett, 1853.

Old South Leaflets. Ed. Directors of the Old South Work. Boston: Old

South Meeting House, 1896–1908.

Stephens, Alexander H. In Recollections of Alexander H. Stephens. Ed.

Myrta Lockett Avary. New York: Doubleday Page, 1910.

16

Secondary Sources

Bates, Ernest Sutherland. American Faith. New York: W. W. Norton,

    1940.

Cole, Arthur Charles. The Irrepressible Conflict, 1850–1865. A History

    of American Life. Vol. VII. New York: Macmillan, 1934.

Lloyd, Arthur Young. The Slavery Controversy. Chapel Hill: Univ. of N.

    Carolina Press, 1939.

Madison, Charles A. Critics and Crusaders. New York: Henry Holt,

    1947.

Nelson, Lawrence Emerson. Our Roving Bible. New York: Abington-

    Cokesbury, 1945.

Stifler, Francis Carr. The Bible Speaks. New York: Duell, Sloan & Pierce,

    1946.

Write a research paper of some five or six typed pages (1250–1500 words) answering a question raised by one of the following general subjects or on a topic your instructor will suggest. (I have included sample questions for some of the topics.)

Hamlet (Why did Hamlet delay so long in "sweeping to his revenge"?)

The Holocaust in World War II (Why were there so few instances of rebellion on the part of the victims of the Nazis?)

Battered Wives (What causes this phenomenon, and how can it be remedied?)

Beowulf (To what extent is it a Christian work?)

The Aztec Indians

Cancer

Men in the Life of Queen Elizabeth I

The Great Depression

Versions of the Faust Legend

REM (Rapid Eye Movements) and Deep-Dream Sleep

Evolution

Charlie Chaplin and the Notion of the Sad Clown

Nuclear Energy

Gregorian Chants

The Rights of Divorced Fathers

Frank Lloyd Wright and His Contribution to Architecture

Political Cartoonists

The Great Schism in the Catholic Church

Jazz

Affirmative Action

The Problem of Evil: Some Answers from Myth and Philosophy

The Homosexual and the Law

Cloning

Paul Robeson: Figure of Controversy

Hemingway: Macho or Mushy

Astrology

President Johnson's "Great Society"

Lizzie Borden: Guilty or Innocent?

Sam Shepherd: Guilty or Innocent?

Salem Witchcraft

Ellis Island

The Creation of Living Organisms for Commercial Use

Alimony Laws

The Insanity Plea in Our Court System

10

The Critical Analysis

Like the research paper, the critical analysis is a specialized form of expository writing. It is specialized both in subject matter, which is limited to works of literature or other art forms, and in approach, which is almost exclusively analytical and interpretative. It is, nevertheless, important to remember that every critical analysis is an expository essay, and everything we have said about expository writing holds true for it as well.

THE NATURE OF A CRITICAL ANALYSIS

A critical analysis is a frequent assignment in college courses. You may be asked to write such a paper about an essay, story, novel, play, movie, or even a composition of music or dance or a work of visual art. Or you may be asked to write a comparative analysis of two or more such works. Sometimes a critical essay is required when the assignment or exam question doesn't mention "critical analysis" at all. You should write a critical analysis, for instance, if you were given an assignment similar to any of these:

- Comment on Lance Morrow's use of imagery and figurative language throughout "In the Beginning: God and Science."
- Tell how Kate Chopin's "The Story of an Hour" fits in with contemporary feminist concepts.
- In many novels and plays, minor characters contribute significantly to the total work. They often have certain functions, in particular, as instruments in the plot, foils for the main characters, commentators on the action or theme, and the like. Write a well-organized essay showing how minor characters function in a work in which they appear importantly. (Adapted from a nationally standardized test question.)

When a critical analysis is called for, what specifically should you expect to write? Despite common misconceptions, you should *not* plan to write simply a summary of the work, nor an evaluation of its merits, nor an expression of the thoughts it raises in your mind—although any of these elements may form a part of your paper. What you should expect to write rather, is an interpretation of the work (or works). And you should expect to do so in terms of the way the author chooses to get his or her meaning across. Whatever kind of literature or art you will be dealing with and whatever the approach you select or are assigned, the heart of your critical analysis will be your answer to these two analytical questions:

1. What is the author trying to say? (meaning)
2. How does he or she go about saying it? (method)

The emphasis you place on your answer to each of these questions will vary, but the presence of both is unavoidable, for they are the essence of the critical analysis.

How do you come to your answers to these questions? By a process that—at least for literature—is known as *close reading*. The first step in planning your critical analysis, then, is to make a close reading of the work that is your subject.

Close Reading

Close reading begins with a concentrated phrase-by-phrase reading of a passage or a work. I recommend that you do this reading aloud. You may also want to take notes as you go along. Professor Elaine Maimon suggests that you even copy down selected passages in order to "get inside the author's rhythms and style."* In any case, take care to mark any word or reference you don't fully comprehend, and be sure that you understand it clearly before you are ready to pull your impressions together.

Be Conscious of the Author   The purpose of close reading is not only to understand the author's meaning fully. It is also to discover what the author does to affect your thinking and your emotions. Reading closely, then, differs from the usual varieties of reading not so much in the more intense attentiveness involved (although this is certainly required) as in the attitudes it demands of the reader. Ordinarily, as a reader, you think of the work you are reading as a vehicle for acquiring knowledge or pleasure. In order to do close reading, however, you will have to train yourself to view the work rhetorically—as the creation of an author for a particular reason or set of reasons. Cleanth Brooks, Robert Penn Warren, and John Thibout Purser label a work of literature "the presentation of an author's way of looking at life."† Your job as a critical reader is to discover what way of "looking at life" is being presented. To do so, you will have to read with the author's purpose foremost in your consciousness. Ask yourself continually: What is the author attempting here? Why would the author include this passage? This effect?

Writing in the Arts and Sciences (Cambridge, Mass.: Winthrop, 1981), p. 162.

†*An Approach to Literature* (N. Y.: Appleton, Century, Crofts, 1964), p. 4.

Read Literally   To do close reading you will have to put aside any tendency you may have to skim over stories quickly just to get the plot or over essays just to find the general meaning. The methodical approach described earlier should help you here. But it may well involve you in the equally unproductive tendency of delving so industriously for hidden meanings and symbolisms that you overlook the author's overall intent. Actually, close reading is first of all a reading for *literal* meaning. Ask yourself as you read, What do the words really say? What do they explicitly mean? What does the syntax literally convey? Only after you have established the literal meaning should you look for hidden interpretation or symbolic significance. Of course, you must delve beneath the surface in order to discover just what the author is trying to get at, but all the clues for a valid interpretation are present right there in the words themselves.

Wonder at the Unusual   As you read, look for anything that seems, on the one hand, part of a pattern, or odd or out-of-place on the other. Notice, for instance, repetition, parallels, metaphors, intriguing openings, interesting conclusions. When anything seems to be calling attention to itself as out of the ordinary, try to reach some conclusion as to why the author put it there and how it fits into the pattern of the work as a whole.

Be Aware of Your Own Reactions   You should also be sensitive to your own reactions and look for the author's purpose behind any unusual response you discover in yourself. Ask yourself, Why do I respond to that tone, situation, character, image, argument in that way? Does the author intend me to feel this way? What did she or he do to provoke this response? By exploring in this way the methods your author uses to influence your relationship with the material, you should be able to arrive at a tentative interpretation of the work.

     Close reading thus is double-edged. You study the author's methods to understand the meaning; and once you have established a tentative meaning you look for methods that will support or argue for your interpretation of it. The guidelines in the accompanying boxed section should be helpful in both searches.

Guidelines for Close Reading

1. *Clues from the overall structure.* Start with the overall structure. How is the work organized? What are the beginning, middle, and end? How does the gross structure contribute to the creation of the overall impression you have decided is the author's purpose?
2. *Clues from the individual parts.* Examine the work part by part. Which parts do you see as most important in contributing to the author's purpose? How do they do so? How do they fit into the whole? Are there portions which do not seem to contribute to, or perhaps seem even to contradict, your interpretation? Can the discrepancies be reconciled? If not, can your interpretation be adjusted to fit the new elements?
3. *Clues from substructures, motifs, patterns.* Within the overall structure, are

there any secondary structures or motifs? Are there unusual elements within the work, ideas or stylistic constructions that catch your attention? Why do you think the author included them? Do they form a pattern? How do they contribute to the author's purpose? to your interpretation?

Planning the Structure of Your Analysis

Your close reading should provide you with preliminary answers to the two analytic questions: What is the author trying to say? and How? These answers can become the foundation for organizing your critical essay. Because the critical analysis is such a specialized form of writing, it is possible to set up a model or format for a thesis that can help organize a wide variety of such essays. The format includes answers to both of the analytic questions:

In *Such-and-Such Work,* Author So-and-So suggests . . . [(1) meaning] by . . . [(2) method].

Since structures are derived from theses, it is even possible to set up a model outline. A typical structural plan will, of course, also reflect the interplay of the two main elements, meaning and method. Here is such a plan:

   I. Introduction leading to thesis.
  II. Interpretation supported by [opening passages, for example]
 III. Interpretation supported by [overall patterns of imagery, for instance]
     Pattern A
     Pattern B
     Pattern C
  IV. Interpretation supported by [for example, resolution of conflict]
   V. Conclusion: Full expression of interpretation with reference to [title, for instance]

In practice, of course, composing your thesis and planning the structure of your critical essay is not nearly so cut-and-dried. Although the basic pattern usually holds, the variations are infinite, determined as they are by the nature of the specific assignment and your specific approach to it. Let's look at variations of the basic thesis and structure that might be produced by writers working from the sample assignments offered at the beginning of this chapter:
• When the assignment places the emphasis upon a specific method:

Assignment: Comment upon Lance Morrow's use of imagery and figurative language throughout "In the Beginning: God and Science."
     Thesis: In "In the Beginning: God and Science," Lance Morrow makes a lively use of imagery to persuade his readers of the importance of the religious and scientific communities at last being forced into dialogue by the new discoveries that bring Biblical and scientific creation theories much closer together.
   I. Introduction—Including explication of Morrow's point
  II. Imagery of hyperbole to convey the enormous improbability of science and religion ever agreeing

    III. Metaphoric introductions to the remarks of scientists and theologians to further the tension between them

    IV. Conclusion: Effect of the imagery—
        To kindle interest in a very technical topic
        To convey a sense of ongoing controversy

- When the assignment places the emphasis upon the meaning: (Here the author's point is to be applied to an externally existing idea.)

    Assignment: Tell how Kate Chopin's "The Story of an Hour" fits in with contemporary feminist concepts.

        Thesis: By portraying Mrs. Mallard's inner acknowledgement of the deep joy that freedom from her kind and loving husband would bring to her, Kate Chopin prefigures an important feminist theme: that even the kindliest "imposition of one person's private will upon another" causes unspeakable agony.

    I. Introduction—including brief summary of plot

    II. Chopin's point: implicit in Mrs. M's feelings
    Nature of Mrs. M's feelings
    Imagery with which it is expressed

    III. How Chopin develops the point: progression of Mrs. M's feelings
      A. Initial response
      B. Gradual awareness
      C. Paradoxical ending

    IV. Conclusion: Application of Chopin's point to contemporary feminist theory

- When the assignment gives you elements to work with, but the subject and emphasis must be your own:

    Assignment: In many novels and plays, minor characters contribute significantly to the total work. They often have certain functions, in particular, as instruments in the plot, foils for the main characters, commentators on the action or theme or the like. Write a well-organized essay showing how minor characters function in a work in which they appear importantly.

        Thesis: In *Hamlet* Shakespeare presents a number of men of action— Fortinbras, Laertes, even Horatio—as foils for his thoughtful hero. In doing so Shakespeare points up the seriousness of Hamlet's struggle with inaction and thus underlines Hamlet's eventual discovery that action itself is not what is important, but rather that "the readiness is all."

    I. Introduction—including explication of Shakespeare's theme of "There is Providence in the fall of the sparrow" and "The readiness is all."

    II. Theme developed through contrast: thoughtful Hamlet vs. active foils
      A. Hamlet and Horatio
      B. Hamlet and Fortinbras
      C. Hamlet and Laertes

    III. Shakespeare's direct statement of theme: Hamlet comes to understand (no longer rejects himself)

    IV. Conclusion

But what about the assignment when you are thrown altogether upon your own resources: "Write a critical analysis of . . . ," for instance? This sort of assignment should not cause you special worry. After all, any one of the previous samples could have been composed for it. What you need to do when the assignment is general in this way is to discover an approach to a work that will permit you to discuss the aspects of it you find the most interesting. When you do your close reading for such an assignment, use a list of the items that caught your attention as an inventory of ideas, and find connections and patterns among them. Then take those patterns that most impressively point to your interpretation of the author's thesis, theme, or meaning, and use them to support it.

Sometimes you will be asked to (or decide to) write a critical analysis in which you will be expected to compare two or more works in some respects. The following question from a standardized exam is typical of such comparative assignments:

> The struggle to achieve dominance over others frequently appears in fiction. Choose two stories in which such a struggle for dominance occurs, and write an essay comparing the purposes for which the author uses the struggle.

In order to plan the structure for a critical analysis coming out of such a question, you might try thinking back to the useful "although clause" format. This format will help you subordinate one work to the other, for it is difficult to produce a unified essay if two important subjects are given equal treatment. Though the word and concept "although" need not, of course, be used, a workable format for such an analysis might go something like this:

> Although many authors, such as Author #1 in "Story #1," focus their stories on the struggle to achieve dominance over others for comedic or lightly satiric purposes, Author #2, especially in "Story #2," explores this topic in order to set forth his particularly brutal view of the nature of the universe.

Solving the Technical Problems

The writing and rewriting stages of the writing process are, as we have said, much the same for critical analyses as they are for the rest of expository writing. There are, however, a few technical problems that you may run into here that are specific to this particular kind of writing. These problems all evolve from the delicate relationship between the material in your critical analysis and the work you are dealing with.

How Much to Summarize?   Perhaps the most difficult problem of this sort you will encounter is deciding how much of the subject work to recount. The least successful attempts at critical analysis are plot summaries with their dull recounting of "and then, and then." You will certainly want to avoid boring your readers in this way. And yet, if you proceed with your interpretative analysis as if the work is as familiar to your readers as it is to you, you run the equally grave risk of utterly confusing them. Your readers then would in the position of a person who joins a group already deep in conversation and tries unsuccessfully to catch enough clues to gather what they are saying—a very frustrating position indeed.

The solution lies in maintaining a delicate balance. A good rule is to assume that your readers have read the work, but that this reading was several years ago. Following this rule, you should summarize whatever material is necessary to make your points clear, but only as much as the demands of your thesis and arguments require. More specifically:

Guidelines for summarizing.

1. Always identify the work (or works) you will be analyzing by title and by author in your introduction.
2. In order to orient your readers, be sure to include somewhere early in your paper a brief summary of the basic points or plot of your work— if only a sentence or two in length.
3. Never introduce a point without giving enough background from the work to make the point comprehensible to your readers. Never attempt to explicate a passage without quoting the passage.
4. On the other hand, do not get caught up in retelling the story, in rearguing the article. Keep your attention focused upon your purpose of developing your *own* critical thesis.

How to Distinguish Your Author's Purpose from Your Own?

Another problem in writing critical analyses is the blending of the two theses involved in this kind of writing: your author's thesis—theme, meaning—and your own. It is not difficult to confuse the two, but it is important that you do not. No matter how heartily you may agree with your author's view of life, your thesis can never be identical with your author's. The following thesis would NOT do for a *critical analysis* of George Will's article, for instance, even though it might lead to a good enough essay on a similar subject:

FAULTY   Israel deserves better treatment than it is getting from the United States government, as George Will points out in "Israel and Munich."

A thesis like the following, on the other hand, would be appropriate for a critical analysis:

In "Israel and Munich" George Will persuasively argues that Israel deserves better treatment than it is getting from the United States government [by drawing a parallel between the current position of Israel and that of Czechoslovakia before World War II].

When you undertake to write a critical analysis, you commit yourself to a purpose that is basically literary or scholarly and whose object is an external work of art.

Inexperienced writers sometimes forget this purpose in another way and use the work as a springboard for expressing their own ideas. The critical analysis one student wrote to answer a question on the significance of Cordelia's death at the conclusion of *King Lear,* for example, was less than successful because the student could not separate her own experience from that of Shakespeare's character:

FAULTY

> The death of Cordelia proves my point that you have to do, think, and say exactly what your elders want you to or you shall perish. . . . It's as though elders need to control your every thought and movement.

Comparisons with your own experience and analogies to other literary works can be helpful to you in explaining your author's meanings, but make sure you do not let such material intrude upon your discussion of the author's intent. Let me suggest some practical ways to help you avoid such difficulties:

1. Get in the habit of speaking in terms of the author. "George Will argues. . . ," "Lance Morrow uses his Romeo and Juliet metaphor to . . . ," "Kate Chopin develops the character of Mrs. Mallard for. . . ."
2. Keep close to the work itself. When you leave it to make comparisons with external experience or other works, be sure that your purpose remains interpretative.
3. Quotations can keep you on the track.* Use them freely—though keep them brief. A well-chosen excerpt can supply irrefutable proof for the point you are making. Furthermore, if you include (in moderation) the words of an author who writes with wit and charm, you cannot help but enhance the effect of your own style.

Guidelines for focusing on author's purpose.

Which Methods or Strategies to Cite?

Some writers inexperienced with critical analyses are so pleased with the strategies they have discovered in their close reading that they are tempted to fill their papers with them in a random "Lookee, here's a metaphor" fashion. This practice has made far too many analyses focusless and inane. To avoid it, take care that every example you include not only demonstrates a point, but that you have clearly drawn the connection between the example and the point it supports.

When to Use Outside Sources?

Unless your instructor tells you otherwise, your critical analysis should be based upon your own reactions to the work in question. Ordinarily, critical analyses are not meant to be research papers and should not involve you in a search of the literature for the critical opinions of others.

This is not to say that all outside sources are forbidden. On the contrary, let me encourage you to use reference books to gain background that will enrich your understanding of the work you will be analyzing. For example, you should certainly use a dictionary to understand an unfamliar word. When you are dealing with the work of an author from an earlier period (or one like James Joyce or Vladimir Nabokov who uses words allusively) it is a good idea to check on key words in the *Oxford English Dictionary*, which provides the literary history of every word in the English language. And you will also want to look

---

*For information on the technical aspects of including quotations in your written work, see Chapter 9, p. 362.

up any references that are unfamiliar to you in an appropriate source. You can find explanations of Greek or Roman gods and goddesses and their stories, for instance, in dictionaries of classical mythology; and you can trace Biblical references through a concordance of the Bible. In certain cases you may find some biographical information about your author helpful to you in making your interpretation of the work. The *Dictionary of National Biography* (British) and the *Dictionary of American Biography* (American) can be useful sources here. There are also dictionaries of literary usage to help you discover the characteristics of such terms as "epic" or "sestina" when they are relevant to your work. There are many such sources. Ask your reference librarian to help you locate the appropriate volume to look up anything that puzzles you in your close reading.

How Much to Evaluate?   Evaluation is not required for a well-written critical analysis (except, of course, for reviews, which are written to advise readers on whether or not the work in question is worth their time). In fact, unnecessary evaluative passages can give a critical essay a less than professional sound. Such comments as the vague "I liked it because it was interesting" or the obvious "I think Faulkner is a pretty good writer" are better left unsaid. And yet an aptly observed evaluative remark can add to the quality of your critical analysis. If you want to include some evaluation in your analysis, here are some practical suggestions:

1. Base your evaluation firmly upon your analytical and interpretative findings.
2. Do not mingle your evaluative comments with analysis and interpretation. The concluding paragraphs are an especially appropriate place for evaluative material.

Suggestions for evaluative comments.

3. Evaluate the work on how well the author succeeds in doing what he or she has set out to do. If you are writing a critical analysis of Wagner's *Lohengrin,* it would be appropriate to comment (if you believed it to be so) that by making the music rise too often to the heights of magnificence, Wagner hardens the listener to the effects of the crescendo and thus loses some of its impact. On the other hand, it would not be appropriate to comment (no matter how truly) that you do not care for the stories about Teutonic mythology that form the basis for Wagner's operas.

The Conventions of Critical Analysis

1. It is conventional to use the present tense for critical analysis. Write "Shakespeare *develops* his theme by . . . " not "Shakespeare *developed* his theme by . . . ."
2. It is conventional to credit the author with conscious manipulation of strategy as, for example: "Shakespeare develops his theme by . . . ."
3. And although you need not hesitate to say "I" where appropriate, your name

standing as the author of the essay is usually sufficient identification for matters of opinion. Therefore, avoid writing "*I think* Shakespeare develops his theme by . . . ." And do not hesitate to write "Shakespeare develops his theme . . . ."

Writing a Review or Critique

In the same way that a critical analysis is a kind of expository writing, a review (or critique, as it is sometimes called) is a kind of critical analysis. It is a critical analysis whose purpose is to provide the reader with a guide to the book, essay, drama, musical performance, or other artistic work it discusses. Because it has this specific purpose, you might call a review an "evaluative critical analysis."

Except for your handling of the summary and the evaluation, you write a review just as you write a critical analysis. The summary of the work that you include in a review is, oddly enough, both more complete and more limited than that you use in writing other critical analyses. It needs to be more complete because the purpose of the review is to acquaint your readers with the work. But on the other hand, if as a reviewer you are recommending the work, you must be careful not to give away so much that your readers will no longer need (or want) to experience it themselves.

The degree of evaluation required is a more serious difference between writing reviews and writing other kinds of critical analyses, because it is the evaluative function that distinguishes the review. In other critical analyses an evaluative passage is optional; in reviews even the thesis itself may well be judgmental:

- This movie is well worth seeing because . . . .
- The world of literature is little enriched by this author's first novel because . . . .

Like all critical analyses, a review is concerned with what the author is trying to say and how he or she goes about saying it, but in the review, as these sample theses indicate, the analytic function backs up the evaluative.

The evaluative techniques tend to differ as well. In reviews, as in all critical analyses, you evaluate a work in terms of its author's goals. In a review, however, it is also appropriate to include your judgment as to the worth of these goals. I have suggested that your personal response to a work has little place in most critical analyses, but in a review you need not hesitate to include personal impressions if you can validate them with evidence from the work.

Analyses of Particular Kinds of Literature

In order to write a good critical analysis of a work, you need to have not only an understanding of the conventions of the critical analysis in general, but also knowledge of the techniques and strategies specific to the kind of art (the *genre*) that you are dealing with. The following sections outline those specific techniques that should be most helpful for your critical writing. Please note, however, that these sections will not attempt a comprehensive discussion of all the valid approaches to literary or artistic analysis or appreciation. Rather my intention is only to augment your instructor's presentation of these matters, and to offer enough examples of techniques specific to each kind of literature to provide a guide for writing critical analyses about each of them.

ANALYZING EXPOSITORY WRITING

Let's begin with expository writing, the subject of this book. In working through *Writing Effectively* you have done a good deal of thinking about how to write expository prose. To compose a critical analysis of this sort of writing, you only have to reverse this thinking from the writer's point of view to that of the reader, from how you can get across what you have to say to how another author has done so. The territory then should already be familiar.

Finding the Author's Meaning

Expository writing may be the easiest kind of writing for you to approach critically when you consider it from another standpoint as well. As you know, the focus of a critical analysis is the author's meaning and methods. For this kind of analysis, expository prose is the most approachable of all the kinds of creative work, because it offers the clearest statement of the author's "way of viewing life." In writing expository essays or longer works of expository prose, authors express themselves directly. Most of the time, as we have seen, authors state their theses in an explicit sentence or two, and where they do not, they imply the thesis so clearly that readers should have no difficulty in formulating it for themselves. Finding the author's meaning, then, is not as central to analysis of expository prose as it is to analysis of other kinds of artistic expression. Consequently, your task in writing an analysis of expository prose is more likely to concern itself with determining your author's way of viewing the thesis and discovering the means by which he or she attempts to persuade you to this point of view.

Determining the Author's Viewpoint

To discover your author's approach, you need to think a bit about the tone of the piece. How literally does your author intend her or his words? What connotations do the words convey? What value judgments are implied? Is your author always speaking to you in a straightforward way or is there some irony (see p. 415) in the tone? Read between the lines. Is your author trying to communicate something that is not written on the paper? Look at the opening sentences of Tom Wolfe's "Down with Sin" essay, for instance:

> The need for a denunciation of sin occurred to me the other day when I read a remark by some young movie star. . . . He had made a picture with Doris Day, and he felt it was time somebody *came to the defense of that girl.* He said,

"You know, Doris is not the nice, sweet, wholesome, Mom's pie, All-American girl everybody makes her out to be. Actually, she is quite a gal." (p. 443, *1*, emphasis Wolfe's)

Wolfe says that he must denounce sin. He means this statement to be startling because he wants his readers to remember that everyone is supposed to be for virtue and against sin; but he never spells out this idea in words. Wolfe would like his readers to find the quotation from the movie star as outrageous as he does. He wants his readers to understand the unconscious irony in the actor's *defense* of Doris Day on the grounds that she is not as virtuous as she is thought to be. The notion that sin now seems to be more acceptable than virtue is central to Wolfe's thesis, and yet he, like many other sophisticated writers, makes his point by implication only. When you prepare to write a critical analysis, you must be sure to catch all such implications.

Discovering the Author's Methods

Once you are clear in your understanding of your author's thesis and of his or her approach to that thesis, you will want to begin looking for the techniques your author uses to persuade you of the truth of that way of thinking. What are the rhetorical techniques specific to expository writing? They are the strategies for writing persuasively and effectively, the very strategies that this book has been concerned with throughout. In order to review them for your work with critical analysis, I can think of no more helpful arrangement than one which has been traditional with rhetoricians since the days of Aristotle. You'll find this arrangement in the accompanying boxed section.

Rhetorical Strategies Available to Composers of Expository Writing

I. Appeal to Ethical Sense (see Part One p. 18, Chapter 1, p. 47, Chapter 4, p. 127)
   A. Presentation of the author as a good person, a likable person, a believable person
   B. Presentation of the author as a knowledgeable person, personally experienced in this area and/or well studied in it
   C. Presentation of the author as a fair-minded, reasonable, understanding person
   D. Presentation of the author somewhere on the scale of objective observer ◄----------► impassioned advocate

II. Appeal to Reason (see Chapter 1, p. 59)
   A. Clear, coherent presentation of thesis
   B. Clear, though less forceful presentation of (or allusion to) the opposing point of view ("although clause" usually preceding thesis presentation)
   C. Logically consistent presentation of supporting material ("arguments")
   D. Supporting material ("arguments") that are internally logical and consistent
   E. "Arguments" based upon fact, statistics, authority, logic

III. Appeal to Emotion
Known in earlier days as "The Flowers of Rhetoric," we now think of many of these techniques as more closely associated with the other kinds of literature.
A. Devices associated with poetry (see Chapter 8, p. 317)
1. Imagery:
a. Metaphor, simile, symbol, connotative language
b. Personification, hyperbole, and allusion
2. Rhythmic, emotion heightening language
3. Repetition and variation
B. Devices associated with fiction (see Chapter 10, p. 408)
1. Narrative, anecdote
2. Dramatization, dialogue
3. Characterization
4. Specific detail (see also Chapter 3, p. 98)
5. Irony
C. Devices of sentence structure (see Chapter 7)
1. Parallelism
2. Balance and antithesis
3. Periodic sentences
4. Cumulative sentences

These are among the most important rhetorical techniques available to the author of expository prose. Before you write your critical analysis, study the work to discover which of these techniques—or what varieties of them—your author employs.

An Example

How might you apply your knowledge of the techniques of expository writing to writing your own critical analysis? The following example, including annotations, outline, and draft analysis, may give you some ideas on how to proceed. The subject of the analysis is Ellen Goodman's "The Cult of Impotence," which you can find on p. 470 of Part Five.

Inventory of Ideas: Notes

Title: Almost a miniature thesis of itself: [We have made a] "Cult of Impotence."
Introduction:
Striking symbol of the isolation tank
Use of precise facts (10 inches of water; 93 degrees)
Use of quotation of inventor (Inventor = a psychiatrist, a doctor, an authority in our society)
Quotation starts as simple explanation; ends in dramatic irony.
First mention of the key phrase: "the universe within"
Allusion to Greta Garbo: "I vant to be alone." (apt, but left unstated)
Brings in readers with "we" (reinforces earlier use of "let's")
Thesis Statement:
The "isolation tank" is as good a symbol as any of a time when we are making

$$+ \qquad\qquad\qquad -$$

• a positive value   out of   our sense of impotence in the world, and

+	–

• a cult   out of   the fragmentation of society and mixed connections of our personal lives

(Note mixed diction, emphasized by antithetically balanced sentence structure.)

Support:

Answers the questions:

A. Why do we "vant to be alone"?
   1. Despair over events beyond our control; feelings of helplessness (Viet-
      nam, Watergate)
   2. Can't even do good without doing bad (Cure typhoid——➤ overpopula-
      tion; raise standard of living ——➤ destroy environment)
B. How is the aloneness manifested in our society?
   1. Statistics on those living alone
   2. Popularity of self-reliance movements ——➤ leads back to the psychiatrist's
      self-absorption tank (and another telling quotation)

Leading to Conclusion: Negative Evaluation

Open criticism built upon earlier preparation
   "Navel gazing"
   "permanent retreat from others and problems"

Leads to restatement of thesis (more strongly—and openly—worded):
   "At a time when we seem in almost perilous need of personal connections and social solutions, the tendency toward the isolation-tank psychology can be a sad perversion of the old American individualism."

Conclusion:

Conclusion introduced by final statement of thesis

Argument summed up by a quoted anecdote
   Contrasts cult view of "the universe within" with "the world without"

Preliminary Outline of Critical Analysis

Thesis: Ellen Goodman, having discovered in Lilly's isolation tank a potent symbol both to explain the me-ness of the Me Decade and to show what is
wrong with it, develops her insight for her readers and persuades us to
share her doubts.

  I. Introduction——➤Thesis
 II. Explains her insight (structure)
III. Persuades us to share her doubts:
    A. Initial surface objectivity
       1. "Let's all look into this together" approach
       2. Use of quotations, facts, and figures
    B. Underlying negative appraisal
       1. Points up "universe within" in quotation
       2. Ironic juxtaposition in initial thesis statement
    C. Forthright negative evaluation
 IV. Conclusion: Anecdote that points up foolishness of "universe within."

Draft: Critical Analysis

We all have moments of insight, sudden flashes of understanding that bring
together the fragments of our existence and, at least for the moment, make

them into a comprehensible whole. Ellen Goodman, who writes a newspaper column of social commentary, must have had just such an insight when she learned of the invention of a California psychoanalyst. In John Lilly's isolation tank Ellen Goodman saw a symbol which summed up and clarified for her the various elements of the "me" decade of the seventies. What is more, it also offered an explanation for her deeply held—but far from universally shared—conviction that there was something inherently wrong in the whole value system underlying it. In "The Cult of Impotence" Goodman explains her insight to her readers and persuades us to share her doubts.

Goodman introduces her article with Lilly's isolation tank and then explains why it is "as good a symbol as any" for the late seventies. To show why, she points out how events like Vietnam and Watergate left Americans with a sense of despair, a sense of living in a world over which they could exercise no control. She shows further how the idealistic belief of the sixties that individuals could really be a force for good ended with the helpless understanding that even good actions have bad results: "When you raise the standard of living," for example, "you destroy the environment." This sense of despair of making a mark for good on the outside world has turned people's attention in upon themselves, Goodman believes. She backs up her belief by citing statistics which point to all of the people who live alone and all those who join "hyper-individualistic" movements, like est, that are "characterized by a frenzied search inward." At this point in her analysis, Goodman has worked her way back to her original symbol, the isolation tank, which is, as she has explained, a therapeutic device of just such a movement.

Goodman's purpose is not simply to describe this phenomenon, however, but to criticize it. And although, as she demonstrates, the society to which her readers belong places high positive value on "finding" oneself or on "doing one's own thing," she makes her point convincingly. She includes her readers immediately in a "Let's all look into this together" approach:

Think what *we* do with it—free *ourselves* from other people and the
environment, enter the "universe within" (p. 470, *3*, emphasis mine).

Note that Goodman carries her readers along, not only by her use of the first-person plural *(we)*, but also by the friendly, conversational quality of her tone and the informality of her diction.

Goodman also wins her readers by her seeming objectivity. She is precise about her facts: The tank has exactly "10 inches of water heated to precisely 93 degrees." She backs up her statements by impressive statistics: "In the years since 1960, the number of primaries . . . has risen by 87 percent . . . . Fifteen million of us live alone. Fifty million . . . are single, widowed or divorced." She does not attempt to paraphrase John Lilly, but through quotation, she lets him speak for himself.

But under the objective veneer, Goodman's point of view is clearly in evidence. What she strives for in the first two-thirds of the essay—and to a large extent succeeds in doing—is to make it seem as if the facts themselves indisputably demonstrate her point of view. Take Lilly's first quotation, for example:

Lying on your back, you can breathe quite comfortably and safely,
freed from sight, sound, people and the universe outside. That way
you can enter the universe within you.

Although Lilly's statement begins in a purely descriptive way, it ends with words that Goodman means to be self-condemning, "the universe within." She takes up this phrase, which to her represents the ridiculous limitation of Lilly's view, and uses it as a motif throughout the essay. Similarly, Goodman's introductory statement of thesis begins with the objective idea of the archaelogically valuable symbolism of the tank, but ends in an ironic juxtaposition of positive values and negative qualities:

> The "isolation tank" is as good a symbol as any of a time when we are
> making a positive value out of our sense of impotence in the world,
> and a cult out of the fragmentation of society and missed connections
> of our personal lives.

Having prepared her readers in this way, Goodman can speak forthrightly in her concluding paragraphs. To Dr. Lilly's final quotation, praising his tank as a "way you can isolate yourself in your deep inner core," Goodman asks rhetorically, "But then where are you?" She supplies her own answer in language more highly charged than she has yet used: at the "dead end of navel-gazing." In this way she leads into an equally highly charged restatement of her thesis that reveals her sense of imminent danger:

> At a time when we seem in almost perilous need of personal connec-
> tions and social solutions, the tendency toward the isolation-tank psy-
> chology can be a sad perversion of the old American individualism.

To reinforce her point and to return to the informal conversational relationship with her readers with which she begins, Goodman concludes by quoting an anecdote that gently pokes fun at another of those "getting in touch with their feelings" types who might well be a user of Dr. Lilly's tank: "I know there is something outside of me . . . I can feel it. I know it is there. But what is it?" When Goodman quotes the response to this fatuous question, she as much as winks at her readers who have already learned quite enough about Dr. Lilly's "universe within." What is this mysterious "other reality" that even this foolish man senses is there? "Perhaps it is the world," Goodman quotes. And her readers cannot help but nod in agreement.

Try It Out

1. Choose an essay from the collection in Part Five (or from another source) and answer each of the questions in *one* of the following sets* in as detailed a manner as you can.

   a. What is the author's thesis? Does he or she state it explicitly or merely imply it? Describe in detail the rhetorical devices he or she employs to develop and sustain the thesis.

   b. What is the author's attitude toward the subject? Do his or her selection and treatment of details contribute to a particular tone that aids in unifying and developing the thesis? What is that tone? Cite specific words, phrases, allusions, and details, and specify their tone and effect.

---

*These questions are adapted from a final examination given to all of the freshman composition classes at a large state university.

    c. What is the relationship between the final paragraph (or paragraph cluster) and the rest of the essay? Show how the structure of the essay prepares us for the author's comments in the final paragraph. Does he or she organize the material in such a way as to create a pattern of development that leads logically to the final comments? Show how.

2. From your answers to the questions, compose a thesis for a critical analysis of the essay.

3. Use the thesis to construct a structural plan for such an analysis.

ANALYZING A NARRATIVE WORK: A STORY, DRAMA, OR NARRATIVE POEM*

In expository writing authors convey their ideas about the world to the reader by stating them more or less directly. In narrative writing, authors convey their ideas more subtly—by telling a story.* As Brooks and Warren put it in one of their insightful definitions:

> A narrative tells of a significant conflict, usually involving human beings, that is resolved in such a way as to imply a comment on human values, feelings, or attitudes. (Adapted from *An Approach to Literature,* p. 9)

To put it into terms associated with fiction, the constituents of narrative writing are *characters* involved in a *plot* that will be resolved to bring out a *theme.* In writing a critical analysis of a narrative work, then, your task is to explain the theme and show how your author uses the characters and plot to arrive at it.

    In order to address the problems of writing a critical analysis of a narrative work in a practical way, we will need to work with a specific example. The following story is especially interesting for one so brief.

Kate Chopin

The Story of an Hour

Knowing that Mrs. Mallard was afflicted with a heart trouble, great care was taken to break to her as gently as possible the news of her husband's death.

    It was her sister Josephine who told her, in broken sentences, veiled hints that

---

*Stories, novels, dramas, and narrative poems are all works of narrative literature and share in the techniques and conventions of story-telling. In addition, narrative poems and enacted drama participate in the techniques and conventions specific to poetry and to the theater. See the later discussions of these forms.

revealed in half concealing. Her husband's friend Richards was there, too, near her. It was he who had been in the newspaper office when intelligence of the railroad disaster was received, with Brently Mallard's name leading the list of "killed." He had only taken the time to assure himself of its truth by a second telegram, and had hastened to forestall any less careful, less tender friend in bearing the sad message.

She did not hear the story as many women have heard the same, with a paralyzed inability to accept its significance. She wept at once, with sudden, wild abandonment, in her sister's arms. When the storm of grief had spent itself, she went away to her room alone. She would have no one follow her.

There stood, facing the open window, a comfortable, roomy armchair. Into this she sank, pressed down by a physical exhaustion that haunted her body and seemed to reach into her soul.

She could see in the open square before her house the tops of trees that were all aquiver with the new spring life. The delicious breath of rain was in the air. In the street below a peddler was crying his wares. The notes of a distant song which someone was singing reached her faintly, and countless sparrows were twittering in the eaves.

There were patches of blue sky showing here and there through the clouds that had met and piled above the others in the west facing her window.

She sat with her head thrown back upon the cushion of the chair quite motionless, except when a sob came up into her throat and shook her, as a child who has cried itself to sleep continues to sob in its dreams.

She was young, with a fair, calm face, whose lines bespoke repression and even a certain strength. But now there was a dull stare in her eyes, whose gaze was fixed away off yonder on one of those patches of blue sky. It was not a glance of reflection, but rather indicated a suspension of intelligent thought.

There was something coming to her and she was waiting for it, fearfully. What was it? She did not know; it was too subtle and elusive to name. But she felt it, creeping out of the sky, reaching toward her through the sounds, the scents, the color that filled the air.

Now her bosom rose and fell tumultuously. She was beginning to recognize this thing that was approaching to possess her, and she was striving to beat it back with her will—as powerless as her two white slender hands would have been.

When she abandoned herself, a little whispered word escaped her slightly parted lips. She said it over and over under her breath: "Free, free, free!" The vacant stare and the look of terror that had followed it went from her eyes. They stayed keen and bright. Her pulses beat fast, and the coursing blood warmed and relaxed every inch of her body.

She did not stop to ask if it were not a monstrous joy that held her. A clear and exalted perception enabled her to dismiss the suggestion as trivial.

She knew that she would weep again when she saw the kind, tender hands folded in death; the face that had never looked save with love upon her, fixed and gray and

---

Kate Chopin (1851–1904). Short-story writer and novelist. Convent educated, Chopin gained her knowledge of the Creole society in New Orleans, which provides the setting for much of her work, as the wife of a successful French businessman in that community and mother of their six children. Widowed at 31, she returned to her girlhood home in St. Louis to care for her mother. She did not begin her writing career until she was 37, three years after her mother's death. Her work is valued for its realistic style and for the keen understanding it displays of the psychology of women struggling with the constraints of the "woman's role."

dead. But she saw beyond that bitter moment a long procession of years to come that would belong to her absolutely. And she opened and spread her arms out to them in welcome.

There would be no one to live for during those coming years; she would live for herself. There would be no powerful will bending her in that blind persistence with which men and women believe they have a right to impose a private will upon a fellow-creature. A kind intention or a cruel intention made the act seem no less a crime as she looked upon it in that brief moment of illumination.

And yet she had loved him—sometimes. Often she had not. What did it matter! What could love, the unsolved mystery, count for in face of this possession of self-assertion which she suddenly recognized as the strongest impulse of her being.

"Free! Body and soul free!" she kept whispering.

Josephine was kneeling before the closed door with her lips to the keyhole, imploring for admission. "Louise, open the door! I beg; open the door—you will make yourself ill. What are you doing, Louise? For heaven's sake open the door."

"Go away. I am not making myself ill." No; she was drinking in a very elixir of life through that open window.

Her fancy was running riot along those days ahead of her. Spring days, and summer days, and all sorts of days that would be her own. She breathed a quick prayer that life might be long. It was only yesterday she had thought with a shudder that life might be long.

She arose at length and opened the door to her sister's importunities. There was a feverish triumph in her eyes, and she carried herself unwittingly like a goddess of Victory. She clasped her sister's waist, and together they descended the stairs. Richards stood waiting for them at the bottom.

Some one was opening the front door with a latchkey. It was Brently Mallard who entered, a little travel-stained, composedly carrying his gripsack and umbrella. He had been far from the scene of the accident, and did not even know there had been one. He stood amazed at Josephine's piercing cry; at Richards' quick motion to screen him from the view of his wife.

But Richards was too late.

When the doctors came, they said she had died of heart disease—of joy that kills.

Preparing to Write

The first step in writing any kind of critical analysis is close reading. In reading narratives closely you will want to go beyond your observation of those interesting parallels, unusual strategies, and symbolic touches that attract attention. You will want, in addition, to make special note of the major elements of narration: plot, characters, theme, and point of view. Let me sketch each of these briefly, using Kate Chopin's story for illustration.

Point of View   Perhaps the most crucial question you can ask when you are trying to gain insight into a story is "From whose point of view are we seeing the action?" What the story actually is varies with the eyes of the beholder. Authors present their stories from points of view that range all the way from the complete subjectivity of one character's perspective to an objectivity that goes beyond the author's view to a strict dramatization of action and dialogue (see Figure 1). The reader's job is to interpret the story in terms of this point of view.

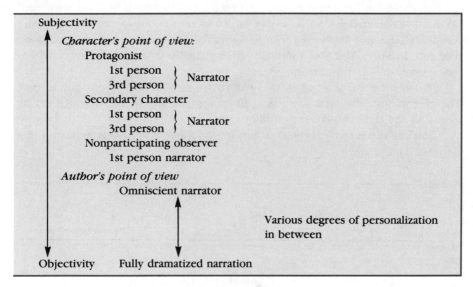

FIGURE 1
Points of View

From what point of view is "The Story of an Hour" written? It begins in the author's own voice:

> Knowing that Mrs. Mallard was afflicted with a heart trouble, great care was taken to break to her as gently as possible the news of her husband's death.

The narration continues in this fairly objective manner until Mrs. Mallard goes to her room alone. At this point, Mrs. Mallard's point of view takes over. Chopin continues using the third-person "she," because with it she can get outside her heroine and provide the reader with external description of her character. But from this time until close to the end, we are not only privy to Mrs. Mallard's thoughts but the narrating voice even takes on the colorations of Mrs. Mallard's own:

> There would be no one to live for during those coming years; she would live for herself . . . . And yet she had loved him—sometimes. Often she had not. What did it matter!

How reliable a narrator is Mrs. Mallard? How close are her views to Chopin's own? This is perhaps the central critical question of the story, and the way you answer it will, to an important extent, determine your interpretation of the story.

Plot Plot begins with *conflict,* the struggle between two (or more) antagonists. In a complex story, determining the central conflict may be difficult; but you must come to a decision in order to understand the story well enough to

Conflict
and plot. write a critical analysis. In "The Story of an Hour," the conflict clearly takes place within Mrs. Mallard, the central character. To state what are the conflicting parties within her requires an interpretation of the story. Is it her own spirit opposed to her internalization of the will of society as represented by her sister, Josephine, and her husband's friend, Richards? Or is her inner antagonist her husband, Brently? Much of the way you eventually interpret the story will be based upon this determination.

Plot can be considered as the way that a conflict is worked out in time. Chronology
and plot. The plot of any particular story is a *chronology* of the incidents which set up, intensify, and then resolve the conflict.

You can often think through a plot more clearly if you diagram it as a time line (see Figure 2).

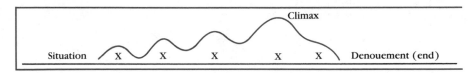

FIGURE 2   Plot as a
Time Line

In Figure 2, the word "situation" stands for the given, the way things are after the introductory passages of the work and before complications in the conflict set in. Each X marks an incident in the conflict, a dramatic episode in the development of the action. The curved line represents the pattern of emotional intensity. The notion of "climax" is a concept about which experts disagree: Some see it as the moment of greatest emotional intensity, others as the point where the outcome becomes inevitable. Where these points in the action do not coincide, you must decide where the climactic point really occurs. As for the "denouement," most stories still have some sort of brief conclusion to round them off and return readers to their own world again. You could work out the plot of "Story of an Hour" along either of the plot lines sketched in Figure 3.

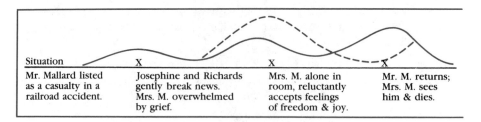

FIGURE 3   Plot Line for
"The Story of an Hour"

Where do *you* place the climax? In "The Story of an Hour" the moment of greatest emotional tension may or may not coincide with the final revelation. Your choice depends upon how much emphasis you feel Kate Chopin puts upon her heroine's death. Does she show that Mrs. Mallard cannot come to terms with the demands that society and her husband place upon her freedom and succumbs to them in death in a final climactic scene? Or does Chopin make a climax of Mrs. Mallard's triumphal moment of understanding of the central importance of personal freedom? If so, then does Chopin mean us to take her heroine's death, interruping only what will once again be a freedomless life, as the denouement rather than the climax of her story? Again a crucial interpretative question.

Another element of plot that Aristotle, for one, considered essential is *reversal*, a sudden turnabout in a major character's thinking or fortunes. Reversal *Reversal* gives tension to a story much as the "although clause" gives tension to an essay. *and plot.* And like the "although clause," it may be implied rather than explicit. Explicit reversal is an important part of the sample story's plot. To the original situation, Brently Mallard's reported death, Mrs. Mallard reacts with a quick, intense grief for her loss. In the second episode, she experiences a reversal of emotion and her grief turns to joy in her new freedom. In the final episode, the situation itself has reversed and Mr. Mallard appears. Mrs. Mallard again experiences a sudden intense grief, this time at the loss of her newfound freedom. Her heart cannot stand the reversal, and she dies. Kate Chopin's story is classic in its plot.

For a plot to succeed it must be plausible. Authors are never completely free in their creativity. In exchange for your "willing suspension of disbelief," as Samuel Taylor Coleridge called it, authors make a silent promise to keep their work within the laws of probability and cause and effect (even though life itself is not always so careful or so neat). Every event, therefore, must be *foreshad-* *Foreshadowing* *owed,* prepared for. Take an example from Chopin's story. People do not usually *and plot.* fall over dead when they hear bad news—as dramatically moving or rhetorically convenient as such sudden demises may be for authors. But Kate Chopin carefully foreshadows her heroine's death, and so we accept it. She tells us in the very first line that "Mrs. Mallard was afflicted with a heart trouble" to such an extent that "great care" needed to be taken in telling her about her husband. She also lets us know that Mrs. Mallard was not one of those people who first greet news "with a paralyzed inability to accept its significance," but rather one who gives herself immediately "with sudden wild abandonment" to a storm of grief. With this foreshadowing, in addition to all the emotional strain the reader knows Mrs. Mallard has undergone within the hour, her death does not seem improbable.

Character

In reading closely you will want to find out as much as you can about each of the characters in the story. You can judge the characters by what the author tells you about them and by what they do. You can also try to understand them by what they say and what other characters say about them—although you cannot always believe what a fictional character says.

What do we know of the characters in Kate Chopin's story? We know that Josephine and Richards are kind, considerate people, who can be counted upon even in an emergency to do the right thing. They broke the sad news to Mrs. Mallard in a kind, capable way, and Josephine was lovingly there for her sister when she needed her. On the other hand, beyond the obvious concern for Mrs. Mallard's health, is there not just a touch of what might be a habitual condescension in Josephine's imploring into her sister's keyhole:

> "Louise, open the door! I beg; open the door—you will make yourself ill. What are you doing, Louise? For heaven's sake open the door."

Is there not just a trace of a stronger personality dominating a weaker one—for her own good?

We know of Brently Mallard only from his wife who comes to believe that she has been wronged by him. Yet even in her perhaps prejudiced eyes he is a "tender" and "loving" man with only "kind intentions." It is clear that Kate Chopin wants to underscore Mallard's basic kindness to make the issue of his dominant will more clear-cut. Though we do not see any example of this dominance, we know from his wife's private thoughts that she, at least, believed that she suffered from it. What is the nature of what Mrs. Mallard refers to as "powerful will bending her in blind persistence"? Perhaps Josephine's speech gives us echoes of it.

And how does Kate Chopin want us to regard her central character? She tells us that Mrs. Mallard is "repressed" and yet "strong." She shows us that she is one who experiences powerful emotions with "wild abandonment." Still we see the reluctance with which she accepts the unconventional insight which comes to her:

> She was beginning to recognize this thing that was approaching to possess her, and she was striving to beat it back with her will . . . .

In Mrs. Mallard, Chopin shows us a woman who has the courage to be completely honest with herself. And yet, what about her moral character? Does Chopin want us to regard her feelings about her loss of her husband as "a monstrous joy"? Or are we to sympathize with them?

Theme   Such questions lead directly to a consideration of the theme, the "what the author is trying to say" that is the heart of the critical analysis. Although the theme does not exactly provide the summary of a work's entire meaning that a thesis does, it is the idea that informs every part of a story and gives it its reason for being. How do you find it? Brooks and Warren's definition points to one good method: If a narrative work consists of "A significant conflict that is resolved in such a way as to imply a comment on human values, feelings or attitudes," then you should be able to find that comment—the theme—by *identifying the conflict* and *noting how it is resolved.* The following procedures should be helpful:

Determining the Theme

1. Precisely identify the conflict in your story. (Do not take a general conflict, such as "man against nature." Choose rather specifics such as "Joe vs. the Antarctic.")
2. Ask yourself, What is the outcome of the conflict? Who wins?
3. Generalize on your answers to (1) and (2) and formulate a tentative theme.
4. Test out your tentative theme to see if it is consistent with all the significant features of the story that you have noted in your close reading. Ask yourself, Is this what all the elements of the story seem to be aimed at? Is this what the author is really trying to say?

Let's work together through the steps listed in the boxed guidelines to try to discover the theme of the Chopin story.

Possible Theme A
1. Conflict: Mrs. Mallard versus (an internalized) Josephine and Richards, or more specifically, Mrs. Mallard's view on marriage versus conventional views.
2. Resolution: Conventional views win.
   No sooner does Mrs. Mallard come to terms with her joyous feelings of freedom from being a wife than she is faced with the continuation of that state. No longer able to face continuing in that role on society's terms, she dies.
3. Generalization (and tentative theme): It is impossible (alternative theme—it is unnatural) for women to try to strive for lives of "self assertion."

Possible Theme B
1. Conflict: Mrs. Mallard versus Louise Mallard.
2. Resolution: Louise wins—at the loss of her life.
3. Generalization (and tentative theme): Freedom of will is the most important value; it alone makes life meaningful or even worthwhile.

Both of these tentative themes—as different as they are—seem to be based on valid interpretations of the story, depending upon how the evidence is read. The question turns on Kate Chopin's use of irony.

Irony   Although irony is not an essential feature of narrative writing, many authors find it a highly effective tool for developing themes in their stories. In the sixteenth century, Wynken de Worde defined the term in a way that has never been bettered: "Ironye," he wrote, is "that which sayeth one thing but giveth to understand ye contrarye." The three basic kinds of irony differ mainly in who presents the irony.

- In *verbal irony,* the *speaker* means the contrary of what he or she says or writes.
- In *dramatic irony,* the *author* means something contrary to what the *speaker* says.
- In *circumstantial irony* (or the *irony of fate*), *fate* sees that events turn out contrary to human expectations—often almost as if in mockery of these expectations.

Kate Chopin uses no **verbal irony** in "The Story of an Hour." Neither she in her own voice nor any of her characters when they speak say anything that is the opposite of what they mean—as, for example, does Flannery O'Connor in this sentence from "Good Country People": "Mrs. Hopewell had no bad qualities of her own, but she was able to use other people's in such a constructive way that she never felt the lack." Chopin does, however, use both of the other kinds of irony to quite remarkable effect.

Irony of fate is deeply ingrained in Chopin's story. There is a grim ironic laughter behind every reversal of the plot. We find it, for example, in the fact that Mrs. Mallard should experience her husband's death—for which she has already mourned—with joy. And we discover even more when, after that forbidden joy, her husband turns out to be alive. The fateful chortle is there again when, after Mrs. Mallard has exchanged a fear of a long life for a wish for it, her original death wish is granted.

As for **dramatic irony,** it is this which gives the final sentence its bite and its pathos:

> When the doctors came, they said she had died of heart disease—of joy that kills.

The doctors thought that Mrs. Mallard's feeling upon seeing her husband alive was a joy so sudden and profound that her heart could not stand the strain. Chopin has given us readers to understand quite the opposite. And yet on second thought, we can see in a final irony of fate that it may well have been joy that killed Louise Mallard—though not the joy the doctors had understood. For had she not experienced the joy of freedom, its loss would not have affected her.

Interpretation   Which of the two proposed themes you favor depends primarily on whether you interpret Chopin's use of Mrs. Mallard's point of view ironically or not. If you read her character ironically, then you will find dramatic irony in passages such as this:

> She did not stop to ask if it were not a monstrous joy that held her. A clear and exalted perception enabled her to dismiss the suggestion as trivial.

You would thus see Mrs. Mallard's joy as monstrous, her feelings toward her kind husband as lacking in gratitude and her ennobling of the idea of self-assertion as selfish and egotistical. To support this interpretation, you would concentrate upon the hysterical quality of such phrases as "feverish triumph in her eyes" and "approaching to possess her." With this interpretation, you might conclude that Chopin wants the reader almost to relish the irony implicit in Mrs. Mallard's final descending the stairs "like a goddess of Victory."

On the other hand, you may choose to identify Kate Chopin's views closely with those of her heroine. Then you would find no irony in her use of the phrase "clear and exalted perception," but see it rather as Chopin's way of overriding any tendency of the reader to echo Mrs. Mallard's fear that hers might be "a monstrous joy." With this interpretation, you would emphasize Chopin's use of spring imagery and note her attaching to it the symbolism of both life and freedom:

> She could see in the open square before her house the tops of trees that were all aquiver with the new spring life. . . . She felt [something coming to her] creeping out of the sky, reaching toward her through the sounds, the scents, the color that filled the air. . . . "Free, free, free." . . . She was drinking in the very elixir of life through that open window.

You might also attach symbolic importance to the way that Chopin at the beginning of the story equates her heroine with her married state by pointedly calling her (alone among the characters) by her married title: *Mrs.* Mallard. Readers do not even learn her given name until after her belief in her husband's death has set her free to be an individual person of her own.

In supporting this interpretation, you would also stress the power of Kate Chopin's insight into a woman's soul. You would back up this view by artful quotation of portions of the story to point out the psychological truth of Mrs. Mallard's experience. First the grief. Then the dazed state. And then the gradual release of the old feelings and the reluctant acceptance of the new freedom. Finally, the passionate embrace of a true sense of self.

With this interpretation, the ecstasy of that "brief moment of illumination" becomes the climax of the story, overshadowing even the ironies of the final scene. For if you see the story in this way, you would understand that the knowledge that comes to Mrs. Mallard in that moment is in itself the theme of the work: that "to impose a private will upon a fellow-creature" is "a crime"; and that it is no less a crime whether it proceeds from "a kind intention or a cruel intention." Viewed in this light, the final scene becomes yet another way for Chopin to reinforce the importance of Louise Mallard's insight. For this scene, so interpreted, dramatically demonstrates that after such a realization, life with her husband on the same basis is no longer possible for Louise Mallard. Reading the story this way adds a final irony, for it makes the doctors righter than they knew when they spoke of the "joy that kills."

A number of differing valid critical analyses could be written for "The Story of an Hour"—as they could for all good short stories. The following is a workable outline for a critical analysis of Chopin's story based upon the second interpretation just sketched:

Thesis: In "The Story of an Hour" Kate Chopin uses a complex system of plot reversals and multiple ironies to convey powerfully to her readers the idea that a life of submission to the will of another—even if the other is a kind and loving person—is not a life that is worth living.

   I. Introduction
  II. Brief summary of plot in terms of its reversals and ironies
 III. Chopin's stress on the importance of Mrs. M's moment of insight:
     A. Creditability of Mrs. M.'s point of view
     B. Her relationship to Richards, Josephine, and Mr. M.
     C. Symbolic building to the moment: spring and life-renewing imagery

      D. Psychological truth of Mrs. M.'s experience
      E. Symbolic use of title: *Mrs.* first and individual name, *Louise,* afterward
  IV. The nature of Mrs. M's insight
   V. Conclusion: The importance of the insight (and final ironies)

Try It Out

1. Choose a piece of narrative writing and identify the parties to the conflict upon which its plot is founded. Who wins the conflict? Suggest a tentative theme by generalizing from the conflict and its resolution.
2. In narrative works that you are familiar with, find examples of (a) verbal irony, (b) dramatic irony, and (c) irony of fate. Explain how each example contributes to its author's purpose in the work as a whole.
3. Find one example of narrative writing in which a character narrates the story. Find another, like "The Story of an Hour," which, though told in the author's own voice, is written from a character's point of view.

ANALYZING A POEM

Some people are intimidated when they are asked to analyze a poem. These people tend to think of poetry as a different species of writing altogether—loaded with conventions that are more technical and more intellectually demanding than those associated with any other genre, but at the same time possessing meanings that are totally emotional, abstract, and otherworldly. Neither of these contradictory impressions comes anywhere near the truth. To begin with, since some of the conventions and techniques of poetry are borrowed frequently by other genres, there is nothing particularly exclusive about them. Furthermore, when these conventions are approached in a unified and logical way, they are not especially difficult to understand.

The techniques of poetry are, for the most part, comprehended under *imagery,* the language of poetry, and *rhythm,* the sound of poetry. All of imagery (sometimes called metaphor) can be understood in terms of comparison—comparing the indescribable thing, feeling, idea that the writer wants to express with a describable object that the reader can comprehend. (You will find a fuller discussion of imagery in Chapter 8, p. 317.) In a similar way, all that is distinctive in the sound of poetry (except onomatopoeia) can be related to the notion of repetition. Although a complete explanation of the conventions of poetry is not appropriate here, the boxed sections, "A Guide to Imagery" and "A Guide to the Sound of Poetry" (p. 423 and 424) do offer a key to the vocabulary of both the language and the sound of poetry that may be helpful to you in writing critical analyses.

As for the mystique about the meaning of poems, I will grant that authors convey their ideas and feelings about life even more subtly in poetry than they do in stories. And because these ideas are more condensed in poems, the form more rhythmical, and the language more imaginative than is ordinarily found in prose, explicating the meaning may be more central to analyzing a poem than to writing about a work of another genre. But the meanings you will be searching for themselves will be far from distantly abstract. All good poetry is deeply rooted in the actual—in the things of the world that you can see, hear, smell, taste, and feel with your hands. Further, in order to get at the full meaning of a poem, you have to come to terms with both the connotative and the denotative meanings of the words actually written upon the page and with the subject-verb-object basic syntax of the clauses and sentences. It is not any airy notion, then, but the linguistic and physical realities behind each poem that make the close reading process for poetry probably the most demanding. The following hints for close reading offer a useful approach.

Reading a Poem Closely

1. **Read the poem aloud.** Poetry is as oral as music and is not meant to be read with the eyes alone. Really listen to the poem as you read it. How does the sound contribute to the poem's meaning? To the emotional atmosphere the poem creates? Be on the lookout for such sound delights as these:

   The breathlessness of Shakespeare's skylark:
   > . . . and then my state,
   > Like to the lark at break of day arising
   > From sullen earth, sings hymns at heaven's gate.

   The nasal quality of Pope's sneeze:
   > Sudden with starting tears each eye o'erflows,
   > And the high dome reechoes to his nose.

2. **Straighten out the poem's syntax.** You cannot begin to comprehend a poem unless you can understand what each of the sentences mean. Take, for example, the first lines of Shakespeare's Sonnet 73:
   > That time of year thou mayst in me behold
   > When yellow leaves, or none, or few, do hang
   > Upon those boughs. . . .

   The first thing to do is to cut through poetic inversion (not to mention four hundred years of language change) and realize that Shakespeare means: You see in me that time of year when a few yellow leaves (or none at all) hang upon the bough. Although it may sound prosaic, the first questions you must ask yourself when you begin reading a poem are What is the subject of the first clause? What is the verb?

3. **Be sure you know the meaning of every word** in the poem—both literal and implied. If you are not really sure, look it up. Since poetry is such a condensed expression, every word counts.

4. **Read literally.** This advice is particularly important when you approach metaphors and other imagery. Ask yourself, What exactly is the comparison? Then try to visualize it (or to imagine its smell, taste, or touch). Let's return to Sonnet 73:

> That time of year thou mayst in me behold
> When yellow leaves, or none, or few, do hang
> Upon those boughs which shake against the cold,
> Bare ruin'd choirs, where late the sweet birds sang.

What does Shakespeare intend us to think of when we read these lines? He compares his time of life with the autumn of the year. But in developing his images to make the time of the year more vivid and more specific, he extends the comparison to include himself as well. How can you get at Shakespeare's imagery? You can picture black, almost leafless branches silhouetted against a grey November sky. Try to feel them "shake against the cold"—as an old man might, perhaps. Then let the image in your mind of the bare boughs in silhouette transform itself into a silhouette of an equally bare "ruin'd choir," that is to say, the choir portion of one of the church or abbey ruins that dot the English countryside. Finally, imaginatively enter into Shakespeare's comparison of the special loneliness shared by the once lively choir loft and the once lively branches. Now that their respective choristers, the choirboys and the birds that once filled them with life and singing, are gone, the choir and the branches—and, by analogy, the poet himself—are left empty and useless and bereft.

5. **Note any unusual play of rhythm or diction,** and decide what the poet means by it. What effect, for instance, does Shakespeare achieve by so frequently breaking up his second line with pauses? And why does he break the logical ordering of the words?

> When yellow leaves, or none, or few, do hang

Might he mean to slow the reader down and add a tone of sadness? And what about the word "cold" at the end of the third line? Is it meant to stand as the object of the phrase "against the cold" in the second line? Or is it the first adjective in the words describing "choirs" in the third line? Or is it meant to "look before and after" and function in both ways? And what does Shakespeare gain by the addition of the adjective "sweet" in "where late the sweet birds sang"?

6. **Decide how the form contributes to the meaning of the poem.** For example, how does the three quatrain-couplet form of the Elizabethan sonnet help Shakespeare to organize his imagery in Sonnet 73? How does Coleridge use the conventions of the medieval ballad to enhance the Gothic effects of his "Rime of the Ancient Mariner?"

When you have satisfied yourself that you have a clear reading of your poem, plan your critical analysis. Back up your interpretation with the formal, metaphoric, and sound effects you have noted. Use these discoveries only in an interpretative way, however; by themselves they have no significance. Do NOT write:

> Shakespeare's "That Time of Year" is a sonnet with 14 lines of iambic pentameter verse and an Elizabethan sonnet rhyme scheme which divides it into a 4/4/4/2 pattern.   FAULTY

Write instead:

> In "That Time of Year," Shakespeare works out a separate comparison to his aging self in each of the three quatrains of the sonnet and concludes with an ironic comment on the rest in the final couplet.

A Sample Critical Analysis

Let's look at a critical analysis published in *Explicator,* a scholarly journal in the field of English literature. First, the poem:

We Real Cool*

> The Pool Players.
>   Seven at the Golden Shovel.
> We real cool. We
> Left school. We
> Lurk late. We
> Strike straight. We
> Sing sin. We
> Thin gin. We
> Jazz June. We
> Die soon.
>   (Gwendolyn Brooks)

The following critical analysis was written by Barbara B. Sims.†

Brooks' *We Real Cool*

The economy of Gwendolyn Brooks' eight-line poem "We Real Cool" parallels the brevity of the lives of her subjects, the pool players of the Golden Shovel.

Each line has two stresses, monosyllabic words in pairs which characterize the players. First, they tell the reader they are "real cool." This one descriptive phrase conjures up an image of the black young man of the streets, lounging before the pool hall, shucking and jiving, attired in a hip costume of colorful slacks, high-heeled boots, and Super Fly hat, playing a transistor radio loudly. At

---

*From *The World of Gwendolyn Brooks,* copyright 1976. Harper & Row, Publishers.
†Reprinted by permission from *Explicator,* vol. 34 (April, 1976) item 58, 39–40.

this point the tone is one of self-congratulation, as if being "real cool" is where it's at. Of course, the players "left school."

The second stanza begins syntactically in the second line of the couplet with the word "We," which is set curiously apart at the end of the line. The "We" is positioned as if to suggest that the identity of the players, individually and collectively, is less important than their clothes and activities.

Stanza 2 tells that the players "lurk late" and "strike straight." The connotations of these phrases tell us that all the activities of the cool people are not as innocent as playing pool and hanging around the set. Mugging, theft, and rape, among other crimes, are suggested by the word "lurk," while "strike" is reminiscent of the gangland "hit," which signifies murder.

The cool people are proud of their way of life, however, for they "sing" (praise) sin. When they drink, they "thin gin" (gin and 7-up?).

The final stanza refers to the players' interest in women—one of insincerity or playfulness. They "Jazz" June. Abruptly, Brooks concludes the poem: "We / Die soon."

Until the last line, the element of bravado in the diction and rhythm has made the activities of the street people seem somehow defendable, if not downright desirable. A certain pride in being outside the conventions, institutions, and legal structures of the predominant society is conveyed. Escaping the drudgery and dullness of school and work has left the lives of these drop-outs open to many romantic possibilities.

However, the tone changes dramatically when the reader learns the street people "Die soon." At once their defiant and complacent attitudes seem quite pathetic, and the reader wonders whom the cool people are trying to kid about the desirability of their disorderly lives.

Comment   In her critical analysis, Barbara Sims sets up her thesis and then explicates Brooks's poem line by line to support it. Her thesis sentence very neatly takes the point the author is trying to make—which Sims sees as an ironic comment on the "brevity of the lives of [Brooks's] subjects"—and ties it together with the most significant and comprehensive of the ways Brooks has gone about saying it—that is, "the economy of the poem" with its eight brief lines, its 24 words.

While explicating the verse, Sims brings in and accounts for each of the curious features she must have noted in her close reading, among them the oddly placed "we" and the increasing repugnance of the sequence of expressions. In such a spare poem, most of the imagery lies in the connotative language, especially in the strong expressions. Sims not only accounts for the meaning of these images but helps us to visualize them.

Sims also attends carefully to the tone of the poem throughout her essay and, at its end, discusses the dramatic—almost paradoxical—change of tone in the poem's closing line. In her account of this change, Sims is able to bring us back to her main point and to conclude with a more precise and more strongly worded restatement of her thesis.

A Guide to Imagery

All imagery is basically comparison, the finding of the most precisely literary notation to serve as the objective correlative for the emotion or idea to be evoked.

Form

1. *Metaphor.* When the objective correlative is equated with the compared item.
   "To see the cherry hung with snow."   (cherry blossom = snow)
2. *Simile.* When the comparison is pointed to explicitly by *like* or *as.*
   "Apple blossoms look *like* snow."
3. *Connotative language.* When the comparison is implied by the connotations of the words employed.
   "I met a traveler from an *antique* land."
4. *Symbol.* When the objective correlative has at least two layers of meaning.
   "And miles to go before *I sleep.*"   (Means both a distance to cover before bed-
                                          time and much to do before death.)

Content

1. *Hyperbole.* When the objective correlative is wildly exaggerated (implying a superlative emotional coloring).
   "He fiddled all the bugs off the sweet-potato vine."
   "Forever and a day."
2. *Allusion.* When the objective correlative refers to a literary source (taking on the emotional coloration of the source).
   "No, I am not Prince Hamlet, nor was meant to be."
3. *Personification.* When the objective correlative is human or has human characteristics.
   "And *Laughter* holding both his sides."
   "He [the eagle] clasped the crag with crooked *hands.*"
4. *Synesthesia.* When the imagery involves a confusion of the senses.
   "*Moulten golden notes*
   And all in tune.
   What a liquid ditty floats"
5. *Metonymy* (including *synecdoche*). When the objective correlative is the part which stands for the whole (or is closely related to it).
   "Your smile had caught fire at Orly."
6. *Paradox* (and *oxymoron*). When the objective correlative expresses a seeming contradiction.
   "And if some lover, such an we,
   Have heard this *dialogue of one.*"

A Guide to the Sound of Poetry

Rhythm
Definition: movement with regular recurrence.

Meter
Definition: patterned rhythm (of English poetry).
1. foot (stressed syllable ´ and unstressed ◡)

     a. *iambic:* soft loud ⌣ ′
       "Shall I compare thee to a summer's day?"
     b. *trochaic:* loud soft ′ ⌣
       "Blessings on thee little man"
     c. *anapestic:* soft soft loud ⌣ ⌣ ′
       "For the moon never beams without bringing me dreams"
     d. *dactyllic:* loud soft soft ′ ⌣ ⌣
       "This is the forest primeval. The murmuring pines and the hemlock."

2. line
    a. dimeter, trimeter, tetrameter (1b & c above), pentameter (1a above), hex-
      ameter (1d above), heptameter, octometer
    b. free verse—irregular rhythm
    c. blank verse—unrhymed iambic pentameter
    d. alexandrine—iambic hexameter

3. stanza
    a. couplet, triplet, quatrain
    b. sonnet: 14 iambic pentameter lines
    c. heroic couplet: iambic pentameter couplet

Variation

1. caesura (a pause in mid line)

     When yellow leaves, or none, or few,

2. non-end-stopped line (making phrase pattern at variance with metric pattern)

     Like to the lark at break of day arising
     From sullen earth, sings hymns at heaven's gate.

3. varying degree of stress on syllables: *Spondee* (′′) and *Pyrrhic* (⌣ ⌣)
4. substitution of feet: *Anacrusis* (+), syllables added, and *Catalexis* (−), sylla-
    bles subtracted from feet

Sound Devices

1. *Onomatopoeia:* the word imitates the sound.
    "How they *clang* and *clash* and *roar.*"
2. *Rhyme*—repetition of final accented sound
    Masculine: bat/cat
    Feminine: batty/catty
    Triple: battiness/cattiness
3. *Alliteration*—repetition of initial sounds
    "What a *t*ale of *t*error now their *t*urbulency *t*ells."
4. *Assonance*—repetition of vowel sounds
    "This b*o*dy dr*o*pt n*o*t d*ow*n"
5. *Consonance*—repetition of consonant sounds.
    "And wa*s* a ble*ss*ed gho*s*t."
6. *Repetition* of words and phrases:
    "I *galloped,* Dirck *galloped,* we *galloped* all three."
    Sometimes used to achieve the effect of a refrain (repetition of a final line or
    lines, as in the old ballads).
    "It's lilac-time in London; it's lilac-time in London."

━━━━━━━━━━━━━━━━━━━━━━━━━━━━━━━ **Try It Out**━━━━━

Write an explication of the following poem:

Jenny Kissed Me

Jenny kissed me when we met
Jumping from the chair she sat in;
Time, you thief, who love to get
Sweets into your list, put that in:
Say I'm weary, say I'm sad,
Say that health and wealth have missed me,
Say I'm growing old, but add,
Jenny kissed me.

(Leigh Hunt, 1784–1859)

ANALYZING A PERFORMANCE

Drama tells a story. Like all narrative literature, a play or a movie consists of characters involved in a plot in order to present a theme. The discussion of narrative literature earlier in this chapter, therefore, can help you write critical analyses of the plays you read. But drama is meant for the stage. And writing a critical analysis of performed literature differs from writing such essays about their literary versions in two important respects.

First, the question "What is the author trying to say" about a performed drama or a movie is not nearly as important as "What is the acting company, or the director or producer, trying to say?" Although the author's story and theme are fundamental to any production, what you really want to get at in your analysis is the meaning of the entire theatrical experience, and that involves the way the author's material is interpreted in actual performance. Second, the methods by which the author and, in this case, the director and the company "go about saying it" must also be expanded to include not only the techniques of story-telling discussed earlier but also the techniques that go into producing the particular sounds, motion, and spectacle of the production. A thorough discussion of these elements is beyond the scope of this work, but the following chart offers examples of the sort of questions you will want to ask yourself when you prepare to write an analysis of a particular performance.

Guidelines for Analysis of a Performance

Background
1. If the work is of an identifiable genre (Theatre of the Absurd, Restoration Comedy, Senecan Tragedy, or other type), what are the characteristics of this form? What are the authors of the works of this kind trying to accomplish by them? Is there anything you should know about the traditional staging or costuming

or musical accompaniment of such drama? How closely does your particular production follow the traditions of the genre? In what ways does it depart from them and why?

2. If the play is written in or set in another time or another place, are there historical, geographical, philosophical, or social facts that would shed light on the performance? Does this presentation try to suggest that other time or place? If so, how? To what extent? If not, why not?

3. If you are familiar with the work in written form, how closely does your production follow the script? How does this performance handle those ambiguous elements that must be interpreted anew with each production (If you are watching *Macbeth,* for example, does the director have the Banquo actor appear as Banquo's ghost at Macbeth's feast or is the ghost to be taken as only a figment of Macbeth's overwrought imagination?).

4. If your production is based upon a drama (or story) that is one of a series, or has a strong autobiographical flavor, are there any essential facts that you should know about your author's life or works? (I would urge you to use such material cautiously, however, and to concentrate your analysis upon the performance itself.)

Action and Characters and Theme

All of the suggestions about analyzing narrative literature are pertinent here. In addition, the following questions may be helpful:

1. How are the acts divided? How are the scenes arranged? Is there any particular pattern in the scenes or sub-scenes? How are subplots handled? What is the function of each scene in the overall pattern?

2. By what gestures, intonations, and attitudes does each actor characterize the character he or she portrays? Is there any interaction between particular characters that is especially telling? How personally or how distantly do the actors relate to the audience? If there are asides, soliloquys, or direct audience address, how are they handled? How does the audience respond to them? Do the comic characters encourage the audience to laugh *at* or *with* them? How much empathy do the noncomic characters elicit? How closely is the audience expected to identify with the protagonists (central characters)? What emotions—sympathy? antipathy? indifference?—do they arouse?

3. If the drama is a tragedy or if it has tragic overtones, what is the basis for the tragedy? Is it caused by a flawed hero? A flawed society? Fate? Some combination of these causes? How does the audience feel at the close of the tragedy? Does a *catharsis* (the washing away of the tragic emotions) take place? Despite the downfall of the leading character(s), is there anything hopeful about the ending (the return of order, for instance)? How is this hope conveyed?

Setting and Stage Business

1. Can you find any motifs or symbolic representations in the dialogue, props, or, perhaps, in a repeated action of one of the characters? What does this motif or symbol seem to mean the first time it appears? Does it take on additional meaning as it is repeated? If so, what?

2. What is the nature of the sets and scenery? Are they realistic or do they merely suggest the place? Is there a symbolic quality about them? If so, what are they meant to express? How does the lighting contribute to the background of the drama? Do any special lighting effects stand out in your memory? What is their significance?

3. How do the costumes affect the mood of the production? Do they help characterize individual characters? If so, how?

4. If there is any particular stage business beyond that which would normally accompany the dialogue, what is its significance? If you have noticed any special patterning in the positioning of the actors upon the stage, what meaning can you give it?

Evaluative Questions
1. How did the audience respond to the play? Were they attentive? Were they fidgety—coughing, fanning, whispering together? Did they laugh in the appropriate places? Were they hushed in the appropriate places? Did they respond warmly and appreciatively at the close?
2. Did you find the action plausible? Did it seem to be true to the laws of logic and of cause and effect? Did the characters seem to act in ways that were psychologically consistent with what you were given of their characters? In short, were you able to suspend your disbelief?
3. Was the production a unified and satisfying experience for you? Why or why not?

Movies

All of the discussion that applies to stage drama applies to motion pictures as well. But film drama adds an extra dimension: the eye of the camera. Dramatic narration is the most objective of all the narrative points of view. When readers read a play or a work that is heavily dependent upon dialogue (such as one of Hemingway's stories), they have a sense of being free to make their own interpretations. When the narrative is produced on the stage, the author's words are given interpretation by the actors and the director. Although playgoers are guided in making their interpretation of the material in this way, the point of view is still usually general and remains relatively objective. Movies, on the other hand, return you to the controlled point of view. Here the camera directs your ideas and guides your thoughts while it focuses your attention.

Thus, in order to analyze movies critically, you must be conscious of where the camera is directing your attention and try to understand why. In addition to the points explored above, you will want to ask yourself questions such as: Why that distant shot? Why that close-up? Why this particular juxtaposition of images? of scenes? of characters? Why a darkening or a lightening? Why the concentration on this curious object? Why is the camera concentrating with such emphasis on the mouth (or the teeth) of the speaker? Why is it not focusing on the speaker at all? Where is it directing our attention instead? Are the listener's reactions more important? Is there something in the setting to which the speaker's words are supposed to relate? Why is this scene hazy? Why is this one so extra sharp in its contrasts? Why is part of the scene out of focus?

The more motion pictures or drama you watch and the more literature you read from the viewpoint described here, the more observant you can train yourself to be. You will become more and more aware of the two kinds of strategies that call attention to themselves: repetitions (or parallels) and deviations from the norm. And you will become more and more insightful in understanding why the author employs these techniques and why they appear where they do. In gaining these skills you should not only be able to write effective critical analyses, you should also find yourself getting even more pleasure from your viewing and your reading.

ASSIGNMENT

Chose one of the essays in Part Five or another essay, story, drama, or poem, as your instructor directs you, and using the tools suggested in this chapter, write a critical analysis of it.

Part Five

A Selection
of Essays

Essays in Part Five

Essays appear in their order of mention in the text.

The essays in Part Five are included for your reading enjoyment. They were selected for their diversity of views and for their interest to readers in general, acknowledging also the quality of the author's reputation. You may also find that they stimulate your thinking about the writing process and serve as a testing ground for your beliefs about writing and for the claims made throughout the book.

Fred Golden

Earth's Creeping Deserts

A tide of ecological refugees from land turning to sand

1   Outside the great conference hall in Nairobi, 16 fountains sent up sparkling plumes of water, and black Mercedes limousines glistened in the bright East African sun. Inside, some 1,500 delegates from 110 nations sat in air-conditioned comfort. The splendid setting of the meeting could hardly have clashed more jarringly with its purpose. At the U.N.'s invitation, the representatives had gathered in the Kenyan capital last week to discuss and devise ways of containing what an increasing number of experts regard as a major environmental danger: the creeping, seemingly relentless spread of the earth's deserts.

2   More than a third of the earth's land mass is desert or desert-like, and one out of seven people—some 630 million—dwell in these parched regions. In the past, they have been able to scratch out a livelihood—barely. Now, largely through man's own folly, their fragile existence is threatened by a deadly disease of the land called, awkwardly but accurately, "desertification."

3   In only half a century, an estimated 251,000 sq. mi. (650,000 sq. km.) of farming and grazing land has been swallowed up by the Sahara along that great desert's southern fringe. In one part of India's Rajasthan region, often called the dustiest place in the world, sand cover has increased by about 8% in only 18 years. In the U.S., so much once fertile farm land has been abandoned for lack of water along Interstate 10 between Tucson and Phoenix that dust storms now often sweep the highway.

4   For most Americans, desertification is not a problem. But for many of the 78 million people who in recent years have had the ground under them turn to dust or sand, there is no easy escape. Washington's Worldwatch Institute estimates that the lives of perhaps 50 million people are jeopardized. As their fields and pastures become no man's lands, the dispossessed add to the tide of ecological refugees who have already swollen the Third World's ranks of unemployed and destitute. Unable to feed themselves, they place new strains on the food supply and create a tinderbox for social unrest. Warns U.N. Secretary General Kurt Waldheim: "We risk destroying whole peoples in the afflicted area."

5   The deserts' cancerous growth came to worldwide attention in the early 1970s with the great drought and famine in Africa's Sahel, the band of impoverished land across the Sahara's southern flank. More than 100,000 people perished before the rains finally came in 1974, and that was not the end of the tragedy. Hundreds of thousands of tribesmen remain in camps, and the desert's

encroachment has not halted. Senegal told the U.N. meeting that it feared its coastal capital, Dakar, would soon be engulfed.

Droughts and crop failures have always been a harsh fact of life in arid regions. But the Sahel's calamity was worsened by distinctly modern factors. Improvements in public health had vastly expanded population. New wells lulled the Africans into thinking they were no longer so completely dependent on the slim rainfall. They enlarged their herds and planted more cash crops like cotton and peanuts. For a while, the land withstood the strains. But when the rains ceased, the crops failed and the cattle stripped the fields of virtually every blade of grass around the overworked wells. Soon the thin layer of topsoil vanished, and there was nothing but rock, sand and dust. The Sahara had won.

6

Though the U.N. conference featured an Arab-led walkout during the Israeli delegate's Negev report and other outbursts of rudeness and rancor, the Nairobi proceedings made some encouraging progress. Scientists presented many carefully prepared technical analyses of desertification and ways to combat it. The U.S. pitched in with an offer to train a cadre of 1,000 Peace Corps volunteers for anti-desertification work. Before the delegates disband this week, they are expected to adopt a 15-point plan that calls for a worldwide effort against the deserts' encroachment with everything from the planting of new vegetation to the settlement of nomads to control grazing.

7

Some scientists feared that the document placed too much faith in technological—rather than "human"—solutions, but the plea nonetheless represents a milestone. For the first time, the international community is committing itself to the fight against the growth of deserts. While the document leaves action up to individual countries, the incentive to collaborate—perhaps even with old enemies—is great. To many countries, doing battle against the deserts is the only alternative to poverty, starvation and chaos.

8

---

(7) *cadre.* A nucleus of trained leaders, around which a larger organization can be developed.

Fred Golden. Journalist and author with a strong scientific bent. A lifelong resident of New York, Golden worked briefly for the *Newark News* and the Associated Press before coming to *Time* where, since 1969, he has headed the Science Section. Among his many books are *The Moving Continent* and *Quasars, Pulsars, and Black Holes: Colonies in Space.* This article was originally published in *Time,* September 12, 1977.

Shana Alexander

Getting Old in Kids' Country

1   Children are a relatively modern invention. Until a few hundred years ago, they did not exist. In medieval and Renaissance painting, you see pint-size men and women wearing grown-up clothes and grown-up expressions, performing grown-up tasks. Children did not exist because the family as we know it had not evolved. In the old days, most people lived on the land, and life was a communal affair.

2   Children today not only exist; they have taken over. God's Country has to an astonishing degree become Kids' Country—in no place more than in America, and at no time more than in the period Halloween-to-New Year's Day. It is during the frantic family skedaddle from pumpkin to holly that Kids' Country runs in its jumpingest high gear.

3   But it is always Kids' Country here. Our civilization is child-centered, child-obsessed. A kid's body is our physical ideal. Weight-watchers grunt and pant. Sages jog from sea to shining sea. Plastic surgeons scissor and tuck up. New hair sprouts, transplanted, on wisdom's brow. One way or another we are determined to "keep in shape," and invariably this means keeping a kid's shape—which we then outfit in baby-doll ruffles, sneakers, blue jeans.

4   The food we live on is kids' food: pizza, hot dogs, fried chicken, ice cream, hamburgers. This bizarre diet is the reason we have such trouble maintaining our kids' bodies. The stuff we now drink has thrown the beverage industry into turmoil. Our consumption of soft drinks has risen 80 percent in a decade. Americans not only are switching *en masse* from hot coffee to iced tea, and from bitter drinks to sweet. The popularity of alcoholic soda pop—the so-called "fun" wines like Thunderbird and apple wine—has jumped 168 percent in five years.

5   Children hate spinach, vitamins, and *haute cuisine.* They like their food kooked, not cooked: you pop, thaw, dissolve, or explode it into eatability. To buy it you push around a wire perambulator, and at the end of the supermarket line you get prizes of colored stamps.

6   In Kids' Country, every day must be prize day. Miss America, Miss Teen-Age America, Miss Junior Miss America, and probably Miss Little Miss America trample each other down star-spangled runways. Volume mail-order giveaways

(3) *from sea to shining sea.* A phrase from the patriotic song, *"America the Beautiful."*
(4) *en masse.* In large numbers; "altogether" (French).
(5) *haute cuisine.* Elegant cookery (French).

will shortly silt up our postal system entirely. All day long TV shows like *Concentration, Dating Game, Hollywood Squares,* and *Jackpot* hand out more toys: wristwatches, washing machines, trips to Hawaii.

The rest of the world may be in fee to the Old Boy Network, carried on to the point of senility, but here there are no elder statesmen left. Seniority in an American politician no longer denotes wisdom, only power or tenure. The old age of the present Congress is a major hindrance. No one considers the Heberts and Eastlands to be Athenian men.   7

Our contemporary heroes are a series of golden boys. A direct line links Charles Lindbergh to Billy Graham to the astronauts to John F. Kennedy—and to his kid brother.   8

The philosopher-kings of Kids' Country are professors like Erich Segal and Charles Reich, who saw in Woodstock and the flower children a new golden age of innocence he called Consciousness III. The totem animal in Kids' Country just now is a talking, philosophizing sea gull who soars on vast updrafts of hot air, and the Kids' Country bogeyman is a wicked movie mafioso with a heart of gold.   9

The ideal of American parenthood is to be a kid with your kid. Take him to Disneyland, take him fishing, take him out to the ball game. Our national pastimes are kids' games, and we are all hooked. When the Redskins are blacked out in Washington, the President holes up in New York so as not to miss the   10

---

(7) *old boy network.* Term referring to the special relationship, particularly useful in business or professional life, that exists between men who share a similar (often elite) background.

(7) *the Heberts and Eastlands* [*not considered*] *Athenian men.* When Alexander wrote this essay, Representative F. Edward Hebert (Democrat, Louisiana) was 75 and Senator James O. Eastland (Democrat, Mississippi) was 73. Although both had served in Congress close to forty years, neither was especially acclaimed for the sort of wisdom that brought renown to ancient Athens.

(8) *Charles Lindbergh, Billy Graham, John F. Kennedy, his kid brother.* All made significant achievements at an early age: Lindbergh, the first solo transAtlantic flight at 25; Billy Graham, a successful evangelist at 28; John Kennedy, the youngest man, 43, ever elected president; Robert Kennedy, Attorney General at 35.

(9) *philosopher kings.* Plato's ideal rulers.

(9) *Erich Segal and Charles Reich.* Professor-authors who idealized youth in such books as Segal's *Love Story,* a tribute to young lovers, and Reich's *The Greening of America,* a book in praise of the ecological and humanitarian passions of youth of the 1960s.

(9) *Woodstock and the flower children.* Woodstock, New York, was the site of a celebrated rock concert and "happening" in July, 1969, attended by an estimated 400,000 flower children.

·(9) *totem . . . is a sea gull . . . and the bogeyman is a . . . mafioso.* The animal symbol of "Kids' Country" is the philosopher sea-gull hero of Richard Bach's best-selling *Jonathan Livingston Seagull.* Its villain is the "Godfather," protagonist of the popular movie of that name.

(10) *take him out to the ball game.* Allusion to the popular song, "Take Me Out to the Ball Game."

big game. Bobby Fischer, the quintessential smart boy of every school, turns the whole country on to chess. *The Boys of Summer* becomes a best-seller. In nostalgia's golden haze, we disremember the poet's full line, "I see the boys of summer in their ruin."

11   In Kids' Country, we do not permit middle age. Thirty is promoted over fifty, but thirty knows that soon his time to be overtaken will come. Middle-aged man must appear to run, even if it is only running in place. Often the big kid outruns his heart. In our over-sixty population, there are ten widows for every man.

12   Like a child's room, Kids' Country is a mess. New York City seems about to disappear under its load of litter, graffiti, and dog droppings. How is it that China can eliminate the house fly, and we can't even clean up Central Park?

13   In Kids' Country, not so ironically, Mommy and Daddy are household gods, and so we have two immense national holidays, elsewhere virtually unknown, called "Mother's Day" and "Father's Day." Without them, the American small businessman would be in even worse shape than he already is.

14   Ours is the first society in history in which parents expect to learn from their children, rather than the other way around. Such a topsy-turvy situation has come about at least in part because, unlike the rest of the world, we are an immigrant society, and for immigrants the only hope is in the kids. In the Old Country, hope was in the father, and in how much family wealth he could accumulate and pass along to his children. In the growth pattern of America and its ever-expanding frontier, the young man was ever advised to Go West. The father was ever inheriting from his son; the topsy-turviness was built-in from the beginning. A melting pot needs a spoon. Kids' Country may be the inevitable result.

15   Kids' Country is not all bad. America is the greatest country in the world to grow up in *because* it's Kids' Country. We not only wear kids' clothes and eat kids' food; we dream kids' dreams, and make them come true. It was, after all, a boys' game to go to the moon.

16   The stirring spoon has done its job. As a people we thrive. By the time they reach sixteen, most American kids today are bigger, stronger—and smarter—than Mommy and Daddy ever were. And if they are not precisely "happier," they may well be more "grown up." But because this is a civilization with no clear rites of passage, life in Kids' Country seems to me to be in many ways the exact opposite of medieval and Renaissance life. If in the old days children did

---

(10) *Bobby Fischer.* United States chess champion at 14, world champion at 28.

(10) *The Boys of Summer.* A series of vignettes about baseball and baseball players by Roger Kahn. The full quotation is from a poem by Dylan Thomas, among whose favorite themes is the sweet brevity of youth.

(14) *the young man was advised to go west.* Allusion to Horace Greeley's famous editorial advice: "Go west, young man" (1859).

not exist, it seems equally true today that adults as a class have begun to disappear, condemning all of us to remain boys and girls forever, jogging and doing push-ups against eternity.

Shana Alexander. Born 1925. Journalist, lecturer, and television commentator. Alexander started out as a reporter and staff writer for such publications as *PM* and *Harper's Bazaar.* She later worked as a columnist and contributing editor for *McCalls* and *Newsweek* and as a commentator for CBS radio and television. She is the author of five books, including *The Feminine Eye* and *Appearance of Evil: The Trial of Patty Hearst.* This article was originally published in *Newsweek,* December 11, 1972.

Joan Didion

On Self-Respect

1   Once, in a dry season, I wrote in large letters across two pages of a notebook that innocence ends when one is stripped of the delusion that one likes oneself. Although now, some years later, I marvel that a mind on the outs with itself should have nonetheless made painstaking record of its every tremor, I recall with embarrassing clarity the flavor of those particular ashes. It was a matter of misplaced self-respect.

2   I had not been elected to Phi Beta Kappa. This failure could scarcely have been more predictable or less ambiguous (I simply did not have the grades), but I was unnerved by it; I had somehow thought myself a kind of academic Raskolnikov, curiously exempt from the cause-effect relationships which hampered others. Although even the humorless nineteen-year-old that I was must have recognized that the situation lacked real tragic stature, the day that I did not make Phi Beta Kappa nonetheless marked the end of something, and innocence may well be the word for it. I lost the conviction that lights would always turn green for me, the pleasant certainty that those rather passive virtues which had won me approval as a child automatically guaranteed me not only Phi Beta Kappa keys but happiness, honor, and the love of a good man; lost a certain touching faith in the totem power of good manners, clean hair, and proven competence on the Stanford-Binet scale. To such doubtful amulets had my self-respect been pinned, and I faced myself that day with the nonplused apprehension of someone who has come across a vampire and has no crucifix at hand.

3   Although to be driven back upon oneself is an uneasy affair at best, rather like trying to cross a border with borrowed credentials, it seems to me now the one condition necessary to the beginnings of real self-respect. Most of our platitudes notwithstanding, self-deception remains the most difficult deception. The tricks that work on others count for nothing in that very well-lit back alley where one keeps assignations with oneself: no winning smiles will do here, no prettily drawn lists of good intentions. One shuffles flashily but in vain through

---

---

(2) *Phi Beta Kappa.* A collegiate honorary association whose members are chosen on the basis of academic achievement.

(2) *Raskolnikov.* Character in Dostoevsky's *Crime and Punishment* who committed a murder in the conviction that his intellectual superiority set him somehow outside of the moral law.

(2) *Stanford-Binet scale.* The original intelligence quotient (IQ) scale.

one's marked cards—the kindness done for the wrong reason, the apparent triumph which involved no real effort, the seemingly heroic act into which one had been shamed. The dismal fact is that self-respect has nothing to do with the approval of others—who are, after all, deceived easily enough; has nothing to do with reputation, which, as Rhett Butler told Scarlett O'Hara, is something people with courage can do without.

To do without self-respect, on the other hand, is to be an unwilling audi-   4
ence of one to an interminable documentary that details one's failings, both real and imagined, with fresh footage spliced in for every screening. *There's the glass you broke in anger, there's the hurt on X's face; watch now, this next scene, the night Y came back from Houston, see how you muff this one.* To live without self-respect is to lie awake some night, beyond the reach of warm milk, phenobarbital, and the sleeping hand on the coverlet, counting up the sins of commission and omission, the trusts betrayed, the promises subtly broken, the gifts irrevocably wasted through sloth or cowardice or carelessness. However long we postpone it, we eventually lie down alone in that notoriously uncomfortable bed, the one we make ourselves. Whether or not we sleep in it depends, of course, on whether or not we respect ourselves.

To protest that some fairly improbable people, some people who *could not*   5
possibly respect themselves, seem to sleep easily enough is to miss the point entirely, as surely as those people miss it who think that self-respect has necessarily to do with not having safety pins in one's underwear. There is a common superstition that "self-respect" is a kind of charm against snakes, something that keeps those who have it locked in some unblighted Eden, out of strange beds, ambivalent conversations, and trouble in general. It does not at all. It has nothing to do with the face of things, but concerns instead a separate peace, a private reconciliation. Although the careless, suicidal Julian English in *Appointment in Samarra* and the careless, incurably dishonest Jordan Baker in *The Great Gatsby* seem equally improbable candidates for self-respect, Jordan Baker had it, Julian English did not. With that genius for accommodation more often seen in women than in men, Jordan took her own measure, made her own peace, avoided threats to that peace: "I hate careless people," she told Nick Carraway. "It takes two to make an accident."

Like Jordan Baker, people with self-respect have the courage of their mis-   6
takes. They know the price of things. If they choose to commit adultery, they do not then go running, in an excess of bad conscience, to receive absolution from the wronged parties; nor do they complain unduly of the unfairness, the undeserved embarrassment, of being named co-respondent. In brief, people with self-respect exhibit a certain toughness, a kind of moral nerve; they display what was once called *character,* a quality which, although approved in the ab-

---

(3) *as Rhett Butler told Scarlett O'Hara.* In a line from the movie *Gone with the Wind* (1939).

(4) *lie . . . in that bed . . . we make ourselves.* Allusion to the folk proverb: "You've made your bed, and now you must lie in it."

stract, sometimes loses ground to other, more instantly negotiable virtues. The measure of its slipping prestige is that one tends to think of it only in connection with homely children and United States senators who have been defeated, preferably in the primary, for reelection. Nonetheless, character—the willingness to accept responsibility for one's own life—is the source from which self-respect springs.

7   Self-respect is something that our grandparents, whether or not they had it, knew all about. They had instilled in them, young, a certain discipline, the sense that one lives by doing things one does not particularly want to do, by putting fears and doubts to one side, by weighing immediate comforts against the possibility of larger, even intangible, comforts. It seemed to the nineteenth century admirable, but not remarkable, that Chinese Gordon put on a clean white suit and held Khartoum against the Mahdi; it did not seem unjust that the way to free land in California involved death and difficulty and dirt. In a diary kept during the winter of 1846, an emigrating twelve-year-old named Narcissa Cornwall noted coolly: "Father was busy reading and did not notice that the house was being filled with strange Indians until Mother spoke about it." Even lacking any clue as to what Mother said, one can scarcely fail to be impressed by the entire incident: the father reading, the Indians filing in, the mother choosing the words that would not alarm, the child duly recording the event and noting further that those particular Indians were not, "fortunately for us," hostile. Indians were simply part of the *donnee.*

8   In one guise or another, Indians always are. Again, it is a question of recognizing that anything worth having has its price. People who respect themselves are willing to accept the risk that the Indians will be hostile, that the venture will go bankrupt, that the liaison may not turn out to be one in which *every day is a holiday because you're married to me.* They are willing to invest something of themselves; they may not play at all, but when they do play, they know the odds.

9   That kind of self-respect is a discipline, a habit of mind that can never be faked but can be developed, trained, coaxed forth. It was once suggested to me that, as an antidote to crying, I put my head in a paper bag. As it happens, there is a sound physiological reason, something to do with oxygen, for doing exactly that, but the psychological effect alone is incalculable: it is difficult in the extreme to continue fancying oneself Cathy in *Wuthering Heights* with one's head

---

(7) *Chinese Gordon . . . held Khartoum against the Mahdi.* Charles George Gordon (1833–1885), popular British general who died valiantly defending Khartoum, the capital of Anglo-Egyptian Sudan, against the siege of Mahmed Ahmed and his Mahdists. Ahmed was believed to be the Mahdi, the Muslim messiah.

(7) *donnee.* Underlying situation (French).

(8) *every day is a holiday. . . .* Allusion to the song, "Every Day's a Holiday with Me."

(9) *Cathy in Wuthering Heights.* Romantic heroine in a novel by Emily Bronte.

in a Food Fair bag. There is a similar case for all the small disciplines, unimportant in themselves; imagine maintaining any kind of swoon, commiserative or carnal, in a cold shower.

But those small disciplines are valuable only insofar as they represent larger   10
ones. To say that Waterloo was won on the playing fields of Eton is not to say that Napoleon might have been saved by a crash program in cricket; to give formal dinners in the rain forest would be pointless did not the candlelight flickering on the liana call forth deeper, stronger disciplines, values instilled long before. It is a kind of ritual, helping us to remember who and what we are. In order to remember it, one must have known it.

To have that sense of one's intrinsic worth which constitutes self-respect is   11
potentially to have everything: the ability to discriminate, to love and to remain indifferent. To lack it is to be locked within oneself, paradoxically incapable of either love or indifference. If we do not respect ourselves, we are on the one hand forced to despise those who have so few resources as to consort with us, so little perception as to remain blind to our fatal weaknesses. On the other, we are peculiarly in thrall to everyone we see, curiously determined to live out— since our self-image is untenable—their false notions of us. We flatter ourselves by thinking this compulsion to please others an attractive trait: a gist for imaginative empathy, evidence of our willingness to give. *Of course* I will play Francesca to your Paolo, Helen Keller to anyone's Annie Sullivan: no expectation is too misplaced, no role too ludicrous. At the mercy of those we cannot but hold in contempt, we play roles doomed to failure before they are begun, each defeat generating fresh despair at the urgency of divining and meeting the next demand made upon us.

It is the phenomenon sometimes called "alienation from self." In its ad-   12
vanced stages, we no longer answer the telephone, because someone might want something; that we could say *no* without drowning in self-reproach is an idea alien to this game. Every encounter demands too much, tears the nerves, drains the will, and the specter of something as small as an unanswered letter arouses such disproportionate guilt that answering it becomes out of the question. To assign unanswered letters their proper weight, to free us from the ex-

---

(10) *Waterloo was won on the playing fields of Eton.* A remark of the Duke of Wellington, who defeated Napoleon at the Battle of Waterloo in 1815, suggesting that the rigorous discipline of elite English boarding schools produced the sort of leadership that carried the day.

(10) *liana.* A tropical vine.

(11) *play Francesca to your Paolo.* Francesca da Rimini deserted her husband and gave herself to his brother Paolo Malatesta. Their story is recorded in Dante's *Inferno* and a number of other literary, dramatic, and musical works.

(11) *Helen Keller to. . . Annie Sullivan.* After a rebellious early childhood, the deaf and blind Helen Keller put herself completely in the competent hands of her teacher, Annie Sullivan.

pectations of others, to give us back to ourselves—there lies the great, the sin-gular power of self-respect. Without it, one eventually discovers the final turn of the screw: one runs away to find oneself, and finds no one at home.

Joan Didion. Born 1934. Essayist, novelist, playwright, and "new" journalist. Didion, a native Californian, has served as columnist and/or contributing editor for *Vogue,* the *Saturday Evening Post* and the *National Review.* She has written a number of books including *The White Album* and *Slouching Towards Bethlehem,* and has collaborated with her husband, John Gregory Dunn, on screenplays for such movies as "Panic in Needle Park" and "A Star is Born." This article was originally published in *Vogue,* August, 1961.

Down with Sin

The need for a denunciation of sin occurred to me the other day when I read a   1
remark by some young movie star, I forget his name, in defense of Doris Day.
He had made a picture with Doris Day, and he felt it was time somebody *came
to the defense of that girl.* He said, "You know, Doris is not the nice, sweet,
wholesome, Mom's pie, All-American girl everybody makes her out to be. Actually, she is *quite a gal.*"

A little later I was over talking to the people at a TV panel show and they   2
showed me a big board with the topics of prospective shows pinned up all over
it. One of the topics was "Adultery, For and Against." One of the TV people told
me, "We're having a problem with that one. We have some terrific people lined
up to talk in favor of it. Norman Mailer and a lot of terrific people, but we
haven't got anybody against."

I don't imagine there are more than two or three people in New York   3
today—a couple of old Presbyterian preachers, maybe, but none of the younger
ones—not more than two or three people in the whole town who would take
a public stand against Adultery. I don't ever recall meeting a girl, over the last
10 years anyway, who would not be acutely embarrassed by any insinuation
that she did not have as flaming a libido as the next girl. One of the worst insults
kicking around today is any word that means, in effect, "wholesome." You are a
wholesome person. How would you like to be called that?

Meantime in the women's colleges, from Vassar, Smith and Radcliffe on   4
down, there is a whole generation of young buds with preRaphaelite hairdos
and black-muslin stockings who worship Guitar Players and Smoking Pot.

This is damned hard on all the guys who planned to grow up and wear   5
hard-finished worsteds and go to Wall Street and take over the country and get
the best girls. Today the girls all talk about going down to the Village and having
affairs with coffeehouse pothead poets, and all the right guys can say is "Aw,
gee." This annoys me, too, because when you make polite conversation with
these girls, and you can't tell them about pot or where to get any, you are not
considered a serious person.

So what this story is against, actually, is not sin exactly, but the Sin Cult. I   6
would like to put forth the thesis that if you want to sin, sin; but don't make so
much noise about it.

(2) *Norman Mailer.* A contemporary novelist almost as well known for his radical
views on moral questions as for his literary prowess.

(3) *libido.* Freudian term for sexual drive.

7   There is a great fascination with evil today. There always has been, but today it takes a funny form. People go around serving notice in one way or another that, "Wow, you may not know it, but I'm a fairly evil person." This is an intriguing frame of mind. What the person is usually saying is, I am not a timid bourgeois. The unspoken premise is that the timid bourgeois does not dare to hang in there with girls with no makeup and long, straight hair in walkup flats on East Sixth Street or hand around the pot pipe in drawing rooms with McIntire moldings or drive black XKE's with nubile bimbos with silk scarves on their heads. It is an obsolete premise. The truth is, the bourgeoisie is taking over sin. There has got to be some other way out to avoid the terrible stigma of being bourgeois.

8   I keep thinking about those poor college girls author Gael Greene interviewed to do her book, *Sex and the College Girl.* They were acutely aware what they ought to be doing, but they didn't quite know how to arrange for the whole thing yet. The sofa at the dormitory wasn't very private, and the turkey-necked night manager with gummy sleepers in his eye at the motel down the highway always made them blush when they drove up with Mr. Wonderful. They could hardly go around asking the other girls because then they'd know the awful truth. You know? These girls end up crying and saying, "I'm the only virgin in Harkney Hall East."

9   Somehow it all recalls a famous line from Jimmy Walker, the erstwhile mayor of New York. Jimmy Walker said, "I never heard of a girl who was seduced by a book." He said that because some censorship issue had come up. People still quote it today on the subject of pornography. The fact is, I haven't met more than six college girls over the past 10 years who weren't undone by a book. Yes, it is a known fact that only six girls east of the Ohio River watershed have survived the junior-year seminar on contemporary literature. They get in there with Lady Brett and all those Hemingway bullfighters and—pow!— half the young bulls from Haverford, Pa., to Bowdoin, Me., have the whole molten case already won for them.

10   Meanwhile, men are not just lollygagging around the Union Club library, either, and they're not only wacked-out, but tough. In fact, the evil that seems to fascinate men most today is violence. A lot of men today have a kind of hairy sentimentality about violence that is somewhat like the girls and Lady Brett.

---

(7) *bourgeois.* "Middle-class person with conservative moral values" (French).

(7) *walkup flats on East Sixth Street. . . drawing rooms with McIntire moldings. . . black XKE's.* "Walkup flats" are apartments in buildings without elevators, often old, rather seedy buildings. "McIntire moldings" are the elaborately carved wall and ceiling decorations originated by Samuel McIntire at the beginning of the nineteenth century. XKE's are expensive automobiles.

(7) *nubile bimbos.* Rather stupid girls, physically ready for mating.

(9) *Lady Brett and all those Hemingway bullfighters.* Lady Brett Ashley, sadly romantic heroine of Ernest Hemingway's novel *The Sun Also Rises* (1926), depicted as a member of the "lost generation" disillusioned by World War I, who has an affair with a bullfighter.

There is a lot of talk currently about how the Mafiosi are moving into big business, Wall Street and everything. I don't know if they are or they aren't. All I know is that a lot of big-business types are ready to invite them into the club car for a couple. It seems to be a way of feeling like you're not a timid bourgeois playing it safe and cozy in a safe and cozy world, after all.

I am at a cocktail party given by an accountant from Downtown, and one of his friends, a Downtown lawyer, tells me in the old confidential tone, "You see that guy over there? That's *Bongo.*"

Bongo?

"Yeah. That guy standing right there is a professional killer. He gets twelve hundred dollars a hit."

A hit?

"That's right. And he doesn't care who it is, either. It's strictly business."

What's he doing here?

"Oh, I've known Bongo for almost a year. I ran into him at a party. You talk to a guy like that and he's a different kind of person. You know what I mean? A different breed. None of the old baloney. You know—God! some days you're talking to people, you're talking all day, and then at the end of the day you suddenly realize it's all been pure baloney. With Bongo it's no baloney. It's all— pow!—right there. He's a really interesting guy."

Five minutes later another guy, the secretary of a large furniture corporation, comes up to me and rocks back on his heels and sucks his eyes in and says, "You see that guy over there? That's a guy I know named Bongo. Twenty-two hundred dollars and—"

I know a guy who can get him for you for twelve beans, I tell him. He doesn't get it.

11

12

13

14

---

(10) *Mafiosi.* Members of the Mafia.

Tom Wolfe. Born 1931. Journalist, scholar, artist, author. Wolfe, a Yale PhD, served as reporter or as contributing editor for the *Washington Post, New York Herald Tribune, New York World Journal, Esquire,* and *Harper's.* An advocate and practitioner of the "new journalism," Wolfe has written ten books on art and contemporary culture, including *The Kandy Kolored Tangerine-Flake Streamline Baby* and *From Bauhaus to Our House.* This article was originally published in *The Saturday Evening Post,* July 1965.

George Will

Israel and Munich

1   Various Jewish religious observances commemorate calamities or narrow deliverance from calamities, and the short history of the Jewish state is replete with such experiences. Today, friction between Israel and the Carter administration is building up a dangerous charge of static electricity. No Israeli government casually risks the U.S. government's displeasure: diminished support for Israel could lead to a calamity from which there would be no deliverance. But the contagious crossness between Washington and Jerusalem that originated in Washington is a compound of Washington impatience and Israeli anxiety. The anxiety is more reasonable than the impatience.

2   For a decade, since the Six Day War of 1967, U.S. policy has been that Israel should trade territory for peace. As President Ford put it, Israel should "dare the exchange of the tangible for the intangible." The secure are always exhorting Israel to be daring. Similarly, the governments of the world constantly insist that Israel be more forthcoming than those governments ever are.

3   Theodore Draper, scholar and journalist, notes that of all the millions of square miles of territory conquered in recent decades, only Israel's occupied territories are expected to be returned. Norman Podhoretz, editor of *Commentary* magazine, notes that of the thirty-five million refugees created since 1945, only the fraction of a million created by Israel's war of independence are expected to be repatriated.

4   Saul Bellow notes: "In this disorderly century refugees have fled from many countries. In India, in Africa, in Europe, millions of human beings have been put to flight, transported, enslaved, stampeded over borders, left to starve, but only the case of Palestinians is held to be permanently open. Where Israel is concerned, the world swells with moral consciousness. Moral judgment, a wraith in Europe, becomes a full-bodied giant when Israel and the Palestinians are mentioned. . . . What Switzerland is to winter holidays and the Dalmatian coast is to summer tourists, Israel and the Palestinians are to the West's need for justice—a sort of moral resort area."

Title. Munich. Ever since Britain's Prime Minister Neville Chamberlain signed a pact with Adolph Hitler in Munich, Germany (1938), the name of that city has become a symbol for cowardly appeasement and betrayal of the weak by the strong. By the Munich pact the Sudeten territory of Czechoslovakia was ceded to Germany in the belief that this land would satisfy Hitler's desire for territory and power and that the world would thereafter enjoy "peace in our time."

(4) *Saul Bellow.* Author of the nonfiction work, *To Jerusalem and Back* (1976).

Today the U.S. government is anxious to bestow upon Israel the honor of 5
leading a life more daring than other nations choose to live. The United States
became a mighty continental nation through conquest in the name of "manifest
destiny." But the U.S. government is irritated because Israel is reluctant to commit itself, before negotiations, to return land it conquered from aggressors who
still deny its right to exist on the coast of Palestine. U.S. security has always
been a function of broad oceans and placid neighbors. But the U.S. government
is irritated because Israel is wary of turning a geographical buffer (the occupied
West Bank of Jordan) into a Palestinian "homeland" that probably would be
dominated by the Palestine Liberation Organization, terrorists committed to the
destruction of Israel.

The U.S. position is that Israel should withdraw to the 1967 borders (per- 6
haps with slight revisions) and the Arab states should take "steps toward" normalization of relations with Israel. But even if Israel were to withdraw in exchange for full peace (recognition of its right to exist, plus free movement of
people, ideas and commerce in the region), there still would be an inherent
asymmetry of risk in a trade of the physical for the political. Arab political
concessions could be repudiated overnight; Israel's physical concessions could
not be reclaimed without war.

Nevertheless, Israel has accepted this asymmetrical policy. It has asked two 7
things. One is that the United States not intrude itself so much that it spares
Arab states the need to negotiate directly with Israel. The second is that the
United States not propose a specific outcome (such as withdrawal in exchange
for "steps toward" normalization). Israel thinks that if Arab states regard withdrawal as a given, they will have no incentive to give anything. After four wars,
Israelis are unmoved by the idea that their security depends less on their toughness than on their malleability. And since the fourth war they are especially
impatient with assurances that the "conscience of the West" will be their shield.
In the October 1973 war Israel not only suffered debilitating losses comparable
to Britain's in the First World War, relative to national strength. Israel also suffered an acute understanding of the "conscience of the West" under oil pressure. Israel was isolated.

Israelis are obsessively interested in U.S. diplomacy, and were fascinated by 8
Jimmy Carter's May meeting in Geneva with Syrian President Assad. Carter
praised Assad's helpfulness, constructive attitude and "intimate knowledge."
That, Carter said, "has helped me a great deal to understand" the Mideast. Now,
diplomacy always involves a lot of solemn nonsense, but Carter went a tad far.
In recent years Assad has called Israel "a basic part of southern Syria," and his
controlled press has asserted that Israel "shall be destroyed." Today the United
States is pleased to regard Assad as a "moderate." Has Assad changed, or has the
United States? Today Assad says "the Palestinian problem has two parts," the

---

(6) *asymmetry.* Without symmetry; one-sided.
(7) *malleability.* Ability to be shaped or formed by pressure.

first concerning the West Bank and the Gaza Strip. "On this territory a Palestinian state might be established, as is now envisaged. This state could not accommodate all the Palestinians. This leads us to the second part of the Palestinian problem, namely the refugee problem. These refugees . . . have a right to return to the land from which they were driven in 1948."

9   The idea that Assad is a moderate, an idea enjoying currency in the U.S. government, is part of a way of perceiving Israel, a way that reminds Podhoretz of autumn 1938 on the eve of Munich:

10   "As Czechoslovakia, a democratic country, was accused of mistreating the German minority in the Sudeten regions, so Israel, also a democratic country, is accused of mistreating the Arab minority within Israel itself and also, of course, in the occupied territories. As the creation of the Czechoslovak state after World War I was called a mistake by Hitler and Neville Chamberlain, so the creation of the Jewish state after World War II is called a crime by contemporary totalitarians and their appeasers. The insistence by the Czechs that surrendering the Sudeten regions to Hitler would leave Czechoslovakia hopelessly vulnerable to military assault was derided, especially on the Left, as a shortsighted reliance on the false security of territory and arms; so a similar insistence by the Israelis with regard to the occupied territories is treated today with lofty disdain by contemporary descendants of these believers in the irrelevance to a nation's security of territorial buffers and arms."

11   Made malleable by diplomatic pounding, Czechoslovakia, by spring 1939, had no shield except "the conscience of the West," and no deliverance.

George Will. Born 1941. Pulitzer prize-winning political columnist. Former college instructor and congressional aide, Will is now a Washington based writer for *Newsweek* and the *National Review* and a syndicated columnist for the *Washington Post.* Will, who comes from a family including scholars and ministers, is known for his intellectual honesty, his wit, and his political conservatism. This article was originally published in *Newsweek,* July 11, 1977.

The Chicago Cubs, Overdue

A reader demands to know how I contracted the infectious conservatism for
which he plans to horsewhip me. So if you have tears, gentle reader, prepare to
shed them now as I reveal how my gloomy temperament received its conservative warp from early and prolonged exposure to the Chicago Cubs.
1

The differences between conservatives and liberals are as much a matter of
temperament as ideas. Liberals are temperamentally inclined to see the world
as a harmonious carnival of sweetness and light, where good will prevails, good
intentions are rewarded, the race is to the swift, and a benevolent Nature arranges a favorable balance of pleasure over pain. Conservatives (and Cub fans)
know better.
2

Conservatives know the world is a dark and forbidding place where most
new knowledge is false, most improvements are for the worse, the battle is not
to the strong, nor riches to men of understanding, and an unscrupulous Providence consigns innocents to suffering. I learned this early.
3

Out in central Illinois, where men are men and I am native, in 1948, at age
seven, I made a mad, fateful blunder. I fell ankle over elbows in love with the
Cubs. Barely advanced beyond the bib-and-cradle stage, I plighted my troth to
a baseball team destined to dash the cup of life's joy from my lips.
4

Spring, earth's renewal, a season of hope for the rest of mankind, became
for me an experience comparable to being slapped around the mouth with a
damp carp. Summer was like being bashed across the bridge of the nose with a
crowbar—ninety times. My youth was like a long rainy Monday in Bayonne,
New Jersey.
5

Each year the Cubs charged onto the field to challenge anew the theory
that there are limits to the changes one can ring on pure incompetence. By
mid-April, when other kids' teams were girding for Homeric battles at the top
6

© 1974, The Washington Post Company. Reprinted with permission.

---

(2) *sweetness and light.* Phrase originated by Jonathan Swift in *The Battle of Books*
(1704) and popularized by Matthew Arnold in *Culture and Anarchy* (1869).

(2) *the race is to the swift.* Allusion to *Ecclesiastes* 9:11: "The race is not to the
swift, nor the battle to the strong . . . nor yet riches to men of understanding."

(3) *the battle is not to the strong.* . . . A contrasting continuation of the allusion
to *Ecclesiastes* 9:11.

(4) *plighted my troth.* Literally, pledged my truth, my loyalty; similar to phrase in
traditional Protestant marriage ceremony.

(6) *Homeric battles.* Battles between the great heroes that Homer describes in the
Iliad and the *Odyssey.*

of the league, my heroes had wilted like salted slugs and begun their gadarene descent to the bottom. By September they had set a mark for ineptness at which others—but not next year's Cubs—would shoot in vain.

7   Every litter must have its runt, but my Cubs were almost all runts. Topps baseball bubblegum cards always struggled to say something nice about each player. All they could say about the Cubs' infielder Eddie Miksis was that in 1951 he was tenth in the league in stolen bases, with eleven.

8   Like the boy who stood on the burning deck whence all but he had fled, I was loyal. And the downward trajectory of my life was set. An eight-year-old could not face these fires without being singed, unless he had the crust of an armadillo, and how many eight-year-olds do?

9   Of the sixteen teams that existed in 1949, all have since won league championships—all but the Cubs. And which of the old National League teams was first to finish in tenth place behind even the expansion teams? Don't ask. Since 1948 the Cubs have played more than 6,000 hours of losing baseball. My cruel addiction continued. In 1964 I chose to do three years of graduate study at Princeton because Princeton is midway between Philadelphia and New York—two National League cities. All I remember about my wedding day in 1967 is that the Cubs dropped a doubleheader.

10   Only a team named after baby bears would have a shortstop named Smalley—a righthanded hitter, if that is the word for a man who in his best year (1953) hit .249. From Roy Smalley I learned the truth about the word "overdue." A portrait of this columnist as a tad would show him with an ear pressed against a radio, listening to an announcer say "The Cubs have the bases loaded. If Smalley gets on, the tying run will be on deck. And Smalley is overdue for a hit."

11   It was the most consoling word in the language, "overdue." It meant: in the long run, everything is going to be all right. No one is really a .222 hitter. We are all good hitters, all winners. It is just that some of us are, well, "overdue" for a hit, or whatever.

12   Unfortunately, my father is a righthanded logician who knows more than it is nice to know about the theory of probability. With a lot of help from Smalley, he convinced me that Smalley was not "overdue." Stan Musial batting .249 was overdue for a hot streak. Smalley batting .249 was doing his best.

13   Smalley retired after eleven seasons with a lifetime average of .227. He was still overdue.

---

(6) *Wilted like salted slugs.* Salting slugs (shell-less snails) draws the moisture from them.

(6) *gadarene descent.* A headlong descent reminiscent of the leap the herd of swine took over the cliff at Gadara after Jesus had driven the demons out of a person and into the swine (Matthew 8:28–32).

(8) *The boy stood on the burning deck whence all but he had fled.* Opening lines of the poem "Casabianca" by Felicia Dorothea Hemans (1793–1838).

Now once again my trained senses tell me: spring is near. For most of the world hope, given up for dead, stirs in its winding linen. But I, like Figaro, laugh that I may not weep. Baseball season approaches. The weeds are about to reclaim the trellis of my life. For most fans, the saddest words of tongue or pen are: "Wait 'til next year." For us Cub fans, the saddest words are: "This is next year." 14

The heart has its reasons that the mind cannot refute, so I say: Do not go gently into this season, Cub fans; rage, rage against the blasting of our hopes. Had I but world enough, and time, this slowness, Cubs, would be no crime. But I am almost halfway through my allotted three-score-and-ten and you, sirs, are overdue. 15

---

(14) *winding linen.* The cloth in which, traditionally, a body was wrapped for burial.

(14) *Figaro.* Hero of Rossini's opera *The Barber of Seville.*

(14) *the saddest words of tongue or pen.* The complete quotation of Whittier reads: "Of all sad words of tongue or pen, / The saddest are these—It might have been."

(15) *The heart has its reasons. Le coeur a ses raisons,* from *Pensées (Thoughts)* by Blaise Pascal (1623–1662).

(15) *Do not go gently into this season. . . . Rage, rage against the blasting of our hopes.* Parody of Dylan Thomas's poem to his dying father, "Do Not Go Gentle": "Do not go gentle into that good night. / Rage, rage against the dying of the light."

(15) *Had I but world enough and time, this slowness, Cubs, were no crime.* Parody of Andrew Marvell's poem, "To His Coy Mistress": "Had we but world enough and time, / This coyness, Lady, were no crime."

(15) *my allotted three score years and ten.* According to the Bible, "The days of man's years are three score and ten, or by reason of strength, four score."

See p. 448 for information about George Will's life and work. This article was originally published in *The Washington Post,* March 20, 1974.

Wayne C. Booth

The Rhetorical Stance*

1 Last fall I had an advanced graduate student, bright, energetic, well-informed, whose papers were almost unreadable. He managed to be pretentious, dull, and disorganized in his paper on *Emma,* and pretentious, dull, and disorganized on *Madame Bovary.* On *The Golden Bowl* he was all these and obscure as well. Then one day, toward the end of term, he cornered me after class and said, "You know, I think you were all wrong about Robbe-Grillet's *Jealousy* today." We didn't have time to discuss it, so I suggested that he write me a note about it. Five hours later I found in my faculty box a four-page polemic, unpretentious, stimulating, organized, convincing. Here was a man who had taught freshman composition for several years and who was incapable of committing any of the more obvious errors that we think of as characteristic of bad writing. Yet he could not write a decent sentence, paragraph, or paper until his rhetorical problem was solved—until, that is, he had found a definition of his audience, his argument, and his own proper tone of voice.

2 The word "rhetoric" is one of those catch-all terms that can easily raise trouble when our backs are turned. As it regains a popularity that it once seemed permanently to have lost, its meanings seem to range all the way from something like "the whole art of writing on any subject," as in Kenneth Burke's *The Rhetoric of Religion,* through "the special arts of persuasion," on down to fairly narrow notions about rhetorical figures and devices. And of course we still have with us the meaning of "empty bombast," as in the phrase "merely rhetorical."

3 I suppose that the question of the role of rhetoric in the English course is meaningless if we think of rhetoric in either its broadest or its narrowest meanings. No English course could avoid dealing with rhetoric in Burke's sense, under whatever name, and on the other hand nobody would ever advocate anything so questionable as teaching "mere rhetoric." But if we settle on the following, traditional, definition, some real questions are raised: "Rhetoric is the art of finding and employing the most effective means of persuasion on any subject, considered independently of intellectual mastery of that subject." As the students say, "Prof. X knows his stuff but he doesn't know how to put it across." If rhetoric is thought of as the art of "putting it across," considered as quite distinct from mastering an "it" in the first place, we are immediately landed in a bramble bush of controversy. Is there such an art? If so, what does it consist of? Does it have a content of its own? Can it be taught? Should it be taught? If it should, how do we go about it, head on or obliquely?

Reprinted by permission of the author and the National Council of Teachers of English.

*This essay was written for English teachers, but what it has to say is important for all writers and students of writing as well.

Obviously it would be foolish to try to deal with many of these issues in twenty minutes. But I wish that there were more signs of our taking all of them seriously. I wish that along with our new passion for structural linguistics, for example, we could point to the development of a rhetorical theory that would show just how knowledge of structural linguistics can be useful to anyone interested in the art of persuasion. I wish there were more freshman texts that related every principle and every rule to functional principles of rhetoric, or, where this proves impossible, I wish one found more systematic discussion of why it is impossible. But for today, I must content myself with a brief look at the charge that there is nothing distinctive and teachable about the art of rhetoric.   4

The case against the isolability and teachability of rhetoric may look at first like a good one. Nobody writes rhetoric, just as nobody ever writes writing. What we write and speak is always *this* discussion of the decline of railroading and *that* discussion of Pope's couplets and the other argument for abolishing the poll-tax or for getting rhetoric back into English studies.   5

We can also admit that like all the arts, the art of rhetoric is at best very chancy, only partly amenable to systematic teaching; as we are all painfully aware when our 1:00 section goes miserably and our 2:00 section of the same course is a delight, our own rhetoric is not entirely under control. Successful rhetoricians are to some extent like poets, born, not made. They are also dependent on years of practice and experience. And we can finally admit that even the firmest of principles about writing cannot be taught in the same sense that elementary logic or arithmetic or French can be taught. In my first year of teaching, I had a student who started his first two essays with a swear word. When I suggested that perhaps the third paper ought to start with something else, he protested that his high school teacher had taught him always to catch the reader's attention. Now the teacher was right, but the application of even such a firm principle requires reserves of tact that were somewhat beyond my freshman.   6

But with all of the reservations made, surely the charge that the art of persuasion cannot in any sense be taught is baseless. I cannot think that anyone who has ever read Aristotle's *Rhetoric* or, say, Whateley's *Elements of Rhetoric* could seriously make the charge. There is more than enough in these and the other traditional rhetorics to provide structure and content for a year-long course. I believe that such a course, when planned and carried through with   7

---

(5) *Pope's couplets.* Alexander Pope (1688–1744), the greatest master of the English couplet, a form of verse in which a pithy, often witty, idea is expressed in two rhyming, ten-syllable lines.

(5) *poll-tax.* A tax for voting, once common in the southern United States.

(7) Aristotle's *Rhetoric.* The *Rhetoric* of the Athenian philosopher and teacher, Aristotle (384–322 B.C.) has been called the single most important text in the history of western education.

(7) Whateley's *Elements of Rhetoric.* Essay on rhetoric written by Archbishop Richard Whateley (1787–1863) that is considered the most influential textbook on the subject throughout the 19th and well into the 20th century.

intelligence and flexibility, can be one of the most important of all educational experiences. But it seems obvious that the arts of persuasion cannot be learned in one year, that a good teacher will continue to teach them regardless of his subject matter, and that we as English teachers have a special responsibility at all levels to get certain basic rhetorical principles into all of our writing assignments. When I think back over the experiences which have had any actual effect on my writing, I find the great good fortune of a splendid freshman course, taught by a man who believed in what he was doing, but I also find a collection of other experiences quite unconnected with a specific writing course. I remember the instructor in psychology who penciled one word after a peculiarly pretentious paper of mine: *bull.* I remember the day when P. A. Christensen talked with me about my Chaucer paper, and made me understand that my failure to use effective transitions was not simply a technical fault but a fundamental block in my effort to get him to see my meaning. His off-the-cuff pronouncement that I should never let myself write a sentence that was not in some way explicitly attached to preceding and following sentences meant far more to me at that moment, when I had something I wanted to say, than it could have meant as part of a pattern of such rules offered in a writing course. Similarly, I can remember the devastating lessons about my bad writing that Ronald Crane could teach with a simple question mark on a graduate seminar paper, or a penciled "Evidence for this?" or "Why this section here?" or "Everybody says so. Is it true?"

8   Such experiences are not, I like to think, simply the result of my being a late bloomer. At least I find my colleagues saying such things as "I didn't learn to write until I became a newspaper reporter." or "The most important training in writing I had was doing a dissertation under old *Blank.*" Sometimes they go on to say that the freshman course was useless; sometimes they say that it was an indispensable preparation for the later experience. The diversity of such replies is so great as to suggest that before we try to reorganize the freshman course, with or without explicit confrontations with rhetorical categories, we ought to look for whatever there is in common among our experiences, both of good writing and of good writing instruction. Whatever we discover in such an enterprise ought to be useful to us at any level of our teaching. It will not, presumably, decide once and for all what should be the content of the freshman course, if there should be such a course. But it might serve as a guideline for the development of widely different programs in the widely differing institutional circumstances in which we must work.

9   The common ingredient that I find in all of the writing I admire—excluding for now novels, plays and poems—is something that I shall reluctantly call the rhetorical stance, a stance which depends on discovering and maintaining in any writing situation a proper balance among the three elements that are at work in any communicative effort: the available arguments about the subject itself, the interests and peculiarities of the audience, and the voice, the implied character, of the speaker. I should like to suggest that it is this balance, this rhetorical stance, difficult as it is to describe, that is our main goal as teachers

of rhetoric. Our ideal graduate will strike this balance automatically in any writing that he considers finished. Though he may never come to the point of finding the balance easily, he will know that it is what makes the difference between effective communication and mere wasted effort.

What I mean by the true rhetorician's stance can perhaps best be seen by contrasting it with two or three corruptions, unbalanced stances often assumed by people who think they are practicing the arts of persuasion.   10

The first I'll call the pedant's stance; it consists of ignoring or underplaying the personal relationship of speaker and audience and depending entirely on statements about a subject—that is, the notion of a job to be done for a particular audience is left out. It is a virtue, of course, to respect the bare truth of one's subject, and there may even be some subjects which in their very nature define an audience and a rhetorical purpose so that adequacy to the subject can be the whole art of presentation. For example, an article on "The relation of the ontological and teleological proofs," in a recent *Journal of Religion,* requires a minimum of adaptation of argument to audience. But most subjects do not in themselves imply in any necessary way a purpose and an audience and hence a speaker's tone. The writer who assumes that it is enough merely to write an exposition of what he happens to know on the subject will produce the kind of essay that soils our scholarly journals, written not for readers but for bibliographies.   11

In my first year of teaching I taught a whole unit on "exposition" without ever suggesting, so far as I can remember, that the students ask themselves what their expositions were *for.* So they wrote expositions like this one—I've saved it, to teach me toleration of my colleagues: the title is "Family relations in More's *Utopia.*" "In this theme I would like to discuss some of the relationships with the family which Thomas More elaborates and sets forth in his book, *Utopia.* The first thing that I would like to discuss about family relations is that overpopulation, according to More, is a just cause of war." And so on. Can you hear that student sneering at me, in this opening? What he is saying is something like "you ask for a meaningless paper, I give you a meaningless paper." He knows that he has no audience except me. He knows that I don't want to read his summary of family relations in *Utopia,* and he knows that I know that he therefore has no rhetorical purpose. Because he had not been led to see a question which he considers worth answering, or an audience that could possibly care one way or the other, the paper is worse than no paper at all, even though it has no grammatical or spelling errors and is organized right down the line, one, two, three.   12

An extreme case, you may say. Most of us would never allow ourselves that kind of empty fencing? Perhaps. But if some carefree foundation is willing to finance a statistical study, I'm willing to wager a month's salary that we'd find at   13

(11) *Ontological and teleological proofs.* Proofs for the existence of God based, respectively, upon the fact of the existence of the created world and upon the purpose that can be discerned within it.

least half of the suggested topics in our freshman texts as pointless as mine was. And we'd find a good deal more than half of the discussions of grammar, punctuation, spelling, and style totally divorced from any notion that rhetorical purpose to some degree controls all such matters. We can offer objective descriptions of levels of usage from now until graduation, but unless the student discovers a desire to say something to somebody and learns to control his diction for a purpose, we've gained very little. I once gave an assignment asking students to describe the same classroom in three different statements, one for each level of usage. They were obedient, but the only ones who got anything from the assignment were those who intuitively imported the rhetorical instructions I had overlooked—such purposes as "Make fun of your scholarly surroundings by describing this classroom in extremely elevated style," or "Imagine a kid from the slums accidentally trapped in these surroundings and forced to write a description of this room." A little thought might have shown me how to give the whole assignment some human point, and therefore some educative value.

14   Just how confused we can allow ourselves to be about such matters is shown in a recent publication of the Educational Testing Service, called "Factors in Judgments of Writing Ability." In order to isolate those factors which affect differences in grading standards, ETS set six groups of readers—business men, writers and editors, lawyers, and teachers of English, social science and natural science—to reading the same batch of papers. Then ETS did a hundred-page "factor analysis" of the amount of agreement and disagreement, and of the elements which different kinds of graders emphasized. The authors of the report express a certain amount of shock at the discovery that the median correlation was only .31 and that 94 percent of the papers received either 7, 8, or 9 of the 9 possible grades.

15   But what *could* they have expected? In the first place, the students were given no purpose and no audience when the essays were assigned. And then all these editors and business men and academics were asked to judge the papers in a complete vacuum, using only whatever intuitive standards they cared to use. I'm surprised that there was any correlation at all. Lacking instructions, some of the students undoubtedly wrote polemical essays, suitable for the popular press; others no doubt imagined an audience, say, of *Reader's Digest* readers, and others wrote with the English teachers as implied audience; an occasional student with real philosophical bent would no doubt do a careful analysis of the pros and cons of the case. This would be graded low, of course, by the magazine editors, even though they would have graded it high if asked to judge it as a speculative contribution to the analysis of the problem. Similarly, a creative student who has been getting A's for his personal essays will write an amusing colorful piece, failed by all the social scientists present, though they would have graded it high if asked to judge it for what it was. I find it shocking that tens of thousands of dollars and endless hours should have been spent by students, graders, and professional testers analyzing essays and grading results totally abstracted from any notion of purposeful human communication. Did no-

body protest? One might as well assemble a group of citizens to judge students' capacity to throw balls, say, without telling the students or the graders whether altitude, speed, accuracy or form was to be judged. The judges would be drawn from football coaches, jai-alai experts, lawyers, and English teachers, and asked to apply whatever standards they intuitively apply to ball throwing. Then we could express astonishment that the judgments did not correlate very well, and we could do a factor analysis to discover, lo and behold, that some readers concentrated on altitude, some on speed, some on accuracy, some on form—and the English teachers were simply confused.

One effective way to combat the pedantic stance is to arrange for weekly confrontations of groups of students over their own papers. We have done far too little experimenting with arrangements for providing a genuine audience in this way. Short of such developments, it remains true that a good teacher can convince his students that he is a true audience, if his comments on the papers show that some sort of dialogue is taking place. As Jacques Barzun says in *Teacher in America,* students should be made to feel that unless they have said something to someone, they have failed; to bore the teacher is a worse form of failure than to anger him. From this point of view we can see that the charts of grading symbols that mar even the best freshman texts are not the innocent time savers that we pretend. Plausible as it may seem to arrange for more corrections with less time, they inevitably reduce the student's sense of purpose in writing. When he sees innumerable W13's and P19's in the margin, he cannot possibly feel that the art of persuasion is as important to his instructor as when he reads personal comments, however few. 16

This first perversion, then, springs from ignoring the audience or overreliance on the pure subject. The second, which might be called the advertiser's stance, comes from *under*valuing the subject and overvaluing pure effect: how to win friends and influence people. 17

Some of our best freshman texts—Sheridan Baker's *The Practical Stylist,* for example—allow themselves on occasion to suggest that to be controversial or argumentative, to stir up an audience is an end in itself. Sharpen the controversial edge, one of them says, and the clear implication is that one should do so even if the truth of the subject is honed off in the process. This perversion is probably in the long run a more serious threat in our society than the danger of ignoring the audience. In the time of audience-reaction meters and pre-tested plays and novels, it is not easy to convince students of the old Platonic truth that good persuasion is honest persuasion, or even of the old Aristotelian truth that the good rhetorician must be master of his subject, no matter how dishonest he may decide ultimately to be. Having told them that good writers always to some degree accommodate their arguments to the audience, it is hard to explain the difference between justified accommodation—say changing *point one* to the final position—and the kind of accommodation that fills our popular magazines, in which the very substance of what is said is accommodated to some preconception of what will sell. "The publication of *Eros* [magazine] represents a major breakthrough in the battle for the liberation of the human spirit." 18

19   At a dinner about a month ago I sat between the wife of a famous civil rights lawyer and an advertising consultant. "I saw the article on your book yesterday in the Daily News," she said, "but I didn't even finish it. The title of your book scared me off. Why did you ever choose such a terrible title? Nobody would buy a book with a title like that." The man on my right, whom I'll call Mr. Kinches, overhearing my feeble reply, plunged into a conversation with her, over my torn and bleeding corpse. "Now with my *last* book," he said, "I listed 20 possible titles and then tested them out on 400 businessmen. The one I chose was voted for by 90 percent of the businessmen." "That's what I was just saying to Mr. Booth," she said. "A book title ought to grab you, and *rhetoric* is not going to grab anybody." "Right," he said. "My *last* book sold 50,000 copies already; I don't know how this one will do, but I polled 200 businessmen on the table of contents, and . . ."

20   At one point I did manage to ask him whether the title he chose really fit the book. "Not quite as well as one or two of the others," he admitted, "but that doesn't matter, you know. If the book is designed right, so that the first chapter pulls them in, and you keep 'em in, who's going to gripe about a little inaccuracy in the title?"

21   Well, rhetoric is the art of persuading, not the art of seeming to persuade by giving everything away at the start. It presupposes that one has a purpose concerning a subject which itself cannot be fundamentally modified by the desire to persuade. If Edmund Burke had decided that he could win more votes in Parliament by choosing the other side—as he most certainly could have done—we would hardly hail this party-switch as a master stroke of rhetoric. If Churchill had offered the British "peace in our time," with some laughs thrown in, because opinion polls had shown that more Britishers were "grabbed" by these than by blood, sweat, and tears, we could hardly call his decision a sign of rhetorical skill.

22   One could easily discover other perversions of the rhetorician's balance—most obviously what might be called the entertainer's stance—the willingness to sacrifice substance to personality and charm. I admire Walker Gibson's efforts to startle us out of dry pedantry, but I know from experience that his exhortations to find and develop the speaker's voice can lead to empty colorfulness. A

---

(21) *Edmund Burke.* (1729–1797) A British statesman and political writer who was considered the finest orator in Parliament.

(21) *Churchill.* Winston Churchill (1874–1965), like Burke, was an author and statesman and considered the finest orator in Parliament as a member and as Prime Minister. Churchill's rhetorical skill evoked the necessary sacrifice during the dark days of World War II when he called for "blood, sweat, and tears."

(21) *"peace in our time".* A phrase associated with Churchill's predecessor, Neville Chamberlain, and interpreted as the rhetoric of appeasement. (See title note to George Will's "Israel and Munich.")

(22) *Walker Gibson.* Contemporary teacher and rhetorician who advocates using imaginative prose.

student once said to me, complaining about a colleague, "I soon learned that all I had to do to get an A was imitate Thurber."

But perhaps this is more than enough about the perversions of the rhetor- **23** ical stance. Balance itself is always harder to describe than the clumsy poses that result when it is destroyed. But we all experience the balance whenever we find an author who succeeds in changing our minds. He can do so only if he knows more about the subject than we do, and if he then engages us in the process of thinking—and feeling—it through. What makes the rhetoric of Milton and Burke and Churchill great is that each presents us with the spectacle of a man passionately involved in thinking an important question through, in the company of an audience. Though each of them did everything in his power to make his point persuasive, including a pervasive use of the many emotional appeals that have been falsely scorned by many a freshman composition text, none would have allowed himself the advertiser's stance; none would have polled the audience in advance to discover which position would get the votes. Nor is the highly individual personality that springs out at us from their speeches and essays present for the sake of selling itself. The rhetorical balance among speakers, audience, and argument is with all three men habitual, as we see if we look at their non-political writings. Burke's work on the Sublime and Beautiful is a relatively unimpassioned philosophical treatise, but one finds there again a delicate balance: though the implied author of this work is a far different person, far less obtrusive, far more objective, than the man who later cried *sursum corda* to the British Parliament, he permeates with his philosophical personality his philosophical work. And though the signs of his awareness of his audience are far more subdued, they are still here: every effort is made to in- volve the *proper* audience, the audience of philosophical minds, in a fundamen- tally interesting inquiry, and to lead them through to the end. In short, because he was a man engaged with men in the effort to solve a human problem, one could never call what he wrote dull, however difficult or abstruse.

Now obviously the habit of seeking this balance is not the only thing we **24** have to teach under the heading of rhetoric. But I think that everything worth teaching under that heading finds its justification finally in that balance. Much of what is now considered irrelevant or dull can, in fact, be brought to life when teachers and students know what they are seeking. Churchill reports that the most valuable training he ever received in rhetoric was in the diagraming of sentences. Think of it! Yet the diagraming of a sentence, regardless of the gram- matical system, can be a live subject as soon as one asks not simply "How is

---

(22) [*James*] *Thurber.* (1894–1961) A witty essayist, short story writer, and hu- morist.

(23) *Burke's work on the Sublime and the Beautiful. The Philosophical Inquiry into the Origin of Our Ideas on the Sublime and Beautiful,* a much praised philosoph- ical essay which Burke wrote in 1756, when he was 27 years old.

(23) cried *sursum corda.* Burke was famous for stirring the emotions of his fellow Members of Parliament with such highly charged phrases as *sursum corda,* "Lift up your hearts."

this sentence put together," but rather "Why is it put together in this way?" or "Could the rhetorical balance and hence the desired persuasion be better achieved by writing it differently?"

25   As a nation we are reputed to write very badly. As a nation, I would say, we are more inclined to the perversions of rhetoric than to the rhetorical balance. Regardless of what we do about this or that course in the curriculum, our mandate would seem to be, then, to lead more of our students than we now do to care about and practice the true arts of persuasion.

Wayne C. Booth. Born 1921. Educator, scholar, rhetorician. Coming from a Utah background, Booth taught at a number of midwestern colleges and universities and is now Professor of English at the University of Chicago. He has served as president of the major professional organizations in his field (MLA, NCTE, CCCC) and is the author of many scholarly articles and six books, including *The Rhetoric of Fiction* and *The Knowledge Most Worth Having.* This article was originally published in *College Composition and Communications,* 14 (October, 1963), 139–45.

Germs

Watching television, you'd think we lived at bay, in total jeopardy, surrounded   1
on all sides by human-seeking germs, shielded against infection and death only
by a chemical technology that enables us to keep killing them off. We are instructed to spray disinfectants everywhere, into the air of our bedrooms and
kitchens and with special energy into bathrooms, since it is our very own germs
that seem the worst kind. We explode clouds of aerosol, mixed for good luck
with deodorants, into our noses, mouths, underarms, privileged crannies—even
into the intimate insides of our telephones. We apply potent antibiotics to minor scratches and seal them with plastic. Plastic is the new protector; we wrap
the already plastic tumblers of hotels in more plastic, and seal the toilet seats
like state secrets after irradiating them with ultraviolet light. We live in a world
where the microbes are always trying to get at us, to tear us cell from cell, and
we only stay alive and whole through diligence and fear.

    We still think of human disease as the work of an organized, modernized   2
kind of demonology, in which the bacteria are the most visible and centrally
placed of our adversaries. We assume that they must somehow relish what they
do. They come after us for profit, and there are so many of them that disease
seems inevitable, a natural part of the human condition; if we succeed in eliminating one kind of disease there will always be a new one at hand, waiting to
take its place.

    These are paranoid delusions on a societal scale, explainable in part by our   3
need for enemies, and in part by our memory of what things used to be like.
Until a few decades ago, bacteria were a genuine household threat, and although
most of us survived them, we were always aware of the nearness of death. We
moved, with our families, in and out of death. We had lobar pneumonia, men-
ingococcal meningitis, streptococcal infections, diphtheria, endocarditis, enteric
fevers, various septicemias, syphilis, and, always, everywhere, tuberculosis. Most
of these have now left most of us, thanks to antibiotics, plumbing, civilization,
and money, but we remember.

    In real life, however, even in our worst circumstances we have always been   4
a relatively minor interest of the vast microbial world. Pathogenicity is not the
rule. Indeed, it occurs so infrequently and involves such a relatively small num-

---

---

(4) *pathogenicity.* Quality of causing disease.

ber of species, considering the huge population of bacteria on the earth, that it has a freakish aspect. Disease usually results from inconclusive negotiations for symbiosis, an overstepping of the line by one side or the other, a biologic misinterpretation of borders.

5   Some bacteria are only harmful to us when they make exotoxins, and they only do this when they are, in a sense, diseased themselves. The toxins of diphtheria bacilli and streptococci are produced when the organisms have been infected by bacteriophage; it is the virus that provides the code for toxin. Uninfected bacteria are uninformed. When we catch diphtheria it is a virus infection, but not of us. Our involvement is not that of an adversary in a straightforward game, but more like blundering into someone else's accident.

6   I can think of a few microorganisms, possibly the tubercle bacillus, the syphilis spirochete, the malarial parasite, and a few others, that have a selective advantage in their ability to infect human beings, but there is nothing to be gained, in an evolutionary sense, by the capacity to cause illness or death. Pathogenicity may be something of a disadvantage for most microbes, carrying lethal risks more frightening to them than to us. The man who catches a meningococcus is in considerably less danger for his life, even without chemotherapy, than meningococci with the bad luck to catch a man. Most meningococci have the sense to stay out on the surface, in the rhinopharynx. During epidemics this is where they are to be found in the majority of the host population, and it generally goes well. It is only in the unaccountable minority, the "cases," that the line is crossed, and then there is the devil to pay on both sides, but most of all for the meningococci.

7   Staphylococci live all over us, and seem to have adapted to conditions in our skin that are uncongenial to most other bacteria. When you count them up, and us, it is remarkable how little trouble we have with the relation. Only a few of us are plagued by boils, and we can blame a large part of the destruction of tissues on the zeal of our own leukocytes. Hemolytic streptococci are among our closest intimates, even to the extent of sharing antigens with the membranes of our muscle cells; it is our reaction to their presence, in the form of rheumatic fever, that gets us into trouble. We can carry brucella for long peri-

---

(4) *symbiosis*. State of living closely together for mutual advantage.

(5) *exotoxins*. Poisons given off by microorganisms.

(5) *bacteriophage*. Virus that feeds on bacteria.

(6) *meningococcus*. Germ (round bacterium) that causes meningitis.

(6) *rhinopharynx*. Back side of the windpipe.

(7) *leukocytes*. White blood cells; the portion of the blood that fights off infection.

(7) *hemolytic streptococci*. Germs (round bacteria) capable of destroying red blood cells.

(7) *antigen*. Substance that stimulates the production of antibodies.

(7) *brucella*. Germ (rod-shaped bacterium) that produces undulant fever.

ods in the cells of our reticuloendothelial system without any awareness of their existence; then cyclically, for reasons not understood but probably related to immunologic reactions on our part, we sense them, and the reaction of sensing is the clinical disease.

Most bacteria are totally preoccupied with browsing, altering the configurations of organic molecules so that they become usable for the energy needs of other forms of life. They are, by and large, indispensable to each other, living in interdependent communities in the soil or sea. Some have become symbionts in more specialized, local relations, living as working parts in the tissues of higher organisms. The root nodules of legumes would have neither form nor function without the masses of rhizobial bacteria swarming into root hairs, incorporating themselves with such intimacy that only an electron microscope can detect which membranes are bacterial and which plant. Insects have colonies of bacteria, the mycetocytes, living in them like little glands, doing heaven knows what but being essential. The microfloras of animal intestinal tracts are part of the nutritional system. And then, of course, there are the mitochondria and chloroplasts, permanent residents in everything.　　8

The microorganisms that seem to have it in for us in the worst way—the ones that really appear to wish us ill—turn out on close examination to be rather more like bystanders, strays, strangers in from the cold. They will invade and replicate if given the chance, and some of them will get into our deepest tissues and set forth in the blood, but it is our response to their presence that makes the disease. Our arsenals for fighting off bacteria are so powerful, and involve so many different defense mechanisms, that we are in more danger from them than from the invaders. We live in the midst of explosive devices; we are mined.　　9

It is the information carried by the bacteria that we cannot abide.　　10

The gram-negative bacteria are the best examples of this. They display lipopolysaccharide endotoxin in their walls, and these macromolecules are read by our tissues as the very worst of bad news. When we sense lipopolysacchar-　　11

---

(7) *reticuloendothelial system.* Our system of antibodies; the bodily system that combines all of the cells (excluding white blood cells) that consume microorganisms or other foreign bodies.

(8) *symbionts.* Members of a symbiotic relationship [see (4)].

(8) *rhizobial bacteria.* Nitrogen-fixing bacteria.

(8) *mitochondria.* Germs (cell particles) that contain the enzymes that convert food to energy.

(8) *chloroplasts.* Germs (plastids) that contain the chlorophyl in green plants.

(11) *gram-negative bacteria.* Bacteria whose walls are formed in such a way that they do not take the purple dye used in Gram's classification system.

(11) *endotoxin.* Toxin secreted within a cell and released with its destruction.

(11) *lipopolysaccharide.* A compound or complex of fats and carbohydrates.

ide, we are likely to turn on every defense at our disposal; we will bomb, defoliate, blockade, seal off, and destroy all the tissues in the area. Leukocytes become more actively phagocytic, release lysosomal enzymes, turn sticky, and aggregate together in dense masses, occluding capillaries and shutting off the blood supply. Complement is switched on at the right point in its sequence to release chemotactic signals, calling in leukocytes from everywhere. Vessels become hyperreactive to epinephrine so that physiologic concentrations suddenly possess necrotizing properties. Pyrogen is released from leukocytes, *adding fever* to hemorrhage, necrosis, and shock. It is a shambles.

12   All of this seems unnecessary, panic-driven. There is nothing intrinsically poisonous about endotoxin, but it must look awful, or feel awful, when sensed by cells. Cells believe that it signifies the presence of gram-negative bacteria, and they will stop at nothing to avoid this threat.

13   I used to think that only the most highly developed, civilized animals could be fooled in this way, but it is not so. The horseshoe crab is a primitive fossil of a beast, ancient and uncitified, but he is just as vulnerable to disorganization by endotoxin as a rabbit or a man. Bang has shown that an injection of a very small dose into the body cavity will cause the aggregation of hemocytes in ponderous, immovable masses that block the vascular channels, and a gelatinous clot brings the circulation to a standstill. It is now known that a limulus clotting system, perhaps ancestral to ours, is centrally involved in the reaction. Extracts of the hemocytes can be made to jell by adding extremely small amounts of endotoxin. The self-disintegration of the whole animal that follows a systemic injection can be interpreted as a well-intentioned but lethal error. The mechanism is itself quite a good one, when used with precision and restraint, admirably designed for coping with intrusion by a single bacterium: the hemocyte would be attracted to the site, extrude the coagulable protein, the microorganism would be entrapped and immobilized, and the thing would be finished. It is when confronted by the overwhelming signal of free molecules of endotoxin, evoking memories of vibrios in great numbers, that the limulus flies into panic, launches all his defenses at once, and destroys himself.

---

(11) *more actively phagocytic.* More intent upon consuming other microorganisms.
(11) *lysosomal enzymes.* An enzyme that is destructive to cells within certain bacteria.
(11) *epinephrine.* Adrenalin.
(11) *necrotizing.* Death-dealing.
(11) *pyrogen.* A fever-producing agent.
(11) *necrosis.* Disease-related death of tissue.
(13) *hemocytes.* Blood cells.
(13) *limulus.* Generic term referring to crabs.
(13) *vibrios.* *S*-shaped or comma-shaped bacteria.

It is, basically, a response to propaganda, something like the panic-producing pheromones that slave-taking ants release to disorganize the colonies of their prey.   14

I think it likely that many of our diseases work in this way. Sometimes, the mechanisms used for overkill are immunologic, but often, as in the limulus model, they are more primitive kinds of memory. We tear ourselves to pieces because of symbols, and we are more vulnerable to this than to any host of predators. We are, in effect, at the mercy of our own Pentagons, most of the time.   15

---

(14) *pheromones.* Subliminal odors sent off by a member of a species to provoke a particular response in another member of the same species.

(15) *Pentagons.* Reference to the five-sided building that houses the United States Department of Defense.

Lewis Thomas. Born 1913. Physician, educator, medical administrator, and author. Having served as Professor or Dean of the College of Medicine at Minnesota, Yale, Cornell, and Rockefeller Universities, Thomas is now with the Sloan-Kettering Cancer Center. He also serves on numerous administrative boards and on the editorial boards of four medical journals. He is the author of many articles on biological subjects and two books: *Lives of a Cell* and *Medusa and the Snail.*

J. H. Plumb

De Mortuis

1   The British have hilarious fun over the quaint funerary habits of the Americans. The death of Hubert Eaton, the world's greatest entrepreneur of death, and the recent discovery of a funeral home for pets, by a wandering British journalist, released another gale of satirical laughter in the English press. The mockery was hearty and sustained; yet was it deserved? Well, certainly much of Mr. Eaton's Forest Lawn is hard to take—the wet, nursery language for the hard facts of dying ("the loved one" for the corpse, "leave taking" for burying, and "slumber" for death), the cosmetic treatment (the contortions of death waxed away, replaced by rouge and mascara and fashionably set hair)—all of this is good for a gruesome joke. The place names of Forest Lawn appall—Lullabyland, Babyland. The piped guff, the music that flows like oil, and the coy fig-leaved art give one goose flesh.

2   One turns, almost with relief, to a harsh fifteenth-century representation of the dance of death—livid corpses, jangling bones and skulls that haunt. How wholesome, after Hubert Eaton, seem the savage depictions by Bonligh of the ravages of plague, or even the nightmares of death painted by Hieronymus Bosch. And how salutary in our own age to turn from Forest Lawn to the screaming, dissolving bodies of a Francis Bacon painting, for surely this is how life ends for most of us, in pain, in agony.

3   And if Forest Lawn nauseates, what of the Pets Parlor? "Blackie" combed and brushed, stretched out on the hearth rug before a log fire, waits for his sorrowing owners. The budgerigar is wired to its perch. The Ming Room houses the Siamese cats, and if you want to do your kitty proud, you can spend three hundred dollars or so on a stately laying out, a goodly coffin (if you're worried about its fun in the afterlife, you can put an outsize rubber mouse in with it), and naturally a special plot in Bide-A-Wee, the memorial park for pets. President Nixon's dog, Checkers, had the treatment: he lies among the immortals in Bide-A-Wee, like Hubert in Forest Lawn.

4   However, this will become a mere second-class death if deep-freezing really catches on, as it shows every sign of doing. The Life Extension Society is spreading, and the entrepreneurs have smelled the profit in immortality. As soon as the breath goes, get yourself encapsulated in liquid nitrogen and stored in one of the specially constructed freezers that are springing up all over America from Phoenix to New York. And so wait for the day when they can cure what you

(3) *budgerigar.* Australian parakeet

died of, or replace what gave way—the heart, the brain, the liver, or the guts—
or rejuvenate your cells.

None of this is cheap: the capsule costs four thousand dollars, and then   5
there are the freezing costs and who knows what they may be in fifty years, so
it would be imprudent not to make ample provision. Forest Lawn may be death
for the rich; this is death for the richer, death for the Big Time. But in America
there are a lot of very rich, so maybe soon now, outside all the large cities,
there will be refrigerators as huge as pyramids, full of the frozen dead. This
surely must be a growth industry.

Perhaps by the year 2000 Hubert Eaton will seem but a modest pioneer of   6
the death industry, for who does not crave to escape oblivion? The rich have
always tried to domesticate death, to make death seem like life. The American
way of death is not novel: seen in proper historical perspective it reaches back
not only down the centuries but down the millenniums, for it is a response to
a deep human need.

Some of the earliest graves of men, dating from paleolithic times, contained   7
corpses decked out with bits of personal finery and sprinkled with red ocher,
perhaps the symbol of blood and life, done in the hope of a future resurrection.
After the neolithic revolution, which created much greater resources and considerable surplus wealth, men went in for death in a very big way. Doubtless
the poor were thrown away, burned or exposed or pushed into obscurity, back
to the anonymous mind from which they came.

The rich and the powerful, high priests and kings, could not die; they   8
merely passed from one life to another. Because the life hereafter was but a
mirror image of life on earth, they took with them everything they needed—
jewels, furniture, food, and, of course, servants. In the Royal Graves at Ur, some
of the earliest and most sumptuous of tombs ever found, a row of handmaidens
had been slaughtered at the burial—death's necessities were life's. No one, of
course, carried this elaboration of funerary activity further than the Egyptians.
And the tombs of Pharaohs and the high officials of the Egyptian kingdom make
Forest Lawn seem like a cheap cemetery for the nation's down-and-outs.

What should we think of vast stone mausoleums outside Washington,   9
stuffed with personal jewelry from Winston's, furniture from Sloane's, glassware
by Steuben, food from Le Pavillon, etc., etc., and in the midst of it all the em-
balmed corpse of a Coolidge or a Dulles? We should roar with laughter. We
should regard it as vulgar, ridiculous, absurd. Pushed back three millenniums,
such habits acquire not only decorum but also majesty, grandeur, awe.

The Egyptians were as portentous in death as in life, and their grave goods   10
only occasionally give off the breath of life, unlike the Etruscans, who domesti-

---

(7) *paleolithic times.* Stone ages, beginning about 7,500,000 years ago when humans began to make simple chipping tools.

(7) *neolithic revolution.* Change that brought on the late Stone Age, about 10,000
B.C., with the invention of farming and of sophisticated stone tools.

cated death more completely and more joyously than any other society. A rich caste of princes built tombs of singular magnificence, filling them with amphorae, jewels, and silver. And they adorned their walls with all the gaiety that they had enjoyed alive. There was nothing solemn about their attitude to death. In their tombs they hunted, played games, performed acrobatics, danced, feasted; their amorous dalliance was both wanton and guiltless. Deliberately they banished death with the recollected gusto of life. No society has brought such eroticism, such open and natural behavior, to the charnel house. But in the annals of death, Etruscans are rare birds.

11   How different the grandiose tombs of medieval barons, with their splendid alabaster or marble effigies. There they lie, larger than life, grave, portentous, frozen in death, a wife, sometimes two, rigidly posed beside them, and beneath, sorrowing children, kneeling in filial piety, the whole structure made more pompous with heraldic quarterings. Yet these are but another attempt to cheat death, to keep alive in stone what was decaying and crumbling below. And even here a breath of life sometimes creeps in. The Earl and Countess of Arundel lie side by side, dogs beneath the feet, pillows under the head, he in armor, she in her long woolen gown. But, movingly enough, they are holding hands. The sons of Lord Teynham cannot be parted, even in death, with their hawk and hound. Nor were these tombs so cold, so marmoreal, when they were first built. They were painted, the faces as alive with color as the corpses in the parlors of Forest Lawn.

12   Seen in the context of history, Forest Lawn is neither very vulgar nor very remarkable, and the refrigerators at Phoenix are no more surprising than a pyramid in Palenque or Cairo. If life has been good, we, like the rich Etruscans, want it to go on and on and on, or at the very least to be remembered. Only a few civilizations have evaded expensive funerary habits for their illustrious rich, and these usually poverty-stricken ones. For all their austerity, the Hindus, burning bodies and throwing the ashes into the Ganges, have maintained distinction in their pyres. Not only were widows coaxed or thrown onto the flames, but rare and perfumed woods were burned to sweeten the spirit of the rich Brahman as it escaped from its corrupt carapace. Cremation a la Chanel!

13   What is tasteless and vulgar in one age becomes tender and moving in another. What should we say if we decorated our tombs with scenes from baseball games, cocktail bars, and the circus, or boasted on the side of our coffins of our amatory prowess, as erect and as unashamed in death as in life. And yet when the Etruscans do just these things, we are moved to a sense of delight that the force of life could be so strong that men and women reveled in it in their graves.

---

(10) *amphorae.* Large clay jars with handles and narrow necks that were used by ancient peoples to carry oil.

(11) *marmoreal.* Like marble: cold, smooth, white, and hard.

(12) *carapace.* Outer shell, such as a turtle's.

(12) *Chanel.* Manufacturer of expensive French perfumes.

So the next time you stroll through Forest Lawn, mildly repelled by its silly   14
sentimentality, think of those Etruscans; you will understand far more easily why
seven thousand marriages a year take place in this California graveyard. After all,
like those Arundels, Eros and Death have gone hand in hand down the ages. The
urge to obliterate death is the urge to extend life, and what more natural than
that the rich should expect renewal. How right, how proper, that Checkers
should be waiting in Slumberland.

---

(14) *Eros.* Greek god of desire.

J. H. Plumb. Born 1911. British scholar, writer, and historian. Currently Professor at
Christ College, Cambridge, Plumb is the author of numerous scholarly and popular articles and of 18 books, including biographies of *Sir Robert Walpole* and *The First Four
Georges* and more general works, such as *Crisis in the Humanities.* This article was
originally published in *Horizon Magazine,* 9 (Spring, 1967), 40–41.

Ellen Goodman

The Cult of Impotence

1   If they ever dig down through layers of future generations, looking for artifacts that tell something about mid-seventies America, let's hope they find John Lilly's isolation tank. It will tell them a great deal.

2   The California physician and psychoanalyst has designed an enclosed tank, with 10 inches of water heated to precisely 93 degrees and room for exactly one person. Why? As he told *People*, "Lying on your back, you can breathe quite comfortably and safely, freed from sight, sound, people and the universe outside. That way you can enter the universe within you."

3   Think what Greta Garbo could have done with that. Think what we do with it—"free" ourselves from other people and the environment, enter the "universe within."

4   The "isolation tank" is as good a symbol as any of a time when we are making a positive value out of our sense of impotence in the world, and a cult out of the fragmentation of society and missed connections of our personal lives. Over the last few years—driven by events more complex than the labels "Vietnam" and "Watergate"—we have turned inward, to the search for personal solutions. We are no longer convinced of the possibility of social change or even the capacity to "do good." Every change reverberates.

5   We have discovered that when you cure typhoid you get overpopulation and when you raise the standard of living you destroy the environment. It is no wonder that we "work on" an area that seems more within our control and power: ourselves.

6   This self-centering is not only a retreat from the world, but a by-product of the current condition of our lives. The newest definition of American individualism is aloneness.

7   In the years since 1960, the number of "primaries"—people living alone—has risen by 87 percent while the number of families has risen only by 23 percent. Fifteen million of us live alone. Fifty million of us are single, widowed or divorced. At least partially in response to this, the new therapies—from the isolation tank on—offer us ways to "get into ourselves." Those who aren't "doing their own thing" or "finding themselves" are "getting in touch with their feelings." The West Coast greeting, "What are you into?" is most aptly answered with one word: myself.

(3) *Greta Garbo.* Swedish film star of the 1930s who, when retiring at the height of her popularity, gave as her reason: "I vant to be alone."

In the hyperindividualism of a movement like est, we are trained to be self-   8
reliant, totally responsible to and for our own lives. The range of the new therapies is characterized by a frenzied search inward. The "isolation tank" seems
to suggest that the road to happiness, peace, fulfillment, understanding, is an
internal route. As Dr. Lilly says, "If you are able to retire deep inside yourself,
you can find the quiet place which nobody can penetrate. This way you can
isolate yourself in your deep inner core."

But then where are you? Then what? The impulses to more self-awareness,   9
self-exploration are positive ones—but not if they lead to a dead end of navel-
gazing, a permanent retreat from others and the problems of the world. At a
time when we seem in almost perilous need of personal connection and social
solutions, the tendency toward the isolation-tank psychology can be a sad perversion of the old American individualism.

I am reminded of a brief exchange Peter Marin had with a man "into"   10
mysticism, and which he repeated in a piece written for *Harper's* last year. He
wrote:

"He was telling me about his sense of another reality. 'I know there   11
is something outside of me,' he said, 'I can feel it. I know it is there. But what
is it?'

" 'It may not be a mystery,' I said. 'Perhaps it is the world.' "   12

---

(8) *est.* Therapeutic program to enhance self-image created by Werner Erhard. Its
program consists of two weekends (sixty hours) of "peak experiences" designed to help
the participant "meet yourself face to face."

Ellen Goodman. Born 1941. Pulitzer prize-winning feature writer and syndicated
columnist. A Bostonian, Goodman has written for the *Detroit Free Press* and *Boston
Globe* and now is published through the *Washington Post* Writer's Group. She writes
primarily on feminist topics and other social and ethical issues. This article was originally
published in *The Boston Globe,* September, 1976.

Alan S. Katz

The Use of Drugs in America:
Toward a Better
Understanding of Passivity

1   When we at Boston University's Mental Health Clinic were first confronted five years ago with the new drug scene, we knew very little about it; all pharmacology books were of little help beyond the chemical analysis which they offered. Although we were well-trained psychiatrists, drugs other than for therapeutic purposes were not part of our training. Drugs had for the most part been a ghetto problem and thus neglected. The very hard-core users were being treated in isolated government hospitals, and the results were worse than a dismal failure. But we were trained in the psychoanalytic model, so we knew that we could learn, that we could see with sufficient experience how and in what way drugs affected personality, if at all.

2   And we talked and we listened in fine detail to a mob of new users who were as ignorant about the drugs as we were but who were demonstrating every kind of personality disturbance that we had ever seen. It was really quite frightening to us for at that time we also had very little knowledge of what pharmaceutic medications were specifically effective to combat the side effects. We did a lot of learning by trial and error. In fact our first task was to use our basic skills and to enlarge our understanding as rapidly as possible. This was incredibly difficult because of the panic that was being caused. At the same time the basic wish of the University was to deny that there was such a problem; it was a kind of philosophy which was universally typical, i.e., don't talk about it and it will go away. However, we were quickly able to show the importance of the problem to the administration of Boston University and received its full support to bring the problem out into the open and to deal with it. . . .

3   Within a year we had a treatment model which was working effectively. The classical psychoanalytic and theoretical formulations were essentially correct but needed expansion, and this we felt was verified by the outstanding success of the treatment model. The Mental Health Unit worked closely with

---

Reprinted by permission from the *Boston University Journal* (Spring, 1971).

---

(1). . . . *trained in the psychoanalytic model.* Psychiatrists are medical doctors who have done further work in psychiatry, the study of mental illness. The psychoanalytic method is the therapeutic technique originated by Sigmund Freud that consists of probing patients' subconscious minds and childhood memories to analyze early developmental traumas in terms of their current symbolic significance.

patients seen in private practice two to three times a week for two to three years. This provided a lot of detail to the uncompleted puzzle.

Our findings represent some 2,000 patient cases. The actual number seen was much greater than that, and it represents some 750 treated from onset to discharge. The treatment time was as short as six sessions and as long as three years. [We also saw a] group [that] was not in treatment, but constituted over four years about 10,000 students meeting in groups of all sizes from 15 to 600 at once to rap about drugs and all other issues which seemed relevant to late adolescence, such as sex and freedom. This allowed us to come into contact with a fairly substantial number of students who were dealing with life well or fairly well, who either did not need or had not sought professional help. This was the closest to a random population to offset the idea that we were only seeing kids who were "upset." . . .   4

What did all of this teach us? We learned that no matter what drug was used, if it was being used for other than occasional social-fun purposes, . . . it was being used to ward off or deal with tension, anxiety, and depression. And we learned what had been theoretically formulated in classical psychiatric literature: that we were dealing with a specific personality type. In psychiatry we call this the passive dependent personality. Conversely we also found that the passive dependent personality types whom we were seeing for non-drug reasons, . . . were tending to become more involved with drugs as their underlying anxieties started to come out in the course of therapy and sought relief by turning on in order to turn off: for us this development again was a validation.   5

There is to my mind, a view I share with almost every colleague I know, no greater jungle of confusion than psychiatric diagnosis, not only because of the abstractness, the differences in clinical training and skills, but also because the psychiatric label changes as the personality changes. Similarly there are few more threatening ideas than that of passivity, because passivity implies *vulnerability, helplessness,* and *dependence* on others. To tell an adolescent that he is passive is to send him up a wall. It is a major insult to his mind. But we have learned, as had others long ago, that one can protest very loudly about "give me my freedom," but if you listen closely there is frequently another little voice that is saying very firmly *"don't you dare."* This is a normal process in adolescence. But it becomes pathologic in drug abuse; I repeat, *abuse,* not just *drug use.*   6

By "passive dependent" we were and are referring specifically to unresolved wishes to remain in a child-like dependent status despite the protestations to the contrary. This wish to remain passive ultimately has to do with anxiety about separation from the nurturing parent. It is crucial to understand the meaning of the patient's passivity.   7

The law of conservation of experience cannot be thwarted or surpassed by any stretch of the imagination, by therapist or patient. To treat as reality the   8

---

(5) *passive dependent personality.* Katz defines this term in paragraph (7).

illusion that one can discard any part of one's experience is foolishness in its most flagrant form. So the student generates anxiety within himself, assuming tacitly that growth will occur by exclusion rather than by acquisition, that one becomes an adult by putting away or discarding childish styles or ways. In reality, growth occurs from within, wherein the entire being grows but where previous ambivalent, ambiguous experiences are retained. Regression, or return to earlier styles of behavioral transactions with the world, figures so prominently in the drug abuser. When adolescents return home on vacation, they begin to bicker, argue, and squabble after a day or so of blissful reunion. This is regression. The more basic truth of passivity is its *healthy intent,* to resist *any advance* which would ignore the important, unsettled, unsatisfied blocks of experience. Passivity may be seen as a self-preserving effort. It has to be seen in terms of its usefulness of value rather than condemned wholesale. The intense threat is that passivity thrusts an individual back to or maintains a position of vulnerability linked to a sense of helplessness. The psychiatrist often becomes angry with the patient, labeling him as "passive aggressive," thereby seeing the passivity as a form of hostility, whereas more often than not in the passive dependent person it is his major defense for survival. That is, the patient in *being ill is not being bad.* The pertinence of these dynamics is crucial in giving direction towards an encompassing understanding of the patient, so that the goal becomes that of accepting the presence of the passivity rather than the rejecting of it. This allows the patient to be released from the stranglehold of his own passivity.

9   As I stated before, such growth ultimately has to do with the separation from the nurturing parent. The whole process begins in infancy, when the really helpless infant through the sound, smell, taste, and touch of the nurturing mother takes into himself and into his very primitive, undifferentiated psyche, or "mind," things from the outside. It is the process by which the infant learns to recognize and remember the outside. For example, when a newborn is hungry he experiences pain, which is relieved by something put into his mouth, and frequently, in the process of feeding, he is touched, and fondled, and cooed to.

10   Some months later the newborn, who is now an infant, has learned that his mother, who is in another room, will come to him if he cries. The amazing thing that has happened is that now he has an image of mother in his head, even though she is not present in the room. Then we begin to see the smiles of recognition. The infant begins to distinguish between different people, different sounds, different smells, and different voices. Slowly all the representations of the outside world, the family, the siblings, the teachers, the society, religion are taken and stored in the unconscious, which is the total memory bank. And they are stored as they are experienced, both good and bad, happy and unhappy. Just as the child develops a sense of I, as separate from you, he must later through a whole series of tasks requiring mastery selectively learn to function independently. When the early development fosters tremendous dependency and does

not allow for independent exploration, error making, and correction, when all tensions are relieved by the parent, the child holds on very intensely to the total parent, whose image he has stored in his mind. To grow, to find his own style, to achieve his own goals and destiny, he must selectively give up parts of the parental image. This is the normal process of adolescence which allows the young adult to have a profound sense of self. If this psychological separation *does not occur,* he remains dependent on his parent. The problem arises when the adolescent fights his own dependent wishes towards the parents who are so firmly entrenched in his own head, even though they may be as far away as 10,000 miles, or even dead. This concept explains the bickering in adolescence, the fighting of "I want"—"no you can't." It is shadow boxing of a kind. The problem is greatly intensified when the parents remain over-protective at a time when the child, now adolescent, should be learning to accomplish on his own. He is searching for independence but he is bound up within himself, fighting his being dependent on the image and the values of the parent in his own mind. So he is constantly expending enormous energy in a battle with those parents. He has not found his own identity, he regresses—he goes backwards under tension. He has not been given the permission to grow up and be different, nor has he utilized it when it was given. So his goal becomes to distinguish himself from his parents by being against them. He denies the meaningfulness of the values of the "straight society" but not selectively. He expresses profound disappointment in his family and this is expanded to include the large family of man. By contrast, the healthier adolescent who has not held on so tenaciously to the parental image, or who has not been held onto so tenaciously, does not feel the perpetual need for battle of dependency-independency. He finds gratification and creative goals to his own liking, to his own talents and style, and has the energy to achieve them. For him being different is not the only way of being free. The implications of this go beyond the drug scene, where origins of rebellion come, not out of ideology and idealism, but out of personal problems.

A second characteristic we found in drug abusers was a withdrawal into   11
the self, and the greater the drug abuse, the greater the withdrawal. Withdrawal means less communication with a varied society, much time spent in reflection which does not imply productive thought but feelings of alienation, and paranoia. As there is usually an increased gap between child and family, and between the student and other peers who have not withdrawn, there is an increased need to huddle together into what we call brotherhoods, which in the last analysis are substitute families, characterized by their permissiveness, the capacity to get close physically, which is warded off in adult children towards their parents, and by the feeling of belonging without restriction and especially belonging without real commitment—commitment to another seen as an equal and not as a parent substitute. In some places these are known as communes. This is not to disparage all communes, for some have very constructive aims, but these brotherhoods can exist in the form of several people living in one room,

or in a house, or in a bus, or in a reconverted hearse, or just a group that is always together.

12   A third characteristic found in virtually all of the patients was a state of clinical depression, with feelings of worthlessness, of loss, of sadness, and an attempt to alleviate these symptoms with various drugs. The heroin user is the extreme example. Although the patient may not recognize this state of depression, *it is always there* to the clinical eye. Some can acknowledge this feeling, for others it is an intriguing and captivating idea worth looking at. In any event, way down deep he knows that he is depressed. He describes his depression in simplistic terms of being "down on the family," "down on society," without greater elaboration. He seems to have achieved liberation from home and is eager to experience, to move, to realize, and to become. Suddenly the adolescent finds that it is lonely out there, and he comes against the unpleasant recognition that life has blockades to plans, disappointments for aspirations, a diminution of importance for aspirations, a diminution of importance and of relevance in an active crowd around him. Here the therapist is presented with the opportunity to exert his most valuable asset: his compassion, his more mature, accepting, *unalarmed* empathic attitude toward all that the human experience includes. To recognize the depression is of enormous value, for it offers the passive depressed patient an avenue of freedom towards seeing himself more realistically. The depressive crisis is not a breakdown, but rather a breakup of insufficient, antiquated ways of dealing with problems in contemporary society. It is never the aim of therapy to reduce the student to anonymity in the crowd. The abuser becomes anonymous. The student is uneradicably singular, his uniqueness is the focus of recognition. To fracture or dismantle the narcissism of the late adolescent is a cruel injustice. The promise of individualism is infinitely more potent than a substitute dependency. That is, "I will help you, but I won't do it for you." The therapy becomes the implementation of these ideas.

13   These were the basic ideas that we formulated to develop our treatment program. The exception to this program is the heroin user who has a particularly severe psychological deterioration and who has very special needs. But we are convinced that many of them can be helped as well, but by other techniques. The only time in our treatment program that a patient was instructed to stop using drugs was when he was prepsychotic, psychotic, or experiencing flashes. Flashing is a particular phenomenon which occurs in some individuals wherein they experience a drug trip spontaneously without having just taken the drug. There is also a cross-over phenomenon: for example, a person smoking some pot might re-experience a past LSD trip. To our minds, this is a warning sign of an impending psychotic episode if the drugs are continued.

14   Very briefly, the four steps to the treatment method are:

1) Make an alliance with the patient to look at the problem, don't moralize, don't probe too deeply or the patient will run from treatment.

---

(12) *narcissism.* Self-absorption.
(13) *psychotic.* Severely disturbed by mental illness.

2) Search for the underlying clinical depression and get the patient involved with this.

3) Clarify the parental relations, not with the goal of breaking up the family, but rather to help the family to grow up, to become adults with one another. This idea has to be frequently reiterated because if the dependent person hears the statement as a threat of breakup, it would mean that there will be no one to depend on.

4) Help the patient to leave the brotherhood, to get re-established with a varied society. This is the most hazardous part of the model.

Incidentally, at this point, without much or any coaxing, the drug user is in the process of voluntarily stopping. The therapist clearly sees the need to give up the drug, but the patient, though he may understand the reason, is magically bound to it. What is rational and logical is unimportant. His sense of control predominates. The passivity has its stranglehold and the patient seems not to be able to budge, for there is still something unaccomplished. With the knowledge that the patient is no longer getting the same pleasure or kind of kicks he once got from drugs, but that he is still clinging to them and their uses as an unenjoyable form of ritual, the therapist then begins to investigate the fear of no longer belonging to the peer group, which is the drug group that makes up the brotherhood. This allows the ritual to become unravelled so that the passivity loses its power. Attention is paid especially to the one, two, or three friends with whom the patient is particularly close, with whom he takes his trips. After all, they belong to the brotherhood and he can believe in the brotherhood because for him it represents the tension-free new kind of adulthood which is better than his parents' adulthood. He is terribly afraid of leaving his friends for he figures that he cannot stand on his own. He is faced with a real dilemma, for although the brotherhood no longer serves the purpose it once did, he had shared in it—in essence he had a sense of existence and meaning in it. His friends as well are threatened if he leaves them, and we see they exert a subtle and sometimes more blatant pressure on him not to believe the "shrink" so that the group will not be diminished. Separating from the brotherhood generally opens a whole vista of ideas concerning the dread of being in a neutral state, of giving up one's only friends, and one's feeling of inadequacy and fear upon entering the "straight society."

Such crises are all derivatives of the task of separation from mother and father; they are the issues of the passivity that has been unresolved but which can now be dealt with, and they are among the reasons that have led to the initial drug use. The exploration of being alone and ultimately confronting one's wishes to be dependent permit the patient to slowly take up the role required for adulthood. It is much like learning to walk. The job of the therapist is, as always, to assist in unstopping the natural growth process, so it may proceed. The new task is a big one, but it is the task which was earlier thwarted: dealing with anxiety and the achievement of goals pleasing to the self. The person is wobbly but there is a mass of energy available for *doing* rather than for just *being.*

17   But the matter becomes further complicated, and I hope what ensues from these ideas is an original contribution to psychiatric literature. During these years of work at the Mental Health Unit, we observed that there was a very distorted idea of what it meant to be aggressive: that competitiveness, striving, and mastery in some manner had become linked up with some destruction; that is, to compete with someone is to destroy the competitor, to achieve is to kill. In some way I came to realize that this concept was inextricably related to drug passivity. In fact, all through this work something had been missing, some factor had been overlooked which was crucial to tying things together. About two years ago it began to make sense and it was very exciting to the scientist-researcher part of me. Small but vital clues had been overlooked in a maze of accumulated data which took on significance only after my working in very intensive therapy with some patients. Obviously I had not heard all things at all times, but I began to hear material that stuck out like a sore thumb, material which I could interpret as meaning "if I take drugs I won't feel so aggressive." The therapist was having an insight. I had often wondered what was at the core of the love movement with the hippies. The hippies and the students whom I have seen and who have used LSD in the largest quantities (such as over 200 times) were in fact the most passive, non-destructive, turned-off group of all drug abusers. Their regression has the most intense infantile character: the wish to be fed, to be protected, and to be carefree. Why had I not thought of this before, because it is classic that one of the aspects of being passive is to ward off being hurt, as I've explained, but also to control the fear of hurting. So I began to review cases and there it clearly was, hundreds of times: "If my parents took drugs, they wouldn't want war." "If you took drugs, you'd understand peace." "If you took drugs you'd see that straight people kill." "When I take drugs, I love everyone." "Man, with drugs you don't have to hassle." "Man, I don't want to hurt anyone" and so forth. The connection between taking drugs to deal with aggressive feeling is now blatantly clear.

18   I profoundly believe that aside from the social-peer purposes, aside from defying the law, aside from the fantasy of warding off depression, tension, and anxiety, the most significant unconscious, unresolved factor in passivity is to ward off the killer in oneself; that is to say, there is a tremendous rage inside, a complicated kind of rage directed at the self, at the figures on whom one is dependent, at the incapacity to bridge the gap between the age groups, a rage at the inequities in society, at the double standards of law and civil rights, against the killer instinct which is cultivated and released by war, at the frustration of not being heard, at the idea competition is war, that achievement is destructive. The drug abuser does not have the freedom to deal with these issues; he is a be-er rather than a doer. He is not a free activist, involved in a creative ideology, in idealism which demands stamina and energy. Instead I contend that he is a very dependent person who is very angry inside, who, ironically, becomes even more passive, more dependent, less aggressive, less striving, and remarkably more depressed. And whenever there is depression there is

rage. So I am stating in conclusion that the use of drugs by the abuser is intended to deal with and put down his rage, over which he has poor control, the use of drugs is to do away with the killer. So he maintains and accentuates his passivity through the drugs, drugs make him more passive, and the rage is put down. Thus we have gone the full circle.

Alan S. Katz. Born 1930. Psychiatrist and teacher. Formerly Head of Boston University's Mental Health Center, Dr. Katz now teaches psychiatry at Boston University's College of Law and College of Medicine and is also in private practice. He has written a number of professional articles and has a forthcoming book.

J. B. S. Haldane

On Being the Right Size

1   The most obvious differences between different animals are differences in size, but for some reason the zoologists have paid singularly little attention to them. In the large textbook of zoology before me I find no indication that the eagle is larger than the sparrow, or the hippopotamus bigger than the hare, though some grudging admissions are made in the case of the mouse and the whale. But yet it is easy to show that a hare could not be as large as a hippopotamus, or a whale as small as a herring. For every type of animal there is a most convenient size, and a large change in size inevitably carries with it a change of form.

2   Let us take the most obvious of possible cases, and consider a giant man sixty feet high—about the height of Giant Pope and Giant Pagan in the illustrated *Pilgrim's Progress* of my childhood. These monsters were not only ten times as high as Christian, but ten times as wide and ten times as thick, so that their total weight was a thousand times his, or about eighty to ninety tons. Unfortunately the cross sections of their bones were only a hundred times those of Christian, so that every square inch of giant bone had to support ten times the weight borne by a square inch of human bone. As the human thigh-bone breaks under about ten times the human weight, Pope and Pagan would have broken their thighs every time they took a step. This was doubtless why they were sitting down in the picture I remember. But it lessens one's respect for Christian and Jack the Giant Killer.

3   To turn to zoology, suppose that a gazelle, a graceful little creature with long thin legs, is to become large: it will break its bones unless it does one of two things. It may make its legs short and thick, like the rhinoceros, so that every pound of weight has still about the same area of bone to support it. Or it can compress its body and stretch out its legs obliquely to gain stability, like the giraffe. I mention these two beasts because they happen to belong to the

(2) *Giant Pope and Giant Pagan in . . . Pilgrim's Progress. Pilgrim's Progress,* John Bunyan's 1678 allegorical description of the spiritual life of a Christian soul in the world of men. Among the dangers its hero, Christian, encounters in his journey to the Celestial City are the Giant Pope and the Giant Pagan, gigantic characters representing what the Evangelical Protestant Bunyan considered the gigantic evils of competing religions.

(2) *Jack the Giant Killer.* Triumphal name given to the hero of the folktale, *Jack and the Beanstalk.*

same order as the gazelle, and both are quite successful mechanically, being remarkably fast runners.

Gravity, a mere nuisance to Christian, was a terror to Pope, Pagan, and Despair. To the mouse and any smaller animal it presents practically no dangers. You can drop a mouse down a thousand-yard mine shaft; and, on arriving at the bottom, it gets a slight shock and walks away, provided that the ground is fairly soft. A rat is killed, man is broken, a horse splashes. For the resistance presented to movement by the air is proportional to the surface of the moving object. Divide an animal's length, breadth, and height each by ten; its weight is reduced to a thousandth, but its surface only to a hundredth. So the resistance to falling in the case of the small animal is relatively ten times greater than the driving force.   4

An insect, therefore, is not afraid of gravity; it can fall without danger, and can cling to the ceiling with remarkably little trouble. It can go in for elegant and fantastic forms of support like that of the daddy longlegs. But there is a force which is as formidable to an insect as gravitation to a mammal. This is surface tension. A man coming out of a bath carries with him a film of water of about one-fiftieth of an inch in thickness. This weighs roughly a pound. A wet mouse has to carry about its own weight of water. A wet fly has to lift many times its own weight and, as every one knows, a fly once wetted by water or any other liquid is in a very serious position indeed. An insect going for a drink is in as great danger as a man leaning out over a precipice in search of food. If it once falls into the grip of the surface tension of the water—that is to say, gets wet—it is likely to remain so until it drowns. A few insects, such as water beetles, contrive to be unwettable; the majority keep well away from their drink by means of a long proboscis.   5

Of course tall land animals have other difficulties. They have to pump their blood to greater heights than a man and, therefore, require a larger blood pressure and tougher blood-vessels. A great many men die from burst arteries, especially in the brain, and this danger is presumably still greater for an elephant or a giraffe. But animals of all kinds find difficulties in size for the following reason. A typical small animal, say a microscopic worm or rotifer, has a smooth skin through which all the oxygen it requires can soak in, a straight gut with sufficient surface to absorb its food, and a simple kidney. Increase its dimensions tenfold in every direction, and its weight is increased a thousand times, so that if it is to use its muscles as efficiently as its miniature counterpart, it will need a thousand times as much food and oxygen per day and will excrete a thousand times as much of waste products.   6

Now if its shape is unaltered, its surface will be increased only a hundredfold, and ten times as much oxygen must enter per minute through each square millimeter of skin, ten times as much food through each square millimeter of intestine. When a limit is reached to their absorptive powers, their surface has   7

---

(5) *proboscis.* Drinking tube, such as an elephant's trunk.
(6) *rotifer.* Microscopic water creature propelled by a rotating wheel of hairs (cilia).

to be increased by some special device. For example, a part of the skin may be drawn out into tufts to make gills or pushed in to make lungs, thus increasing the oxygen-absorbing surface in proportion to the animal's bulk. A man, for example, has a hundred square yards of lung. Similarly, the gut, instead of being smooth and straight, becomes coiled and develops a velvety surface, and other organs increase in complication. The higher animals are not larger than the lower because they are more complicated. They are more complicated because they are larger. Just the same is true of plants. The simplest plants, such as the green algae growing in stagnant water or on the bark of trees, are mere round cells. The higher plants increase their surface by putting out leaves and roots. Comparative anatomy is largely the story of the struggle to increase surface in proportion to volume.

8   Some of the methods of increasing the surface are useful up to a point, but not capable of a very wide adaptation. For example, while vertebrates carry the oxygen from the gills or lungs all over the body in the blood, insects take air directly to every part of their body by tiny blind tubes called tracheae which open to the surface at many different points. Now, although by their breathing movements they can renew the air in the outer part of the tracheal system, the oxygen has to penetrate the finer branches by means of diffusion. Gases can diffuse easily through very small distances, not many times larger than the av-erage length traveled by a gas molecule between collisions with other mole-cules. But when such vast journeys—from the point of view of a molecule—as a quarter of an inch have to be made, the process becomes slow. So the portions of an insect's body more than a quarter of an inch from the air would always be short of oxygen. In consequence hardly any insects are much more than half an inch thick. Land crabs are built on the same general plan as insects, but are much clumsier. Yet like ourselves they carry oxygen around in their blood, and are therefore able to grow far larger than any insects. If the insects had hit on a plan for driving air through their tissues instead of letting it soak in, they might well have become as large as lobsters, though other considerations would have prevented them from becoming as large as man.

9   Exactly the same difficulties attach to flying. It is an elementary principle of aeronautics that the minimum speed needed to keep an aeroplane of a given shape in the air varies as the square root of its length. If its linear dimensions are increased four times, it must fly twice as fast. Now the power needed for the minimum speed increases more rapidly than the weight of the machine. So the larger aeroplane which weighs sixty-four times as much as the smaller needs one hundred and twenty-eight times its horsepower to keep up. Applying the same principles to the birds, we find that the limit to their size is soon reached. An angel whose muscles developed no more power weight for weight than those of an eagle or a pigeon would require a breast projecting for about four feet to house the muscles engaged in working its wings, while to economize in weight, its legs would have to be reduced to mere stilts. Actually a large bird such as an eagle or kite does not keep in the air mainly by moving its wings. It is generally to be seen soaring, that is to say balanced on a rising column of air.

And even soaring becomes more and more difficult with increasing size. Were this not the case eagles might be as large as tigers and as formidable to man as hostile aeroplanes.

But it is time that we passed to some of the advantages of size. One of the 10 most obvious is that it enables one to keep warm. All warm-blooded animals at rest lose the same amount of heat from a unit area of skin, for which purpose they need a food-supply proportional to their surface and not to their weight. Five thousand mice weigh as much as a man. Their combined surface and food or oxygen consumption are about seventeen times a man's. In fact a mouse eats about one quarter its own weight of food every day, which is mainly used in keeping warm. For the same reason small animals cannot live in cold countries. In the arctic regions there are no reptiles or amphibians, and no small mammals. The smallest mammal in Spitzbergen is the fox. The small birds fly away in the winter, while the insects die, though their eggs can survive six months or more of frost. The most successful mammals are bears, seals, and walruses.

Similarly, the eye is a rather inefficient organ until it reaches a large size. 11 The back of the human eye on which an image of the outside world is thrown, and which corresponds to the film of a camera, is composed of a mosaic of "rods and cones" whose diameter is little more than a length of an average light wave. Each eye has about half a million, and for two objects to be distinguishable their images must fall on separate rods or cones. It is obvious that with fewer but larger rods and cones we should see less distinctly. If they were twice as broad two points would have to be twice as far apart before we could distinguish them at a given distance. But if their size were diminished and their number increased we should see no better. For it is impossible to form a definite image smaller than a wave length of light. Hence a mouse's eye is not a small-scale model of a human eye. Its rods and cones are not much smaller than ours, and therefore there are far fewer of them. A mouse could not distinguish one human face from another six feet away. In order that they should be of any use at all the eyes of small animals have to be much larger in proportion to their bodies than our own. Large animals on the other hand only require relatively small eyes, and those of the whale and elephant are little larger than our own.

For rather more recondite reasons the same general principle holds true of 12 the brain. If we compare the brain weights of a set of very similar animals such as the cat, cheetah, leopard, and tiger, we find that as we quadruple the body weight, the brain weight is only doubled. The larger animal with proportionately larger bones can economize on brain, eyes, and certain other organs.

Such are a very few of the considerations which show that for every type 13 of animal there is an optimum size. Yet although Galileo demonstrated the contrary more than three hundred years ago, people still believe that if a flea were as large as a man it could jump a thousand feet into the air. As a matter of fact the height to which an animal can jump is more nearly independent of its size than proportional to it. A flea can jump about two feet, a man about five. To jump a given height, if we neglect the resistance of the air, requires an expenditure of energy proportional to the jumper's weight. But if the jumping muscles form a constant fraction of the animal's body, the energy developed per ounce of muscle is independent of the size, provided it can be developed quickly enough in the small animal. As a matter of fact an insect's muscles, although they can contract more quickly than our own, appear to be less efficient; as otherwise a flea or grasshopper could rise six feet into the air.

14   And just as there is a best size for every animal, so the same is true for every human institution. In the Greek type of democracy all the citizens could listen to a series of orators and vote directly on questions of legislation. Hence their philosophers held that a small city was the largest possible democratic state. The English invention of representative government made a democratic nation possible, and the possibility was first realized in the United States, and later elsewhere. With the development of broadcasting it has once more become possible for every citizen to listen to the political views of representative orators, and the future may perhaps see the return of the national state to the Greek form of democracy. Even the referendum has been made possible only by the institution of daily newspapers.

15   To the biologist the problem of socialism appears largely as a problem of size. The extreme socialists desire to run every nation as a single business concern. I do not suppose that Henry Ford would find much difficulty in running Andorra or Luxembourg on a socialistic basis. He has already more men on his payroll than their population. It is conceivable that a syndicate of Fords, if we could find them, would make Belgium Ltd. or Denmark Inc. pay their way. But while nationalization of certain industries is an obvious possibility in the largest of states, I find it no easier to picture a completely socialized British Empire or United States than an elephant turning somersaults or a hippopotamus jumping a hedge.

---

(15) *Andorra . . . Luxembourg.* Andorra, with its population of 12,000, and Luxembourg, with its population of 315,000, are very small European countries.

J. B. S. Haldane. 1892–1964. British scholar, socialist, writer and lecturer on scientific, social, and political affairs. For many years Professor of Biometry at London University, Haldane is the author of many books including *Science and Ethics, Animal Biology* (with J. S. Huxley) and *My Friend, Mr. Leakey,* a children's text.

Lance Morrow

In the Beginning:
God and Science

Sometime after the Enlightenment, science and religion came to a gentleman's   1
agreement. Science was for the real world: machines, manufactured things, med-
icines, guns, moon rockets. Religion was for everything else, the immeasurable:
morals, sacraments, poetry, insanity, death and some residual forms of politics
and statesmanship. Religion became, in both senses of the word, immaterial.
Science and religion were apples and oranges. So the pact said: render unto
apples the things that are Caesar's, and unto oranges the things that are God's.
Just as the Maya kept two calendars, one profane and one priestly, so Western
science and religion fell into two different conceptions of the universe, two
different vocabularies.

This hostile distinction between religion and science has softened in the   2
last third of the 20th century. Both religion and science have become self-consciously aware of their excesses, even of their capacity for evil. Now they find
themselves jostled into a strange metaphysical intimacy. Perhaps the most extraordinary sign of that intimacy is what appears to be an agreement between
religion and science about certain facts concerning the creation of the universe.
It is the equivalent of the Montagues and Capulets collaborating on a baby
shower.

According to the *Book of Genesis,* the universe began in a single, flashing   3
act of creation; the divine intellect willed all into being, *ex nihil.* It is not surprising that scientists have generally stayed clear of the question of ultimate

---

---

(1) *the Enlightenment.* Eighteenth-century philosophical movement whose purpose
was to throw off the in-faith religious acceptance of the past and try to understand the
universe in a completely rational way; "The Age of Reason."

(1) *apples and oranges.* Proverbial analogy indicating that the items in question are
too diverse for reasonable comparison.

(1) *render unto apples.* . . . Allusion to the Biblical verse, "Render unto Caesar the
things that are Caesar's, and unto God the things that are God's" (*Mark* 12:17 and *Matthew* 22:21).

(1) *Maya.* Indians of the Yucatan Peninsula, whose civilization reached its impressive height around 1000 A.D.

(2) *Montagues and Capulets.* Feuding families of Shakespeare's "star-crossed lovers," Romeo and Juliet, from his play of the same name.

(3) *Ex nihil.* "From nothing" *(Latin).*

authorship, of the final "uncaused cause." In years past, in fact, they held to the Aristotelian idea of a universe that was "ungenerated and indestructible," with an infinite past and an infinite future. This was known as the Steady State theory.

4   That absolute expanse might be difficult, even unbearable, to contemplate, like an infinite snow field of time, but the conception at least carried with it the serenity of the eternal. In recent decades, however, the Steady State model of the universe has yielded in the scientific mind to an even more difficult idea, full of cosmic violence. Most astronomers now accept the theory that the universe had an instant of creation, that it came to be in a vast fireball explosion 15 or 20 billion years ago. The shrapnel created by that explosion is still flying outward from the focus of the blast. One of the fragments is the galaxy we call the Milky Way—one of whose hundreds of billions of stars is the earth's sun, with its tiny orbiting grains of planets. The so-called Big Bang theory makes some astronomers acutely uncomfortable, even while it ignites in many religious minds a small thrill of confirmation. Reason: the Big Bang theory sounds very much like the story that the Old Testament has been telling all along.

5   Science arrived at the Big Bang theory through its admirably painstaking and ideologically disinterested process of hypothesis and verification—and, sometimes, happy accident. In 1913, Astronomer Vesto Melvin Slipher of the Lowell Observatory in Flagstaff, Arizona, discovered galaxies that were receding from the earth at extraordinarily high speeds, up to 2 million m.p.h. In 1929, the American astronomer Edwin Hubble developed Slipher's findings to formulate his law of an expanding universe, which presupposes a single primordial explosion. Meantime, Albert Einstein, without benefit of observation, concocted his general theory of relativity, which overthrew Newton and contained in its apparatus the idea of the expanding universe. The Steady State idea still held many astronomers, however, until 1965, when two scientists at Bell Telephone Laboratories, Arno Penzias and Robert Wilson, using sophisticated electronic equipment, picked up the noise made by background radiation coming from all parts of the sky. What they were hearing, as it turned out, were the reverberations left over from the first explosion, the hissing echoes of creation. In the past dozen years, most astronomers have come around to operating on the assumption that there was indeed a big bang.

6   The Big Bang theory has subversive possibilities. At any rate, in a century of Einstein's relativity, of Heisenberg's uncertainty principle (the very act of observing nature disturbs and alters it), of the enigmatic black holes ("Of the God who was painted as a glittering eye, there is nothing now left but a black socket," wrote the German Romantic Jean Paul), science is not the cool Palladian temple of rationality that it was in the Enlightenment. It begins to seem

---

(6) *Palladian Temple of rationality.* Referring to a temple devoted to Pallas Athena, Greek goddess of wisdom.

(6) *the Enlightenment.* See note for paragraph (1).

more like Prospero's island as experienced by Caliban. Some astronomers even talk of leftover starlight from a future universe, its time flowing in the opposite direction from ours. A silicon-chip agnosticism can be shaken by many puzzles besides the creation. Almost as mysterious are the circumstances that led, billions of years ago, to the creation of the first molecule that could reproduce itself. That step made possible the development of all the forms of life that spread over the earth. Why did it occur just then?

7   A religious enthusiasm for the apparent convergence of science and theology in the Big Bang cosmology is understandable. Since the Enlightenment, the scriptural versions of creation or of other "events," like the fall of man or the miracles of Jesus Christ, have suffered the condescension of science; they were regarded as mere myth, superstition. Now the faithful are tempted to believe that science has performed a laborious validation of at least one biblical "myth": that of creation.

8   But has any such confirmation occurred? Robert Jastrow, director of NASA's Goddard Institute for Space Studies, has published a small and curious book called *God and the Astronomers,* in which he suggests that the Bible was right after all, and that people of his own kind, scientists and agnostics, by his description, now find themselves confounded. Jastrow blows phantom kisses like neutrinos across all chasms between science and religion, seeming almost wistful to make a connection. Biblical fundamentalists may be happier with Jastrow's books than are his fellow scientists. He writes operatically: "For the scientist who has lived by his faith in the power of reason, the story ends like a bad dream. He has scaled the mountains of ignorance; he is about to conquer the highest peak; as he pulls himself over the final rock, he is greeted by a band of theologians who have been sitting there for centuries."

9   Isaac Asimov, the prodigious popularizer of science, reacts hotly to the Jastrow book. "Science and religion proceed by different methods," he says. "Science works by persuasive reason. Outside of science, the method is intuitional, which is not very persuasive. In science, it is possible to say we were wrong, based on data." Science is provisional; it progresses from one hypothesis to another, always testing, rejecting the ideas that do not work, that are contradicted by new evidence. "Faith," said St. Augustine, "is to believe, on the word of God, what we do not see." Faith defies proof; science demands it. If new information should require modification of the Big Bang theory, that modification could be accomplished without the entire temple of knowledge collapsing. Observes Harvard University Historian-Astronomer Owen Gingerich: "*Genesis* is not a book

---

(6) *Prospero's Island as experienced by Caliban.* Caliban, man monster in Shakespeare's *The Tempest,* was frustrated by his inability to understand and served Prospero and his magic isle while filled with passionate rage.

(6) *silicon-chip agnosticism.* Computer-age, scientifically based questioning of the existence of God.

(8) *Neutrinos.* Subatomic particles.

of science. It is accidental if some things agree in detail. I believe the heavens declare the glory of God only to people who've made a religious commitment."

10   A number of theologians concur that the apparent convergence of religious and scientific versions of the creation is a coincidence from which no profound meaning can be extracted. "If the last evidence for God occurred 20 billion years ago," asks Methodist W. Paul Jones of Missouri's St. Paul School of Theology, "do we not at best have the palest of deisms?" Jesuit Philosopher Bernard Lonergan goes further: "Science has nothing to say about creation, because that's going outside the empirical. The whole idea of empirical science is that you have data. Theologians have no data on God." There comes a point, somewhere short of God, at which all computers have no data either. With the Big Bang theory, says Jastrow, "science has proved that the world came into being as a result of forces that seem forever beyond the power of scientific description. This bothers science because it clashes with scientific religion—the religion of cause and effect, the belief that every effect has a cause. Now we find that the biggest effect of all, the birth of the universe, violates this article of faith."

11   Some scientists matter-of-factly dismiss the problem of creation. Says Harvey Tananbaum, an X-ray astronomer at the Harvard-Smithsonian Astrophysical Laboratory: "That first instant of creation is not relevant as long as we do not have the laws to begin to understand it. It is a question for philosophers and religionists, not for scientists." Adds Geoffrey Burbidge, director of Kitt Peak National Observatory: "Principles and concepts cannot be measured. A question like 'Who imposed the order?' is metaphysical." Still, virtually everyone—both scientists and laymen—is taken by the sheer unthinkable opacity of the creation and what preceded it. Says Jastrow: "The question of what came before the Big Bang is the most interesting question of all."

12   One immense problem is that the primordial fireball destroyed all the evidence; the temperature of the universe in the first seconds of its existence was many trillion degrees. The blast obliterated all that went before. The universe was shrouded in a dense fog of radiation, which only cleared after 1 million years, leaving the transparent spangled space we see in the night sky now. The first million years are as concealed from us as God's face. There are many forms of knowing: science, experience, intuition, faith. Science proceeds on the theory that there is method in all mysteries, and that it is discoverable. It obeys, reasonably, what is called the "first law of wingwalking": "Never leave hold of what you've got until you've got hold of something else." Faith, by definition, is a leap. It must await its verification in another world.

13   If it has done nothing else, however, the new coincidence of scientific and theological versions of creation seems to have opened up a conversation that has been neglected for centuries. Roman Catholic Theologian Hans Küng detects the beginning of a new period, which he calls "pro-existence," of mutual assistance between theologians and natural scientists. People capable of genetic engineering and nuclear fission obviously require all the spiritual and ethical guidance they can get. As for theologians, the interchange between physics and

metaphysics will inevitably enlarge their ideas and give them a more complex grounding in the physically observed universe. The theory of the Big Bang is surely not the last idea of creation that will be conceived; it does suggest that there remain immense territories of mystery that both the theologian and the scientist should approach with becoming awe.

Lance Morrow. Born 1941. Journalist. After distinguishing himself at Harvard and working for a time as a reporter on the *Washington Star,* Morrow joined *Time* magazine, where he is now a contributing editor, valued especially for his agility with words. He has written poetry, plays, and numerous essays and articles. This article was originally published in *Time,* February 5, 1979.

Walter Williams

U.S. Blacks and a Free Market

1   Does black socioeconomic progress necessarily depend upon whether blacks
are liked by whites? Does it depend on the continuance of massive federal expenditures?

2   Well, if you asked the self-appointed black spokesmen, the answer to these
questions would be "yes." But before we all agree, there are some important
issues that must be raised. One issue is why is it that black entry, *en masse,* into
the mainstream of American society has these requirements, when it was not a
condition for other racial groups? How do blacks differ from these other minorities?

3   One of the most distinguishing features of American society is that we are
a nation of racial minorities. What's more, casual reading of American history
will show that none of these minorities was welcomed to our shores with open
arms. They all faced varying degrees of open hostility and disadvantage. One
need not go back too far in history to see in ads, "No Irish need apply," or, "Any
color or country, except Irish." At one time Orientals were denied land ownership through the Alien Exclusion Act. Japanese citizens were imprisoned. Jews
faced centuries of persecution and discrimination which was not completely
relieved when they came to our country.

4   The point of these observations is not that of determining who received
the worst treatment. Nor is it to minimize the legacy of black slavery and disen-
franchisement. The point *is* to question propositions concerning black socioeconomic progress which have now received an axiomatic status.

5   Some people attempt to explain away black difficulties by pointing out that
blacks are a readily identifiable group and hence easily discriminated against.
Well, what about Orientals? They are easily identified. But by virtually any standard of socioeconomic success, Orientals are at the top of the ladder. Twenty-
five percent of Orientals are professional workers compared to 15 percent for
the general population. They have the second highest level of educational

---

Reprinted by permission from *Antheum Syndicate.*

---

(2) *en masse.* As a group (French).
(3) *Alien Exclusion Act.* The Alien Land Acts of 1913 and 1920 in California (and
similar acts in other states) provided that orientals who were not citizens could not own
property.
(3) *Japanese . . . imprisoned.* In the fear-filled days following the Japanese bombing
of Pearl Harbor, Japanese Americans on the West Coast were forced to go to internment
camps.

achievement. In addition, social disorganization among Orientals, as manifested by crime, juvenile delinquency and dependency, is lower than any other population group.

It is fairly certain that societal love cannot explain the assimilation of past disadvantaged groups. It is without any doubt at all that massive Department of Health, Education and Welfare (HEW) expenditures and affirmative action did not play a role. If we are not to subscribe to racist doctrines of group inferiority and dependence, the question still remains: How do blacks differ from past disadvantaged groups? 6

One of the major differences between blacks and other minorities is the kind of economic system they faced when they became franchised and urbanized. Minorities of the past faced a system of unfettered free enterprise. For example, a poor, uneducated Italian immigrant in the 1920s in New York could own and operate a taxi as a means to upward mobility. All he needed was industry, ambition and a used car with the word "Taxi" written on it. Today, a black, Hispanic, or for that matter anyone else, seeking the same path to upward mobility would find that he needs more than a car, industry and ambition. He would have to buy a taxi license which costs $60,000. 7

Yesterday's disadvantaged could effectively acquire skills. Many jobs used a piece rate as a form of compensation and there was no federally mandated minimum-wage law. What this meant was that a person could be low-skilled and still employable. Being employable meant a chance of upgrading skills and income. For today's disadvantaged minorities such a chance is reduced. The minimum-wage law has the full force of a law which says, "If you cannot produce $3.10 worth of goods and services per hour, you shall never be employed." The effect of this law is revealed by the scandalous rate of unemployment among black youths. 8

A low-skilled person of the past could just walk up to a building site and offer his labor services. Today he must be a member of a union which has little incentive to grant him membership. Similarly, occupational licensing has an exclusionary effect. Historically, only the learned professions were licensed (doctors, lawyers and ministers); today there are over 500 licensed occupations—including poodle trimmers, peddlers and tree-trimmers. Numerous economic studies show that the effect of licensing is that of restricting entry and raising incomes of practitioners. 9

Therefore, what has happened is that when blacks received the franchise, they found that many markets were closed and hence the traditional sources of upward mobility. For too many blacks dependency has been substituted for self-initiative for lack of a better insight into the problems that they face. This misunderstanding has led their leadership to preside over the formulation of the first permanent welfare group in America's history. Ironically, this leadership, perhaps unwittingly, solidly supports labor laws that seriously handicap the most disadvantaged while it vociferously supports other laws which increase dependence. 10

11   What disadvantaged people need are freer markets and a return to the principles of the Bill of Rights—principles which the Supreme Court of the 1930s threw out when they gave the state and federal governments greater control over the individual's economic life. Black people need a fair chance to compete—nothing more and nothing less.

Walter Williams. Teacher and writer. Williams serves as Professor of Economics at Temple University, writes a syndicated newspaper column, and has been acclaimed as a leading voice for the new black conservatives. This article was originally published in the *Cincinnati Enquirer* (May, 1980).

Judith Crist

Gentlemen and Scholars of the Press

Much as I would like to be a keeper of my profession's flame, a herdsman of its sacred cows, a minstrel of its mythology, I think it is time to announce publicly that the newspaper business is not what it was. Hildy Johnson is no more and *The Front Page* is history. Journalism is my profession, factual reporting is my function, and my mission, for the moment, is iconoclasm. For an inside story, then, of what the newspaper business has become, step into my city room and let me shatter your last illusion.   1

Here you will find no one rushing about shouting "Stop the presses!" or even "Hold Page One for a hot exclusive!" The managing editor does not stand glued to a telephone listening to a leg man ("Here's your Page One headline, boss!"). There are no crap games going on in corners, no fedora-topped drunkards tippling from desk-drawer bottles, no wily reporters solving crimes with evidence they have stolen from the scene, no practical jokers reveling in writing fake stories or merely in throwing bags of water out of windows.   2

I look about me at the clean-shirted, barbered, shaven, and sober commuters who are my colleagues and I ought to be ashamed. Child of the thirties that I am, and an admitted lover of legends and popular images, I should call them, one and all, "bourgeois." But I am one of them, a member indeed of a relatively new element of the bourgeoisie, the post-war newspaperman who has come into his own at last as a professional.   3

Many choose to think that the romance has gone out of newspapering, taking with it all the life and lust and adventure immortalized by Ben Hecht and Charles MacArthur and perpetuated in old men's tales of escapades and capering characters. Yes, the romance is gone—but only if romance is the stuff of economic insecurity and the personal, professional, and ethical carelessness bred by such insecurity.   4

The transition that has taken place on metropolitan newspapers—and I am speaking primarily of the New York City newspapers—was summed up recently   5

(1) *Hildy Johnson . . . and The Front Page.* Hildy Johnson is the reporter hero of the play, *The Front Page,* written by Ben Hecht and Charles MacArthur in 1928. This play portrays the hard-bitten journalistic world of popular fantasy that Crist describes in paragraph (2).
   (1) *iconoclasm.* Idol smashing; in Crist's words, "illusion shatter[ing]."
   (3) *bourgeois.* Middle class (French).
   (4) *Ben Hecht and Charles MacArthur.* See *The Front Page* note to paragraph (1).

by a *Herald Tribune* editor. Time was, a mere 20 years ago or so, he remarked, when two telephone calls could solve any midnight emergency. One to Bleeck's downstairs and another to Chumley's in Greenwich Village would bring more than a score of reporters to the scene in minutes. Today it would take 20 suburban phone calls and the combined timetables of the New York Central, the New Haven, and the Pennsylvania railroads to produce a dozen reporters in a matter of hours; only a handful of *Tribune* reporters still live in Manhattan and they can be found in saloons only in the event of special celebrations—if, that is, a babysitter has been found for the occasion.

6   Besides, he added bemusedly, today some careful thinking and going-through-channels would be in order before 20 newspapermen were summoned to work after hours: there is, after all, the matter of time-and-a-half for overtime, extra pay for working on a day off. . . .

7   The basic change in newspapering these 20 years has indeed been an economic one and it has changed the character of the typical reporter. In the past he held on to his job from day to day, by the quality of his daily product as proof of his worth and by the whim of his employer. He knew that competition for his job was keen, for the glamor that has always attached itself to newspapering has ever drawn an endless flood of applicants, and the law of labor supply rather than the cost of living kept salaries at a sub-subsistence level.

8   Financial and professional insecurity turned the newspaperman into a bohemian who made a virtue of his lack of worldly status, a vice of such personal securities as education or professional training or even domesticity. If only for lack of money, the typical reporter was unmarried, an habitue of furnished rooms and cheap saloons, seeking solace among his fellows. He tended, naturally enough, to repay in kind the insecurity his employer offered, by moving on from job to job, by insouciance and prankishness that was charming but often disastrous, by kicking in the competitive clinches for temporary survival, and by an irresponsibility that caused him to regard his work as an end unto himself alone. The tramp printer of an earlier era was godfather to the tramp newspaperman.

9   For the young and gifted, reporting became a sort of Left Bank training ground, a preparation for the non-newspaper writing jobs to which contacts or talents would lead them. Those who remained, middle-aged and leg weary, could only grow old ungracefully as copy readers or desk men on the "lobster shift."

10   Certainly, as a list of newspaper alumni of those days would prove, there were giants in those city rooms. Many of them fled while they still had their youth. A dedicated few stayed on to be today's sages. But I speak of the rank and file, and for them the living was wild and woolly and gay, or so the story goes. But was it? Ben Hecht recently began a bit of lush reminiscence about

---

(8) *bohemian.* "Arty," unconventional.

(9) *Left Bank.* Refers to the colony of struggling young artists and writers who have traditionally lived on the Left Bank of the River Seine in Paris, France.

(9) *"lobster shift."* Early morning working shift (midnight to 8:00).

Chicago journalism of the twenties by declaring, "We were a newspaper tribe of assorted drunkards, poets, burglars, philosophers and boastful ragamuffins— we were supermen with soiled collars and holes in our pants," glorying in a fourteen-hour work day, arrogant and sodden. But even Hecht had to conclude, "On the whole, we were a somewhat pathetic crew of paupers and ignoramuses. . . ."

This, at the very least, will never be said of the newspaperman of today. Making an unscientific survey of my colleagues, I would say the not-atypical reporter is married and has 2.1 children, in all likelihood a mortgage, and a college degree of which he is not ashamed. In fact, we have reached the point where some will speak voluntarily of school of journalism degrees, once considered the very credentials of the mama's boy or the publisher's pet.   11

Today the reporter's fondness for shop talk in the nearby saloon is regulated by his commuting-train schedule, for his hours are regular; the seven-hour day rules in New York City. He has two days off a week, eight holidays a year, and two to four weeks annual vacation, depending on length of service. He can be fired only for "good and just" cause, not by whim. He is given paid sick-leave, a pension or a retirement-with-severance plan. These days he can start as a cub at about $85 a week and, even without merit raises, count on almost doubling his salary with automatic annual increases in six years. In short, he does well, as any young doctor or lawyer would agree.   12

But more important, today's reporter pays for his security with skill and responsibility. Because he has tenure he can weigh values beyond the cutthroat competitive scoop of the moment; because he has a future he can devote himself to the refinement of his craft, to specialization and expertise, so that not only does his value to his employer increase, but also his own opportunities for advancement broaden. Thus—from police reporter to foreign correspondent, from messenger boy to science editor, from college correspondent to Washington staffer—these are the paths my friends have followed and not mere dreams of glory.   13

Where did he come from, this "average" reporter with a respect for facts, a consolidated cultural background acquired in an orderly fashion, an interest in implications and inner workings, a concern beyond the headline and an involvement beyond the by-line? Quite simply, he is a product of the economic revolution brought to newspapering by the American Newspaper Guild, a "professional" union founded exactly 25 years ago under the leadership of Heywood Broun, one of the great newspaper men of modern times. A "professional" union presents an anomaly, for certainly it is a popular prejudice that professionals should not or cannot be organized. But it took a union to make a profession out of newspaper reporting simply because the union achieved the economic security that frees a man to work in a truly professional manner in any field.   14

In passing, I'd like to protest the cliché that so "personal" a skill as writing cannot be subject to set hours and wages, nor should genius be hamstrung thereby. It cannot be and it isn't. But the fact is that newspaper writers are not   15 inspired "creative" artists. Theirs is a skill, partly instinctive and partly acquired, in the gathering of facts and the transmission of those facts in words. Nevertheless, the man who possesses that increasingly rare skill is entitled to a fair price for its sale. A minimum—and this is the only limit the Guild has set—is essential for the beginning of bargaining. After that, it's up to the seller to prove his superiority for a superior price. The merit raise is still with us.

16   Economic security has proved a magnet for bright young men who in the past could not afford to linger purely for the fun of wearing a press card in their hats. A growing sense of responsibility on the part of the publisher and a more thoroughly educated public have helped to make his stay worthwhile. Reporting no longer begins with sex slayings and ends with political scandal. The era of the expert—in science, education, art, housing, medicine, social service, foreign affairs, music—is at hand. Nor has the day of the all-around news reporter passed.

17   The copy desk is no longer the graveyard for old reporters with no place else to go. Like the make-up and other editing desks, it is now the goal for those interested in the technical aspects of editorial production. It offers higher starting salaries than reporting, and there is a Guild-instituted apprentice system for aspiring desk men, indicating that the copy desk is now the chosen area of expert craftsmen.

18   The "security system" works two ways. Not only does it attract and hold men of higher caliber but it also brings higher hiring standards. The publisher realizes that he is hiring for keeps and tends, therefore, to pick the cream of the ever-flourishing crop of applicants. He develops, too, a greater sense of responsibility toward his employees. It's not sentiment, merely good business. He has a far greater investment in a $150-a-week worker than in a $25-a-week floater and tends, therefore, to be more concerned about his work and his welfare.

19   And so a profession comes of age.

20   Most newspapermen stay put nowadays. Ten, 15, 20 years service on one paper is no rarity. But fidelity is inspired as much by a sense of professional pride and loyalty as by a liking for security. True, from time to time some of the young or the perennially debt-ridden or the restless will yield to the rich or glamorous seduction of television and publicity jobs and depart, leaving the field to the professionals. But for the most part, our roving days are over.

21   Has the change been for the better? Compare today's newspapers with those of 25 or 30 years ago and try to deny that it has.

22   One characteristic of the newspaper business has not changed. As each year the number of newspapers decreases and therefore fewer jobs remain, every reporter lives more and more with the awareness that there are at least a score of highly qualified applicants for his job. The publishers, needless to say, share this awareness and would not hesitate, given a free hand, to reap the obvious benefits. I started out in 1945 when the Guild had raised beginning pay to $27 a week, and I turned down a $65-a-week non-newspaper job to grab it. Were it not for the Guild, I doubt that starting salaries today would be much higher— nor do I doubt that I'd jump at the chance regardless of price.

For sane, sober, and secure though this business has become, it has lost none of the glory that is its essence, the glory of transmitting the fact, of telling the truth so that the people will know it, and—one must confess—of being on the inside when news is made. I have to say this deprecatingly within earshot of colleagues who likewise affect to be cynics, lest we be seen as men and women with a mission or dedication.   23

But none of the fun has gone out of newspapering either. If anything, the company is better, the wit is more sophisticated, the joking less juvenile, the iconoclasm more judicious, and the occasional bender all the better for its occasion. And something has been added, a sense of service beyond one's self and a consciousness of craft: in short, professional pride.   24

Hildy Johnson never had it so good.   25

Judith Crist. Born 1922. Reporter, theater critic, and teacher of journalism. Crist began her career as a reporter and critic for the *New York Herald Tribune* and served as film and theater critic for the *Ladies Home Journal, TV Guide, The Washingtonian,* the *Saturday Review,* the *New York Post,* and the *Today* television show. Her essays have twice been collected and published as books.

E. B. White

The Distant Music of the Hounds

1   To perceive Christmas through its wrapping becomes more difficult with every year. There was a little device we noticed in one of the sporting-goods stores—a trumpet that hunters hold to their ears so that they can hear the distant music of the hounds. Something of the sort is needed now to hear the incredibly distant sound of Christmas in these times, through the dark, material woods that surround it. "Silent Night," canned and distributed in thundering repetition in the department stores, has become one of the greatest of all noisemakers, almost like the rattles and whistle of Election Night. We rode down on an escalator the other morning through the silent-nighting of the loudspeakers, and the man just in front of us was singing, "I'm gonna wash this store right outa my hair, I'm gonna wash this store . . . ."

2   The miracle of Christmas is that, like the distant and very musical voice of the hound, it penetrates finally and becomes heard in the heart—over so many years, through so many cheap curtain-raisers. It is not destroyed even by all the arts and craftsness of the destroyers, having an essential simplicity that is ever-lasting and triumphant, at the end of confusion. We once were out at night with coon-hunters and we were aware that it was not so much the promise of the kill that took the men away from their warm homes and sent them through the cold shadowy woods, it was something more human, more mystical—something even simpler. It was the night, and the excitement of the note of the hound, first heard, then not heard. It was the natural world seen at its best and most haunting, unlit except by stars, impenetrable except to the knowing and the sympathetic.

3   Christmas in this year of crisis must compete as never before with the dazzling complexity of man, whose tangential desires and ingenuities have created a world that gives any simple thing the look of obsolescence—as though there were something inherently foolish in what is simple, or natural. The human brain is about to turn certain functions over to an efficient substitute, and we hear of a robot that is now capable of handling the tedious details of psychoanalysis, so that the patient no longer need confide in a living doctor but

---

---

(1) *"I'm gonna wash this store. . . ."* Parody of "I'm Gonna Wash that Man Right Out of My Hair" from the musical comedy *South Pacific* (1949) by Richard Rodgers and Oscar Hammerstein.

(3) *tangential.* Only superficially relevant.

can take his problems to a machine, which sifts everything and whose "brain" has selective power and the power of imagination. One thing leads to another. The machine that is imaginative will, we don't doubt, be heir to the ills of the imagination; one can already predict that the machine itself may become sick emotionally, from strain and tension, and be compelled at last to consult a medical man, whether of flesh or of steel. We have tended to assume that the machine and the human brain are in conflict. Now the fear is that they are indistinguishable. Man not only is notably busy himself but insists that the other animals follow his example. A new bee has been bred artificially, busier than the old bee.

So this day and this century proceed toward the absolutes of convenience, of complexity, and of speed, only occasionally holding up the little trumpet (as at Christmas time) to be reminded of the simplicities, and to hear the distant music of the hound. Man's inventions, directed always onward and upward, have an odd way of leading back to man himself, as a rabbit track in snow leads eventually to the rabbit. It is one of his more endearing qualities that man should think his tracks lead outward, toward something else instead of back around the hill to where he has already been; and it is one of his persistent ambitions to leave earth entirely and travel by rocket into space, beyond the pull of gravity, and perhaps try another planet, as a pleasant change. He knows that the atomic age is capable of delivering a new package of energy; what he doesn't know is whether it will prove to be a blessing. This week, many will be reminded that no explosion of atoms generates so hopeful a light as the reflection of a star, seen appreciatively in a pasture pond. It is there we perceive Christmas—and the sheep quiet, and the world waiting.

4

E. B. White. Born, 1899. Pulitzer prize-winning man of letters and writer of essays and poems. White was a contributing editor of the *New Yorker* and columnist for *Harper's.* He has written 21 books including essay collections such as *One Man's Meat,* books of humor, such as *Is Sex Necessary?* (with James Thurber), children's classics like *Charlotte's Web,* and perhaps the most famous rhetoric ever, *The Elements of Style* (with William Strunk).

Wallace E. Stegner

Good-bye to All T--t

1   Not everyone who laments what contemporary novelists have done to the sex act objects to the act itself, or to its mention. Some want it valued higher than fiction seems to value it; they want the word "climax" to retain some of its literary meaning. Likewise, not everyone who has come to doubt the contemporary freedom of language objects to strong language in itself. Some of us object precisely because we value it.

2   I acknowledge that I have used four-letter words familiarly all my life, and have put them into books with some sense that I was insisting on the proper freedom of the artist. I have applauded the extinction of those d--d emasculations of the Genteel Tradition and the intrusion into serious fiction of honest words with honest meanings and emphasis. I have wished, with D. H. Lawrence, for the courage to say shit before a lady, and have sometimes had my wish.

3   Words are not obscene: naming things is a legitimate verbal act. And "frank" does not mean "vulgar," any more than "improper" means "dirty." What vulgar does mean is "common"; what improper means is "unsuitable." Under the right circumstances, any word is proper. But when any sort of word, especially a word hitherto taboo and therefore noticeable, is scattered across a page like chocolate chips through a tollhouse cookie, a real impropriety occurs. The sin is not the use of an "obscene" word; it is the use of a loaded word in the wrong place or in the wrong quantity. It is the sin of false emphasis, which is not a moral but a literary lapse, related to sentimentality. It is the sin of advertisers who so plaster a highway with neon signs that you can't find the bar or liquor store you're looking for. Like any excess, it quickly becomes comic.

4   If I habitually say shit before a lady, what do I say before a flat tire at the rush hour in Times Square or on the San Francisco Bay Bridge? What do I say before a revelation of the inequity of the universe? And what if the lady takes the bit in her teeth and says shit before *me*?

5   I have been a teacher of writing for many years and have watched this problem since it was no bigger than a man's hand. It used to be that with some Howellsian notion of the young-girl audience one tried to protect tender female

---

---

(2) *Genteel Tradition.* Term first used by George Santayana, philosopher and literary critic, who used it to criticize a number of late nineteenth-century American writers whom he considered over-conventional and prissy.

(2) *D. H. Lawrence.* Early twentieth-century British novelist, whose works are much acclaimed, but were once censured (and censored!) for prurience.

(5) *Howellsian notion.* The sort of idea likely to be held by William Dean Howells, a writer at the turn of the 20th century who was regarded by his later contemporaries as a "genteel sentimentalist."

members of a mixed class from the coarse language of males trying to show off. Some years ago Frank O'Connor and I agreed on a system. Since we had no intention whatever of restricting students' choice of subject or language, and no desire to expurgate or bowdlerize while reading their stuff aloud for discussion, but at the same time had to deal with these young girls of an age our daughters might have been, we announced that any stuff so strong that it would embarrass us to read it aloud could be read by its own author.

It was no deterrent at all, but an invitation, and not only to coarse males. For clinical sexual observation, for full acceptance of the natural functions, for discrimination in the selection of graffiti, for boldness in the use of words that it should take courage to say before a lady, give me a sophomore girl every time. Her strength is as the strength of ten, for she assumes that if one shocker out of her pretty mouth is piquant, fifty will be literature. And so do a lot of her literary idols.   6

Some acts, like some words, were never meant to be casual. That is why houses contain bedrooms and bathrooms. Profanity and so-called obscenities are literary resources, verbal ways of rendering strong emotion. They are not meant to occur every ten seconds, any more than—Norman Mailer to the contrary notwithstanding—orgasms are.   7

So I am not going to say shit before any more ladies. I am going to hunt words that have not lost their sting, and it may be I shall have to go back to gentility to find them. Pleasant though it is to know that finally a writer can make use of any word that fits his occasion, I am going to investigate the possibilities latent in restraint.   8

I remember my uncle, a farmer who had used four-letter words ten to the sentence ever since he learned to talk. One day he came too near the circular saw and cut half his fingers off. While we stared in horror, he stood watching the bright arterial blood pump from his ruined hand. Then he spoke, and he did not speak loud. "Aw, the dickens," he said.   9

I think he understood, better than some sophomore girls and better than some novelists, the nature of emphasis.   10

---

(5) *Frank O'Connor.* Irish writer of short stories of great humor and charm.

(6) *Her strength is as the strength of ten.* . . . Ironic allusion to Sir Galahad's claim that "My strength is as the strength of ten / Because my heart is pure" from Alfred Lord Tennyson's poem, "Sir Galahad."

(7) *Norman Mailer.* Contemporary American writer, some of whose autobiographical works contain allusions to his sexual prowess. [See also Tom Wolfe's "Down with Sin," paragraph (2)].

Wallace E. Stegner. Born 1909. Scholar, teacher, and Pulitzer prize-winning author. Midwestern in background, Stegner is currently Professor of English at Stanford University. He is author of many articles and more than 13 books, including *Angle of Repose and Recapitulation.* This article was originally published in *The Atlantic Monthly,* 215 (March, 1965), 119.

William Raspberry

Children of Two-Career Families

1   Maybe you have to be crazy to argue with two Harvard psychiatrists—particularly two such insightful psychiatrists as Barrie Greiff and Preston Hunter.

2   So before I register my small objection to their article in the May-June issue of *Harvard Magazine,* let me say that nearly everything these two doctors have to say about the strains and stresses of dual-career families makes sense to me.

3   The only paragraph that arched my eyebrows included this sentence: "Dual-career parents . . . shouldn't overburden their children with responsibility for themselves or their siblings, or for running the household; that only cheats them out of their childhood and confuses them about parental roles."

4   "Dual-career" families are defined as families in which both husband and wife have careers (as opposed to jobs) that require separate, major commitments outside the marriage.

5   The advice in the paragraph cited is calculated to help the children of these families deal with "the anger, hostility, rebellion and feelings of abandonment" caused by their parents' absence.

6   My fear is that the advice may feed another set of problems: the problems that stem from a general sense of uselessness.

7   It is my belief that many of the difficulties America's young people face today are the result of their sense of unnecessity. They are not needed to produce income, to maintain the family routine, to help in any serious way. As a result, they are likely to see themselves as part of no vital enterprise which they deem to be of overriding importance.

8   They may feel loved and well-provided for, but they are also likely to feel unnecessary.

9   This sense of uselessness, I am convinced, lies behind the shocking statistics on teen-age pregnancy, youthful homicide and suicide, crime, alcoholism, drug abuse—the whole range of things we refer to when we talk about the decline in character among young Americans.

10   And because it is harder for children of affluent families to feel necessary, it had seemed to me vital that they at least be given some responsibility for "themselves or their siblings, or for running the household."

11   Can it be only coincidental that teenage suicide, drug abuse, etc., were practically nonexistent when most American families lived on farms, or in non-urban settings, where their children's contributions to the families' general welfare was taken for granted?

These children worked on the farm, or gathered firewood, or looked after livestock and performed a whole variety of chores, not because their parents were concerned about developing in them a sense of responsibility but because their contributions were in fact necessary. Nor was there any concern that the performance of these necessary tasks would "cheat them out of their childhood." 12

But most of these tasks have no obvious counterpart in the typical affluent, urban or suburban household. If they live in apartments or townhouses, today's youngsters don't even have lawns to mow. 13

Nor is it a problem only for the well-off. The children of urban tenements may see themselves as equally unnecessary, playing no important role in their families' welfare. 14

Under the circumstances, it seems to me that the problem for modern parents is to find ways to give their children a sense of usefulness, to make them feel that they are a vital part of a general family enterprise, and not just impediments to their parents' careers. It seems obvious to me that if children don't see themselves as valuable to others, they are unlikely to feel that they are valuable to themselves. 15

The Harvard psychiatrists worry about cheating children out of their childhood. I worry about cheating them out of something more profoundly important: their self-respect as responsible, contributing human beings. 16

William Raspberry. Born 1935. Journalist, lecturer and syndicated columnist. Formerly with the *Indianapolis Recorder,* Raspberry now is contributing editor of the *Washington Post.* He is also a television commentator and panelist and an instructor at Howard University. Raspberry writes mainly about racial issues, public education, and urban affairs. This article was originally published in *The Washington Post,* May 19, 1980.

Carll Tucker

On Splitting

1   One afternoon recently, two unrelated friends called to tell me that, well, their marriages hadn't made it. One was leaving his wife for another woman. The other was leaving her husband because "we thought it best."

2   As always after such increasingly common calls, I felt helpless and angry. What had happened to those solemn vows that one of the couples had stammered on a steamy August afternoon three years earlier? And what had happened to the joy my wife and I had sensed when we visited the other couple and their two children last year, the feeling they gave us that here, in this increasingly fractionated world, was a constructive union?

3   I did not feel anger at my friends personally: Given the era and their feelings, their decisions probably made sense. What angered me was the loss of years and energy. It was an anger similar to that I feel when I see abandoned foundations of building projects—piled bricks and girders and a gash in the ground left to depress the passerby.

4   When our grandparents married, nobody except scandalous eccentrics divorced. "As long as we both shall live" was no joke. Neither was the trepidation brides felt on the eves of their wedding days. After their vows, couples learned to live with each other—not necessarily because they loved each other, but because they were stuck, and it was better to be stuck comfortably than otherwise.

5   Most of the external pressures that helped to enforce our grandparents' vows have dissolved. Women can earn money and may enjoy sex, even bear children, without marrying. As divorce becomes more common, the shame attendant on it dissipates. Some divorcees even argue that divorce is beneficial, educational; that the second or third or fifth marriage is "the best." The only reasons left to marry are love, tax advantages, and, for those old-fashioned enough to care about such things, to silence parental kvetching.

6   In some respects, this freedom can be seen as social progress. Modern couples can flee the corrosive bitterness that made Strindberg's marriages night-

(5) *kvetching.* Persistent complaining (Yiddish).

(6) *Strindberg's marriages.* Despite the fact that August Strindberg (1849–1912) considered his first wife to be ruthless, aggressive, and emasculating almost from the first, the Swedish playwright remained married to her from 1877 to 1891. His second marriage, though shorter, was equally unfortunate and was probably a partial cause of his emotional breakdown that coincided with it.

mares. Dreiser's Clyde Griffiths might have abandoned his Roberta instead of drowning her.

In other respects, our rapidly-rising divorce rate and the declining marriage rate (as more and more couples opt to forgo legalities and simply live together) represent a loss. One advantage of spending a lifetime with a person is seeing each other grow and change. For most of us, it is not possible to see history in the bathroom mirror—gray hairs, crow's feet, yes, but not a change of mind or temperament. Yet, living with another person, it is impossible not to notice how patterns and attitudes change and not to learn—about yourself and about time—from those perceptions.

Perhaps the most poignant victim of the twentieth century is our sense of continuity. People used to grow up with trees, watch them evolve from saplings to fruit bearers to gnarled and unproductive grandfathers. Now, unless one is a farmer or a forester there is almost no point to planting trees because one is not likely to be there to enjoy their maturity. We change addresses and occupations and hobbies and life-styles and spouses rapidly and readily, much as we change TV channels. In our grandparents' day one committed oneself to certain skills and disciplines and developed them. Carpenters spent lifetimes learning their craft; critics spent lifetimes learning literature. Today, the question often is not "What do you do?" but "What are you into?" Macrame one week, astrology the next, health food, philosophy, history, jogging, movies, est—we fly from "commitment" to "commitment" like bees among flowers because it is easier to test something than to master it, easier to buy a new toy than to repair an old one.

I feel sorry for what my divorced friends have lost. No matter how earnestly the former spouses try to "keep in touch," no matter how generous the visiting privileges for the parent who does not win custody of the children, the continuity of their lives has been broken. The years they spent together have been cut off from the rest of their lives; they are an isolated memory, no more integral to their past than a snapshot. Intelligent people, they will compare their next marriages—if they have them—to their first. They may even, despite not having a long shared past, notice growth. What I pray, though, is that they do not delude themselves into believing like so many Americans today, that happiness is only measurable moment to moment and, in the pursuit of momentary contentment, forsake the perspectives and consolation of history.

There is great joy in watching a tree grow.

---

(6) *Dreiser's Clyde Griffiths might have abandoned his Roberta instead of drowning her.* In Theodore Dreiser's *An American Tragedy* (1925), the protagonist, Clyde Griffiths, unwilling either to leave the girl he has seduced to her fate as an unwed mother or to marry her himself, takes her out in a rowboat and permits her to drown.

(8) *est.* Werner Erhard's *Erhard Seminar Training* movement. [See also Ellen Goodman's "The Cult of Impotence," note to paragraph (8)].

Carll Tucker. Born, 1951. Author and columnist. Formerly a reporter for the *Village Voice,* Tucker is now a contributing editor of the *Saturday Review,* for which he writes a regular column. This article was originally published in *The Saturday Review,* January 21, 1978.

Meg Greenfield

The Trappings Trap

1   The more I ponder it, the less surprised I think any of us should be that the determined intruder made it up the drainpipe and into the royal bedchamber. Startled, yes—in particular, the Queen of England was surely entitled to have been somewhat taken aback at the sight of the uninvited Mr. Fagan standing by her bed at dawn. But surprised that it could have happened? No. The episode is just one more in an ever enlarging array of examples of the vast distance between myth and reality where the competence of organizations is concerned. The organization in this case was nothing less formidable than the security apparatus designed to protect the Queen of England—which turned out to have been, as it seems, on a several-years-long tea break. What a perfect metaphor for the characteristic revelation of our time.

2   There is, of course, something universally and eternally appealing to people in the idea of a single determined individual's confounding a formidable official barrier and making it to the other side, provided no harm is done to anything but the dignity and vanity of the officials who were trying to keep him out. Folks always cheer the lone protesting figure who manages to outwit the forces of exclusion and end up on the VIP side of the wrought-iron gate or velvet rope or whatever. And I think, too, that there is often at least a little mixed feeling, if not an actual whisper of reassurance, in confirmation of the truth that the guys with the guns—the police, the soldiers, the investigators and operatives and guards—are not 100 percent efficient, not supermen who can do whatever they want.

3   **Lore and Nonsense:** But I don't think the caption to this story is the daring and enterprise of a lone, romantic scaler of walls. And I don't think the major message is: thank God the authorities aren't too good (for our own good) at what they do. I think the Buckingham Palace caper is just another element in the crash of our assumptions about power and the trappings of power and the look of power. "Assumptions" is the key word here. We keep learning, though not necessarily believing, that daddy is not all powerful, that the most masterful-seeming and authoritative-looking protectors of the general well-being are often neither masterful nor authoritative, that what seems safe or certain isn't.

(1) *intruder into the Royal bed-chamber.* At dawn on July 9, 1982, Michael Fagan, a 31-year-old, unemployed Londoner with a history of mental problems, climbed the drainpipe at Buckingham Palace unobserved by the Royal Guards, entered Queen Elizabeth's bed chamber unchallenged, and had 12 minutes of uninterrupted conversation with the Queen before the police finally responded.

Clearly we are using wrong standards of judgment, entranced by a veritable
bouquet of romantic lore and nonsense. I mean: all those redcoats and the bear-
skin hats and the changing of the guard and the aura of invincibility and time-
lessness—it all transmits a powerful, if subliminal, signal that things are under
control here, however chaotic they may be somewhere else. I don't know about
you, but I fell for it, and I don't mind saying that I am getting a little embarrassed at the number of times this has happened over the past two decades.   4

For me, it began with the Bay of Pigs, right after the rumors of an impending American-supported action had been confirmed. I well remember sitting
around with a bunch of young friends arguing passionately among ourselves as
to whether this was a justified military action, whether we as a country should
do what John F. Kennedy had authorized. We assumed and did not even bother
to stipulate an American victory. It simply did not occur to us that all those
confident-looking government people with their much vaunted access to secret
information and all those spiffy-looking military types could have it absolutely
wrong, could blow it. Certain things one learned about the frailty and jerry-built
enterprises of the security people during the Watergate years had the same
capacity to astonish. And so, of course, did the information that came out in the
aftermath of the failed hostage-rescue mission at Desert One. The quality of the
Queen's protection fits in nicely with all of this; it gives it a touch of class, puts
a diamond crown on its head.   5

It is true that we all know that our own organizations—the clubs, businesses and bureaucracies within which we work—are not nearly so deliberate
or controlled as they tend to look when the fruit of a series of accidents, confusions and general dishevelments is revealed to the outside world as "policy."
The wry, self-disparaging one-liners that adorn our office-hours coffee mugs and
desk calendars attest to this. So it isn't just the security people. And I suppose
it is also true that the press has played some part in reinforcing these illusions
of omnipotence on the part of uniformed authority, even though we are more
often charged with "tearing it down." We are, after all, blessed with the ability   6

---

(5) *Bay of Pigs.* In April, 1961 President John F. Kennedy authorized an unsuccessful invasion of Cuba at the Bay of Pigs. The attack was planned during the preceding
Eisenhower administration and was carried out by U.S. trained Cuban refugees.

(5) *Watergate Years.* The years between the bungled burglary of the offices of the
Democratic National Committee in the Watergate office and apartment complex, Washington D.C. on June 17, 1972 by exC.I.A. agents in the pay of the Nixon administration
and August 9, 1974 when President Richard Nixon resigned in disgrace. Throughout
those years American television and newspapers gradually revealed an unsavory history
of illegal undercover activity on the part of government officials, often including security
people.

(5) *failed hostage rescue mission at Desert One.* On April 25, 1980, President
Jimmy Carter sponsored an attempt to rescue the diplomats and aides who had been
imprisoned in the American Embassy in Iran since November, 1980. Both the planning
and the execution of the rescue mission, which was to have been accomplished by hel-
icopters landing at an isolated spot in Iran, code-named Desert One, are generally conceded to have been badly bungled.

to characterize our own misapprehensions as universal, calling something a "surprise development" and thus sharing the burden of having been surprised with others. Still, I think that we are talking here about something distinctively to do with military and security forces and that people's widespread illusions on the subject are something more than merely what the press has encouraged us to believe over the years.

7   **Mystique:** It is the "trappings trap" we have all fallen into; we are suckers for the apparatus and appurtenances of power. After Watergate there was a lot of discussion about whether our presidents were enjoying such things too much, and Jimmy Carter declined to make use of many of them. But no one thought to ask whether the all-seeing, all-knowing machinery we have created, the thing with the siren on top and the scowling, chevroned personnel inside, knew what in the hell it was doing. Our perception of life abroad is susceptible to the same confusions: everyone knew the Iraqis would beat the Iranians because they were well-armed and -trained martial-looking third-worlders against a bunch of ululating weirdos carrying pictures of the Ayatollah Khomeini. Everyone knew the Cambodian hadn't been invented who had anything mean or military to him: they all wore pale, loose cotton clothes and smiled a lot and ate squooshy fruit—what kind of a soldier is that?

8   We fall for a uniform, for an air of occidental-style proficiency, for a tough, mean look, for a shako headdress, for the mystique of regimental or magisterial tradition. We better look out. The calculations we base all this on concern a great deal more than drainpipes and people who fantasize about the Queen.

---

(7) *Iraqis would beat the Iranians.* In September, 1980 Iraq invaded Iran. By summer of 1982, when Greenfield wrote her article, Iran had pushed the Iraqi army out of Iran and was itself invading Iraq.

(7) *Ayatollah Khomeini.* After the Iranian revolution of February, 1979, the devout Muslim victors recalled Ruhollah Khomeini, an octogenarian ayatollah (holy man) from exile in Paris to be their political and spiritual leader.

(7) *Cambodian . . . soldier.* Although the Cambodians have long had the reputation of a gentle, nonwarlike people, in 1977 Cambodian insurgents with their Vietnamese allies militarily overpowered the murderous Pol Pot and his followers, all of whom were also Cambodian.

Meg Greenfield. Born 1930. Pulitzer prize-winning editorial writer, editor, and columnist. Greenfield began her career as a reporter and eventually Washington editor for *Reporter Magazine.* Since 1968 she has been with the *Washington Post,* where she is now Editorial page editor. And since 1974 she has written a biweekly column for *Newsweek.* This article was originally published in *Newsweek,* 100 (July 26, 1982), 80.

Part Six

Revision Guide

A/An

A and *an* are both indefinite articles. Use *a* before nouns that begin with consonant sounds and *an* before nouns that begin with vowel sounds.

> EX: *a* sample; *an* example
>
> EX: *an* apple, *a* banana, *an* orange, *a* pear, and two grapes
>
> EX: *a* horse; *an* honest man

See **Article.**

Abbreviations

Although abbreviations are immensely useful in bibliographic and technical
writing and in note taking and personal correspondence, they are rarely appropriate in expository prose. In this sort of writing you should avoid abbreviations
except for those few forms that have become standard. These include:

Abbreviations Followed by Periods

1. Titles when followed by a name (Mr. Benson, Ms. Steinem, Dr. Einstein)
2. Degrees after a name (Jane Pitt, Ph.D., or M.D., or M.S.W.)
3. Initials (R. W. Kane, M. Dorinda Young)
4. Others, such as a.m. and p.m. (which may be capitalized if you choose);
   Jr., Sr.; m.p.h. (miles per hour), r.p.m. (revolutions per minute)

Abbreviations without Periods

1. Government agencies (FBI, CIA, HUD)
2. Radio or television call letters (WKRP, WNRK, CBS)
3 Acronyms (initials which spell a pronounceable word—CORE, WAVES,
   VISTA)

Abbreviations That You Should NOT Use in Formal Writing

1. Days (Sun.) or months (Jan.)
2. Given names (Geo. or Chas.) unless that is how a well-known person
   identifies himself or herself
3. Cities and states (N.Y.C. or Cal.), except the commonly used D.C. for
   District of Columbia
4. Words in addresses (St., N. Blvd.)
5. Courses of instruction (Soc. 101)
6. Words preceding a number (vol., p.)
7. Military, religious, or political titles (Col., Rev., Hon.)
8. Latin abbreviations. *For example* is preferred to *e.g., that is* to *i.e.* Even
   in bibliographical work, *Ibid.* and *op. cit.* have, for the most part, become obsolete.

Rules for Using Abbreviations

1. Abbreviations should not interfere with the regular punctuation of the
   sentence. If an abbreviation falls at the end of a sentence, regular punctuation prevails, except for the period which is not added.

EX: We shall arrive at 6 p.m.
     Shall we come at 6 p.m.?
     It's already 6 p.m.!

Do not space between the period and the final punctuation mark.

2. Identify abbreviations that may be unfamiliar. Most readers would recognize WAVES as the women's branch of the United States Navy, but in using less well-known initials or acronyms, write the title fully once with the initials, and then abbreviate all further references. Two alternatives are:

EX: Mr. Jenkins took over the DPW (Department of Public Works) in December. The DPW now employs four hundred people.

EX: Mr. Jenkins took over the Department of Public Works (DPW) in December.

Above/Below

Writers sometimes refer to their work as if it were written on a single long page. When they say, "We have already discussed this point *above*," they mean that they have discussed it earlier in the work; and when they say "We will have cause to refer to this point *below*," they are suggesting a later discussion. Because the metaphor of a single long page can be confusing, this usage is becoming obsolete, and you should probably avoid it in your own work.

Absolutes

Absolutes are adjective phrases with subjects of their own. You might also think of them as clauses without verbs.

EX: The word processor raced across the page, *its keys rising and falling* with incredible speed.

For a more detailed discussion, see Chapter 6, p. 226.

Accept/Except

Accept means to take or receive. *Except* refers to an exclusion.

EX: We *accept* everything *except* personal checks.

Access/Excess

Access is a noun which means "the ability to get at or use" or "to get into something or some place." It can also refer to the door or entrance itself. *Excess* means "more than enough" (*excess* energy) or "more than a certain amount or degree" (in *excess* of a million dollars).

EX. In an *excess* of misplaced creativity, she gained *access* to the only copy of the final exam.

Acronyms
See **Abreviations, without Periods.**

Active/Passive

A sentence is in the *active* voice when it contains a verb that tells that its subject is actively doing or being something.

> EX: The *dog chased* his tail.

A sentence is in the passive voice when it contains a verb that tells that something is being done to or being suffered by its subject.

> EX: The *tail was chased* by the dog.

The passive version of a sentence is often more awkward than the active version, and frequently confusing and less direct. Because the agent of the action can be omitted in the passive, writers sometimes use this construction deliberately to obscure.

> EX: (active) The political *candidate suggested* that his opponent, J. S. Bigsby, was not as circumspect about his finances as he should be.
> EX: (passive) *It was suggested* that J. S. Bigsby was not as circumspect about his finances as he should be.

Avoid the passive whenever you can. Use it only when you really mean to put the emphasis on the deed rather than upon the doer:

> EX: The man *had been killed* in the night by a person or persons unknown.
> EX: The courtyard *had been ransacked.*

Adjectives

An adjective is a part of speech used to describe a noun. In a sentence an adjective occurs either before the noun it describes (*several* violations, *big* nose, *purple* hat) or in a complementary position. Adjective complements (predicate adjectives) complete forms of the verb "to be":

> EX: His nose is *big.* We were *hungry.* The mouse will be *quick.*

Or they can follow sensory verbs:

> EX: The table feels *smooth.* Pizza tastes *delicious.* Sulfur smells *nasty.*

Even when adjectives follow the verb, as in the preceding examples, they continue to describe the noun or subject.

Articles *(the, a, an),* demonstrative pronouns *(this, that, these, those),* and possessive pronouns *(my, her, his, your, their, its)* also function as adjectives.

Adjective Clauses

An adjective clause is a subordinate (dependent) clause that functions as an adjective in a sentence; that is to say, the clause as a whole describes a noun. Like all clauses, an adjective clause has a subject and a verb. The feature of the adjective clause that keeps it subordinate—that prevents it from standing on its own as a full sentence—is the presence of a relative pronoun. Relative pronouns include *who, which, that, whom,* or *whose* (see **Pronouns: Relative**).

> EX: The hockey player, *who was a surly, ill-tempered man,* was put out of the game.

EX: The man *whose raincoat could not be found* continued in an ill humor for the rest of the day.

Which is appropriate only as a substitute for inanimate objects.

EX: The raincoat, *which had not yet been discovered,* belonged to the ill-humored man.

That, a pronoun that many prefer to *which,* may be used to substitute for any noun—animate or inanimate.

EX: A man *that the world had forgotten* looked sadly at a discarded teddy bear *that sported a well-chewed ear.*

Punctuating Adjective Clauses

Set off adjective clauses with commas when the material they contain is parenthetical and not essential to the meaning of the sentence. Do not use commas when the descriptive material in the clause is essential to identifying the particular person or thing described.

ESSENTIAL—no commas: Gert would never forget *the dog that wagged its tail* so pathetically.
NONESSENTIAL—use commas: Gert would never forget *Rover, who wagged his tail* so pathetically.

(See **Commas: Parenthetical**.)
For a more detailed discussion of adjective clauses, see Chapter 5, pp. 179 ff.

Adverbs

An adverb is a part of speech that describes or modifies a verb. By telling when *(afterwards, now, then),* where *(there, near, far),* how *(fully, slowly, well),* or how often *(often, frequently, seldom),* adverbs mark a sentence for time, place, manner, or frequency. The largest group of adverbs is formed by adding *-ly* to adjectives *(quickly, softly, prettily).*

Unlike nouns, verbs, or adjectives, adverbs can be placed almost anywhere in the sentence. *(The squirrel climbed quickly. Quickly the squirrel climbed. The squirrel quickly climbed.)*

Intensifiers such as *very, most, quite, somewhat,* and *fairly,* which modify adjectives and adverbs, are also traditionally classified as adverbs.

Adverb Clauses

An adverb clause is a subordinate (dependent) clause that functions as an adverb in the sentence; that is to say, the clause as a whole completes the verb and/or marks the sentence for time, place, condition, or cause. As an adverb, the adverb clause can be placed equally well at the beginning or end of a sentence and may also be used in midsentence. The feature of the adverb clause that keeps it subordinate—that prevents it from standing on its own as a full sentence—is the adverbial conjunction with which it begins. Among the most common of these terms are *because, when, if, after, before, since,* and *although.* When an adverb clause follows a sentence, no special punctuation is needed.

When it begins a sentence, however, or is placed in the middle, you should set it off with commas.

> EX: *Because the dance was over,* the orchestra went home.
> EX: The orchestra went home *when the dance was over.*
> EX: The orchestra, *after the dance was over,* went home.

For a more detailed discussion, see Chapter 6, p. 201 ff.

Adverbial Conjunctions
See **Conjunctions.**

Advice/Advise
Advice is a noun.

> EX: My *advice,* Raquel, is to avoid contact sports.

Advise is a verb.

> EX: I would *advise* you to learn to play bridge.

Affect/Effect
When used as verbs, *affect* and *effect* have similar—though not identical—meanings. *Affect* means "to influence" and is used primarily in the emotional sense. *Effect* means to bring about.

> EX: How did Marjorie's speech *affect* you?
> EX: He lowered prices to *effect* economic change.

Affect is not used as a noun except in a narrow, technical sense (in the field of psychology). *Effect,* when used as a noun, means "result":

> EX: The price change had little economic *effect.*

Aggravate/Irritate
Irritate means to annoy or to chafe.

> EX: Try not to *irritate* your boss before you request a raise.
> EX: The buckle on the shoe began to *irritate* the child's foot.

Aggravate means to make worse an already bad situation or irritation.

> EX: His boss's irritation was *aggravated* by his request for a raise.
> EX: The sore on the child's foot was *aggravated* by the rubbing of the buckle.

Remember, *aggravation* occurs only when a situation is already painful, angry, or unpleasant.

Agreement: Pronouns with Antecedents
A pronoun takes the place of a noun. (See **Pronoun; Pronouns, Demonstrative; Pronouns, Indefinite; Pronouns, Interrogative; Pronouns, Personal; Pronouns, Reflexive;** and **Pronouns, Relative.**) Somewhere in the words preceding a pronoun there must be a definite word (or phrase) for which the pronoun is a substitute. The pronoun must point definitely to that word or

phrase and, in the case of personal pronouns, must resemble this antecedent in number (singular—*she, he*—or plural—*they*) and gender (masculine—*he, him, his*—or feminine—*she, her*). In the case of relative pronouns, the pronoun must also agree in humanity (human—*who, whom*—or nonhuman—*which*).

> EX: Jack, *who* was dressed in *his* red jacket, Jill, *who* wore *her* knitted cap, and *their* dog, *which* was clad in *its* warm blanket, shivered in the biting wind which greeted them on *their* winter walk.

Compound Antecedents

Agreement in gender is clear when both elements of a compound antecedent are of the same sex.

> EX: Neither *Jack* nor *Tom* could find *his* shoes.

The gender of the pronoun becomes a problem, however, when the sex of the antecedents differ.

> EX: Neither *Jack* nor *Jill* could find *his or her* shoes.

His or her can become awkward. *Their,* being plural, would be incorrect in a *neither/nor* context (see **Agreement: Subject and Verb**). In such cases, it is better to rewrite, making the antecedent clearly plural:

> EX: *Both Jack and Jill* searched for *their* shoes without success.

Hazy Antecedents

When your reader cannot be quite sure which of two nouns is the antecedent for a pronoun, you have a hazy antecedent.

> EX: Dad told John *he* had an appointment with the dentist.

He could mean either *Dad* or *John.* Rephrase: Dad mentioned *John's* dental appointment to *him.*

Ghostly Antecedents

A ghostly antecedent must be made to appear in sentences like these:

> INCORRECT: Sally saw all her friends at Christmas. It had all the qualities of a
> class reunion.

It refers to a meeting or party which is never mentioned. The antecedent of *it* is a "ghost" which might appear in this form:

> CORRECT: Sally saw all her friends at Christmas at a *party that* had all the quali-
> ties of a class reunion.

Ghosts of this sort, like all ghosts, should be avoided wherever possible.

Never use pronouns to mean, vaguely, "all the stuff I just said." Constructions like the following should be carefully edited to make them more specific and more clear.

> INCORRECT: Jan has long wanted to spend a summer in Italy. *This* was on her
> mind all the time. *It* kept interfering with her studies. She finally
> made up her mind to take the trip, *which* surprised no one.

CORRECT: Jan had long wanted to spend a summer in Italy. *This desire* was on her mind all the time. *Dreams of Roman fountains and Venetian canals* kept interfering with her studies. She finally made up her mind to take the trip, *a decision which* surprised no one.

Gender Related Antecedents
See **Gender.**

Agreement: Subject and Verb

Subject and verb must agree in number; that is to say, a singular subject takes a singular verb and a plural subject takes a plural verb.

EX: This *student likes* classes. These *students like* weekends.

When a sentence is inverted to begin with *here* or *there,* the verb still agrees with the subject—even though the subject now follows the verb:

EX: Here *is* your *coat.* Here *are* your *coats.*
EX: There *are* two *people* in the boat. There *is* one *person* in the boat.

There are four situations where errors in agreement commonly occur: when a phrase comes between a subject and verb, when the subject is compound, when the subject is a pronoun, and when a singular subject appears to be plural.

Subject Accompanied by a Phrase
RULE: The subject of a sentence CANNOT be part of a prepositional phrase. And, of course, the verb must match the subject.

EX: All the *legs* of the lamb <u>*were broken.*</u> (*Of the lamb* is a prepositional phrase.)

Compound Subject
RULE A: When a sentence has two or more subjects (either singular or plural) that are connected by *and,* make sure the verb is plural:

EX: Both *Janet and Phil fail* to realize how much their whispering annoys their professor.

EXCEPTION: When two nouns are coupled together in such a way that they represent one thing, they take a singular verb:

EX: *Peanut butter and jelly is* my favorite sandwich.

RULE B: When two or more singular subjects are connected by *or, nor,* or *but,* use a singular verb.

EX: Neither *Washington nor Jefferson is* my favorite president.
EX: Not only *Mr. Perry,* but also *his partner,* <u>*was*</u> away.

RULE C: When one of the subjects connected by *or, nor,* or *but* is singular and the other plural, the verb agrees with the closer subject.

EX: Neither *George nor* the *dragons <u>are</u>* ready to fight.
EX: Neither the *dragons nor George <u>is</u>* ready to fight.
EX: <u>*Is*</u> either *George or* the *dragons* really going to fight?

RULE D: Singular subjects followed by *as well as, in addition to, no less than,* or *together with* require a singular verb.

EX: *John* as well as his friend *regrets* the incident.

Pronoun Subject

RULE A: Pronouns that refer to a single being take a singular verb: *each, every, everyone, everybody, somebody, anybody, nobody, no one, any, anyone, anybody, either, neither.*

EX: *Everybody seems* happy today.

RULE B: *None* and *all* may take either singular or plural verbs depending upon what they refer to.

EX: *None* of the soldiers *are* willing to volunteer.
EX: *None* of the pie *has* been eaten yet.

RULE C: Pronouns that take a plural verb include *several, both, many,* and *few.*

EX: *"Many are called,* but *few are chosen."*

RULE D: When *it* is the subject of a sentence, the verb is always singular, regardless of what follows the verb.

EX: *It is* the New York Yankees.

RULE E: Personal Pronouns. When personal pronouns are used with the verb *to be (am, is, are, was, were),* the verb must also agree with its subject in person:

EX: *She was* saying again and again: *"I am* to be Queen of the Prom. *You are* to be my partner."

In the case of a compound subject, the verb agrees in person with the closer pronoun.

EX: Neither she nor *I am* wrong.

Singular Subject Which Appears Plural

RULE: All singular subjects, however they appear, take singular verbs.

1. *Singular words that end in "s."* Examples of such nouns that are singular in meaning include *dynamics, electronics, ethics, news, economics, mumps.*

   EX: *Electronics has become* a major field of study.

2. *Titles.* A title takes a singular verb even though it uses a plural noun or pronoun.

   EX: *"Sixty Minutes" is* aired on Sundays.

3. *Numbers.* Plural numbers take a singular verb when they are used to indicate a total or a unit.

   EX: *A million dollars is* the prize.

4. *Collective Nouns.* Collective nouns (singular forms which represent more than one person or thing considered as a unit) take a singular verb.

> EX: The *swarm* of bees *is* heading this way.

EXCEPTION: Collective nouns take a plural verb when they are not considered as a unit, but this syntax seldom occurs.

> EX: The *jury were* not in agreement.

If that sort of sentence sounds awkward to you, rewrite is as: The *members* of the jury *were* not in agreement.

Allegory

Allegory may be thought of as expanded symbolism. (See **Symbol.**) An allegory is a narrative which, in addition to having its own validity when read literally, uses its characters and situations as interrelated symbols that present a different message on the figurative level. (See **Figurative Language.**)

Although we usually associate allegory with such narrative writing as Swift's *Gulliver's Travels,* Orwell's *Animal Farm,* and Aesop's fables, expository essayists, such as James Thurber, sometimes include allegorical passages that help them support their theses.

Alliteration

Alliteration is the repetition of the sounds at the beginning of syllables.

> EX: The grim, ungainly, ghostly, gaunt, and ominous bird of yore.   (Poe)
> EX: A trumpet that hunters hold to their ears so that they can hear the distant music of the hounds.   (White)

See **Assonance** and **Consonance.**

All of

Do not use *all of* when you mean *all.*

> EX: *all the money, all the children, all the time.*

Only use *all of* before pronouns.

> EX: *all of us, all of you, all of them.*

All Ready/Already

Each of these expressions has its own meaning. They are not interchangeable. *All ready* means completely prepared.

> EX: He is *all ready* for Saturday's game.

Already refers to time.

> EX: She had *already* studied for the quiz.

All Right

There is no word spelled *alright.*

EX: It was *all right* with Attila if his troops were too tired to loot, but he did insist on a little pillaging.

All Together/Altogether

These two expressions have different meanings and are not interchangeable. *All together* means collectively, everyone at one time or place.

EX: *All together* now—pull!

Altogether means completely.

EX: Your proposal is *altogether* unacceptable.

Allusion

Allusion is a kind of imagery (in whatever form—metaphor, simile, symbol, connotative language) in which the describable thing (objective correlative) to which the author's indescribable feeling or abstract idea is being compared involves reference to a literary or historical situation. Through allusion authors can include the world of the other situation (or literary work) in their own and can call upon whatever emotions their readers associate with that other situation or work to enrich their own.

EX: It is the equivalent of the Montagues and the Capulets collaborating on a baby shower.   (Morrow allusion to Shakespeare's *Romeo and Juliet.*)

Allusion/Illusion

An *illusion* is something that appears to be, but does not really exist. *Allusion* comes from the verb *to allude* and means "the act of making a reference" or the reference itself. *Allusion* also refers to imagery that contains this sort of reference. See **Allusion.**

EX: In her lecture the professor made an *allusion* to Macbeth's *illusion* of Banquo's ghost.

A Lot

A lot consists of two words. Though it is proper to write such sentences as "He ate a lot of beans," the expression is too informal for most serious essays.

Although Clause

"Although clause" is a shorthand way of referring to that portion of the working thesis statement that sets up the point of view that the thesis itself refutes. By extension, the term *although clause* can also refer to that portion of the composition which presents an alternative way of thinking. The model "although clause" fits the format:

Although others say *x*, *y* is closer to the truth.
or
Despite *x* to the contrary, *y* is true.

While identifying the "although clause" is highly useful in discovering a thesis and setting up the structure of a composition, you will not necessarily want to use it in its exact phrasing in your finished compositions.

Alumna/Alumnus

Both of these words refer to a graduate of a school, or even to a person who once attended a particular school. *Alumna* is feminine (plural, *alumnae*). *Alumnus* is masculine (plural, *alumni*).

> EX: Karen is an *alumna* of Oberlin, Ann and Sue are *alumnae* of Chicago, Dan is an *alumnus* of Michigan, and George and David are *alumni* of Case Western Reserve. They are all *alumni* of midwestern universities.

(When sexes are mixed, use the masculine form.)

Ambiguity

An ambiguous sentence is one that can be understood in more than one way.

> FAULTY: The doctor told him that weekly visits would no longer be a good idea.

Without further explanation of that ambiguous sentence, the patient might deduce either that he need not see the doctor again or that he needs to see the doctor more often or less often. In such situations, rewrite.

Ambiguity can also result from faulty punctuation.

> EX: Marty said, "Sally is dead." "Marty," said Sally, "is dead."

In such instances, punctuation changes everything—especially for Marty and Sally.

Among/Between

Between is used when referring to two people or things. If more than two are involved, you must use *among*.

> EX: Richie and Lynn made plans to divide the money *between* them, but Robbie, Russ, and Ruth decided the money should be divided *among* all of them.

Although some people think that *between you and I* sounds more elegant, the correct form is *between you and me*. It is true that, although correct, *between him and her* sounds terrible. Reword such awkward phrases.

An

See **A/An.**

Analogy

An analogy is an extended simile that is usually used to support an argument (see **Simile**). In an analogy the explicit comparison of the simile is extended to show a point by point likeness between the two objects, events, or ideas.

The validity of the conclusion to be drawn from an analogy is completely dependent upon (1) how many points of comparison can be made and, even more important, (2) how closely related these similarities are to the point of the argument.

Take, for instance, the two examples of analogy given on p. 319. In the first Morrow uses the fact that the Maya kept both a profane and a priestly calendar to suggest that it is natural for "Western science and religion [to] fall into two different conceptions of the universe, two different vocabularies." In the second, Will gives a long and impressive list of similarities in the situations of the Czechs just before Munich and of the Israelis today to suggest that the Israelis have sound historic reasons to be wary of depending on "the conscience of the West." The connection between the Mayan calendar and Western ideology is tenuous at best and Morrow's sketchy linkage of the two does little to enhance the connection. Will's extended and carefully drawn analogy is much more convincing.

However, because there are always some differences in analogous situations and ideas, argument from analogy can never be completely valid. Nevertheless, analogies do permit readers to understand one set of ideas in terms of another and, when used cautiously, can be highly effective.

Angry/Mad

If you want to convey in writing the idea of rage, irritation, or fury, you should use *angry* and not *mad. Mad* means "mentally ill or deranged."

> EX: I am *angry* about his treatment of the poor. I must have been *mad* to have voted for him.

Antecedents

See **Agreement: Pronouns with antecedents.**

Antithetical Balance

See **Balanced and contrasting parallelism.**

Antonym

An antonym is a word which means the opposite or almost the opposite of another word. The antonym of *big* might be *little, small, tiny, diminutive,* or any other word with similar meaning.

Antonyms may reflect opposite action (lose-find), qualities (light-dark), or sex (boy-girl, rooster-hen).

Anxious/Eager

Both words refer to anticipation, but *anxious* implies a worried, fearful anticipation and *eager* refers to a joyful and enthusiastic anticipation.

> EX: Cheryl was *anxious* about her test scores.
> EX: Chris was *eager* to learn to drive.

Apostrophe

An apostrophe (') is a mark of punctuation that has two functions: to replace the missing letters in contractions and to indicate possession.

1. Use the apostrophe to punctuate contractions.

EX: cannot = can't; has not = hasn't; do not = don't; would not = wouldn't; he is = he's; we have = we've; it is = it's; they are = they're

EXCEPTION: will not = won't

2. Use an apostrophe to signify ownership by adding it *after* the person(s) or thing(s) that the object(s) belongs to. Add an *s after* the apostrophe if the owner is single or has a non-*s* plural. You do not need to add an *s* if the plural already has one.

EX: John's dog; Harry's hats; a house's chimney; a dog's tail; a woman's magazine; the houses' chimneys; the dogs' tails; women's magazines

EXCEPTION: Omit the apostrophe from *its* when it is used as a possessive pronoun.

EX: *Its* fur was mussed.

See **Double Possessive.**

Around

Do not use *around* before a number. Use *about* or *approximately.*

EX: He was *about* thirty years old.

EX: It was *approximately* fifteen centimeters away from the edge.

Articles

An article is a part of speech, one of three words *(a, an,* and *the)* which modify a noun. Articles are often classed with adjectives as modifiers of nouns. *The* is a definite article. *A* is indefinite. *An* is the indefinite article used with nouns which begin with a vowel.

EX: Jan drove *the* car.

The makes the sample sentence refer to a particular car, one that has been identified earlier in the composition. This is not the case in the following examples:

EX: Jan drove *a* car. Jan drove *an* automobile.

Here no particular car or automobile is intended. It is the general idea of this kind of motor transportation that is important.

As/Like

As and *like* both convey the idea of comparison. *Like,* however, is a preposition that is followed by an object. *As* is a conjunction that introduces a clause containing a subject and a verb—although sometimes the verb is "understood."

EX: She doesn't type *as* neatly as George [does].

EX: He has a voice *like* a German shepherd's.

EX: He looks *like* his father.

EX: He does not work day and night *as* his father [does].

If you use *like his father* in the preceding sentence, you might mean that he does not work hard just like his father [does not work hard]. The intended meaning is that his father does work hard, of course.

    Like cannot mean *as if* or *as though.*

       INCORRECT: He raised his fist like he was going to hit him.

Use *as if he were* to correct the sentence.

As/Since

As is an adverbial conjunction that either indicates comparison (see **As/Like**) or suggests the passing of time. It does not imply causality. *As,* therefore, can mean *while,* but it should never be used to mean *since* or *because.*

    INCORRECT: *As I had to wait,* I brought along a book.
    CORRECT: I read a book *as I was waiting* in order to pass the time.
    CORRECT: *Since I had to wait,* I brought along a book.

Assonance

Assonance is the repetition of vowel sounds.

    EX: From the molten golden notes
        What a liquid ditty floats (Poe)
    EX: This week, many will be reminded that no explosion of atoms generates so
        hopeful a light (White)

See **Alliteration** and **Consonance.**

Assure/Ensure/Insure

All of these words have the sense of providing sureness, certainty. *Assure* carries the idea of a promise; it is frequently used to suggest avoiding worry or concern.

    EX: I *assure* you that the monster is really dead.

Ensure means to make certain.

    EX: This pass will *ensure* your admittance to the trial.

Insure almost always refers to the business of paying to protect the value of a life or property.

    EX: We tried to *insure* our house against mud-slides, but the cost in California
        is too high.

Asterisk

An asterisk (*) is sometimes used instead of a number reference in writing where only a few footnotes appear.

    EX: Sarah Jones had played many roles by the time she was forty.*

The "footnote" would then look like this:

    *She was most acclaimed for her work in *Candide* in 1945, *Hedda Gabler* in 1947,
    and in *Romeo and Juliet* in 1949.

Auxiliary Verbs

Auxiliary verbs combine with action verbs so that these verbs can express a greater variety of times and purposes. There are two kinds of auxiliary verbs: helping verbs and modals. Helping verbs are the forms of *be* and *have* that combine with present and past participles.

> EX: Joey *was fighting.* Jane *has been playing* in the mud. Gina's mittens *were left* behind. Aunt Selma *will be tempted* to spank.

Modals include such verbs as *should, would, may, can, must, do.* They are used before the present-tense form of verbs as well as before those verbs that have helping-verb attachments.

> EX: Aunt Selma *would have been tempted* to spank the children, and *might have* even *spanked* them, if she *did* not *remember* the old saying: "You *can catch* more flies with honey than with vinegar."

Await/Wait

Await takes an object. You can *await* my *arrival,* *await* the baby's birth, *await* the *holidays. Wait* does not take an object. You just *wait.* But if there is an object to deal with, you can *wait for* something. *Wait on* means to serve (as in a restaurant). *Wait on* never means the same as *wait for.*

> INCORRECT: Let's not *wait on* him to get here.
> CORRECT: Let's not *wait for* him to get here.

Bad/Badly

Bad is an adjective, *badly* an adverb.

> EX: The painter had done a *bad* job, and so the house was *badly* painted.

Problems arise when the word is used with verbs like *feel.* When *feel* is used as a linking verb, it takes a predicate adjective, Thus, *I feel bad* means I feel ill. (*I feel badly* implies there is something wrong with my sense of touch.)

Balanced and Contrasting Parallelism

Balanced parallelism, like serial parallelism, is the repetition of similar syntactic constructions (parts of speech, phrases, clauses) with similar sound and meaning. In balanced parallelism, however, the parallels are constructed in pairs, the two items balancing one another with a conjunction or mark of punctuation acting as a balance point.

> EX: Eat not to dullness; drink not to elevation.   (Franklin)

In contrasting parallelism (or antithetical balance) the balanced items are the contradiction or the antithesis of each other.

> EX: The urge to obliterate death is the urge to extend life.   (Plumb)

For a more complete discussion, see Chapter 7, p. 242 ff. See **Parallelism.**

Be

The verb *to be* is an irregular verb that, alone among the verbs in our language, has retained most of the Old English inflections. Even today, both the present and the past tense forms change with first, second, and third person in the singular and the plural.

I *am*	I *was*
You *are*	You *were*
He, she, or it *is*	He, she or it *was*
We *are*	We *were*
They *are*	They *were*

The past participle is (*have, has*) *been*. The verb *to be* is particularly important because not only is it the verb most often used in English, but it also combines with the participles of the other verbs to form other tenses and the passive voice. (See **Auxiliary Verbs; Active/Passive.**)

Begin—Irregular Verb
They begin; they began; they have begun.

Behalf of
In behalf of and *on behalf of* mean two different things. *On behalf of* means in someone's place. Miles Standish proposed to Priscilla *on behalf of* John Alden or in John's place for John.

   In behalf of implies for the good of or for the benefit of. We raise funds *in behalf of* charities. We speak *in behalf of* his candidacy. When we replace the candidate and speak his thoughts, we are speaking *on his behalf.*

Below
See **Above/Below.**

Beside/Besides
Beside means "at the side of." *Besides* means "furthermore" or "in addition to."

   EX: I like to walk *beside* you. *Besides,* I have no other friends.

Between/Among
See **Among/Between.**

Biannual/Bimonthly/Biweekly
Biannual means once every two years. *Biennial* means the same. A *biennium* is a two-year period. *Bimonthly* means every two months. *Biweekly* means once every two weeks.

   EX: Tony owned so many pieces of property that he could inspect them only *biannually.*

(See also **Semiannual**.)

Bite—Irregular Verb
They bite; they bit; they have bitten.

Blame for/Blame on
Blame on is incorrect.

   INCORRECT: He *blamed* his stiffness *on* the required daily exercise. (He does not really mean to blame his stiffness.)

> CORRECT: He *blamed* the required daily exercise *for* his stiffness. (Here the exercise rightly takes the blame.)

Brackets

Use brackets ([]) when you are quoting another author and wish to include your own editorial comment or to add a word or words to make that author's syntax conform to your own in the surrounding material.

In the Quotation

> EX: By mid-April, when other kids' teams were girding for Homeric battles at the top of their league, my heroes [the Cubs] had wilted like salted slugs and begun their gadarene descent [like the headlong descent of the herd of swine at Gadara after Jesus had transferred to them the demons who had been bedevilling the local populace] to the bottom.   (Will)
> or
> My heroes had wilted like salted slugs and begun their gadarene descent to the bottom. [Note Will's use of classical and biblical imagery.]

In Your Text:

> EX: In "Chicago Cubs, Overdue," George Will speaks of the Cubs baseball team of his childhood as "[his] heroes [wilting] like salted slugs."

See **Ellipsis Points.**

Break—Irregular Verb

They break; they broke; they have broken.

Bring—Irregular Verb

They bring flowers; they brought flowers; they have brought flowers.

Bring/Take

You *bring* something *here.* You *take* something *there.*

> INCORRECT: Red Riding Hood, *bring* your Grandma some goodies.
> CORRECT: Red Riding Hood, *take* your Grandma some goodies, and don't *bring* the wolf home with you.

Can/May

Can indicates ability; *may* indicates permission.

> EX: I *can* climb to the top of that tree if my mother says that I *may*.

Capital/Capitol

The only time you use *capitol* is when you refer to the center of government, the building itself. All other uses are spelled *capital.*

> EX: We visited the *Capitol* when Congress was in session.
> EX: That is a *capital* idea. I should reinvest my *capital.*
> EX: He committed a *capital* crime.
> EX: Do we need *capital* letters?
> EX: Is Austin the *capital* of Texas?

Capitalization

Use capital letters only when absolutely necessary. There are a number of occasions when they are necessary:

1. Capitalize the proper names of particular persons, places, or things.

    EX: We drove our Chevrolet Impala to see Uncle James and my three aunts in South Dakota.

2. Capitalize beginnings of sentences and lines of verse.

    EX: Little Bo Peep
    Has lost her sheep
    And can't tell where to find them.
    EX: Some girls are very careless.

3. Capitalize the pronoun "I" and the interjection "O."

    EX: And then I prayed, "Help us, O Lord."

4. Capitalize important words in titles. Do not capitalize articles or conjunctions and prepositions less than five letters long unless they are the first word of the title.

    EX: *A Man for All Seasons, Catcher in the Rye,* "Rock Around the Clock," *All About Eve*

5. Capitalize personal titles and titles of high office.

    EX: Mr. and Mrs. Abercrombie met the Secretary of State and his private secretary.

6. Capitalize the first word of outline headings.
7. Capitalize names of days, months, holidays, and holy days.

    EX: This year Yom Kippur fell on Thursday.
    EX: St. Patrick's Day is always on March 17.

8. Capitalize school courses but not general areas of study.

    EX: She always enjoyed geography, but Geography 101 was a difficult course.

9. Capitalize adjectives derived from proper nouns.

    EX: "Has anyone seen an American ship?" asked Cho Cho San.
    EX: I have studied my English for hours.

10. Capitalize directional words only when they designate a specific area.

    EX: The South has always been noted for its hospitality, but birds fly north in the spring.

11. Capitalize nouns or pronouns referring to the Deity.

    EX: Do not lightly invoke the name of God.
    EX: The priest called to Him in prayer.

12. Capitalize seasons only when personified.

> EX: Here comes Old Man Winter again.
> EX: A winter in Buffalo is a numbing experience.

Some "don'ts" and "not necessaries":

1. Sometimes a.m., p.m., jr., and sr. are capitalized, but it is unnecessary.
2. Never capitalize the word *the* before a periodical title, such as the *Cincinnati Post,* the *Philadelphia Inquirer.*
3. Some writers capitalize the first word after a colon, but you need not unless a question follows.

> EX: There are three things you must do: Pay attention to directions, trust the leader, and bring insect repellent.

Catch—Irregular Verb

They catch balls; they caught balls; they have caught balls.

Center Around/Circle Around

Center around is incorrect usage. *Center* is a point and cannot circle anything. You might use *center on* or *center at.* You may also find it appropriate to use *revolve around* or *gather around.*

Similarly do not use *circle around. Circle* means *travel around.*

> INCORRECT: The Indians were always shown *circling around* the wagon train.
> CORRECT: The Indians were always shown *circling* the wagon train.

Cite/Sight/Site

Cite, sight, and *site* are unrelated words that happen to be pronounced the same.

> EX: I can *cite* the article in the zoning laws that prohibits a construction *site* from filling up with rubbish and becoming a distasteful *sight.*

Clauses

A clause contains a subject, its verb, and their modifiers. When a clause stands on its own (and begins with a capital letter and concludes with a period—or question mark or exclamation point), it is a sentence.

> EX: Many birds fly south in winter.

When such a clause forms part of a sentence, it is called a *main clause (independent clause):*

> EX: Many birds fly south in winter; their migrating is a delight to see.
>
>   main clause   main clause

When a clause has an element about it that prevents it from standing on its own, it is called a *subordinate clause (dependent clause)* and must be attached to a main clause to be a part of a sentence. Subordinate clauses function as adjectives, adverbs, or nouns in their sentences and are called by those names.

ADJECTIVE CLAUSE: Birds (which) *cannot stand the cold* fly south in winter.
ADVERB CLAUSE: (Because) *some birds cannot stand the cold,* they fly south in winter.
NOUN CLAUSE: Everyone knows (that) *many birds fly south in winter.*

(Circled in each example is the element that keeps the clause subordinate.)
See **Adjective Clauses, Adverb Clauses, Noun Clauses.**
See also Chapter 5, p. 161.

Collective Nouns

A collective noun names a class of person or things: *family, convention, herd, jury.* It is plural in meaning and singular in form. When it refers to a unit, it requires a singular verb. When its parts are not acting as a unit, it requires a plural verb.

> EX: The committee is in agreement. The committee are not in agreement.

The singular verb is most often used.
See **Noun.**

Colloquial Language

Colloquial language is informal language used in everyday speech but seldom appropriate to formal writing. The more colloquialisms you use in writing, the more informal your writing becomes.

> EX: If Harvey *totals* his father's car again, he will really be *in a jam.* He's definitely *spacy.*

Colons

The colon (:) is a mark of punctuation that has a limited use. It signifies "namely," "to wit," "that is," or "Let me explain" and thus is used to introduce examples or to set up explanations. The following instances are typical:

> EX: The food we live on is kids' food: pizza, hot dogs, fried chicken, ice cream, and hamburgers." (Alexander) (The colon here may be translated "namely.")
> EX: None of this is cheap: the capsule costs four thousand dollars, and then there are the freezing costs. (Plumb) (Translate this colon "that is.")
> EX: The American way of death is not novel: seen in proper historical perspective, it reaches back not only down the centuries but down the millenniums, for it is a response to a deep human need. (Plumb) (Here the colon could be translated "Let me explain.")

You should also use colons in the following technical ways:

1. Follow the salutation of a formal letter with a colon (Dear Sir or Madam:)
2. Separate with a colon hour and minutes (9:45), biblical chapter and verse (Acts 2:27), act and scene numbers (II:iii), volume and page of a periodical (*Saturday Review* 16: 197), and place of publication and publisher (Columbus, O.: Charles E. Merrill Publishing Co.).

3. In dialogue follow the speaker's name with a colon:

EX: Penny: The sky is falling!
Foxy: Come hide in my cave, my dear.

4. In typing, double space after a colon (except with time, biblical citations, play citations, and volume/page citations). Use a capital letter after a colon when a question follows.

EX: The question must be asked: What will be done about these homeless immigrants?

Comma

The comma (,) is a mark of punctuation that is used to signify a pause, but not a full stop, within a sentence. Note the following rules for its use.

Main Clauses

RULE: Use a comma to separate the main clauses of a compound sentence when the second (or further) clause is introduced by a coordinating conjunction *(but, and, or, nor, for,* or *yet)*. Unless such a sentence is very short, insert a comma after the first clause, before the conjunction.

EX: The Scout leader tried to keep the boys together, for he did not want to search the zoo at closing time ever again.

CAUTION:

Do not use a comma between main clauses that are not also separated by a coordinating conjunction. Such sentences require a full stop, that is, a semicolon or a period.

EX: The Scout leader tried to keep the boys together; he did not want to search the zoo again.

It is also wiser to use a semicolon for this central separation if you have used commas within the clauses. See **Comma Splice.**

Introductory Phrases and Clauses

RULE: Use commas to set off introductory phrases and clauses.

EX: After the rain, (or "After the rain was over,") the team returned to the practice field.

Parenthetical, Extraneous, or Interrupting Sentence Elements

RULE: Use commas to surround interrupting material to set it off from the rest of the sentence. (Always use two commas for such interruptions unless one side is already marked by some other mark of punctuation or the beginning of the sentence.) Some examples:

1. Interrupting phrases (*Limping badly,* Jan ran, *or tried to run,* all the way around the stadium.)
2. Adverbials (Harry returned, *nevertheless,* and brought the money with him. He had already spent some of it, *however.*)

3. Nonessential *who, which, that* clauses (The book, *which was written in eight months,* has been a best-seller since December.)
4. Appositives (Beatrice, *the waitress in the smart beige uniform,* spilled the punch on Dr. Miller.)
5. Mild interjections (*Well,* let's go. *Why,* here's Charley.)
6. Direct address (*Bill,* wait for us.)

Quotations
RULE: Use commas to set off direct quotations.

> EX: "Why," she asked, "are you always late?"

Elements in a Series
RULE: Use commas to separate parts of a series. The comma is optional before the final conjunction.

> EX: We brought pots, pans, dishes, and glasses.

Miscellaneous
RULE: Use commas in certain more technical situations:

1. Between the day and year in dates (Sunday, December 7, 1941)
2. Between places in addresses (Philadelphia, Pennsylvania)
3. Between names and titles or degrees (Patrick Sanders, Jr., or Jane Killane, Ph.D.)
4. To divide numbers of over four and sometimes over three digits, separating groups of three (6345; 6,345; 1,233,987)
5. After the salutation and closing in letters (Dear Grandma, and Yours truly, Marie)

Clarity
RULE: Use a comma to promote clarity.

> EX: Mr. Smith, our dean has been arrested.
> EX: Mr Smith, our dean, has been arrested.

In the case of the comma, fewer is better. Use commas only as needed. Many novice writers overdose on commas.

Comma Splice (Comma Fault)
A comma splice, sometimes called a "comma fault," produces a run-on sentence when a comma is incorrectly used in place of a period or in place of a semicolon between independent clauses. See **Comma, Semicolon,** and **Run-On Sentence.**

When two independent clauses are not connected with a coordinating conjunction *(and, but, or, nor, yet, for,* or *so),* you have separate sentences and should divide with a period or a semicolon, not a comma.

> INCORRECT: Everyone applauded Paul, he was a star.
> CORRECT: Everyone applauded Paul. He was a star.
> CORRECT: Everyone applauded Paul, *for* he was a star.

When two independent clauses are joined by an adverbial connective *(indeed, therefore, however, nevertheless),* a semicolon is called for.

INCORRECT: Her dress was perfect, nevertheless the bride looked unhappy.
CORRECT: Her dress was perfect; nevertheless, the bride looked unhappy.

EXCEPTION: If a sentence has three or more independent clauses which are parallel, the comma is an acceptable divider.

EX: "Children disobey their parents, students ignore teachers, teens sneer at police, and young men ignore the draft registration laws," said Grandpa.

Common Noun
See **Noun.**

Compared to/Compared with
Use *compared to* when you are showing that you consider two things are alike. Use *compared with* to show relationships, either alike or different.

EX: Her bedroom could be *compared to* the third day of a four-day rummage sale. But *compared with* her brother's room, hers belonged in *House Beautiful.*

Comparison of Modifiers
Most adjectives and adverbs have two degrees of comparison: comparative and superlative.

EX: Adjective: pretty, prettier, prettiest
Adverb: beautifully, more beautifully, most beautifully

Most adjectives of one or two syllables form comparatives and superlatives by adding *-er* and *-est.* Longer adjectives are preceded by *more* and *most.*

EX: tall, taller, tallest; beautiful, more beautiful, most beautiful

Some adjectives use both forms.

EX: This was the *happiest* day of her life. She was the *most happy* bride we had ever seen.

Some adjectives have irregular forms of comparison.

EX: good, better, best; little, less, least; bad, worse, worst.

When comparing two persons or things, use a comparative adjective. When comparing three or more persons or things, use a superlative adjective.

EX: Meg is the *smarter* of the two. Jane is the *smartest* girl in our class.

Remember always to complete comparisons.

INCORRECT: Scrooge was certainly the stingiest.
CORRECT: Scrooge was certainly the stingiest man in London.

See **Modify/Modifier.**

Complected

Complected is heard in spoken language, but it is not a word. The correct word is *complexioned.* It is an awkward word and there are better ways of expressing your thought.

> CORRECT: Dark-*complexioned* people do not sunburn as quickly as fair people.
> BETTER: People with dark *complexions . . .*

Complement

The complement, as its name implies, is the part of the sentence that completes the verb. Most frequently it takes the action of the verb and serves as its object. *Ball* is the *direct object* of the verb *hit* in this example:

> EX: Ray hit the *ball.*

Sometimes, however, the complement refers to the subject. If it is an adjective describing the subject, it is called a *predicate adjective:*

> EX: Ray was *courageous.*

If the complement is a noun (or pronoun) equated with the subject by a form of the verb "to be," it is called a *predicate nominative:*

> EX: The ball was a hard-hitting *missile. (ball = missile)*

In sentences with a predicate nominative, the predicate nominative and the subject may be reversed without changing the meaning of the sentence.

> EX: Your trash may be my *treasure.* My treasure may be your *trash.*
> EX: The caller is *he.* He is the *caller.*

See **Predicate.**

Complement/Compliment

A *complement* is that which completes. In grammar it refers to the part of the sentence that completes the verb (see the preceding discussion). It can also mean the full quota, of a ship's crew or an army unit, for instance. Although pronounced the same, *compliment* is an unrelated word meaning words of courtesy or praise or, when used as a verb, the giving of such words.

> EX: He *complimented* the Captain on filling his ship's *complement* so quickly.

Complex Sentence

A complex sentence contains one independent (main) clause and one or more dependent (subordinate) clauses (see **Clauses**). Adjective, adverbial, and noun clauses can all form complex sentences.

> EX: Jerry, *who could not be lazier,* sat on the dock all day. (Adjective clause)
> EX: *When Jerry sat on the dock all day,* he could not have been lazier. (Adverb clause)
> EX: *That Jerry could not have been lazier* was clear to all. (Noun clause)

See **Sentence.**

Compound Sentence

A compound sentence has two or more main (independent) clauses, joined by coordinating conjunctions *(and, but, or, nor, for, yet)* or by a semicolon and an adverbial conjunction (*therefore, besides,* etc.) or by a semicolon alone.

> EX: Jerry sat on the dock all day; he caught a cold and two fish.

See **Clauses** and **Sentence.**

Compound-Complex Sentence

The compound-complex sentence has two or more independent (main) clauses and one or more dependent (subordinate) clauses.

> EX: Jerry, who had never been lazier, sat on the dock all day; yet he still caught two delicious fish.

See **Clauses, Complex Sentence, Compound Sentence, Sentence.**

Conjunctions

A conjunction is a part of speech used to join words, phrases, or clauses.

1. Coordinating conjunctions join words, phrases, and clauses of equal grammatical rank such as two independent clauses. They are *and, but, or, nor, for, yet,* and *so.*
2. Subordinating conjunctions introduce subordinate clauses. Some of these are *after, although, as, because, unless,* and *while.*
3. Correlative conjunctions are always used in pairs: *either/or, neither/ nor, both/and, not only/but also,* and *whether/or.*
4. Adverbial conjunctions are used as conjunctions between independent clauses (*therefore, however, furthermore, nevertheless, thus,* and others).

Connotative Language

Connotative meaning is *implied* meaning as opposed to denotative meaning, which is *literal* meaning. All words and phrases have both kinds of meaning, and both are important. For example, the words *stench* and *fragrance* both denote "smell" or "odor," but their connotations are so diverse that they cannot appropriately be interchanged.

Connotative language is a form of imagery in which the author's idea (objective correlative) is described in the connotations of his language rather than in a specific word or phrase to which it is equated (metaphor) or to which it is compared by the use of *like* or *as* (simile).

> EX: The landlord's *red-lipped* daughter.   (Noyes, "The Highwayman")

In the following passage George Will explains the rhetorical function of one example of connotative language commonly used by sportscasters:

> ". . . And Smalley is overdue for a hit."
>
> It was the most consoling word in the language, "overdue." It meant: in the long run everything is going to be all right. No one is really a .222 hitter. We are all good hitters, all winners. It is just that some of us are, well, "overdue" for a hit or whatever.   (Will)

See **Denotative Language.**

Consist in/Consist of

Consist in refers to abstract elements which contribute to a complete effect.

> EX: His charm *consists in* an open smile and a kind disposition.

Consist of is more often used to refer to parts of a whole list.

> EX: The dessert *consists of* egg, chocolate, sugar, and whipped cream.

Consonance

Consonance is the repetition of consonant sounds.

> EX: Our throats were tight as tourniquets.   (Shapiro)
> EX: It was the night, and the excitement of the note of the hound, first heard, then not heard.   (White)

See **Alliteration** and **Assonance.**

Contact

Contact is a noun which is frequently used as a verb. Its use as a verb will probably be generally accepted in the future, but now it is best to avoid it in most formal writing.

> AVOID: She expects you to *contact* her by Thursday.
> CORRECT: She expects you to *make contact* with her by Thursday.
> BETTER: She expects you to *call* (or *telephone* or *write*) her by Thursday.

Continual/Continuous

Continual means "repeated over and over, but with pauses or breaks." *Continuous* means "without interruption." Drumbeats are *continual.* Droning is *continuous.*

> EX: Their *continual* bickering bored their friends.
> EX: The *continuous* downpour stopped the game.

Contractions

A contraction is a shortened form of a word in which an apostrophe takes the place of the omitted letter or letters.

> EX: *Isn't* that your dog, *Ma'am?*
> EX: *He's goin'* on down the road.
> EX: *It's* time to go.

See **Apostrophes.**

Contrast to/Contrast with

When *contrast* is used as a verb meaning "to compare," it is followed by *with.*

> EX: Coaches should not *contrast* a girl's ability *with* that of her teammates.

When *contrast* is used as a noun, it is followed by *to.*

> EX: Barry's work was slovenly in *contrast to* his partner's.

Coordinating Conjunction
See **Conjunction.**

Copulative Verbs
See **Linking Verbs.**

Correlative Conjunction
See **Conjunction.**

Could Have/Could of
See **Would Have.**

Council/Counsel
Council is a noun that means a group of advisers or people who deliberate. *Counsel* as a noun means advice. *Counsel* as a verb means to give advice.

> EX: The city *council* is in session every Thursday.
> EX: Your *counsel* on marriage problems has always been helpful.
> EX: When you *counsel* your clients, remember their economic problems.

Councilor and *counselor* are preferred spellings, although *councillor* and *counsellor* are also correct. *Counselor* is also used to mean attorney.

Crass
Crass is a frequently misused word. It does not refer to greed or penny-pinching or the tasteless display of wealth. It refers to stupid insensitivity.

> EX: We were appalled by her *crass* treatment of the handicapped students in our class.

Criteria/Criterion
The singular form is *criterion*; the plural is *criteria.* Say the *criterion is,* the *criteria are.*

Cumulative Sentence
A cumulative sentence is composed of a base sentence (subject-verb-complement) occurring at or near the beginning, followed by a number of phrase or clause modifiers.

> EX: There lay Humpty-Dumpty, who had once looked so jaunty, smashed beyond repair into a hundred bits of eggshell, his white in globs, his yolk beginning to congeal on the pavement.

For a thorough discussion, see Chapter 7, p. 261 ff.

Dangling Modifiers
Dangling modifiers are parts of sentences which become so disconnected from the words they are meant to describe that the sense of the sentence is changed or lost.

Dangling Participles

> INCORRECT: Jumping into bed, the sheets were cold.

The sheets, in this sentence, are jumping into bed. The actual word being modified is omitted.

CORRECT: Jumping into bed, John found that the sheets were cold.

Now John is jumping, not the sheets

Dangling Adverbial Modifiers

INCORRECT: When he was six years old, Pat's teacher taught him to read.

(That's not bad for a six-year-old teacher.)

CORRECT: When Pat was six years old, his teacher taught him to read.

INCORRECT: After being out until 2 A.M., Paul's mother grounded him.

(Being out late made her cranky.)

CORRECT: Because Paul stayed out until 2 A.M., his mother grounded him.

The noun and pronoun being modified must be clearly identified and be placed as close as possible in the sentence to the modifier.

Dash

The dash (—) is a mark of punctuation which should be used sparingly in formal writing. It is used instead of the colon in informal writing and instead of the comma for added emphasis. It may be used to include incidental information:

EX: Some scientists feared that the document placed too much faith in technological—rather than "human"—solutions.   (Golden)

It may also be used to set up an informal series:

EX: Because the life hereafter was but a mirror image of life on earth, [the Egyptians] took with them everything they would need—jewels, furniture, food, and, of course, servants.   (Plumb)

Or it may be used to achieve emphasis, contrast, or change in the sentence's direction:

EX: Only a handful of reporters still live in Manhattan, and they can be found in saloons only in the event of special celebrations—if, that is, a babysitter has been found for the occasion.   (Crist)

The dash is typed by making *two* unspaced hyphens. Do not space before or after the dash.

Deadly/Deathly

Deadly means death-causing. *Deathly* means death-like.

EX: After Juliet took the *deadly* poison, there was a *deathly* stillness in the tomb once again.

Demonstrative Pronouns
See **Pronouns: Demonstrative; This/That.**

Denotative Meaning

The *denotative meaning* of a word or phrase is its explicit meaning as compared to its connotative or implied meanings. For example, the denotative meaning of the phrase "a traveling salesman and a farmer's daughter" ignores the overtones suggested by the long lineage of off-color jokes on the subject. The words simply denote their stated meaning: an itinerant mechandiser and an agriculturalist's female offspring. See **Connotative Language.**

Dependent Clauses

See **Clauses, Adjective Clauses, Adverb Clauses, Noun Clauses.**

Differ from/Differ with

Differ from means "not the same as." *Differ with* means "disagree."

> EX: The Quakers and the Catholics in our organization *differ from* one another in their form of worship but do not *differ with* one another in their belief in religious freedom.

Different from/Different than

Different from is always correct although it may sound awkward at times. *Different than* is possible only when *different* precedes a clause in which some words are understood rather than stated.

> EX: Angie found that she felt no *different* being in love for the eighth time *than* [she felt being in love] the first.

In all other instances, stay with *different from.*

> EX: My dreams are *different from* yours. Our style is *different* in every way *from* yours.

Direct Object

See **Complement.**

Discover/Invent

These words are not synonymous. *Discover* means to find something that was already in place. *Invent* means to make something new or find a new use for something.

Sometimes *discover* means to identify a new use for something already in place. For example, a certain mold had always occurred under certain conditions. The *discovery of penicillin* refers to a new use for an extract of that mold.

Although wheels were already in existence, as were engines and many other elements of the automobile, they had to be put together in a certain way with the addition of new elements, including fuel, for the *invention of the automobile.*

Disinterested/Uninterested

A *disinterested* person has no personal connection, no opinion, is neutral. An *uninterested* person just doesn't care, although he may or may not have a stake in an issue.

EX: They looked for a *disinterested* person to act as referee. When they found someone, he was *uninterested* in the job.

Dive—Irregular Verb
They dive; they dived or they dove; they have dived.

Doesn't/Don't
Does and *Doesn't* are singular. *Do* and *Don't* are plural.

EX: Sally *doesn't* look her best in red. Her sisters *don't* either.

Be especially careful not to use *don't* with a single subject because it is one of the nonstandard constructions that people find most distracting.

Do—Irregular Verb
He does; they do; they did; they have done. See **Doesn't/Don't.**

Done/Finished
Use *finished* unless you are referring to completely cooked meat.

EX: Our work is *finished;* the hamburgers are *done.*

Dots
See **Ellipsis Points.**

Double Negative
Although speakers of standard English in Shakespeare's day believed that the more negative words one used in a sentence the more emphatically negative it became, today's standard English abides by the theory that negative words cancel each other out and thus turn a statement positive. You should, therefore, be careful to avoid a double negative (an error that readers find especially bothersome).

INCORRECT: No one never came. [Means "Somebody always came"]
CORRECT: No one ever came.

There is one construction, however, in which a double negative subtly reinforces a positive meaning:

EX: It is *not uncommon* to hear crying from the Kindergarten on the first day of school.
EX: She sold the set for a *not inconsiderable* sum.

Not uncommon is a cautious way to say *common. Not inconsiderable* means "considerable."

Double Possessive
Possessive case can be expressed with an apostrophe or by using *of* (John's brother, brother of John). In some sentences, you will need to use a double possessive, an apostrophe and *of,* in order to make your meaning clear.

EX: *We saw a painting of Whistler* means that Whistler was the subject of the painting.
EX: *We saw a painting of Whistler's* means that Whistler was the painter.

There is also room for choice. The following examples are both correct.

> EX: He was a friend of Whistler.
> EX: He was a friend of Whistler's.

See **Apostrophe.**

Doubt

Doubt can be followed by *that* and *whether* as they seem appropriate.

> EX: I *doubt that* he has enough money to invest.
> EX: I *doubt whether* she is sincere.

It is less commonly accepted to follow *doubt* with *if.*

> EX: I *doubt if* she is sincere.

In most cases, *whether* would be a better choice than *if.*

Due to

Due to is acceptable when describing a noun. It follows a linking verb.

> EX: Her success was *due to* working hard—and being the President's daughter.

Due to may NOT be used as an adverb explaining a verb.

> INCORRECT: He died *due to* an extreme cold.

Instead use *because of, on account of, owing to.*

> CORRECT: He died *because of* an extreme cold.

Due to the fact that is wordy and pretentious. Avoid using it.

Eager
See **Anxious/Eager.**

Effect
See **Affect/Effect.**

Elicit/Illicit

Elicit means "to draw out."

> EX: Try to *elicit* more information from that witness.

Illicit means illegal or not allowed.

> EX: She was engaged in the *illicit* manufacture of alligator belts.

Ellipsis Points

Use ellipsis points—that is, three periods (. . .)—when you interrupt a quotation in order to indicate the omission of a word, words, or sentences. Ellipses help you make the syntax of the quoted material conform with your own writing. (See **Brackets,** punctuation often useful in this connection.) Ellipses also permit you to leave out those portions of the quotation that are not relevant to the point you are making.

Whenever you omit part of a quotation, be sure that you do not alter the author's essential message. Sometimes advertisements use ellipses to deceive.

EX: (Original quotation) The *Times* critic called it "The biggest mess of a movie this season."

(Advertisement using a misleading ellipsis) The *Times* critic called it "The biggest . . . movie this season."

Rules for Use

1. When you type an ellipsis, space between the dots.
2. When the omission is at the end of the sentence or includes the end of a sentence, you need a fourth dot (the period).

   EX: The President said, "Ask not what your country can do for you. . . ."

3. An unfinished or interrupted sentence in recorded conversation, however, ends with only three dots.

   EX: Marion began, "But if only I . . ."

4. The ellipsis should not be used to indicate a pause in speech.

   WEAK: Tom mumbled, "I . . . uh . . . I don't . . . uh . . . think so."
   BETTER: Tom mumbled, "I—uh—I don't—uh—think so."

See **Dash.**

Emigrate/Immigrate

Migration refers to moving from place to place. The move may or may not be permanent. You can *migrate to* a place or *migrate from* a place. "Migrate to" is *immigrate.* "Migrate from" is *emigrate.*

EX: Stanislaus *emigrated from* Poland in 1923. He *immigrated to* the United States.

EX: Stanislaus was an *emigrant from* Poland. He was an *immigrant to* the United States.

Ensure
See **Assure/Ensure/Insure.**

Equally as

Because the comparative meaning of *as* is included in the word *equally, as* is unnecessary and should not be used with it.

INCORRECT: His job is important, but there are others equally as important.
CORRECT: His job is important, but there are others equally important.

Euphemism

A euphemism is a more pleasant or less offensive way to state what the speaker or writer considers an unpleasant or unmentionable idea.

When the word *pregnant* was too blunt for sensitive company, euphemisms included "she has something in the oven," "they are expecting a bundle of joy," "the stork will arrive with a package from heaven," and other sayings today considered more offensive than *pregnant.*

Doctors call pain *discomfort.* Teachers call children *socially immature* when they bite each other. When a weight lifter gets fat, he claims he is *bulking up.*

The use of euphemisms presents a moral issue when it is intended to blur the reality of something a writer does not wish to admit. For example, many thoughtful people believe it is immoral to call the destruction of vast areas of vegetation *defoliation* or to refer to munitions which are used to kill people as *anti-personnel materials.*

It is usually wiser to avoid using euphemisms when the plainly stated original idea would do as well.

Everyday/Every Day

Everyday is a compound word when used as an adjective.

> EX: Just wear your *everyday* clothing.

When referring to a frequency in time, write *every day* as two words.

> EX: We shall help you *every day* until you finish.

Except

Some grammarians consider *except* a conjunction which should be followed by the subject of an understood clause:

> EX: They all arrived early *except she* [did not].

Others consider *except* a preposition to be followed by an object:

> EX: They all arrived early *except her.*

While they try to decide, stick with the objective. Use *except me, except us, except him.*
See **Accept/Except.**

Exclamation Point

The exclamation point (!) is a mark of punctuation that indicates excitement. It may also signal fear or surprise or other strong emotions. Overused, however, the exclamation point loses its impact. Save it only for moments of strongest excitement. Such moments are very rare in expository writing.

The same sentence may take on new meaning if it is followed by an exclamation point.

> EX: Who is singing *Thunder Road?* It's Bruce Springsteen.
> EX: Who is that in the lobby? It's Bruce Springsteen!

Expository Writing

Expository writing is a setting forth of meaning or intent in prose. Unlike narrative writing, its purpose is not to tell a story but rather to explain ideas or to expound a point. It is characterized by the presence of a thesis, either explicit or implicit; and it is structured by the development or support of that thesis.

Extended Metaphor

An extended metaphor is a metaphor where the comparison is expanded so that the qualities of the describable objective correlative (see **Objective Correlative**) are spoken of in terms of the qualities related to the indescribable feeling or idea the author wishes to convey.

EX: The plane *cut* across the sky, *slashing* through clouds, a swift silver *knife* against the blue.

See **Metaphor.**

Fall—Irregular Verb
They fall; they fell; they have fallen.

Farther/Further
Farther and *further* both mean "more" or "to a greater extent." *Farther* only refers to actual distance in space which can be measured. *Further* refers to time or other abstract measurement.

EX: Which family lives *farther* from the railroad tracks?
EX: I changed my opinion upon *further* consideration.
EX: *Further,* as a condensed version of *furthermore, "further"* has an additional or *further* use as an adverbial connective.

Faulty Parallelism
See **Parallelism: Faulty.**

Fewer/Less
Fewer is used with number; *less* is used with quantity.

EX: There were *fewer* than six people on the sign-up sheet.
EX: There was *less* noise tonight.
EX: We had hoped for *fewer* cases of chicken pox this year.
EX: We had hoped there would be *less* chicken pox this year.

With *fewer,* you can count the number of cases.
EXCEPTION: You can use *less* with a number when it refers to a collective sum (*less* than 30 years old or a salary *less* than $25,000).

Fiancé/Fiancée
A woman's *fiancé* is the man she is engaged to marry. The engaged woman is his *fiancée.* Although these are foreign words, they are frequently used and need not be italicized (or underlined).

Figurative Language
Figurative language is language used to express meaning that goes beyond its literal interpretation. Historically, figurative language is considered to be composed of individual "figures of speech" (or "flowers of rhetoric," as they were known for centuries) that served the masters of rhetoric as persuasive tools in their appeal to the emotions of their audience. Of the more than 200 such figures that were once codified, writers still find a good number that remain useful today. Among these are the **Rhetorical Question, Parallelism, Balanced** and **Contrasting Parallelism, Inversion,** and **Irony,** all of which are separately defined here.

In recent years, however, the term *figurative language* is ordinarily equated with *imagery,* the discussion of one idea or thing in terms of another. **Imagery** is discussed separately here along with some of the best-known figures. These include the images of form—**Metaphor, Simile, Connotative Language, Symbol, Allegory, Analogy**—and some major images of content—**Personification, Hyperbole, Allusion, Synesthesia, Metonymy, Synecdoche, Paradox,** and **Oxymoron,** all of which are also listed separately.

Figures of Speech
See **Figurative Language.**

Finished
See **Done/Finished.**

Firstly
This is not an acceptable form. Many people use *firstly, secondly, thirdly.* It is better to use *first, second,* and *third* as adverbs.

> EX: *First,* I don't know how to drive. *Second,* I have no car. *Third,* I'm afraid of driving in traffic.

Flammable/Inflammable
Both words mean the same thing: flame-able, easily ignited.

Flied
See **Fly.**

Flowers of Rhetoric
See **Figurative Language.**

Fly—Irregular Verb
They fly; they flew; they have flown. *Flied* is correct only in sentences about the ball park where Pete *flied out* to third.

Fragment
A fragment is a portion of a sentence that is punctuated as if it were a sentence.

> EX: Though it is not a sentence.
> EX: Which was a surprise.

Occasionally, an experienced writer employs a fragment effectively.

> EX: What's wrong with nondiscrimination, with simple fairness? *Two things really.*   (Raspberry)

But, in general, fragments—like all structural errors of the sentence—are especially distracting to readers and thus are best avoided.

Funny
Funny is best used to mean "amusing," rather than "peculiar" or "suspicious" or "unusual." If you do not mean "amusing," find a more precise word than *funny.*

Further
See **Farther/Further.**

Gender

Gender is an attribute of nouns and pronouns designating masculine, feminine, or neuter. Neuter words usually refer to inanimate objects.

Some male-female designations are necessary, such as rooster/hen, gentleman/lady, and bull/cow. Other male-female differences are less important but still used, such as actor/actress and host/hostess. Others have become obsolete, such as aviator/aviatrix, author/authoress, poet/poetess.

Words such as *councilman* have, in this time of almost equal opportunity, called forth such terms as *councilwoman*. Unfortunately, such gender words have spawned awkward plurals such as *councilpersons* or *congresspersons*. When you can, it is wiser to avoid such awkwardness and choose terms such as *councilors* or *legislators (senators, representatives)*.

Pronouns also have gender. *He, his,* and *him* are masculine; *she, her,* and *hers* are feminine; and *it* and *its* are neuter. Plural pronouns are the same for all three genders: *they, their, theirs, them, we, our, ours, us, you, your, yours.* Problems arise when singular pronouns must agree in gender with their antecedents. When the subject is of mixed or unknown gender, things become tricky. Since the old rule, so offensive to many, of using the masculine term in such cases is now obsolete, it is better to avoid the problem altogether and stick with a plural subject: "The students, they. . . ." In the rare cases where the plural simply cannot be used, *he or she,* though awkward, is correct.

Gender/Sex

Be careful in using the word *gender.* It refers only to the masculine, feminine, or neuter quality of words. It does not mean the same as *sex.*

INCORRECT: You may not discriminate in hiring on the basis of *gender.*
CORRECT: You may not discriminate on the basis of *sex.*
INCORRECT: She had to do twice as well because of her *gender.*
CORRECT: She had to do twice as well because of her *sex.*

Gerund

When the *-ing* form of a verb is used as a noun, it is called a *gerund.*

EX: The *ringing* of the bell seemed to go on forever.

See **Noun Phrase.**

Get—Irregular Verb

They get hives; they got hives; they have gotten hives.

Go—Irregular Verb

They go; they went; they have gone.

Good/Well

Good is an adjective, modifying nouns and pronouns. *Well* is an adverb, modifying verbs and adjectives.

After linking or sensory verbs, *good* is usually used because it describes the subject rather than the verb.

EX: Gardenias smell *good.* Pizza tastes *good.* Country music sounds *good* to many people.

In all of those sentences, a more descriptive or precise word than *good* might have been found *(fragrant, delicious, pleasant),* but in no case should *well* have been used.

In referring to physical well-being, *well* usually follows *feel.*

EX: He feels *well* for the first time since football season.

Well follows most other verbs.

EX: He eats *well,* sleeps *well,* dances *well,* and lies *well.*

Got/Gotten

Got is incorrectly used to mean "to have." Since "have" itself always accompanies it, *got* in this sense is redundant.

INCORRECT: Jerry *has got* thirty-five horses.
CORRECT: Jerry *has* thirty-five horses.

Gotten, when used to mean "acquire" or "purchase," however, is not incorrect—although it is considered a bit awkward.

EX: Jerry *has gotten* thirty-five horses.
BETTER: Jerry has acquired thirty-five horses.

Great

Great should be reserved for occasions for which the meanings "extensive," "remarkable," or "very large" are required. Do not use *great* to describe the way one feels or one's skill at something. These uses are too informal for writing.

INCORRECT: He played a *great* game of tennis today. It's *great* to be here with you. This is a *great*-looking office.

Hail/Hale

Hale can mean either *healthy* (adjective) or *haul* (verb.).

EX: He felt *hale* and hearty until he was *haled* into court by his wife.

Hail means to greet or call out.

EX: Try to *hail* a cab for us. *Hail,* Caesar!

The expression *hail fellow, well-met* does not mean healthy fellow, but one who is friendly and apt to greet you. Or call a cab for you.

Hang/Hanged, Hang/Hung

When discussing *hanging* as a means of executing a person, the past tense and the participle forms are *hanged.*

EX: He *was hanged* for the murder of his mother-in-law. The *hanged* man was revived and lived a long life.

When using *hang* in any other sense, use *hung* for the past and participle forms.

EX: She *hung* the picture upside down.

EX: The picture *was hung* upside down.

Hanging Hyphen

The hanging hyphen is acceptable and looks like this: She is a *six-* or seven-time winner.

See **Hyphen.**

Healthful/Healthy

Healthful foods, activities, and environments contribute to your health. They keep you *healthy*.

Helping Verb

See **Auxiliary Verb.**

Historic/Historical

Historic things are a part of history. Mt. Vernon is a *historic* home, Gettysburg is a *historic* battleground, segregation is part of a *historic* struggle.

Historical things are based on history. We have *historical* novels, *historical* research, *historical* studies.

Use *a,* not *an,* before *historic.*

Homonym

A homonym or homophone is a word which sounds the same as another word but is different in spelling and meaning.

EX: The *knight* rode out each *night* in search of dragons.

EX: Charlie *threw* the discus *through* a window.

Hopefully

Hopefully is rapidly becoming the most misused word in the language. *Hopefully* is not an adverbial conjuction like *however.* It is an adverb that modifies a verb. Although it is becoming acceptable to many in its conjunctive form, here is the strict interpretation: In the sentence, "Hopefully, I will run five miles tomorrow," *hopefully* must modify run. Unfortunately, the writer does not really mean that she will run full of hope. She means that she hopes she will be able to run that far, and that is what she must state:

CORRECT: I hope that I shall be able to run five miles tomorrow.

I hope I have made this clear.

Hyperbole

Hyperbole is a kind of imagery (in whatever form—**metaphor, simile, symbol, connotative language**) in which the describable thing (**objective correlative**) to which the author's indescribable feeling or abstract idea is being compared is a gross exaggeration. Writers use hyperbole when the emotion they want to express is inexpressible because it is so big, so vast, so overwhelming that any regular image would seem an understatement.

EX: He could fiddle all the bugs off a sweet-potato vine. (Benét)

EX: My youth was like a long rainy Monday in Bayonne, New Jersey. (Will)

Hyphen

Hyphens (-) join two or more words or parts of words together to form a compound word (father-in-law, good-bye, ex-champion). But since not all compound words or prefixed words take hypens, your dictionary will have to be your guide for words that include hyphens in their regular spelling.

Compound Adjectives

Always use a hyphen, however, when you use two or more words as a single adjective—even when these words are not ordinarily punctuated in this way:

> EX: Marcia enjoyed sentence combining.
> Marcia enjoyed her sentence-combining course.
> EX: Joseph was well dressed.
> Joseph was a well-dressed representative of his company.
> EX: It was a good talk between mother and daughter.
> It was a good mother-and-daughter talk.

Avoiding Confusion

Be sure to use a hyphen when it is needed to avoid confusing similar words:

> EX: The International House co-op.   The chicken coop.
> EX: Re-cover the furniture.   Recover from your illness.

See **Hanging Hyphen.**

Hyphenation in Word Division

If you must continue a word on the next line of type, you should follow some rules for dividing.

1. Divide between syllables.
2. Never divide a one-syllable word.
3. The part of the word on each line must have one vowel sound and must be pronounceable (not *ear-th*).
4. Do not leave one letter alone on a line (*a-gent*).
5. Leave a single long vowel at the end of a syllable (*ho-tel, ta-ble, fa-mous*).
6. Do not permit a short vowel sound to end a syllable (*bas-ket, wag-on, plan-et*).
7. Words ending in *le* keep the consonant preceding *le* with the *le* (*sta-ble, ma-ple, mar-ble, am-ple*).

Whenever possible, go to the next line and write the whole word. You will avoid confusing errors and your work will be easier to read.

If . . . Were

When *if* or *as if* or *as though* is used to express a condition that does not exist or a situation that is only wished for or desired, you should follow the subject by *were* even if that subject is singular:

> EX: *If* the world *were* flat . . .
> EX: . . . led the prayers *as if* he *were* the Pope.
> EX: . . . *wished* she *were* Queen Elizabeth.

Illicit
See **Elicit/Illicit.**

Illusion
See **Allusion/Illusion.**

Imagery
Imagery is figurative language used to express otherwise inexpressible feelings or abstract ideas through comparisons. The author draws the comparisons to objects or ideas with which readers can be expected to have had some previous experience. (See **Objective Correlative.**) These comparisons can take the form of **Metaphors, Similes, Symbols,** or **Connotative Language** (see separate listings). When these comparisons are expanded and compounded, they produce **Extended Metaphors, Analogies** (expanded simile), and **Allegories** (expanded symbol).

Images are classified by content as well as by form. In content, a metaphor, for instance, can be **Allusion, Hyperbole, Metonymy, Paradox (Oxymoron), Personification, Synecdoche,** or **Synesthesia** (all separately indexed).

Immigrate
See **Emigrate/Immigrate.**

Imply/Infer
The speaker or writer *implies* (suggests, hints). The listener or reader *infers* (draws his or her own conclusions).

> EX: He *implied* that he was wealthy by mentioning that his wife had left her sable coat outside Gucci's in the Rolls Royce.
>
> EX: We *inferred* from his remarks that he was wealthy.

Indefinite Antecedent
See **Agreement: Pronouns with Antecedents.**

Indefinite Pronouns
See **Pronouns: Indefinite.**

Indefinite Reference
See **Agreement: Pronouns with Antecedents.**

Independent Clauses
See **Clauses.**

Indirect Object
An indirect object is the noun or pronoun *to whom* or *for whom* a thing is done. Sometimes the words *to* and *for* are not written but are understood.

> EX: Paula gave the present to *me.*
>
> EX: Paula gave *me* the present.
>
> EX: He gave [to] *Kim* all the help she needed.

The indirect object takes the objective form of the pronoun. You cannot say: He gave *she* and *I* his blessing. You must use *her* and *me.*

Individual

The word *individual,* both as an adjective and as a noun, carries with it the sense of singleness, of separate entity. It should not be used synonymously with a word as general as *person.* Avoid usage such as "Joe is a terrific individual."

Infer

See **Imply/Infer.**

Infinitive

The *to* form of the verb is called an *infinitive.*

> EX: to run, to write.

See **Noun Phrase.**

Inflammable

See **Flammable/Inflammable.**

Ingenious/Ingenuous

Ingenious means *inventive.*

> EX: Kathleen devised many *ingenious* ways for avoiding Latin class.

Ingenuous means *unworldly, innocent,* and *artless.*

> EX: The sophisticated bachelor found the young singer's *ingenuous* frankness irresistible.

The noun *ingenuity* is derived from *ingenious. Ingenue* has the same root as *ingenuous.*

Input/Output

Input and *output* are part of the jargon of the computer world, and are not usually appropriate in any other context. Under no circumstances should they be used as verbs.

Inside/Inside of

Use *inside* (meaning "within") without adding *of.*

> INCORRECT: He is *inside of* the house.
> CORRECT: He is *inside* the house.

Use *inside of* only when referring to limitations of time or distance.

> EX: We can be with you *inside of* an hour. We saw six leveled homes *inside of* a two-block area.

Insure

See **Assure/Ensure/Insure.**

Intensifiers

See **Adverbs.**

Interjections

Interjections are words that are grammatically unnecessary to the rest of the sentence, but are used to express emotions such as surprise, dismay, fear, or pain *(Oh! Wow! Hallelujah! Ow!).*

Intransitive and Transitive Verbs

A *transitive* verb takes a direct object.

> EX: He *punched* his little brother.
> EX: His mother *saw* him do it.
> EX: He will not *do* it again.

(*Brother, him,* and *it* are objects.)

An *intransitive* verb does not take a direct object.

> EX: Birds *fly.*
> EX: The man *died.*

Most verbs can be used as either transitive or intransitive.

> EX: The gourmand *ate* his *dinner.* (transitive)
> EX: The gourmand *ate* for hours and hours. (intransitive)

Most dictionaries list verbs as *vt* or *vi* immediately following the entry.

Inversion

Inversion is a figure of speech which involves inverting (or reversing) the normal syntax of the English sentence. Authors sometimes use this figure to achieve an almost poetic emotional quality:

> EX: But her long fair hair was girlish; and girlish and touched with the wonder of mortal beauty her face.   (James Joyce, *Portrait of the Artist as a Young Man)*

As effective as this figure can be, take care to use it with restraint. Its inappropriate use can lead to ludicrous effects:

> FAULTY: The two teams continued to play the football game, though down the rain fell until deteriorated were the conditions.

Irony

Irony is a rhetorical strategy in which the intended meaning is opposite from what is said or implied. Scholars distinguish three kinds of irony:

1. *Verbal Irony.* Here the speaker means the contrary of what he or she says or writes.

   > EX: One of the *worst insults* kicking around today is any word that means in effect *'wholesome.'* You are a wholesome person. How would you like to be called that?   (Wolfe, emphasis mine)

2. *Dramatic Irony.* Here the author means something contrary to what the speaker says.

   > EX: In the October 1973 war Israel . . . also suffered an acute understanding of the *'conscience of the West'* under oil pressure.   (Will, emphasis mine)

3. *Circumstantial Irony* (the "Irony of Fate"). Fate sees to it that circumstances turn out contrary to human expectations—almost as if in mockery of these expectations.

EX: *"Silent Night,"* canned and distributed in thundering repetition in the department stores, has become one of the greatest of all *noisemakers,* almost like the rattles and whistles of Election Night. (E. B. White, emphasis mine)

Irregardless
See **Regardless.**

Irregular Verbs
See **Regular Verbs** and the separate listings of the most common irregular verbs, individually alphabetized throughout the Revision Guide.

Irritate
See **Aggravate/Irritate.**

Italics (Underlining)
Underlining in a manuscript or typescript indicates italic script in print. Such underlining has a number of uses.

1. *Titles.* Always underline the title of a separately published work: *Tom Sawyer, Macbeth.* (See also **Titles.**)
2. *Foreign Words.* If you use a word or a phrase from a foreign language, you must underline it. Many words from foreign sources, such as *kimono, chauffeur, spaghetti,* or *poltergeist,* have come into such customary use that they are now considered to be English words as well and need not be italicized. Occasionally, however, you will need to use a foreign word or phrase that has not yet become assimilated into English and for which there is no precise English equivalent. Examples of such terms might include *chutzpah* (Yiddish), or *sturm und drang* (German), or *in medias res* (Latin). A word of caution: If you overuse foreign expressions, some readers may charge you with affectation.
3. *Words as Words.* Underline words or phrases when you are discussing them as words.

   EX: What is the meaning of *sincerity?*

4. *Emphasis.* Underlining can also be an effective way of calling attention to a word or phrase you may want to emphasize. Use this sort of italicization sparingly, however. Like the exclamation point, it can easily be overdone and become counterproductive. Sometimes a portion of a quotation you are using may be italicized and sometimes you may choose to emphasize a part of a quotation in this way yourself. In either case, be sure to let your reader know whether you or the author is the source of the italics: (Emphasis mine) or (Emphasis Smith's).

Its/It's
It's is a contraction meaning *it is* or *it has* and should not be confused with the possessive *its.*

EX: The lion has a thorn in *its* paw, but *it's* not my job to remove it.

Judge

Correct spellings are *judge, judging, judged. Judgment* is preferred, but *judgement* is also correct.

Kind/Kinds

The singular form is usually used but causes some confusion in verb agreement. Most grammarians would accept "What *kind* of clothes *are* these?" Some writers try to avoid the problem by using "What *kinds* of clothes *are* these?" This is not a correct use of *kinds.* The plural form should be used only for classifying things specifically.

> EX: How many *kinds* of birds are in Farleigh Woods?

A more precise word might be *species,* but *kinds,* if used, should be plural.

This *kind* of problem *keeps* cropping up (not "These *kinds* of problems *keep* cropping up").

Kind of/Sort of

Although it is always appropriate to speak of "this kind of scholar" and "that sort of apple," the use of *kind of* and *sort of* as qualifiers should be restricted to informal occasions. Edit out such expressions if they occur in your formal written work.

> WEAK: This kind of writing is *sort of* sloppy and its content is *kind of* vague.
> BETTER: This kind of writing is sloppy and its content is rather vague.

Know—Irregular Verb

They know; they knew; they have known.

Lay—Irregular Verb

Hens lay eggs; hens laid eggs; hens have laid eggs.

Lay/Lie

Lie can mean "to tell an untruth." It can also mean "to recline." In either case, it does not take an object.

> EX: The gangster *lied* to the judge.
> EX: The judge will *lie* on the couch.

Lay means "to put" and always takes an object.

> EX: *Lay* your coat down.
> EX: *Lay* your bets.

People sometimes are confused by these two verbs because their parts are irregular and *lay* is the past of *lie* (Today I *lie* down; yesterday I *lay* down). See **Lay—Irregular Verb** and **Lie—Irregular Verb.**

Leave/Let

Leave means to withdraw or go away. *Let* means to allow or permit. If you say, "*Leave* me alone," you mean "Remove yourself from my presence." If you say "*Let* me alone," you are saying, "Allow me to be by myself," either physically or symbolically.

EX: *Let* her go to the movies. *Let* them stay out until midnight.

EX: *Leave* the notes on the desk. Be sure you *leave* early.

Lend/Loan

You might *lend* me ten dollars or *loan* me ten dollars. Either is acceptable (twenty would be even more acceptable), but *lend* has a more formal sound and would be a better choice when you need a verb. *Loan* is always the correct noun.

EX: He tried to get a *loan* from the bank.

Do not say, "He tried to get the loan of Joe's car." Say, "He tried to borrow Joe's car."

Lets/Let's

Lets means *allows.*

EX: Becky *lets* her sister borrow her clothes.

Let's means *let us.*

EX: *Let's* try to get there early.

Never use *let's us,* as in *let's us* be there early.

Lie—Irregular Verb

They lie down; they lay down; they have lain down.

See also **Lay/Lie.**

Like

See **As/Like.**

Linking Verbs

Linking verbs (also known as copulative verbs) are verbs that take a predicate adjective or a predicate nominative instead of a direct object: they link rather than act. Linking verbs include all the forms of the verb *be* and other verbs such as *seem, appear, feel, look, remain, become.*

EX: Jane *seems* so confident and *appears* so self-possessed that I *become* all elbows and knees whenever she *is* around, *remain* miserable while she *is* near, and *feel* totally foolish as soon as she *is* away.

Loose Sentence

See **Cumulative Sentence.**

Literal Language

In literal language, the words mean exactly what they say. Such is not the case with figurative language.

LITERAL: His lying destroyed the relationship.

FIGURATIVE: His lies were the worm in the apple of love.

The word *literally* is misused when used like this: She was *literally* as big

as a house. He *literally* turned green with envy. These things are done figuratively, not literally.
See **Figurative Language.**

Lowercase
Lowercase, often marked *lc,* refers to the small letters of the alphabet as opposed to capital letters.

> EX: The author e. e. cummings always used lowercase for his name.

Mad/Angry
See **Angry/Mad.**

Main Clauses
See **Clauses.**

Majority
Majority means more than half the total. Fifty-one votes out of one hundred is a *majority.* If you are comparing more than two totals, be careful. The largest total may not be a majority. If Sally has twenty votes, George has twenty-seven, and Charlie has thirty-two, Charles has the most (a *plurality*), but not more than half (a *majority*).

> The usage *great majority* is correct; *greater majority* is not.

> As is the case with most collective nouns, *majority* takes a singular verb when unified, a plural verb when divided.

> EX: The *majority* of Irishmen *is* for unification.

> EX: The *majority* of Irishmen *disagree* about how to achieve unification.

May
See **Can/May.**

Media/Medium
Media is the plural form of *medium.* Television *is* a *medium* of communication. So is radio. So is the newspaper. They *are* all communications *media.*

> It is incorrect to say "The *media is* treating the President harshly."

Memento/Momentum
These are two totally unrelated words which are frequently jammed together to form a nonword, *momento.* A *memento* is a remembrance or souvenir. *Momentum* popularly means "forward push" but has precise technical definitions as well. There is no such word as *momento!*

Metaphor
A metaphor is a form of imagery where the indescribable feeling or abstract idea is equated with the describable thing or idea (**objective correlative**) to which it is compared.

> EX: His eyes were hollows of madness.   (eyes = hollows of madness)
> The fog came in on little cat feet.   (fog = cat)

The ship plowed the waves. (ship going through waves = plow going through field)

The term *metaphor* is sometimes also used in a general way to mean any image or imagery in general.

See also **Extended Metaphor.**

Metonymy

Metonymy is a kind of imagery (in whatever form—**metaphor, simile, symbol, connotative language**) in which the describable thing (**objective correlative**) to which the author's feeling or abstract idea is being compared is not the thing itself, but rather something closely associated with it. For example, in order to convey the emotion associated with a noted soldier giving up his *military career,* an author might write:

> EX: He abandoned his *sword* forever.

See **Synecdoche.** In recent years the term *metonymy* has been used also to include synecdoche.

Misplaced Modifier
See **Dangling Modifier.**

Mixed Metaphor

A mixed metaphor consists of two or more implied, unrelated comparisons of the same thing.

> EX: The plane *shot* across the heavens, a great *bird tearing* through clouds, a silver *knife* in the sky.

In revision, the writer must first choose between bird and knife metaphors (and bullet, if you want to include *shot*), and then continue with that single comparison. Mixed metaphors are usually a sign of an inept writer.

Modals
See **Auxiliary Verbs.**

Modify/Modifier

To modify is a grammatical term that means to describe or shape the meaning of. Adjectives, adjective phrases, and adjective clauses are modifiers whose function is to describe nouns. An important part of the function of adverbial modifiers—adverbs, adverb phrases and adverb clauses—is to shape the meaning of verbs.

It is especially important to place adjectival modifiers as close as possible to the noun they modify. (See **Dangling Modifiers** and **Comparison of Modifiers.**)

Myself

Myself is used primarily when the first person (I) is acting.

> EX: I gave [to] *myself* the injection. (indirect object)
> EX: I hurt *myself.* (object)

EX: I felt sorrow within *myself.* (object of preposition)

Myself should never be used in place of *I* or *me.*

INCORRECT: Jerry and *myself* were the only ones who cared.
INCORRECT: They invited Joanne and *myself* to come with them.

Nauseated/Nauseous

Nauseated means to feel sick. *Nauseous* means sickening or disgusting.

EX: His *nauseous* humor made us *nauseated.*
INCORRECT: He made me *nauseous.* That means: *He made me disgusting.*

Negative

Negative words deny the verb. They include *not, never, no,* and *none.* If you use two in one clause, you will cancel the denial.

EX: I *don't* have *no* tuition. I *never* had *no* tuition.

These sentences as they stand mean "I do have tuition," "I had tuition." See **Double Negative.**

Neither/Nor

Neither . . . nor can be used only when referring to two elements.

EX: *Neither* she *nor* her mother, *neither* soccer *nor* tennis.

When both elements are singular, the verb is singular.

EX: Neither *she* nor her *mother is* angry.

When both elements are plural, the verb is plural.

EX: Neither the *cowboys* nor the *Indians were* depicted realistically.

When one is singular and the other is plural, the verb agrees with the closest one.

EX: Neither the doctor nor his *instruments were* prepared.

None

None is considered singular because it means *no one.*

EX: *None* of the boys *is* able to sing.

In some cases it is considered acceptable to use *none* as a plural when it means no persons.

EX: *None* of the two hundred victims *were* from our town.

When the number meant by *none* is unclear, use the singular. Be consistent throughout the sentence.

INCORRECT: None of the girls has their purses.
CORRECT: None of the girls has her purse.

Nonrestrictive Clause
See **Comma; Adjective Clauses.**

Nothing

Nothing always takes the singular verb.

> EX: *Nothing* but pain and injuries *has* plagued him all season.

Nouns

A noun is the part of speech that functions as a subject or an object in a sentence, clause, or phrase. A proper noun is a capitalized word which designates a particular person, place, or thing. A common noun is nonparticular and not capitalized. Proper nouns might be *Washington, Richard, Crest.* Common nouns might be *city, boy, toothpaste.*
See **Collective Nouns.**

Noun Clauses

A noun clause is a subordinate (dependent) clause that functions as a noun in a sentence; that is to say, the clause as a whole serves as the subject or the complement (object) of the sentence or clause, as or the object of a prepositional phrase. The feature of the noun clause that keeps it subordinate—that prevents it from standing on its own as a full sentence—is the presence of introductory words, such as *that* or *what, where, when.*

> EX: *That the man was drowning* was immediately apparent. (as a subject)
> EX: He said *that he had forgotten to bring his water wings.* (as a complement)
> EX: The doctor knew *what he had to do.* (as a complement)
> EX: She took the doctor to *where the accident could be seen clearly.* (as the object of a preposition)

Never set off a noun clause with punctuation because noun clauses act as subjects or objects and no punctuation should ever come between a subject and its verb or a verb and its object.

Noun Phrase

A noun phrase is a group of two or more related words acting as a single noun. Noun phrases can be gerund phrases:

> EX: *Getting a license* is the first step.

Noun phrases can be infinitive phrases:

> EX: *To teach someone to drive* requires patience.

Number

When the word *number* is used as a noun, it usually takes a singular verb.

> EX: The *number* of unemployed *is* appalling.

When the article *a* is used, as in *a number,* use a plural verb.

> EX: *A number* of unemployed *are* planning disturbances.

See **Plurals.**

Numbers

Under most circumstances, spell out numbers from one to twelve and write larger figures (13, 874, 69,998,303) in numeral form. Dates and times (December 2, 1931 at 2:40 A.M.) should, as a rule, be given in numerals; and if you must begin a sentence with a number, it is usually wiser to spell it out.

Objective Correlative (O.C.)

Objective correlative is T. S. Eliot's way of referring to the objective part of a literary comparison that the author uses to bring home to the reader the indescribable feeling or idea that he or she has in mind.

> EX: My luve is like a *red, red rose.* (Burns)
> EX: The road was *a ribbon of moonlight.* (Noyes)

In the second example, it is not the objective road, but rather the author's indescribable feelings about that particular road and that particular time, that the o.c. *ribbon of moonlight* is meant to convey.

For a more complete discussion, see Chapter 8, p. 316 ff.

Object of a Preposition

Pronouns that are objects of prepositions are always in the objective form. People who do not understand grammar and who want to sound genteel or elegant make some common errors.

> INCORRECT: There was bad feeling *between she and I.*

Although it may sound awkward to say *between her and me,* it is correct. The objects of the preposition *between* must be objective *(her* and *me).* If it sounds too bad, say *between Mary and me, between us,* or reword in some other way.

Object of a Verb
See **Complement.**

Only

When *only* is used to mean *no more than,* it should be placed as close as possible to the word it limits.

> INCORRECT: He *only* has *an hour.*
> CORRECT: He has *only an hour.*
> CORRECT: Phil jumped from the bridge *only an hour ago.*
> INCORRECT: Phil *only jumped* from the bridge an hour ago.

The incorrect version implies that the only thing Phil got around to doing an hour ago was jumping from the bridge, although there were other things he might have done besides.

Only should not be used as a conjunction.

> INCORRECT: He wanted to sing, *only* he had a sore throat.

Use instead *but, however,* or whatever conjunction seems appropriate.

Onomatopoeia

Onomatopoeia is the use of words and phrases where the sound evokes the meaning.

EX: How they *clang* and *clash* and *roar!* (Poe)

EX: The *buzz saw snarled* and *rattled* in the yard. (Frost)

EX: Man not only is notably *busy* himself but insists that the other animals follow his example. A new bee has been bred artificially, *busier* than the old bee. (White)

Opportunity

Opportunity can be followed by *of, for,* or *to.*

EX He had the *opportunity to* steal the emeralds.

EX: The police used that *opportunity for* questioning him.

EX: It was the *opportunity of* a lifetime.

You can see that *opportunity for* is followed by a noun or noun form (gerund). *Opportunity to* is followed by a verb.

Opposite

See **Antonym.**

Output

See **Input/Output**

Oxymoron

An oxymoron is a paradox in a phrase. It is a figure of speech in which two contradictory terms are juxtaposed: *deafening silence, blind vision, frigid warmth.*

   An oxymoron can also be considered a sort of imagery in which the describable thing (**objective correlative**) the author's indescribable feeling or abstract idea is being compared to involves a contradiction.

EX: And if some *lover such as we*
   Have heard this *dialogue of one. . .* (Donne)

See **Paradox.**

Pair

Pair takes a singular verb when both parts act as one *(pair* of socks *is). Pair* takes a plural verb when the two parts are not acting as one.

EX: That *pair are* always arguing.

When speaking of more than one pair, it is correct to use *pairs.*

EX: She owns six *pairs* of jeans.

Paradox

Paradox is a kind of imagery (in whatever form—**metaphor, simile, symbol, connotative language**) in which the describable thing (**objective correlative**) to which the author's indescribable feeling or abstract idea is being compared is a contradiction. Authors often rely upon paradox to get across a normally incomprehensible mystery, such as the nature of God or of love.

   John Donne uses the paradox in his sonnet "Batter My Heart" to show the inexplicable freedom that the pious can find in obedience—even a forced obedience—to the will of God.

EX: Take me to You, imprison me, for I,
    Except You enthrall me, never shall be free,
    Nor ever chaste, except You ravish me.   (Donne)

See **Oxymoron.**

Parallel

When *parallel* is used as a noun, it can be followed by *with* or *between.*

EX: There are no *parallels with* his situation.

EX: Do you see the *parallels between* acting and teaching?

When *parallel* is an adjective, it is followed by *to.*

EX: Palo Alto Drive runs *parallel to* Irvine Avenue.

Parallelism

Parallelism is the repetition of similar syntactic constructions (parts of speech, phrases, clauses) with similar sound and meaning so as to emphasize the repetitive feature. The repetition makes the content of the parallelism more memorable, and the rhythmic effects provided by the repetition can evoke an emotional response.

EX: A *keeper of* my profession's flame, a *herdsman of* its sacred cows, a *minstrel of* its mythology.   (Crist)

EX: He tended, naturally enough, to pay in kind the insecurity his employer offered
    by moving on from job to job,
    by insouciance and prankishness that was charming but often disastrous,
    by kicking in the competitive clinches for temporary survival, and
    by an irresponsibility that caused him to regard his work as an end unto himself alone.   (Crist)

For a more detailed discussion, see Chapter 7, p. 242 ff.
See **Balanced and Contrasting Parallelism; Parallelism, Faulty.**

Parallelism, Faulty

Whenever you use parallel constructions, it is important to make sure that the parallel elements are syntactically alike. Awkward, even ludicrous, effects result from faulty parallelism. When parallel verbs are in different tenses, for instance:

INCORRECT: Lady Macbeth *urged* her husband to kill, *had seduced* him into the deed, and continually *washes* her guilty hands.

Or if parallel phrases are of different kinds:

INCORRECT: *With* heavy hearts, *with* stout resolve, and *having been* up all night, the Siamese twins decided to part their ways.

Parentheses

Parentheses ( ) are marks of punctuation used to enclose a word or phrase that qualifies or explains what has gone before or to repeat what has gone before in a different way.

EX: My cousin will arrive (unless he loses his way again) in time for dinner.

EX: My little brother (a pest as usual) told my date I planned to marry for money.

Parenthetical remarks tend to interrupt the text, however; so be careful not to overuse them.

Participles

The *-ed* form of a verb is called a *past participle* and may be used as an adjective: *respected* banker, well-*founded* respect, *funded* reserves, *driven* snow (note the irregular participle form). When the *-ing* form of a verb is used as an adjective, it is called a *present participle.* (It is called a *gerund* when it is used as a noun.) Examples include *singing* bird, *jesting* Pilate, *annoying* itch.

Participles are also used to dominate adjective phrases.

EX: *Clapping* its wee hands, the baby cooed for joy.

EX: The baby, *cooing* for joy, clapped its wee hands.

EX: Suddenly *puzzled,* the professor scratched her head.

Keep your participles and participle phrases as close as you can to the nouns they modify so that they will not "dangle" awkwardly. (See **Dangling Modifier.**)

INCORRECT: The retiring man accepted the gift of a punch bowl, *pleased as punch.*

This construction makes it seem as if the bowl is pleased. Also be very sure that the subject of your introductory participle phrase is also the subject of your sentence.

INCORRECT: Having reached the lovable age of three, the mother planned a birthday party for her little daughter.

INCORRECT: Tattered and worn, the lawyer shoved his favorite briefcase under his arm.

Parts of Speech

See **Nouns, Verbs, Adjectives, Adverbs, Conjunctions, Prepositions, Interjections, Articles.**

Passive Verbs and Sentences

See **Active/Passive.**

Period

A period (.) is a mark of punctuation used at the end of a complete statement or command. It is also used to conclude most abbreviations.
See **Abbreviations.**

Periodic Sentence

A periodic sentence is one in which its base sentence (subject-verb-complement) is preceded by a number of phrase or clause modifiers.

EX: When his nose is drippy and his throat is scratchy, when his supervisor seems unreasonable and the work piles high, and after two unsuccessful attempts to get the radiator to function, a fellow begins to wish that he were home in bed.

For a thorough discussion of the periodic sentence, see Chapter 7, p. 270.

Personal Pronoun
See **Pronouns: Personal.**

Personification
Personification is a kind of imagery (in whatever form—**metaphor, simile, symbol, connotative language**) in which the describable thing (**objective correlative**) to which the author's indescribable feeling or abstract idea is being compared is human or has human characteristics.

Personifications are of two kinds. One kind involves turning an abstraction into a human being:

EX: *Sport* that wrinkled *Care* derides
And *Laughter* holding both its sides.   (Milton)

The other kind of personification ascribes human characteristics to the non-human:

EX: Smile, O voluptuous cool-breathed *earth.*   (Whitman)
EX: From my mother's sleep I fell into *the State,*
And I hunched in its belly till my wet fur froze.   (Jarrell)

Picnic
In adding endings, a *k* must be inserted so that the *c* followed by *i* will not have the sound of *s.* Correct spellings are *picnicked, picnicking, picnickers.*

Plurals
Most plural nouns are formed by adding *-s* to the singular. Exceptions: Nouns which end in a consonant and *y* form the plural by changing *y* to *i* and adding *-es (hobbies, parties).* Nouns which end in *s, sh, ch, x,* and *z* add *-es* to form the plural *(buses, matches, foxes, buzzes, pushes).* Some nouns ending in *f* add *-s (chiefs).* Others change the *f* to *v* and add *-es (thieves. leaves).*

A final group of nouns form plurals irregularly *(children, geese, deer, women).* When in doubt, look them up.

Compound Nouns
Although most compound nouns form their plurals regularly by adding *-s* to the end *(spoonfuls, cross-examinations),* a few where the significant word comes first add the *-s* to that portion of the word *(fathers-in-law, senators-elect).*

Populace/Populous
Populace refers to the people, the population. It is a noun. *Populous* is an adjective meaning having many people.

EX: Only a small part of the *populace* was permitted to vote.
EX: Houston is becoming one of the most *populous* cities in the nation.

Possession or Possessives
See **Apostrophe; Double Possessive.**

Possessive Pronouns
See **Pronouns: Personal.**

Practically
Practically means *in a practical way.* Do not use it to mean *almost.*

CORRECT: Let us think *practically* upon that problem.
INCORRECT: We were *practically* there by six o'clock.
INCORRECT: He was *practically* my brother-in-law.

Use *almost* in those sentences. When you mean a stage has for all practical purposes been reached, you might use *virtually.*

EX: Her delivery was *virtually* flawless.
EX: He was *virtually* an expert on paleontology.

Precede/Proceed
Precede means to go before. *Proceed* means to continue on or to go forward.

EX: The Queen *preceded* the Crown Prince as the Royal party *proceeded* down the marble hall.

Predicate
The predicate is that part of a sentence which indicates what the subject is doing or being. It always includes a verb and may also include its modifiers and complements.

EX: Jack *selects.* Sally *shovels.* Artie *is never ready.* Perry *is running away.*

A simple predicate is the verb alone. A compound predicate is two or more verbs having the same subject and joined by a conjunction.

EX: Manuel *studied* and *wrote* for hours each day.

See **Complement.**

Predicate Adjective
See **Complement.**

Predicate Complement
See **Complement.**

Predicate Nominative
See **Complement.**

Prejudice/Prejudiced
Because the *d* sound at the end of *prejudiced* is difficult to pronounce, people sometimes think that the passive verb *to be prejudiced* is spelled the same way as the noun *prejudice.*

CORRECT: Her heart was filled with *prejudice.* For one reason or another she was *prejudiced* against almost everyone on her corridor.

Prepositions

A *preposition* is a part of speech which relates its object, a noun or pronoun, to another element in a sentence.

> EX: He sings *in* the church choir. *In* relates *choir* to *sings.* (adverb phrase)
> EX: He is part *of* the mob. *Of* relates *mob* to *part.* (adjective phrase)

Never make the mistake of using the preposition twice.

> INCORRECT: *With* whom did you come *with? To* what do you attribute your long
> life *to?*

Here is a list of common prepositions:

about	at	by	inside	outside	under
above	before	down	into	over	until
across	behind	during	like	past	up
after	below	except	near	since	upon
against	beneath	for	of	through	with
along	beside	from	off	to	within
among	between	in	on	toward	without
around	beyond				

Preposition at End of Sentence

It is sometimes correct form to end a sentence with a preposition. Some prepositions might fall at the ends of sentences: for example, *what it's all about, a chair to stand on, a pace to keep up with.*

To paraphrase Winston Churchill, the old rule of never putting a preposition at the end of a sentence often causes unwieldy constructions "up with which no one should have to put."

Prepositional Phrase

The prepositional phrase is made up of the preposition, its object, and any modifiers of the object: *within six years, in certain related cases, by careful and diligent searching.* Prepositional phrases function in a sentence as an adjective by describing a noun. (The fisherman *with the broad-brimmed hat* . . .) or as an adverb by marking the action of the sentence for time or place or quality (*In the morning* the fisherman sat fishing *on the bank*).

Prevent

Prevent can be followed by *from* or by the possessive noun or pronoun.

> EX: We tried to *prevent* Ray *from* escaping. We tried to *prevent* his escaping.
> We also tried to *prevent Joe's* escaping.
> INCORRECT: We tried to *prevent Ray* escaping.

Principal/Principle

Principal means "first" or "head" or "most important" and can be used in this meaning both as a noun and as an adjective. It can also refer to a sum of money that earns dividends.

EX Mr. Steinmetz is *principal* of Jimmy's school. (noun)

EX: He had one of the *principal* roles in *Brigadoon.* (adjective)

EX: She lived on the interest and did not have to use the *principal* in her account.

A *principle* is a rule by which a person lives or by which an organization is conducted.

EX: Loyalty to her employers was a guiding *principle.*

Proceed
See **Precede/Proceed.**

Prodigy/Protégé/Protégée
A *prodigy* is a person who has some exceptional talent or ability. He or she is often considered exceptional because he or she is very young, and the word is often used with *child.*

EX: Mozart was a child *prodigy.* He composed fine music at the age of eight.

Protégé (masculine) or *protégée* (feminine) refers to a person whose talent or career is being furthered by and often supported by a person of means or influence.

EX: Mozart was a *protégé* of the composer Haydn.

Pronoun
A pronoun is a word used in place of a noun. Pronouns are classified as **personal, relative, interrogative, indefinite, demonstrative, reflexive.** See individual listings.
See also **Agreement: Pronouns and Antecedents and Gender.**

Pronouns: Demonstrative
Demonstrative pronouns imply that the speaker or writer is pointing at a specific object or person. They may be used as nouns, but are usually more effective when you use them as demonstrative adjectives. The demonstrative pronouns are *this* (plural: *these*) and *that* (plural: *those*).

EX: *This plate* is wet. *That towel* is dry. Why not dry *this* with *that*?

See **This/That.**

Pronouns: Indefinite
There are a number of indefinite pronouns. They include such terms as *such, any, some, each, all, either, none, one, somebody, something.*
See **Agreement: Subjects and Verbs.**

Pronouns: Interrogative
Interrogative pronouns, which are almost identical with the relative pronouns, introduce questions.

EX: *Who* is in charge here? *Which* is the right direction?

Pronouns: Personal

In ancient days all English nouns and pronouns used to be inflected—that is, used to have different endings or forms to indicate the person they represented and to show their syntactic function in a sentence. But now only our personal pronouns change form to correspond with the person represented, and only these and the relative pronouns signify whether they are serving a subjective or objective or possessive function.

In speaking of yourself as the subject of a clause or sentence, use *I.* When joined together with others, use *we.* To make these pronouns the object of a verb or of a preposition, use *me* and *us.* When substituting a pronoun for other people and using it as a subject, choose (as appropriate) *he, she, they.* If you want one of these for an object, use *him, her, them.* (See also **Gender.**)

Choosing Subjective or Objective Forms

Most of the time choosing the correct form is fairly straightforward. Few speakers of English would ever say "*Me* went to the store" or "Pat took *I* to the picnic." But some people have problems when another name or phrase intrudes:

> EX: Jane and *I* went to the store. Pat took Joe and *me* to the picnic.

If you are ever troubled by a pronoun decision of this sort, simply remove the extra words and test out the construction with the pronoun standing alone in its place.

With the Verb "To Be"

The verb "to be" acts as an equal sign, equating the subject on one side with the complement on the other. Therefore, when the complement is a pronoun, traditionally, it should be written as a subject:

> EX: *It was he* who had saved the cat from the flames.

You should follow this rule in your writing, although in recent years speakers of Standard English have become more relaxed about following it in their speech. Many of them would not hesitate to answer a telephone query with "It's *me.*"

With Than and As

Than and *as* are not prepositions that take objects, but conjunctions that begin clauses where the verb is often not stated, but understood. When the subject of such understood verbs is a pronoun, it should, naturally, be in its subject form:

> EX: Joan is a better swimmer *than I* [am]. Roy is almost as tall *as he* [is].

Occasionally, the subject and the verb are both understood and the pronoun is meant to be the verb's object. Be careful with your choice of pronoun in such cases. The meaning can differ markedly:

> EX: She likes Jody better than I [like Jody]. She likes Jody better than [she likes] me.

With Between

Since *between* is a preposition, it should be followed by an object. Thus the correct form should be *between you and me* or *between her and me.* If this construction persists in sounding awkward to you, you might choose rather to reword and write *between Mary and me*.

Possessive Pronouns
The correct forms are:

My hat. It's *mine*.	*Your* hat. It's *yours*.
Her hat. It's *hers*.	*His* hat. It's *his*.
Its hat. It's *its*.	*Our* hats. They're *ours*.
Their hats. They're *theirs*.	

The main point to notice is that even though *its, hers, yours,* and *theirs* add *-s* to signify possession, none of them takes an apostrophe.

Please note also that forms common to a number of dialects, such as *youse, you-all, mines,* and *his'n,* are not included in the standard personal pronouns.

Pronoun Reference
See **Agreement: Pronouns and Antecedents.**

Pronouns: Reflexive
Reflexive pronouns are formed by adding *self* (or *selves*) to personal pronouns. They include *myself, himself, themselves, itself,* and so on. A reflexive pronoun is used to emphasize a noun or pronoun by repeating it within the sentence in another form.

> EX: *I* inspected the property *myself.*
> EX: I couldn't believe that the *star himself* had arrived.

Reflexive pronouns should never be used as a substitute for an appropriately used personal pronoun.

> INCORRECT: She taught Larry and *myself* to swim.
> CORRECT: She taught Larry and *me* to swim.

Pronouns: Relative
Relative pronouns include *who, whoever, which, whichever, that, whom, whomever, what, whatever, whose.* Like all pronouns they take the place of nouns. Relative pronouns serve as the subject or complement of adjective clauses describing the noun for which they substitute. (Exception: the noun that *whose* modifies serves as the subject or the complement of the clause which contains it.)

Use *who* and *whom* for persons and animals with personality, *which* for inanimate things and other animals, and *that* for any of these.

> EX: The cat, *which* was red, began to purr.
> EX: The small ancient lady, to *whom* it belonged, began to purr also.

See also **Who/Whom.**

Proper Nouns
See **Nouns.**

Protégé
See **Prodigy/Protégé/Protégée.**

Proved/Proven

Prove is no longer an irregular verb. The regular *-ed* form, *proved,* is now preferred to *proven* when combined with *has* or *had.*

> EX: He *has proved* his point. It *has been proved* to my satisfaction.

Proven is still the appropriate adjective, however: *proven* facts, *proven* ability.

Punctuation

See **Apostrophe, Brackets, Colon, Comma, Dash, Hyphen, Parentheses, Question Mark, Quotation Marks, Semicolon.**

Question Mark

A question mark (?) is used to indicate a question or an uncertainty.

1. Use a question mark at the end of a sentence that asks a question. (Where will you be on Tuesday?)
2. Do not use a question mark after an indirect question. (He asked what I wanted for my birthday.)
3. A question mark may be used to indicate that the writer is uncertain or questions the truth of a statement, such as "The war raged from 1812(?)–1815" or "The movie queen was born in 1952 (?)."

A question mark shows the end of a question. It therefore goes inside quotation marks when a question is being quoted and outside the marks when the sentence containing the quotation is a question itself.

> EX: The child asked, "Why is the sky blue?"
> EX: Have you ever heard the saying, "All in good time"?

Quite/Really/Very

Quite, really, and *very* are intensifiers; that is, they are meant to emphasize the adjective they describe and make it stronger. They are so overused, however, that in most cases it is questionable whether they achieve that end. Like exclamation points, they can add a gushy rather than an emphatic quality.

> LESS EFFECTIVE: Professor Jones is *really (quite, very)* well known.
> STRONGER: Professor Jones is well known.

When you are tempted to prop up a colorless or weak adjective in this way, try substituting a more expressive or colorful adjective. You might, for instance, replace *very funny* with *hilarious, quite silly* with *ridiculous, really big* with *mammoth* or *colossal.*

Quotation Marks

Quotation marks (" ") are punctuation marks used to enclose short direct quotations.

> EX: As Teresa Ferster Glazier reminds us, "Every quotation begins with a capital letter."

Do not use quotation marks for indirect quotations, which are usually introduced by *that* (unless you are including the exact words of your source).

EX: Professor Glazier reminds us that we should begin our quotations with capital letters.

Use quotation marks around the title of a poem or short story or song or any piece of writing that is not separately published.

EX: "The Barefoot Boy" is a poem by John G. Whittier.

Use single quotation marks (' ') as substitutions when you need to use quotation marks within a quotation.

EX: "Recite 'The Barefoot Boy' for me," Aunt Matilda demanded.

Use quotation marks to begin and end all parts of quotations that are interrupted by nonquoted material, but do not insert them at the end of each sentence when the quotation continues on.

EX: "Play hard," the coach advised, "and don't be afraid to block the other side. But always keep strictly to the rules of the game."

See **Quotations** and **Italics.**

Quotations

Be sure that you indicate all quoted material, even if it is only a phrase. Enclose short quotations within quotation marks, and block off with wide margins any quotations that are longer than three lines of type or script. In double-spaced typescript you will ordinarily single space your quotations. Quotation marks are unnecessary when you use whole blocks of quoted material.

EX: George Will insists that "the differences between conservatives and liberals are as much a matter of temperament as ideas," and goes on to detail these differences:

Liberals are temperamentally inclined to see the world as a harmonious carnival of sweetness and light, where good will prevails, good intentions are rewarded, the race is to the swift, and a benevolent Nature arranges a favorable balance of pleasure over pain. Conservatives . . . know better. (p. 449)

If you omit any part of a quotation, use ellipses (three dots) to indicate the omitted material (see **Ellipsis Points**). If you need to add any words of your own to a quotation, enclose them in brackets [ ].

Whenever possible, identify the source of your quotation. If such attribution is not possible or desirable, you still must not burst into quotation as birds burst into song, but use such introductions as "Authorities agree that . . ." or even "It has often been said. . . ." For a more detailed discussion, see p. 362 in Chapter 9.

Raise

Raise is a regular verb.

They raise sheep; they raised sheep; they have raised sheep.

Raise/Rise

Raise takes an object; *rise* does not. Things *rise* unassisted, but if they need help, they must be *raised.* You can *raise* the window, *raise* the roof, *raise* Lazarus. Steam can *rise;* heat and bread can *rise.*
See **Raise** and **Rise—Irregular Verb.**

Rarely

Use *rarely,* not *rarely ever.*

> INCORRECT: He *rarely ever* sees his family.
> CORRECT: He *rarely* sees his family.

Really/Real

Real and *really* are not interchangeable. *Real* is correctly used only as an adjective.

> EX: My pearl came from a *real* oyster.

In writing, *real* should not be used as an intensifier.

> INCORRECT: Joe was *real* impressed with my pearl.
> CORRECT: Joe was *really* impressed with my pearl.

Usually it is more effective to eliminate the *really* altogether.

> BETTER: Joe was impressed with my pearl.

See **Quite/Really/Very.**

Reason Is Because

Although this construction is used in a number of oral dialects, it is *not* Standard English and must be avoided in written work. Write "The reason is *that.*"

> EX: *The reason* Lisa did not come to the square dance *is that* her new shoes pinched her feet.

Reason Why

Reason why is incorrect usage because *why* is unnecessary.

> INCORRECT: I wish I knew the *reason why* he stopped calling Dorothy.
> CORRECT: I wish I knew *why* he stopped calling Dorothy.
> CORRECT: I wish I knew his *reason for* not calling Dorothy.
> CORRECT: I wish I knew the *reason* he stopped calling Dorothy.

Redundancy

Redundancy refers to unnecessary repetition, a form of wordiness to watch for as you edit your work.

> EX: 6 *a.m.* in the *morning* (a.m. *is* morning).
> EX: *Dr.* Phillips, *M.D.*
> EX: his *honest sincerity*
> EX: the *sickly invalid*
> EX: *each* and *every*
> EX: *three different* attorneys

The accompanying list of common redundancies may help in revising your writing.

adequate *enough*
advance planning
am in possession of (use "have")
a percentage of (use "some")
appear *to be*
appointed *to the post of*
ascend, hoist, raise, lift *up*
as never before *in the past*
as to whether
at an early date (use "soon")
atop *of,* inside *of*
at some time *to come*
attach, assemble, collaborate, cooperate, fuse, join, merge, unite *together*
barracks (or dormitory) *buildings*
best of health (use "well" or "healthy")
big *in size*
biography *of his life*
blue *in color*
but nevertheless
christened *as*
classified *into groups*
close proximity
consensus *of opinion*
continue *to remain*
descend *down*
due to the fact that (use "because")
during the time that (use "while")
entirely complete
final completion, settlement, outcome
first priority
frown, smile *on his face*
give due consideration to (use "consider")
give rise to (use "cause")
good benefit
grateful thanks
habitual custom

invited guest
joint cooperation
last *of all*
little duckling, baby, sapling, smidgeon
lonely isolation
made an approach to (use "approach")
made a statement saying (use "stated" or "said")
made *out* of
more superior, preferable
mutual advantage *of both*
never *at any time*
new beginning, creation, innovation, record, recruits
one *and the same*
over *with*
passing phase, fad, fancy
past history
penetrate *into*
protrude *out*
quite unique
recall, recoil, return, revert *back*
results so far *achieved*
separate and distinct (use "separate" or "distinct")
separate *apart*
serious danger
sink, swoop *down*
take action on the plan (use "act")
termed *as*
the house in question (use "this house")
body of *the late . . .,*
widow of *the late*
throughout *the length and breadth*
today's modern woman (use "today's" or "modern")
total annihilation, extinction, reversal
true facts
usual customs

had occasion to be (use "was")
important essentials
in this day and age (use "today")

violent explosion
weather *conditions*
young infant, baby, teen-ager

Referent
See **Agreement: Pronouns with Antecedents.**

Reflexive Pronouns
See **Pronouns: Reflexive.**

Regard
With regard to and *in regard to* are both correct usage.

> EX: Our conversation *with regard to* financing your project has been recorded.
> EX: *In regard to* your ideas, we are in total opposition.

Do not use *in regards to* or *with regards to.*

Although some writers use *regarding* and *as regards,* many grammarians consider these terms to be less acceptable as a stylistic choice.

When *regard* is used as a verb, it is followed by *as.*

> EX: I *regard* this *as* a damaging statement.
> EX: He will *regard* your interest *as* an invasion of his privacy.

You would not say "*regard it* an invasion" or "*regard it to* be an invasion." Just use *as.*

Regardless
The word *regardless* must be followed by *of.*

> EX: My parents will send me to college *regardless of* my poor grades.

Irregardless is not a word.

Regular Verbs
Most verbs are regular verbs. They are called *regular* because they form the past tense and past participle by adding *-d* or *-ed* to the present form.

> EX: They *seem;* they *seemed;* they *have seemed.*
> EX: They *walk;* they *walked;* they *have walked.*

Irregular verbs form the past tense and past participle in a variety of ways. The forms of the more common irregular verbs are included alphabetically within this guide.

Relative Clauses
See **Adjective Clauses.**

Respectful/Respective
Respectful refers to the state of showing honor or deference to someone (*respectful* to Grandma) or something (*respectful* towards the flag). *Respective* means belonging to each individual.

EX: She was *respectful* to all her teachers.

EX: State your *respective* qualifications when your names are called.

Restrictive/Nonrestrictive Elements

See **Commas: Parenthetical, Extraneous, or Interrupting Elements** and **Adjective Clauses: Punctuating Adjective Clauses.**

Reverend

Reverend cannot be used in place of a name (Incorrect: What time is the *Reverend* coming? Hello, *Reverend*). *Reverend* is an adjective and should precede a full name, including Mr., Mrs., Miss, Ms., or Father.

INCORRECT: The Reverend Peter Marshall

CORRECT: The Reverend *Mr.* Peter Marshall

Reverend should never be used in the plural (the Reverends John and Margaret Phillips).

Rhetorical Question

A rhetorical question is a figure of speech in which authors ask questions not to elicit answers but rather to make their points. A rhetorical question not only attracts readers' eyes because it is syntactically different from the surrounding prose, but it engages readers' minds because, though it expects no overt answer, it is directed to each reader personally.

EX: " 'If you are able to retire deep inside yourself, . . . you can isolate yourself in your deep inner core.' But then *where are you? Then what?"*(Goodman. Emphasis mine.)

EX: "One of the worst insults kicking around today is any word that means in effect 'wholesome.' You are a wholesome person. *How would you like to be called that?*" (Tom Wolfe. Emphasis mine.)

Authors sometimes provide answers for their rhetorical questions themselves.

EX: *"Does black socioeconomic progress necessarily depend upon whether blacks are liked by whites? Does it depend on the continuance of massive federal expenditures?* Well, if you asked the self-appointed black spokesmen, the answer to those questions would be 'yes.' But before we all agree, there are some important issues that must be raised."(Walter Williams. Emphasis mine.)

Ride—Irregular Verb

They ride; they rode; they have ridden.

Ring—Irregular Verb

Bells ring; bells rang; bells have rung.

Rise—Irregular Verb

The sun rises; the sun rose; the sun has risen.

Run-On Sentence

A run-on sentence is a group of words that contains more than one main (independent) clause but is punctuated as if it were a single sentence.

INCORRECT: When the air had cleared, we saw our favorite car still coming on strong it still had a chance to win!

CORRECT: When the air had cleared, we saw our favorite car still coming on strong. It still had a chance to win!

CORRECT: When the air had cleared, we saw our favorite car still coming on strong; it still had a chance to win!

Substituting a comma for the period or the semicolon in the edited versions would be as incorrect as the first example.

See **Comma Splice.**

Semiannual/Semimonthly/Semiweekly

Semiannual means happening or appearing twice a year. *Semimonthly* means twice each month. *Semiweekly* means twice a week. Our newspaper will appear *semiweekly* on Tuesdays and Fridays.

See also **Biannual.**

Semicolon

A semicolon (;) is a mark of punctuation that joins two or more closely related independent clauses when no coordinating conjunction (such as *and, but, or, nor, yet, for,* or *so*) is used. It is particularly valuable when an adverbial connective, ordinarily followed by a comma *(therefore, however, indeed, nevertheless),* is present.

> EX: Marcia has always been athletic; she plays tennis and golf well.
> EX: Marcia plays tennis and golf well; however, her basketball skills are only mediocre.

A semicolon can also separate the elements of a series if one or more of those elements contain commas.

> EX: In reading, many children have trouble with comprehension; with phonics, especially vowel sounds; and with visual memory, including the learning of sight words.

WARNING: A semicolon indicates a full stop—much as a period does. Be careful NOT to use it as a substitute for a comma, but confine your use of it to the two situations just outlined.

Sensual/Sensuous

The differences in usage between *sensual* and *sensuous* are subtle. *Sensual* is most often used when the senses under discussion involve sexual gratification. *Sensuous* is used to mean appealing to all or any of the five senses.

> EX: The director suggested the *sensual* pose, the breathy voice, the provocative smile.
> EX: We enjoyed the *sensuous* fragrance of magnolias.

Sentence

A sentence consists of a subject doing or being something. More technically, a sentence consists of a subject and its predicate—that is, a subject and verb, which may or may not have a complement. The subject, verb, and complement all may or may not have modifiers.

Grammarians distinguish four kinds of sentence structures: **simple, compound, complex,** and **compound-complex** (see individual listings). Sentences are also classified by their end punctuation. There is the declarative sentence, a statement that ends in a period:

> EX: Birds fly. The boy hit the ball.

The interrogative sentence is a question that ends in a question mark:

> EX: Do birds fly? What hit the ball?

The exclamatory sentence is an expression of surprise or emotion, that closes with an exclamation point:

> EX: Fly, birds, fly! It's a hit!

And the imperative sentence, a command, may end with either a period or an exclamation point—depending upon the vigor with which the command is given. (Note: when a command appears to have no subject, "you" is always the understood subject):

> EX: Fly away, little birds. [You] Hit the ball.

Sentence Fragment
See **Fragment.**

Serial Parallelism
See **Parallelism.**

Set—Irregular Verb
They *set* the table today; yesterday they *set* the table; they have *set* the table.

Set/Sit
Set takes an object. *Sit* does not take an object. You cannot *sit* something; you must *set* it.

> EX: *Set* the books on that chair, and *sit* over here with us.
> EX: *Set* the clock, *set* the table, *set* the child on his bench.
> EX: *Sit* down.

See **Set—Irregular Verbs** and **Sit—Irregular Verb.**

Shake—Irregular Verb
They shake; they shook; they have shaken.

Shall/Will, Should/Would.
Originally, *shall* and *should* were used to express future intent when their subjects were *I* or *we* (first person). *Will* and *would* were used the rest of the time. If writers or speakers wanted emphasis, they could reverse these combinations *(I will. He should.)* Now the distinction is fading and *will* and *would* are used most of the time in speech and less formal writing. Although it is no longer essential, in formal writing you might still want to maintain the distinction. And

in one case of *should,* you should do so. For when *should* is combined with a second-, or third-person subject, it still retains some of the emphatic sense of *ought;* and if you use *should* indiscriminately, it can give an officious mandatory tone to your work.

Shine—Irregular Verb

Without an object: The sun shines; the sun shone; the sun has shone.

With an object: They shine their shoes; they shined their shoes; they have shined their shoes.

Should

See **Shall/Will, Should/Would.**

Should Have

See **Would Have.**

Sight

See **Cite/Sight/Site.**

Simile

A simile is a form of imagery where the indescribable feeling or abstract idea is compared with a describable thing or idea **(objective correlative)** by means of the words *like* or *as.*

> "My luve is *like* a red, red rose." (Burns)
> "Our throats were tight *as* tournequets." (Shapiro)
> "Scattered across a page like chocolate chips through a toll-house cookie." (Stegner)

See also **Analogy,** an expanded simile.

Simple Sentence

A simple sentence consists of a single main clause with its subject and verb— and no additions to prevent it from standing on its own. It can be as brief as: *Jerry sat.* Or it can be very long—lengthened almost indefinitely by compounding the subject, verb, and complements and by the addition of adjectives (and adjective phrases), adverbs (and adverb phrases), appositives, absolutes, and so on. As long as no other *clause* is added on, the sentence remains simple:

> EX: Jerry, whistling a merry tune and wearing a pair of ragged overalls with a red-checked handkerchief in the pocket, and Joan, similarly garbed and just as lazily happy, sat on the dock all day long, fishing from time to time, but mainly watching the clouds roll by, too absorbed in each other to pay much attention to anything else.

See **Sentence.**

Sing—Irregular Verb

Birds sing; birds sang; birds have sung.

Singular

See **Plurals.**

Sink—Irregular Verb
Ships sink; ships sank; ships have sunk.

Sit—Irregular Verb
They sit down; they sat down; they have sat down.
See also **Set/Sit.**

Site
See **Cite/Sight/Site.**

Slang
See **Colloquial Language.**

So
In more formal writing, *so* should be used not as an intensifier, but as a comparative.

> WEAK: Jane was *so* pretty.
> BETTER: Jane was *so* pretty that I could not take my eyes off her.

So/So That
So stands alone when it expresses a consequence of some action.

> EX: He smashed the car, *so* he has to walk.

So is followed by *that* when it means *in order that.*

> EX: He needed a ride *so that* he could get there by Friday.

Sort of
See **Kind of.**

Spelling
Because the spelling of English words does not always coincide in any universally regular manner with the way they are pronounced, memorization of the spelling of individual words and the determination to look up the rest is the only sure method. There are, nevertheless, a number of rules that you may find helpful:

Double Vowels
The following rules, which will probably have the vaguely familiar ring of your early school days, can still be of use when you can't remember which way to order your vowels.
1. For most double vowels
   > RULE: When two vowels go walking,
   >   The first one does the talking.

   > EX: p<u>ea</u>ch, b<u>oa</u>t, p<u>ou</u>r.

   > EXCEPTIONS: Diphthongs such as *ou* and *oi* and the *i* and *e* combination.

2. For *i* and *e* combinations

   RULE: *I* before *e*

   Except after *c.*

   Or when sounding like "ay,"

   As in *neighbor* or *weigh.*

   EX: fr*ie*nd, bel*ie*f, rec*ei*ve, th*ei*r

Adding Suffixes That Begin with Vowels (*-ed, -ing, -able,* and so on)

1. For words that end in *e*

   RULE: Drop the *e* before adding the suffix.

   Explanation: The final vowel *e* serves to keep the central vowel sound long, and the vowel in the suffix will serve the same purpose.

   EX: *mope, moping, moped.* Chris sat around and *moped.*

2. For final accented words that do NOT end in *e*

   RULE: Double the final consonant before adding the suffix.

   Explanation: The double consonant prevents the vowel in the suffix from turning the central vowel sound long. The doubling thus keeps the vowel sound short.

   EX: *mop, mopping, mopped.* Chris *mopped* the floor.

3. For words that end in *y*

   RULE: Change *y* to *i* and add suffix. When the suffix is *-s,* change it to *-es.*

   EX: marry, married, marries

   EXCEPTIONS: (a) keep the *y* when the suffix is *-ing.*

   EX: marrying

   (b) Keep the *y* when the word is a proper noun.

   EX: Jenny's

The K Sound and the S Sound

Problem: In English the letters *k* and *c* both carry the K sound, and *s* and *c* both carry the S sound. It is difficult to sound out the spelling of words with these sounds in them. Part of the problem can be handled by rules, however.

1. For syllables beginning with a K sound

   RULE: Spell with a *k* when followed by *i* or *e.*

   Spell with a *c* when followed by *a* or *o* (and usually *u*).

   EX: *ki*tchen *ke*ttle, *ca*tching *co*ld, *cu*bs

2. For words ending with a K sound

   RULE: Spell with *-ck* when the final syllable is stressed.

   Spell with *-c* when the final syllable is unstressed.

   EX: si*ck*, pi*c*nic.

For adding suffixes (beginning with *i* or *e*): You can keep the K sound if you begin the suffix with a *k*.

EX: picni*cking,* picni*cker*

3. For words with S sounds
   RULE: Spell with *s* whenever the S sound is followed by an *a* or an *o* or a *u*.

EX: sat [cat], sot [cot], sub [cub]

Unfortunately, both *s* and *c* can be used before *i* and *e*; so when you are not sure here, you will have to look up the spelling.

Combined Words
RULE: Words formed by combining two words retain all the letters of both words, even if a letter repeats.

EX: roommate, withheld, overrule

Words formed by adding a prefix retain all the letters of both prefix and base, even if a letter repeats.

EX: misspell, unnatural, interracial, dissatisfied

The accompanying list of commonly misspelled words will also help you in revising. Memorize the spelling of any that are troublesome to you.
See also **Apostrophes.**

Spelling List

The following is a list of everyday words that have been found to be most frequently misspelled. These words are in such common use that people rarely take the time to look them up in a dictionary. Unfortunately, these words are also so commonplace they are considered "simple," and thus when they are misspelled, they leave readers with a particular negative impression of the writer. If spelling is a problem for you, you can clear up a large proportion of it by a procedure that has worked for many others with a similar problem: First, identify your own particular troublemakers by having someone test you on this list. Then, make a deliberate effort to memorize the words you have missed. (You can use such memory tricks as closed-eyed visualization, idea-letter association, and repeated writing.) Finally, test out your troublemakers as many times as it takes for you to be sure you will not misspell them again.

absence	accept	achieve	acknowledged	advertisement
alter	argument	assistance	athlete	beautiful
beginning	believe	benefit	business	characteristic
circumstances	committee	conscious	decision	definition
describe	description	difference	effect	embarrass
especially	exercise	experience	familiar	February
forty	fourth	friend	hoping	immediately
intelligence	its	judgment	knowledge	library

maintenance	necessary	neighbor	ninety	ninth
occasionally	opportunity	parallel	personal	persuade
planned	possession	presence	principle	privilege
psychology	receive	recognize	rhythm	science
shining	similar	society	studying	succeed
surprise	their	there	they're	thoroughly
too	traveling	Tuesday	usually	Wednesday

Stationary/Stationery

Stationary means not moving, remaining in one place. *Stationery* refers to paper, cards, and envelopes used to correspond by note or letter.

> EX: The cabinets were *stationary*. She ordered monogrammed *stationery* to go on one of the shelves.

Steal—Irregular Verb

Thieves steal; thieves stole; thieves have stolen.

Sting—Irregular Verb

Bees sting; bees stung; bees have stung.

Stuff

Shakespeare said, "We are such *stuff* as dreams are made of." And if you also want to use the word in its original sense of "primary substance," you would be using it appropriately. But *stuff* used in its usual vague conversational sense is too informal for most writing situations. Search out and use a word that more exactly expresses your thought.

> INCORRECT: We put all our *stuff* in one box.

If you can be precise, use *clothing, tools, supplies,* or whatever describes what is in the box. If you cannot be precise, use *belongings* or *materials.*

Subject-Verb Agreement
See **Agreement: Subject and Verb.**

Subordinate Clause
See **Clauses, Adjective Clauses, Adverb Clauses, Noun Clauses.**

Subordinating Conjunctions
See **Conjunctions.**

Swim—Irregular Verb
Fishes swim; the fishes swam; the fishes have swum.

Swing—Irregular Verb
They swing; they swung; they have swung.

Syllabication
See **Hyphenation in Word Division.**

Symbol

A symbol is a form of imagery where the describable thing or idea (**objective correlative**) to which the indescribable feeling or abstract idea is equated takes on both a literal and a figurative meaning (sometimes more than one figurative meaning).

EX: John Lilly's isolation tank in the following passages:

Literal meaning
{ John Lilly's isolation tank . . . [is] an enclosed tank, with 10 inches of water heated to precisely 93 degrees and room for exactly one person . . . [where] freed from sight, sound, people and the universe outside, . . . you can enter the universe within you.

Figurative (symbolic) meaning
{ The "isolation tank" is as good a symbol as any of a time when we are making a positive value out of our sense of impotence in the world, and a cult out of the fragmentation of society and missed connections of our personal lives.   (Goodman)

Synecdoche

Synecdoche is a kind of imagery (in whatever form—**metaphor, simile, symbol, connotative language**) in which the describable thing (**objective correlative**) to which the author's indescribable feeling or abstract idea is being compared is not the thing itself, but rather a single part of it which substitutes for the whole.

EX: Is football still a-playing
Along the river shore,
With lads to chase the *leather*   (leather = football)
Now I stand up no more?   (A. E. Housman)

EX: The *hippocratic eye* will see/In nakedness, anatomy.   (hippocratic eye = doctor)
(Robert Graves)

See **Metonymy.**

Synesthesia

Synesthesia is a kind of imagery (in whatever form—metaphor, simile, symbol, connotative language) in which the describable thing (objective correlative) to which the author's indescribable feeling or abstract idea is being compared involves stretching or bending the sensory experience beyond the limits of the single sense that would seem to be logically appropriate. Such images are often particularly striking and effective.

EX: The sunlight on the garden/Hardens and grows cold.   (Louis MacNeice)
EX: Wild men caught and sang the sun in flight.   (Dylan Thomas)

Synonym

A synonym is a word that means the same (or almost the same) as another word. *Rich* is a synonym for *wealthy, sick* for *ill, healthy* for *well, hurry* for *rush, swiftly* for *rapidly.*

Although words can be similar in meaning, the good writer is able to choose the word with the exact shade of meaning required. The best word is usually not the longest or most impressive word. It is the word that most precisely expresses the idea and the connotation you want to convey.

Syntax

Syntax refers to the way words, phrases, and clauses work together in a sentence. Syntax which is faulty or complicated leaves the reader confused.

Faulty syntax can be seen when subjects do not agree with predicates, when pronouns do not match antecedents, and when professors do not agree with students on sentence structure.

Take
See **Bring/Take.**

Than and Pronouns Following
You can decide which pronoun you want to use following *than* more easily if you try to complete the thought. Mentally add in the missing words:

> EX: Everyone has more money *than he* [has].
> EX: He is taller *than she* [is tall].

By changing the pronoun after *than,* you might change the whole meaning of the sentence, so be careful.

> EX: She loved music more *than he* [loved music].
> EX: She loved music more *than* [she loved] *him.*

That/This
This and *that* and their plurals, *these* and *those,* are demonstrative pronouns which point to or substitute for *specific* objects or persons.

> EX: This tree. Those trees. That player. Those players.

Do not use demonstrative pronouns to signify "all this," "all that I have just said."

> INCORRECT: We could all dress in costume, carve a pumpkin, and bob for apples as we used to do when we were children. *This* would be fun.
> CORRECT: *This plan* would be fun.

See also **Agreement: Pronouns with Antecedents.**

That/Which/Who
See **Pronouns: Relative** and **Who/Whom.**

Their/There/They're
Their and *theirs* are possessives. They express the idea of "belonging to."

> EX: This is *their* furniture. The house is also *theirs.*

There can be used as an introductory word or as a word to tell the place.

> EX: *There* can be only twelve members. *There's* no reason to involve more people. Only the twelve members were *there.*

They're is a contraction which means "they are."

> EX: *They're* leaving to pick up *their* notes which they left *there* overnight. *There's* no doubt that *they're theirs.*

Thesis and Thesis Statement

The thesis of an expository work is the point the author is trying to develop within the work. It is the organizational focus of the work about which all the rest is planned. It is the major idea of the work to which all other ideas are subordinated.

A thesis statement is a sentence (or possibly two) in which the thesis is embodied. Although all well-written expository works have a thesis, occasionally they do not have an explicit thesis statement. The great majority of expository works have at least one such statement, however, and frequently have two. The places where you will be most likely to find such statements are in the final sentences of the introductory paragraph(s) and in the conclusion of the work.

However you eventually plan to handle the thesis in your own writing, it is wise for you to compose a working thesis statement at the start to help you plan the structure of your composition. Ways of arriving at your thesis statement are discussed in "Writing the First Paper" and in Chapter 1.

See **Although Clause.**

Thing or Things

Unless your purpose is to convey vagueness, try to avoid using the word *thing* (or *things*). Substitute a more precise word for it wherever you can in editing your work.

> WEAK: Robin finished the *thing* she was working on.
> BETTER: Robin finished the *project* she was working on.
> OK: It was just a *thing* of rags and tatters. (purposely vague)

Till/Until

Until is more often used than *till,* but either is acceptable and the meanings are the same. *'Til* is a seldom used contraction for *until. 'Till* is not a word.

> EX: Until tomorrow then.
> EX: " . . . Till the end of time."

Titles

1. Capitalize the first and every other significant word in a title: *The Decline and Fall of the Roman Empire.*
2. Underline (italicize) the title of every separately published work. These include full-length books *(Catch-22, The Third Reich);* magazines and journals *(The Ladies' Home Journal, College English);* operas or symphonies *(La Traviata);* plays, movies, and television shows *(Hamlet, The Attack of the Killer Tomatoes);* anthologies and encylopedias *(The Encyclopaedia Brittanica).*
3. Put quotation marks around the titles of portions of books, such as chapters, works anthologized or otherwise included within books,

short stories, essays, articles, songs, poems: "The Story of an Hour";
"Goodbye to All T--t"; "The Rime of the Ancient Mariner."

> EX: Ellen Goodman's essay "The Cult of Impotence" is one of the reprinted
> essays in Beth Neman's text, *Writing Effectively.*

4. When you place a title at the beginning of a work of your own, you
   should neither underline it nor put quotation marks around it—except
   those portions, of course, that you would normally italicize or enclose
   with quotation marks.

To/Too/Two

Errors in using these words are probably the result of carelessness rather than
lack of understanding. Watch for them when you proofread.

Two is always a number. *Too* means "also" and "overly" or "excessive." In
other situations, *to* is the correct spelling.

> EX: The *two* farmers walked *too* far *to* go *to* the store and *to* the market *too.*

Transitive Verbs
See **Intransitive and Transitive Verbs.**

Try and/Try to

Do not substitute *try and* for *try to.* Although this construction is often heard
in conversation, it is not correct in writing.

> INCORRECT: We should *try and* remember the way back," she said conspiratori-
> ally.
>
> CORRECT: "Yes, we should *try to* remember the way," he repeated ironically.

Underlining
See **Italics.**

Uninterested
See **Disinterested/Uninterested.**

Unique

Since *unique* means that the idea or thing it describes is the only one in the
world, such expressions as *very unique* or *especially unique* are more than a
little excessive and should be avoided.

Until
See **Till/Until.**

Used To

Never say *we use to* or *we didn't used to.* Say *we used to* and *we didn't use to.*

> CORRECT: We *used to* enjoy homemade ice cream, but we *didn't use to* get it
> in large quantities because no one *used to* have a freezer.

Verbs

A verb is the part of speech that carries the action of a sentence. It tells what
the subject does or is. Verbs can be **regular** or irregular, transitive or **intran-**

sitive, and they can be used in the **active** or the passive voice. (See individual listings.)

See also **Auxiliary Verbs** and **Linking Verbs.**

Verbals, Verbal Phrases

When a form of a verb is not used as a verb, but as another part of speech, it is called a "verbal." When a verbal dominates a phrase, it is known as a "verbal phrase."

See **Gerund, Infinitive,** and **Participle.**

Very

See **Quite/Really/Very.**

Wait/Wait on

See **Await.**

Want/Wish

Want should be used when a direct object follows.

> EX: Did she really *want* the mink *coat?*

Wish should be used with an indirect object.

> EX: We *wish you* luck on your exams.

The English butler who asks, "Does madam *wish* her *tea* now?" is using incorrect grammar.

> You may use *wish for* or *wish to* in appropriate situations.

> EX: We all *wish for* peace.
> EX: Did Sandra always *wish to* be Miss Nebraska?

Well

See **Good/Well.**

When/Where

When and *where* should not be used after *is* to form a definition.

> INCORRECT: A civil war *is when* two parts of the same government oppose each other with violence.
> INCORRECT: A hole in one *is where* a golfer sinks the ball with one driving stroke.
> CORRECT: A Civil War is a war in which . . .
> CORRECT: A hole in one occurs when a golfer . . .

Where at

At is not appropriate after *where.*

> INCORRECT: Where's it at?
> CORRECT: Where is it?
> INCORRECT: He always knows where it's at.
> CORRECT: He always knows where it is.

Which

See **Pronouns: Relative.**

Who's/Whose
Who's means *who is* or *who has.*

> EX: *Who's* sending these threatening letters?
> EX: *Who's* been eating my porridge?

Whose is a possessive form.

> EX: *Whose* math paper is this?
> EX: We know *whose* tapes are being pirated, but we don't know *who's* doing it?

Who/Whom
Who is used as the subject of a sentence or clause. *Whoever* follows the same rules. *Whom* and *whomever* are used as objects of verbs or prepositions or indirect objects. *Whomever* is awkward and seldom seen.

> CORRECT: *Who* is your best friend? Your best friend is *whoever* has a car for Saturday night.
> CORRECT: The person to *whom* you owe the most money is not always the person *whom* you want to see.
> CORRECT: We asked *who* had been here longest. He is the one *whom* we wanted to interview.
> CORRECT: We will present the keys to *whoever* wins the raffle.

In this sentence, a clause, *whoever wins the raffle,* is the indirect object, but *whoever* is the subject of the clause.

If the use of *whom* is correct but sounds stilted or awkward to you, try to rewrite the sentence, avoiding it altogether.

See **Pronouns: Relative.**

Will
See **Shall/Will, Should/Would.**

Win
Win as a noun is acceptable in informal or journalistic writing. In formal writing, *win* is a verb and *victory* might be the noun you choose.

> WEAK: Paul tried once more for a *win* at Indianapolis.
> BETTER: Paul tried once more *to win* at Indianapolis.
> > or
> Paul tried once more for a *victory* at Indianapolis.

Wish/Want
See **Want/Wish.**

With
Do not use *with* to add a further thought to a sentence.

> WEAK: Janice and Albert always led the class *with* Patty trailing in third place.
> BETTER: Janice and Albert always led the class; Patty trailed in third place.

Would

See **Shall/Will, Should/Would.**

Would Have/Would of

Would have is correct. Never use *would of.*

> CORRECT: We *would have* come earlier. He *would have* helped you.
> CORRECT: We *would've* come earlier.
> INCORRECT: We *would of* come earlier.

The same rule applies to *could have* and *should have.*

Write—Irregular Verb

They write; they wrote; they have written.

Your/You're

Your is a possessive. *You're* is a contraction which means *you are.*

> EX: *You're* always leaving *your* coat on that chair.